Thinking: Psychological Perspectives on Reasoning, Judgment and Decision Making

Thinking: Psychological Perspectives on Reasoning, Judgment and Decision Making

Edited by

David Hardman
London Metropolitan University, UK
and
Laura Macchi
University of Milan-Bicocca, Italy

JOHN WILEY & SONS, LTD

First published in paperback September 2005

This publication is designed to provide accurate and authoritative information in regard to the
subject matter covered. It is sold on the understanding that the Publisher is not engaged in
rendering professional services. If professional advice or other expert assistance is required, the
services of a competent professional should be sought.

Other Wiley Editorial Offices

John Wiley & Sons Inc., 111 River Street, Hoboken, NJ 07030, USA

Jossey-Bass, 989 Market Street, San Francisco, CA 94103-1741, USA

Wiley-VCH Verlag GmbH, Boschstr. 12, D-69469 Weinheim, Germany

John Wiley & Sons Australia Ltd, 33 Park Road, Milton, Queensland 4064, Australia

John Wiley & Sons (Asia) Pte Ltd, 2 Clementi Loop #02-01, Jin Xing Distripark, Singapore 129809

John Wiley & Sons Canada Ltd, 22 Worcester Road, Etobicoke, Ontario, Canada M9W 1L1

Wiley also publishes its books in a variety of electronic formats. Some content that appears
in print may not be available in electronic books.

Library of Congress Cataloging-in-Publication Data

Thinking: psychological perspectives on reasoning, judgment and decision making /
edited by David Hardman and Laura Macchi.
  p.   cm.
Includes bibliographical references and index.
ISBN 0-471-49457-7
1. Thought and thinking. 2. Reasoning (Psychology) 3. Judgment. 4. Decision making.
I. Hardman, David. II. Macchi, Laura, 1961–
BF 441.T466   2003
153.4—dc21   2003003951

British Library Cataloguing in Publication Data

A catalogue record for this book is available from the British Library

ISBN 10: 0-471-49457-7 (H/B)   ISBN 13: 978-0-471-49457-7 (H/B)
ISBN 10: 0-470-02572-7 (P/B)   ISBN 13: 978-0-470-02572-7 (P/B)

Typeset in 10/12pt Times by TechBooks, New Delhi, India
Printed and bound in Great Britain by Antony Rowe Ltd, Chippenham, Wiltshire
This book is printed on acid-free paper responsibly manufactured from sustainable forestry
in which at least two trees are planted for each one used for paper production.

Contents

List of Contributors   vii

Introduction   xi

Part I: Reasoning   **1**

Chapter 1   A Theory of Hypothetical Thinking   3
             Jonathan St. B.T. Evans, David E. Over and Simon J. Handley

Chapter 2   Individual Differences in the Development of Reasoning Strategies   23
             Maxwell J. Roberts and Elizabeth J. Newton

Chapter 3   Generalising Individual Differences and Strategies Across
             Different Deductive Reasoning Domains   45
             Padraic Monaghan and Keith Stenning

Chapter 4   Superordinate Principles, Conditions and Conditionals   63
             Neil Fairley and Ken Manktelow

Chapter 5   Premise Interpretation in Conditional Reasoning   79
             Guy Politzer

Chapter 6   Probabilities and Pragmatics in Conditional Inference: Suppression
             and Order Effects   95
             Mike Oaksford and Nick Chater

Part II: Judgment   **123**

Chapter 7   Verbal Expressions of Uncertainty and Probability   125
             Karl Halvor Teigen and Wibecke Brun

Chapter 8   Possibilities and Probabilities   147
             *Paolo Legrenzi, Vittorio Girotto, Maria Sonino Legrenzi and
             Philip N. Johnson-Laird*

Chapter 9   The *Partitive* Conditional Probability   165
             Laura Macchi

Chapter 10   Naive and yet Enlightened: From Natural Frequencies to Fast and
             Frugal Decision Trees   189
             *Laura Martignon, Oliver Vitouch, Masanori Takezawa and Malcolm
             R. Forster*

Chapter 11   More is not Always Better: The Benefits of Cognitive Limits   213
              Ralph Hertwig and Peter M. Todd

Chapter 12   Correspondence and Coherence: Indicators of Good Judgment in
              World Politics   233
              Philip E. Tetlock

Part III: Decision Making   251

Chapter 13   Cognitive Mapping of Causal Reasoning in Strategic Decision
              Making   253
              A. John Maule, Gerard P. Hodgkinson and Nicola J. Bown

Chapter 14   Belief and Preference in Decision Under Uncertainty   273
              Craig R. Fox and Kelly E. See

Chapter 15   Medical Decision Scripts: Combining Cognitive Scripts and
              Judgment Strategies to Account Fully for Medical Decision
              Making   315
              Robert M. Hamm

Chapter 16   On the Assessment of Decision Quality: Considerations Regarding
              Utility, Conflict and Accountability   347
              Gideon Keren and Wändi Bruine de Bruin

Author Index   365

Subject Index   375

List of Contributors

Dr Nicola J. Bown, *Centre for Decision Research, Leeds University Business School, Maurice Keyworth Building, University of Leeds, Leeds LS2 9JT, UK*

Dr Wändi Bruine de Bruin, *Department of Social and Decision Sciences, Carnegie Mellon University, Pittsburgh, PA 15213, USA*

Dr Wibecke Brun, *Department of Psychosocial Science, University of Bergen, Christiesgt 12, Bergen, N5015, Norway*

Professor Nick Chater, *Department of Psychology, University of Warwick, Coventry, CV4 7AL, UK*

Professor Jonathan St. B.T. Evans, *Centre for Thinking and Language, Department of Psychology, University of Plymouth, Drake Circus, Plymouth, Devon PL4 8AA, UK*

Dr Neil Fairley, *Department of Psychology, University of Leicester, University Road, Leicester LE1 7RH, UK*

Professor Malcolm R. Forster, *Department of Philosophy, University of Wisconsin-Madison, Madison, WI 53706, USA*

Professor Craig R. Fox, *Anderson School of Management and Department of Psychology, UCLA, 110 Westwood Plaza, Box 951481, Los Angeles, CA 90095-1481, USA*

Professor Vittorio Girotto, *LPC CNRS, University of Provence, Aix-en-Provence 13100, France, and Department of Arts and Design, University of Architecture, Venice, Italy*

Professor Robert M. Hamm, *Clinical Decision-Making Program, Department of Family and Preventive Medicine, University of Oklahoma Health Sciences Center, 900 NE 10th Street, Oklahoma City, OK 73104, USA*

Dr Simon J. Handley, *Centre for Thinking and Language, Department of Psychology, University of Plymouth, Drake Circus, Plymouth, Devon PL4 8AA, UK*

Dr David Hardman, *Department of Psychology, London Metropolitan University, Calcutta House, Old Castle Street, London E1 7NT, UK*

Dr Ralph Hertwig, *Center for Adaptive Behavior and Cognition, Max Planck Institute for Human Development, Lentzeallee 94, 14195 Berlin, Germany*

Professor Gerard P. Hodgkinson, *Leeds University Business School, Maurice Keyworth Building, University of Leeds, Leeds LS2 9JT, UK*

Professor Philip N. Johnson-Laird, *Department of Psychology, Princeton University, Green Hall, Princeton, NJ 08544, USA*

Professor Gideon Keren, *Faculty of Technology Management, Eindhoven University of Technology, PO Box 513, 5600 MB, Eindhoven, The Netherlands*

Professor Paolo Legrenzi, *Professor of Cognitive Psychology, Faculty of Architecture, University Institute of Architecture of Venice, Italy*

Professor Maria Sonino Legrenzi (now retired)

Professor Laura Macchi, *Facoltà e Dipartimento di Psicologia, Università degli Studi di Milano-Bicocca, Piazza dell'Ateneo Nuovo, 1, 20126 Milan, Italy*

Professor Ken Manktelow, *Psychology Division, MC Block, University of Wolverhampton, Wulfruna Street, Wolverhampton, West Midlands WV1 1SB, UK*

Dr Laura Martignon, *Fachbereich 17, Mathematik und Informatik, Universität Kassel, Postfach 101380, D-34109 Kassel, Germany*

Dr A. John Maule, *Leeds University Business School, Maurice Keyworth Building, University of Leeds, Leeds LS2 9JT, UK*

Padraic Monaghan, *Department of Psychology, University of Warwick, Coventry CV4 7AL, UK*

Dr Elizabeth J. Newton, *Department of Human Communication Science, University College London, Chandler House, 2 Wakefield Street, London WC1N 1PF, UK*

Professor Mike Oaksford, *School of Psychology, Cardiff University, PO Box 901, Cardiff CF10 3YG, UK*

Professor David E. Over, *Psychology Department, St Peter's Campus, University of Sunderland, Sunderland SR6 ODD, UK*

Dr Guy Politzer, *Centre National de la Recherche Scientifique (CNRS)—Psychologie Cognitive, Université de Paris 8, 2, rue de la Liberté, 93526 Saint-Denis, France*

Dr Maxwell J. Roberts, *Department of Psychology, University of Essex, Wivenhoe Park, Colchester, Essex CO4 3SQ, UK*

Kelly E. See, *Fuqua School of Business, Duke University, Box 90120, Durham, NC 27708, USA*

Professor Keith Stenning, *Division of Informatics, University of Edinburgh, 2 Buccleuch Place, Edinburgh EH8 9LW, UK*

Dr Masanori Takezawa, *Max Planck Institute for Human Development, Center for Adaptive Behavior and Cognition, Lentzeallee 94, 14195 Berlin, Germany*

Professor Karl Halvor Teigen, *Department of Psychology, University of Oslo, PO Box 1094 Blindern, N-0317 Oslo, Norway*

Professor Philip E. Tetlock, *Hass School of Business, University of California, Berkeley, CA94720–1900, USA*

Dr Peter M. Todd, *Center for Adaptive Behavior and Cognition, Max Planck Institute for Human Development, Lentzeallee 94, 14195 Berlin, Germany*

Professor Oliver Vitouch, *Department of Psychology, University of Klagenfurt, Universitätsstrasse 65–67, A-9020 Klagenfurt, Austria*

Introduction

This book is concerned with reasoning, judgment and decision making. Reasoning is concerned with making inferences, judgment is about the formation of beliefs about the likelihood of uncertain events, and decision making is about choosing between alternatives. These three aspects of cognition are overlapping and interlinked: we may reason when attempting to form a judgment, and our judgments may inform our decision making. For the sake of convenience, we have organised the book into three major sections corresponding to each of these topics.

Reasoning, judgment and decision making each have a normative theory (respectively, logic, probability theory and utility theory) that predicts what a rational thinker should do in some particular circumstance, but in each of these areas people are frequently observed to violate the rational norms. Following Simon's (1956) notion of bounded rationality, as well as the heuristics and biases programme from the 1970s onwards (Kahneman, Slovic & Tversky, 1982), much recent work has suggested that there may be good reasons why people violate rational norms. This theme runs through a number of the chapters presented here—for example, Chapters 6, 10 and 11.

The use of strategies and heuristics, as well as the role of individual differences, is also discussed in several chapters across the three sections. In reasoning, most theorists in recent years have focused on universal mechanisms, such as mental logic or mental models. Others have questioned whether there is a universal mechanism, and focus on the acquisition and use of different strategies (see Chapters 2 and 3). Chapter 1 suggests that deductive thinking itself may be a strategy that experimental participants have to be persuaded to adopt. Recent work in judgment has proposed that people may choose from a range of "fast and frugal" heuristics, sometimes referred to as "one-reason decision making". The focus of this research programme has been to show that such heuristics are "ecologically rational": judgments based on a single environmental cue can be highly accurate and involve little cognitive effort (see Chapters 10 and 11; for an alternative view of these results, see Chapter 9).

In Chapter 13, Maule, Hodgkinson and Bown distinguish between heuristic (short cut) strategies and more elaborate strategies in strategic decision making, and in Chapter 15, Hamm discusses the role of scripts and strategies in medical decision making. Dual processes in thinking are also discussed by Evans et al. in Chapter 1. Although they largely cite the reasoning literature (and are included in the reasoning section), they propose a theory that they believe also applies to other areas of thinking.

Individual differences are examined in relation to strategy use (Chapters 2 and 3), as well as need for cognition (Chapter 13) and need for cognitive closure (Chapter 12).

Another theme that occurs in various chapters is that of beliefs and background knowledge, and the role that these play in thinking. For example, background knowledge is clearly seen to affect the inferences we draw from conditional statements (as in Chapters 4, 5 and 6), and the use of fast and frugal heuristics in judgment is also based on knowledge of the environment (Chapters 10 and 11). Several chapters in the decision-making section are concerned with knowledge-based decision making, but we particularly draw readers' attention to Chapter 14 by Fox and See, who show that people's beliefs play a key role in making decisions where there is uncertainty.

A final theme that runs through a number of chapters is the prevalence of causal thinking. This occurs in the last three chapters of the reasoning section and in the discussion of fast and frugal decision trees (Chapter 10), expert political judgment (Chapter 12), and decision making (Chapters 13 and 15).

In the remainder of this introduction, we present a short summary of each of the chapters.

REASONING

In Chapter 1, the first chapter of the Reasoning section, Evans, Over and Handley present a theory of hypothetical thinking based on the idea that both an implicit and an explicit cognitive system is involved in thinking. They also argue that thinking about hypothetical possibilities is guided by the three principles of singularity, relevance and satisficing. A single possibility is considered (singularity principle) after being generated by the implicit cognitive system in line with the relevance principle (what is most plausible in the current context). The explicit cognitive system then evaluates this possibility and accepts it if it is satisfactory (the satisficing principle). Although the authors draw upon data from the reasoning literature to support their theory, they consider that the theory itself can also be applied in other areas of thinking, such as decision making.

In Chapter 2, Roberts and Newton discuss the use of strategies in reasoning. They describe a number of ways in which the term "strategy" can be defined, including whether or not "strategy" implies some element of consciousness. Having specified their own interpretation of what is meant by "strategy", Roberts and Newton go on to investigate how and why people differ in their strategy use. Their research into spatial and verbal strategies indicates that a key step in strategy discovery is the identification and deletion of redundant steps in problem solution. Furthermore, the people who are most competent in using some task-general strategy are most likely to drop them in favour of some task-specific short cut.

By contrast, in Chapter 3, Monaghan and Stenning argue that what is needed is a computational description of the processes operating on different representations. According to their account, spatial representations are less able to express abstractions than are verbal representations, but which kind of representation will be most appropriate depends on the task and how much information needs to be expressed in order to do the task. Individual differences relate to a person's ability to select the kind of representation that is most appropriate for the performance of a given task.

The next three chapters examine reasoning about conditional statements ("If p then q"). The degree to which we accept that the consequent q follows from the antecedent p is dependent on our background knowledge. According to Fairley and Manktelow, in Chapter 4, our background knowledge includes principles that specify the conditions that must be satisfied in order for some goal to be achieved. These are referred to as "superordinate principles" ("SuperPs"). Where the antecedent of a conditional statement fails to include a salient condition, or where we are led to doubt the existence of a normally taken-for-granted condition, we may fail to doubt that the consequence of the statement follows. Fairley and Manktelow argue that the evidence of SuperPs across a variety of domains is problematic for domain-specific theories of reasoning, but that domain-general theories would also need some modification. For example, the explicitness of a mental model may depend on the goals of the problem in question.

In Chapter 5, Politzer adopts a similar approach to that of Fairley and Manktelow in explaining content effects in reasoning. However, whereas Fairley and Manktelow refer to SuperPs, Politzer refers to the concept of a causal field. The causal field contains all the possible candidates for the role of a cause in a particular context. The notion is taken from Mackie's (1974) theory of causality, but is also extended to non-causal reasoning problems. Mackie's theory also provides a formalism for describing the relationship between the explicit elements of a problem and the relevant parts of background knowledge.

In Chapter 6, Oaksford and Chater investigate both the suppression of conditional inferences and the order effects that can occur when, for example, "q only if p" is used instead of "if p then q". In order to explain the data, they develop their probabilistic computational level model of conditional inference (Oaksford, Chater and Larkin, 2000). This model outlines the computational problem that people are trying to solve when given a conditional inference task. Oaksford and Chater assume that the problem is not about which logical rule to apply, but how to use one's knowledge of the probabilities involved (How probable is the antecedent? How probable is the consequent? What is the probability that there are exceptions to if p then q?). They show that a probabilistic model provides a good fit to previously published findings on conditional inference.

JUDGMENT

The section on probabilistic judgment begins with Chapter 7, in which Teigen and Brun review research into verbal expressions of uncertainty and probability. Although numerical probabilities are more precise and can be used within systems of calculation, we do not always know how to obtain them or whether, indeed, they are correct. By contrast, although verbal terms can to some degree be mapped onto a probability dimension, they also have properties that cannot be captured by numbers.

In Chapter 8, Paolo Legrenzi, Girotto, Maria Legrenzi and Johnson-Laird describe how the theory of mental models can, with some additional assumptions, be applied to thinking about probabilities and possibilities. When judging the probability of an event, the reasoner constructs models and derives a probability from the proportion of the models in which the event holds true. Errors may occur when a person fails to construct fully explicit models. In addition, models may sometimes include numerical "tags" and a solution is arrived at through simple arithmetic.

In Chapter 9, Macchi addresses the topic of Bayesian reasoning. Early evidence for base-rate neglect has been attributed to the use of heuristics. However, recent approaches have challenged this body of work, suggesting that people are capable of Bayesian reasoning when probabilities are stated in the form of natural frequencies rather than percentage probabilities that apply to a single event. Macchi offers a pragmatics alternative explanation of those phenomena. Bayesian reasoning tasks include several items of numerical information, and what is crucial for correct reasoning is that the text does not hide the relationship between sets and subsets. Mistakes occur when the relationship between set and subset is not clearly described.

In Chapter 10, Martignon, Vitouch, Takezawa and Forster show how decision trees can be developed for both fully Bayesian and "fast and frugal" decision making. Different trees can be constructed for different heuristics, and the predictive performance of each relates to how costly misses and false positives are. In line with the general ethos of the fast and frugal approach, the fast and frugal trees are shown to perform well on predictive tasks.

In Chapter 11, Hertwig and Todd show that cognitive limitations can enable important cognitive functions. Moreover, the simple strategies that are used in judgment can lead to surprisingly high levels of accuracy. After giving examples of these, Hertwig and Todd turn an old idea on its head. Whereas it is typically argued that simple processing strategies arise as a result of our cognitive limitations, Hertwig and Todd suggest that the very success of simple strategies in evolution is the reason why we have limited processing capacity.

In Chapter 12, Tetlock describes some results from a 15-year research programme on expert political judgment. He identifies many of the same biases among professionals that have previously been found in laboratory studies with undergraduate students. Tetlock also finds that individuals who show a preference for explanatory closure and parsimony are more prone to a range of biases, although the more open-minded experts also showed a bias in that they assigned too much probability to too many alternative scenarios (the result of being too imaginative). As in Fox and See's Chapter 14 in the next section, Tetlock also uses support theory to explain some biases in probability judgment. However, he also shows how difficult it is to prove error in the political domain, as experts are often willing to defend their thinking when they have apparently been inaccurate.

DECISION MAKING

In Chapter 13, the first chapter in the section on decision making, Maule, Hodgkinson and Bown examine the cognitive processes involved in strategic decision making. They do this by asking people to write down all the thoughts and ideas that occur to them while considering a decision, and then deriving causal cognitive maps from these protocols. By analysing the degree of complexity of the different maps, the authors are able to investigate the influence of time pressure on decision making. They are also able to compare the complexity of causal maps in relation to whether or not the participant chose a particular alternative. The authors relate their work to theories that distinguish between two types of information-processing strategy: heuristic and elaborative.

In Chapter 14, Fox and See review work from two areas: decision making under risk, and uncertainty and probability judgment. Prospect theory claims that cognitive functions relating to the integration of values and probabilities in our decision representations lead to the systematic violations of classical decision theory. More recently, support theory has been developed to explain why judged probabilities frequently fail to conform to the laws of chance. In essence, support theory proposes that we do not judge events; rather, we judge *descriptions* of events, called hypotheses. Fox and See provide evidence for a two-stage model of decision making that incorporates both theories. They then go on to develop an extended version of the two-stage model that incorporates the role of people's beliefs. To be more specific, it seems that people are more willing to bet on uncertain events when they have some knowledge about the *source* of uncertainty.

In Chapter 15, Hamm also is concerned about the way in which decision makers represent and use knowledge, although his chapter is specifically about decision making within medicine. He argues that research into medical decision making has tended to neglect the routine nature of most decisions made by physicians. Thus, in most cases, they instigate a course of action without consideration of decision theoretic concepts. More deliberative thinking may occur, however, when there is a mismatch between a patient and an activated script. Hamm goes on to discuss the implications of the scripts approach, including the role of decision aids in medicine.

In Chapter 16, Keren and Bruine de Bruin take up an issue raised in Chapter 12 by Tetlock, that of a possible lack of compatibility between the decision maker and the person judging decision quality. A lack of compatibility may result from the use of different values held by the decision maker and judge, or it may result from the use of different frameworks used to structure the decision problem. The authors focus on the latter difficulty and address three approaches to decision making: the gambling paradigm (every problem can be seen as a choice between gambles), the conflict model (decision making involves the resolution of emotional conflict) and the accountability model (the decision maker's main goal is to defend decisions if held accountable). The authors suggest that in the absence of unequivocal standards for judging decision quality, we can justify our decisions only through the use of arguments—a conclusion that is consistent with the accountability model.

REFERENCES

Kahneman, D., Slovic, P. & Tversky, A. (1982). *Judgment Under Uncertainty: Heuristics and Biases*. Cambridge: Cambridge University Press.

Mackie, J. L. (1974). *The Cement of the Universe*. Oxford: Oxford University Press.

Oaksford, M., Chater, N. & Larkin, J. (2000). Probabilities and polarity biases in conditional inference. *Journal of Experimental Psychology: Learning, Memory, and Cognition*, 26, 883–899.

Simon, H. A. (1956). Rational choice and the structure of environments. *Psychological Review*, 63, 129–138.

PART I

Reasoning

CHAPTER 1

A Theory of Hypothetical Thinking

Jonathan St. B.T. Evans
University of Plymouth, UK
David E. Over
University of Sunderland, UK
and
Simon J. Handley
University of Plymouth, UK

Human beings engage in a kind of thinking that requires consideration of hypothetical possibilities. For example, we may imagine a possible world resulting from some action or choice that is before us. We may entertain an hypothesis and consider its implications, or we may attempt to forecast the most plausible states of affairs given some scenario. Hypothetical thinking, we assume, is a uniquely human facility that is a distinguishing characteristic of our intelligence.

We became interested in hypothetical thinking when developing our ideas about dual processes in thinking and reasoning (Evans & Over, 1996). According to the dual-process theory, there are distinct cognitive mechanisms underlying implicit and explicit thinking (see also Reber, 1993). The implicit system (termed "System 1" by Stanovich, 1999) provides automatic input to human cognition in the form of pragmatic processes whose tendency is to contextualise the current environment in the light of background beliefs and knowledge, a process which Stanovich (1999) describes as the "fundamental computational bias". We see the implicit system as comprising largely localised, domain-specific neural networks reflecting the learning history of the individual, although any innate "input modules" of the type envisaged by Fodor (1983) would also operate implicitly. The explicit system—or "System 2"—we see as uniquely human, linked to language and reflective consciousness, and providing the basis for reasoning. Explicit thinking requires working memory and is therefore sequential and sharply limited in processing capacity compared with the implicit system. Effective functioning of the explicit system is also linked to measures of general intelligence (Reber, 1993; Stanovich, 1999).

Thinking: Psychological Perspectives on Reasoning, Judgment and Decision Making. Edited by David Hardman and Laura Macchi.
© 2003 John Wiley & Sons, Ltd.

Our theory of hypothetical thinking reflects an attempt to understand the interplay of these two systems in human cognition and to identify the functions which System 2 thinking—uniquely human—adds to our intelligence. We know that one function of the implicit system is to utilise pragmatic cues to direct the locus of attention of the explicit system. This idea is central to the heuristic-analytic theory of reasoning (Evans, 1984, 1989). According to this theory, observed errors and biases in reasoning may underestimate the logical competence of our analytic (explicit) reasoning because preconscious heuristic (implicit, pragmatic) processes lead us to represent the wrong information as relevant. Our cognitive representations may thus be biased by prior experience which, for example, may foreground a feature of the problem which is logically irrelevant to its solution (see Evans, 1989, for discussion of many examples). This argument is similar to Stanovich's (1999) discussion of a fundamental computational bias. Stanovich demonstrates, however, that a small number of individuals—high in general intelligence—can resist pragmatic influences and reason in a logical, abstract manner to achieve normative solutions on a range of reasoning and judgment tasks.

More recently, we have taken a more positive view of the implicit system, regarding pragmatic influences as being generally adaptive in achieving our ordinary everyday goals (Evans, Over & Manktelow, 1993; Evans & Over, 1996). The automatic introduction of background beliefs and personal goals into our thinking is valuable in the ordinary world (if not the psychological laboratory), since we normally wish to reason from all relevant belief. This still leaves the question of how the explicit system operates and what precisely it does. We were led by a review of the tasks requiring explicit processing resources to the view that the representation of hypothetical possibilities is the common factor (Evans & Over, 1996). Hence our interest in developing a theory of hypothetical thinking.

THE THREE PRINCIPLES OF HYPOTHETICAL THINKING

We will use the term "mental model" to describe the representations that people form of hypothetical possibilities. Our use of the terms is thus broadly compatible with Johnson-Laird's (Johnson-Laird, 1983; Johnson-Laird & Byrne, 1991) except that we do not accept the limited propositional formats that Johnson-Laird proposes to describe the content of such models. The relationship of the hypothetical thinking theory to the mental model theory of deduction will be discussed in some detail later in this chapter.

Our theory of hypothetical thinking involves three principles, defined as follows:

- *The singularity principle*. People consider a single hypothetical possibility, or mental model, at one time.
- *The relevance principle*. People consider the model which is most relevant (generally the most plausible or probable) in the current context.
- *The satisficing principle*. Models are evaluated with reference to the current goal and accepted if satisfactory.

The operation of the three principles is illustrated by the diagrammatic representation of the hypothetical thinking model shown in Figure 1.1. A single hypothetical possibility or mental model is generated in line with the relevance principle (see below) by the implicit cognitive system. This model is then evaluated by the explicit system and accepted if it is satisfactory (satisficing principle). Once models are accepted, they are then processed by

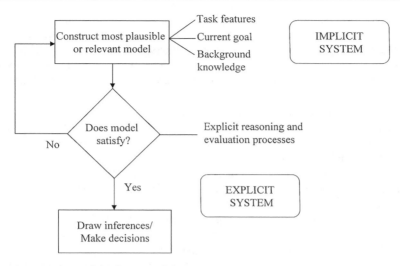

Figure 1.1   Hypothetical thinking model

the explicit system with regard to the task in hand in order to generate judgments, decisions or inferences.

The Singularity Principle

The singularity principle derives not simply from consideration of the limited capacity of working memory, but from observations in the various psychological paradigms used to study hypothesis testing. One such paradigm is that of concept identification or concept learning. In these studies, participants are shown positive or negative instances of logical rules from which they have to infer what the rule is. One of the classical findings in this area (Bruner, Goodnow & Austin, 1956; Levine, 1966) is that people adopt a single hypothesis which is consistent with the initial information. As further instances are examined, the hypothesis is maintained until or unless evidence which contradicts it is encountered. A falsifying case leads people to abandon their hypothesis—and within memory constraints— to adopt a new one consistent with evidence already presented.

This hypothesis-testing framework actually describes a simple example of the operation of the whole system, as illustrated in Figure 1.1. An hypothesis is generated as being plausible (consistent with current evidence) and serves the role of the model in this example. The explicit system evaluates the hypothesis against evidence and accepts it if it satisfies (is consistent with the evidence). Only when a falsifying case is encountered is the evaluation unsatisfying, and the model (hypothesis) abandoned and a new one generated. Both relevance and satisficing principles come into play here, in the model-generating and model-evaluation stages, respectively.

Of course, this very general model needs to be supplemented for any particular task by proposals about the final stage concerning how inferences are drawn or decisions made. In the case of hypothesis testing, there seems to be some kind of inductive reasoning mechanism (possibly Bayesian confirmation) that leads people to accept an hypothesis as true if they fail to encounter a falsifying case within a reasonable number of tests. This is well illustrated by research on Wason's (1960) "2 4 6" problem (reviewed by Evans, 1989; Manktelow, 1999). The 2 4 6 task is so devised that people will generally keep encountering confirming evidence of a wrong (insufficiently generalised) initial hypothesis so long as they test positive instances (see Klayman & Ha, 1987). As tests continue to satisfy, participants become convinced of the correctness of their hypothesis, and even when told that it is wrong, they find it very difficult to consider alternatives. This has been described as a "confirmation bias", although the term is controversial since it is not clear that people are deliberately trying to confirm their hypotheses (see Evans, 1989; Klayman, 1995). Evidence from the "pseudodiagnosticity" task of Doherty et al. (1979) also supports the singularity principle with an explicit claim by Mynatt, Doherty and Dragan (1993) that people can consider only one hypothesis at a time. Research on this task is considered in some detail later in the chapter.

Another form of evidence for the singularity principle is the demonstrable difficulty people have in learning or processing disjunctive rules. A classical finding in the concept-learning literature (Bruner et al., 1956) is that people find it very hard to learn rules which are defined disjunctively. In the reasoning literature, this is best illustrated by reference to Wason's notorious THOG problem (Wason & Brooks, 1979). In this task, participants are shown four designs: a black square, a white square, a black circle and a white circle. They are then given the following rule: *if, and only if, any of the designs includes either the colour I have written down or the shape I have written down, but not both, it is called a THOG.*

Participants are told that the black square is a THOG and asked to classify the other three designs. Readers who have not encountered this problem before might like to attempt its solution before reading on.

In order to solve the THOG, one needs to consider a disjunction of hypotheses. If the black square is a THOG, the value written down must be

Either black and circle
Or white and square

If the rule is "black or else circle", the white circle must be a THOG, but the other shapes may not be THOGS. The same conclusion follows if the rule is "white or else square". Hence, although one does not know which rule was written down, one can classify just the white circle as a THOG. Intelligent student participants find this problem very difficult, however, and the majority give incorrect answers.

What of decision making? The normative theory of decision making apparently requires us to consider simultaneously the outcomes of alternative actions. Suppose we are making a decision by choosing between, say, two tempting job offers, A and B. Standard decision theory is a normative account of how such a choice is made, and, according to it, we should coherently consider two possible states of affairs, or possible worlds. We should compare the possible world in which we choose job A with the possible world in which we choose job B, assessing the expected utility of A and the expected utility of B. If we select the job that yields the highest expected utility, we are said to engage in *consequential* decision making.

This normative account of decision making suggests that people can hold in mind two or more possibilities at the same time, and simultaneously weigh all of their respective probable benefits and costs—an idea at odds with the singularity principle. This unbounded normative theory has many limitations as a descriptive account of ordinary decision making, or even as a rational ideal for it (Evans & Over, 1996). In contrast, according to our descriptive account of hypothetical thinking, people represent only one relevant possible world at a time as a mental model. If they are making a decision, they may model two or more possible worlds sequentially, but not simultaneously. Moreover, they tend to focus quickly on one of these possibilities and to draw out only some of its consequences, and they give it up, or switch attention from it, only if they discover a negative consequence. According to our view, decision making does not involve any systematic attempt at optimising choice, as people often focus on the most immediately plausible, attractive or relevant option.

The Relevance Principle

A key idea in our theory is that the models people consider are preconsciously cued by the implicit system in accordance with the relevance principle. This pragmatic process reflects the interplay of three factors, as illustrated in Figure 1.1. First there are the features of the task or the environment that need to be processed by the participant. The second influence is the current *goal* that the person has adopted. The final input comes from long-term memory or stored knowledge. By a process which remains a great mystery in cognitive science (the "frame" problem), the human brain is able automatically and rapidly to extract from vast stores of knowledge just those items relevant to the problem at hand. The interaction of these three factors ensures that the most relevant model is the one that gets represented. Pragmatic relevance does not necessarily equate to logical relevance, however, especially on artificial experimental tasks. Hence, this preconscious determination of relevance can be the cause of observed errors and biases in the reasoning literature (Evans, 1989).

Relevance theory in the context of pragmatics and discourse comprehension has been best developed in the work of Sperber and Wilson (1986). In a recent revision of the theory, Sperber and Wilson (1995, see also Sperber, Cara & Girotto, 1995) distinguish not one but two principles of relevance as follows:

- *First (cognitive) principle of relevance.* Human cognition tends to be geared towards the maximisation of relevance.
- *Second (communicative) principle of relevance.* Every act of ostensive communication communicates a presumption of its own optimal relevance.

The second principle is that described as *the* principle of relevance in the 1986 theory. This principle has influence on reasoning and decision tasks in so far as problem information is communicated verbally. However, we are largely concerned with relevance effects in thinking outside a directly communicative context. For this reason, we welcome the explication and discussion of the first principle, which was only implicit in the original theory. Relevance, for us, is always related to the current goals, both practical and epistemic, of the individual. Sperber and colleagues have recently applied their relevance theory directly to work in the reasoning tradition (Sperber et al., 1995).

In recent writings about the mental model theory of reasoning, Johnson-Laird (e.g., Johnson-Laird & Savary, 1999) has proposed a *principle of truth* which leads people to represent true rather than false possibilities. Although Johnson-Laird finds this principle useful in accounting for the various phenomena that he describes as "cognitive illusions", we are not convinced that there is any such principle. For example, people can very easily and quite accurately represent false possibilities if instructed to do so, as shown in many experiments designed to elicit subjective truth tables (see Evans, Newstead & Byrne, 1993, for a review of the truth-table task; Evans, Legrenzi & Girotto, 1999, for a recent exam-ple of such experiments). Although we think that people do generally tend to represent what is probable or plausible, we believe that this is simply the default operation of the relevance principle. In everyday hypothetical thinking, it is generally adaptive to consider the most plausible scenarios, as, for example, when evaluating the outcome of a potential decision.

The default representation of likely possibilities can easily be changed, however, if the goal adopted by the individual makes other possibilities more relevant to the task in hand. Such a goal may be set by experimental instructions to identify false cases of conditional rules, as in the truth-table task. To take a more "real-life" example, insurance salespeople are adept at getting customers to imagine low-probability (but costly) events, such as houses burning down or premature death by accident. This illustrates a problem with the "principle of truth"—it ignores altogether the *utility* of possibilities or models that people may need to consider. We also know that the cases which people represent are highly sensitive to the context in which problems are presented. Numerous examples are provided by research on the thematic version of the (Wason, 1966) selection task.

In one such experiment, Manktelow and Over (1991) asked participants to evaluate the rule employed by a department store: if a customer spends more than £100, they may take a free gift. When given the perspective of a customer, people were concerned to check people spending more than £100 and not receiving gifts. When given the perspective of a store manager, however, participants wanted to check customers who spent less than £100 and still took the gift. It is evident that the customers' goal is to make sure that the store is not cheating (there are no cases where people spend the money and do not receive the gift), but the store manager's goal is to ensure that customers do not cheat (by taking a gift while spending less than £100). Hence, it is clear that pragmatic relevance is driving card selections on these problems.

The Satisficing Principle

The notion of "satisficing" arises from the bounded rationality research programme of Herb Simon (e.g., Newell & Simon, 1972; Simon, 1982). It can be contrasted with the notion of optimisation that arises in various contexts, including behavioural decision theory. Opti-misation requires an algorithm capable of examining all logical possibilities and choosing the one that is best. Satisficing, however, means employing heuristics that find solutions which are satisfactory, or good enough, but are not guaranteed to be optimal. The point is, of course, that in a world of unlimited complexity and with brains of limited information-processing capacity, optimisation is usually a practical impossibility. It has been shown, for example, that engineers use satisficing strategies in design problems where very complex search spaces are involved (Ball, Evans & Dennis, 1994; Ball et al., 1997).

The notion of bounded rationality and satisficing persists in some major current research programmes on reasoning and decision making. For example Gigerenzer (Gigerenzer & Goldstein, 1996; Gigerenzer & Todd, 2000) has argued, with the aid of computer simula-tions, that "fast and frugal" heuristics can provide surprisingly accurate solutions to decision problems with a fraction of the computational costs of optimisation methods. Oaksford and Chater (1998) have argued against logicism in psychology on the grounds that logical analy-sis becomes computationally intractable once more than a few premises are involved (as with real-world belief systems), and that real-world reasoning is non-monotonic, or *defeasible*. That is to say, we make inferences which we later give up when new information comes to light. These authors have also proposed that performance in deductive reasoning tasks is driven by simple heuristics (e.g., Chater & Oaksford, 1999).

Our theory of hypothetical thinking incorporates the notion of a satisficing principle at the stage of explicitly evaluating models, as shown in Figure 1.1. (Although the operation of the implicit system could also be regarded in a sense as satisficing rather than optimising, that process is described by the relevance rather than satisficing principle.) Specifically, we propose that mental models delivered as relevant, plausible candidates by the implicit system are subjected to evaluation by the explicit system. There can be no question of optimising possibilities because only one is considered at a time (singularity principle). Hence, the current model is examined to see whether it is good enough to achieve the current goal in line with the satisficing principle. If it fails, it is rejected and an alternative model is generated for consideration. It follows that intelligent action requires effective heuristic generation of models as well as effective evaluation, requiring both implicit and explicit systems to function well. What constitutes satisfaction will depend upon the particular task that is being addressed, but, in general, models will be explicitly evaluated against the current goals that the individual is pursuing and, in the case of hypothetical reasoning, for consistency with other relevant knowledge.

As explained earlier, decision-making processes will not optimise, as people will tend to choose an action with satisfying consequences without continuing to search for alternatives. While this apparently violates the rationality principles of normative decision theory, this theory has serious deficiencies, as discussed by Evans and Over (1996, Chapter 2). The theory contains no prescriptions for how many possibilities should be searched and to what depth of consequences. In most real-world situations of any complexity, an attempt at exhaustive and optimal search would be computationally intractable. Of course, we do not imply that there is no consideration of alternatives in decision making, although this happens sequentially and is influenced by recency biases, fatigue and the limited time available. For example, someone searching for a flat in London may initially evaluate options for reasonable rent, convenient travel and spacious layout. None of the early options satisfy, but after weeks of fruitless search, the buyer may well end up accepting a flat inferior to one rejected earlier!

Our proposals also entail that reasoning is by default probabilistic, and that pure deductive inference from assumptions, just taken as true, is exceptional. Given some premises, people will generally construct the most plausible model of the world consistent with those premises and use this as the basis for inference. However, these inferences will be defeasible, as new information may cause people to reject, or at least to doubt, any model they have constructed. A good example arises in the research on suppression of the modus ponens inference, originally demonstrated by Byrne (1989). If participants are given the following premises

If Ruth has an exam tomorrow, she will work late in the library
Ruth has an exam tomorrow

they will usually infer, following the valid inference form modus ponens, the conclusion that Ruth will work late in the library. The hypothetical possibility that people model, given both premises, is as follows:

Ruth has an exam; Ruth works late in the library.

From here the truth of the conclusion follows trivially, as long as the model is assumed to be true or held to be certain. However, people's reasoning being defeasible, they will not maintain their confidence in the original model if later premises tend to undermine it. For example, if the following additional premise follows the above:

If the library stays open, Ruth will work late in the library

fewer participants will draw the modus ponens conclusion. The additional premise causes people to doubt, or feel uncertain about, the original conditional premise, and they will lower any probability they assign to the conclusion (Politzer & Braine, 1991; Stevenson & Over, 1995). Related research has shown that people's willingness to draw conditional inferences is affected by the availability of "disabling conditions", which prevent the consequent of the conditional from holding when its antecedent is true (Cummins et al., 1991; Thompson, 1994; Thompson & Mann, 1995).

These findings suggest that mental models are not simply truth-table cases asserted or denied, as in the standard mental theory of propositional reasoning (Johnson-Laird & Bryne, 1991). Rather, the representation of a hypothetical possibility includes some indicator of its own plausibility or probability. In the above example, the initial model is revised to include the condition that the library stays open, but its probability drops in the process, with a corresponding reduction in confidence in the conclusion drawn. Standard deductive logic does not specify how this should happen, but only what validly follows from assumptions or from premises held to be certain. Moreover, what the participants are doing does not conform to deductive reasoning instructions, which tell them to assume that the premises are true. However, Bayesian probability theory does apply to uncertain premises in both deductive and non-deductive inference, and taking account of uncertain premises makes a great deal of sense from the point of view of personal rationality in the everyday world (Evans & Over, 1996).

HYPOTHETICAL THINKING IN DEDUCTIVE REASONING TASKS

A small field of work on the psychology of deductive reasoning (reviewed by Wason & Johnson-Laird, 1972) had already become massive by the time of the review some 20 years later by Evans et al. (1993), and it has continued to gather pace since then. An intermediate review of the field was provided by Evans (1982), whose opening paragraph (p. 1) is as follows:

> In one sense this book is only about deductive reasoning. In another sense it is about language comprehension, mental imagery, learning processes, memory organisation and the nature of human thought. The first sense is defined by the *paradigms* employed; the second by the psychological *processes* which the paradigms evoke.

This point was emphasised because many researchers thought that employing the deductive reasoning paradigm meant that they were studying deductive reasoning. This idea derived from the logicism which produced the paradigm in the first place, but which has been discarded by most reasoning researchers since Evans (2002). The paradigm itself consists of presenting people with some premises and asking them to generate or evaluate a conclusion as being logically valid, given precisely those premises (and no others) as assumptions. Research conducted since the Evans (1982) review has confirmed that many things other than deductive reasoning are going on in the minds of the participants, and the paradigm has been increasingly used in recent years to demonstrate non-logical pragmatic influences, as in some examples already quoted above.

Since the publication of Johnson-Laird's seminal work on mental models (Johnson-Laird, 1983), there has been a major debate between rival model-based and rule-based theories of deduction (see Evans et al., 1983, Chapter 3, for a review of this controversy). The rule theory proposes that people possess a "mental logic" comprised of some inbuilt inference rules and some general strategies for indirect or suppositional reasoning (see Rips, 1994; Braine & O'Brien, 1998). Hence, reasoning deductively takes the form of a mental proof, similar to a logician's proof, except that not all features of standard logic are included. The model theory, by contrast, assumes that people have a deductive competence based upon understanding a simple semantic principle: a valid conclusion must be true in all situations where the premises are true.

The general theory of mental models (Johnson-Laird, 1983; Johnson-Laird & Byrne, 1991) proposes three stages in deductive reasoning. First, reasoners form a mental model to represent a situation in which all of the premises are true. Next, they formulate a provisional conclusion that is true in this model but semantically informative (not a repetition of a premise, for example). Finally, they validate the conclusion by searching for counterexample cases—models in which the premises hold, but the conclusion does not. If no such counterexample is found, the argument is declared valid.

In reviewing the models versus rules debate, Evans and Over (1996, 1997) came to the view that neither theory was sufficiently well formulated to constitute a falsifiable theory, and that attempts to distinguish the theories empirically may well prove futile. However, viewed as a framework or paradigm, the models approach is more plausible and attractive, as it is capable of being applied to a wide range of phenomena in reasoning, judgment and decision making. The theory can also be mapped into our hypothetical thinking model as a special case where the goal of the thinker is to solve a deductive problem. However, some of the specific proposals in the standard mental model theory appear to conflict with our principles of hypothetical thinking, especially the singularity principle. We examine these issues in detail below.

Syllogistic Reasoning

The mental model theory was first applied to reasoning with classical syllogisms (Johnson-Laird & Bara, 1984). It was argued that although people search for counterexamples when asked to make deductions, limitations in working-memory capacity make this a hazardous and error-prone process. Therefore, Johnson-Laird and Bara (1984) classified syllogisms into three categories, according to whether the premises supported one, two or three mental models of the premises (this system has been queried by later authors, but we let this point pass). It was predicted and observed that more reasoning errors would be associated with problems where more models of the premises would be constructed. Whether this should be interpreted as evidence for a search for counterexamples or a lack of such search is moot. The basic data on syllogisms show that people endorse many fallacies on what Johnson-Laird calls multimodel invalid problems.

Recent evidence from a large-scale study of syllogistic reasoning suggests that people do not ordinarily consider counterexample cases, at least when asked to evaluate whether a particular conclusion follows from some premises (Evans et al., 1999). In this study—uniquely in psychological literature, to our knowledge—participants were given every possible pair of syllogistic premises in combination with every possible conclusion and asked to decide whether the conclusions necessarily followed from the premises. The syllogisms were classified a priori into three types:

- *Necessary.* The conclusion must be true if the premises are true. These are normally termed valid syllogisms.
- *Possible.* The conclusion could be true if the premises are true.
- *Impossible.* The conclusion cannot be true if the premises are true.

After the data had been collected, it was noticed that there appeared to be a bimodal distribution in the endorsement rate of possible syllogisms (normally known as fallacies), some being accepted very frequently and others very infrequently. We termed these "possible strong" and "possible weak". These endorsement rates were confirmed in a replication study also. The key point is that possible strong fallacies are endorsed as often as necessary problems, and possible weak as infrequently as impossible problems. This finding strongly suggests that people consider only a single model of the premises when reasoning. If the model includes the conclusion, the problem is evaluated as valid; otherwise, it is evaluated as invalid, without any search for counterexamples. Possible problems have models of the premises that are both compatible and incompatible with the premises. Hence, it seems that on possible strong problems the first model which comes to mind is the one that supports the conclusion, but on possible weak problems, the model participants think of is the one that excludes the conclusion.

We regard these findings as strong evidence for the hypothetical thinking model. Even when instructed to make necessary conclusions, participants still tend to base their conclusion on consideration of a single model of the premises, in line with the singularity principle. The conclusion that participants do not ordinarily consider counterexamples was also supported in a separate study using different methodology by Newstead, Handley and Buck (1999). However, we have evidence that people can generate alternative models when explicitly instructed to do so (Bucciarelli & Johnson-Laird, 1999), and that strong instructional emphasis on logical necessity can reduce the rate at which they endorse fallacious syllogistic conclusions (Evans et al., 1994). Our interpretation of these findings is that default probabilistic reasoning is so powerful that it persists even in the face of standard deductive reasoning instructions. However, strong instructional emphasis on necessity will cause people not to be satisfied with the first model they consider and to generate others. This is far from the original idea in the model theory that people have deductive competence based upon routine searching for counterexamples, and much better support for the claim of Evans (2000a) that deduction is a *strategy* which participants have to be persuaded to adopt.

Evidence for mental model theory in syllogistic reasoning has also been claimed in interpretation of the "belief-bias" effect (Evans, Barston & Pollard, 1983; Klauer, Musch & Naumer, 2000), in which people endorse more believable than unbelievable conclusions as valid, regardless of the logical validity of the syllogism. We now know that the effect is principally due to the suppression of fallacies that people would otherwise make—possible strong syllogisms—when the conclusion presented for evaluation is unbelievable (Evans, 2000b; Evans, Handley & Harper, 2001). The interpretation of this finding by mental model theorists (for example, Oakhill, Johnson-Laird & Garnham, 1989) is that an unbelievable conclusion stimulates a more effective search for counterexample models. However, the recently formulated selective processing model of belief bias (Evans, 2000b) provides an account more compatible with the hypothetical thinking model. According to this model, the initial process of constructing a model is biased by the conclusion presented. In line with the relevance principle, people try to construct a model which is plausible or probable given their background beliefs. Hence, if the conclusion is believable, they tend to construct a model which supports it, but if it is unbelievable, they tend to construct a model which excludes the conclusion.

On this interpretation, people again construct only a single, plausible mental model. The suppression of fallacies with unbelievable conclusions is due to people finding from the start the alternative model which refutes the conclusion on possible strong problems, rather than searching for counterexample cases. Evidence from a recent study by Evans et al. (2001) supports this argument, because the authors investigated (for the first time in the literature) belief bias on possible weak problems also. Recall that these normally have very low endorsement rates. Possible weak conclusions were endorsed significantly more often when they were *believable*, but with little difference between unbelievable and neutral conclusions. This positive belief-bias effect also suggests that people find the model which is compatible with the belief from the outset. If they thought first of the model they usually find—which refutes the conclusion—they would know the problem to be invalid and have no reason to consider other models.

Propositional Reasoning

The mental model theory of reasoning with propositional connectives such as "if" and "or" (Johnson-Laird & Byrne, 1991; Johnson-Laird, Byrne & Schaeken, 1992) is built around the idea that people can represent multiple mental models corresponding to different lines in a truth table. This appears to conflict with the singularity principle, so we will consider the proposals in a little detail. The connective *if p then q* is typically represented *initially* by a single explicit model:

$[p]$ $\quad q$

$\quad \ldots$

This representation is distinguished from that of a conjunction (*p* and *q*) in two ways. First of all, there is an exhaustivity marker, or "mental footnote", in the form of the square brackets around *p*, indicating that it is exhaustively represented with respect to *q*. That is, *p* must appear in any mode that in which *q* does. Second, there is an implicit model " ... " which indicates that other models are possible but not explicitly represented at this time. Thus, modus ponens, given *p*, conclude *q*, could be made immediately from this initial representation. However, the theory also proposes that the representation can be "fleshed out" to include explicit representation of other truth-table cases compatible with the rule. Modus tollens, given not-*q*, conclude not-*p*, is a valid inference made by about 60 per cent of student participants (see Evans et al., 1993). According to the theory, presentation of not-q leads to an inference only if people succeed in fleshing out the fully explicit model set:

$$p \qquad q$$
$$\neg p \qquad q$$
$$\neg p \qquad \neg q$$

The premise "not-q" eliminates all but the last model, so enabling the conclusion "not-p" to be drawn. One problem with this proposal is that it commits the model theory to an interpretation of the conditional as material implication, with all the paradoxes that entails (Edgington, 1995; Evans, Handley & Over, 2003). However, we also find it implausible that people will consider three models at once. Worse still from the viewpoint of the hypothetical thinking model, Johnson-Laird and Byrne (1991) proposed that some connectives were initially represented by two explicit models. For example, in order to explain differences in inference rates between (logically equivalent) "if then" and "only if" conditionals, they suggested that the statement "p only if q" was represented as

$$[p] \qquad q$$
$$\neg p \qquad \neg q$$
$$\ldots$$

Moreover, in order to account for matching bias observed with the Wason selection task and the conditional truth-table task, they proposed that negated conditionals had added fragments in their initial models. For example, "If p then not-q" might be represented as:

$$[p] \qquad \neg q$$
$$\qquad q$$
$$\ldots$$

The singularity principle proposes that people consider only one mental model at a time, so there is an apparent conflict with these proposals. In fact, we can argue strongly that Johnson-Laird and Byrne's mental model theory of propositional reasoning is mistaken in proposing these multimodel representations. For example, Evans, Clibbens and Rood (1995) argued that the model theory account of matching bias contradicted the account offered by Johnson-Laird of the "negative conclusion bias" associated with negated conditionals in a different reasoning task. Evans and Handley (1999) showed how a coherent account of both phenomena could be made on the assumption that people model only the true-antecedent and true-consequent case in their initial representations. In their argument, both matching bias and negative conclusion bias arise in the process of drawing inferences from these representations.

The multiple model representation of "p only if q" was questioned by Evans (1993), who argued that it was incompatible with experimental literature. This claim has been strongly substantiated in subsequent studies also. People do not offer more cases of $\neg p$ and $\neg q$ as confirming "p only if q" than "if p then q" in the truth-table task (e.g., Evans & Newstead, 1977; Evans et al., 1999). Nor do they include more such cases in representations of imaginary worlds in which the rules are true (Evans, Ellis & Newstead, 1996). In line with the mental model theory of the selection task (Johnson-Laird, 1995), the proposal also predicts that people should select all four cards. Not only do they not do so, but also they do not even select more false-antecedent and false-consequent cards with "only if" than "if then" conditionals (Evans, Legrenzi & Girotto, 1999, Experiment 3).

But how would the hypothetical thinking model account for the moderate competence to perform the modus tollens inference? The argument is as follows. Given the premise "If p then q," people consider the most relevant case: p and q. Given the second premise "not-q", however, this model no longer satisfies and is rejected. There is then an attempt to generate a new model consistent with the added information as well as the original conditional premise. If the model $\neg p \ \neg q$ is found, the modus tollens conclusion is endorsed. This requires an inference based on the fact that any p's must be with q's, and hence in the possible world in which there is no q there is no p either. Johnson-Laird (see Evans & Handley, 1999, p. 744) has suggested this kind of process in order to account for double-negation effects in modus tollens reasoning. However, on close inspection, we note that the mechanism of reasoning here is *not* based on the semantic principle that supposedly underlies deduction in the mental models account. In fact, it is very similar to the kind of suppositional account that mental logicians have proposed for modus tollens inference: suppose p were the case; then q would have to be present, but q is absent, so p cannot be the case. When we recall that the "direct" inferences of the mental logicians are those that can be made from initial representations, and that the "indirect" inferences—requiring suppositions—are those which require fleshing out in the models account, it seems that the distinction between the two proposed mechanisms of inferences may be more apparent than real.

The difficulty here lies in the mental models theory's concept of "fleshing out". Supposedly, deductions in the model theory are based upon the observation that all the models (that the reasoner has thought of) are consistent with the conclusion. However, in cases such as modus tollens, the model that supports the inference can be discovered only by fleshing out where *fleshing out is itself an inferential process*. This problem arises whether one accepts the current argument that people are "fleshing out" an alternative model to the one rejected, or the original claim that people flesh out three explicit models. Let us consider a related problem for the model theory of propositional reasoning: accounting for people's reasoning on the truth-table task. If people are asked to classify the four truth-table cases for a conditional *If p then q* (see Evans et al., 1993), they tend to answer as follows:

p and q	TT	true
p and $\neg q$	TF	false
$\neg p$ and q	FT	irrelevant
$\neg p$ and $\neg q$	FF	irrelevant

To our knowledge, no theory has been put forward by mental model theorists to explain how these responses are produced. It is clear, however, that the true case is the one explicitly represented initially, that the irrelevant cases are the "true possibilities" that might be fleshed out, and the false case (TF) is the one that would never be fleshed out. The problem is this: how do people know the difference between false and irrelevant cases unless they flesh out all true cases? Or if they do flesh them out, why are not "irrelevant" cases regarded as true? Morever, why—if there is a principle of truth—do people find it easy to identify the correct falsifying case as TF? It seems to us that one would have to argue that people can solve the falsification truth-table task because they construct this case from the true case they habitually consider: TT. Now the situation is very similar to the modus tollens problem. The reasoner can certainly discover TF by arguing as follows: every case with a p must have a q, so we cannot have a case with a p and no q. But, again, the reasoning is conducted in order to generate the model from which the conclusion is derived. In other words, people are reasoning *to* the models, not from them.

Suppositional Reasoning

Handley and Evans (2000) have recently presented a detailed study of propositional reasoning involving suppositions. As this study provided findings of direct relevance to the hypothetical thinking model, we will consider it in some detail. The suppositional strategy of interest was based on a logical principle known as *reductio ad absurdum*. According to this principle, if a supposition, or temporary assumption, leads to a contradiction, the negation of that supposition can be drawn as a logical conclusion. For example, Handley and Evans presented the problem in a geological context, where the key premises were the following:

If the sample contains mineral p, it contains mineral q.
The sample contains either mineral p or mineral q but not both.

If we suppose that the sample does contain mineral p, it follows from the first premise that it contains mineral q, but from the second premise that it does not contain mineral q. This is a contradiction, from which it follows that the sample does *not* contain mineral p. *Reductio* reasoning of this kind is postulated as a fundamental principle in reasoning by theorists in the mental logic tradition (Rips, 1994; Braine & O'Brien, 1998). Suppositional reasoning is not, however, an intrinsic principle in the mental models theory. The above problem could be solved in the model theory only by the difficult means of fleshing out fully explicit representations of both rules. In this case, one would discover only one model compatible with both, in which the sample does not contain p, but does contain q.

In their first experiment, Handley and Evans presented several problems of this type, varying also the presence of negated components. Participants were asked to choose between answers in the form of "p", "not-p" or "can't tell". All of the problems proved to be very difficult, with very low rates of correct responses. Moreover, on some problems, a common response was the *opposite* of the correct answer. This happened on problems where the form of the leading proposition in both premises was congruent. The form of the following example is a congruent one:

If p then q
p or q but not both

In this case, only 10 per cent of participants chose not-p—the correct answer—but a staggering 43 per cent endorsed p as the valid conclusion.

An example of an incongruent problem was

If not p then q
p or not q, but not both

Note here that the leading proposition is negative in the conditional and affirmative in the disjunctive. *Reductio* reasoning here would lead to the valid conclusion "p". On incongruent problems, participants were indifferent between the valid conclusion and its opposite. In this case, 20 per cent chose p, and 17 per cent chose not-p. Handley and Evans were led to propose an explanation along the lines of the hypothetical thinking model presented in this chapter. They argued that people might be proposing a single model based on the conditional premise, and, due to superficial reasoning with the disjunctive premise, would accept this model (on congruent problems) as the basis for their answers.

Hence, on the congruent problem, the conditional premise, if p then q, suggests the model

p q

(Our system assumes concrete mental models, so we omit the abstract exhaustivity marker [].) The disjunctive premises, according to Johnson-Laird and Byrne (1991), might be represented initially in a way which does not distinguish inclusive and exclusive readings, and in which only propositions corresponding to true cases are represented:

p

   q

The two lines here indicated, in a rudimentary way, the presence of multiple models. However, we do not need to assume that participants consider such alternative models. Rather, we can propose simply that the participants evaluate the current model, p and q, against the disjunctive premise and are erroneously satisfied by it (failing to notice the import of the "but not both"). Thus, the p and q model is maintained and provides the basis of the inferences drawn. On incongruent problems, the initial model may be abandoned, as superficial processing of the disjunctive premise does not appear to be consistent with the p and q case. In support of this, Handley and Evans observed significantly higher rates of "can't tell" responses on incongruent problems, as well as the disappearance of the opposite answer bias.

To test this hypothesis, Handley and Evans designed a second experiment in which correct answers could in some cases be derived by maintaining an initial model based on congruent lead propositions. These problems combined a biconditional with an inclusively disjunctive premise. An example of a congruent problem is as follows:

If and only if p then q
p or q, or both

Here the *reductio* argument required is as follows: suppose not-p; it follows from the first premises that not-q, but from the second premise that q. Hence, not-p must be false, so conclude p. This sounds very difficult. However, if people simply assume the model p and q, given the conditional, and maintain it, given the disjunctive premise, this masterly non-reasoning will lead them to the correct answer, p. In fact, very high correct solution rates were observed for problems of this type, 80 per cent for the example shown, in stark contrast to Experiment 1. Experiment 2 also used incongruent problems, such as:

If and only if p then q
not-p or not-q, or both

In this case, the supposition of p leads to a contradiction, so that not-p is a valid conclusion. Despite the incongruence here, solution rates were high relative to Experiment 1 (59 per cent for the problem shown), although significantly lower than on congruent problems. Handley and Evans proposed an explanation of the relative ease of these incongruence problems, again couched in terms of the hypothetical thinking model. They suggested that the pragmatics of the biconditional are such that although the initial model that would be considered is p and q, once this is eliminated, a second model would come to mind, namely, not-p and not-q. Thus, in terms of the model (Figure 1.1), the process of reasoning is as follows:

- Examine the biconditional premise: represent the model p and q.
- Examine the disjunctive premise: discard the model p and q.
- Cycle back to the biconditional premise and generate an alternative model: not-p and not-q.
- The new model satisfies with regard to the second premise, so maintain model and read off conclusion, not-p.

Of course, it is intrinsic to the hypothetical thinking model that models may be discarded and replaced if they fail to satisfy. This will only work, however, if there is another relevant, plausible model available. In the case of the biconditional (but not conditional), we think this is plausibly the case, as people are cued to think about one-to-one correspondence—or lack of it.

The process described by Handley and Evans implies that people are making suppositions, but not in the sense assumed by mental logic theorists. Rather than supposing individual propositions, they are supposing whole states of affairs, or mental models. Moreover, suppositions are not temporary assumptions leading only to conclusions if they are contradicted. By contrast, the models supposed form the basis of conclusions drawn, *unless* they are contradicted. One predictive consequence of this difference is that if people are supposing whole models, they should be just as easily able to draw conclusions about both embedded propositions—q as well as p—as about one. In the mental logic approach, any conclusion about the truth of q would involve additional reasoning to that required to derive a conclusion about the truth of p. In their Experiment 3, participants were required to give conclusions about both p and q. Their solution rates were not significantly lower than in the equivalent problems of Experiment 2 where conclusions only about p were required. This finding strongly supports the hypothetical thinking model and poses many problems for the rule theory.

CONCLUSIONS

In this chapter, we have proposed a general model of hypothetical thinking and provided specific evidence for its principles within the literature on reasoning. The proposed mechanism is that people consider one mental model at a time representing some hypothetical state of the world. The model considered is that which is relevant given the context and current goals, and is by default a probable or plausible model. This model is maintained unless it fails to satisfy when explicitly evaluated. An unsatisfying model is discarded and replaced, if possible, by an alternative, relevant possibility. The model which is accepted forms the basis for inferences drawn or judgments or decisions made.

The mechanism proposed is not a deductive or logical one, although it could manifest the limited deductive competence shown in the literature, provided that the evaluation of models is motivated by understanding of the logic of the problems. In practice, however, we argue that people normally reason probabilistically rather than deductively. In support of this, we have shown evidence from the syllogistic reasoning literature that people generally consider only one model of the premises when reasoning, and we have also shown how evidence on the belief-bias effect is compatible with the hypothetical thinking model. In the area of propositional reasoning, we have shown that the proposals of Johnson-Laird and his colleagues that people represent propositional connectives, sometimes with multiple mental models, not only are unnecessary but also lead to inconsistencies and failed empirical predictions. Finally, we have considered at some length a recent study of suppositional reasoning whose findings are highly compatible with the hypothetical thinking model, but are most difficult to account for in terms of either the mental logic theory or the standard mental models approach.

While we have concentrated, in the limited space available, on accounting for findings in the deductive reasoning literature, we believe that the model presented potentially has a much wider application to the study of other kinds of hypothetical thinking, including decision making, hypothesis testing and forecasting.

REFERENCES

Ball, L. J., Evans, J. St. B. T. & Dennis, I. (1994). Cognitive processes in engineering design: a longitudinal study. *Ergonomics*, *37*, 1653–1786.

Ball, L. J., Evans, J. St. B. T., Dennis, I. & Ormerod, T. C. (1997). Problem-solving strategies and expertise in engineering design. *Thinking and Reasoning*, *3*, 247–270.

Braine, M. D. S. & O'Brien, D. P. (eds) (1998). *Mental Logic*. Mahwah, N.J: Erlbaum.

Bruner, J. S., Goodnow, J. J. & Austin, G. A. (1956). *A Study of Thinking*. New York: Wiley.

Bucciarelli, M. & Johnson-Laird, P. N. (1999). Strategies in syllogistic reasoning. *Cognitive Science*, *23*, 247–303.

Byrne, R.M.J. (1989). Suppressing valid inferences with conditionals. *Cognition*, *31*, 61–83.

Chater, N. & Oaksford, M. (1999). The probability heuristics model of syllogistic reasoning. *Cognitive Psychology*, *38*, 191–258.

Cummins, D. D., Lubart, T., Alksnis, O. & Rist, R. (1991). Conditional reasoning and causation. *Memory and Cognition*, *19*, 274–282.

Doherty, M. E., Mynatt, C. R., Tweney, R. D. & Schiavo, M. D. (1979). Pseudodiagnosticity. *Acta Psychologica*, *43*, 11–21.

Edgington, D. (1995). On conditionals. *Mind*, *104*, 235–329.

Evans, J. St. B. T. (1982). *The Psychology of Deductive Reasoning*. London: Routledge.

Evans, J. St. B. T. (1984). Heuristic and analytic processes in reasoning. *British Journal of Psychology*, *75*, 451–468.

Evans, J. St. B. T. (1989). *Bias in Human Reasoning: Causes and Consequences*. Brighton: Erlbaum.

Evans, J. St. B. T. (1993). The mental model theory of conditional reasoning: critical appraisal and revision. *Cognition*, *48*, 1–20.

Evans, J. St. B. T. (2000a). What could and could not be a strategy in reasoning. In W. Schaeken, G. DeVooght & A. D. G. Vandierendonck (eds), *Deductive Reasoning and Strategies* (pp. 1–22). Mahwah, NJ: Erlbaum.

Evans, J. St. B. T. (2000b). Thinking and believing. In J. Garcia-Madruga & N. C. Gonzalez-Labra (eds), *Mental Models in Reasoning* (pp. 41–55). Madrid: UNED.

Evans, J. St. B. T. (2002). Logic and human reasoning: an assessment of the deduction paradigm. *Psychological Bulletin*, *128*, 978–996.

Evans, J. St. B. T. & Handley, S. J. (1999). The role of negation in conditional inference. *Quarterly Journal of Experimental Psychology*, *52A*, 739–769.

Evans, J. St. B. T. & Newstead, S. E. (1977). Language and reasoning: A study of temporal factors. *Cognition*, *5*, 265–283.

Evans, J. St. B. T. & Over, D. E. (1996). *Rationality and Reasoning*. Hove: Psychology Press.

Evans, J. St. B. T. & Over, D. E. (1997). Rationality in reasoning: The case of deductive competence. *Current Psychology of Cognition*, *16*, 3–38.

Evans, J. St. B. T., Barston, J. L. & Pollard, P. (1983). On the conflict between logic and belief in syllogistic reasoning. *Memory and Cognition*, *11*, 295–306.

Evans, J. St. B. T., Clibbens, J. & Rood, B. (1995). Bias in conditional inference: implications for mental models and mental logic. *Quarterly Journal of Experimental Psychology*, *48A*, 644–670.

Evans, J. St. B. T., Ellis, C. E. & Newstead, S. E. (1996). On the mental representation of conditional sentences. *Quarterly Journal of Experimental Psychology*, *49A*, 1086–1114.

Evans, J. St. B. T., Handley, S. H. & Harper, C. (2001). Necessity, possibility and belief: A study of syllogistic reasoning. *Quarterly Journal of Experimental Psychology*, *54A*, 935–958.

Evans, J. St. B. T., Handley, S. H. & Over, D. E. (2003). Conditionals and conditional probability. *Journal of Experimental Psychology: Learning, Memory, and Cognition*, *29*, 321–335.

Evans, J. St. B. T., Legrenzi, P. & Girotto, V. (1999). The influence of linguistic form on reasoning: the case of matching bias. *Quarterly Journal of Experimental Psychology*, *52A*, 185–216.

Evans, J. St. B. T., Newstead, S. E. & Byrne, R. M. J. (1993). *Human Reasoning: The Psychology of Deduction*. Hove and London: Erlbaum.

Evans, J. St. B. T., Over, D. E. & Manktelow, K. I. (1993). Reasoning, decision making and rationality. *Cognition*, *49*, 165–187.

Evans, J. St. B. T., Allen, J. L., Newstead, S. E. & Pollard, P. (1994). Debiasing by instruction: the case of belief bias. *European Journal of Cognitive Psychology*, *6*, 263–285.

Evans, J. St. B. T., Handley, S. J., Harper, C. & Johnson-Laird, P. N. (1999). Reasoning about necessity and possibility: A test of the mental model theory of deduction. *Journal of Experimental Psychology: Learning, Memory and Cognition*, *25*, 1495–1513.

Fodor, J. (1983). *The Modularity of Mind*. Scranton, PA: Crowell.

Gigerenzer, G. & Goldstein, D. G. (1996). Reasoning the fast and frugal way: models of bounded rationality. *Psychological Review*, *103*, 650–669.

Gigerenzer, G. & Todd, P. M. (2000). *Simple Heuristics That Make Us Smart*. New York: Oxford University Press.

Handley, S. J. & Evans, J. St. B. T. (2000). Supposition and representation in human reasoning. *Thinking and Reasoning*, *6*, 273–312.

Johnson-Laird, P. N. (1983). *Mental Models*. Cambridge: Cambridge University Press.

Johnson-Laird, P. N. (1995). Inference and mental models. In S. E. Newstead & J. St. B. T. Evans (eds), *Perspectives in Thinking and Reasoning* (pp. 115–146). Hove: Erlbaum (UK) Taylor & Francis.

Johnson-Laird, P. N. & Bara, B. G. (1984). Syllogistic inference. *Cognition*, *16*, 1–61.

Johnson-Laird, P. N. & Byrne, R. (1991). *Deduction*. Hove & London: Erlbaum.

Johnson-Laird, P. N. & Savary, F. (1999). Illusory inferences: a novel class of erroneous deductions. *Cognition*, *71*, 191–299.

Johnson-Laird, P. N., Byrne, R. M. J. & Schaeken, W. (1992). Propositional reasoning by model. *Psychological Review*, *99*, 418–439.

Klauer, K. C., Musch, J. & Naumer, B. (2000). On belief bias in syllogistic reasoning. *Psychological Review*, *107*, 852–884.

Klayman, J. (1995). Varieties of confirmation bias. *The Psychology of Learning and Motivation*, *32*, 385–417.

Klayman, J. & Ha, Y. W. (1987). Confirmation, disconfirmation and information in hypothesis testing. *Psychological Review*, *94*, 211–228.

Levine, M. (1966). Hypothesis behaviour by humans during discrimination learning. *Journal of Experimental Psychology*, *71*, 331–338.

Manktelow, K. I. (1999). *Reasoning and Thinking*. Hove: Psychology Press.

Manktelow, K. I. & Over, D. E. (1991). Social roles and utilities in reasoning with deontic conditionals. *Cognition*, *39*, 85–105.

Mynatt, C. R., Doherty, M. E. & Dragan, W. (1993). Information relevance, working memory and the consideration of alternatives. *Quarterly Journal of Experimental Psychology*, *46A*, 759–778.

Newell, A. & Simon, H. A. (1972). *Human Problem Solving*. Englewood Cliffs, NJ: Prentice-Hall.

Newstead, S. E. Handley, S. H. & Buck, E. (1999). Falsifying mental models: Testing the predictions of theories of syllogistic reasoning. *Journal of Memory and Language*, *27*, 344–354.

Oakhill, J., Johnson-Laird, P. N. & Garnham, A. (1989). Believability and syllogistic reasoning. *Cognition, 31*, 117–140.

Oaksford, M. & Chater, N. (1998). *Rationality in an Uncertain World.* Hove: Psychology Press.

Politzer, G. & Braine, M. D. S. (1991). Responses to inconsistent premises cannot count as suppression of valid inferences. *Cognition, 38*, 103–108.

Reber, A. S. (1993). *Implicit Learning and Tacit Knowledge.* Oxford: Oxford University Press.

Rips, L. J. (1994). *The Psychology of Proof.* Cambridge, MA: MIT Press.

Simon, H. A. (1982). *Models of Bounded Rationality.* Cambridge, MA: MIT Press.

Sperber, D. & Wilson, D. (1986). *Relevance.* Oxford: Basil Blackwell.

Sperber, D. & Wilson, D. (1995). *Relevance* (2nd edn). Oxford: Basil Blackwell.

Sperber, D., Cara, F. & Girotto, V. (1995). Relevance theory explains the selection task. *Cognition, 57*, 31–95.

Stanovich, K. E. (1999). *Who Is Rational? Studies of Individual Differences in Reasoning.* Mahwah, NJ: Erlbaum.

Stevenson, R. J. & Over, D. E. (1995). Deduction from uncertain premises. *Quarterly Journal of Experimental Psychology, 48A*, 613–643.

Thompson, V. A. (1994). Interpretational factors in conditional reasoning. *Memory and Cognition, 22*, 742–758.

Thompson, V. A. & Mann, J. (1995). Perceived necessity explains the dissociation between logic and meaning: the case of "only if". *Journal of Experimental Psychology: Learning, Memory and Cognition, 21*, 1554–1567.

Wason, P. C. (1966). Reasoning. In B. M. Foss (ed.), *New Horizons in Psychology I* (pp. 106–137). Harmondsworth: Penguin.

Wason, P. C. & Brooks, P. G. (1979). THOG: the anatomy of a problem. *Psychological Research, 41*, 79–90.

Wason, P. C. & Johnson-Laird, P. N. (1972). *Psychology of Reasoning: Structure and Content.* London: Batsford.

CHAPTER 2

Individual Differences in the Development of Reasoning Strategies

Maxwell J. Roberts
University of Essex, UK
and
Elizabeth J. Newton
University College London, UK

INTRODUCTION

This chapter discusses how people discover and select among reasoning strategies, and why individuals differ. Although this is a minority topic, there are signs that it is currently gaining in importance. However, there have been numerous false starts in this field in the past. Interesting results (e.g., Sternberg, 1977; MacLeod, Hunt & Mathews, 1978; Lohman & Kyllonen, 1983; Cooper & Mumaw, 1985) generate a flurry of activity, along with books and conference symposia. Then, instead of the topic moving into the mainstream, enthusiasm fades away, researchers move to other fields and findings cease to be cited. The reasons for this are not clear, but probably reflect the additional work necessary for good individual differences research, coupled with the lack of perceived glamour in investigating strategies, compared with those researchers seeking to identify the fundamental cornerstones of reasoning. Irrespective of the exact reasons for its fading away, the next generation of researchers is faced with the daunting task of recreating the momentum of the past. With the knowledge that the current interest in reasoning strategies could have a similar fate awaiting it, we would like to begin by outlining some general conclusions implicated by research to date:

(1) People discover new methods and principles as a result of their successes. Failure prevents such discovery.
(2) Creativity is hindered if the basics of a task have not been mastered.
(3) Undirected "learning by discovery" is a poor educational strategy when foisted on the less able.

Thinking: Psychological Perspectives on Reasoning, Judgment and Decision Making. Edited by David Hardman and Laura Macchi.
© 2003 John Wiley & Sons, Ltd.

(4) But giving people external aids to assist their performance simultaneously inhibits discoveries.

One purpose of this chapter is to try to show that these conclusions follow naturally from current findings in the field, and we will return to them again at the end. As we hope the reader will recognise, they have profound implications for the ways in which people are educated, and so the need for a more widespread acceptance of the importance of this domain of research cannot be overemphasised.

BACKGROUND

How do people make inferences? When researchers attempt to answer this question, the hypotheses entertained by them depend crucially on their assumptions about the nature of higher cognitive processes. Traditionally, it has been assumed that there exists a monolithic *fundamental reasoning mechanism*, a device called into play whenever triggered by appropriate material (e.g., Johnson-Laird & Byrne, 1991; Rips, 1994). The task of the researcher is therefore simply to identify its cognitive processes, and specify them via a *universal reasoning theory*. Unfortunately, this is complicated by the fact that people are adept at applying varied methods, even for solving simple deduction problems. It is therefore necessary to determine whether the observed processes are genuinely fundamental, or have overlaid and obscured those that are more basic. Elsewhere, Roberts (1993) has argued that there are insurmountable difficulties associated with this, and hence the existence of individual differences in the use of reasoning strategies derails the search for the fundamental reasoning mechanism. Space considerations rule out repeating the arguments here, but their logical implication is that in the domain of human reasoning, no cognitive processes can be identifiable as fundamental. Instead, people possess a range of strategies that can be applied to various tasks. To date, this position has not been refuted in print (e.g., Roberts, 2000a).

Whether or not the extreme position above is accepted, the existence of individual differences in people's reasoning strategies cannot be denied, and their study is again gaining importance in its own right (e.g., Schaeken et al., 2000). It seems scarcely possible that we could ever claim to have a full understanding of human cognition without taking them into account. Of course, the study of individual differences in cognition and, in particular, in strategy usage, is not new. However, until recently, studies have tended to be isolated, and there has been little attempt to integrate the findings across domains (for exceptions, see Crowley, Shrager & Siegler, 1997; Kuhn & Pearsall, 1998). One consequence of this is that there are still disagreements to be resolved, even for such basics as the definition of the word *strategy*.

Definitions of "Strategy"

In general, there are two categories of definition for the word "strategy". *Broad definitions* assert that any self-contained set of goal-directed procedures constitutes a strategy, as long as these are optional, so that their utilisation by any given person is not guaranteed. Hence, Siegler & Jenkins (1989) suggest that a strategy is "any procedure that is non-obligatory and goal directed" (p. 11). In a similar vein, Roberts (1993) defines a reasoning strategy as "a set of cognitive processes which have been shown to be used for solving certain types of deductive reasoning tasks, but for which there is not sufficient evidence to assert that these processes themselves constitute all or part of the fundamental reasoning mechanism" (p. 576). This follows from his argument that optional processes cannot be asserted to be fundamental in the domain of deduction. *Narrow definitions* additionally assert that only self-contained sets of procedures that are *not* fundamental processes can be said to be strategies. Generally, a conscious element to their selection and/or execution is also specified, closely linking this category to the literature on metacognition (e.g., Brown, 1987; Schoenfeld, 1987). Other optional extras may also be added to the definition. For example, the principle that a strategy should require more effort to implement than a non-strategy. Hence, Bjorklund, Muir-Broaddus and Schneider (1990) define a strategy as an "effortful, deliberately implemented, goal directed process that is potentially available to consciousness" (p. 119). Alternatively, Evans (2000) defines a strategy as "thought processes that are elaborated in time, systematic, goal-directed, and under explicit conscious control" (p. 2).

What are the consequences of these alternative definitional categories? At first sight, they appear simply to invoke subtle differences in the use of language. Hence, a researcher using a broad definition might investigate *which* strategies are used in particular circumstances, but, with a narrow definition, might investigate *whether* strategies are used in particular circumstances. However, narrow definitions have many difficulties without conferring any particular benefits. They carry the implicit assumption that it is easy to distinguish between fundamental and non-fundamental processes, and this may well not be the case in some domains (Roberts, 1993, 2000a). More seriously, for a set of processes to constitute a strategy, the requirement of a conscious component runs the risk of creating a domain with movable boundaries. In other words, whether or not a set of processes constitutes a strategy can depend upon the latest piece of research and the extent to which its findings are accepted. For example, Reder and Schunn (1996) argue that much of what is considered to be metacognitive activity takes place without conscious awareness, while Siegler and Stern (1998) suggest that the discovery and implementation of a new strategy may take place before a person has any awareness of this. Defining a concept according to its phenomenological status therefore runs the risk of the field as a whole becoming mired, with people expending effort into debating what could and could not be a strategy in a given domain, rather than trying to understand why people use different strategies. In addition, if there are general principles underlying why people differ in the processes that they apply, irrespective of their phenomenological status, then the debate is irrelevant, adds nothing to our understanding, and creates an unnatural and pointless divide. This will apply equally to any other arbitrary extras when defining strategy.

For the current chapter, a broad definition will be assumed, minimally specifying a strategy as any set of self-contained cognitive processes that can be dispensed with in favour of alternatives. Any narrowing of the definition runs the risk of detracting from what we consider be the major issue: How, and why do people differ? However, the use of broad definitions has also been criticised, both for going against common-sense notions, and for their redundancy (e.g., Bisanz & LeFevre, 1990; Bjorklund & Harnishfeger, 1990), and so it is necessary to question whether these are serious problems. Taking the common-sense issue first, dictionary definitions of "strategy" tend to emphasise planning rather than procedure (in line with its military origins). However, such definitions tend to be diffuse and multifaceted, and are seldom adequate when set in the context of the more rigorous use of language entailed by scientific study. Furthermore, they were not devised with the intention of informing category boundaries in psychology; therefore, insisting on rigid dictionary compatibility when identifying domains of research is unlikely to offer any benefits. Considering the redundancy issue, if we are going to use a broad definition of strategy, then, at first sight, it could be argued that we should retitle this chapter "Individual Differences in the Development of Reasoning Procedures". However, it should be noted that even with a broad definition, there are still important differences between "strategy" and "procedure/process". The broad definition still entails that a strategic set of procedures is optional, and that it is self-contained. Furthermore, use of the term in this way emphasises a position of neutrality, at the very least, concerning whether fundamental processes exist, and their exact nature.

Types of Reasoning Strategy

Underlying this chapter is the issue of how and why people differ in their reasoning strategies. In order to simplify matters, it will be helpful first to outline a taxonomy. This is based upon Roberts (2000a), but with an additional category which may assist in the interpretation of some findings. The basis for this taxonomy is that strategies differ in (i) how information is represented and manipulated, (ii) how widely they may be applied, and (iii) how accurate they are likely to be under ideal conditions (that is, ignoring constraints such as working memory requirements). The first two types of strategy to be described are both *generally* applicable: They have been proposed for a wide range of reasoning tasks, and will give an accurate answer if executed correctly. In addition, they are *domain-free*: The processes operate identically on represented information irrespective of content and context. However, their versatility goes hand in hand with a tendency for inefficiency: They can be demanding and error-prone to execute in many situations.

For *spatial strategies*, information is represented in arrays akin to mental diagrams, such that the configural information on the representation corresponds to the state of the affairs in the world. Relationships between objects can be inferred from their relative positions on the representation. For example, the heights of a set of objects might be represented as a linear array, with the tallest entity at the top. It is then possible to infer which is tallest and shortest even if this information has not been given explicitly. The mental models theory of Johnson-Laird and Byrne (e.g., 1991) has a spatial strategy as its basis. For *verbal* strategies, information is represented in the form of verbal or abstract propositions, and the application of various content/context-free syntactic rules enables new conclusions to be drawn from the represented information. For example, it is often proposed that, given the knowledge *if A is true, then B will happen*, and given that *A is true*, a modus ponens rule will automatically activate, producing the conclusion that *B has happened*. These rules are taken to form a closed system which is generally applicable, domain-free, and cannot easily be modified with practice. Deduction-rule theories of reasoning (e.g., Rips, 1994; Braine & O'Brien, 1997) come into this category. Although proponents of verbal and spatial strategies sometimes assert that these categories are mutually exclusive, data suggest that for many tasks, users of either can be identified, and that individuals can switch between the two.

In addition to the generally applicable strategies above, various *narrowly applicable* strategies have also been identified. Their use potentially confers a number of advantages.

In particular, this can reduce the amount of effort necessary for problem solving, either improving performance, or not worsening it to any significant degree. For example, if knowledge can be applied in order to perform a task, this can offer a great saving in resources, either reducing the complexity of, or bypassing, generally applicable processes altogether. However, this can make a person susceptible to belief bias (e.g., Evans, 1989; Roberts & Sykes, 2003). It has also been proposed that context-dependent rules may be important components of performance, for example, the pragmatic reasoning schemas advocated by Holyoak & Cheng, 1995. Neither of these domain-specific procedures will be discussed further in this chapter. Where appropriate context permits these methods, it is not clear that reliable individual differences in their adoption can be identified (e.g., Evans, Barston and Pollard, 1983). Of more interest for the current discussion are two categories of narrowly applicable strategy which can potentially reduce task demands, but which are usually not universally adopted, and are hence associated with individual differences in strategy usage.

For some reasoning tasks, sometimes only if items are appropriately formatted, certain people utilise *task-specific short-cut* strategies which can both reduce effort and result in massive gains in performance. For example, consider the following categorical syllogism:

Some of the artists are not beekeepers.
Some of the chefs are beekeepers.
Therefore, some of the chefs are not artists. TRUE or FALSE.

However difficult this problem may appear, it is trivially easy if the *two-somes* rule is applied: If the quantifier *some* appears in each of the first two premises, a syllogism never has a valid conclusion (see Galotti, Baron & Sabini, 1986). As another example, consider the following compass-point directions task problem: Where would a person end up, relative to the starting point, after taking one step north, one step east, one step north, one step east, one step south, one step west and one step west and one step west? The modal strategy is to attempt to trace the path, mentally if no external means of representation are available (a spatial strategy). A generally faster, more accurate and less stressful approach is to use cancellation: Opposite directions cancel, and those that remain constitute the correct answer (see Roberts, Gilmore & Wood, 1997; Newton & Roberts, 2000). The action of task-specific short-cut strategies may often resemble simple rules, and it is important to emphasise that they are conceptually distinct from verbal strategies. These rules are only narrowly applicable, are not innate features of cognition and may be learned rapidly.

Roberts (2000a) included a variety of effort-reducing algorithms and heuristics under the heading of *task-specific short-cut strategy*, but here we will make a distinction between algorithms—which are guaranteed to yield the correct answer—and heuristics—which will not necessarily do so. Algorithmic procedures will continue to be named "task-specific short cuts", while heuristic procedures will be termed "coping strategies". Coping strategies are applied by people who are unable or unwilling to invoke a generally applicable strategy for a task, usually because this is too demanding, and are unable to identify task-specific short cuts, but do not wish to guess. Sometimes this may be achieved by pruning the number of processing steps for a generally applicable strategy. For example, a problem describing the relative locations of objects might be ambiguous: two or more permutations of layouts may be possible. Even if the task requires the representation of all layouts in order to obtain a correct answer, considering only one of these will reduce the memory load (e.g., Roberts, 2000b). Alternatively, task-specific coping strategies may be applied, the best-known of which is the atmosphere strategy for solving categorical syllogisms (e.g., Gilhooly et al., 1993). Here, if either premise contains a negation, a negation will be reported for the conclusion, and if either premise contains the word *some*, the conclusion will likewise contain *some*. For a traditional multiple-choice task with five answer options (as used by Dickstein, 1978), the chance score is 20 per cent, but the atmosphere strategy can yield a modest gain over this (23 per cent correct). Alternatively, returning to the compass-point directions task, subjects very occasionally report using a "last-two" strategy, in which the last two directions of a problem are reported as the answer, ignoring all previous ones. With a chance score at this task of approximately 3 per cent, this strategy can also offer a benefit over guessing: typically 10–15 per cent correct depending on the nature of the trials used.

Whether the distinction between task-specific short-cuts and coping strategies will prove useful remains to be seen. One potential problem is that the differences between the two may not be entirely clear-cut. For example, if a task-specific short-cut is applied beyond its range of applicability, then, technically, it becomes a coping strategy. For example, consider adding redundant premises to a categorical syllogism:

Some of the artists are not beekeepers.
Some of the beekeepers are not artists.
All of the beekeepers are chefs.
All of the chefs are beekeepers.
Therefore, some of the chefs are not artists. TRUE or FALSE.

Applying the two-*somes* rule (or the similar two-negatives rule) here is inappropriate; the given answer is correct. Alternatively, in the right circumstances, coping strategies will give correct answers. It is easy to devise sets of compass-point directions task trials in which the "last-two" strategy always gives the correct answer. Nonetheless, we believe that the distinction will be useful for at least two reasons which will be discussed later: (i) people who devise task-specific short cuts are likely to differ in their ability from people who devise coping strategies; (ii) people who adopt coping strategies may prevent themselves from discovering task-specific short-cuts.

After outlining a taxonomy of strategies for reasoning tasks, the next step is to see the extent to which there are individual differences in their adoption within this domain. Roberts (2000a) provides a full discussion of this, and Table 2.1 provides a summary here, but with the addition of coping strategies. For a fuller description of the tasks themselves, the reader should also consult Evans, Newstead and Byrne (1993). Clearly, there are considerable differences both within and between tasks, and these must be explained if a full understanding of *all* reasoning phenomena is to be achieved. To date, the majority of research into individual differences in reasoning strategies has been concerned with identifying differences rather than explaining them. As long as it is accepted that the majority of findings are sound, and that people's strategies can be reliably identified in a reasonable number of domains, work now needs to address how and why these individual differences arise, and how they are influenced by task variables. More specifically, we can ask such questions as the following:

Why do some people use verbal and others use spatial strategies to make inferences?
Why do only some people use generally applicable strategies, while others use narrowly applicable strategies?

Table 2.1   Strategies identified for various deduction tasks

	Example references	Verbal	Spatial	Mixed	TSSC	Coping
Sentence-picture verification	MacLeod, Hunt & Mathews (1978); Coney (1988)	N	✓	✓	?	
Categorical syllogisms	Gilhooly et al. (1993); Ford (1995)	✓	✓		✓	✓
Linear syllogisms	Quinton & Fellows (1975); Wood (1978); Sternberg & Weil (1980)	✓	✓	N	✓	
2D relational inference	Roberts (2000b)	?	N			?
Conditional reasoning	Dieussaert et al. (1999)			???		
Truth-teller problems	Schroyens, Schaeken & d'Ydewalle (1996); Byrne & Handley (1997)			???		
Family relationship	Wood & Shotter (1973); Wood (1978)		N		✓	
Compass-point directions	Roberts, Gilmore & Wood (1997); Newton & Roberts (2000)		N		✓	?

The example references are just a selection from the many pieces of work investigating individual differences in reasoning strategies. Others are mentioned in the text. Spatial and verbal strategies may both be considered to be *generally applicable*. Mixed strategies are a combination of verbal and spatial processes. Task-specific short-cuts (TSSC) and coping strategies may both be considered to be *narrowly applicable*. The symbols denote the following:
✓   Researchers have claimed that users of this type of strategy have been identified for a task.
N   This appears to be the natural strategy for a task: the majority of people use it or are aware of its existence, and that it will give the correct answer if executed correctly.
?   This type of strategy may be used for a task, but further evidence is required.
???   Further research is required before we can be certain that people in different strategy categories can be identified.

INDIVIDUAL DIFFERENCES IN THE USE OF REASONING STRATEGIES

We would like to begin this section by suggesting that in order to answer fully questions concerning why people use different strategies, it is necessary to take a developmental perspective. In other words, we need to understand how and why children's and adults' use of strategies changes with experience—whether in the course of a few seconds, or over many weeks. In order to construct this review, we will be drawing freely on both adult and child literature. There is little evidence to suggest that strategy development procedures differ with age (e.g., Kuhn, 1995; Siegler & Lemaire, 1997).

The phrase, "strategy development", subsumes several different, potentially separable phenomena. To begin with, we need to identify mechanisms of *strategy selection*: how do people choose between different options, and how does experience with the use of a strategy affect the likelihood that it will be used in the future? However, an understanding of this by itself is not enough: People can only select between strategies which are available to them (Roberts, Gilmore & Wood, 1997). A full account of strategy availability will almost certainly entail an understanding of *strategy discovery*: how do people identify new methods? In some circumstances, strategy availability may depend upon the correct execution of an evaluation procedure in order to determine whether a newly discovered strategy is valid. If this is not carried out with precision, the outcome could be an incorrect rejection of a task-specific short cut, so that a strategy is present in the repertoire, but nonetheless is not available. Alternatively, evaluation errors could result in a person's applying a coping strategy in the mistaken belief that it is highly accurate. In the past, most research has focused on the different aspects of strategy development in isolation from each other, with strategy selection receiving the most attention. Only occasionally will an ambitious theory tackle more than one aspect (e.g., Crowley, Shrager & Siegler, 1997).

Strategy Selection

The main point of difference for theories of strategy selection concerns the extent to which these processes are sensitive to experience, current task demands and performance. At one extreme are cognitive style accounts (e.g., Sternberg, 1997). Here, choice of strategy is determined by an individual tendency, or preference, to represent and/or process information in a particular way. For example, with the visualiser-verbaliser distinction, some people will have a tendency to form spatial representations of information, while others will tend to form verbal representations (e.g., Riding, Glass & Douglas, 1993).

Stylistic accounts of strategy selection have widespread intuitive appeal, but Roberts and Newton (2001) identify a number of problems with this approach. In particular, the phrase "stylistic preference" has connotations of both choice and some degree of flexibility. However, one apparent demonstration of cognitive styles in action is where people use a suboptimal strategy which is apparently in line with their style, as when people persist with a particular learning strategy even though a task has been structured in order to make it particularly difficult to apply (e.g., Scott, 1993). If people genuinely have a choice of strategies in such circumstances, their selections have effectively sabotaged their performance. This is a curious state of affairs that demands a better explanation than a mere preference to think in a certain way. Alternatively, if a suboptimal strategy is used because no others are available, this lack of choice indicates that no strategy selection procedure has taken place at all, let alone one that is stylistically based. Where this occurs, we need to understand why people differ in their strategy repertoires. Even where people do appear to show stylistic preferences, these can usually be subsumed under other explanations. For example, where strategy usage is directly linked to levels of ability—as when people with high spatial ability reason spatially while people with low spatial ability reason verbally—this can simply be seen as an adaptive choice based upon a cost-benefit analysis (e.g., MacLeod, Hunt & Mathews, 1978).

Overall, Roberts and Newton (2001) conclude that cognitive style accounts have little to offer in the way of predictive or explanatory power. At best, all they can achieve are redescriptions, rather than explanations, of strategy selection phenomena under certain circumstances. Any attempt to offer a general account can be easily defeated by showing circumstances where strategy selections are counterintuitive with respect to notional style; for example, where people with high spatial ability tend to avoid the use of spatial strategies (e.g., Cooper & Mumaw, 1985; Roberts, Gilmore & Wood, 1997).

More sophisticated theories of strategy selection take account of the characteristics of the task itself, together with a person's current performance, ability and experience, and perhaps also desired level of precision (for example, via speed–accuracy trade-offs). The most straightforward models posit some sort of cost-benefit analysis. Where two or more strategies are available for performing a task, the selected strategy will be the one that gives optimum performance, taking into account the individual qualities of the person (e.g., Christensen-Szalanski, 1978). One example of research compatible with this utilised the sentence-picture verification task (MacLeod, Hunt & Mathews, 1978). Here, verbal and spatial strategies did not differ particularly in their effectiveness, and people with high spatial ability tended to use the spatial strategy while people with low spatial ability tended to use the verbal strategy.

Although straightforward in their predictions, these simple accounts of strategy selection leave a lot of questions unanswered. For example, the precise specification of how costs and benefits are estimated tends to be fuzzy, and there is little evidence to suggest that people cycle through various options systematically before settling on a final choice. In addition, the selection of non-optimal strategies, particularly where better alternatives are available, requires a more sophisticated theory for an explanation. One example discussed by Siegler (1996, p. 153) was children being successfully taught a rehearsal strategy which improved their memory. However, very few children continued to use this strategy when given the option not to. Another example is the finding that, although, with practice, more sophisticated and effective strategies tend to become more prevalent, newly discovered strategies are rarely implemented abruptly, unless prompted by external events. Instead, many tasks are characterised by high trial-by-trial variability, and an ebb and flow of strategies, giving wavelike patterns of adoption. This is particularly apparent in the domain of children's arithmetic: Siegler and Jenkins (1989) found only sporadic use, after discovery, of the effective "min-strategy" for addition. For this, a sum is calculated by counting up from the larger addend. For example, 2 and 5 are added together by starting from 5 and counting two upwards: "5, 6, 7". Its use among children who discovered it became widespread only after impasse problems—in which one addend was too great to represent on fingers—had been presented (for example, 24 +2).

Siegler's Adaptive Strategy Choice Model (ASCM) for selecting between arithmetic strategies (e.g., 1996) is one example of a mechanism that can account for these phenomena. It is entirely associative and so dispenses with the need for a metacognitive, let alone conscious, decision-making mechanism. Effectively, a strategy selection decision is made for every trial, based upon previous experience with the task:

> Each time a strategy is used to solve a problem, the experience yields information regarding the strategy, the problem and their interaction. This information is preserved in a database on each strategy's speed and accuracy for solving problems in general, problems with particular features, and specific problems. (p. 235)

Hence, the selection of a strategy is based upon the strength with which it can be associated with success with a particular problem in relation to its competitors. This model is able to account for why new strategies—whether discovered or taught—are often generalised slowly, even when superior to their competitors. With little experience, there can be little associated success, so that a well-practised, reasonably successful strategy may, in the short term, be preferred to a little-practised strategy that could boost success.

Reder and Schunn (1996) likewise suggest that strategy selection depends upon a wholly associative mechanism. They focus on the role of intrinsic variables in invoking strategies (such as problem features) and extrinsic variables (such as knowledge about past success of strategies, and wording of instructions). For example, their studies into metamemory have investigated the circumstances under which people will either attempt to retrieve the answers to problems, or attempt to compute answers. Results suggest that familiarity with the question elements influences strategy selection, rather than familiarity with actual problems and the answers previously generated from them. They therefore suggested that information about the past success of particular strategies need not be necessary for strategy selection.

In general, the current models of strategy selection are sophisticated and successful, although there are some differences concerning precisely which variables are important. One issue likely to recur for the foreseeable future is that of whether the control processes associated with strategy selection entail a metacognitive component, and whether this is conscious. Recently, one or even both have been denied. For example, Reder and Schunn (1996) suggest that strategy selection processes are implicit not just for metamemory tasks: "Much of the processing that is called metacognitive typically operates at an implicit level; that is, without conscious awareness" (p. 73), and the models described above reflect this. However, the use of the word "much" here is vague, and open to subjective interpretation. A more powerful theory would be one that specified when strategy selection processes entail metacognition, and when this, in turn, entails conscious control. Hence, Kuhn and Pearsall (1998) suggest that strategy selection can have a substantial metacognitive component, and they make the general observation that the properties of theories may be closely linked to the tasks investigated: the recall of information would be expected to be a rapid, well-practised, relatively automated process, with little time for planning and reflection. In contrast, Kuhn and colleagues investigated "scientific" discovery tasks, which subjects performed over a period of several weeks, giving much more scope for metacognition, reflection and conscious control. In addition, Crowley, Shrager and Siegler (1997) suggest that without metacognition, models of strategy development can account for *either* strategy selection *or* discovery. In order to account for both, it is necessary to include a metacognitive component that can monitor and overrule the action of the associative component. This has been successfully modelled by Shrager and Siegler's (1998) Strategy Choice and Discovery Simulation (SCADS).

Another issue to consider is whether high trial-by-trial strategy variability is a general feature of cognition, or whether this is confined to tasks with certain characteristics. This is important because it reflects on how we should view strategy transitions. If trial-by-trial variability is low, strategy change becomes a rarer and more mysterious event. Many researchers take the high-variability view (e.g., Kuhn et al., 1995, for a "scientific" discovery task; Lohman & Kyllonen, 1983, for spatial reasoning; Siegler & Jenkins, 1989, for arithmetic), although the data are not all one way, and Newton and Roberts (2000) point out that for the compass-point directions task, trial-by-trial strategy variability appears to be low, and that cancellation, once discovered, propagates rapidly (see also Alibali, 1999). Newton and Roberts suggest that this is because of the relatively great advantage of cancellation compared with the spatial strategy. In other words, trial-by-trial variability may be a function of the relative benefits of available strategies, and possibly a person's knowledge of this (which can be modified by feedback and practice, as in the widespread generalisation of the min-strategy after the presentation of impasse trials). However, another possibility is that the methodology of identifying subjects' strategies is important. The highest trial-by-trial variability is typically observed during microgenetic studies. These involve the intensive observation of individuals over an extended period of time. Subjects report strategy usage on a trial-by-trial basis, and errors/response times are used as corroboration (e.g., Siegler & Crowley, 1991; Kuhn, 1995). While this reveals high trial-by-trial variability, there is the risk that requiring subjects to report strategy usage in this way alerts them to the point of interest of the study, thus encouraging more experimentation than would normally be the case. In addition, where subjects externalise thinking for each trial via the use of pencil and paper, this has been shown to disrupt strategy discovery (Roberts, Gilmore & Wood, 1997; Newton & Roberts, 2000).

Strategy Availability

It is difficult to gain a full understanding of strategy selection without knowing the likely strategies that a person will choose between on commencement of a task, and how new strategies may be added while performing it. "Strategy availability" encompasses several different aspects. A person's strategy repertoire is the sum total of the strategies currently possessed, suitable for applying to the current task. These may be added to with experience at a task as a result of strategy discovery and evaluation. However, not all strategies in the repertoire may be available. If a person considers a strategy to be inappropriate for a given task, not because it is too difficult to apply, but because it is believed that it will generate incorrect answers for an unacceptably high proportion of trials, then that strategy will not be available for use unless further events cause a modification of this belief.

On commencement of a task, we can make some reasonable guesses about the sorts of strategies that will be present in a strategy repertoire, and these must exist as a result of relevant past experience with similar or related tasks. Unfortunately, the current authors are not aware of any reliable, non-invasive, diagnostic procedures for determining precisely an individual's strategy repertoire prior to commencement of a task for any domain. The difficulty that this presents can be illustrated by considering the compass-point directions task again. Suppose that a person solves several trials, perhaps taking 15 seconds per problem. Without warning, a very long trial occurs, perhaps over 30 seconds long, then a short trial, less than 10 seconds, then another very long trial, and after that every single trial takes less than 10 seconds, along with a considerable improvement in accuracy. A retrospective report will invariably indicate that a person first started by using the spatial strategy, and then suddenly changed to cancellation. An indication of the point at which the transition took place will correspond closely with the very long trials. The question is, what exactly happened at this point, and why?

An extreme knowledge-based account of strategy usage would assert that at the transition point above, the person suddenly utilised a strategy that had been present in the repertoire all along. This position is primarily derived from studies of expertise (e.g., Glaser, 1984; Ericsson & Lehmann, 1996). These typically confirm the entirely reasonable notion that, for a particular recognised domain of expertise (such as chess, physics or computer programming), the experts will possess more domain-relevant knowledge than the novices. More controversial is to infer from this that, for *any* given task (such as categorical syllogisms, the compass-point directions task or intelligence tests), those with superior performance—the notional experts—must have had more past experience relevant to the task, *and this is the only reason for the differences* (e.g., Schiano et al., 1989; Simon, 1990). For example, "problem solving, comprehension, and learning are based upon knowledge . . . and people continually try to understand and think about the new in terms of what they already know" (Glaser, 1984, p. 100), and "the study of individual differences is closely tied to the study of learning and transfer of training" (Simon, 1990, p. 15). Hence, in general terms relevant to our discussion, the strategy repertoire of an individual is determined only by knowledge, acquired as a result of previously encountering either an identical task or related tasks. In the above example, one possible reason for the delay in the implementation of cancellation for the directions task is that the relevant analogous procedure, perhaps acquired when learning a superficially dissimilar task, did not transfer easily. However, we should note that without converging evidence, this position is tautological. Why did the person use cancellation? Because he or she possessed the relevant knowledge. How do we know that the person possessed the relevant knowledge? Because he or she used cancellation.

Although a person who has a larger strategy repertoire due to past experience will obviously be more likely to use effective strategies than other people, it is straightforward to show that not all strategy usage phenomena can be explained by knowledge differences. In the compass-point directions task, the majority of people who use cancellation do so from the first trial. It is quite possible that these subjects arrive at the task without explicit knowledge of cancellation—discovering this strategy quickly during practice—but a knowledge-based explanation would assert that these people already had cancellation present in their strategy repertoires. It is highly unlikely that they had encountered this task before, and so any relevant knowledge must have been transferred from experience elsewhere. However, Newton and Roberts (2000) gave subjects a task that involved the cancellation of nonsense words. Although they were able to learn this relatively easily and perform well at it, there was absolutely no evidence of transfer of the cancellation procedure from this to the directly analogous compass-point directions task administered immediately afterwards. Clearly, a transfer explanation of strategy usage should be applied only with care and with evidence. In addition, Roberts, Gilmore and Wood (1997) found that giving subjects the option to use pencil and paper suppressed the use of cancellation, *with the result that they performed worse than had cancellation been adopted*. One possible explanation of this is that the reduced task demands suppress the *knowledge* of cancellation. However, it is also possible that they suppress the *discovery* of cancellation. Newton and Roberts (2000) went on to show that if subjects were required to practise using cancellation, the subsequent offer of pencil and paper was not taken up, and cancellation was universally adopted. Together, these findings suggest that pencil and paper did not suppress knowledge, and so must have suppressed discovery instead.

Given that new strategies can be discovered while performing a task, we need to understand how this occurs and why individuals differ. Hence, we need to know what a person can learn about a task from the way in which information is encoded, represented and manipulated, and how this may be affected by the level of performance. Assuming that the discovery of new methods is a good thing, we need to be able to identify the situations in which this is most likely to be triggered, so that in the classroom the frequency of these circumstances can be increased. Broadly, there are two categories of theory of how problem-solving events lead to strategy discovery: failure-based and success-based. An example of a failure-based theory is that of VanLehn (1988), in which it is suggested that *all* learning, including strategy discovery, takes place as a result of the failure of a current strategy to generate a satisfactory answer when solving a problem, that is, an impasse (see also Newell, 1990). When encountering an impasse, a problem solver focuses on overcoming it, and the outcome is incorporated into the knowledge base. However, evidence for the sole importance of this type of event for strategy discovery is mixed (e.g., VanLehn, 1991) and does not withstand microgenetic analysis. For example, when investigating children's addition strategies, Siegler and Jenkins (1989) found that impasse problems could trigger the adoption of the min-strategy, but *only* if this had been discovered on previous trials. No trace of impasse-related behaviour (such as many errors) could be identified just before the point where the min-strategy was *really* discovered.

Intuitively, a failure-based approach to learning must be flawed. Such a theory should predict that the best performers would experience few failures and learn relatively slowly, while the worst performers would experience many failures and catch up. The opposite of this can be observed in any classroom (Roberts & Newton, 2001). Likewise, Roberts, Gilmore and Wood (1997) suggest that people who are most likely to experience impasses are those who are least likely to be able to resolve them.

Success-driven strategy discovery has been implicated by numerous past studies. For example, Wood (1978) found that the people who discovered task-specific short-cuts for linear syllogisms were those who were initially best at solving them by spatial strategies, while Galotti, Baron and Sabini (1986) found that good reasoners at categorical syllogisms were more likely to discover task-specific short-cuts—such as the two-*somes* rule—than bad reasoners. Roberts, Gilmore and Wood (1997) found that people with high spatial ability were more likely to use the cancellation strategy for the compass-point directions task, and were also better able to reason by the use of a spatial strategy when given problems that inhibited the use of cancellation. Finally, Siegler (e.g., 1996) has found that, in general, successful execution of arithmetic strategies is more likely to lead to the recall of answers on subsequent presentations of the same problems. All of these findings indicate that the best performers are also the more likely to improve their performance still further by discovering more effective strategies. The worst performers at a task are hence doubly penalised; these people would benefit the most from implementing more effective strategies, yet they are least likely to discover them.

The key to explaining the above findings appears to be that the more successful problem solver is better able to represent information accurately and stably. Hence, while one cause of success may be the presence of appropriate knowledge, success may also depend upon appropriate levels of relevant general abilities, that is, the domain-general skill, or skills, necessary for the optimal execution of a strategy. Levels of ability are frequently linked to representational quality and/or working memory capacity, and relevant abilities may include spatial ability, verbal ability, numerical ability or intelligence, depending on the strategy, the task and its presentation.

More fundamentally, successful performance equals consistent performance. For example, if a person finds that taking one step east, one step north and one step west always results in a heading of due north, it is straightforward to infer that opposite steps are redundant, and may be cancelled no matter how many others intervene, and hence that the entire process of constructing the spatial representation is also redundant. Compare this with a person whose answers range from north-east to north-west for the same steps—these errors are not unknown even among university students. Similarly, a child who finds that $9 + 7$ always gives the answer 16 will be far more likely to memorise this solution, so that counting procedures become redundant, especially compared with a child who finds that the same item gives answers that range from 14 to 18. Finally, only a person who can solve categorical syllogisms successfully is likely to be able to identify the repeating pattern that two *somes* always yield no valid conclusion. Hence, in general, the successful performer is better able to detect regularities, remove redundant solution steps and create less cumbersome, more elegant strategies. Conversely, while unsuccessful performance may lead to an awareness of the need for new strategies, it will also prevent their discovery: the "noisy" representations which lead to poor performance mean that regularities are less detectable. Overall, underlying all of these points is the fact that consistency provides its own feedback, enabling strategy refinement and learning to take place. Simultaneously, the effectiveness of strategies can also be evaluated. The best are those that give consistent, precise answers with the minimum of effort (for other accounts of success-based strategy discovery, see Wood, 1978; Karmiloff-Smith, 1992; Crowley, Shrager & Siegler, 1997).

One important point to note is that the above discussion has focused on *strategy reduction*: how overcomplex strategies are simplified such that processing is reduced and accuracy increased. This should be contrasted, for example, with research by Kuhn and colleagues in which *strategy expansion* has been studied: how are simple strategies increased in sophistication to cope with task demands? For example, how does trial and error change into a strategy where all variables are held constant except the one of interest, which is manipulated systematically? Although there will be differences in the mechanisms of strategy discovery between the two categories, the limiting principle of success is still likely to apply: it is unlikely that current strategies can be successfully expanded unless they are being utilised successfully. However, it is unlikely that expansion processes will be based upon consistency, leading to the detection and deletion of redundancies, so much remains to be learnt about strategy discovery.

A final aspect of strategy availability, not always acknowledged, concerns the occasional need to evaluate the validity of newly discovered strategies. For example, subjects sometimes report identifying cancellation while solving compass-point directions task problems, experimenting with this—with a corresponding increase in solution times—but eventually rejecting the strategy as invalid. A newly discovered strategy whose validity is uncertain is therefore potentially not available despite being present in the strategy repertoire. Incorrect evaluation may thus act as a barrier to adoption for some, even when the new strategy is very effective. Roberts, Gilmore and Wood (1997) again suggest that this need to evaluate newly identified strategies is more likely to present a problem to people less able to execute the original strategies successfully. This is because, where necessary, the only means of evaluation is to compare the output of the new strategy with one that is known to be valid—the one from which it was derived. Even if the answers generated by the new strategy are the more accurate, the people who are unable to execute the original strategy successfully will find a persistent disagreement in answers. This must inevitably lead to the rejection of the new strategy. Evidence in support of the importance of the evaluation process comes from Newton and Roberts (2000), who found that, for the compass-point directions task, the level of feedback affected the frequency with which cancellation was adopted. Partial feedback (correct/incorrect) led to no more cancellation than no feedback at all, while full feedback (the correct answer if an error was made) led to significantly more people adopting cancellation. It was argued that full feedback was unlikely to be increasing the likelihood that cancellation was discovered, and hence this was facilitating its evaluation. Partial feedback is unlikely to assist to the same extent: knowing that an answer is incorrect need not mean that a conflicting answer found by using a different strategy must be correct.

The need to evaluate the validity of a strategy may at first sight appear to be odd, particularly given Siegler's suggestion that strategy discovery is constrained by the "goal sketch". This is a representation of the subgoals that must be satisfied in order to solve a problem, along with the requirement that all new strategies must satisfy these subgoals. Hence, as long as the goal sketch represents valid goals, only valid strategies are discovered. The presence of the goal sketch was suggested as the reason why children competent at addition were never observed to use pathological strategies (Siegler & Jenkins, 1989). Also relevant is children's ability to evaluate the elegance not just of strategies that they discover by themselves (e.g., Siegler & Jenkins, 1989) but also strategies that are described to them but are too cognitively demanding for them to use (e.g., Siegler & Crowley, 1994). The assumption that the goals of the compass-point directions task are well understood and are represented on a goal sketch should likewise constrain the discovery of new strategies for this task. Why, then, might some students be unaware of, or have difficulty in evaluating, the validity of cancellation? A closer look at the findings suggests that the conflict may be more apparent than real. Siegler and Jenkins (1989) found that, for addition strategies, awareness of elegance was linked to how extensively and rapidly a new strategy would be generalised. This suggests individual differences in the ability to evaluate strategies, and is similar to the observation that occasionally cancellation is discovered but then rejected. Hence, although strategy discovery may be constrained by a goal sketch, people are not necessarily aware that this is the case. We therefore need to determine when strategy evaluation is likely to be an important determinant of availability.

The existence of coping strategies in the deduction literature must make us pause for thought concerning the general principle of the goal sketch: some people *do* generate pathological strategies that cannot possibly work reliably. This should not be taken as being an irrational act in its own right. The people who execute generally applicable strategies successfully will identify task-specific short-cuts, and it is likely that the least successful people will resort to coping strategies. For the latter, there is likely to be little to lose in adopting an error-prone strategy that reduces effort. However, the use of faulty strategies, especially where task-specific short-cuts are potentially discoverable, suggests either an incorrect representation of the task goals leading to the potential to identify and accept a coping strategy, or that a goal sketch does not always constrain strategy discovery. One interesting observation is that the generation of coping strategies is not completely unprincipled. For example, although the "last-two" strategy is very occasionally reported for the compass-point directions task, no subject has ever reported the use of a "first-two" strategy or a "first-and-last" strategy. Clearly, coping strategies are not plucked out of thin air, but the factors that constrain their derivation will inevitably be harder to identify compared with task-specific short-cuts. Overall, this is an area in which more research is urgently required. Deduction tasks are likely to provide a particularly suitable domain for this, given the frequent suggestion that task misconstrual is an important source of errors (e.g., Evans, Newstead & Byrne, 1993; Roberts, Newstead & Griggs, 2001) indicating the possibility that many people represent inappropriate goals on the goal sketch.

IMPLICATIONS FOR THEORIES OF REASONING

What implications do the findings outlined have for reasoning researchers? When we consider models of strategy selection, it is apparent that irrespective of their exact details, the use of any particular strategy for a given task is by no means guaranteed. Even if people know a wide variety of strategies, the precise characteristics of a task, coupled with the experience and ability of the people solving it, may cause certain strategies to be favoured to the extent that competitors are rarely adopted, even by people with the highest levels of relevant ability. Hence, the absence of a type of strategy in a particular experiment cannot be used to rule out its use with other task formats, other tasks, other people or even the same people after extended practice. Also of importance are the findings concerning trial-by-trial variability. Overall means averaged over numerous trials may be concealing highly varied strategy usage, as indicated by Bucciarelli and Johnson-Laird (1999) when looking at externalisations for solving categorical syllogisms. We simply do not know what processes may be being hidden if our only measure per subject is, say, two or three error rates derived from numerous trials. However, it would be no exaggeration to say that while we really do not know what the strategy variability phenomena are that need to be accounted for by deduction theories, this is also true for cognition in general. Base levels of trial-by-trial variability, and the variables that influence these, are yet to be identified in any systematic way.

Considering issues of strategy discovery, the key events appear to be the identification and deletion of redundant steps. These will enable inefficient but generally applicable strategies (whether verbal or spatial) to be converted into task-specific short-cuts, for which the lack of generalisability to new tasks, or even to new formats, is a risk worth taking for the gains in productivity on the current task. Overall, the findings indicate that the best performers at generally applicable strategies are among those most likely to cease to use them, because task-specific short cuts have been identified. We also suggest that the worst performers at generally applicable strategies may also dispense with them, but this time switching to coping strategies. To capture all aspects of deduction, it therefore appears that a very wide cross-section of ability is required, much wider than could be expected to be achieved from a typical sample of university students. Virtually nothing is known about how coping strategies are devised, and whether these are subject to any evaluation at all. The very fact that they usually offer better performance than guessing implies that these processes are not trivial, and are based upon some understanding of the task, and it would be of particular interest to determine how individual differences in task understanding lead to different pathways of strategy development.

One consequence of the success-based model of strategy discovery is that research into this topic has become much harder. Impasse problems, or at least extremely difficult problems, are easy to devise, and, having administered the task, the experimenter knows where to look for the behaviour of interest. However, if strategy discovery is a comparatively rare event that takes place with ordinary trials, and only among particular people, the investigation of this becomes much harder. The location of the interesting event becomes more or less under the control of the subject, so that task measures have to be devised such that a strategy change is detectable at any point in the experiment. It is also likely to be advisable to screen people, using appropriate ability tests, so that those most likely to discover new strategies can be identified. Research into these phenomena is undoubtedly hard to do well, but this should never be taken as a criterion when deciding upon a project. Easy questions to answer are not necessarily the most interesting questions.

SOME SPECULATIONS

Pathways of Strategy Development

Having linked strategy discovery to success at executing current strategies, we would like to suggest that one fruitful avenue of research is to consider which strategies are likely to mutate into others. If we take the view that, when approaching a reasoning task for the first time, the starting point for most people will be a generally applicable strategy, whether verbal or spatial, and that success may lead to its modification into a task-specific short cut, while failure may lead to its modification into a coping strategy, it is then possible to speculate concerning pathways of strategy development.

Suppose that a person devises and adopts a task-specific short-cut. If the task is then altered to disrupt its use, changing back to a generally applicable strategy should be straightforward. The person must have been adept at executing such a strategy to begin with (this successful reversion has been demonstrated by Roberts, Gilmore and Wood, 1997). It is also possible for task-specific short-cuts to be further refined with practice. Indeed, Wood (1978) identified a progression of such strategies for linear syllogisms (see also Siegler & Stern, 1998). It is highly unlikely, although technically possible, that a person using a task-specific short cut would convert it into a coping strategy. The poor performance and possible poor understanding that lead to the use of a coping strategy would have prevented the discovery of a task-specific short-cut to begin with. Hence, one type of person will perform well at generally applicable strategies, and will also discover, relatively rapidly, improvements for particular circumstances, enabling a flexible, adaptive and effective approach to reasoning.

Moving down the ability range slightly, we may find people who can execute generally applicable strategies sufficiently well for reasonable performance, but not so well that task-specific short cuts can be easily generated or evaluated. Such people will appear to be relatively inflexible in their strategy approach, although performance will at the very least be adequate, and task modifications (such as the provision of appropriate feedback) may be able to assist in the development of a new strategy.

Next, we would predict that coping strategies can be dangerous to apply because they can block strategy development. Once a pathological strategy has been adopted, even if it is executed faultlessly, it is likely to conceal the patterns necessary for identifying genuine task-specific short-cuts. For example, use of the atmosphere strategy for categorical syllogisms will prevent the discovery of the two-*somes* rule, because this strategy never yields "no valid conclusion" as an answer. This is not the case with all coping strategies. For example, Roberts, Newstead and Griggs (2001) showed that in solving categorical syllogisms, the majority of premise misinterpretations still enable the two-*somes* rule to be discovered because *some* in both premises would continue to lead to "no valid conclusion".

Simultaneously, such premise misinterpretations simplify problem solving by reducing the numbers of meanings that need to be considered. Hence, in this particular case, a coping strategy makes the discovery of the task-specific short cut more likely than if a generally applicable strategy was persisted with. Overall, though, any coping strategy that conceals the necessary repeating patterns will prevent the discovery of task-specific short-cuts, but any coping strategy that inadvertently reveals them will enhance their discovery. We suspect that the latter situation is the less common of the two. Hence, if we assume that the poorer performers at generally applicable strategies are the more likely to use coping strategies, they are less likely to discover task-specific short-cuts to improve their performance, not only because of the poor execution of generally applicable strategies, but also because of the risk that they will instead adopt strategies that will actually block their discovery. It is therefore quite possible that poor performers at generally applicable strategies, like the best performers, will also show highly varied strategy usage, but this will reflect their trying a variety of coping strategies in a doomed attempt to find some sort of method that is reasonably effective. This suggests that high strategic variability can manifest itself in very different people, but for different reasons. The consequence of this is that variability should not be considered as a single individual difference dimension, without a simultaneous consideration of adaptivity.

In sum, a consideration of which strategies may mutate into which others, coupled with a consideration of trial-by-trial variability, could prove to be particularly valuable for researchers when trying to make sense of strategy development, and it may prove equally fruitful for educators to be alert to the possibility that some people may be at risk of adopting strategies that hinder learning.

The Window of Opportunity for Strategy Discovery

Success-based strategy discovery implies a simple progressive model. If we make tasks easier, strategy discovery will increase, and if tasks are made harder, strategy discovery will decrease. Currently, it is not clear whether the level of difficulty should be considered globally or locally. For example, considering the compass-point directions task, a 20-step trial should be harder than an 8-step trial, and so might be associated with fewer people discovering cancellation. However, the solution procedures for either trial are essentially the same. Both could contain the same cancellation-triggering combination of, say, one step north, one step east, one step south and one step west. Hence, extending the trial length may not interfere with the discovery of cancellation, but could still disrupt its evaluation: In theory, any redundant steps can lead to its discovery, but an accurate answer to the entire problem may be required if this strategy is to be evaluated (Newton & Roberts, 2000). It may therefore be the case that in order to manipulate the discovery of cancellation, it is necessary to vary the difficulty of execution of the component strategy steps rather than the trial length (for example, by using concurrent interference tasks, or by allowing pencil and paper for working). The problem with this is that the pencil and paper manipulation has been shown by Roberts, Gilmore and Wood (1997), together with Newton and Roberts (2000), to suppress the discovery of cancellation. Therefore, making a task easier in this way, and hence boosting success, does not seem to increase strategy discovery. Newton and Roberts (2000) conclude from this that success will lead to strategy discovery only if there is a need for more effective strategies: making people more successful at a task will not necessarily lead to better methods if this removes the need to identify them.

Overall, these findings suggest that, for any given person, there exists a window of opportunity at which strategy discovery will be the most likely. The task must be sufficiently easy such that success and hence consistency can lead to the identification and deletion of redundant steps, but not so easy that the incentive to apply this process vanishes. The optimum level of difficulty will vary from person to person, depending upon his or her proficiency at a task. Of course, it is possible that pencil and paper are a special case, and that other ways of making tasks easier do not suppress strategy discovery. Perhaps it is simply the opportunity to externalise thinking that reduces learning in this case. However, in today's high-technology society, in which the goal appears to be to externalise as much thinking as possible via personal computers, this finding by itself is not without consequence for educators. Either way, a success-based model of strategy discovery must imply either a simple progressive model (easier versions of a task equals more discovery; harder versions equals less discovery) or a window-of-opportunity model, and so an important current research goal is to identify positively one pattern or the other.

CONCLUSIONS

In the Introduction, we made several claims concerning the educational implications following from findings in the strategy development literature. We hope that the reader can see how we arrived at these, and we will end by returning to them and making some final comments. To begin with, we believe that current research overwhelmingly supports our first conclusion: *people discover new methods and principles as a result of their successes*; *failure prevents such discovery*. Hence, while failure can make a person aware that new methods are required, this same failure usually prevents their identification. Of course, other evidence may be around the corner to suggest an important role to failure, but this is unlikely to nullify previous research, and so dual models of strategy discovery may be required.

We believe that generalising these findings to our second conclusion, *creativity is hindered if the basics of a task have not been mastered*, is fully justified. Equating creativity with the discovery of new methods is no worse than other definitions that have been proposed in the past, and we would hope that a teacher would prefer a child to discover a task-specific short cut than a coping strategy. Hence, not all creative acts have equal utility, and those with the highest utility require the greatest initial proficiency. This principle seems to be self-evident in every walk of life except in certain classrooms.

In general, these findings show that self-guided learning must be implemented with great care. Our third conclusion, *undirected "learning by discovery" is a poor educational strategy when foisted on the less able*, is again a reflection of the finding that people performing poorly at a task are less able to discover new strategies other than coping strategies, which can hinder matters still further. Clearly, a person in such a position requires vigilant monitoring and assistance, but care is required concerning this, leading to our fourth and last conclusion, that *giving people external aids to assist their performance simultaneously inhibits discoveries*. Even giving the simplest possible assistance, pencil and paper, has had dramatic effects in our research, and the effect of this and other aids on strategy discovery is clearly an important issue to consider in the future.

REFERENCES

Alibali, M. W. (1999). How children change their minds: Strategy changes can be gradual or abrupt. *Developmental Psychology*, *35*, 127–145.

Bisanz, J. & LeFevre, J. (1990). Strategic and nonstrategic processing in the development of mathematical cognition. In D. F. Bjorklund (ed.), *Children's Strategies* (pp. 213–244). Hillsdale, NJ: Erlbaum.

Bjorklund, D. F. & Harnishfeger, K. K. (1990). Children's strategies: Their definition and origins. In D. F. Bjorklund (ed.), *Children's Strategies* (pp. 309–323). Hillsdale, NJ: Erlbaum.

Bjorklund, D. F., Muir-Broaddus, J. E. & Schneider, W. (1990). The role of knowledge in the development of strategies. In D. F. Bjorklund (ed.), *Children's Strategies* (pp. 93–128). Hillsdale, NJ: Erlbaum.

Braine, M. D. S. & O'Brien, D. P. (1997). *Mental Logic*. Mahwah, NJ: Erlbaum.

Brown, A. (1987). Metacognition, executive control, self-regulation and other more mysterious mechanisms. In F. E. Weinert & R. H. Kluwe (eds), *Metacognition, Motivation and Understanding* (pp. 65–116). Hillsdale, NJ: Erlbaum.

Bucciarelli, M. & Johnson-Laird, P. N. (1999). Strategies in syllogistic reasoning. *Cognitive Science*, *23*, 247–303.

Byrne, R. M. J. & Handley, S. J. (1997). Reasoning strategies for suppositional deductions. *Cognition*, *62*, 1–49.

Christensen-Szalanski, J. J. J. (1978). Problem solving strategies: A selection mechanism, some implications, and some data. *Organizational Behaviour and Human Performance*, *22*, 307–323.

Coney, J. (1988). Individual differences and task format in sentence verification. *Current Psychological Research and Reviews*, *7*, 122–135.

Cooper, L. A. & Mumaw, R. J. (1985). Spatial aptitude. In R. F. Dillon (ed.), *Individual Differences in Cognition* (vol. 2) (pp. 67–94). Orlando, FL: Academic Press.

Crowley, K., Shrager, J. & Siegler, R. S. (1997). Strategy discovery as a competitive negotiation between metacognitive and associative mechanisms. *Developmental Review, 17*, 462–489.

Dickstein, L. (1978). The effect of figure on syllogistic reasoning. *Memory and Cognition, 6*, 76–83.

Dieussaert, K., Schaeken, W., Schroyens, W. & d'Ydewalle, G. (1999). Strategies for dealing with complex deduction problems: Combining and dividing. *Psychologica Belgica, 39*, 215–234.

Ericsson, K. A. & Lehmann, A. C. (1996). Expert and exceptional performance: evidence of maximal adaptation to task constraints. *Annual Review of Psychology, 47*, 273–305.

Evans, J. St. B. T. (1989). *Bias in Human Reasoning*. Hove: Psychology Press.

Evans, J. St. B. T. (2000). What could and could not be a strategy in reasoning? In W. Schaeken, G. De Vooght, A. Vandierendonck & G. d'Ydewalle (eds), *Deductive Reasoning and Strategies* (pp. 1–22). Mahwah, NJ: Erlbaum.

Evans, J. St. B. T., Barston, J. L. & Pollard, P. (1983). On the conflict between logic and belief in syllogistic reasoning. *Memory and Cognition, 11*, 295–306.

Evans, J. St. B. T., Newstead, S. E. & Byrne, R. M. J. (1993). *Human Reasoning: The Psychology of Deduction*. Hove: Psychology Press.

Ford. M. (1995). Two models of mental representation and problem solving in syllogistic reasoning. *Cognition, 54*, 1–71.

Galotti, K. M., Baron, J. & Sabini, J. P. (1986). Individual differences in syllogistic reasoning: Deduction rules or mental models? *Journal of Experimental Psychology: General, 115*, 16–25.

Gilhooly, K. J., Logie, R. H., Wetherick, N. E. & Wynn, V. (1993). Working memory and strategies in syllogistic-reasoning tasks. *Memory and Cognition, 21*, 115–124.

Glaser, R. (1984). Education and thinking: The role of knowledge. *American Psychologist, 39*, 93–104.

Holyoak, K. J. & Cheng, P. W. (1995). Pragmatic reasoning with a point of view. *Thinking and Reasoning, 1*, 289–313.

Johnson-Laird, P. N. & Byrne, R. M. J. (1991). *Deduction*. Hove: Psychology Press.

Karmiloff-Smith, A. (1992). *Beyond Modularity: A Developmental Perspective on Cognitive Science*. Cambridge, MA: MIT Press.

Kuhn, D. (1995). Microgenetic study of change: What has it told us? *Psychological Science, 6*, 133–139.

Kuhn, D. & Pearsall, S. (1998). Relations between metastrategic knowledge and strategic performance. *Cognitive Development, 13*, 227–247.

Kuhn, D., Garcia-Mila, M., Zohar, A. & Andersen, C. (1995). Strategies of knowledge acquisition. *Monographs of the Society for Research in Child Development, 60* (Serial no. 245).

Lohman, D. F. & Kyllonen, P. C. (1983). Individual differences in solution strategy on spatial tasks. In R. F. Dillon & R. R. Schmeck (eds), *Individual Differences in Cognition* (vol. 1) (pp. 105–135). New York: Academic Press.

MacLeod, C. M., Hunt, E. B. & Mathews, N. N. (1978). Individual differences in the verification of sentence–picture relationships. *Journal of Verbal Learning and Verbal Behaviour, 17*, 493–507.

Newell, A. (1990). *Unified Theories of Cognition*. Cambridge, MA: Harvard University Press.

Newton, E. J. & Roberts, M. J. (2000). An experimental study of strategy development. *Memory and Cognition, 28*, 565–573.

Quinton, G. & Fellows, B. J. (1975). "Perceptual" strategies in the solving of three-term series problems. *British Journal of Psychology, 66*, 69–78.

Reder, L. M. & Schunn, C. D. (1996). Metacognition does not imply awareness: Strategy choice is governed by implicit learning and memory. In L. M. Reder (ed.), *Implicit Memory and Metacognition* (pp. 45–77). Mahwah, NJ: Erlbaum.

Riding, R. J., Glass, A. & Douglas, G. (1993). Individual differences in thinking: cognitive and neuropsychological perspectives. *Educational Psychology, 13*, 267–280.

Rips, L. J. (1994). *The Psychology of Proof*. Cambridge, MA: MIT Press.

Roberts, M. J. (1993). Human reasoning: Deduction rules or mental models, or both? *Quarterly Journal of Experimental Psychology, 46A*, 569–589.

Roberts, M. J. (2000a). Individual differences in reasoning strategies: A problem to solve or an opportunity to seize? In W. Schaeken, G. De Vooght, A. Vandierendonck & G. d'Ydewalle (eds), *Deductive Reasoning and Strategies* (pp. 23–48). Mahwah, NJ: Erlbaum.

Roberts, M. J. (2000b). Strategies in relational inference. *Thinking and Reasoning*, 6, 1–26.

Roberts, M. J. & Newton, E. J. (2001). Understanding strategy selection. *International Journal of Human–Computer Studies*, 54, 137–154.

Roberts, M. J. & Sykes, E. D. A. (2003). Belief bias and rational inference. *Quarterly Journal of Experimental Psychology*, 56A, 131–154.

Roberts, M. J., Gilmore, D. J. & Wood, D. J. (1997). Individual differences and strategy selection in reasoning. *British Journal of Psychology*, 88, 473–492.

Roberts, M. J., Newstead, S. E. & Griggs, R. A. (2001). Quantifier interpretation and syllogistic reasoning. *Thinking and Reasoning*, 7, 173–204.

Schaeken, W., De Vooght, G., Vandierendonck, A. & d'Ydewalle, G. (2000). *Deductive Reasoning and Strategies*. Mahwah, NJ: Erlbaum.

Schiano, D. J., Cooper, L. A., Glaser, R. & Zhang, H. C. (1989). Highs are to lows as experts are to novices: Individual differences in the representation and solution of standardised figural analogies. *Human Performance*, 2, 225–248.

Schoenfeld, A. H. (1987). What's all the fuss about metacognition? In A. H. Schoenfeld (ed.), *Cognitive Science and Mathematics Education* (pp. 189–215). Hillsdale, NJ: Erlbaum.

Schroyens, W., Schaeken, W. & d'Ydewalle, G. (1996). Meta-logical reasoning with knight-knave problems: The importance of being hypothesised. *Psychologica Belgica*, 36, 145–170.

Scott, B. C. E. (1993). Working with Gordon. *Systems Research*, 10, 167–192.

Shrager, J. & Siegler, R. S. (1998). SCADS: A model of children's strategy choices and strategy discoveries. *Psychological Science*, 9, 405–410.

Siegler, R. S. (1996). *Emerging Minds: The Process of Change in Children's Thinking*. New York: Oxford University Press.

Siegler, R. S. & Crowley, K. (1991). The microgenetic method: A direct means for studying cognitive development. *American Psychologist*, 46, 606–620.

Siegler, R. S. & Crowley, K. (1994). Constraints of learning on non-privileged domains. *Cognitive Psychology*, 27, 194–226.

Siegler, R. S. & Jenkins, E. A. (1989). *How Children Discover New Strategies*. Hillsdale, NJ: Erlbaum.

Siegler, R. S. & Lemaire, P. (1997). Older and younger adults' strategy choices in multiplication: Testing predictions of ASCM using the choice/no-choice method. *Journal of Experimental Psychology: General*, 126, 71–92.

Siegler, R. S. & Stern, E. (1998). Conscious and unconscious strategy discoveries: A microgenetic analysis. *Journal of Experimental Psychology: General*, 127, 377–397.

Simon, H. A. (1990). Invariants of human behaviour. *Annual Review of Psychology*, 41, 1–21.

Sternberg, R. J. (1977). *Intelligence, Information Processing, and Analogical Reasoning*. Hilldale, NJ: Erlbaum.

Sternberg, R. J. (1997). Are cognitive styles still in style? *American Psychologist*, 52, 700–712.

Sternberg, R. J. & Weil, E. M. (1980). An aptitude × strategy interaction in linear syllogistic reasoning. *Journal of Educational Psychology*, 72, 226–239.

VanLehn, K. (1988). Towards a theory of impasse driven learning. In H. Mandl & A. Lesgold (eds), *Learning Issues for Intelligent Tutoring Systems* (pp. 19–41). New York: Springer-Verlag.

VanLehn, K. (1991). Rule acquisition events in the discovery of problem-solving strategies. *Cognitive Science*, 15, 1–47.

Wood, D. J. (1978). Problem solving—the nature and development of strategies. In G. Underwood (ed.), *Strategies in Information Processing* (pp. 329–356). London: Academic Press.

Wood, D. J. & Shotter, J. (1973). A preliminary study of distinctive features in problem solving. *Quarterly Journal of Experimental Psychology*, 25, 504–510.

CHAPTER 3

Generalising Individual Differences and Strategies Across Different Deductive Reasoning Domains

Padraic Monaghan
University of Warwick, UK
and
Keith Stenning
University of Edinburgh, UK

INTRODUCTION

Observations of individual differences in reasoning present a challenge to specifying the mechanisms of human reasoning. Investigations that attempt to unearth the nature of the fundamental reasoning mechanism (FRM) are challenged by evidence that different representations and strategies are used in reasoning. Particularly clear evidence comes from studies of reasoners' use of contrasting external representations (e.g., Roberts, Gilmore & Wood, 1997; Ford, 1995; Stenning, Cox & Oberlander, 1995). Distinguishing external representations is not subject to the problems that beset the identification of the internal representations on which the FRM is supposedly based (Stenning & Oberlander, 1995; Stenning & Yule, 1997). Evidence from observations of external representations is only indirect evidence about internal ones, but it is stronger evidence than that based on distinct-sounding representations which turn out to be indistinguishable for the kinds of evidence collected. Studies of reasoning with external representations show robust individual differences in both representation selection and strategies for deployment.

The minimising response to such arguments is that external representations are unrelated to internal ones, and that different strategies for the use of internal ones consist of "noise" in accounts of reasoning mechanisms. So, for categorial syllogisms, the ongoing debate over whether the FRM operates with spatial, verbal or mental model representations is claimed to be settled by a majority verdict. The FRM is described by the system that explains

Thinking: Psychological Perspectives on Reasoning, Judgment and Decision Making. Edited by David Hardman and Laura Macchi.
© 2003 John Wiley & Sons, Ltd.

most responses for most people. Johnson-Laird and Byrne (1991) admit that "each theory accounts for how some people reason some of the time", but claim that their theory fits the most data. Using the supposedly contrasting representation of deductive rules, then, will be a strategy for reasoning that merely interferes with the use of mental models in reasoning, even if it seems to fit performance on certain reasoning tasks.

Consonant with this minimising approach is the idea that all individual differences in reasoning performance can be fitted by adjusting the parameters of the system posited as the FRM. So, for mental models, different responses are due, for example, to the different abilities of subjects to maintain multiple models, related to measures of working memory capacity. This assumes that differences in response are merely quantitative rather than qualitative. Ford's (1995) data throw this view into doubt. Groups of subjects spontaneously produce diagrammatic or algebraic representations for solving categorial syllogisms, and find different problems difficult according to the representation they seem to be using. No parameter setting has been shown to be able to account for this variation.

The alternative response is to accept the existence of a variety of representations and strategies, and attempt to describe and explain the nature of representational and strategic variation and change. There are several accounts that have posted descriptions of strategy variation, but few that expand these descriptions into *explanations* of performance.

This chapter will develop an alternative, more computational approach to analysing individual differences. Representational and strategic variation will be embraced as an opportunity to enhance computational analyses of reasoning. Our approach is to develop representational and strategic distinctions that can be shown to be generalisable across different reasoning domains.

GENERALISING STRATEGIES ACROSS REASONING TASKS

Roberts (1993) has classified strategies across a range of tasks in terms of their use of either spatial or verbal representations. But "spatial" and "verbal" are concepts which are themselves notoriously in need of analysis. We will argue that the data he presents can be more systematically accounted for by a computational characterisation of the properties of the representational systems used.

Roberts (1993) has suggested that the alternative strategies spontaneously developed in reasoning problems can be described in terms of whether they use representations that are primarily spatial or verbal in nature. In linear syllogisms, Wood (1978) discovered that subjects either constructed a spatial array of the items in the problems, or searched through the verbal statements for particular items in relation to each other. In the sentence-picture verification task, subjects either encoded the sentence as a spatial array and compared it to the presented picture, or made a verbal encoding of the sentence and then encoded the picture to match against the sentence encoding (Macleod, Hunt & Mathews, 1978). In categorial syllogisms, Ford (1995) has noted two strategies that depend on quite different types of representation. Some subjects developed a method that represents the information in the syllogism in terms of spatially organised sets of properties. Other subjects operated on the verbal form of the problem, substituting information "algebraically" from one statement to another.

The compass directions task (Roberts, Gilmore & Wood, 1997) also exhibits alternative strategies as subjects learn to solve problems. Subjects either mentally trace a path according to the directions, and work out the direction of the final point with respect to the starting point on some quasi-map, or they use a "cancellation" method, where east-moves and west-moves cancel each other out, and the answer depends on reading off the remaining moves that have not been cancelled. Subjects learn to use the cancellation strategy only if a "window of opportunity" for changing strategy presents itself (Chapter 2, this volume).

Alternative strategies for different reasoning tasks can be described in terms of whether they employ spatial or verbal representations. Generalisations are further supported by the direction of change from spatial to verbal strategies. If a subject uses both a spatial and a verbal strategy, the verbal strategy tends to succeed the spatial strategy. Furthermore, measures of spatial ability seem to reflect the fluency of this strategy change. Scoring high on spatial ability tests relates to quicker development of a verbal strategy, or appropriate changes to more effective strategies (Roberts, Gilmore & Wood, 1997).

However, as it stands, the spatial/verbal strategy distinction is problematic. First, representations are classified on the basis of phenomenology, and determining the differences between an internal verbal representation and a spatial representation is at least problematic (Pylyshyn, 1973; Anderson, 1978). However, whole subfields, such as the study of working memory, have been based, at least initially, on the verbal/spatial distinction (e.g., Baddeley, 1990). Still, determining the differences between spatial and verbal by reference to the processes that these representations invoke would enable a computational account to be squared with the descriptions of different strategy use (Paivio, 1986).

A second problem with Roberts' account is that the *direction* of strategy change is not always the same. For linear syllogisms and the compass directions task, the "privilege of occurrence" is from spatial to verbal strategies. But there is no such privilege of occurrence for categorial syllogisms, as subjects tend to use one strategy or the other (the subjects that do use both vary as to which they use first, but quickly settle on using one or the other method). More problematically, for the sentence-picture verification task, some students change from using the verbal strategy to using a spatial strategy[1] (Clark & Chase, 1972).

The approach of Roberts has been to tally strategy change with psychometric measures of ability. So, for example, more *spatially* able subjects (as measured by performance on the Saville–Holdsworth Advanced Test Battery Spatial Reasoning Test [Saville & Holdsworth Ltd, 1979]) tend to use the more efficient verbal strategies sooner in the compass directions task. But, in the sentence-picture verification task, high spatial ability related to using the spatial strategy (Macleod, Hunt & Mathews, 1978). However, in Ford's (1995) syllogism study, each strategy seems to be equally appropriate, and so the use of one or other strategy is unlikely to relate to higher ability.

These mixed results suggest that there may be better ways of classifying different strategies than in terms of the verbal/spatial distinction. Different strategies are seen to be more or less appropriate given the task constraints. A version of the compass directions task, for example, which provides moves for two individuals, and requires their relative positions to be reported, is a very difficult problem to solve with the cancellation strategy. Wood (1978) interprets the patterns of strategy change in terms of being from less effective to more efficient strategies, and Roberts speaks of strategies becoming more task specific. But

---

[1] The change is actually from a verbal strategy to a "flat" strategy, where the encoding of the sentence takes the same length of time whether it is affirmative or negative—behaviourally, it is indistinguishable from a spatial strategy, though introspective accounts suggest that the representations are not spatial (Marquer & Pereira, 1990). This indeed further indicates the great difficulties over postulating alternative accounts of internal representations in terms of their phenomenology without recourse to the computational properties of the representations.

John is taller than Paul
Dave is taller than Paul
Tom is taller than Dave
Ian is taller than Tom
Dave is taller than John

Figure 3.1   The linear syllogisms problem

Ian
Tom
Dave
John
Paul

Figure 3.2   The "unified" representation for the linear syllogisms problem

Ian
Tom
Dave

Figure 3.3   The "search" strategy representation for the linear syllogisms problem

what makes one strategy more effective, efficient, appropriate or task specific than another? Such terms beg a computational description of the processes operating on the different representations.

If a characterisation of "efficiency" can be provided, the following generalisations of strategy change should hold:

- There is a privilege of occurrence from less effective to more effective strategies.
- Subjects with "high ability" tend to develop more effective strategies sooner.

Our characterisation is in terms of the expressiveness or specificity of the system from which the representations are drawn (e.g., Levesque, 1988; Stenning & Oberlander, 1995; Stenning, 1999, 2002). Spatial representations tend to be more specific, whereas verbal representations are more expressive, or, rather, inexpressive verbal sublanguages tend to be parts, not well demarcated, of more expressive languages. An efficient strategy, then, is one where the representation system employed has the optimal level of expressiveness for the task at hand.

To see this exemplified, consider linear syllogisms strategies for the problem shown in Figure 3.1. The subject has to say who is taller, Ian or Dave. The "unified" or "spatial" representation will be something like that shown in Figure 3.2. From this representation, the subject can answer that Ian is taller. However, a "search" strategy will look for Ian in the left column of the statements, and then resolve all individuals between Ian and John, producing a representation something like Figure 3.3.

The relations between the other individuals is left unexpressed. More information than is minimally necessary for solving the problem has to be resolved into the "unified", or spatial, representation, because it is less able to express abstractions. This means extra effort is expended in assimilating all the information in order to express the relations between all individuals. The more expressive verbal representation does not have to express as much information about the individuals—only the relations between the two target individuals and any intervening individuals are specified.

Figure 3.4 Three situations consistent with the verbal representation in the sentence-picture verification task

In other tasks, it may be more efficient to specify more information in order to solve the problem. The verbal strategy in the sentence-picture verification task, for example, takes more steps to operate (and is therefore less efficient) for negative problems (that is, problems where the sentence contains a negative term), and this is because the information is not so specific as with the spatial strategy, and so requires some additional unpacking. A "spatial" encoding of the sentence, "The star is not above the cross", would look like the diagram on the left of Figure 3.4. The verbal strategy encoding is consistent with situations where stars and crosses are alongside one another—possibilities excluded by the specification of relations in the spatial, or flat, strategy. These situations are shown in the centre and right of Figure 3.4. When the subject is then presented with the picture, a contradiction with the sentential encoding is less immediate than with the spatial, or flat, encoding.

Strategic flexibility, then, is determined by the subject's ability to select appropriate representational systems that are conducive to solving the task. An overexpressive system means that relations that need to be assessed between individuals may not be readily available— further resolutions of the relations between individuals may be required. An overspecific system will mean that unnecessary effort is spent in expressing the relations between all elements in the representation, and storing this information. This is the essence of measures of "ability" that determine strategic flexibility: it is the ability to select a representation that has the correct balance between specifying information and permitting sufficient range of expression. Kyllonen, Lohman and Snow's (1984) review of strategies used by subjects on spatial ability tests supports such a view. Subjects that score highest on spatial ability measures tend to be more flexible in their use of different strategies on the tasks. Snow (1980) indicated that subjects that scored the highest on the paper-folding test used combinations of "mental construction" of the stimulus with "feature extraction". These strategies reflect again whether the representation used is specific (in the former case) or drawn from a more expressive system (in the case of the latter strategy).

Abilities and Styles of Reasoning

The discussion so far has concerned abilities in adapting and using strategies that employ differently expressive systems of representation to solve problems. Ford's (1995) study of different strategies for solving syllogisms showed that there are alternative ways of representing information which are not different in their appropriateness for the task. Each strategy is more or less appropriate for different syllogistic problems, but across the range of problems they cannot be distinguished in terms of effectiveness. The question of what determines *preference* for using particular strategies is a separate challenge to accounting for individual differences in the ability of subjects to select an appropriate representation. Again, the approach of using a computational analysis of the representations proposed here can encompass both kinds of observations.

We have been particularly interested in accounting for aptitude-treatment interactions (ATIs) in reasoning tasks. ATIs occur when different treatments benefit subject populations that can be distinguished in terms of their performance on an independent measure. In the educational research literature, most studies of ATIs have focused on "general scholastic ability" as the aptitude dimension, while analysing different methods of teaching some topic. In other words, the studies look at different effects of teaching methods on able and not so able students. This focus on general ability is understandable (if debatable) from an applied point of view, but will not be our focus. The ATIs we examine here are cases where two groups of highly able students show opposite responses to two teaching methods. This choice is theoretically important. We stand a much better chance of finding replicable ATIs if we split groups on the basis of a measure that reflects something about kinds of mental process, than if we split on some conglomerate measure such as scholastic ability. If we can show that different subgroups of able students nevertheless show opposite responses to different teaching "treatments", that is some indication that we are dealing with styles of thinking rather than general measures of ability.

Such ATIs are challenging for three reasons. Firstly, the cases where some subjects get worse and others get better at performing the same task would be difficult to square with parametrised models of strategy variation. Why should the reverse pattern of benefits and deficits hold when the training regime is altered? If subjects differ only in terms of their capacity along particular dimensions of ability, how can training either benefit the group with high ability or prove detrimental to them? It seems that the patterns of change are far more subtle than can be handled by such descriptions of behaviour.

The second challenge that ATIs present is to theories of strategy variation that consider only unidimensional accounts of behaviour. Roberts has concentrated on explaining strategy change in terms of "ability". When subjects have difficulties following one teaching intervention, and the same subjects benefit from another intervention, this suggests that the effects cannot be entirely explained in terms of abilities. Otherwise, the same subjects would benefit no matter what form the training took.

The third challenge is actually to find replicable instances of ATIs, which are notoriously difficult to replicate (Snow, 1980). Stenning and Monaghan (1998) argue that at least a part of the problem stems from fundamental features of the psychometric approach. Without a characterisation of *mechanism* and *mental process*, we should expect ATIs to fail to replicate when we change populations, tasks and teaching methods. A prerequisite for finding ATIs and replicating them is that a correct interpretation of the effects of training is available and the basis of the distinction between groups is correctly established.

We have applied the computational account of strategy variation to two reasoning domains. The following discussion summarises the ATIs that we found in both domains. The characterisation of the tests and tasks that determine the ATIs is necessary in order to provide an explanatory account of this strategy variation.

ATIS IN TEACHING REASONING

An ATI in Teaching First Order Logic

Hyperproof is a multimodal logic program developed by Barwise and Etchemendy (1994). The interface is shown in Figure 3.5. It combines a graphical situation (the chessboard at the top of the window) with sentential expressions (listed below the chessboard) of the

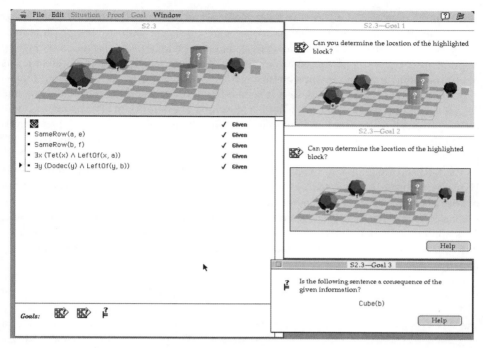

Figure 3.5 The Hyperproof interface. From Barwise and Etchemendy (1994). *Hyperproof.* CSLI Publications, reproduced with permission

relations in the graphics. Students construct proofs by combining graphical situations with sentential expressions in order to achieve goals that can be presented either as sentences or graphics. The graphical situations can contain abstraction, so the size, shape, position and name of the objects can be left unspecified. In Figure 3.5, the position of two objects is left unspecified by positioning them to the right of the chessboard (icons off the board stand for objects which are on the board but in unknown positions). Two objects have shape and size unspecified by being indicated as cylinders (objects are one of three sizes and one of three shapes). Finally, three objects have their labels unspecified.

Stenning, Cox and Oberlander (1995) compared students that followed a 14-week course taught with Hyperproof to another group that used Hyperproof with the graphics window disabled. These courses, then, differed in that one course provided graphical expressions of situations, and students were required to work with graphically abstract situations in order to solve problems, whereas the other course required students to learn to reason by Fitch-style natural deduction rules.

Students were classified according to their performance on the analytical (as opposed to logical) subscale of the Graduate Record Examination (GRE) analytical reasoning test, derived from a GRE primer (for further details, see Stenning, Cox & Oberlander, 1995). These problems are constraint-satisfaction problems. Although the test is verbally set and verbally responded to, many of the problems are usefully solved by constructing graphical representations (Cox, 1996). Problems on the GRE varied in terms of the level of abstraction useful in the representations used to solve them. Some problems constrained the solution to a single situation, whereas other problems were consistent with several, or sometimes many, states of affairs. Diagrammatic representations tend to be useful for the former group of problems. Successful performance on this test related to selective use of different levels of abstraction in the representations used.

Students were divided into those that scored high on this test (GRE-Hi) and those that scored less well (GRE-Lo). Students took a reasoning test before and after taking the logic course. This test required the student to reason with Hyperproof-type graphical situations, except that the problems were set in natural language. We called this the "blocks-world" (BW) test.

The GRE-Hi students improved their score on the BW test as a result of following the Hyperproof course, but their scores worsened if they followed the non-graphical Hyperproof course. The GRE-Lo students demonstrated the opposite effect: they benefited from the non-graphical course, but their performance was impaired by following the Hyperproof course. This aptitude-treatment interaction between performance on the GRE and learning from different logic courses required further exploration in order to provide an *explanation* of the effect.

Fortuitously, Hyperproof offers a unique insight into the types of representations that students are using as they solve problems, as whenever a graphical situation is constructed by the student the exact level of abstraction in the representation can be measured. So, if a shape is left unspecified in terms of its size, shape or position, this means that a certain level of graphical abstraction is used in the representation. The proofs of GRE-Hi and GRE-Lo students were analysed in the Hyperproof course (Oberlander et al., 1999). GRE-Hi students tended to use more graphical abstraction in their proofs than did GRE-Lo students, at least for situations introduced as assumptions in the proofs.

This difference in proof style bears a strong resemblance to the distinction between serialist and holist learning behaviours, as described by Pask (1976). Serialists like to construct fully specified situations one by one, and build up a sense of the whole after working through individual examples. Holists prefer to structure their learning so as to gain an overall impression of the whole before focusing on details. The GRE-Lo students construct graphical situations that have little or no abstraction. The GRE-Hi students' graphical situations tend to cover the space of possibilities at a higher level of granularity, and contain more abstraction. More abstract representations relate to using a more expressive system, and Hyperproof reveals this as a stylistic preference in addition to, or rather than, an ability. Furthermore, the GRE reflects this distinction and can be seen as a *stylistic* measure rather than an ability *per se*, as scoring low on this test correlates with performing better as a result of following the non-graphical Hyperproof course. Ironically, it is the students that score high on the GRE that seem to be disadvantaged by following a traditional logic course, the type normally taught at universities in order to provide a formal basis to argumentation and reasoning.

An ATI in Learning Syllogisms

We replicated the GRE aptitude by logic course treatment interaction in a very different domain, a domain where the teaching intervention is extremely short. Students were taught one of two methods for solving syllogisms, which used either Euler's circles representations of the information contained in the premises, or natural deduction type representations.

Table 3.1 "Natural deduction" representations of syllogism premises

Premise	Translation
Some As are Bs	A and B
All As are Bs	A → B
Some As are not Bs	A and ¬B
No As are Bs	A → ¬B

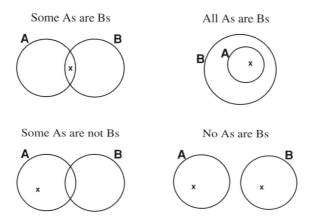

Figure 3.6 Euler's circles representations of syllogism premises

The representations used for each method are shown in Figure 3.6 and Table 3.1. The representations were accompanied by a method for combining the representations of each premise to reach a conclusion. These methods were theoretically derived from formal equivalence results (Stenning & Yule, 1997), but bear close resemblance to the spatial and verbal strategies identified by Ford (1995). For further details of the study, see Monaghan and Stenning (1998).

As with the Hyperproof study, students were classified into GRE-Lo and GRE-Hi groups according to their score on the GRE pre-test. All tutoring was done blind, in the sense that the tutor did not know anything about the students' pre-test scores. The ease with which students acquired the methods for solving syllogisms was assessed by counting the number of errors that the student made in applying the method, and the number of interventions the student required in order to apply the method successfully.

The GRE-Lo students made fewer errors and required fewer interventions in learning the ND method than the GRE-Hi students. For the EC method, the opposite pattern emerged: the GRE-Hi students made fewer errors and required fewer interventions for this method. The ANOVAs of the interaction between teaching method and GRE group were significant in each case. For errors, $F(1, 13) = 5.64$, $p < 0.05$; for interventions, $F(1, 13) = 5.26$, $p < 0.05$. Figures 3.7 and 3.8 indicate the different errors and interventions made by each group for the two methods.

The same ATI was found as with the Hyperproof teaching study. The GRE median split predicts the relative ease or difficulty that students will have with different teaching interventions, both in terms of what they learn from a course in the case of Hyperproof,

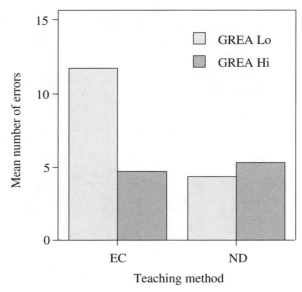

Figure 3.7 Number of errors by GRE group for the teaching methods: $F(1, 13) = 5.64$, $p < 0.05$

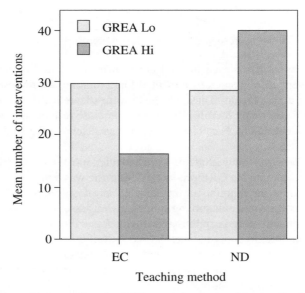

Figure 3.8 Number of interventions by GRE group for the teaching methods: $F(1, 13) = 5.26$, $p < 0.05$

and in terms of how easily they acquire and make use of a representational system in the case of solving syllogisms. There is, in fact, no main effect of teaching method—the two theoretically equivalent methods are equally effective in this study.

Any account in terms of the conventional psychometric spatial/verbal distinction is inadequate for describing the ATIs demonstrated here. It does not capture the nature of strategy development shown in a range of reasoning tasks. Moreover, in the use of Hyperproof, students use graphical representations *differently*, and this difference is essentially the level of abstraction employed in the representations used. This explanatory framework also applies to the syllogism ATI result.

In the case of the two methods for teaching syllogisms, the difference in level of abstraction in the representations used is more deeply hidden than in the Hyperproof case. Essentially, the equivalence of the two methods is due to their implementing the same algorithm (Stenning & Yule, 1997) where individuals are identified and described in terms of the three properties, A, B and C. Though there is an overall equivalence, there is, of course, the possibility of variations in implementation within each method; for example, in when and how individuals are described. For the natural deduction method as used here, an individual is selected at the outset of the method and then fully described in terms of the three properties. For the Euler's circles method as used here, a greater degree of abstraction is at play—several individuals are resolved simultaneously, but their properties remain abstract until one is selected for full description. This property of abstraction is independent of the spatial/verbal distinction, as shown by the existence of an adapted version of the Euler's circles method (see below), which fully specifies a pre-selected individual just as the natural deduction method does. As with using different representations in Hyperproof, the GRE-Hi students are more comfortable with using more abstraction in their representations, and the GRE-Lo students are disadvantaged unless they have the opportunity to use more specific representations.

So our goal is to replace analyses in terms of spatial/verbal differences with one based on the level of abstraction. We have argued that strategy change in reasoning tasks is best described in terms of the level of abstraction used in the representations, and that this ties directly with the *expressivity* of the system from which these representational tokens are drawn. The selection or development of an "efficient" level of abstraction in representation has been seen as an ability measure, predicted by scores on spatial ability measures. But our ATI results indicate that there is a stylistic dimension to the use of different levels of abstraction in chosen representation systems. Subjects have preferences for a level of abstraction in their reasoning.

But this account in terms of abstraction still needs to be related to the modality of information presentation (sentence or diagram) because either modality can be abstract or concrete. In order to account for these preferences, we return to a spatial/verbal distinction but with a very different characterisation from previous accounts. The distinction is based on differences between the modalities in how representation systems are related to each other. A useful metaphor is that of "landscapes" of representational systems. As reasoners narrow down to a particular system to reason in, they can be thought of as navigating in a highly structured landscape of related systems. Our proposal is that the structures of the landscape of diagrammatic systems is rather different from the landscape of sentential language fragments.

STRATEGY CHANGE AND REPRESENTATIONAL LANDSCAPES

We have proposed one way of describing strategy development in reasoning tasks in terms of adjusting the level of abstraction of representations. Using a representation that is too specific means that more work has to be done during construction and maintenance of the representation than is necessary for solving the task. This is the case with the "spatial" strategy in linear syllogisms. However, a representation that is not specific enough means that information that is implicit may have to be specified in order to solve the task, and this is the case in the "verbal" strategy for the sentence-picture verification task when the subject is faced with negative problems.

This way of presenting the situation does not emphasise the distinction between abstraction adjustments which might take place within a single representation system by choosing token representations which are more or less abstract. Once we take the latter metarepresentational point of view seriously, however, there are other ways of describing differences between spatial and verbal representations and strategies. We can think of the small contextualised representation systems involved in laboratory tasks as fragments of larger systems—either sentential or graphical. These fragments bear complex family relationships to other systems. Navigating around these landscapes of systems to find one in which to solve the problem then becomes a large part of the learning process. Differences between the navigation problem for sentential and graphical systems may explain individual differences.

Moving to a smaller, more specific fragment may inherit schemata that are practised with regard to the larger system. When expressed within a larger more general system, problems can be recast so as to bring to bear previously learned responses to situations. This tendency can be observed in expert/novice distinctions in a number of domains. In physics (Chi, Feltovitch & Glaser, 1981), geometry (Koedinger & Anderson, 1990) and computer programming (McKeithen et al., 1981), novices tended to rely upon superficial features of the task. Experts' deeper representations tended to uncover commonalities between problems in the domain. This makes problem solving quicker within predetermined structures that facilitate problem solution. However, occasionally, the expert may be disadvantaged by embedding the problem within a practised system, as, then, creative approaches to problems that do not quite fit established schemata are suppressed (Wiley, 1998).

The methods for teaching syllogisms exemplify the nature of this nesting of fragments of languages. Both the graphical and the verbal systems we have described are fragments nested within larger systems. This is most obvious in the graphical case. For example, Euler's circles as specified in our teaching study is a member of a family of systems which use closed curves to represent sets. Some well-known members of the family are Venn diagrams and Carroll diagrams (see Stenning, 2002, for a review of some of the relations in this family tree). There are closer relatives of Euler which extend the system, for example, by allowing the complements of sets to be enclosed in circles. This latter system (perhaps it should be called Euler-inside-out) is an only slightly larger fragment of logic than Euler *tout simple*. Figure 3.9 shows the two expressions of the premise "No As are Bs" within the Euler-inside-out system. With sentential systems, this nesting is hidden, especially in natural language. The transitions from fragment to fragment are invisible transitions between sublanguages of an apparently homogeneous universal language—English or whatever. But we believe that this is an illusion as far as mental representation and process are concerned.

The interpretation of fragments of discourse (like those involved in setting and solving reasoning problems) takes place within tiny fragments of languages. This is one aspect which formalisation reveals. Formal logics are well known to be nested within other formal logics—propositional calculus inside monadic predicate logic, monadic predicate logic within first-order logic, first order within higher order, non-modal logics inside modal logics and so on. The fragments in play in the solution of typical laboratory reasoning problems are much finer grained than this well-known large-scale landscape. For example, the fragment

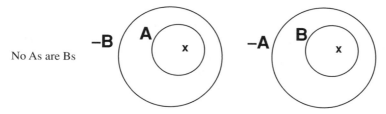

No As are Bs

Figure 3.9 Euler-inside-out representations of the syllogism premise "no As are Bs"

of propositional calculus which we use to model Euler (in creating our equivalent sentential teaching system) is also nested within a very slightly larger system which corresponds to the graphical Euler-inside-out system.

One possible key to differences between the metasystemic landscapes of graphical and sentential systems is in terms of the theorem provers that come with the systems. In the sentential case, it is the procedures for guiding derivations (the theorem prover) which demarcate the fragment of the larger language that is actually "in play". If the theorem prover simply never takes certain paths of derivation, the parts of the language that are down those paths are simply "out of play". The procedures which we taught for solving syllogisms sententially, in order to model Euler *tout simple*, work by ensuring that the premises receive the right encoding so that the theorem prover can be a one-pass process with no backtracking (just like the graphical system).

But a natural relaxation of this theorem prover yields an equivalent fragment to the Euler-inside-out system.[2] This system does require backtracking—that is, it is possible wrongly to encode the premises in a way which cuts off solution and requires backtracking to a different encoding. Euler-inside-out is just the same. Graphically, one may encode the two premises so that the middle term, "B", is represented by the things *within* a circle in one premise (as on the right of Figure 3.9), and *outside* a circle in the other premise (as on the left of this figure). The two premise diagrams will not then unify into a composite diagram, and one has to backtrack to choose a different representation of one or other premise.

It is a feature of graphical systems that they tend to be less separable from their theorem provers. The Euler system does not naturally decompose into a "language" and a proof mechanism. Indeed, "proof" in Euler is not the discursive process reflected in sentential calculi. This contrast is less obvious in Euler than in more expressive systems such as Peirce's existential graphs (see Stenning, 2000, for a discussion of the contrast between agglomerative and discursive uses of representations). Recent work by Shin (2002) has shown how alternative reading algorithms can play a distinctive role in reasoning with graphical systems.

So although the graphical and the linguistic nestings of related systems can be lined up entirely equivalently at one formal level, they may yet be distinct at finer-grained levels of description. These finer-grained levels may be the ones needed to analyse the individual differences in representational behaviour which concern us here. The feel of travelling about in the space of graphical fragments is rather different from the feel of getting about between the language fragments—the latter is a much more seamless process, and because

---

[2] It is equally possible to adapt the Euler-inside-out system, so that no backtracking is required, by adding rules about how premises should be represented initially.

of the relation between theorem prover and language, it is harder to distinguish strategic from representational change. At any rate, *learning* a method for solving problems of some class is not just a matter of constructing a new fragment. It is very much a matter of locating that fragment in the landscape of its family relations—the larger landscape of systems. From this perspective, we have presented evidence that different subjects find it easier or harder to perform this location of a new fragment in graphical or sentential "space".

The individual differences in learning from different representations are in terms of *recognising* the landscape of representational systems within which the particular system being used for a reasoning problem is nested. Without recognition of the landscape, one cannot make adaptations to the language fragment that make problem solving more effective or appropriate for the task at hand. High "spatial ability", then, relates to the ability of the subject to navigate within the representational landscape and come up with an appropriate fragment of the system for the given problem. The high-ability subjects in spatial tasks use a variety of fragments for solving the problems.

Recognising the representational landscape is also closely akin to appropriate application of the inherited schemata—a mistaken conception of the relationship between fragments will mean that inappropriate schemas will be applied. Stanovich's (1999) discussion of the variable ability of subjects to decontextualise information in reasoning tasks is one such expression of the difficulties inherent in determining which aspects of the larger language are appropriate within the fragment.

Stanovich suggests that there are two reasoning systems that contribute to problem solving. System 1 is fundamental, automatic, heuristic (Evans, 1989), implicit, associative (Sloman, 1996) and holistic. System 2 is controlled, analytic, explicit and rule-based. System 1 processing is inclined to import a context when interpreting problems, whereas a feature of System 2 processing is that it is decontextualised. The extent to which a subject can decontextualise information, or override the basic System 1 processes, is a matter of individual differences. There is a "fundamental computational bias" to contextualise information, and the extent to which this influences problem solving in a range of domains is a generalisable individual difference.

Applying a conversational context is a common response to artificial, laboratory-based reasoning tests, with the subjects attempting to maintain a modicum of normality in their responses. A large part of formal education is learning to control the embedding of communication in different contexts. Therefore, many psychometric tests of the success of students' acquisition of this formal skill are themselves replete with implicit assumptions that would be naturally applied in cooperative, communicative situations. The GRE is a prime example of this, the test requiring the subject to master the implicit balance between what is supposed to be assumed and what is to be tested.

The subjects that are good at the GRE are those that are good at performing this selective application of context in determining which assumptions to make implicitly and which have to be made explicit in resolving the problems. These GRE-Hi subjects are also good at selecting appropriate schemata, and selecting an appropriate level of abstraction in the representations used to solve the problems. What is perplexing, though, are the ATI results with respect to teaching the GRE groups. The GRE-Hi subjects actually seem to be worse at recognising the representational landscape, and applying appropriate schemata, when the language fragment is embedded in a sentential landscape. The ability to decontextualise, then, appears to be bound to a representational landscape—graphical decontextualisation is a different skill from sentential decontextualisation. Elsewhere, we have shown that this preference for one or the other approach to learning is related to subjects' implicit models of communication, as evidenced by their naive logical intuitions about quantifiers (Monaghan, 2000). For example, a substantial number of subjects (about 40–50 per cent) who, before being taught syllogisms, reject the inference from "no As are Bs" to "no Bs are As", learn better from the graphical system; subjects who accept this inference learn better from the sentential method for solving syllogisms. This inference is one of those which allow reformulation of premises to avoid backtracking in reasoning in Euler-inside-out. Students who do not command the inference pattern benefit from the graphical help, probably because graphical symmetry makes the inference obvious. This shows the interrelationship between accounts in terms of abstraction and accounts in terms of grasp of the relations between representation systems.

CONCLUSION

There do seem to be differences in the reasoning styles of subjects who prefer spatial and verbal representations to support reasoning. But we have argued that accounts of these differences that rest on phenomenology are theoretically unsatisfactory, and differences that refer only to the tokens of the representational systems (e.g., Larkin & Simon, 1987) are, at best, incomplete. We have identified abstraction as the critical property of strategic variation in using different representations, and this leads to a conceptualisation of abilities and styles in terms of representational landscapes. Our focus has been on the nature of the landscapes of representational systems and the relationship between languages and theorem provers. We suggest that, to generalise individual differences in reasoning and provide explanatory rather than descriptive accounts of behaviour, psychometric approaches have to be understood in computational terms.

Recognition of the relationship between fragments within a representational system seems to be an ability measure. But there is also a significant style in play: navigating within a graphical representational system is somewhat different from navigating around a sentential system. This is due to the different correspondence between the tokens of the language and the theorem prover operating on the symbols. Such differences reflect the "fundamental computational bias" in reasoning, in that subjects vary in terms of the extent to which they can appreciate the applicability of a generalised schema to a fragment of the representational system.

In conclusion, it is clear that we need methods for relating the various representations and strategies which the same subject may use during the course of acquiring expertise at solving a class of problems. Logic provides some of the methods, though they need adapting to the small, finite problems that make up most of the experimental repertoire. We have argued that the key to understanding the individual differences between subjects is understanding these different trajectories toward expertise. All of these different aspects of the computations which go on are susceptible to logical/computational analysis, and only such an analysis will yield a systematic account of the data.

ACKNOWLEDGEMENTS

The support of the McDonnell Foundation and the Economic and Social Research Council, UK, under Fellowship Grant no. R 000271074, is gratefully acknowledged.

REFERENCES

Anderson, J.R. (1978). Arguments concerning representations for mental imagery. *Psychological Review*, *85*, 249–277.

Baddeley, A.D. (1990). *Human Memory: Theory and Practice*. Hove: Psychology Press.

Barwise, J. & Etchemendy, J. (1994). *Hyperproof*. Stanford, CA: CSLI Publications.

Chi, M.T.H., Feltovich, P.J. & Glaser, R. (1981). Categorization and representation of physics problems by experts and novices. *Cognitive Science*, *5*, 121–152.

Clark, H.H. & Chase, W.G. (1972). On the process of comparing sentences against pictures. *Cognitive Psychology*, *3*, 472–517.

Evans, J.St.B.T. (1989). *Bias in Human Reasoning: Causes and Consequences*. Hove: Erlbaum.

Johnson-Laird, P.N. & Byrne, R.M.J. (1991). *Deduction*. Hillsdale, NJ: Erlbaum.

Koedinger, K.R. & Anderson, J.R. (1990). Abstract planning and perceptual chunks: Elements of expertise in geometry. *Cognitive Science*, *14*, 511–550.

Kyllonen, P.C., Lohman, D.F. & Snow, R.E. (1984). Effects of aptitudes, strategy training, and task facets on spatial task performance. *Journal of Educational Psychology*, *76*, 130–145.

Larkin, J.H. & Simon, H.A. (1987). Why a diagram is (sometimes) worth ten thousand words. *Cognitive Science*, *11*, 65–100.

Levesque, H.J. (1988). Logic and the complexity of reasoning. *Journal of Philosophical Logic*, *17*, 355–389.

Macleod, C.M., Hunt, E.B. & Mathews, N.N. (1978). Individual differences in the verification of sentence–picture relationships. *Journal of Verbal Learning and Verbal Behavior*, *17*, 493–507.

Marquer, J.M. & Pereira, M. (1990). Reaction times in the study of strategies in sentence–picture verification: A reconsideration. *Quarterly Journal of Experimental Psychology*, *42*, 147–168.

McKeithen, K.B., Reitman, J.S., Rueter, H.H. & Hirtle, S.C. (1981). Knowledge organization and skill differences in computer programmers. *Cognitive Psychology*, *13*, 307–325.

Monaghan, P. (2000). Representation and Strategy in Reasoning, an Individual Differences Approach. PhD thesis, Division of Informatics, University of Edinburgh.

Monaghan, P. & Stenning, K. (1998). Effects of representational modality and thinking style on learning to solve reasoning problems. In *Proceedings of the 20th Annual Conference of the Cognitive Science Society* (pp. 716–721). Madison, WI: Erlbaum.

Oberlander, J., Monaghan, P., Cox, R., Stenning, K. & Tobin, R. (1999). Unnatural language discourse: an empirical study of multimodal proof styles. *Journal of Logic, Language and Information*, *8*, 363–384.

Paivio, A. (1986). *Mental Representations: A Dual Coding Approach*. Oxford: Oxford University Press.

Pask, G. (1976). Styles and strategies of learning. *British Journal of Educational Psychology*, *46*, 128–148.

Pylyshyn, Z. (1973). What the mind's eye tells the mind's brain. *Psychological Bulletin*, *80*, 1–24.

Roberts, M.J. (1993). Human reasoning: Deduction rules or mental models, or both? *Quarterly Journal of Experimental Psychology*, *45A*, 569–589.

Roberts, M.J. Gilmore, D.J. & Wood, D.J. (1997). Individual differences and strategy selection in reasoning. *British Journal of Psychology*, *88*, 473–492.

Saville & Holdsworth Ltd. (1979). *Advanced Test Battery: Manual and User's Guide*. Thames Ditton, Surrey.

Shin, S. (2002). *The Iconic Logic of Peirce's Graphs*. Cambridge, MA: MIT Press.

Sloman, S.A. (1996). The empirical case for two systems of reasoning. *Psychological Bulletin*, *119*, 3–22.

Snow, R.E. (1980). Aptitude processes. In R.E. Snow, P.-A. Federico & W.E. Montague (eds), *Aptitude, Learning and Instruction* (vol. 1, pp. 27–60). Hillsdale, NJ: Erlbaum.

Stanovitch, K.E. (1999). *Who Is Rational? Studies of Individual Differences in Reasoning*. Mahwah, NJ: Erlbaum.

Stenning, K. (1999). The cognitive consequences of modality assignment for educational communication: The picture in logic. *Learning and Instruction*, *9*, 391–410.

Stenning, K. (2000). Distinctions with differences: comparing criteria for distinguishing diagrammatic from sentential systems. In M. Anderson, P. Cheng & V. Haarslev (eds), *Theory and Application of Diagrams: Lecture Notes in Artificial Intelligence, 1889* (pp. 132–148). Heidelberg: Springer-Verlag.

Stenning, K. (2002). *Seeing Reason: Image and Language in Learning to Think.* Oxford: Oxford University Press.

Stenning, K. & Monaghan, P. (1998). Linguistic and graphical representations and the characterisation of individual differences. In S. Ó'Nualláin (ed.), *Spatial Cognition* (pp. 299–313). Amsterdam: John Benjamins.

Stenning, K. & Oberlander, J. (1995). A cognitive theory of graphical and linguistic reasoning: logic and implementation. *Cognitive Science, 19,* 97–140.

Stenning, K. & Yule, P. (1997). Image and language in human reasoning: a syllogistic illustration. *Cognitive Psychology, 34,* 109–159.

Stenning, K., Cox, R. & Oberlander, J. (1995). Contrasting the cognitive effects of graphical and sentential logic teaching: reasoning, representation and individual differences. *Language and Cognitive Processes, 10,* 333–354.

Wiley, J. (1998). Expertise as mental set: The effects of domain knowledge in creative problem-solving. *Memory and Cognition, 26,* 716–730.

Wood, D.J. (1978). Problem solving—the nature and development of strategies. In G. Underwood (ed), *Strategies in Information Processing* (pp. 329–356). London: Academic Press.

CHAPTER 4

Superordinate Principles, Conditions and Conditionals

Neil Fairley
University of Leicester, UK
and
Ken Manktelow
University of Wolverhampton, UK

CONTENT EFFECTS

The role of problem content in human reasoning has been the prime focus of the psychology of reasoning throughout its recent, and not so recent, history. The oldest reported "content effect" was the belief-bias effect in syllogistic reasoning, stemming from early work by Wilkins (1928), and followed by similar studies in the succeeding decades. Although the belief-bias effect is often construed as showing that people are likely to accept conclusions consonant with their beliefs and reject those dissonant with them, irrespective of their logical validity, Evans and Over (1996, 1997) have shown that the effect is more one of debiasing than of bias: its major effect is to bring about a lower rate of acceptance of unbelievable invalid conclusions.

However, far more research effort has been directed at forms of reasoning where problem contents seem to facilitate rather than inhibit inferences, and most of this work has been on conditional reasoning. Historically, logical validity has often been considered to be the "gold standard" against which our reasoning should be measured. This approach has had a huge influence on psychological accounts of deduction, and the fact that when people reason, they often do not follow logical prescriptions has raised questions regarding human rationality (Evans & Over, 1996, 1997). Hence the idea of "facilitation" effects, as some content effects on conditional reasoning have been labelled: certain contents raise the likelihood that people will endorse logically valid conclusions.

One familiar example of this is the facilitation effect in performance on Wason's selection task (see Manktelow, 1999, for a summary). The task, in its original version (Wason, 1968), asks people to test the truth status of a conditional claim about four cards, stated in the general form, "If p then q". The cards are known to show an instance of p or not-p on

Thinking: Psychological Perspectives on Reasoning, Judgment and Decision Making. Edited by David Hardman and Laura Macchi.
© 2003 John Wiley & Sons, Ltd.

one side, and q or not-q on the other side, and the solvers can see the values p, not-p, q and not-q on the cards before them. Assuming a reading of the stated conditional consistent with the material conditional of logic, and the norm of falsificationism in hypothesis testing, the correct solution is to select the cards which could reveal the combination of p and not-q: the p card, in case it has not-q on its reverse, and the not-q card, in case it has p on its reverse. However, as is well known, participants in such experiments tend not to do this: they choose the p card alone, or the p card with the q card. As is equally well known, the apparently correct solution can be "facilitated" in a number of ways, usually involving changing both the content and the instructional frame from the abstract contents and bald true-or-false goal which comprised the original form of the task.

Numerous demonstrations of the facilitation effect followed its first report by Wason and Shapiro in 1971; they are extensively reviewed in many places (e.g., Griggs, 1983; Evans, Newstead & Byrne, 1993; Oaksford & Chater, 1994; Sperber, Cara & Girotto, 1995; Manktelow, 1999), and we shall not repeat such an exercise here. We merely note at this stage that the initial characterisation of the facilitation effect and similar content effects has run into trouble. This trouble has led to a wholly different and more fruitful approach to the use of different problem contents in the study of reasoning. It concerns the question of appropriateness of norms, and can be stated for present purposes in two related forms.

Consider again the facilitation effect in Wason's selection task, that is, forms of the task which lead to a greater proportion of the "correct" $p +$ not-q selection compared to the usual patterns of the p card alone or $p + q$. Are these latter patterns necessarily mistakes? No, is the answer. Lowe (1993, 1997) has developed a logical argument in favour of the modal pattern while preserving the status of the selection task as a deductive (or metadeductive) problem. More radically, Oaksford and Chater (1994, 1998) have argued that naive reasoners are really approaching the selection task as a task of optimal data search with the aim of updating their beliefs. Using a Bayesian framework, they have shown how it is possible to predict patterns of performance on the selection task in various guises, on the assumption that it is a task of information gain, not of deduction.

Thus, the normative status of the standard and modal solutions is not a settled matter (the question of appropriate norm allocation for this and a wider range of reasoning problems is considered in detail by Stanovich, 1999). The issue of "correct" reasoning has also been addressed from a more empirical standpoint. Beginning in the late 1980s, patterns of performance were predicted and observed which were reliable and rationally justifiable, but not consistent with the narrow "logical" reading of a conditional reasoning task. In the case of the selection task, this is best illustrated by the perspective effect in the deontic task.

FROM CONTENTS TO CONTEXTS

Reasoning research took a new step in the 1980s with the advent of systematic studies of deontic thinking, which began with an effort to explain the facilitation effect in the selection task. Deontic thinking is the kind we engage in when we think about what we are permitted or obliged to do or not do, so common forms of deontic reasoning are those involved in inferences about rules, promises, prohibitions, warnings, threats and so on. As such, deontic reasoning falls under the philosophical definition of practical reasoning, being concerned with action, as opposed to pure or theoretical reasoning, which is concerned with matters of fact, that is, truth and falsity.

Turning the selection task from a task of pure reasoning to one of deontic reasoning was found to have a dramatic effect on performance, as was first clearly demonstrated in a seminal paper by Cheng and Holyoak (1985). Prior to this work, facilitation of the "correct" selection task solution had been found with contents to do with postal regulations, drinking age rules and shopping, among others. Cheng and Holyoak's work suggested that such facilitation is due to our particular expertise in deontic reasoning, which, they argued, results from the use of domain-specific schemas, abstracted from experience.

Cosmides (1989) also put forward a domain-specific theory to explain our facility in deontic reasoning, but this time it was based on an evolutionary rationale. Cosmides argued that people come ready equipped with innate thinking modules which have evolved to deal with age-old adaptive problems whose solution is necessary for survival. She called these Darwinian algorithms. The one she focused on was the social contract algorithm. She held that people innately understand that if you take a benefit, you pay a cost, and are also instinctively prepared to look for cheaters: those who try to take a benefit without paying the cost. This was an evolutionary necessity in a social species, she argued, since without it, those who kept to the contract would be quickly exploited, and ultimately extinguished, by the cheaters.

Two important points of direct relevance to us arose from this work. Firstly, these domain-specific approaches mark the beginning of a shift towards actively using content to study different kinds of reasoning. Secondly, the research led to the empirical problem mentioned earlier, whereby rational patterns of inference emerge which do not accord with the strict logical prescription for correctness.

This was first shown by Cosmides (1989). She argued that people would tend to look for cheaters irrespective of the formal logic of the case. For instance, when the target rule is switched from the standard "If you take a benefit, you pay a cost" to read "If you pay a cost, you may take a benefit", a cheater will be detected by discovering not-p + q cases: the mirror image of the standard correct pattern. She duly found this pattern with a switched rule in the selection task. However, it proved possible to elicit this response without switching the conditional. Manktelow and Over (1991) gave people the deontic rule, "If you spend more than £100, you may take a free gift", in the context of four possible forms of violation: where the customer cheats the store (by taking the gift without spending enough), where the store cheats the customer (by not giving the gift despite the money having been spent), where the store is inefficient (by handing out gifts although not enough has been spent) and where the customer is self-denying (in not taking the gift even though enough has been spent). Only the first and third of these cases correspond to Cosmides' cheater, and yet all four produced highly reliable inference patterns in the predicted directions.

This phenomenon has become known as a perspective effect, and has been confirmed by a number of independent studies (e.g., Gigerenzer & Hug, 1992; Politzer & Nguyen-Xuan, 1992). These other theorists have explained the effect in terms of domain-specific schema theories, Cosmides' in the first case, and Cheng and Holyoak's in the second. Manktelow and Over, however, offered an explanation which made a connection between deontic reasoning and decision theory. They proposed that people think about, say, compliance with a rule of permission in terms of mental models of possible situations and the preferences they have between them. In this view, each type of violation of the shop rule above is a violation of the assumed preferences of one or other party involved in the transaction conveyed by the rule. For instance, the first case is a violation because the customer's preferred model, where a gift is due, is negated. Thus, deontic rules function because they express a relation between utilities: I utter such a rule because I want something from you (for example, to spend more than £100), and you accept it because you will get something from me (a gift). Each party must assume the other's preferences for the transaction to proceed.

A decision-theoretic approach to deontic reasoning is more general than a domain-specific schema approach. It emphasises the role of wider sorts of knowledge, rather than that belonging to isolated domains (e.g., Manktelow & Over, 1991, 1995; Over & Manktelow, 1993). To give one example, it would predict that deontic inferences would be affected by knowledge of probabilities as well as of utilities, and this has been confirmed (Manktelow, Sutherland & Over, 1995). It has also enabled a more general view of more general kinds of reasoning, consistent with work in other areas by other research groups. In the rest of this chapter, we shall report some recent work on these.

KNOWLEDGE AND REASONING: EXTENDING THE PERSPECTIVE EFFECT

From this point, we elaborate our consideration of the role of knowledge in certain forms of reasoning, firstly, by looking briefly at related studies by independent research groups; secondly, by looking at how this work has led to a reformulation of the perspective effect. In the next section, we follow up this line of thought and survey some recent work in which we begin to detail the form this knowledge might take, and how it may be involved in inference.

Categorising the kind of knowledge involved in reasoning was attempted for one species of everyday inference—causal reasoning—by Cummins and her colleagues (Cummins et al., 1991; Cummins, 1995). These researchers suggested that causal inference is mediated by two kinds of factors: disabling conditions and alternative causes. A disabling condition is any factor which prevents an otherwise sufficient cause from producing its effect. For example, a reasoner who is considering the relationship between "studying hard" (a cause) and "doing well in exams" (an effect) may be able to bring to mind factors, such as exam nerves, which they believe could prevent hard study from producing good performance. Such a factor is classed as a disabling condition. In contrast, alternative causes cast doubt on the causal necessity, rather than sufficiency, of cause for effect. In this example, these might include such things as cheating in the exam: an alternative cause of achieving the outcome in question.

Similar factors had previously been advanced in the literature on the suppression of inferences, pioneered by Byrne (e.g., 1989). For instance, Byrne noted that in some conditional reasoning contexts, alternative antecedents were possible which were each sufficient, and hence not individually necessary, for the consequent. Byrne also pointed to the possibility of additional conditions; that is, where an antecedent case might not be sufficient in itself for the consequent (Byrne & Johnson-Laird, 1992). Additional conditions (which, in essence, are additional requirements to be met before the consequent can be achieved) play a similar role to Cummins' disabling conditions: they disrupt the relation of sufficiency between antecedent and consequent. Additional conditions do so when they are absent; disabling conditions do so when they are present.

Thus, in causal inference, there appear to be two general categories of mediating factors, which can be distinguished on the grounds of their respective impact on beliefs about causal sufficiency or necessity. On the one hand, there are disabling conditions together with their counterpart additional requirements, which influence beliefs about causal sufficiency; on the other hand, there are alternative causes, influencing beliefs about causal necessity.

The concepts of necessity and sufficiency have proved useful not only in categorising mediating factors in causal inference, but in explaining aspects of deontic reasoning as well. Thompson (1995), for instance, applied these constructs critically to Cheng and Holyoak's pragmatic schema theory, arguing that all the effects predicted by Cheng and Holyoak, plus some effects not so predicted, could be accounted for in terms of variations in people's perceptions of the condition relations of necessity and sufficiency. Perceptions of condition relations were held by Thompson to be determined by the availability of counterexamples, in the shape of alternative antecedents and additional consequents, with this availability, in turn, governed by knowledge.

Such ideas have recently been extended to the deontic perspective effect, and used to extend that effect beyond deontic reasoning. The deontic perspective effect had been explained by all theorists in terms of the different social roles (parent/child; shopkeeper/shopper, and so on) which participants are cued to take in a deontic reasoning task (e.g., Manktelow & Over, 1991; Gigerenzer & Hug, 1992). However, Fairley, Manktelow and Over (1999) offered an alternative analysis of the perspective effect in terms of necessity and sufficiency. In this analysis, it was proposed that one social role, that of the "agent", or utterer of the rule, induced participants to focus on the necessity of a precondition's being satisfied before an action could be taken; while the other role, that of the "actor", or the target of the rule, resulted in a focus on the sufficiency of the precondition for the action.

This analysis was also applied to predict "perspective" effects in causal reasoning, and these predictions were confirmed. Thus, both deontic and non-deontic perspective effects could be accounted for in the same way, strongly implying that the perspective effect is not decisive evidence that deontic reasoning is somehow special and distinct from other forms of reasoning, as has sometimes been claimed (for independent demonstrations of non-deontic perspective effects, see Beller and Spada, 1998, who also used causal contexts; Ahn and Graham, 1999; and Staller, Sloman and Ben-Zeev, 2000, who used specified biconditional target sentences). Rather, the condition relations explanation suggests that reasoners understand both causal and deontic relationships through perceptions of necessity and sufficiency, which they see as linking some physical cause with an effect or some social precondition with an action. Thus, a condition relations analysis has the potential to unite apparently disparate domains of everyday reasoning under a common theoretical framework. It therefore becomes important to understand how knowledge, in the shape of mediating factors, influences beliefs about necessity and sufficiency.

KNOWLEDGE AND REASONING: STUDIES OF SUPERORDINATE PRINCIPLES (SuperPs)

Let us begin with causal mediating factors, and ask why it is that some factors are effective at mediating inference while others are not. To clarify this question, we return to the example of causal inference introduced above, which relates studying hard to doing well in exams. We can express this relation as a conditional: "If you study hard, you do well in exams", and use it in a syllogism in modus ponens (MP) form:

If you study hard, you do well in exams.
You study hard.
Therefore: you do well in exams.

As we argued earlier, it would be relatively easy to understand people withholding this inference if they can bring a disabling condition (say, exam nerves) to mind: doubt about the sufficiency of the antecedent for the consequent is induced. It would be much more difficult to understand their withholding it on other grounds (say, that the examinee wears blue socks). Why does the former factor, but not the latter, count as a disabling condition?

A similar question can be raised with regard to alternative causes. Recasting the syllogism into a denial of the antecedent (DA) argument yields:

If you study hard, you do well in exams.
You do not study hard.
Therefore: you do not do well in exams.

Here, some factors (say, cheating) would count as alternative causes, and if they can be brought to mind may well cause the conclusion to be withheld by introducing doubt about the necessity of the antecedent for the consequent, while once again other factors (wearing blue socks) would not be expected to affect this inference. Again, the question arises as to why this should be the case.

There is a clear relation here between knowledge and implicit negation. From a strictly logical point of view, all negations of a stated item should be equivalent: they are not the stated item. This should apply to implicit as well as explicit negations, so cheating and blue socks should be alike in their logical status: they are both implicit negations of studying hard. However, there are strong intuitive grounds for doubting this: blue socks and cheating seem to be quite different sorts of denial of studying hard.

Manktelow and Fairley (2000) argued that the distinction between implicit negations as active and inactive candidate mediating factors can be explained by invoking the concept of superordinate principles (SuperPs) in everyday reasoning. In essence, this explanation holds that when reasoners are faced with everyday inferences such as the MP and DA examples above, they are being invited to think about a situation to which they can bring their own knowledge and experience. This knowledge may suggest to them a superordinate antecedent which, to their minds, properly captures the necessary and sufficient conditions for the outcome asserted in the given conditional. In our example, where the stated outcome is "do(ing) well in exams", this antecedent might be something like "writing down good answers", as in "If you write down good answers, you do well in exams". When applied to a specific inference, such as the DA one above, in which the conditional is taken to assert that "studying hard" is necessary for "doing well", this SuperP allows a determination to be made of whether there are, in fact, alternative ways of achieving the stated outcome. This determination is made in terms of whether any candidate alternative causes could plausibly cause or allow the relevant superordinate antecedent to become an actual state of affairs. Factors such as cheating in the exam, which do allow this, count as alternative causes: other candidate factors, such as wearing blue socks, do not.

The notion of SuperP can be applied equally easily to inferences such as MP, in which the conditional is taken to assert the sufficiency of antecedent for consequent. In this case, the determination is made in terms of whether, given that the stated antecedent is an actual state of affairs, any plausible factors can be brought to mind which could prevent the superordinate antecedent ("writing down good answers") from also becoming an actual state of affairs. Familiar factors such as exam nerves, which are able to do this, are classed as disabling conditions: factors whose absence has the same effect are classed as additional requirements; other factors (such as wearing blue socks) that have no known

Table 4.1 The full set of alternative causes and disabling conditions used in the "Study hard" experiment

Condition 1: Sufficiency condition		
Disabling condition (DC)	Arrived 5 minutes late for exam	Is nervous
Explicit negation of DC	Did not arrive late	Is not nervous
Irrelevant to SuperP	Wore blue socks	Is friendly
Exaggerated DC	Arrived 15 minutes late for exam	Is very nervous
Condition 2: Necessity condition		
Alternative cause (AC)	Cheated by doing Y*	Is intelligent
Explicit negation of AC	Did not cheat	Is not intelligent
Irrelevant to SuperP	Wore blue socks	Is friendly
Exaggerated AC	Cheated by doing Y and Z[†]	Is very intelligent

*Y: managing to see a copy of the question paper before the exam.
[†]Z: sneaking a look at a neighbour's answer during the exam.

impact on the actuality or otherwise of the superordinate antecedent have no effect on inference.

Thus, the SuperP construct begins to explain how reasoners might include background knowledge in everyday inference. Predictions arising from this construct were tested in a series of experiments reported in Manktelow and Fairley (2000).

In one of these, participants were presented with a brief scenario based on the content above, in which they were invited to imagine that a lecturer had said to her students:

If you study hard, you will do well in the next test.

Their task was to judge how well each of a number of imaginary students was likely to have done in this test. The object of this experiment was to introduce a range of candidate alternative causes and disabling conditions which differed in their relation to the presumed SuperP ("writing down good answers"), in order to test how these different relations would affect inferences drawn from the target conditional.

Accordingly, for each of two different candidate alternative causes and disabling conditions, four instances were devised: a plain form, an exaggerated form, an explicit negation, and an item irrelevant to SuperP. These are set out in full in Table 4.1. Each candidate mediating factor was presented as an additional premise (placed between the second premise and the conclusion) in the appropriate conditional syllogism: MP for the disabling conditions and DA for the alternative causes. Each syllogism was said to refer to a different imaginary student. Participants rated how well each student was likely to have done on a seven-point rating scale, ranging from 1 (did exceptionally badly) through 4 (a bare pass) to 7 (did exceptionally well), and these ratings were compared to those given for a baseline MP or DA conditional syllogism in which no candidate mediating factors were mentioned.

Results from the MP syllogisms confirmed that the irrelevant items and explicit negations of the disabling condition had no significant effect on the level of endorsement of the MP inference, while the exaggerated disabling conditions suppressed the conclusion significantly more strongly than did the plain forms. Results from the DA syllogisms tell a similar story: in this case, the irrelevant items and explicit negations of the alternative cause led to a significantly higher level of endorsement of DA (that is, rejection of the conclusion) than did the plain or exaggerated alternative causes.

These findings provide evidence consistent with the proposal that when the presumed SuperP is satisfied, either by the stated cause or by an alternative unstated cause, an inference that the effect has occurred is accepted. The complement of this is that when SuperP is not satisfied, either by overt denial or implicit disabling, the inference is accepted markedly less readily.

A second experiment extended the study to additional requirements, alongside disabling conditions and alternative causes. Results again confirmed predictions. Both the plain and exaggerated additional requirements produced significantly higher levels of endorsement of MP than baseline, with the exaggerated additional requirements producing significantly higher levels than the plain forms. Results from the DA condition provided further evidence that a SuperP is being taken into account. One of the disabling conditions from the MP task was also included in the DA condition as an explicit negation of an alternative cause. Interestingly, in the DA condition, this explicit negation produced acceptance ratings which were so low that they closely approached the minimum possible rating. It appears, then, that this factor acted as a disabling condition in the DA task, just as it did in the MP task. Disabling conditions, which suppress conclusions about causal sufficiency, should, of course, not have any effect on the DA inference, which is concerned with necessity. That they do affect this inference provides further support for the proposal that participants are endorsing inferences in the light of a SuperP which they believe asserts both the necessary and sufficient conditions for the consequent.

These experiments confirm that SuperPs have an important influence on causal reasoning. Two further experiments reported in Manktelow and Fairley (2000) extended the SuperP analysis to deontic reasoning. As in the causal experiments described above, the object was to investigate the capacity of the SuperP construct to explain the effects of mediating factors—in this case, to do with the concepts of permission and obligation rather than causation.

Deontic reasoning also seems well suited to this kind of analysis. Consider, for example, a child who has been told, "If you tidy your bedroom, you may go out to play", and who tidies his room but simply piles up the rubbish he has collected outside his door. Here, even though the specific obligation set out in the rule has been satisfied, the parent may well insist that the rubbish is disposed of properly before allowing the child out to play. In this case, disposing of the rubbish properly is an additional requirement, and failing to do this will count as a disabling condition. Similarly, consider a child who fails to tidy his bedroom but instead performs some other action. One possibility is that the child performs some other useful task: say, cleaning the oven or washing the dishes. Another—perhaps more realistic—alternative might be for the child to watch TV or talk to friends on the phone. Intuitively, the former actions are more readily condoned than the latter. In the extreme, the child may perform so many useful actions that these are viewed as fully mitigating his failure to fulfil the specific obligation set out in the rule. In this case, we have an alternative condition under which the child is allowed out to play.

As in the causal case, the distinctions between these factors make sense in terms of a SuperP, which in this instance might be something like "help round the house" or "be a good boy", and, again, the SuperP appears to operate through beliefs about necessity and sufficiency. Thus, alternative conditions cast doubt on the deontic necessity of fulfilling a stated precondition before a certain action is permitted, while additional requirements or disabling conditions cast doubt on whether the way in which the precondition has been satisfied is sufficient for the action to be permitted.

Manktelow and Fairley (2000) report two experiments in which these ideas were tested, using the parent–child content described above. Results from the first experiment confirmed that actions which satisfied the presumed SuperP, such as "tidied the living room" or "washed the dishes", were endorsed more frequently than were ambiguous actions ("did homework" or "made a cake"). In turn, these ambiguous items were endorsed more frequently than actions which clearly do not satisfy SuperP, such as "watched TV" or "phoned friends". Endorsement was measured simply by asking participants whether they would let the child out to play, given one or other of the candidate antecedent values. A second experiment used a more sensitive measure. The target rule was altered to "If you tidy your bedroom, you may go out to play for an hour". This allowed a graded response scale to be used in which the available options represented lengths of time. Results again confirmed that actions which satisfied the presumed SuperP were endorsed more frequently than were ambiguous ones, which, in turn, were endorsed more frequently than actions which do not satisfy the SuperP. Furthermore, this experiment allowed a new and strong prediction to be made. In the case of a child who goes beyond what is required in the rule (that is, has tidied the bedroom and washed the dishes, too), it was predicted that an "Ultra-Q" response would be obtained: time allowed out in this case would exceed that for any other case, including the case where the rule was explicitly satisfied. This prediction was upheld, the first time that a response going beyond the stated consequent has been reported, or even allowed.

EXTENDING SuperP: CONTEXTS AND CONSEQUENCES

These experiments confirm that in both deontic and causal reasoning, the SuperP construct allows the effects of mediating factors to be explained and novel effects predicted, as well as elaborating what counts as an implicit negation or a pragmatic equivalent of a stated value. In this section, we report some further studies in which the questions arising from these ideas and results are explored. They are reported in detail by Fairley and Manktelow (2000).

One ready prediction is that different contents should establish different contexts, which is another way of saying different SuperPs. In one experiment, we made a one-word change to a deontic task in order to achieve this difference. Again, we adapted the parent–child rule; in this case, it was altered to "If you don't tidy your bedroom today, you're grounded". Two scenarios were used: in one, the rule was said to have been uttered by a parent who was concerned about the child's increasing laziness. In the other, it referred to his increasing disobedience. This single change in wording was the only difference between the two scenarios, which were given to different groups. The scenarios were intended to invoke two different SuperPs, to do with laziness and disobedience, respectively, and hence produce different response profiles: laziness is to do with inaction, while disobedience is more to do with defiance. A range of violations was provided, varying in their distance from the stated precondition of tidying the bedroom, as in the previous studies. Participants responded to each violation by stating whether, and for what period of time, the boy should be grounded.

As can be seen from Table 4.2, the results confirmed that the two scenarios produced markedly different patterns of responses. The conceptually closest value to the precondition ("cleans living room") was treated alike in both conditions, but the more distant values were treated differently: in the laziness condition, all remaining violations attracted a similar level of sanction (the scores are not significantly different), perhaps because they all

Table 4.2   Altered SuperPs: disobedience versus laziness: mean "grounding" scores (in days) for each activity

	Activity	Cleans bedroom	Cleans living room	Makes cake	Watches TV	Phones friends
Category of concern	Laziness	0	1.63	1.86	2.72	2.50
	Disobedience	0	1.84	2.95	4.54	5.09

show at least some measure of activity. However, in the disobedience condition, there was an increasing level of sanction as values became more distant from the stated precondition. This latter finding indicates a possible discontinuity, consistent with a presumed SuperP boundary, in the case of disobedience: here, a distinction appears to exist between "allowable" violations—those which still satisfy SuperP—and non-allowable violations, which was not apparent when laziness was the framing principle.

One element which all the scenarios used so far have in common is that they all concerned with "practical" reasoning. That is, participants are required to reach conclusions about courses of action which would enable, say, an exam to be passed or a troublesome child to be dealt with. As we pointed out earlier, this kind of reasoning has been connected with decision making, and thus may be analysed in terms of subjective utility and probability. All normative accounts of decision making specify that decisions among options are to be taken with regard to their consequences (see Baron, 1994, 1996, for a review of the principle of consequentialism from a psychological perspective). It follows that the consequences of practical inferences, as well as their context, should affect the ways they are drawn. From this, it follows that SuperP boundaries may be open to change by perceived consequences.

Fairley and Manktelow (2000) tested this proposition with a courtroom scenario, under the prediction that, where a conclusion is seen as having unfair or unjust consequences, people would set particularly strict criteria for SuperP satisfaction, as reflected in a relative reluctance to assent to such a conclusion. Participants took on the role of an appeal-court judge whose task was to decide, on the basis of specified evidence, whether certain "guilty" verdicts reached by a lower court should be allowed to stand. The key manipulation was of the consequences of endorsing the verdict: participants were told that a "three strikes and out" law was in operation, under which a third conviction for any offence entailed an automatic life sentence. For first offences, the sentence which followed a guilty verdict varied with the seriousness of the charge. The seriousness of the offences in these imaginary cases ranged from the minor (shoplifting) through the progressively more serious crimes of car theft, armed robbery, and attempted murder.

Participants were required to determine the status of the MP syllogism shown below, in which "X" was instantiated as the type of evidence on which the lower court had convicted the suspect: either "a witness identification" or "a signed confession":

If there is X, the defendant must be guilty.
There is X.
Therefore: the defendant must be guilty.

We predicted that in making their determinations, participants would take into account a SuperP: "If there is sufficient evidence, the defendant must be guilty", and that this SuperP

Table 4.3 Proportionate versus disproportionate sentences: mean levels of endorsement for each offence

	Offence	Shoplifting	Car theft	Armed robbery	Attempted murder
Type of sentence	Proportionate	5.75	5.05	5.45	5.30
	Disproportionate	2.80	4.65	4.55	5.80

would be more likely to be deemed satisfied in the case of proportionate sentences (for example, one month's probation for shoplifting) than in the case of disproportionate ones (for example, life imprisonment for shoplifting). On this basis, we predicted that, as sentences became more and more disproportionate, their rejection would become increasingly likely. Participants made their judgments on a labelled, 7-point scale, ranging from 1 (the sentence definitely should not stand), through 4 (completely uncertain whether the sentence should stand), to 7 (the sentence definitely should stand).

The results, set out in Table 4.3, confirmed this prediction. Proportionate sentences were endorsed with little variation between offences, while participants tended to be increasingly unwilling to endorse sentences as these became more disproportionate.

In the context experiment described previously, we showed that boundaries differ between SuperPs: the results of this experiment go beyond that in that they demonstrate that the boundaries of a single SuperP can be drawn differently in the light of the consequences of endorsing an inference. Knowledge of consequences has clearly affected people's propensity to endorse an inference, consistent with an analysis of practical reasoning in terms of decision making rather than deduction: normatively, consequences should affect decisions, but should not affect deductions.

Having established the existence of SuperP boundary effects in "practical" contexts, where the endorsement or otherwise of an inference has consequences in terms of specifying a course of action, we shall now report a final experiment in which we followed up the previous point by attempting to discover whether such boundary effects generalise to epistemic contexts, where no course of action is implied by the endorsement of an inference, and in which the target conditional is treated simply as a hypothesis about the way the world works.

Whether or not boundary effects are to be found in epistemic contexts is an open question. Practical and epistemic inferences can be clearly distinguished in terms of their different functions: practical inferences are concerned with deciding what to do, while epistemic ones are concerned with establishing what is the case. This distinction mirrors the philosophical distinction, mentioned earlier, between practical reasoning (about actions) and pure or theoretical reasoning (about facts and truths). However, what one decides to do is very closely bound up with what one believes to be the case. The decision not to start smoking, for instance, may well be arrived at as a result of considering the truth status of some purported facts: the health risks faced by smokers. Conversely, committed smokers may interpret the facts in a different way, so as to allow them to be comfortable with the habit (Chater and Oaksford, 1996, used a similar argument in criticising proposals for the primacy of deontic over epistemic reasoning). Issues such as this suggest that inferences which, strictly, are epistemic may be subject to influences from practical considerations.

Fairley and Manktelow (2000) investigated this possibility by comparing the patterns of endorsement generated by inferences which have practical consequences with those from an otherwise identical inference which does not. They used a scenario involving an imaginary hormone, called "Alpha-Levodine", supposedly believed by researchers to be produced at high levels by the body in response to certain foods. The target conditional was "If you eat lamb, you produce more Alpha-Levodine", said to be a prediction made by these researchers. The participants' task was to check whether the researcher's hypothesis was correct or not. They did this by selecting appropriate cards from a large-array version of Wason's Selection Task (LAST), in which the eight cards represented hormone test results from eight individuals, each of whom had been given a different food to eat (in this experiment, only antecedent values were displayed). These eight foodstuffs were intended to vary in their conceptual distance from lamb, and included two other kinds of meat (beef and pork), two kinds of fish (mackerel and cod), two plant foodstuffs which are generally regarded as healthy (cabbage and apple) and finally a food which is generally regarded as unhealthy (chocolate cake).

Three independent experimental conditions were provided. In the first of these, it was stated that raised levels of Alpha-Levodine had been found to have positive consequences for health, while, in the second condition, these consequences were said to be negative. Thus, conclusions reached in these conditions are bound up with practical consequences. In contrast, in the third condition, the target conditional was presented simply as a research hypothesis, with no suggestion that finding the hypothesis true or false would have any practical consequences at all: any consequences were purely to do with the truth status of the target sentence. Thus, the comparison between results in this condition and those in the other two allowed the researchers to determine whether any boundary effects found in the first two conditions would also be found in epistemic contexts. No prior predictions were made about what such effects would look like.

The results are shown in Table 4.4. The most immediate result was that, although there were differences in response profiles between the three conditions, these differences were not between the epistemic condition and the practical ones. In both the positive outcome and the epistemic condition, there was a similar decline in card selections as the conceptual distance of foodstuffs from the stated antecedent (lamb) increased, and the results from these conditions were statistically indistinguishable. The results from the negative outcome condition also demonstrated a decline, but here participants chose significantly more "meat" cards than in the other conditions. The SuperP in this experiment was presumed to be "eating foods like lamb", and this latter finding suggests that the SuperP boundary in the negative outcome condition was drawn less tightly than in the other conditions. This may reflect an understandable caution on the part of participants who believe that foods such as lamb may have negative consequences for health, and so include a wider range of foods within the SuperP of "like lamb". However, this is the only way in which the conditions differed, and the difference is not along the epistemic-practical borderline. Psychologically, there is little evidence for such a borderline here.

CONCLUDING REMARKS

This chapter has been concerned with the role of knowledge in inference. The proposal that knowledge is used when making inferences is uncontroversial, but the nature of this influence

Table 4.4 SuperPs in practical and epistemic contexts: percentage of participants choosing cards within postive-outcome, negative-outcome and epistemic contexts

	Card	Lamb	Beef	Pork	Mackerel	Cod	Apple	Cabbage	Chocolate cake
	Positive	100	50	50	22	44	28	33	33
Context:	Negative	100	90	84	47	47	37	31	42
	Epistemic	100	61	56	28	39	28	28	22

has not been well understood. We believe that the SuperP construct is a step forward in this understanding. In the experiments described here, we have shown that SuperPs can predict and explain the effects of mediating factors in both causal and deontic reasoning contexts, that they can cast light on the nature and role of implicit negation and pragmatic equivalence in reasoning, that SuperPs can help explain connections between everyday reasoning and decision making, and that the construct can be extended to epistemic as well as practical inference.

SuperPs can be viewed as principles which, in context, properly specify the conditions for membership of the category expressed in the consequent part of a conditional sentence. Thus, in the "exam" experiment described earlier, the target conditional, "If you study hard, you will do well in the next test", asserts that satisfying a certain condition (hard study) will lead to membership of the category, "people who do well in the next test". As we have seen, however, background knowledge can lead people to question this assertion, and to hold instead that a SuperP akin to "writing down good answers" better captures the conditions for membership of this category, such that that same inference can be made or withheld depending on the way these more general conditions are brought into play.

However, despite its capacity to account for much in our data, this approach has an obvious limitation: in our "lazy/disobedient" experiment, we were able to produce significant changes in participants' responses by leading them to believe that a child's behaviour arose from disobedience as opposed to laziness. While this finding is perfectly consistent with the view that we sensitised participants to two different categories of concern, such a view has nothing to say about why violations within one of these categories should be subject to different penalties than the same violations in the other category. In this respect, understanding SuperPs purely in terms of category ascription tells only half the story: it fails to incorporate the different motivations and goals which, presumably, are what lead to violations within these different categories being treated differently.

Because of this, SuperPs may perhaps be better described as principles which specify the conditions which will lead to some goals being achieved. In the case of the "lazy/disobedient" experiment, the relevant goal is, of course, the prevention of either disobedience or laziness; these different goals may be held more or less strongly, and perceived ways of achieving them may differ, thus accounting for the differences in the way in which violations were treated within the different contexts. This goal-based approach can be applied to each of the SuperPs proposed to explain findings in the current experiments: even in the epistemic condition of the "foodstuff" experiment, in which no practical consequences followed from confirmation or disconfirmation of the target conditional, an epistemic goal (of "understanding which foods contain Alpha-Levodine" as a means of arriving at the SuperP "foods like lamb") could explain the "distance" effects observed.

Note that this goal-based approach is not an alternative to the category-based approach mentioned above: rather, in this view, goals provide an incentive to discover whether, and how, category membership can be achieved. This goal-based approach is also, of course, fully consistent with an important point which we made earlier: that "everyday" deduction is very closely related to decision making.

In the kinds of everyday, semantically rich contexts explored here, then, reasoners appear to invoke SuperP in goal-directed inferences. The relevance of a candidate SuperP instance (of which the stated antecedent is just one of the possible cases) is given by the overlap between the features of the instance and those of the goals inherent in the consequent of the target conditional. Whatever one's goals might be, the principles which maximise the chances of achieving them are those that fully specify the conditions under which they will occur, and these are ones that state the necessary and sufficient conditions for their occurrence. This is not to say, however, that when people reason with a conditional containing a SuperP, they are necessarily reasoning with a biconditional. Logical biconditionals state that the antecedent is necessary and sufficient for the consequent, and vice versa. The kinds of inferences we have explored here, however, indicate two departures from this model.

Firstly, there is no evidence for this bidirectionality; that is, for inference from consequent to antecedent. That much would follow in any case from the notion that the goals inherent in the consequent specify the relevant features of the SuperP: the goals determine that the direction of inference is from antecedent to consequent. Secondly, we have seen how the particular inference task (for example, MP versus DA) leads to a focusing on either the sufficiency or the necessity, respectively, of antecedent for consequent. This idea of focusing recalls the similar notion put forward by Legrenzi, Girotto and Johnson-Laird (1993) that people focus on the explicit elements of a mental model when making an inference or a decision. Our proposal adds to this idea: reasoners may also focus selectively on one or other of the possible relations between them.

This does not mean that the results reported here can be interpreted only in the terms of mental model theory. As pointed out by Manktelow and Fairley (2000), these results do not sit comfortably with any of the current major theories of reasoning. The model theory would have to be modified to allow that elements in models have features which can be made explicit or left implicit, depending on the goals of the inferential problem; at present, the construct of implicit/explicit representation applies only to the problem elements themselves. Similarly, the theory would have to deal with the ways in which the condition relations (necessity and sufficiency) can also be selectively attended to. The same problems beset the mental logic approach (e.g., Braine & O'Brien, 1991; Rips, 1994), which would need to account for the ways in which implicit negations sometimes may, and sometimes may not, stand for a stated positive instance, and would also need to account for selective focusing on necessity and sufficiency. SuperPs pose the question for the information gain theory of how to express its integral rarity assumption, and also imply a greater role for utility (including epistemic utility) in addition to probability (cf. Evans & Over, 1996, on this point). Lastly, the current findings are also troublesome for domain-specific theories, such as pragmatic reasoning schema theory (Cheng & Holyoak, 1985; Holyoak & Cheng, 1995) and social contract theory (e.g., Cosmides, 1989). This is because we have found that the same patterns of influence of SuperPs, and of necessity and sufficiency (see Fairley, Manktelow & Over, 1999), can be detected across causal, deontic and epistemic domains. In the time-honoured tradition of concluding sentiments, we can only assert that further research will be needed before these patterns are clarified, let alone explained.

REFERENCES

Ahn, W. & Graham, L.M. (1999). The impact of necessity and sufficiency in the Wason four-card selection task. *Psychological Science, 10,* 237–242.

Baron, J. (1994). *Thinking and Deciding,* 2nd edn. London: Cambridge University Press.

Baron, J. (1996). Nonconsequentialist decisions. *Behavioral and Brain Sciences, 17,* 1–42.

Beller, S. & Spada, H. (1998). Conditional reasoning with a point of view: The logic of perspective change. In M.A. Gernsbacher & S.J. Derry (eds), *Proceedings of the Twentieth Annual Conference of the Cognitive Science Society* (pp. 138–143). Mahwah, NJ: Erlbaum.

Braine, M.D.S. & O'Brien, D.P. (1991). A theory of If: A lexical entry, reasoning program, and pragmatic principles. *Psychological Review, 98,* 182–203.

Byrne, R.M.J. (1989). Suppressing valid inferences with conditionals. *Cognition, 31,* 61–83.

Byrne, R.M.J. & Johnson-Laird, P.N. (1992). The spontaneous use of propositional connectives. *Quarterly Journal of Experimental Psychology, 44A,* 89–110.

Chater, N. & Oaksford, M. (1996). Deontic reasoning, modules and innateness: A second look. *Mind and Language, 11,* 191–202.

Cheng, P.W. & Holyoak, K.J. (1985). Pragmatic reasoning schemas. *Cognitive Psychology, 17,* 391–416.

Cosmides, L. (1989). The logic of social exchange: Has natural selection shaped how humans reason? Studies with the Wason selection task. *Cognition, 31,* 187–276.

Cummins, D.D. (1995). Naive theories and causal deduction. *Memory and Cognition, 23,* 646–658.

Cummins, D.D., Lubart, T., Alksnis, O. & Rist, R. (1991). Conditional reasoning and causation. *Memory and Cognition, 19,* 274–282.

Evans, J.St.B.T. & Newstead, S.E. & Byrne, R.M.J. (1993). *Human Reasoning: The Psychology of Deduction.* Hove: Erlbaum.

Evans, J.St.B.T. & Over, D.E. (1996). *Rationality and Reasoning.* Hove: Psychology Press.

Evans, J.St.B.T. & Over, D.E. (1997). Rationality in reasoning: the problem of deductive competence. *Current Psychology of Cognition, 16,* 3–38.

Fairley, N. & Manktelow, K.I. (2000, August). Contexts, consequences and superordinate principles in practical inference. Paper presented at the Fourth International Conference on Thinking, University of Durham, UK.

Fairley, N., Manktelow, K.I. & Over, D.E. (1999). Necessity, sufficiency and perspective effects in causal conditional reasoning. *Quarterly Journal of Experimental Psychology, 52A,* 771–790.

Gigerenzer, G. & Hug, K. (1992). Domain-specific reasoning: Social contracts, cheating and perspective change. *Cognition, 43,* 127–171.

Griggs, R.A. (1983). The role of problem content in the selection task and in the THOG problem. In J.St.B.T. Evans (ed.), *Thinking and Reasoning: Psychological Approaches.* London: Routledge.

Holyoak, K.J. & Cheng, P.W. (1995). Pragmatic reasoning with a point of view. *Thinking and Reasoning, 1,* 289–313.

Legrenzi, P., Girotto, V. & Johnson-Laird, P.N. (1993). Focussing in reasoning and decision making. *Cognition, 49,* 37–66.

Lowe, E.J. (1993). Rationality, deduction and mental models. In K.I. Manktelow & D.E. Over (eds), *Rationality.* London: Routledge.

Lowe, E.J. (1997). Whose rationality? Logical theory and the problem of deductive competence. *Current Psychology of Cognition, 16,* 140–146.

Manktelow, K.I. (1999). *Reasoning and Thinking.* Hove: Psychology Press.

Manktelow, K.I. & Fairley, N. (2000). Superordinate principles in reasoning with causal and deontic conditionals. *Thinking and Reasoning, 6,* 41–65.

Manktelow, K.I. & Over, D.E. (1991). Social roles and utilities in reasoning with deontic conditionals. *Cognition, 39,* 85–105.

Manktelow, K.I. & Over, D.E. (1995). Deontic reasoning. In S.E. Newstead & J.St.B.T. Evans (eds), *Perspectives on Thinking and Reasoning: Essays in Honour of Peter Wason*. Hove: Erlbaum.

Manktelow, K.I., Sutherland, E.J. & Over, D.E. (1995). Probabilistic factors in deontic reasoning. *Thinking and Reasoning*, *1*, 201–219.

Oaksford, M. & Chater, N. (1994). A rational analysis of the selection task as optimal data selection. *Psychological Review*, *101*, 608–631.

Oaksford, M. & Chater, N. (1998). A revised rational analysis of the selection task: Exceptions and sequential sampling. In M. Oaksford & N. Chater (eds), *Rational Models of Cognition*. Oxford: Oxford University Press.

Over, D.E. & Manktelow, K.I. (1993). Rationality, utility and deontic reasoning. In K.I. Manktelow & D.E. Over (eds), *Rationality*. London: Routledge.

Politzer, G. & Nguyen-Xuan, A. (1992). Reasoning about conditional promises and warnings: Darwinian algorithms, mental models, relevance judgements or pragmatic schemas? *Quarterly Journal of Experimental Psychology*, *44*, 401–412.

Rips, L.J. (1994). *The Psychology of Proof*. Cambridge, MA: MIT Press.

Sperber, D., Cara, F. & Girotto, V. (1995). Relevance theory explains the selection task. *Cognition*, *57*, 31–95.

Staller, A., Sloman, S.A. & Ben-Zeev, T. (2000). Perspective effects in non-deontic versions of the Wason selection task. *Memory and Cognition*, *28*, 396–405.

Stanovitch, K.E. (1999). *Who Is Rational? Studies of Individual Differences In Reasoning*. Mahwah, NJ: Erlbaum.

Thompson, V.A. (1995). Conditional reasoning: The necessary and sufficient conditions. *Canadian Journal of Experimental Psychology*, *49*, 1–58.

Wason, P.C. (1968). Reasoning about a rule. *Quarterly Journal of Experimental Psychology*, *20*, 273–281.

Wason, P.C. & Shapiro, D. (1971). Natural and contrived experience in a reasoning problem. *Quarterly Journal of Experimental Psychology*, *23*, 63–71.

Wilkins, M.C. (1928). The effect of changed material on the ability to do formal syllogistic reasoning. *Archives of Psychology*, *102*.

CHAPTER 5

Premise Interpretation in Conditional Reasoning

Guy Politzer

Centre National de la Recherche Scientifique, Saint-Denis, France

Conditional sentences are pervasive in human communication. Many arguments contain conditional premises or a conditional conclusion. The expression "conditional reasoning" could appropriately be applied to such arguments. However, there is a tradition in psychological research, which will be followed here, of restricting the application of this expression to two-premise arguments that have one conditional premise (called the major), and a second premise (called the minor) made of either the antecedent of the conditional or its negation, or the consequent of the conditional or its negation. This leads to the following four arguments:

Two deductively valid arguments:
Modus ponendo ponens (MP):
if p then q; p; therefore q.
Modus tollendo tollens (MT):
if p then q; not-q; therefore not-p.

Two deductively invalid arguments:
The fallacy of affirming the consequent (AC):
if p then q; q; therefore p.
The fallacy of denying the antecedent (DA):
if p then q; not-p; therefore not-q.

Conditional reasoning is, on par with Wason's selection task, the most investigated paradigm in the psychology of reasoning (Wason, 1966; for reviews, see Evans, Newstead & Byrne, 1993; Manktelow, 1999). The general trend of performance with formal material (in which arguments are presented in their symbolic form) seems robust, even though there is some variability due to factors such as instructions and response format. The conclusion of MP is endorsed by nearly everybody; that of MT by around two-thirds of the participants only, while both fallacies are committed by around one-half of them (for a review, see Evans, 1982; Evans, Newstead & Byrne, 1993). It is hard to have as clear a picture of performance with thematic material, that is, material in which the symbols p and q are instantiated by

Thinking: Psychological Perspectives on Reasoning, Judgment and Decision Making. Edited by David Hardman and Laura Macchi.
© 2003 John Wiley & Sons, Ltd.

short meaningful sentences. Some early studies (e.g., Matalon, 1962; T.C. O'Brien, 1972; Staudenmayer, 1975) had already observed that the rate of endorsement was a function of the semantic content of the sentences, but this observation was rather incidental. More recent studies of conditional reasoning, with planned observations, have shown that the effects may be of considerable magnitude; they will be reviewed below. These results are not surprising given that investigations of conditionals have regularly shown differences in interpretation as a function of content (Legrenzi, 1970; Wason & Johnson-Laird, 1972; Fillenbaum, 1975, 1978; Politzer, 1981). Such effects have been given greater emphasis in the context of research on the thematic version of Wason's selection task, where they soon became the main centre of interest.

"Content effect" is the name traditionally given to the variation of responses and consequently of reasoning performance as a function of the semantic content of the premises. The present chapter aims to propose a theoretical framework to explain these effects in conditional reasoning. It will not concern itself with issues that oppose theories of deductive reasoning (such as the mental model–mental logic debate). The reason is that in focusing on the interpretative step (in particular, the pragmatic processes involved in utterance interpretation) that precedes the inferential step proper, it is orthogonal to such a debate: This interpretative step yields the final semantic representation (be it a mental model or a syntactic expression) which serves as the input to the deductive step.

A FORMALISATION OF CONDITIONALS IN CONTEXT

When we look for a formal description of conditionals that could at the same time account for content effects, one area suggests itself, namely, causality. The search for causal factors and the formation of a good hypothesis rely crucially on knowledge of the domain under investigation. Mackie's (1974) theory of causality provides two important concepts within a formalism that seems susceptible to generalisation to other conditionals. The first concept is that of a "causal field". A cause acts in a context that contains other factors which formally are possible candidates for the role of a cause. However, they are not usually considered as a cause. They are not even mentioned in causal statements because it is tacitly accepted that they are present in the normal state of the world. This set of factors constitutes the causal field against which the factor identified as a cause is extracted by virtue of its difference in the field. A classical example of a factor that belongs to the causal field is the presence of oxygen in the air in the case of an accidental explosion. Although, physically, a cause (in the sense that it is necessary for the explosion to occur), it is usually not considered as a cause and usually need not be mentioned.

Second, Mackie (1974) pointed out that a cause often has a fine-grained structure that can be described formally as a disjunctive form, so that the causal relation can be written as follows:

$$[(A_m \& \ldots \& A_1 \& A) \lor (B_n \& \ldots \& B_1 \& B) \lor \ldots] \rightarrow Q$$

While the whole disjunctive form is both necessary and sufficient for the effect Q to occur, each disjunct as a whole, such as $(A_m \& \ldots \& A_1 \& A)$, is sufficient, and each conjunct $(A, A_1, \ldots, A_m)$ separately is necessary with respect to the disjunct in which it appears. $A_1, \ldots, A_m$, and $B_1, \ldots, B_n$ play the role of background conditions in the causal field with respect to

A and B (the focal factors), respectively. Mackie did not explicitly combine both analyses; that is, the disjunctive form structure of a cause and the causal field.[1] But given that any factor in the causal field has the same logical status as the cause, it is clear that these factors can be formally integrated conjunctively within the disjuncts of a normal form.

If one generalised to other conditionals than causals (with possible exceptions such as analytically true conditionals), *if A then Q* could also be formalised as above. The factors with a subscript constitute what could be called by analogy a "conditional field". The following abridged form, restricted to only two disjuncts of two conjuncts each, will be more manageable for the purpose of exposition:

$$[(A_1 \& A) _v (B_1 \& B)] \rightarrow Q$$

Conjunctive Components

A is the only factor in the antecedent that appears in the verbalisation of the conditional sentence, *if A then Q*. A_1 is a background condition which is assumed to be satisfied in the normal state of the world. Since its satisfaction is necessary to complement the antecedent and turn the conjunct into a sufficient compound factor, it will be called a "complementary necessary condition" (CNC). In conversation, A_1 is assumed to be part of common knowledge. The necessity status of many such conditions is assumed by the speaker to be indisputable; their satisfaction is tacitly assumed in the same manner as factors in the causal field remain unmentioned. The existence of such conditions was recognised long ago, as suggested by the following statements, the first from Ramsey (1931): "In general we can say with Mill that 'if P then Q' means that Q is inferrable from P, that is, of course, from P together with certain facts and laws not stated but in some way indicated by the context". The second is from Goodman (1947): "The assertion that a connection holds is made on the presumption that certain circumstances not stated in the antecedent obtain." The status of these facts or circumstances can nowadays be clarified on the basis of pragmatic theory. It is not the aim of the present chapter to develop it. Suffice it to say that the assumption of satisfaction of CNCs comes as an epistemic implicature. Conditionals are typically uttered with an implicit ceteris paribus assumption to the effect that the speaker believes that the normal conditions of the world (the satisfaction of the CNCs that belong to common knowledge) hold. Should further information deny or just raise doubt of this assumption, the implicature is cancelled and the conditional premise no longer conveys a sufficient condition.[2]

The properties of CNCs need to be analysed in some more detail. First, CNCs vary in their degrees of necessity. Consider, for example, *if Mary needs bread, she goes to the supermarket*. Among the various CNCs some are sine qua non conditions (call them "strong conditions"; for example, *Mary is not bedridden*), and others are less indispensable ("weak conditions"; for example, *she has the time, she has got small change*). As this example shows, necessity is a matter of degree, and the degree is immediately suggested by knowledge of the domain.

---

[1] Mackie may have had reasons for this, linked with a concern to distinguish particular causal events from general ones. This need not concern us here.
[2] Artificial systems, such as default logics, require the search for exceptions in the whole database, which soon becomes intractable. This formidable problem is solved in human communication by the speaker's guarantee of normality: any exception ought to be mentioned and an absence of qualification means that the normal state of the world obtains. In a sense, the "burden of the proof" is reversed.

Second, there are two kinds of CNCs. Some of them are such that it cannot be the case (or it is less likely) that Q in their absence (they are called "enablers" in the domain of causality) and some others are intrinsically negative in the sense that it cannot be the case (or it is less likely) that Q in their presence (they are called "disablers" in the domain of causality). By "satisfaction" of a CNC is meant their presence (or truth) in the first case, or their absence (or falsity) in the second case.[3]

Third, although it is easier for purposes of exposition to consider CNCs as discrete, this need not be the case. Referring again to the domain of causality, recall that Mill's methods (Mill, 1988/1843) concern first the discrete case and subsequently the continuous case (in the method of concomitant variation). Similarly, in a conditional field, the CNCs (as well as the focal factors) can vary by degree, so that there can be a functional relation between a CNC and the consequent Q. This often gives rise to rules of the type *the more A_i, the more Q*, called "topoi" in studies of argumentation (Anscombre, 1995).

Finally, the CNCs vary in their availability. Some have low or very low availability; these may be virtually unlimited in number. They can be described as "preconditions" for the sentence to be asserted. Some others have high availability but are usually limited in number. For a causal sentence such as *if one turns the ignition key, the engine starts*, an example of the first kind is *the engine has not been removed from the car* (a prerequisite before one even thinks of starting the engine), while *the battery has not run down* is an example of the second kind. Besides the objective knowledge of the domain, there is a psychological criterion to distinguish between the two. If asked what is necessary for the engine to start after the ignition key has been turned, most people would propose the same few "conditions" (such as the state of the battery, petrol or plugs) after a rapid search of memory, whereas different people would generate different "preconditions" (the engine is in the car, the car is not on the moon, etc.) after a rather long process of *abduction*. In brief, the assumption of satisfaction of the preconditions is not questionable; without it, the sentence would not be assertable, or, at the very least, it would be deceptive. The assumption of satisfaction of the conditions is questionable on the part of the hearer, and it is the one which concerns us. It is at the basis of the possibility that a conditional sentence is susceptible to controversy. Except for cases where there is a lack of relation between antecedent and consequent (to be considered below), most disputes over the credibility of a conditional statement revolve around the question of the satisfaction of a CNC, and, more precisely, of the extent to which the speaker is right in assuming the satisfaction of a CNC. The relevance of an indicative conditional statement stems principally from the fact that one is licensed to infer the consequent, the antecedent being granted, or reasonably likely (Sperber, Cara & Girotto, 1995). Given that, like any other statement, a conditional is uttered with a guarantee of relevance, the speaker must be credited with belief in the satisfaction of the CNCs; failing this, the truth of the compound antecedent and that of the whole sentence could not be assumed, and the inference from the antecedent to the consequent would fail. However, the hearer may have independent reasons to question this satisfaction, due to diverging or new sources of information, consideration of plausibility and so on.

---

[3] Mackie (1974) described the antecedent as

(A & B & ⁻C) ᵥ (D & F & ⁻G) ᵥ . . .

where A (and D) are INUS conditions (each is an insufficient but non-redundant part of an unnecessary but sufficient condition), B (and F) are enablers and C (and G) are disablers (or counteracting causes in Mill's terms [Mill, 1988/1843]) marked by an explicit negation.

Disjunctive Components

There are usually supplementary factors like those in the second disjunct $(B_1 \& B)$ whose conjunction, if satisfied, would be sufficient for Q to hold. With respect to B, B_1 is also a CNC. The status of disjuncts such as $(B_1 \& B)$ with respect to $(A_1 \& A)$ is that of an alternative sufficient condition. A and B, which are the factors of interest in the conditional field, are "antecedents". Given that B_1, like A_1, is tacitly assumed, B acts as an "alternative antecedent".

If the hearer has some reason to believe that A is the only antecedent, or that the alternative antecedents are not satisfied, he is licensed to infer *if it is not the case that A, it is not the case that Q*. This is the well-known "invited inference". Technically, it is also an implicature, but notice that it need not be a default assumption. It is essentially dependent on the context, part of which is determined by the knowledge base, and another part by preceding utterances that constitute the dialogue. Nevertheless, if the implicature has been generated, it can be cancelled by an additional piece of information. All this can be illustrated by the classic example from Geis and Zwicky (1971), *if you mow the lawn, I'll give you five dollars*. In this underspecified context, there is a lack of cues that could suggest alternative antecedents and reasons to assume their satisfaction. It is the intuition of most people that the inference, *if you don't mow the lawn, I will not give you five dollars*, is implied, an implicature that could be cancelled if the speaker added, for example, *there are also a number of things to repair in the house*. As Lilje (1972) argued, the invited inference is less likely to occur if the sentence is uttered in response to *how can I earn five dollars?*, which triggers a search for, and retrieval of, alternatives in the knowledge base. In brief, the possible interpretation of *if* as a biconditional stems from an implicature which the hearer generates or not on the basis of the knowledge base, given the aim of the talk exchange.[4]

Relation Within the Conditional Link

The antecedent should be related to the consequent, in the sense that knowing the antecedent should be a good reason to believe the consequent. The various antecedents (including the main antecedent A) may be more or less strongly linked to the consequent in that sense, and here again the connection is indicated by knowledge of the domain. In the case of *if Mary needs bread, she goes to the supermarket*, there are many alternative antecedents, some of which are strongly linked to the consequent (*Mary needs matches*), some moderately (*Mary feels bored*) and yet others weakly or not at all (*Mary is looking for a new house*). In the last case, that Mary needs a new house is not a good reason to believe that she goes to the supermarket; but such judgments are defeasible upon revelation of a new piece of information; for example, that there is an advertisement board in the supermarket where she can find offers of houses to rent. In brief, background knowledge is a determinant of belief in the conditional as a whole through the appraisal of the link between antecedent and consequent. This differs from the process considered under the heading Conjunctive Components, where background knowledge provides conditions whose satisfaction determines belief in the compound antecedent.

---

[4] Pragmaticists do not all agree on the mechanism of generation of this implicature. For two recent (and diverging) accounts, see Horn (2000) and van der Auwera (1997, of which the present account is a variation).

In summary, the judgment of the sufficiency of the antecedent may be revised if the satisfaction of the CNC is doubted, denied or partial. The judgment of the necessity of the antecedent results from the assumption of non-satisfaction or of the absence of alternative antecedents. This judgment may be cancelled if new information arouses doubt or brings denial of this assumption, and both judgments of the sufficiency and necessity of the antecedent may be questioned right away if the antecedent is not strongly related to the consequent.

The foregoing framework enables us to derive the following general consequences for conditional reasoning arguments.

(D_1) *The rate of endorsement of MP and MT will decrease*
   (i) if the satisfaction of a CNC is denied;
   (ii) if a doubt of the satisfaction of a CNC is suggested (in particular, when a new piece of information enters the context) or stated;
   (iii) if it is stated or known that the CNC is not fully satisfied.
        In these cases, belief in the consequent of the conditional is not warranted, by virtue of the definition of a CNC. Consequently, MP fails to deliver a sure conclusion; so does MT because its conclusion is *not $(A_1 \& A)$*: since A_1 is now uncertain, one cannot conclude about *A* with certainty.
   (iv) with weak CNCs, the effect of these manipulations will be weaker because the consequent is less dependent on weak than on strong CNCs.

(D_2) *The rate of endorsement of AC and DA*
   (i) *will increase* as a function of the ease with which the context invites the implicature;
   (ii) *will decrease* as a function of the salience of alternative antecedents in the context;
   (iii) *will decrease* with knowledge of additional information that emphasises the existence or the satisfaction of alternative antecedents (so leading to the cancellation of the implicature).
        This is because the rate of acceptance of the two arguments under consideration is known to be an increasing function of the rate of biconditional interpretation (which is assumed to depend on the implicature).

(D_3) *The rate of endorsement of the conclusion of the four arguments* should be an increasing function of the relatedness of the antecedent to the consequent. This derivation will not be considered in the rest of this chapter because, to the best of the author's knowledge, it has not been addressed experimentally.

A REVIEW OF THE LITERATURE

Interest in the phenomena which, from the present point of view, are linked to the manipulation of alternative antecedents or of CNCs is relatively recent: it dates back to the early 1980s in the first case and to the late 1980s in the second case.

Studies of Valid Arguments

Byrne (1989) is the first author to have applied to valid arguments a manipulation similar to the one which Rumain et al. (1983, reviewed below) used only for invalid arguments. One group of participants solved standard arguments such as, for MP: *if she has an essay to write, she will study late in the library; she has an essay to write*; therefore: (a) *she will study late in the library*; (b) *she will not study late in the library*; (c) *she may or may not study late in the library.* Another group solved the same arguments as the first group, modified by the addition of a third premise; this premise was a conditional that had the same consequent as the major and an antecedent that was a CNC with regard to the major, such as *if the library stays open, she will study late in the library.* While, for the first group, a high level of correct responses on MP and MT was observed, for the second group (with mention of a CNC) this rate collapsed to around 35 per cent for both MP and MT; that is, the majority did not endorse the conclusion. As claimed by D_1(ii), the addition of the conditional premise (for example, *if the library stays open...*) casts doubt on the CNC which constitutes its antecedent through an epistemic implicature; hence the observed effect.

Chan and Chua (1994) used various non-causal conditional rules with MP and MT arguments. For each conditional premise, they defined three necessary conditions for the consequent of the conditional to hold; these conditions varied in strength (that is, in degree of necessity or importance as estimated by judges). For example, with a MP whose major was *if Steven is invited, he will attend the party*, the three levels of necessity were introduced each time by an additional premise following Byrne's (1989) paradigm: *if Steven knows the host well, he will attend the party* (or *if Steven knows at least some people well, he will attend the party*, or *if Steven completes the report tonight, he will attend the party*). The response options were *he will attend the party; he will not attend the party; he may or may not attend the party.* It was observed that the endorsement rate of the conclusion of these three-premise arguments was a decreasing function of the degree of necessity. In brief, the statement of an additional conditional premise which contained a CNC in its antecedent diminished the rate of endorsement of the conclusion all the more sharply as the condition was strong, in accordance with D_1(iv).

Stevenson and Over's (1995) first experiment had two controls and five experimental conditions. The first control was a standard argument, such as (for MP) *if John goes fishing, he will have a fish supper; John goes fishing*, whose conclusion was evaluated on a five-option scale: *John will have a fish supper; will probably have... may or may not have... probably won't have... won't have....* The second control had a third premise with a CNC as antecedent (as in Byrne's experimental condition): *if John catches a fish, he will have a fish supper.* The five experimental conditions had a fourth premise that informed the subject about the likelihood of the satisfaction of the CNC: *John is always lucky; almost always... sometimes... rarely... very rarely....* While, in the second control condition, Byrne's results were replicated, the effect of the fourth premise on both MP and MT was to decrease the rate of endorsement of the conclusion and correlatively to increase the uncertainty ratings in a near-monotonic fashion across conditions. This shows that the manipulation of degrees of necessity results in functionally related degrees of belief in the conclusion of the arguments, again supporting D_1(ii).

In their second experiment, the same authors used three-premise arguments in which the second premise was a categorical sentence that introduced various levels of frequency directly into the necessary condition. For example, given the major premise, *if John goes fishing, he will have a fish supper*, there were five levels in the second premise: *John always catches a fish when he goes fishing; almost always... sometimes... almost never... never....* For both MP and MT, the rate of endorsement of the conclusion decreased monotonically as the frequency mentioned in the second (categorical) premise decreased (with a floor effect on the two smallest frequencies). In brief, in agreement with

D_1(i) and (ii), the denial and explicit introduction of various degrees of doubt on a CNC diminished the endorsement of the conclusion; moreover, the greater the doubt, the greater the decrease.

Cummins' studies (Cummins et al., 1991; Cummins, 1995) focused on arguments with causal conditionals. She demonstrated that the acceptance rate of the conclusion depended on the number of disabling conditions for MP and MT. For example, of the following two MP arguments, *if the match was struck, it lit; the match was struck / it lit* and *if Joe cut his finger, it bled; Joe cut his finger / it bled*, people are less prone to accept the conclusion of the first, which can be shown to have many disabling conditions, than the conclusion of the second, which has few. Thompson (1994, 1995) obtained similar results not only with causals, but also with non-causal rules, such as obligations, permissions and definitions, by using conditionals that varied in perceived sufficiency (as independently rated by judges). She defined a sufficient relationship as one in which the consequent always happens when the antecedent does. The following sentences exemplify a high and a low level of sufficiency, respectively, for permissions: *If the licensing board grants it a licence, a restaurant is allowed to sell alcohol. If athletes pass the drug test at the Olympics, the IOC can give them a medal.* The author observed that the rate of endorsement of the conclusion was an increasing function of the level of sufficiency. As these examples show, the Thompson manipulation can also be described in terms of sentences with a high or a low number of CNCs, whether positive or negative (whereas Cummins' disablers were necessarily negative). Consequently, CNCs are less likely to be all satisfied when this number is high than when it is low; hence the difference in the acceptance rate of the valid conclusion, in line with D_1(ii).

More direct evidence of the effect of the assumption of satisfaction of CNCs on the willingness to endorse the conclusion was provided by George's (1995) third experiment. Two groups of participants received contrasting instructions. One group was asked to assume the truth of debatable conditionals such as *if a painter is talented, his/her works are expensive*, while the other group was invited to take into consideration the uncertain status of the statements. As a result, 60 per cent in the first group endorsed the conclusion of at least three of the four MP arguments, while in the second group only 25 per cent did so. By asking them to asssume the truth of such conditionals, participants were invited to dismiss possible objections such as *the painter must be famous*, whereas stressing the uncertainty of the statement is a way to invite them to take such objections into account.

Manktelow and Fairley (2000) manipulated the extent to which a CNC is satisfied. With a low degree of satisfaction, the consequent was less likely to occur and with a high degree it was more likely to occur (a disabling condition and an additional requirement, respectively, in their terminology). A standard MP argument with the major premise *if you pass your exams, you will get a good job* served as a control, while the other arguments were made of this MP to which one of the following premises was added: (i) got very low grade; (ii) got low grade; (iii) got respectable grade; (iv) got excellent grade. The conclusion had to be assessed on a 7-point scale (from very low to very high certainty to be offered a good job). For the first two conditions, the certainty ratings were below the control (and lower for the *very low grade* condition than for the *low grade* condition). For the last two conditions, the certainty ratings were above the control (and higher for the *excellent grade* condition than for the *respectable grade* condition). In brief, the degree of certainty of the conclusion is an increasing function of the degree to which a necessary condition is satisfied, in keeping with D_1(iii).

Recent papers on conditional reasoning (Newstead et al., 1997) have reported differences in the rate of endorsement of the conclusion as a function of the type of speech act associated with the conditional; in particular, promises and threats, on the one hand, and tips and warnings, on the other hand, seem to constitute two contrasted groups, the former giving rise to more frequent endorsements of the conclusion than the latter on all arguments (a result confirmed by Evans and Twyman-Musgrove, 1998). As noted by the authors, the key factor seems to be the extent to which the speaker has control over the occurrence of the consequent, which is higher for promises and threats than for tips and warnings. This result is in agreement with the present framework. On the one hand, weaker control implies greater difficulty to ensure the satisfaction of the CNCs; hence, according to D_1(ii), less certainty that the consequent will follow. On the other hand, weaker control implies the possibility that uncontrolled alternative antecedents exist; hence, according to D_2(ii), fewer endorsements of the conclusion on invalid arguments, to which we now turn.

Studies of Invalid Arguments

In a pioneering study, Rumain, Connell and Braine (1983) demonstrated the effect of alternative antecedents on the endorsement of AC and DA. This was done by using additional premises that stated explicitly the existence of alternative antecedents. When adult participants were presented with a standard argument made of a major premise, such as *if there is a dog in the box, there is an orange in the box* (and the appropriate minor premise), they commited the fallacies 70 per cent of the time; but when these two premises were presented together with two additional conditional premises, such as *if there is a tiger in the box, there is an orange in the box* and *if there is a pig in the box, there is an apple in the box*, they commited the fallacies only 30 per cent of the time. The manipulation was specially designed to alert the participants in the second condition to the plurality of antecedents (*dog, tiger*) for a single consequent (*orange*), so that the invited inferences of the type *if there is not a dog, there is not an orange* or *if there is an orange, there is a dog* were countermanded, in agreement with D_2(iii).

This claim is also supported by the results of a similar experiment by Markovits (1985): The conditional premise (for example, *if there is a snowstorm during the night, school will be closed the next day*) was preceded by a scenario referring to a few alternative causes (teachers' strike, a fault in the plumbing), a procedure that resulted in improved performance.

The results of another experiment by Markovits (1984) support derivation D_2(ii). He used an apparatus that had five cups at the top and five cups at the bottom, rubber tubes connecting the top and the bottom cups. The connections between the top and the bottom cups were not visible, except for one of them (3-top to 3-bottom). In order to know participants' assumptions about the connections, they were asked where a marble put in cup 1-top would go, after which they were asked analogues of the conditional reasoning questions; that is, which bottom cup they expected a marble to reach if it had been introduced in cup 3-top and similarly if it had been introduced in cup 5-top; which top cup they thought the marble came from, if it had reached cup 5-bottom or if it had reached cup 3-bottom. The answer to each of these questions is equivalent to the conclusion of one of the four arguments (MP, DA, MT and AC, respectively), while the information provided is equivalent to the minor premise, and knowledge of the visible connection provides the major premise. The results were more or less correct depending on whether or not participants assumed that any top cup would lead to any bottom cup. In brief, participants committed fewer fallacies when they assumed that there were alternative trajectories leading to the same outlet. The author argued that performance on conditional reasoning is mediated by an awareness of the existence of alternative antecedents to the consequent, as claimed by D_2(ii).

In Cummins' studies of causal conditionals described above, the role of alternative causes in invalid arguments was also investigated. For example, comparing two AC arguments, such as *if the match was struck, it lit; the match lit / it was struck* and *if Mary jumped into the swimming pool, she got wet; Mary got wet / she jumped into the swimming pool*, people were more prone to accept the conclusion of the first, which has few alternative causes, than that of the second, which has many. Thompson (1994, 1995) defined a necessary relationship as one for which the consequent occurs only when the antecedent occurs. A sentence such as *if athletes pass the drug test at the Olympics, the IOC can give them a medal* is also an example of a high level of necessity, whereas *if a people have a PhD in astrophysics, they are allowed to teach at a university* is an example of a low level of necessity.[5] The author observed that the rate of endorsement of invalid arguments was an increasing function of the level of necessity. These studies show, in line with D_2(ii), that the more available the alternative antecedents (high level of necessity, low number of alternative causes), the less likely the invited inference that leads to the endorsement of the conclusion.

Quinn and Markovits' experiment (1998) was restricted to causals. They compared conditionals that differed in the strength of the association between antecedent and consequent defined as follows. Given an effect, judges were requested to produce as many causes as they could in a limited time. Considering two causes produced for an effect, the more frequent was considered as the more strongly associated to the effect, so that the authors could define two groups of conditionals, a stong group (for example, *if a dog has fleas, it will scratch constantly*) and a weak group (for example, *if a dog has a skin disease, it will scratch constantly*). No significant effect was observed for the valid arguments, but for invalid arguments, there were fewer endorsements of the conclusion. Within the present framework, this result is in agreement with D_2(ii). With the weak association, the antecedent is not the most available; therefore, it is relatively easy for a more available antecedent to be retrieved and play the role of an alternative cause. In contrast, with the strong association, the antecedent is the most available; it is therefore relatively difficult for a less available antecedent to be retrieved and play the role of an alternative cause.

In Byrne's (1989) experiment described above, one group of participants solved standard arguments modified by the addition of a conditional premise that had the same consequent as the major and an antecedent that was an alternative antecedent to the major; for example, *if she has an essay to write, she will study late in the library* (major); *if she has some textbooks to read, she will study late in the library* (additional). The rate of endorsement of the AC and DA collapsed from about 60 per cent for the control group to 8 per cent for the group with an alternative antecedent, confirming the Rumain et al. manipulation. Notice that, when the additional premise is added to the invalid arguments, its conditional expression suggests the existence of an alternative antecedent (for example, *if she has some textbooks to read...*); hence, the observed effect as expected on the basis of D_2(ii).

Using the same major premise as above, *if you pass your exams, you will get a good job*, Manktelow and Fairley (2000) manipulated the extent to which the factor "performance on

---

[5] High level of necessity as defined by Thompson should not be confused with strong CNCs as defined here. The former characterise A antecedents (with regard to the consequent); the latter are A_1 conditions complementary to A.

interview" was satisfied. There was a control (a standard DA argument), while the other arguments were made of this DA argument, to which one of the following premises was added: (a) did not perform well on interview, (b) performed well, (c) performed brilliantly. The expressed certainty of the conclusion decreased across conditions from (c) to (a), the level for the latter group being close to the minimum of the scale. In keeping with $D_2(iii)$, the additional premises that mention alternative antecedents (conditions b and c) diminished the rate of acceptance of the conclusion of DA (and the greater the degree of satisfaction, the greater the decrease in acceptance rate). For condition (a), it is interesting to note that, since "good interview" is an alternative antecedent, "bad interview" (which is potentially a disabling condition) qualifies as well as the denial of an alternative antecedent. In agreement with $D_2(i)$, the explicit statement of the non-satisfaction of an alternative antecedent (bad interview) reinforces the presumption that the antecedent (pass the exams) is the only factor at work, and it does so better than if no alternative antecedent was mentioned.

Manktelow and Fairley took the observation that a disabling condition seems to affect DA, and other observations reported in their paper as evidence in favour of the existence of superordinate principles. In the job scenario, participants would be guided by a principle such as "produce favourable evidence of suitability", which is more general than the stated antecedent of the conditional. Similarly, with a permission rule such as *if you tidy up your room, you may go out to play for one hour*, participants chose to allow the boy out for half an hour, knowing that he had washed the dishes, and for more than an hour, knowing that he had both tidied the bedroom and washed the dishes; the superprinciple would be "be a good boy". Within the present framework, it is fully agreed that the endorsement of the conclusion requires more information than the antecedent; it has been hypothesised explicitly that a conditional is uttered in a context, part of which exploits the knowledge base. What has been called the conditional field precisely provides a formalisation of the notion that a consequent follows from a structured set of factors (organised as a disjunctive form), the stated antecedent being just one member of the set. Take, for example, a causal conditional such as *if a match is struck, the gas will explode*. The causal field contains alternative causes such as *sparkler, incandescent objects*, etc. These are easily accessed and can be extensionally listed; at a metacognitive level, they can be intensionally labelled as, and subsumed under, the notion "combustion catalytic starter", which could also be called a superprinciple, but is nothing else than the set of alternative causes.

The notions of superprinciple and of conditional field share a common idea, but the latter has several advantages: while it is rooted in a long philosophical tradition, it has a formal description, and it has the potential to give an explanation of virtually all the content effects known to affect conditional reasoning, as shown by this review.

Truth-Table Evaluation Tasks

Finally, a few studies which used the paradigm of truth-table evaluation are highly relevant to the present review. Hilton, Jaspers and Clarke (1990) presented their subjects with three sets of arguments. The first set consisted of a number of instances of the four standard arguments. An example for MP was *if he works hard, he will pass; he works hard/he will pass*. To constitute the second set, these arguments were modified by the introduction of an additional categorical premise that *affirmed* an alternative antecedent: *if he works hard, he will pass; the exam is easy; he works hard/he will pass.* Similarly, in the third set of arguments, there was an additional categorical premise that *denied* a CNC: *if he works hard, he will pass; the exam is difficult; he works hard/he will pass.*[6] For each set of arguments, on the basis of the responses (the conclusion was evaluated as true; sometimes true and sometimes false; false) it was possible to infer participants' interpretation of the conditional premise. The authors classified these interpretations as expressing (i) sufficient (but not necessary) conditions; (ii) sufficient and necessary conditions; (iii) necessary (but not sufficient) conditions. If we take the standard two-premise arguments as a basis of comparison, arguments in which an alternative antecedent was asserted gave rise to fewer "necessary" interpretations of the conditional (and to more "sufficient" interpretations); and arguments in which a CNC was denied gave rise to fewer "sufficient" interpretations of the conditional (and to more "necessary" interpretations). These results are in line with D_1(i) and D_2(iii). Notice that since it is claimed that performance on conditional argments is determined by the interpretation of the conditional premise, this experiment is particularly interesting; in effect, in showing that the interpretation of the conditional premise can be inferred from performance on conditional arguments and coincides with the one predicted, it supports the general claim.

Direct support of the rationale that underlies the derivation D_1(ii) can be found in the results obtained by O'Brien, Costa and Overton (1986) with another truth-table evaluation task. Participants were presented with conditional sentences that expressed an hypothesis in the frame of medical or mechanical scenarios (for example, *if the thermostat is replaced, the car will not overheat*). They were then given the result of an observation: it stated that an operation was performed [p] (or not performed [not-p]) and the patient recovered [q] (or did not recover [not-q]) or that a part was replaced (or not replaced) and the engine still overheated (or no longer overheated); all four combinations were proposed. Participants were then asked about the doctor's (or mechanic's) certainty that the hypothesis was correct (the options were certain that correct; certain that incorrect; cannot be certain) in each of the four cases. Two results of interest are that (i) the hypothesis was more often estimated as uncertain in the medical scenario than in the mechanical one (although to a lesser extent than in the [not-p, q] case), after the observation of the [p, q] case (operation and recovery or part replaced and engine working); and (ii) the hypothesis was less often estimated as falsified by the [p, not-q] observation in the medical scenario (operation and no recovery) than in the mechanical one (part replaced and engine not working). As argued by the authors, the medical domain is generally viewed as less deterministic than the mechanical one, so that, medically, there may be hidden internal causes that prevent an action from being efficacious. It seems that the causal link between the antecedent and the consequent of the conditional may be less predictable in some domains than in others: The satisfaction of the salient CNCs is more open to doubt (because they are less controlable, or even assumed to be hidden).

D_2(i) and (ii) also get direct support from the same experiment. The hypothesis was more often estimated as uncertain in the medical scenario than in the mechanical one for the [not-p, q] case (no operation and recovery or no part replaced and engine working). A likely explanation put forward by the authors lies in the notion of spontaneous recovery, applicable to the medical domain, but not to the mechanical one. This is an instantiation of the concept of alternative causal antecedent, which is more available in the medical

---

[6] Under normal conditions, an exam is neither too easy nor too difficult, so that easiness acts as an alternative antecedent, and difficulty as a disabler.

domain than in the mechanical one. In brief, this experiment shows that information with the same logical status can affect belief in a conditional sentence differently depending on the conceptual domain involved.

CONCLUSION

It is basic to the distinction between induction and deduction that while the conclusion of the former contains factual assertions not included in the premises, the conclusion of the latter is free from any fact not already included in the premises. Although it is also widely agreed that inductive activity depends more on knowledge of the domain than on formal properties of the premises, but deduction depends entirely on the formal properties of the premises, the second part of this assertion seems questionable as far as human reasoning is concerned. In deduction, content plays a role that is complementary to form: the knowledge base is the source of implicated premises that are cancellable or of explicit, uncertain premises. In conditional reasoning, the former may lead to the affirmation of an invalid conclusion; the former and the latter may also give rise to a doubt or a denial of a valid conclusion, depending on their degree of uncertainty. Premises constitute a skeleton that is fleshed out by other premises imported from the knowledge base. Talking—and wondering about—"content effects" in deductive reasoning is as tautological as talking of "form effects" would be. Human deduction is a process by which the reasoner exploits the context jointly with the explicit premises in order to yield new information. One implication is that one of the commonest arguments directed at proponents of formal treatment of human deduction fails. This argument says that if deduction was based on a formal analysis of the premises, no effect of content should occur. But this is to forget the premises provided by the knowledge base. In fact, "content effects" do occur because deduction is not only based on a formal analysis of the premises *explicitly provided*, but also on premises dictated by world knowledge (and on the interpretation of the explicit premises based on pragmatic principles). The phenomena reviewed in the present chapter also exhibit "content effects". Conditional arguments are uttered in a context for some purpose. Their conditional premise is embedded in a conditional field whose factors are determined by world knowledge. When this is accepted, the "content effects" become understandable and explicable.

ACKNOWLEDGEMENT

The author thanks Denis Hilton for his comments on a first draft of this chapter.

REFERENCES

Anscombre, J.-C. (1995). *Théorie des topoï.* [Theory of topoi]. Paris: Kimé.
Byrne, R. M. J. (1989). Suppressing valid inferences with conditionals. *Cognition, 31,* 61–83.
Chan, D. & Chua, F. (1994). Suppression of valid inferences: Syntactic views, mental models, and relative salience. *Cognition, 53,* 217–238.
Cummins, D. D. (1995). Naive theories and causal deduction. *Memory and Cognition, 23,* 646–658.
Cummins, D. D., Lubart, T., Alknis, O. & Rist, R. (1991). Conditional reasoning and causation. *Memory and Cognition, 19,* 274–282.

Evans, J. St. B. T. (1982). *The Psychology of Deductive Reasoning.* London: Routledge & Kegan Paul.

Evans, J. St. B. T., Newstead, S. E. & Byrne, R. M. J. (1993). *Human Reasoning. The Psychology of Deduction.* Hove: Erlbaum.

Evans, J. St. B. T. & Twyman-Musgrove, J. (1998). Conditional reasoning with inducements and advice. *Cognition, 69,* B11–B16.

Fillenbaum, S. (1975). IF: Some uses. *Psychological Research, 37,* 245–260.

Fillenbaum, S. (1978). How to do some things with *if.* In J. W. Cotton & R. L. Klatzky (eds), *Semantic Factors in Cognition.* Hillsdale, NJ: Erlbaum.

Geis, M. L. & Zwicky, A. M. (1971). On invited inferences. *Linguistic Inquiry, 2,* 561–566.

George, C. (1995). The endorsement of the premises: Assumption-based or belief-based reasoning. *British Journal of Psychology, 86,* 93–111.

Goodman, N. (1947). The problem of counterfactual conditionals. *Journal of Philosophy, 44,* 113–128.

Hilton, D. J., Jaspars, J. M. F. & Clarke, D. D. (1990). Pragmatic conditional reasoning: Context and content effects on the interpretation of causal assertions. *Journal of Pragmatics, 14,* 791–812.

Horn, L. R. (2000). From *if* to *iff*: Conditional perfection as pragmatic strengthening. *Journal of Pragmatics, 32,* 289–386.

Legrenzi, P. (1970). Relations between language and reasoning about deductive rules. In G. B. Flores d'Arçais & W. J. M. Levelt (eds), *Advances in Psycholinguistics* (pp. 322–333). Amsterdam: North-Holland.

Lilje, G. W. (1972). Uninvited inferences. *Linguistic Inquiry, 3,* 540–542.

Mackie, J. L. (1974). *The Cement of the Universe.* Oxford: Oxford University Press.

Manktelow, K. (1999). *Reasoning and Thinking.* Hove: Psychology Press.

Manktelow, K. I. & Fairley, N. (2000). Superordinate principles in reasoning with causal and deontic conditionals. *Thinking and Reasoning, 6,* 41–65.

Markovits, H. (1984). Awareness of the "possible" as a mediator of formal thinking in conditional reasoning problems. *British Journal of Psychology, 75,* 367–376.

Markovits, H. (1985). Incorrect conditional reasoning among adults: Competence or performance? *British Journal of Psychology, 76,* 241–247.

Matalon, B. (1962). Etude génétique de l'implication. In E. W. Beth, J. B. Grize, R. Martin, B. Matalon, A. Naess & J. Piaget (eds), *Implication, formalisation et logique naturelle. Etudes d'Epistémologie Génétique* (pp. 69–93). Vol. 16. Paris: P.U.F.

Mill, J. S. (1988/1843). *A System of Logic.* New York: Harper.

Newstead, S. E., Ellis, M. C., Evans, J. St. B. T. & Dennis, I. (1997). Conditional reasoning with realistic material. *Thinking and Reasoning, 3,* 49–76.

O'Brien, D. P., Costa, G. & Overton, W. F. (1986). Evaluations of causal and conditional hypotheses. *Quarterly Journal of Experimental Psychology, 38A,* 493–512.

O'Brien, T. C. (1972). Logical thinking in adolescents. *Educational Studies in Mathematics, 4,* 401–428.

Politzer, G. (1981). Differences in interpretation of implication. *American Journal of Psychology, 94,* 461–477.

Quinn, S. & Markovits, H. (1998). Conditional reasoning, causality, and the structure of semantic memory: strength of association as a predictive factor for content effects. *Cognition, 68,* B93–B101.

Ramsey, F. P. (1931). *The Foundations of Mathematics and Other Logical Essays.* R. B. Braithwaite (ed.). London: Routledge and Kegan Paul.

Rumain, B., Connell, J. & Braine, M. D. S. (1983). Conversational comprehension processes are responsible for reasoning fallacies in children as well as adults: *If* is not the biconditional. *Developmental Psychology, 19,* 471–481.

Sperber, D. & Wilson, D. (1986). *Relevance: Communication and Cognition.* London: Blackwell.

Sperber, D., Cara, F. & Girotto, V. (1995). Relevance theory explains the selection task. *Cognition, 57,* 31–95.

Staudenmayer, H. (1975). Understanding conditional reasoning with meaningful propositions. In R. J. Falmagne (ed.), *Reasoning: Representation and Process in Children and Adults* (pp. 55–79). Hillsdale, NJ: Erlbaum.

Stevenson, R. J. & Over, D. E. (1995). Deduction from uncertain premises. *Quarterly Journal of Experimental Psychology, 48A,* 613–643.

Thompson, V. A. (1994). Interpretational factors in conditional reasoning. *Memory and Cognition*, *22*, 742–758.

Thompson, V. A. (1995). Conditional reasoning: The necessary and sufficient conditions. *Canadian Journal of Experimental Psychology*, *49*, 1–60.

van der Auwera, J. (1997). Conditional perfection. In A. Athanasiadou & R. Dirven (eds), *On Conditionals Again* (pp. 169–190). Amsterdam: John Benjamins.

Wason, P. C. (1966). Reasoning. In B. M. Foss (ed.), *New Horizons in Psychology 1*. Harmondsworth: Penguin.

Wason, P. C. & Johnson-Laird, P. N. (1972). *Psychology of Reasoning. Structure and Content*. London: Batsford.

CHAPTER 6

Probabilities and Pragmatics in Conditional Inference: Suppression and Order Effects

Mike Oaksford
Cardiff University, UK
and
Nick Chater
University of Warwick, UK

INTRODUCTION

Over the last few years, we have been developing a probabilistic approach to human reasoning which suggests that many of the so-called errors and biases seen in deductive reasoning are the result of applying everyday uncertain reasoning strategies to these laboratory tasks (see Chater & Oaksford, 2000, 2001). We initially applied this approach to the Wason selection task. We argued that participants are making decisions about whether the benefits of selecting certain types of data, in terms of information gain (indicative task) or utility (deontic task), outweighed the costs (Oaksford & Chater, 1994, 1995a, 1996, 1998a, 1998b; Oaksford et al., 1997; Chater & Oaksford, 1999a; Oaksford, Chater & Grainger, 1999). More recently, we have applied this approach to syllogistic reasoning (Chater & Oaksford, 1999b).

Both of these inferential forms are complex compared to the standard conditional inference task, where participants are provided with a conditional premise *if p then q* and a range of categorical premises, *p*, not-*p*, *q* and not-*q*. Inferring *q* given *p*, and not-*p* given not-*q* correspond to the logically valid inferences of modus ponens (MP) and modus tollens (MT), respectively. Inferring not-*q* given not-*p*, and *p* given *q* correspond to the logical fallacies of denying the antecedent (DA) and affirming the consequent (AC), respectively. Because it was clear that a simplified version of the probabilistic approach we applied to the selection task could also be applied to conditional inference, we have recently shown how the model can explain polarity biases (Evans, Newstead & Byrne, 1993) in the conditional inference

Thinking: Psychological Perspectives on Reasoning, Judgment and Decision Making. Edited by David Hardman and Laura Macchi.
© 2003 John Wiley & Sons, Ltd.

task (Oaksford, Chater & Larkin, 2000). This bias occurs when negations are used in the antecedent and consequent of a conditional. The principal result is that people are biased towards negative conclusions. According to our model and Oaksford and Stenning's (1992) contrast set account of negations, this bias occurs because negations define high-probability categories. Oaksford et al. (2000) showed that when manipulating probabilities instead of negations, a high-probability conclusion effect is observed analogous to negative conclusion bias. Consequently, their application of a probabilistic model to conditional inference seems to explain one of the principal biases observed in a rational probabilistic framework.

However, there are other effects in conditional inference that Oaksford et al. (2000) did not address and that may be understood from a probabilistic perspective. Our goal in this chapter is to speculate on whether this is feasible. The two effects we look at are suppression effects (e.g., Byrne, 1989; Cummins et al., 1991; Cummins, 1995; Byrne, Espino & Santamaria, 1999) and order effects (Evans, 1977; Evans & Newstead, 1977; Evans & Beck, 1981; Thompson & Mann, 1995; Girotto, Mazzocco & Tasso, 1997; Evans, Handley & Buck, 1998). Suppression effects occur when further information reduces the degree to which a participant is willing to endorse an inference. For example, if you are told that *if the key is turned, the car starts* and that *the key is turned*, you are likely to endorse the MP inference to the conclusion that *the car starts*. However, if you are also told, *if the petrol tank is not empty, the car starts*, you are less likely to endorse this conclusion because the car may not start if the petrol tank is empty. The petrol tank being empty provides an *exception* to the rule. Byrne (1989), who called such cases "additional antecedents", showed that they suppress the valid inferences of MP and MT. Other information can suppress DA and AC. For example, if you are told that *if the key is turned, the car starts* and that *the key is not turned*, you might endorse the DA inference to the conclusion that *the car does not start*. However, if you are also told, *if the car is hot-wired, the car starts*, you are less likely to endorse this conclusion because the car may start because it has been hot-wired. Byrne (1989), who called such cases "alternative antecedents", showed that they suppress the fallacies of DA and AC.

Order effects occur when, for example, the order of clauses is reversed, as in the conditional *q only if p*. When this is done, participants tend to endorse more AC and MT inferences and fewer MP and DA inferences. In this chapter, we argue that our simple probabilistic model can provide quite detailed accounts of suppression effects. Our account of order effects derives the connection between conversational pragmatics and subjective probability that we first discussed in Oaksford and Chater (1995a).

However, before we turn to our account of these effects, we first outline the reasons why we believe that a probabilistic approach to conditional inference is required. This involves a brief discussion of the inadequacy of the material conditional of standard logic in providing an account of the conditional as it used in everyday inference.

LOGICISM AND UNCERTAINTY

Within philosophy, linguistics, logic and computational theory, there is general convergence on the view that standard first-order logic is inadequate to capture everyday reasoning about the real world. Although some psychologists are well aware of these literatures, we believe that their implications concerning the scope of first-order reasoning have not been fully recognised. Indeed, the very fact that the two leading formal psychological theories of reasoning, mental logic (e.g., Rips, 1994) and mental models (e.g., Johnson-Laird & Byrne,

1991), both retain the standard logical apparatus suggests that the inadequacies of first-order logic as a model for human reasoning are not universally accepted. We first sketch the standard logical treatment of the conditional, and then consider its problems and attempted solutions to these problems within a logical framework.

Problems with the Material Conditional

The standard approach within the formal semantics of natural or logical languages is to provide a recursive definition of the truth of complex expressions in terms of their parts. The natural language phrase *if p then q* is usually rendered as the material conditional of logic. The material conditional $p \rightarrow q$ is true if and only if p is false or q is true (or both). This semantics licenses the valid rules of inference, modus ponens (MP) and modus tollens (MT). There are certain well-known counterintuitive properties of this semantics. For example, it means that any conditional with a false antecedent is true—thus, the sentence, "if the moon is striped, then Mars is spotted", is true according to the material conditional. But, intuitively, it is either false or nonsensical.

Further problems arise because the material conditional allows "strengthening of the antecedent". That is, given the premise *if p then q*, we can conclude that *if (p and r) then q*, for any *r*. Strengthening of the antecedent seems appropriate in mathematical contexts. *If it is a triangle, it has three sides* does imply that *if it is a triangle and it is blue, it has three sides*. Indeed, this is a crucial feature of axiomatic systems in mathematics—axiomatisation would be impossible if adding new axioms removed conclusions that followed from the old axioms. However, strengthening of the antecedent does not apply to most natural language conditionals, which, as we have argued, are uncertain. For example, *if it's a bird, it flies* does not allow you to infer that *if it's a bird and it's an ostrich, it flies*. That is, for natural language conditionals, conclusions can be lost by adding premises; that is, strengthening the antecedent does not hold. Furthermore, note that whether some additional information *r* has this effect or not is content dependent; for example, if you learn that this bird is a parrot, the conclusion that *it can fly* is not lost. The distinction between inference systems in which strengthening of the antecedent does or does not hold is of central importance to knowledge representation in artificial intelligence. Roughly, inference systems where strengthening of the antecedent holds are known as monotonic systems (continuously adding premises leads to continuously adding conclusions, without removing any); inference systems where strengthening of the antecedent does not hold are non-monotonic. In artificial intelligence, it is universally accepted that human everyday reasoning is uncertain and thus non-monotonic, and that developing systems for non-monotonic reasoning is a major challenge (e.g., McCarthy & Hayes, 1969; Ginsberg, 1987).

Regarding our first problem with material implication, that a false antecedent guarantees the truth of a conditional, an intuitive diagnosis is that material implication fails to specify that there be any connection between the antecedent and the consequent—they can simply be any two arbitrary propositions. Within the logical literature, there have been two general approaches to capturing this intuition—relevance logic and modal logic.

Solutions?: Relevance and Modality

Relevance logic, as its name implies, demands that there be a relationship of "relevance" between antecedent and consequent, where this is defined in terms of the proof of the consequent involving the antecedent (Anderson & Belnap, 1975). From a logical point of view, systems of relevance logic are not well developed. For example, it has been very difficult to provide a semantics for relevance logics (Veltman, 1985); this means that it is not clear quite what notion of relevance is being coded by the syntactic rules used in particular relevance logics. But, in any case, the relation of relevance would not appear to be reducible to notions of proof, particularly not in everyday contexts, because the uncertain character of reasoning means that proofs are never possible. So relevance logics do not appear to be a useful direction for developing a notion of the conditional which applies to everyday reasoning. However, in the psychology of reasoning, Braine (1978) has advanced a relevance-based account, arguing that people naturally only assert conditionals when the consequent is deducible from the antecedent.

The second approach to the conditional employs modal notions, such as necessity and possibility. Syntactic systems of modal logic and so-called strict implication based on them were first suggested by C.I. Lewis (1918). Semantic theories for modal logics were developed much later by Kripke (1963), permitting an understanding of the notions of necessity and possibility that were being encoded in the syntactic rules. Specifically, Kripke provided a semantics in terms of "possible worlds". The idea is that different modal logics can be understood in terms of different relations of "accessibility" between possible worlds. In these terms, a proposition is necessary if it is true in all accessible possible worlds, and it is possible if it is true in some accessible possible worlds.

The most philosophically important account of conditionals is given by the Lewis–Stalnaker possible world semantics for the counterfactual conditional (Stalnaker, 1968; D. Lewis, 1973). A counterfactual conditional is one in which the antecedent is known to be false: for example, *if the gun had gone off, he would have been killed*. According to material implication, such claims are always true, simply because their antecedents are false. But, clearly, this cannot be correct—under most circumstances, the counterfactual *if he had stubbed his toe, he would have been killed* will be judged unequivocally false. Looking at the Lewis–Stalnaker semantics for such claims reveals all the problems that logical approaches to everyday reasoning must confront in philosophy and in artificial intelligence (AI).

The intuitive idea behind the Lewis–Stalnaker semantics for a conditional such as *if the gun had gone off, he would have been killed* is based on the idea that in the world maximally similar to the actual world but in which the gun went off, he died. Clearly, the major issue here is what counts as the world maximally similar to the actual one. One important criterion is that the physical laws are the same, so that speeding bullets still tend to kill people, the gun is pointing in the same direction, and so on—the only difference is that the gun went off in this world, whereas it did not in the actual world. But there is a vast range of specific problems with this account. For example, it is not at all clear how to construct a world where only a single fact differs from the actual world. This is problematic because for this to be true (assuming determinism) the difference in this crucial fact implies either a different causal history (the bullet was a dud, the gun was faulty, etc.) or different causal laws (pulling triggers does not make guns go off in this possible world). Moreover, a different causal history or different causal laws will have different causal consequences, aside from the single fact under consideration. Thus, it appears inevitable that the so-called maximally similar world differs in many ways, rather than just about a single fact, from the actual world. So, by changing one thing, we automatically change many things, and it is not at all clear what the inferential consequences of these changes should be. The problem of specifying the ramifications of a single change to a world (or in an agent's knowledge about its world) is immensely difficult—in AI, this problem has been called the frame problem (Pylyshyn, 1987), and it has bedevilled AI research for the last 30 years. Hence, a theory of conditionals which presupposes a solution to the frame problem is unlikely to prove satisfactory as a basis for a psychology of conditional reasoning.

These problems aside, this semantics for the counterfactual (that is, where the antecedent—the gun going off—does not apply in the actual world) has also been applied to the indicative case (where the gun may or may not have gone off). Simplistically, the hypothetical element of an indicative statement, such as *if the gun goes off, he is dead*, seems to be captured by the same semantics—the only difference is that we do not know whether the actual world is one in which the gun goes off or not. Nonetheless, this kind of semantic account does avoid some of the absurdities of material implication. Thus, for example, sentences such as *if the moon is striped, then Mars is spotted* are now clearly false—in worlds maximally similar to the actual world in which the moon is striped, Mars will still look red. Crucially, it is intuitively clear that strengthening of the antecedent can no longer hold. For example, *if it's a bird, it flies* does not allow you to infer that if it's a bird and it's an ostrich, it flies. The worlds in which the antecedents are evaluated will clearly differ—the world most similar to the actual world in which something is a bird is not the same as the world most similar to the actual world in which something is an ostrich. In particular, in the first world, the thing will most likely fly (because most birds fly); but in the second world, the thing will not fly (because ostriches cannot fly). These examples suggest that the Lewis–Stalnaker semantics may provide a more descriptively adequate theory of conditionals than the material conditional.

However, for psychological purposes, we need an account of the formal processes that could implement this semantics. People do not have access to possible worlds—instead, they have access to representations of the world, which they can productively recombine to produce different representations of the way the world might be or might not have been. The programme of attempting to mechanise reasoning about the way the world might be has been taken up by the study of knowledge representation in AI. The starting point is the notion of a knowledge base that contains representations of a cognitive agent's beliefs about the world. This approach involves formal representations and formal proof procedures that operate over these representations which can be implemented computationally. However, it is far from clear that formal attempts in AI can adequately capture the Lewis–Stalnaker semantics.

Let us reconsider strengthening the antecedent and perhaps the best-known approach to this problem within AI. Problems for strengthening the antecedent arise when the inferences that can be made from one antecedent intuitively conflict with the inferences that can be made from another. For example, knowing that *Tweety is a sparrow* leads to the conclusion that *Tweety flies*, whereas knowing that *Tweety is one second old* leads to the conclusion that *Tweety cannot fly*. This leads to the problem of what we infer when we learn that *Tweety is a one-second-old sparrow*; that is, the problem of what we infer when the antecedent is strengthened. It is intuitively obvious that a one-second-old sparrow cannot fly; that is, that when Tweety is one second old, the possible world in which Tweety cannot fly is more similar to the actual world than any other possible world where Tweety can fly. Although this is intuitively obvious, formally, it is not obvious how to capture this conclusion. Formally, we can regard these two pieces of information as two conditional rules, *if something is a bird it can fly*, and *if something is one second old it cannot fly*. Formal proposals in AI (e.g., Reiter, 1985) appear unable to break the symmetry between these rules and specify which of these conflicting conclusions we should accept. That is, these proposals do not respect our intuitive understanding of how the Lewis–Stalnaker semantics should be applied. The point here is that in the example it is our knowledge of what the rules mean and how the world works that indicate that a one-second-old sparrow is not going to fly. More generally, it is not the formal properties of conditionals that determine the subsets of possible worlds in which they are evaluated in the Lewis–Stalnaker semantics. What matters is the content of the rules, to which the formal procedures for inference in logicist AI do not have access.

There have been various alternative proposals within the AI literature to deal with the problem of strengthening the antecedent, or default reasoning. The best known are McCarthy's (1980) circumscription, McDermott and Doyle's (1980) non-monotonic logic I, McDermott's non-monotonic logic II (1982) and Clark's predicate completion (1978). However, the problems that we have described above appear to apply equally to all of these approaches (McDermott, 1987; Shoam, 1987, 1988). Moreover, approaches based on formal logic within the psychology of reasoning, such as mental logics (e.g., Rips, 1994) and mental models (e.g., Johnson-Laird & Byrne, 1991), also fail to address these issues, because the approach they adopt formalises the conditional by the standard logic of material implication. However, as we have seen, the material conditional completely fails to capture the use of conditionals in everyday inference.

A Probabilistic Approach

We have seen that conditional inference is of fundamental importance to cognitive science, as well as to AI, logic and philosophy. We have suggested that the problems that arise in capturing conditional inference indicate a very profound problem for the study of human reasoning and the study of cognition at large. This is that much of our reasoning with conditionals is uncertain, and may be overturned by future information; that is, they are non-monotonic. But logic-based approaches to inference are typically monotonic, and hence are unable to deal with this uncertainty. Moreover, to the extent that formal logical approaches embrace non-monotonicity, they appear to be unable to cope with the fact that it is the content of rules, rather than their logical form, which appears to determine the inferences that people draw. We now argue that perhaps by encoding more of the content of people's knowledge, by probability theory, we may more adequately capture the nature of everyday human inference. This seems to make intuitive sense, because the problems that we have identified concern how uncertainty is handled in human inference, and probability theory is the calculus of uncertainty.

Before we outline how a probabilistic approach can account for some of the effects seen in experiments on conditional inference, we briefly consider how it can avoid some of the problems we have just introduced for the material conditional. From a probabilistic point of view, the natural interpretation of conditionals is in terms of conditional probability. Thus, the statement that birds fly (or more long-windedly, if something is a bird, it flies) can be regarded as claiming that the conditional probability of something flying, given that it is a bird, is high. Probability theory naturally allows non-monotonicity. If all we know about a thing is that it is a bird, the probability that it flies might be, say, .9 ($P(\text{flies}|\text{bird}) = .9$). However, the probability of its flying given that it is both a bird and an ostrich is 0 or nearly 0 ($P(\text{flies}|\text{bird, ostrich}) = 0$), and the probability of its flying given that it is both a bird and a parrot may be, say, .96 ($P(\text{flies}|\text{bird, parrot}) = .96$). All these statements are completely compatible from the point of view of probability theory. So, from a probabilistic perspective, the result of strengthening the antecedent in these cases leads to intuitively acceptable results. This approach to the meaning of conditional statements has been proposed in philosophy by Adams (1966, 1975), and has also been adopted in AI (Pearl, 1988). There have been some problems raised with this probabilistic interpretation of the conditional. These concern the rather unnatural scenario in which conditionals are embedded; for example, *if (if p then q) then r* (Lewis, 1976). However, the relevance of these problems to the design of AI systems and to human cognition is unclear (Pearl, 1988). Certainly, as we now argue, they do not seem to impinge on our ability to provide probabilistic interpretations of conditional reasoning in the laboratory.

A PROBABILISTIC APPROACH TO CONDITIONAL INFERENCE

Several authors have suggested that human conditional inference has a significant proba-bilistic component (Chan & Chua, 1994; Anderson, 1995; Stevenson & Over, 1995; Liu, Lo & Wu, 1996; George, 1997). Here we outline Oaksford, Chater and Larkin's (2000) probabilistic computational level model (Marr, 1982) of the inferences that people should make in these experiments.

A Computational Level Model

In this model, rules are represented as 2×2 contingency tables, as in Table 6.1. In this table, with respect to a rule *if p then q*, $a = P(p)$, the probability of the antecedent; $b = P(q)$, the probability of the consequent; and $\varepsilon = P(\text{not-}q \mid p)$, the probability that the consequent does not occur given the antecedent. ε is the exceptions parameter, as used by Oaksford and Chater (1998b). For example, if p is *turn the key* and q is *the car starts*, ε is the probability that the car does not start even though you have turned the key. Following previous accounts (Chan & Chua, 1994; Stevenson & Over, 1995; Liu, Lo & Wu, 1996), Oaksford et al. (2000) assumed that people endorse an inference in direct proportion to the conditional probability of the conclusion given the categorical premise. The following expressions for the conditional probabilities of each inference can be derived from Table 6.1:

MP: $P(q \mid p) = 1 - \varepsilon$ (1)   DA: $P(\neg q \mid \neg p) = \dfrac{1 - b - a\varepsilon}{1 - a}$ (2)

AC: $P(p \mid q) = \dfrac{a(1 - \varepsilon)}{b}$ (3)   MT: $P(\neg p \mid \neg q) = \dfrac{1 - b - a\varepsilon}{1 - b}$ (4)

We show the behaviour of the model relevant to explaining suppression effects in Figure 6.1. This figure shows how the probability that each inference should be drawn varies as a function of ε, that is, the probability of exceptions. This probability is directly related to the suppression of the valid inferences MP and MT by the introduction of exceptions. If ε is high, this corresponds to a rule with many exceptions. Figure 6.1 shows that, as would be predicted, the probability that MP or MT should be endorsed falls as ε rises.

Figure 6.1 also shows that DA and AC seems to be affected by exceptions in a similar way. However, as we mentioned in the discussion, DA and AC seem to be most affected by the probability of alternatives; for example, the probability that a car can be started

Table 6.1   The contingency table for a conditional rule, *if p then q*, when there is a dependency between the p and q that may admit exceptions (ε). $a = P(p)$, $b = P(q)$, and $\varepsilon = P(\text{not-}q\,|\,p)$

	q	not-q
p	$a\,(1-\varepsilon)$	$a\varepsilon$
not-p	$b - a\,(1-\varepsilon)$	$(1-b) - a\varepsilon$

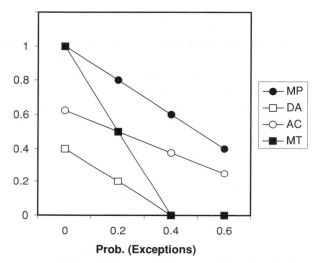

Figure 6.1   How the probability that a conclusion should be drawn varies as a function of the probability of exceptions ($P[\text{not-}q\,|\,p]$: Prob.[Exceptions]). The probability of the antecedent (a [$P(p)$]) and the probability of the consequent (b [$P(q)$]) were held constant at .5 and .8, respectively

other than by turning the key. This corresponds to the probability of the car's starting even though the key has not been turned; that is, $P(q\,|\,\text{not-}p)$. We call this probability DA$'$ because it is the complement of DA ($P(\text{not-}q\,|\,\text{not-}p)$; consequently, as the probability of DA$'$ increases, the probability of drawing DA decreases. DA$'$ is linearly related to ε, with $\frac{b-a}{1-a}$ as the intercept and $\frac{a}{1-a}$ as the slope. This reveals that, according to the model, if the probability of exceptions is kept constant, changes in DA$'$ will involve changes in the probabilities of the antecedent and consequent, that is, in a and b ($P[p]$ and $P[q]$). We could have treated DA$'$ as a primitive parameter of the model. However, we chose only to parameterise exceptions for two reasons. First, we wished to be parsimonious: the model already contains three parameters. Second, linguistically, the structure of if . . . then rules reflects the causal ordering of events in the world (Comrie, 1986), allowing us to predict what will happen next. These predictions go awry only because of exceptions. Thus, MP and the reasons why it might fail are particularly cognitively salient (Cummins et al., 1991), and that is why we treat exceptions as a primitive. As we will see when we model the data on the suppression effect, this choice makes experimentally testable predictions.

Oaksford et al.'s (2000) model is defined at Marr's computational level; that is, it outlines the computational problem people are attempting to solve when they are given conditional inference tasks to perform. It also specifies the knowledge that they bring to bear on the problem, that is, knowledge of the probabilities of exceptions and of the antecedents and consequents of the rules they are given. That is, we abandon the conventional view that the problem people confront is one of which logical rules to apply to these conditional statements.

EXPLAINING SUPPRESSION EFFECTS

Oaksford et al. (2000) concentrated on showing how their probabilistic model could account for polarity biases in conditional inference. However, the model can also be applied to the standard pattern of results on the task and to suppression effects. We now look at how the model applies to these data.

The Standard Results

We first show how this account explains the standard abstract data on conditional inference. To model the data, we need to find appropriate values for $P(p)$, $P(q)$ and ε. However, for the abstract material normally used in these tasks, it is difficult to know what values people would normally assume. Some constraints can be derived by looking at the base rates of natural language predicates, as it seems reasonable to assume that, when confronted with incomplete information, people will use their prior knowledge to fill in the gaps. That is, they will assume that new cases will be pretty much like those they have already seen. Most natural language predicates cut up the world into relatively small subsets; for example, most things are not birds, are not black, are not coffee pots and so on. That is, the probability that any randomly selected object is a bird, is black or is a coffee pot is very low. We exploited this "rarity" assumption in modelling Wason's selection task (Oaksford & Chater, 1994, 1996, 1998b).

However, as Oaksford et al. (2000) observe, in the context of conditional inference, a rarity assumption is probably not appropriate. They pointed out that inferences are specific to contexts. So, for example, you are only likely to need to make inferences about donkeys being stubborn in contexts where you are likely to encounter donkeys. That is, even though the base rate of donkeys is likely to be very low, in contexts where it would be appropriate to draw inferences about them, the probability of encountering a donkey is likely to be higher, possibly a lot higher than the base rate. Consequently, to model the standard data, we averaged conditional probabilities over the whole parameter space but excluding values of $P(p)$ and $P(q)$ that were less than .1, that is, the rare values. Moreover, to be able to infer reliably that a particular animal is stubborn, given that it is a donkey, there had better be more stubborn things than donkeys. If this were not the case, our inferences could go awry; that is, we would quite often encounter non-stubborn donkeys. So, for the rule *if something is a donkey* (p), *it is stubborn* (q), whatever the absolute values of $P(p)$, it is likely that $P(q) > P(p)$. To model the standard data, we therefore calculated conditional probabilities averaged only over the region of the parameter space where $P(q) > P(p)$.

To compute the predicted values, we sampled the parameter space where $P(q) > P(p)$ between .1 and .9, in steps of .1 with $\varepsilon = .1$. For each set of parameter values, we computed the predicted probability of each inference, using Equations 1–4. Overall, this meant that 36 values were calculated for each inference. Finally, we averaged over all 36 values for each inference to obtain the predicted proportion of those inferences people should make. For MP, the mean, in percentage (data mean in brackets), was 90.00 (97.36) because this probability relies only on ε. For DA, the mean was 42.86 (42.09); for AC, the mean was 45.00 (42.64); and for MT, the mean was 82.14 (62.18). Although we made no attempt to optimise these values, they agree reasonably well with the standard data, especially for DA and AC. Thus, it would appear that the standard pattern of results on the conditional inference task, which appears irrational from a logical point of view, may be a reflection of a rational probabilistic strategy. Only two assumptions were needed, (i) that participants sample quite broadly in the parameter space outside the rarity region, and (ii) that they assume $P(q) > P(p)$.

Suppression Effects

In this section, we show how our simple probabilistic model can account for suppression effects. These effects involve the way additional information, either explicitly given in the experimental set-up (e.g., Byrne, 1989) or implicitly available from prior knowledge (e.g., Cummins et al., 1991), can affect the inferential process. In either case, we assume that this information has the effect of altering the subjective probabilities that are then entered into Equations 1–4 to calculate the probability that an inference will succeed. Additional antecedents (or exceptions), for example, the information that there is petrol in the tank with respect to the rule *if you turn the key, the car starts*, concern the probability of the car's not starting even though the key has been turned—that is, they concern ε. If you do not know that there is petrol in the tank, you cannot unequivocally infer that the car will start (MP). Moreover, bringing to mind other additional factors that need to be in place to infer that the car starts—for example the battery must be charged—will increase this probability. ε is a primitive parameter of Oaksford et al.'s (2000) model and can be derived directly from the data for the MP inference. It is therefore an immediate consequence of our model that if there are many additional antecedents, that is, ε is high, the probability that the MP inference should be drawn will be low. That is, suppression of MP by additional antecedents is a direct prediction of the model.

Alternative antecedents, such as the information that the car can also be started by hot-wiring with respect to the rule *if you turn the key, the car starts*, concern the probability of the car starting even though the key has not been turned; that is, $P(q \mid \text{not-}p)$. If you know that a car can be started by other means, you cannot unequivocally infer that the car will not start although the key has not been turned (DA). Moreover, bringing to mind other alternative ways of starting cars, such as bump-starting, will increase this probability. $P(q \mid \text{not-}p)$ is DA', the converse of DA ($P[\text{not-}q \mid \text{not-}p]$). It is therefore an immediate consequence of our model that if there are many alternative antecedents, that is, $P(q \mid \text{not-}p)$ is high, the probability that the DA inference should be drawn will be low. That is, suppression of DA by alternative antecedents is a direct prediction of the model.

Suppression effects are just what would be predicted if people regard conditional reasoning as non-monotonic and defeasible, as we discussed in the section *Logicism and*

Uncertainty. There, following suggestions especially in the AI knowledge representation literature (e.g., Pearl, 1988), we proposed that conditional sentences were represented in terms of conditional probabilities. This suggestion has the consequence that, for example, the probability that *the car starts* if *the key is turned* is less than 1, say, .9; that is, P(*starts* | *key-turned*) = .9. If all we know is that *the key is turned*, the probability that *the car starts*, that is, the probability of endorsing MP, would be .9. However, the probability of its starting given that the key is turned and the petrol tank is empty is 0 (P[*starts* | *key turned, empty*] = 0). Our theoretical model amounts to applying this resolution of the conceptual problems, with strengthening the antecedent, to the empirical evidence on conditional reasoning performance.

Modelling the Suppression Effect I: Byrne (1989)

Figure 6.2 shows the overall fit of the model to Byrne's (1989) data. The observed proportions of inferences endorsed in Byrne's Experiment 1 are shown with filled diamonds (data), and the proportions predicted by the model are shown with unfilled squares (model). The three graphs correspond to the three conditions in Byrne's (1989) experiment. The *simple* condition that provided the baseline in which there was no manipulation of alternative or additional antecedents. In the *alternative antecedent condition*, participants were provided with an alternative rule; for example, *if hot wired, the car starts.* This graph reveals that this manipulation suppressed both DA and AC, but not MP or MT. In the *additional antecedent condition*, participants were provided with an additional rule; for example, *if there is petrol in the tank, the car starts.* This graph reveals that this manipulation suppressed both MP and MT, but not DA or AC. We fitted the model to the data by looking for the values of $P(p)$ and $P(q)$ that maximised the log of the likelihood (L) of the data given the model. L is given by the joint binomial distribution:

$$L = \prod_{j=1}^{J} \binom{F_j}{f_j} p_j^{f_j} (1 - p_j)^{F_j - f_j} \tag{5}$$

where J is the number of inferences (that is, 4), f_j is the frequency with which an inference is endorsed, F_j is the total number of responses (that is, N), and p_j is the probability of drawing an inference according to our probabilistic model. To estimate the best-fitting parameter values, we minimised the log of (5), using a steepest descent search implemented in Mathematica's (Wolfram, 1991) *MultiStartMin* function (Loehle, 2000), which supplements the Newton–Raphson method with a grid-search procedure to ensure a global minimum. The log-likelihood ratio test statistic G^2, which is asymptotically distributed as χ^2, was used to assess the goodness of fit (Read & Cressie, 1988). This statistic evaluates the model fit by comparing the predicted values to a saturated model where all the values of p_j are set to the empirically observed proportions of cards selected. Within each condition in Byrne's Experiment 1, $P(p)$, $P(q)$ and ε were estimated from the data. As there were four data points and three parameters, G^2 was assessed against one degree of freedom. For model comparisons, the conventional 5 per cent level of significance is regarded as unreasonably large (Read & Cressie, 1988). The level of significance for rejection was therefore set at the 1 per cent level. The model could not be rejected for any of the three conditions (the best-fit parameter values are shown in parentheses), simple: $G^2(1) = .04$,

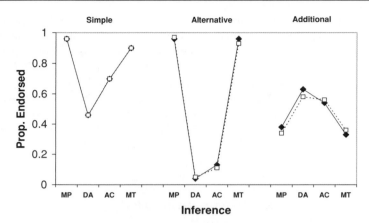

Figure 6.2   Fit between the model and Byrne's (1989: Experiment 1) suppression data, showing the probability of endorsing each inference observed (data) and predicted by Oaksford et al.'s (2000) probabilistic model (model)

$p > .50$ ($P(p) = .57$, $P(q) = .78$, $\varepsilon = .04$); alternative: $G^2(1) = .40$, $p > .50$ ($P(p) = .11$, $P(q) = .95$, $\varepsilon = .03$); or additional: $G^2(1) = .38$, $p > .50$ ($P(p) = .61$, $P(q) = .37$, $\varepsilon = .66$). Moreover, collapsing across conditions, the model could also not be rejected: $G^2(3) = .82$, $p > .50$.

According to probability theory, the conditional probabilities, $P(\text{not-}q \mid p)$ and $P(q \mid \text{not-}p)$, are independent of $P(p)$ and $P(q)$. However, according to our probability model, manipulating alternative and additional antecedents leads to changes in people's assessments of $P(p)$ and $P(q)$ (see Equations 2–4), as can be seen in the best-fit parameter values. It is important therefore that the changes in these parameters in response to manipulations of alternative and additional antecedents make intuitive sense. Let us look first at alternative antecedents. There are two cases to consider. First, how should being told that there are many different ways of starting a car affect one's assessment of the probability of its starting? Intuitively, it seems it should raise the probability: the more ways there are of making something happen, the greater the probability that it does happen. This common-sense principle seems to be based on the fact that people interpret events as part of a causal nexus rather than as isolated and independent. Second, how should being told that there are many different ways of starting a car affect one's assessment of the probability that the key is turned? Intuitively, it seems it should lower the probability: the more ways there are of making something happen, the lower the probability that any particular way need be invoked (but see below). These intuitions seem to be captured by Oaksford et al.'s (2000) model. In the simple condition in Experiment 1, the best fitting value for $P(p)$ was .57 and for $P(q)$ it was .78, but in the alternative antecedents condition, $P(p)$ fell to .11 and $P(q)$ increased to .95.

We now look at the effects of additional antecedents. Again, there are two cases to consider. First, how should being told that there are many different factors affecting whether a car will start affect one's assessment of the probability that the key is turned? Intuitively, it seems it should leave this probability unaffected: knowing that other factors are required for an action to succeed does not affect the probability that that action is performed. Second, how should being told that there are many different factors affecting whether a car will start affect one's assessment of the probability of its starting? Intuitively, it seems it should lower the probability: the more things that can prevent an action from producing the desired effect, the less likely that effect is to occur. Again, these intuitions seemed to be captured by Oaksford et al.'s (2000) model. In the additional antecedents condition, $P(p)$ stayed roughly the same at .61, while $P(q)$ decreased to .37. The suggestion that the model's behaviour may be consistent with various common-sense principles of reasoning is a prediction that is open to experimental test.

Modelling Suppression Effects II: Cummins et al. (1991)

Denise Cummins very kindly provided us with the raw data from her 1991 paper on suppression effects. In that experiment, a variety of causal conditionals were pre-tested for number of alternative and additional antecedents. These factors were also fully crossed in a 2×2 design; that is, rules were used that had many alternative and many additional antecedents (MM), many alternative and few additional antecedents (MF), few alternative and many additional antecedents (FM), and few alternative and few additional antecedents (FF). Participants rated each inference for each rule on a 6-point scale (1–6). To model these data, we re-scaled these ratings into the 0–1 probability scale by taking away 1 and dividing by 5. To fit the model to the data using the same procedure as above, we then multiplied each proportion by the sample size (27). This number was then rounded to the nearest integer, to obtain the frequency of participants endorsing an inference. We then fitted the model to the data, for each rule-type (MM, MF, FM and FF), as we described above. The model could not be rejected for any of the four rules (the best-fit parameter values are shown in parentheses), MM: $G^2(1) = 2.14, p > .10$ ($P(p) = .48, P(q) = .66, \varepsilon = .29$); MF: $G^2(1) = 5.58, p > .01$ ($P(p) = .49, P(q) = .67, \varepsilon = 25$); FM: $G^2(1) = .92, p > .20$ ($P(p) = .52, P(q) = .64, \varepsilon = .23$), or FF: $G^2(1) = 1.66, p > .10$ ($P(p) = .46, P(q) = .63, \varepsilon = .16$). Collapsing across conditions, the model could also not be rejected: $G^2(4) = 10.30, p > .02$. Consequently, as for Byrne (1989), the model provides good fits to Cummins et al.'s (1991) results.

We also fitted the model to each individual participant's results. We did this by first re-scaling the ratings as above, and then minimising the sum of squared differences between the data and the model, as in Oaksford et al. (2000). This procedure meant that best-fitting parameter values could be calculated for each rule type for each participant. These parameters could then be analysed statistically. First, however, we assessed the goodness of fit. We used the best-fit parameter values to calculate the probability of drawing each inference for each participant. We then compared the mean of these values to the re-scaled data means. We illustrate the fit in Figure 6.3, which shows the mean probabilities of each inference calculated from the data and calculated from the model. The error bars show the 95 per cent confidence intervals for the data. For this comparison, $R^2 = .84$, a result which shows that the model captures the general trend in the data quite well. We also computed the root mean squared scaled deviation (RMSSD) (Schunn & Wallach, 2001), which provides a scale-invariant estimate of how much the model diverges from the exact location of the data points in standard error units. RMSSD = 1.62, which means that, on average, the model deviated from the data values by only 1.62 standard error units. Thus, the model provides a good fit to the location of each data point.

Having established that the model provided a good fit to the data, we then asked whether the model's parameters vary in the way the model predicts. The model may fit the data

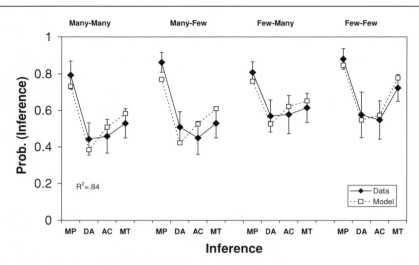

Figure 6.3 Fit between the model and Cummins et al.'s (1991) suppression data, showing the mean probability of endorsing each inference observed (Data) and mean value predicted by Oaksford et al.'s (2000) probabilistic model (Model). Error bars show 95% confidence intervals

very well, but not necessarily for the right reasons. For example, our model predicts that variation in additional antecedents should affect ε, the exceptions parameter. When there are many additional antecedents, ε should be higher than when there are few additional antecedents. Figure 6.1 also shows that there should be a relationship between ε and the number of alternative antecedents. As the number of exceptions increases, the probability that DA should be endorsed falls, and so the probability of alternative antecedents (DA') rises. So, when there are many alternative antecedents, ε should be higher than when there are few alternative antecedents.

We analysed the best-fitting values of ε in a 2 × 2, within-subjects ANOVA with alternative (many vs. few) and additional (many vs. few) antecedents as factors (see Table 6.2). There was a significant main effect of additional antecedents: $F(1, 26) = 18.72$, $MSE = .006$, $p < .0005$. ε was significantly higher when there were many (mean = .25, SD = .16) than when there were few (mean = .19, SD = .13) additional antecedents. There was also a significant main effect of alternative antecedents: $F(1, 26) = 7.44$, $MSE = .010$, $p < .025$. ε was significantly higher when there were many (mean = .25, SD = .16) than when there were few (mean = .20, SD = .13) alternative antecedents. These results confirm the predictions of our model.

There was also a very close to significant interaction effect: $F(1, 26) = 4.19$, $MSE = .004$, $p = .051$. Simple effects comparisons showed that although alternative antecedents had a significant effect on ε when there were few additional antecedents—$F(1, 26) = 14.44$, $MSE = .006$, $p < .001$—they did not have a significant effect on ε when there were many additional antecedents: $F(1, 26) = 1.24$, $MSE = .008$, $p = .275$. According to our model, it would seem that when there are many additional antecedents, alternative antecedents must influence inference via $P(p)$ and $P(q)$ rather than ε. The other simple effects comparisons revealed that additional antecedents significantly influenced ε at both levels of alternative antecedents (few: $F(1, 26) = 17.02$, $MSE = .006$, $p < .001$, many: $F(1, 26) = 5.44$, $MSE = .004$, $p < .05$), although the effect was weaker when there were many alternative antecedents.

Table 6.2 Mean values of the best-fit parameters (ε, $P(p)$ and $P(q)$) for Cummins et al.'s (1991) experiment by alternative antecedents (Alts.: many vs. few) and additional antecedents (Adds.: many vs. few)

| | Many Alts. | | | | Few Alts. | | | |
| | Many Adds. | | Few Adds. | | Many Adds. | | Few Adds. | |
Parameter	Mean	SD	Mean	SD	Mean	SD	Mean	SD
ε	.27	.18	.23	.13	.24	.13	.15	.12
$P(p)$	.47	.19	.45	.19	.49	.20	.41	.22
$P(q)$	.68	.15	.67	.15	.62	.16	.63	.21

We also analysed the $P(p)$ and $P(q)$ parameters (see Table 6.2). There are a couple of predictions about how these parameters should vary. In modelling Byrne's (1989) results above, we found quite marked changes in these parameters. In the best-fit parameter values, many alternative antecedents led to increases in $P(q)$ and decreases in $P(p)$, whereas many additional antecedents led to decreases in $P(q)$ but no changes in $P(p)$. We motivated these changes by appeal to various common-sense principles. We tested to what extent these patterns are present in Cummins et al.'s (1991) results. However, Byrne's (1989) explicit manipulation produced stronger effects (compare Figures 6.2 and 6.3), and she did not use a fully crossed design, so possible interaction effects could not be assessed. Consequently, any effects are likely to be weaker. Moreover, the interaction for ε suggests that the predicted differences for alternative antecedents will be seen only when there are many additional antecedents.

We analysed the best-fitting values of $P(p)$ and $P(q)$ in a $2 \times 2 \times 2$, within-subjects ANOVA with parameter ($P(p)$ vs. $P(q)$), alternative antecedents (many vs. few) and additional antecedents (many vs. few) as factors (see Table 6.2). There was a significant main effect of parameter: $F(1, 26) = 14.71$, $MSE = 145$, $p < .001$. $P(q)$ (mean $= .65$, SD $= .17$) was significantly higher than $P(p)$ (mean $= .45$, SD $= .20$). This simply reflects the general constraint on our model that $P(q) > P(p)(1 - \varepsilon)$, so that when $\varepsilon = 0$, $P(q) > P(p)$. There was also a significant two-way interaction between parameter and alternative antecedents, $F(1, 26) = 4.88$, $MSE = .006$, $p < .05$, which was modified by a three-way interaction: $F(1, 26) = 4.67$, $MSE = .005$, $p < .05$. The three-way interaction partly reflects the prediction that the differences for alternative antecedents will be seen only when there are many additional antecedents. When this is the case, $P(q)$ was significantly higher—planned contrast: $F(1, 26) = 10.12$, $MSE = .006$, $p < .005$—when there were many alternative antecedents than when there were few alternative antecedents (see Table 6.2). Moreover, when there were many additional antecedents, there was a trend, although not significant, for $P(p)$ such that it was lower when there were many alternative antecedents than when there were few (see Table 6.2). These results are consistent with the changes in these parameter values observed in Byrne (1989), which we suggested may reflect various common-sense principles of reasoning.

However, there were other changes in parameters reflected in the three-way interaction. Specifically, when there were few alternatives, $P(p)$ was higher when there were many additional antecedents than when there were few. This difference was significant in a planned contrast: $F(1, 26) = 14.28$, $MSE = .005$, $p < .001$. This means, for example, that if you know a car can be started only by turning the key (few alternative antecedents), then the more conditions that need to be satisfied for turning the key to start the car (many additional antecedents), the more likely you are to turn the key (higher $P(p)$). The only intuitive motivation we can think of for such a principle is that, the more conditions that might need to be checked before taking an action, the more likely someone is not to bother and perform the action regardless, just to see if it works. Such a principle may be of limited generality.

In this section, we have shown how our model can provide detailed fits to the data on the suppression effect. Moreover, we have demonstrated that to achieve the fits the best-fit parameter values behave pretty much as would be expected. In the following sections, we explore some further suppression effects in conditional inference that can also be explained by this model.

Suppression Effects: Further Findings

In this section, we address a range of further findings on the suppression effect that would appear to be compatible with Oaksford et al.'s (2000) probabilistic model. We first look at the possible consequences of experiments such as those reported by Cummins et al. (1991), and Thompson (1994), where information about alternative and additional antecedents is provided implicitly.

Implicit Presentation

Cummins et al. (1991), Cummins (1995) and Thompson (1994) report results that were very similar to Byrne's (1989). However, they left information about additional and alternative antecedents implicit. That is, unlike Byrne (1989), these authors pre-tested rules for how many alternative and additional antecedents they allowed, and used these rules in the experimental task with no further explicit cueing as to the relevance of alternative and additional antecedents. These results seem directly to contradict Byrne, Espino and Santamaria (1999, p. 369), who have recently argued that people do *not* have, "a general insight into the idea that there may be alternatives or additional background conditions that are relevant to inferences". Byrne et al. (1999) appear to be arguing that, in the absence of explicitly provided information about alternative or additional antecedents, people do not retrieve it from long-term memory of world knowledge to decide whether to draw an inference. This view is not consistent with Cummins et al. (1991) or Thompson (1994), where, even when such information was left implicit, suppression effects were still observed. Consequently, participants must be accessing appropriate world knowledge to determine the likelihood that an inference can be drawn. This conclusion is further supported by the recent results of Liu et al. (1996). In their "reduced" inference condition, they presented participants with contentful material but without an explicit conditional premise; for example *knowing that the key has been turned, how probable is it that the car starts*? They found similar suppression effects as when they provided an explicit conditional premise. As Liu et al. (1996) argue, in the reduced inference condition, participants *must* be basing their inferences on accessing prior knowledge. *Pace* Byrne et al. (1999), that similar suppression effects were observed means that information about additional and alternative antecedents was being implicitly accessed.

Facilitating DA and AC

Byrne (1989) also showed that suppression effects can be removed by providing more information in the categorical premise. For example, given *if p then q* and *if r then q*, participants would be given the categorical premise, *p and r*. In Experiment 2, Byrne found that using materials like this removed all suppression effects. Indeed, using this manipulation produced a facilitation effect for DA and AC. We can explain this effect by the different ways additional and alternative antecedents affect the appropriate conditional probabilities. Only the number of alternative antecedents independently affects these probabilities, whereas the number of additional antecedents does not. For example, take the rule *if the key is turned, the car starts*. There are many exceptions to this rule: the car will not start if there is no petrol (*if there is petrol in the tank, the car starts*), if the battery is flat (*if the battery is charged, the car starts*) and so on. To make the MP inference in the first place, one must assume that all these possible additional conditions are *jointly* satisfied. Consequently, being told that *the key is turned and the battery is charged* is not going to affect people's estimate of the probability of MP, nor, by parity of reasoning, that of MT, as they have already assumed that this jointly necessary condition applies. Conversely, there are other ways to start cars, hot-wiring (*if hot-wired, the car starts*), jump-starting (*if jump-started, the car starts*) and so on. Each is individually sufficient to start the car; consequently, the more that are ruled out, the less likely the car is to start. Consequently, being told that *the key was not turned and the car was not hot-wired*, will increase someone's estimate of the probability of DA, and, by parity of reasoning, that of AC. In terms of Oaksford et al.'s model, this means that this manipulation decreases the probability that the car starts even though the key has not been turned. This explanation accounts for the facilitation effect for DA and AC that Byrne (1989) observed in her Experiment 2.

Graded Suppression of MP and MT

Stevenson and Over (1995) have shown variation in MP and MT inferences by concentrating not on the number of additional antecedents but on their likelihood. So participants could be told that,

If the key is turned, the car starts,	(1)
If the battery is charged, the car starts, and that	(2)
The battery is always (almost always, sometimes, rarely, very rarely) charged	(3)

Participants are then given the categorical premise *the key is turned*. The manipulation in the third premise directly manipulates the likelihood of an exception; that is, ε ($P(\text{not-}q \,|\, p)$). Participants' willingness to endorse MP and MT tracked this manipulation, as would be predicted by our probabilistic account. If we look at Equations 1 and 4, for MP and MT, it is clear that as ε increases, the probability of MP decreases. A similar effect is also predicted for MT, although, if a and b are kept constant, the slope for MT will be steeper than for MP (see Figure 6.1). Interestingly, in Stevenson and Over's data, using the *always* instruction leads to a facilitation effect compared to the condition in which premise 3 is absent. This is because, although in premise 2 participants are told that further conditions need to apply to make the inference in premise 1, they are then told in premise 3 that these conditions always apply!

Chan and Chua (1994) used a similar manipulation to Stevenson and Over (1995) to reveal graded suppression of MP and MT. However, rather than use a further premise, like 3 above, they used different additional antecedents that varied in their relative salience for achieving the conclusion. For example, premise 2 is quite salient to whether the car starts or not. However, other less salient conditions can be imagined:

If the engine has not been removed overnight, the car will start, or   (2′)
If it was not foggy last night, the car will start   (2″)
(damp points can prevent ignition)

Chan and Chua (1994) observed the same graded suppression of MP and MT as observed by Stevenson and Over (1995).

George (1997) has also investigated graded suppression effects in conditional inference by directly introducing information in the conditional about the probability of the consequent given the antecedent. For example, he used rules such as *if Pierre is in the kitchen, it is (not) very probable that Marie is in the garden*. This manipulation directly affects ε; when the consequent includes "very probable", ε is low, and when it includes "not very probable", ε is high. Predictably, in his Experiment 1, there were more MP inferences in the very probable than in the not very probable condition.

Sufficiency and Suppressing DA and AC

George (1997) also found suppression effects for DA and AC when perceived sufficiency was reduced (for "valid arguments", see George, 1997, Table 6.1); that is, when ε is high. These effects are not predicted by a simple model based on the effects of additional and alternative antecedents. However, they are predicted by our probabilistic model. Examining Equations 2 and 3, for DA and AC, reveals that increasing ε while keeping a and b constant will also lead to reductions in the relevant conditional probabilities (see Figure 6.1). Intuitively this also makes sense because the numbers of exceptions and alternatives are related. For example, the rule *if the key is turned, the car starts* captures the *normal* and *most reliable* way (ε is as low as it can get) of starting cars. Alternative methods of starting cars are generally less reliable; for example, *if the car is bump-started, the car starts*, relies on further factors such as the speed being sufficiently high when you take your foot off the clutch and so on. So this alternative way of starting a car is also a less reliable way of starting a car; that is, ε is higher. Our probabilistic model captures this intuition and so can explain the suppression of DA and AC when perceived sufficiency is low.

Summary

Oaksford et al.'s simple probabilistic model appears to be capable of accounting for many of the suppression and facilitation effects in conditional inference. The key factor is that people's prior knowledge can be interpreted as affecting the subjective probabilities assigned to events or to their occurrence conditional on other events occurring. Most of our arguments for how the model explains these effects result from showing why, intuitively, a particular manipulation should affect the relevant probabilities in a way that is consistent with our simple probabilistic model. In the next section, we see whether this pattern of explanation can be extended to order effects in conditional inference.

ORDER EFFECTS

Other important determinants of performance on conditional inference are the order of clauses within the conditional premise, that is, the difference between *if p then q* and *q only if p*, and the order of presentation of the premises and conclusion of a conditional inference. These manipulations are important and interesting, and we argue that they may also be amenable to a probabilistic treatment.

Clause Order

There are two consistent effects of the change of clause order. First, *the car starts only if the key is turned* leads to more AC and MT inferences and fewer MP and DA inferences than *if the key is turned, the car starts* (Evans, 1977; Roberge, 1978; Evans & Beck, 1981). Second, it has been found that paraphrasing a rule *if p then q*, using *only if* depends on two factors: temporal precedence, that is, which of *p* and *q* occurs first, and perceived necessity, that is, is *p* necessary for *q* or *q* necessary for *p*? (Evans, 1977; Evans & Newstead, 1977; Evans & Beck, 1981; Thompson & Mann, 1995). Note that in our example, turning the key (*p*) both precedes and is causally necessary for the car to start, and hence is best paraphrased as *q only if p*; the opposite paraphrase, *the key is turned only if the car starts*, seems pragmatically infelicitous. Thompson and Mann (1995) have also observed that these effects seem independent of content domain; that is, they occur for conditionals expressing causes, permissions, definitions or co-occurrence relations.

Our model clearly does not address the psycholinguistic findings on paraphrasing. However, we can look to see whether the principal effect of the *q only if p* rule revealed by these results, to emphasise the necessity of *p* for *q*, is amenable to a probabilistic treatment. Probabilistically, this effect seems to correspond to a situation where the probability of the consequent given that the antecedent has not occurred ($P[q \mid \text{not-}p]$) is lowered; that is, there are fewer alternative ways of achieving the effect. This immediately gives rise to the problem that if this probability decreases, the probability of the DA inference increases. But the observation in this literature is that DA and MP inferences decrease while AC and MT increase (Evans, 1977; Evans & Beck, 1981). However, an alternative interpretation is that the *q only if p* rule lowers the joint probability of *q* and not-*p* ($P[q, \text{not-}p]$). Under these circumstances, it is possible to rearrange the marginals, that is, $P(p)$ and $P(q)$, so that the probability of DA falls and the probability of AC rises. However, to model the increase in MT requires a fall in ε. This predicts an increase in MP inferences. But, in the data, the move to the *q only if p* rule leads to decreases in the frequency of MP endorsements, not increases. Consequently, however one tries to capture the effect of the *q only if p* rule, it seems that the model is bound to get the direction of change wrong for at least one inference. This is further borne out in fitting the model to Evans' (1977) results. The model could not be rejected for the *if p then q* rule, $G^2(1, N = 16) = 4.92, p > .02$, or for the *q only if p* rule, $G^2(1, N = 16) = 1.02, p > .30$ (see Figure 6.4). Moreover, although the predicted proportion

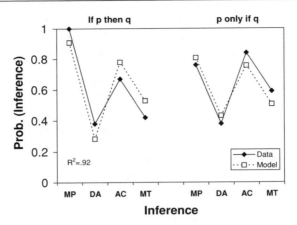

Figure 6.4   The observed and predicted probability of endorsements of each inference for the *if... then* and *only if* rules in Evans (1977)

of endorsements minimised the differences between rules, the direction of change was correct for MP, AC and MT. However, the model predicted an increase in DA inferences for the *q only if p* rule where either no change (Evans, 1977) or decreases were found (Evans & Beck, 1981).

Clause Order, Utilities and Conversational Pragmatics

It would appear that a straightforward probabilistic account of clause order effects is not available in our simple model. However, we believe that this may be because order manipulations have pragmatic functions that may be better captured via changes in utilities rather than probabilities. Oaksford, Chater and Grainger (1999) made a similar suggestion in the selection task. Order effects are usually discussed in terms of their direct effect on the construction of mental representations for the premises (Johnson-Laird & Byrne, 1991; Girotto et al., 1997; Evans et al., 1998). However, ordering of information may have pragmatic effects other than affecting the order in which a discourse representation is assembled. For example, order typically encodes the *topic* or focus of a discourse. For example, in an active sentence, the subject is the topic—hence the subject is mentioned first—whereas in a passive sentence the object is the topic—hence the object is mentioned first. Consequently, in interpreting even the relatively restricted discourse provided by a conditional syllogism, it is important to understand the normal communicative function of different sentential and clausal orderings.

Ordering manipulations may change the topic of a discourse. Changing the clausal ordering from *if p then q* to *q only if p* switches the topic from *p* to *q*. Communicative functions can be revealed by posing questions where one or the other linguistic form would be the most appropriate reply. For example, in response to the query, "What happens if I turn the key?", one might respond, "If you turn the key, the car starts." However, in response to the query, "Why did the car start?", one might reply, "Well, that happens only if you turn the key." Switching responses to these two queries would be pragmatically infelicitous. These examples suggest that the pragmatic function of *if p then q* is to focus attention on what can be predicted given that p is known, whereas the pragmatic function of q *only if* p is to focus attention on explaining why q happened. Assuming that p temporally precedes q, as is normal (Comrie, 1986), MP and DA are the predictive inferences that are suppressed for the q *only if* p form, and AC and MT are the explanatory inferences that are facilitated for this form. This pattern of suppression and facilitation is consistent with the explanatory function of the q *only if* p form of the rule. The effect here is not to alter the relevant probabilities, but rather to alter the importance attached to the different inferences. Consequently, we argue that the utility to a reasoner of the different classes of inference is altered by the clause order manipulation. For the q *only if* p rule, people assign higher utility to the explanatory, AC and MT inferences, and a lower utility to the predictive, MP and DA inferences.

Premise and Conclusion Order

A further manipulation of order involves altering the order of premises and conclusion (Girotto, Mazzocco & Tasso, 1997; Evans, Handley & Buck, 1998). Girotto et al. (1997) showed that people are more willing to draw MT when the premises are presented in order (PCR) rather than in the standard order (PCS):

(PCR) The car has not started	(PCS) If the key is turned, the car starts
If the key is turned, the car starts	The car has not started
(The key was not turned (C))	(The key was not turned (C))

(The labels derive from Evans et al. (1998): "PC" means the conclusion (C) comes after the premises (P); "S" means that the premises are in standard order, conditional before categorical premise; and "R" means that this premise order is reversed.) The conclusion (in parentheses) was not presented in Girotto et al. (1997), as they used a production task where participants must spontaneously produce a conclusion rather than evaluate the validity of particular conclusions provided by the experimenter. Girotto et al. (1997) found no effect of this manipulation on MP, DA or AC, nor does it affect q *only if* p conditionals or biconditionals.

Evans, Handley and Buck (1998) used a similar manipulation but also varied the position of the conclusion. They used the orders in PCR and PCS (including the conclusion because Evans et al. used an evaluation task) and the following orders:

(CPR) The key was not turned (C)	(CPS) The key was not turned (C)
The car has not started	If the key is turned, the car starts
If the key is turned, the car starts	The car has not started

Evans et al. (1998) failed to replicate Girotto's et al.'s (1997) finding of increases in MT inferences with premise order reversals (PCR and PCS). What they did find was that both presenting the conclusion first (CPR and CPS vs. PCS) and reversing the premises (PCR and CPR vs. PCS) led to a reduction in negative conclusion bias, as we discussed in the introduction to this chapter. It was possible for Evans et al. (1998) to discover this because they used all the four conditions fully crossed with Evans' (1972) negations paradigm, where the four rules, *if p then q*, *if p then not-q*, *if not-p then q*, and *if not-p then not-q*, are presented. Evans et al.'s (1998) failure to replicate Girotto et al. (1997) suggests that it

Table 6.3 Mean values of the best-fit parameters ($P(p)$ and $P(q)$) for Evans et al.'s (1998) Experiment 2 by premise and conclusion order (PC vs. CP), premise order (standard vs. reverse), and whether the clause was negated or affirmative

	PC				CP			
	Standard		Reverse		Standard		Reverse	
	Mean	SD	Mean	SD	Mean	SD	Mean	SD
Negated	.85	.07	.78	.05	.82	.04	.67	.04
Affirmative	.59	.10	.73	.01	.76	.01	.73	.11

may be too simplistic to attempt an interpretation that concentrates only on variation in MT inferences. We therefore concentrate on the effects described by Evans et al.

Probabilities and Conversational Pragmatics

Oaksford and Chater (1995a) suggested that conversational pragmatics may influence reasoning by affecting subjective probabilities. In that paper, we were concerned with accounting for the effects of relevance manipulations in Wason's selection task (Sperber, Cara & Girotto, 1995). We suggested that increasing the relevance of particular instances of a rule may result in increasing the degree of belief that such instances exist. Consequently, order effects that alter the topic of a sentence may also serve to increase the relevance and hence the subjective probability of a described property or event. This reasoning suggests investigating the probabilistic effects of ordering manipulations. We have done this by fitting our probabilistic model to the results from Evans et al.'s (1998) Experiment 2 that used the fully crossed design outlined in PCR to CPS. We fitted the model to the data for each of the four rules in the negations paradigm in each of the four conditions. We allowed all three parameters (a, b and ε) of the model to vary. The model could not be rejected for any of the 16 rule-condition pairs: average $G^2(1, N = 20) = 1.54$ (SD $= 1.65$), $p > .20$. Moreover, overall, the model could not be rejected: $G^2(16) = 24.63$, $p > .05$.

We investigated whether there were significant changes in parameter values dependent on the experimental manipulations. We first looked at the values of a and b, that is, of the probability of the antecedent ($P(p)$) and consequent ($P(q)$), respectively. To do this, we treated the parameters as our unit of analysis. $P(p)$ and $P(q)$ were estimated for each of the four rules in each of the four conditions, PCR to CPS.[1] Table 6.3 shows the mean values of the best-fit parameter values split by premise and conclusion order (PC vs. CP), premise order (S vs. R) and negation, that is, whether the parameter corresponds to a negated or an affirmative clause. According to Oaksford et al.'s (2000) model of the negations paradigm, negated clauses should correspond to high-probability categories. For example, our model predicts that $P(q)$ should be higher for the rule *if p then not-q* than for *if p then q*.

---

[1] In the analyses for the affirmative group the $P(q)$ value for the HL rule was omitted. This was because this rule is pragmatically odd. For example, it is like suggesting that *if something is black, it is a raven*, a statement known to be false because there are far more black things besides ravens. In Oaksford et al.'s (2000) model, the best fit values of $P(q)$ value for this rule were always high, and that is why we removed them from the analysis. However, this left too few data points in each cell (3). Consequently, we added a further data point corresponding to the mean of the remaining data points.

Consequently, we should see an effect of negation: negated clauses should correspond to higher probabilities.

We conducted a 2×4, mixed ANOVA with condition as a between-subjects factor and negation as the within-subjects factor.[2] There were main effects of negation, $F(1, 12) = 23.72$, $MSE = .002$, $p < .0005$, and of condition, $F(3, 12) = 3.27$, $MSE = .005$, $p = .059$, which were both modified by a significant interaction, $F(3, 12) = 19.51$, $MSE = .002$, $p < .0001$. Simple effects comparisons revealed that the best-fit parameters were significantly higher when they corresponded to a negated rather than an affirmative clause only for the PCS condition, $F(1, 12) = 70.44$, $MSE = .002$, $p < .0001$. This analysis really just redescribes Evans et al.'s (1998) finding that these order manipulations remove negative conclusion bias, in terms of our probabilistic model. However, why this happens in the model is interesting.

The difference between affirmative and negated clauses has narrowed for the non-standard orders mainly because of *increases* in the probabilities of the affirmative clause. The simple effect comparison for the affirmative clauses was significant: $F(3, 21) = 7.17$, $MSE = .003$, $p < .002$. To analyse this effect further, we carried out a one-way ANOVA on just the affirmative data. In post hoc Newman–Keuls tests, all the non-standard conditions had affirmative clauses that had significantly higher probabilities than the standard PCS condition at the 5 per cent level. No other differences approached significance. A very different pattern of results was found for the negated clauses. Again the simple effect comparison was significant: $F(3, 21) = 8.94$, $MSE = .003$, $p < .001$. However, now in post hoc Newman–Keuls tests, there were no significant differences between the PCS, PCR and CPS conditions; that is, the probabilities of the negated clauses remained high. However, all three of these conditions had negated clauses that had significantly higher probabilities than the CPR condition at the 5 per cent level.[3]

How could these order manipulations lead to these changes in subjective probability? We have suggested that making some piece of information relevant (Sperber, Cara & Girotto, 1995) may increase the subjective probability of an event (Oaksford & Chater, 1995a), and that making something the topic of a discourse may have the same effect. We should not be surprised at such changes in our subjective probabilities because in inference they are all relative to context. So, for example, the probability of encountering a llama on the streets of Cardiff is extremely low by our estimation. However, the probability of such an encounter at London Zoo is far higher. In all but the standard PCS condition, instead of the rule, one of the antecedent or consequent clauses is the first sentence of the limited discourse provided by these argument forms. That is, one of the antecedent or consequent clauses acts as the topic of the discourse. This explains why the probabilities of the affirmative clause rise. No corresponding increases in the probabilities of negated clauses occur because they are already high. This seems to make sense. For example, the probability that people are *not* going to encounter a llama on the streets of Cardiff is already very high. Telling them that they are not going to encounter one, that is, making *not* encountering llamas the topic of some discourse, is unlikely to increase their subjective estimate of this event.

Another aspect of the ordering manipulation concerns the coherence of the resulting discourse. PCS, PCR and CPS all seem to be coherent, whereas CPR does not. We illustrate

---

[2] We used a repeated-measures ANOVA because each parameter-rule combination occurs in each condition; for example, $P(p)$ for the *if p then q* rule was estimated for each of the four conditions.

[3] We cannot offer any explanation for the decline in the probability of categories corresponding to negated clauses in the CPR conditions.

this point by providing discourse examples of these different orders. We use the MP argument form throughout.

PCS'   When there is heavy rain in the Welsh Marches, there are often floods
        along the river Severn. In summer 1999, there was heavy rain in the
        Welsh Marches. Towns along the river Severn were flooded for days.

Here the causal relation between rain in the Welsh Marches and flooding on the Severn is the topic. After the second sentence, the invited inference is clearly what is stated in the final sentence, that is, the conclusion. So the function of this ordering seems to be to consider the consequences of the truth of the relationship described in the conditional.

PCR'   In summer 1999, there was heavy rain in the Welsh Marches. When
        there is heavy rain in the Welsh Marches, there are often floods along
        the river Severn. That year, towns along the river Severn were flooded
        for days.

Here the topic is the heavy rain in the Welsh Marches in the summer of 1999. Introducing the causal relation in the second sentence clearly invites the reader to consider the consequences of this fact. So the function of this ordering seems to be to consider the consequences of the fact described in the first sentence, that is, of the topic of the discourse.

CPS'   In summer 1999, towns along the river Severn were flooded for days.
        When there is heavy rain in the Welsh Marches, there are often floods
        along the river Severn. There was heavy rain in the Welsh Marches
        that year.

Here the topic is clearly the flooding along the river Severn in the summer of 1999. Introducing the causal relation in the second sentence clearly invites the reader to consider possible explanations of this fact. So the function of this ordering seems to be to consider possible explanations of the fact described in the first sentence, that is, of the topic of the discourse.

Note that PCR' and CPS' are interchangeable; for example, if we presented AC in CPS form, the resulting discourse would be identical to MP in PCR form. This predicts that MP and AC inferences in both PCR' and CPS' should be endorsed at similar levels, whereas normally MP inferences are endorsed much more strongly. In Evans et al.'s (1998) results, the difference between endorsements of MP and AC was 21 per cent in the PCS condition, whereas in the PCR and CPS conditions it was only 5 per cent and 6 per cent, respectively (DA and MT inferences were at similar levels overall in all conditions).

?CPR'   In summer 1999, towns along the river Severn were flooded for days.
        There was heavy rain in the Welsh Marches that year. When there is
        heavy rain in the Welsh Marches, there are often floods along the river
        Severn.

We have put a question mark before CPR' because, although the discourse is not nonsensical, it is not wholly coherent. The first sentence introduces a fact. For the second sentence to be coherent, it must be regarded as relevant to this fact. The only way it seems this can come about is when the fact in the second sentence is explanatory of (or can be predicted from) the first. That is, the second sentence is a tentative attempt to suggest a causal relation between the facts described in these juxtaposed sentences (see Comrie, 1986, on the use of sentential juxtaposition to suggest causation). The final conditional sentence then states that there is such a relation. This seems to violate the pragmatic maxim of quantity (Levinson, 1983): a statement should be as informative as is required for the current discourse. The problem here is that the first two sentences in CPR' suggest only that there *may* be a causal relation between these two facts. However, the final sentence makes the more informational statement that there actually is such a relationship. According to the maxim of quantity, if someone knew that such a relationship existed, there was no point in just suggesting that it did in the first two sentences. Rather, as in the other orders, this should be stated upfront.

What effects might we predict from this apparent violation of the maxim of quantity? The most obvious effect of stating only that a causal relation *may* exist in the first two sentences is to weaken participants' belief in the conditional describing that relation in the final sentence. Although we have argued that there is not always a relation between the degree to which a rule is believed and exceptions (Chater & Oaksford, 1999a), this is often the case. For example, your degree of belief that *if something is a widget, it is blue* would probably be severely reduced if you are told that *most widgets are not blue*. This suggests that the effect of CPR' may be to increase the probability of exceptions; that is, this pragmatic account of order effects suggests that ε rises in the CPR' condition. We therefore statistically compared the best-fit values of ε between conditions in a one-way, within-subjects ANOVA. The result was significant: $F(3, 9) = 5.57, MSE = .003, p < .025$. In post hoc Newman–Keuls tests, the CPR condition (mean = .21, SD = .08) had a higher mean probability of exceptions than all other conditions at the 5 per cent level (PCS: mean = .08, SD = .02; PCR: mean = .08, SD = .03; CPS: mean = .10, SD = .03). No other differences approached significance. Consequently, it would seem that Evans et al.'s (1998) results are consistent with the likely probabilistic effects of our pragmatic account of the premise-conclusion ordering manipulation.

Summary

We have argued that the pragmatic effects of ordering manipulations are compatible with Oaksford et al.'s (2000) probabilistic account of conditional inference. In the case of premise and conclusion order effects (Girotto et al., 1997; Evans et al., 1998), the explanation is mediated by the pragmatic effects of these manipulations. This is consistent with Oaksford and Chater's (1995a) arguments about the probabilistic effects of pragmatic phenomena. In explaining the effect of clause order changes (e.g., Evans, 1977; Roberge, 1978; Evans & Beck, 1981), we argued that a decision theoretic perspective may be required to capture the different explanatory and predictive functions of the *if p then q* and *q only if p* rule forms.

CONCLUSIONS

We have argued that a probabilistic approach can resolve many of the problems of logic-based approaches to non-monotonic or defeasible reasoning. These problems are revealed by phenomena such as the failure of strengthening of the antecedent for everyday conditionals. Adopting a probabilistic approach leads naturally to the expectation of suppression effects in conditional inference, which we modelled, using a simple contingency table approach to the meaning of conditional statements. We also showed how the same model accounts for a variety of other suppression and facilitation effects. We also looked at order effects. We argued that these phenomena can be explained in a rational, probabilistic framework as long as close attention is paid to the pragmatic function of these different ordering manipulations and their likely probabilistic effects. In sum, together with Oaksford et al.'s (2000) account of negative conclusion bias, we have shown that a rational probabilistic model may explain many of the major effects in the psychology of conditional inference. This is important because previous commentators in this area have seen these data as providing evidence of systematic bias or of the operation of suboptimal algorithms for conditional reasoning.

REFERENCES

Adams, E. (1966). Probability and the logic of conditionals. In J. Hintikka & P. Suppes (eds), *Aspects of Inductive Logic*. Amsterdam: North-Holland.

Adams, E. (1975). *The Logic of Conditionals: An Application of Probability to Deductive Logic*. Dordrecht: Reidel.

Anderson, A. R. & Belnap, N. D. (1975). *Entailment: The Logic of Relevance and Necessity*, vol. 1. Princeton, NJ: Princeton University Press.

Anderson, J. R. (1995). *Cognitive Psychology and Its Implications*. New York: W. H. Freeman.

Braine, M. D. S. (1978). On the relationship between the natural logic of reasoning and standard logic. *Psychological Review*, *85*, 1–21.

Byrne, R. M. J. (1989). Suppressing valid inferences with conditionals. *Cognition*, *31*, 1–21.

Byrne, R. M. J., Espino, O. & Santamaria, C. (1999). Counterexamples and the suppression of inferences. *Journal of Memory and Language*, *40*, 347–373.

Chan, D. & Chua, F. (1994). Suppression of valid inferences: Syntactic views, mental models, and relative salience. *Cognition*, *53*, 217–238.

Chater, N. & Oaksford, M. (1990). Autonomy, implementation and cognitive architecture: A reply to Fodor and Pylyshyn. *Cognition*, *34*, 93–107.

Chater, N. & Oaksford, M. (1999a). Information gain and decision-theoretic approaches to data selection. *Psychological Review*, *106*, 223–227.

Chater, N. & Oaksford, M. (1999b). The probability heuristics model of syllogistic reasoning. *Cognitive Psychology*, *38*, 191–258.

Chater, N. & Oaksford, M. (2000). The rational analysis of mind and behaviour. *Synthese*, *122*, 93–131.

Chater, N. & Oaksford, M. (2001). Human rationality and the psychology of reasoning: Where do we go from here? *British Journal of Psychology*, *92*, 193–216.

Clark, K. L. (1978). Negation as failure. In *Logic and Databases* (pp. 293–322). New York: Plenum Press.

Comrie, B. (1986). Conditionals: A typology. In E. C. Traugott, A. ter Meulen, J. S. Reilly & C. A. Ferguson (eds), *On Conditionals* (pp. 77–99). Cambridge: Cambridge University Press.

Cook, S. A. (1971). The complexity of theorem proving procedures. In *Proceedings of the Third Annual ACM Symposium on the Theory of Computing* (pp. 151–158). New York: Association for Computing Machinery.

Cummins, D. D. (1995). Naïve theories and causal deduction. *Memory and Cognition*, *23*, 646–658.

Cummins, D. D., Lubart, T., Alksnis, O. & Rist, R. (1991). Conditional reasoning and causation. *Memory and Cognition*, *19*, 274–282.

Evans, J. St. B. T. (1972). Interpretation and "matching bias" in a reasoning task. *Quarterly Journal of Experimental Psychology*, *24*, 193–199.

Evans, J. St. B. T. (1977). Linguistic factors in reasoning. *Quarterly Journal of Experimental Psychology*, *29*, 297–306.

Evans, J. St. B. T. & Beck, M. A. (1981). Directionality and temporal factors in conditional reasoning. *Current Psychological Research*, *1*, 111–120.

Evans, J. St. B. T. & Newstead, S. E. (1977). Language and reasoning: A study of temporal factors. *Cognition*, *8*, 265–283.

Evans, J. St. B. T., Handley, S. & Buck, E. (1998). Order effects in conditional reasoning. *British Journal of Psychology*, *89*, 383–403.

Evans, J. St. B. T., Newstead, S. E. & Byrne, R. M. J. (1993). *Human Reasoning*. Hillsdale, NJ: Erlbaum.

George, C. (1997). Reasoning from uncertain premises. *Thinking and Reasoning, 3*, 161–190.

Ginsberg, M. L. (ed.) (1987). *Readings in Nonmonotonic Reasoning*. Los Altos, CA: Morgan Kaufmann.

Girotto, V., Mazzocco, A. & Tasso, A. (1997). The effect of premise order in conditional reasoning: A test of the mental model theory. *Cognition, 63*, 1–28.

Johnson-Laird, P. N. & Byrne, R. M. J. (1991). *Deduction*. Hillsdale, NJ: Erlbaum.

Kripke, S. (1963). Semantical considerations on modal logic. *Acta Philosophica Fennica, 16*, 83–94.

Levinson, S. (1983). *Pragmatics*. Cambridge: Cambridge University Press.

Lewis, C. I. (1918). *A Survey of Symbolic Logic*. Berkeley, CA: California University Press.

Lewis, D. (1973). *Counterfactuals*. Oxford: Oxford University Press.

Lewis, D. (1976). Probabilities of conditionals and conditional probabilities. *Philosophical Review, 85*, 297–315.

Liu, I., Lo, K. & Wu, J. (1996). A probabilistic interpretation of "If-then". *Quarterly Journal of Experimental Psychology, 49A*, 828–844.

Loehle, C. (2000). Global Optimization 4.0 [computer program]. Naperville, IL: Loehle Enterprises.

Marr, D. (1982). *Vision*. San Francisco, CA: W. H. Freeman.

McCarthy, J. M. (1980). Circumscription: A form of non-monotonic reasoning. *Artificial Intelligence, 13*, 27–39.

McCarthy, J. M. & Hayes, P. (1969). Some philosophical problems from the standpoint of artificial intelligence. In B. Meltzer & D. Michie (eds), *Machine Intelligence* (vol. 4.) New York: Elsevier.

McDermott, D. (1982). Non-monotonic logic II: Non-monotonic modal theories. *Journal of the Association for Computing Machinery, 29*, 33–57.

McDermott, D. (1987). A critique of pure reason. *Computational Intelligence, 3*, 151–160.

McDermott, D. & Doyle, J. (1980). Non-monotonic logic I. *Artificial Intelligence, 13*, 41–72.

Oaksford, M. & Chater, N. (1994). A rational analysis of the selection task as optimal data selection. *Psychological Review, 101*, 608–631.

Oaksford, M. & Chater, N. (1995a). Information gain explains relevance which explains the selection task. *Cognition, 57*, 97–108.

Oaksford, M. & Chater, N. (1995b). Theories of reasoning and the computational explanation of everyday inference. *Thinking and Reasoning, 1*, 121–152.

Oaksford, M. & Chater, N. (1996). Rational explanation of the selection task. *Psychological Review, 103*, 381–391.

Oaksford, M. & Chater, N. (1998a). *Rationality in an Uncertain World: Essays on the Cognitive Science of Human Reasoning*. Hove: Psychology Press.

Oaksford, M. & Chater, N. (1998b). A revised rational analysis of the selection task: Exceptions and sequential sampling (pp. 372–398). In M. Oaksford & N. Chater (eds), *Rational Models of Cognition*. Oxford: Oxford University Press.

Oaksford, M. & Stenning, K. (1992). Reasoning with conditionals containing negated constituents. *Journal of Experimental Psychology: Learning, Memory and Cognition, 18*, 835–854.

Oaksford, M., Chater, N. & Grainger, B. (1999). Probabilistic effects in data selection. *Thinking and Reasoning, 5*, 193–243.

Oaksford, M., Chater, N. & Larkin, J. (2000). Probabilities and polarity biases in conditional inference. *Journal of Experimental Psychology: Learning, Memory and Cognition, 26*, 883–899.

Oaksford, M., Chater, N., Grainger, B. & Larkin, J. (1997). Optimal data selection in the reduced array selection task (RAST). *Journal of Experimental Psychology: Learning, Memory and Cognition, 23*, 441–458.

Pearl, J. (1988). *Probabilistic Reasoning in Intelligent Systems*. San Mateo, CA: Morgan Kaufman.

Pylyshyn, Z. W. (ed.). (1987). *The Robot's Dilemma: The Frame Problem in Artificial Intelligence*. Norwood, NJ: Ablex.

Read, T. R. C. & Cressie, N. A. C. (1988). *Goodness-of-Fit Statistics for Discrete Multivariate Data*. Berlin: Springer-Verlag.

Reiter, R. (1985). On reasoning by default. In R. Brachman & H. Levesque (eds), *Readings in Knowledge Representation* (pp. 401–410). Los Altos, CA: Morgan Kaufmann.

Rips, L. J. (1994). *The Psychology of Proof*. Cambridge, MA: MIT Press.

Roberge, J. J. (1978). Linguistic and psychometric factors in propositional reasoning. *Quarterly Journal of Experimental Psychology, 30*, 705–716.

Schunn, C. D., & Wallach, D. (2001). Evaluating goodness-of-fit in comparison of models to data. Unpublished manuscript. Learning Research and Development Center, University of Pittsburgh, US.

Shoam, Y. (1987). *Reasoning About Change*. Boston, MA: MIT Press.

Shoam, Y. (1988). Efficient reasoning about rich temporal domains. *Journal of Philosophical Logic, 17*, 443–474.

Sperber, D., Cara, F. & Girotto, V. (1995). Relevance explains the selection task. *Cognition, 57*, 31–95.

Stalnaker, R. (1968). A theory of conditionals. In N. Rescher (ed.), *Studies in Logical Theory*. Oxford: Oxford University Press.

Stevenson, R. J. & Over, D. E. (1995). Deduction from uncertain premises. *Quarterly Journal of Experimental Psychology, 48A*, 613–643.

Thompson, V. A. (1994). Interpretational factors in conditional reasoning. *Memory and Cognition, 22*, 742–758.

Thompson, V. A. & Mann, J. M. (1995). Perceived necessity explains the dissociation between logic and meaning: The case of "only if". *Journal of Experimental Psychology: Learning, Memory and Cognition, 21*, 1554–1567.

Veltman, F. (1985). Logics for Conditionals. PhD Thesis, Faculteit der Wiskunde en Natuurwetenschappen, University of Amsterdam.

Wolfram, S. (1999). Mathematica 4.0 [computer program]. Cambridge: Cambridge University Press.

PART II

Judgment

CHAPTER 7

Verbal Expressions of Uncertainty and Probability

Karl Halvor Teigen
University of Oslo, Norway
and
Wibecke Brun
University of Bergen, Norway

Few decision makers are prophets; most of us have to admit that our knowledge is incomplete and our foresight limited. Hence, our claims and predictions have often to be qualified with expressions indicating degrees of confidence or uncertainty. We use qualifiers such as "possibly", "perhaps", "most likely" and "almost certainly" to express how much we believe in a given proposition, and phrases such as "uncertain", "doubtful", "unlikely" and "improbable" to indicate how much we doubt it. From a quantitative, probabilistic perspective, such degrees of belief and doubt can be expressed on a numeric probability scale from 0 to 1; hence, the linguistic phrases have often been called "verbal probabilities".

Numeric probabilities have several advantages over linguistic phrases. One is their preciseness, making predictions and comparisons based on numeric probabilities easy to perform. Even when numerical probabilities are not exact, as with chances "around 50 per cent", or "between .6 and .8", their degrees of inexactitude are relatively clearly defined. They also have straightforward interpretations; for instance, in the frequentistic case, we know that a probability of .7 for T implies that T should occur, on average, in 7 out of 10 cases. Finally, as they are parts of a well-developed system of calculation, there are explicit rules for how they should be combined, and how they can enter normative models of decision.

The main drawback of numeric probabilities seems to be that we often do not know how to get hold of them; and when we get hold of them, we often do not know whether we got them right. On my way through a foreign city, I come to a junction where I start to feel uncertain about directions. I am most inclined to continue straight ahead, but I feel I might be wrong. Perhaps I should turn left, but I am far from sure. These inclinations and uncertainties may easily be put into words; they do not arrive in my head as a set of numbers. I may, however, be asked to "produce" numbers matching my subjective state of uncertainty. Or, alternatively, a listener may try to "translate" my verbal expressions into

Thinking: Psychological Perspectives on Reasoning, Judgment and Decision Making. Edited by David Hardman and Laura Macchi.
© 2003 John Wiley & Sons, Ltd.

corresponding numeric probabilities. For instance, one might conclude that the phrase "I am most inclined" corresponds to a probability around .7, "perhaps" could mean anything from .2 to .8 and "I am far from sure" could refer to all subjective probabilities below .6.

We begin this chapter by briefly reviewing previous attempts to coordinate verbal and numeric probabilities by mapping verbal phrases onto a probability dimension. We then argue that such attempts will remain only partly successful because of inherent differences between words and numbers. Specifically, verbal terms are *directional*: they can be classified as either positive or negative, drawing attention to the occurrence or non-occurrence of a target outcome. In communicating probabilities, choice of verbal terms reflects and determines perspective and may thus guide reasoning and decision making.

CAN VERBAL PROBABILITIES BE TRANSLATED INTO NUMBERS?

The research literature of verbal probabilities is replete with translation attempts, beginning with a study by Lichtenstein and Newman (1967). The "first two decades" of such research was reviewed by Clark (1990). Later translation studies have been performed by Reagan, Mosteller and Youtz (1989), Hamm (1991), Mullet and Rivet (1991), Clarke et al. (1992) and others. Some of these studies have been directed at specific contexts where verbal probabilities are routinely used by experts, as in auditing (Davidson, 1991; Amer, Hackenbrack & Nelson, 1994), in management (Trinkaus, 1989) and in medicine (Bryant & Norman, 1980; Kong et al., 1986; Sutherland et al., 1991). In a typical translation study, participants are presented with a set of verbal expressions, and are asked to state their numeric equivalent on a probability scale from 0 to 1, or from 0 to 100 per cent. Some studies follow a complementary procedure: presenting numeric probabilities and asking the participants to select appropriate verbal terms.

The recurrent findings in these studies are (1) a reasonable degree of between-group consistency, combined with (2) a high degree of within-group variability. In other words, mean estimates of "very probable", "doubtful" and "improbable" are reasonably similar from study to study, supporting the claim that probability words are translatable; but, at the same time, the interindividual variability of estimates is large enough to represent a potential communication problem. If, for instance, the doctor tells the patient that a cure is "possible", she may mean a 5 per cent chance, but it may be interpreted to mean a 70 per cent chance, or vice versa. This variability is typically underestimated by the participants themselves. Brun and Teigen (1988) asked medical doctors to specify a range within which would fall 90 per cent of other doctors' interpretations. This interval included on the average (for 14 verbal phrases) less than 65 per cent of the actual individual estimates. Amer, Hackenbrack and Nelson (1994) found that auditors' 90 per cent ranges included, on average, only 56 per cent of the individual estimates (for 23 phrases). In other words, the problem posed by interindividual variability appears to be aggravated by a low degree of variability awareness.

To improve communication, several attempts have been made to construct standard lists of verbal expressions, where each phrase is coordinated with an appropriate numeric probability (Beyth-Marom, 1982; Hamm, 1991; Tavana, Kennedy & Mohebbi, 1997; Renooij & Witteman, 1999). It is, however, difficult to legislate word usage. One problem is that such standardisations are easiest to accept for words (and in areas) where they are least needed, that is, for phrases that have a fairly standard meaning anyway ("50/50 chance", "certain" or "impossible"), but they are most difficult to accept for words with great interindividual variability (such as "uncertain" and "possible") where they would be most helpful.

CAN VAGUENESS BE QUANTITATIVELY REPRESENTED?

Why are verbal probabilities so difficult to translate into numbers? Most researchers seem to agree that this is because words are vague. Such vagueness is not restricted to probability words. We run into the same problem with other quantifiers. How many is "many" people? How tall is a "tall" man? In a classic paper, Bertrand Russell (1923) claimed that, denotatively, all language is vague. We nowhere find clear and distinct boundaries between cases where a particular word (such as "red") does absolutely not apply, and cases where it applies 100 per cent. However, we could try to be more exact about its vagueness. Indeed, the logician Max Black (1937) suggested the possibility of drawing a "consistency profile" for concepts, in the shape of a curve describing the relation between a measurable variable (such as height) and the application of a predicate (such as "tall"). A vague predicate would be described by a gentle slope. The more precise a predicate, the steeper its consistency profile (for a review of the philosophical debate on the concept of vagueness, see Williamson, 1994).

A similar way of describing vagueness has more recently been applied to verbal probabilities by Budescu and Wallsten and their associates (for an overview, see Budescu & Wallsten, 1995). Budescu and Wallsten assume that individual phrases can be characterised by their membership functions over the probability scale. Membership values range from a minimum value of 0, for probabilities that are absolutely not included in the concept, to a maximum value of 1, for probabilities that are typical or perfect exemplars of the concept. According to this model, vagueness is reflected in the range and spread of the membership function. Membership functions can also be positively or negatively skewed. The meaning of a particular probability expression for a particular individual can, according to this model, best be described by the location, spread and shape of its membership function. Budescu and Wallsten show how membership functions can be derived from experiments with spinners (Wallsten et al., 1986) and lotteries (Budescu & Wallsten, 1990) representing different probabilities, in which participants compare the applicability of different phrases. Wallsten and Budescu draw a distinction between intraindividual vagueness and interindividual variability, claiming that individuals are consistently different from each other in their use of probability terms, so that, ideally, membership functions should be determined for each phrase on an individual level. Individual membership functions have been constructed by asking how well different numbers describe a particular probability word, to be rated on a scale ranging from "not at all" to "absolutely". This method requires each probability phrase to be rated in conjunction with several numeric probabilities, spanning the range from 0 to 1 (Karelitz, Budescu & Wallsten, 2000).

The vagueness of probability terms makes them susceptible to context effects. One explanation of the interindividual variability in numeric translations would be that different respondents have had different contexts in mind. However, providing a context does not take variability away; if anything, respondents appear to disagree more on the interpretation of expressions embedded in a meaningful statement than when the same expressions are presented out of context (Beyth-Marom, 1982; Brun & Teigen, 1988). This could be due to divergent opinions on the issue represented by the statement (its probability as well as its desirability), which, in turn, would colour the way the expression is interpreted. It has been demonstrated that the interpretations of probability terms are influenced by prior probabilities, or base rates (Wallsten, Fillenbaum & Cox, 1986); for instance, a "likely" snowfall in December will be assigned a higher probability than a "likely" snowfall in October. Interpretations are also affected by outcome severity (Weber & Hilton, 1990), and by outcome valence (Cohen & Wallsten, 1992), making a "likely" win more probable than a "likely" loss. Interpretations can even be affected by the introduction of an irrelevant numeric anchor. Subjects who were asked to give numerical interpretations of "slight chance", "chance", "possible" and "likely", in a context of medical diagnoses, produced higher numerical estimates after being exposed to a high, randomly drawn percentage than after a low random percentage (McGlone & Reed, 1998).

DO WORDS REPRESENT THE SAME PROBABILITIES AS NUMBERS?

The translation approach presupposes that verbal probabilities can be meaningfully placed on a numeric probability scale, whereas the membership function approach rests on the assumption that all probability expressions (words as well as numbers) can be mapped onto the same, underlying probability dimension. Both approaches focus on the similarities, or the common ground, between linguistic and numeric expressions, even when allowing for differences in variability, vagueness, and susceptibility to context effects.

However, research in the field of subjective probabilities has revealed that probability is, for most people, a "polysemous" concept allowing for several interpretations (Kahneman & Tversky, 1982; Teigen, 1994; Hertwig & Gigerenzer, 1999). Some of these interpretations may be more easily triggered by numbers, whereas others are more closely linked to particular verbal phrases. For instance, Hacking (1975) claimed that the word "uncertain" typically refers to epistemic, or internal, probability, whereas "probably" typically refers to probabilities of an aleatory, or external, kind. Windschitl (Windschitl & Wells, 1996, 1998; Windschitl, 2000) argues that numeric probabilities tend to encourage analytical and rule-based reasoning, whereas verbal responses allow for more associative and intuitive thinking. Thus, numeric and verbal probabilities may reflect different systems of reasoning (Denes-Raj & Epstein, 1994; Sloman, 1996) and hence be influenced by different aspects of the situation. For instance, the numeric probability of winning a raffle was solely determined by the number of tickets held by the participant, relative to the total number of tickets, in general agreement with objective rules for computing chances. However, when participants rated their winning probabilities on a verbal uncertainty scale, the perceived likelihood was also influenced by the distribution of tickets among the other players. When another player held more tickets than the target player, the latter was considered less likely to win than when no other players held more tickets. This "alternative-outcomes effect" influenced not only verbal probability ratings, but also lottery preferences, indicating that verbal probability ratings may predict actual choice behaviour better than numeric probabilities.

A related, but even stronger demonstration of a dissociation between numeric and verbal probabilities is evidenced by the "equiprobability effect". In a situation with n equiprobable outcomes, the probability of each is $1/n$. This classical principle of probability calculus appears to be easy to understand and obey for numeric probabilities, but not for linguistic expressions. A study of probability expressions (Teigen, 1988a) showed that people tend to prefer high-probability phrases (such as "great chances", "high probability" and "not improbable") to low-probability phrases when asked to characterise the chances of equiprobable outcomes with objective p values from 1/8 to 1/3. With non-equivalent outcomes, the same chances were referred to as "small chances", "low probability" and "improbable".

In a recent study (Teigen, 2000), numeric and verbal phrases were obtained from the same participants, who judged the probability of either equal or unequal outcomes. One scenario described a job applicant, Tom, who was competing with two other, equally qualified candidates. Most participants correctly estimated Tom's numeric probability as 1/3, but accepted high-probability phrases, such as "not improbable" (p = .56),[1] "entirely possible" (p = .71), and "good chance" (p = .71), as appropriate verbal descriptions of his chances, whereas the low-probability phrases "rather improbable" (p = .12), "somewhat doubtful" (p = .25) and "quite uncertain" (p = .32) were considered inappropriate. Participants told that Tom was competing with *five* other candidates adjusted his numeric chances downward towards 1/6, but still considered the high-probability phrases to be appropriate verbal descriptions of the situation. Participants in two other conditions, who were asked to describe Tom's chances in an *unequal* situation (one better applicant, who is said to have a probability of 1/3 or 1/6 to withdraw his application), considered low-probability phrases to be more appropriate than high-probability phrases.

The equiprobability effect may be due to a variant of causal (dispositional) thinking. An applicant who has the necessary qualifications for the position, and with no stronger competitor to prevent him from being selected, is considered to have a good chance, whereas an applicant who has to compete with a stronger candidate is considered to be in an inferior position. In the latter case, success is considered improbable, doubtful, or, at best, uncertain, being dependent upon the competitor's unlikely withdrawal. When, however, numeric probabilities are requested, this type of causal or case-based reasoning is swayed by rule-based, distributional calculations.

TWO KINDS OF VERBAL PROBABILITY EXPRESSIONS

As observed by Moxey and Sanford (1993), linguistic expressions of frequency and quantity are of two kinds, some referring to the target set (called the "refset"), and others to its complement (the "compset"). A teacher may say that "some students" attended the lecture, referring to the students actually present, whereas a colleague may report that "not many students" attended, directing the listener's attention to the complementary set of absent students. Similarly, in the opening sentence of this chapter, the word "few" ("few decision makers are prophets") naturally prepared the reader for a description of the non-prophetic compset ("most of us"). If we had instead written "a few", the effect would have been the opposite. "A few decision makers are prophets" would create expectations about some sensational disclosures of what it takes to be a member of the prophetic minority (the refset), unless the continuation were be preceded by "but", suggesting a narrative turn of the sentence.

---

[1] Probabilities in parentheses are numeric equivalents offered by participants in a control group, who were asked to translate the verbal expressions into numbers.

This focus, or perspective distinction, also applies to verbal probability expressions. Probability is in itself a Janus-faced construct, as all probabilities between 0 and 1 carry two messages in one: they indicate that a particular outcome may happen, but not necessarily so; we are told that something may be the case, but again, maybe not. It is only natural that some words and phrases are particularly appropriate to indicate the positive possibility, whereas others refer to the negative, flip side. Positive and negative are used here not in an evaluative sense (as good or bad), but in the linguistic and logical sense of affirming or negating a target outcome. For instance, "T is possible" clearly refers to the potential occurrence of T, whereas "T is uncertain" refers to its potential non-occurrence. Positive phrases are thus, in a sense, pointing upwards, directing our focus of attention to what might happen, whereas negative phrases are pointing in a downward direction, asking us to consider that it might not happen after all. Choice of phrase determines whether we are talking about the content of the celebrated glass in terms of how full it is or rather in terms of how empty.

Tests for Directionality

The positive or negative direction of probabilistic expressions can be determined in the following ways.

Adding Adverbial Quantifiers

Adverbial quantifiers such as "a little", "somewhat", "rather", "entirely" and "very" serve to weaken or intensify the message of a probability phrase in various degrees. According to Cliff (1959), such adverbs function as "multipliers", moving the meaning of an adjectival or adverbial phrase up or down the dimension in question. Positive phrases will accordingly become more positive by adding a strong quantifier (such as "very" or "extremely"), whereas negative phrases will become more negative. So if the probability equivalent of "extremely doubtful" is perceived to be lower than the probability of "somewhat doubtful", *doubtful* must be a negative term. Similarly, if "very uncertain" indicates a lower probability than "a little uncertain", *uncertain* has also a negative directionality. In contrast, *likely* has a positive direction, as "highly likely" corresponds to a higher value on the probability scale than "somewhat likely" or just "likely".

Introducing Linguistic Negations

Once we know the directionality of a phrase, a phrase with opposite directionality can be created by linguistic negations; either by lexical negation (adding "not"), or by affixal negation (for instance, by adding the prefix "un-" or "in-"). Thus, if "completely certain" is a positive phrase, "not completely certain" must be negative. If "probable" and "possible" are positive, "improbable" and "impossible" will be negative, and "not improbable" and "not impossible" will be positive again, being negations of negated positives.

The two main forms of linguistic negations are not equivalent. Whereas a phrase P and its complement not-P are logical contradictions, in the sense that both cannot be false (law of the excluded middle), P and un-P are contraries, or opposites, which cannot both be simulta-neously true; but both may be false, if we allow for something in between (Horn, 1989). For instance, there is a middle ground between being "efficient" and being "inefficient": I can admit I am not efficient without labelling myself an inefficient person. From this, one would expect affixal negations to have a stronger impact than lexical negations on the meaning of probability words. In a translation study by Reyna (1981), this was actually found to be the case. For instance, "improbable" was associated with a lower probability value than "not probable". A limitation of this study was that all un-negated phrases were at the same time directionally positive, high-probability expressions. Thus, less is known about negations that change negative phrases into positive (as, for instance, when "doubtful" is changed to "doubtless" or "not doubtful").

Combined Phrases

Positive verbal phrases can easily be combined with other, stronger positive expressions; for instance, we may say, "it is *possible*, even *probable*", or "it is *probable*, yes, indeed, *almost certain*". Similarly, negative phrases go together with other negatives, as "it is *improbable*, in fact, *almost impossible*". Positive and negative phrases cannot be joined unless their contrast is explicitly acknowledged, for instance, by "but": "it is *possible*, but *rather uncertain*", or "it is *unlikely*, but *not impossible*". Thus, the way phrases are combined can tell us whether they belong to the same or to different categories; it can also give information about the relative strength of the phrases.

Continuation Tasks

Moxey and Sanford (1987) suggested that the attentional focus of quantifiers can be em-pirically determined by asking subjects to continue incomplete sentences; for instance, "not many MPs attended the meeting, because they ...". This sentence was typically com-pleted with reasons for the absence rather than for the presence of MPs at the meeting, showing that "not many" directs the reader's attention to the non-present set of MPs (the compset). The continuation task was adapted for verbal probabilities by Teigen and Brun (1995). Participants in one experiment were given 26 incomplete statements containing different verbal probability expressions; for instance, "It is very improbable that we left the keys in the car, because ...", or "It is almost certain that Clinton will become a good president, because ...". The sentence completions were then categorised as pro-reasons (if they contained reasons for the occurrence of the target issue—for example, reasons for the keys being left in the car), con-reasons (reasons against the target issue—why the keys would *not* be in the car) or mixed reasons (reasons both for and against the target).

The results showed that nearly all phrases could be unambiguously classified as either positive or negative. Only the phrases "a small probability" and "a small chance" were am-biguous, as some participants completed them with pro-reasons (probabilities and chances being positive words), whereas others gave reasons against (presumably because of their smallness). Phrases involving the term "uncertain" were also distinct by being evaluated either as purely negative or mixed.

Moxey and Sanford (2000) also suggest other continuation tests. For instance, a negatively valenced target event must be combined with a negative probability expression if the proposition is to be evaluated as "good", but combined with a positive probability expression if it has to be evaluated as "bad", as in the following examples:

"It is possible that someone will die, which is a bad/good* thing"
"It is improbable that anyone will die, which is a bad*/good thing"
(asterisks indicate unacceptable propositions)

The point here is that the relative pronoun "which" has an opposite reference in these two cases, depending upon the attentional focus created by the probability term.

Answering Words

In a communicative context, answers containing positive words will naturally be preceded by "yes", whereas negative words go naturally together with "no". For instance, if someone says, "I think we left the keys in the car", and receives the answer "——, it is possible", we would expect the answer to contain "yes" rather than "no". If the answer is "——, it is improbable", the first (missing) word would be "no". This was confirmed in a second experiment, reported by Teigen and Brun (1995). This experiment also showed that the combination "no, but" was mostly acceptable in conjunction with positive phrases, such as "no, but there is a chance", whereas "yes, but" preceded (mildly) negative phrases ("yes, but it is somewhat uncertain").

The general picture emerging from this research is that verbal probability phrases are not at all vague as far as their directionality is concerned. Their location on the probability scale may be debatable, but their categorisation as either positive or negative expressions leaves, with few exceptions, little room for doubt.

From the overview of representative positive and negative expressions, portrayed in Table 7.1, it is evident that most, but not all, directionally negative phrases also contain linguistic negations (lexical or affixal). Furthermore, most of them, but not all, describe low probabilities. Positive phrases seem generally to be more numerous, more common and more applicable to the full range of probabilities; in typical lists of verbal phrases designed to cover the full probability scale, positive phrases outnumber the negatives in a ratio of 2:1 (Beyth-Marom, 1982; Kong et al., 1986; Reagan et al., 1989; González-Vallejo & Wallsten, 1992).

WHEN ARE POSITIVE AND NEGATIVE PHRASES CHOSEN?

What determines the choice of verbal phrase? According to the traditional approach, speakers choose expressions matching the probabilities they bear in mind. With a probability approaching certainty, we say it is "highly probable" or "almost certain". Probabilities around 50 per cent will be characterised as "50/50" or "uncertain". Generally, one might think that positive phrases will be used to characterise probabilities above 5, whereas negative phrases will be used to characterise probabilities below .5.

From a linguistic point of view, this model appears to be overly simplistic. Affirmations and negations are not simply mirror images of each other, dividing the world between them like the two halves of an apple. Linguistically and logically, as well as psychologically, the

Table 7.1 Examples of directionally positive and negative probabilistic expressions

Positive expressions (pointing to occurrences)	Negative expressions (pointing to non-occurrences)
Probable	Improbable
Very probable	Highly improbable
Somewhat probable	Rather improbable
Quite probable	Quite improbable
Not improbable	
Likely	Unlikely
Highly likely	Somewhat unlikely
Not unlikely	
Possible	Impossible
Entirely possible	Almost impossible
A slight possibility	
Not impossible	Not sure
A chance	No chance
Good chance	
	Not quite certain
Certain	Uncertain
Almost certain	Somewhat uncertain
Not uncertain	Very uncertain
Not doubtful	Doubtful
Doubtless	Very doubtful
A risk	Not very risky
Some risk	
Perhaps	Perhaps not
A small hope	Almost no hope
Increasing hope	

positive member of a positive/negative pair of adverbs or adjectives has priority over the negative; it is mentioned first (we say "positive or negative", not "negative or positive"; "yes and no", not "no and yes"), it is usually unmarked (probable vs. *im*probable, certain vs. *un*certain) and it requires shorter processing time (Clark & Clark, 1977). Negations seem to presuppose an implicit affirmation, which is then denied. In line with this, Wason (1965) asserted that the function of negative statements is "generally to emphasize that a fact is contrary to expectation" (p. 7). President Nixon's famous saying, "I am not a crook", exemplifies the duplicity of negations: by denying something, they imply and induce the opposite expectation.

It follows that the chances for aversive events (negatively valenced outcomes) are not typically described by directionally negative probability phrases. We speak of the probability, possibility or risk of a loss rather than saying that the loss is doubtful or uncertain. The reason appears to be that directionally negative phrases, by denying the target outcome (here: the failure or loss), tacitly assume this as the expected, default outcome. To announce that a failure is "doubtful" implies that someone has maliciously prepared for (or even planned) a failure that somehow may not be attained. Thus, Teigen and Brun (1995) found that directionally positive expressions apply equally well to positive and negative outcomes, whereas directionally negative expressions are more appropriate for describing successes than failure. We can speak of a "highly uncertain success", but rarely about "a highly uncertain failure".

If focus of attention, or perspective, is a decisive characteristic of the two classes of probability phrases, then positive phrases should be chosen whenever we want to stress the potential attainment of the target outcome (regardless of its probability), and negative phrases should be chosen when we, for some reason or another, feel it is important to draw attention to its potential non-attainment. Imagine a medical situation in which the patient displays three out of six diagnostic signs of a serious disease. How should we describe the patient's likelihood of disease? Regardless of the actual (numeric) probability, a doctor who wants to alert the patient, and perhaps request that further tests be administered, would choose a positive phrase, saying, for instance, that there is "a possibility of disease", or "a non-negligible probability" or "a significant risk". If, however, the doctor has the impression that the patient has lost all hope, or that his colleague is about to draw a too hasty conclusion, he might say that the diagnosis is "not yet certain", or that there is still "some doubt". In the same vein, the three diagnostic signs may be characterised as "some" or "several" in the positive case, and as "not many" or "not all" in the negative case.

This prediction was tested by presenting three groups of introductory psychology students at the universities of Oslo and Bergen with the following scenario (Teigen & Brun, 2003).

> Polycystic syndrome (PS)[2] is a quite serious disease that can be difficult to detect at an early stage. Diagnostic examination includes six tests, all of which must give positive reactions before PS can be confirmed. (Note: Positive reactions here mean indication of disease; negative reactions indicate absence of disease.)
>
> Here follow the statements from six different doctors that have each examined one patient suspected of having PS.
>
> *Group A:* Your task is to estimate the number of positive tests you think each of these doctors has in mind.
>
> *Group B:* Your task is to estimate the probability of PS you think each of these doctors has in mind.
>
> *Group C:* Your task is to complete the statements to make them as meaningful as possible, choosing the most appropriate expression from the list below each statement. You may, if you choose, use the same expression in several statements.

All groups were then given the following six statements:

1. The examination showed positive reactions to some of the tests.
2. The examination showed negative reactions to some of the tests.
3. The examination did not show positive reactions to all the tests.
4. The examination did not show negative reactions to all the tests.
5. The examination showed positive reactions to several of the tests.
6. The examination showed negative reactions to several of the tests.[3]

---

[2] This is a fictitious disease. We owe the name to Julie Hatfield, who, in a talk given at the XXVII International Congress of Psychology (Stockholm, July 2000), reported that most people think they are less at risk than most other people of developing this syndrome, thus extending the concept of unrealistic optimism to a nonexistent diagnostic entity.

[3] The Norwegian terms employed were *Noen av testene* ["some of the tests"], *alle testene* ["all the tests"] and *flere av testene* ["several of the tests"].

Table 7.2 Numeric and verbal probabilities of polycystic syndrome (PS) based on verbal descriptions of the outcome of six medical tests

Results of medical examination	Group A (n = 46) Mean estimated number of positive tests	Group B (n = 35) Mean estimated probability of disease	Group C (n = 34) Choices of verbal probabilistic phrases[a]	
			Positive	Negative
Positive reactions				
On *some* of the tests	2.48	46.4%	25	9
Not on *all* the tests	3.98	53.7%	3	31
On *several* tests	3.67	61.3%	32	2
Negative reactions				
On *some* of the tests	3.09	44.0%	4	30
Not on *all* the tests	2.59	39.2%	16	18
On *several* tests	2.56	27.1%	0	34

[a]Positive phrases: certain, probable, possible, no doubt; Negative phrases: uncertain, improbable, impossible, doubtful. Adapted from Teigen & Brun, 2003.

For group C, each statement was followed by a second, incomplete sentence, "It is thus ———— that the patient has PS", to be completed with one of the following expressions: certain / uncertain / probable / improbable / possible / impossible / doubtful / no doubt.

Positive reactions to "some" or to "several" tests direct the reader's attention to tests that indicate PS. How many are they? According to the answers from group A, "some of the tests" typically refer to two or three of the six tests, whereas "several tests" typically mean three or four tests (mean estimates are presented in Table 7.2, first column). Both these estimates are lower than "not . . . all the tests", which was usually taken to mean four out of six tests. But the latter expression is directionally negative, pointing to the existence of tests that did *not* indicate disease. The question now is whether this change of attention would have any impact on (1) the numeric probability estimates produced by group B and, more importantly, on (2) the choices of verbal phrases designed to complete the phrases by group C.

Table 7.2, second column, shows the mean probability estimates for PS given by group B. Participants in this group thought that a doctor who refers to positive reactions on "some of the tests" has a mean disease probability of 46.4 per cent in mind, whereas a doctor who refers to "several tests" has a significantly higher probability of 61.3 per cent in mind. These results are clearly in line with the number of tests corresponding to "some" and "several", as estimated by group A. However, the probability estimate for "not all of the tests" was lower than for "several", despite the higher number of tests it implies.

The three statements about negative test reactions formed a mirror picture. "Some" tests with negative reactions imply positive reactions on three or four tests, whereas "several" and "not all" tests showing negative reactions imply two or three positive tests. Translated into probabilities, "not all" lies again between the other two, with significantly higher probability for disease than in the case of "several" negative tests. Thus, even if probability estimates are in general correspondence with the estimated number of positive or negative tests, there is an indication that the numeric probabilities are influenced by the (positive or negative) way the test results are presented.

When we turn to group C, who were asked to choose appropriate verbal expressions, the way the test results were described turns out to be of central importance (Table 7.2, last two columns). When "some" test results are positive, most participants thought it most appropriate to conclude, "It is thus *possible* that the patient has PS." Some participants said it is *probable*, whereas only 26 per cent preferred one of the negative phrases (*uncertain, improbable*, or *doubtful*). With "several" positive test results, PS was considered *probable* by a majority of the participants, and only 6 per cent chose any of the negative phrases. However, when "not all" test results are positive, more than 90 per cent of the participants switched to a negative phrase, claiming that it is *uncertain* (14), *doubtful* (12), *impossible* (3) or *improbable* (2) that the patient has PS.

With "some" or "several" *negative* test results, a complementary pattern emerges, as nearly all respondents concluded that PS is, in these cases, *improbable, doubtful* or *uncertain*. But again, if "not all" tests are negative, the picture changes. In this case, about half of the respondents preferred a positive characteristic (it is *possible*).

These results demonstrate that choices of phrase are strongly determined by how the situation is framed. The way the evidence is described appears to be more important than the strength of the evidence. Thus, the half-full/half-empty glass metaphor strikes again. If the glass is half-full, the outcome is possible. If it is half-empty, the outcome is uncertain. Perhaps we could go one step further and claim that any degree of fullness, or just the fact that the glass is *not* (yet) *completely empty*, prepares us for possibilities rather than uncertainties; whereas all degrees of emptiness, including the claim that the glass is just *not full*, suggest uncertainties and doubts.

CONSEQUENCES OF CHOICE OF TERMS

The above study demonstrates how similar situations can be framed in positive as well as in negative verbal probability terms. This will draw attention either to the occurrence or the non-occurrence of a target outcome, or, in Moxey and Sanford's (2000) terminology, determine the reader's perspective. But does it matter? If I know that "possible" and "uncertain" can both describe a 50/50 probability, I could mentally switch from one expression to the other, and more generally translate any positive phrase into a corresponding negative one, or vice versa. However, the extensive research literature on framing (Tversky & Kahneman, 1981; Levin, Schneider & Gaeth, 1998) suggests that the original formulation of a judgment or decision task can strongly influence subsequent inferences and choices. Thus, we may legitimately expect perspective effects (or framing effects) also in the case of positive versus negative verbal probability expressions. Three variants of such effects are described below (based on Teigen & Brun, 1999).

Effects on Probabilistic Reasoning

The rules of probability calculus dictate that a conjunction of two events must be less prob-able than each of the individual events. Thus, the chances that the Eagles will win both their last two games of the season are lower than the Eagles' chances of winning each separate game. People seem sometimes to be intuitively aware of this rule, as for instance, when discussing the improbability of coincidences, but in other cases they incorrectly assume that the combination of a high-probability event (for example, that Björn Borg will win a decisive game) and a low-probability event (that he will lose the first set in the game) should be assigned an intermediate rather than a still lower probability (Tversky & Kahneman, 1983). Tversky and Kahneman originally attributed this "conjunction fallacy" to an inappropriate use of the "representativeness heuristic". According to this interpretation, the conjunction "Björn Borg will lose the first set and win the game" appears in some ways representative (he usually wins), and in some ways not so representative (he rarely loses the first set); this mix of representative and unrepresentative elements will combine into an impression of medium representativeness, and hence give rise to a medium-probability judgment. This and similar interpretations of the conjunction effect imply that people evaluate the *match* between the described event and their picture of reality, rather than the mismatch. After all, we evaluate the representativeness of the target event, not its non-representativeness. Sanbonmatsu, Posavac and Stasney (1997) have suggested that probabilities generally tend to be overestimated, due to selective hypothesis testing. The outcomes or events to be evaluated serve as temporary hypotheses, to be confirmed or disconfirmed by the available evidence. From the research on hypothesis testing, we know that people often bias their search towards confirming evidence. Such a bias inevitably leads to inflated probability estimates.

If *probability* judgments selectively favour a search for supportive, confirmatory evidence, what are we to expect from *uncertainty* judgments? More generally, will a perspective change from positive to negative verbal terms have an effect on the tendency to overestimate probabilities? In one experiment (Teigen & Brun, 1999, Experiment 4), participants were asked to evaluate the chances of two conjunctive events (the Eagles' chances of winning their two next games, the chances that both the Czech Republic and Slovakia would apply for EU membership, the chances that two friends would be able to move together to the same city, and the chances that the Liberal Party would gain two seats in parliament). These chances were described either on positive verbal scales, in terms of probabilities or possibilities, or on negative verbal scales, in terms of uncertainties or doubts. For instance, a referendum outcome favouring EU membership could be described as "somewhat uncertain" in the Czech Republic and "quite uncertain" in Slovakia. Participants were then asked to rate the uncertainty of the combined event on a scale from "very uncertain" to "not uncertain" (with "quite uncertain", "somewhat uncertain" and "a little uncertain" as intermediate values).

The results showed a strong perspective effect. On the positive verbal probability and possibility scales, a substantial number of participants committed conjunction errors (about 50 per cent with a mild criterion, increasing to 80 per cent with a strict criterion for a correct conjunctive response). On the negative uncertainty and doubtfulness scale, the number of conjunction errors was at least 20 per cent lower on both criteria. In other words, two intermediate uncertainties are readily seen to yield a "very uncertain" conjunction, and the combination of "a little doubtful" and "somewhat doubtful" event is typically considered to be "quite doubtful", that is, less probable, compared to the individual events.

Negative phrases thus appear to counteract the conjunction fallacy. But this does not make people better probabilistic thinkers in all respects. The experiment included also a disjunction task, which asked participants to estimate the Eagles' chances of winning at least one of their two last games, or the chances that at least one of the above mentioned countries would say yes to the EU. Correct disjunctive responses require the probabilities to be higher, or at least as high as the probability of the individual events. Such answers appeared to be facilitated by positive verbal probabilities, but hindered by negative verbal phrases.

Effects on Predictions

Windschitl and Wells (1996) have argued that verbal probabilities sometimes better reflect people's actual behaviour than their numeric probability estimates do. If so, we should pay more attention to people's words than to their numbers. Moreover, since they appear to have a choice between two types of words, we should perhaps be especially sensitive to how they frame their message.

Imagine asking two students at a driving school about their chances of passing the driving test without additional training. One says, "It is a possibility." The other says, "It is somewhat uncertain." What are their subjective probabilities of success? And will they actually take the test?

Teigen and Brun (1999, Experiment 2) asked one group to answer the first of these questions (along with several other, similar questions), whereas another group received the second type of questions. The positive phrases in this study were translated into probabilities between 44 per cent and 69 per cent, whereas the negative phrases were estimated to lie between 36 per cent and 68 per cent. In the above example, "a possibility" received a mean estimate of 57.5 per cent whereas "somewhat uncertain" received a mean estimate of 52 per cent. These differences in probability estimates were, however, minor compared to the differences in predictions. More than 90 per cent of participants predicted that the first student would take the test, whereas less than 30 per cent believed that the "uncertain" student would do the same. Similar results were found for a scenario in which employees gave verbal statements about their intentions to apply for promotion. Positively formulated intentions ("a chance", "possible", or "not improbable") led to 90 per cent predictions that they would apply, whereas negatively formulated intentions ("not certain", "a little uncertain", or "somewhat doubtful") led to less than 25 per cent apply predictions.

In a second study (Teigen & Brun, 1999, Experiment 2a), the same participants gave numeric probability estimates as well as predictions, based either on the driving school scenario or the application scenario. This made it possible to compare predictions based on positive phrases with predictions based on negative phrases, with matching numeric probabilities. The results clearly showed that the same numeric probabilities are associated with positive predictions in the first case, and negative predictions in the second. For instance, positive phrases believed to reflect a probability of 40 per cent were believed to predict positive decisions (taking the test or applying for promotion) in a majority of the cases, whereas negative phrases corresponding to a probability of 40 per cent were believed to predict negative decisions (put off test and fail to apply).

Effects on Decisions

Despite the vagueness and interindividual variability of words, decisions based on verbally communicated probabilities are not necessarily inferior to decisions based on numeric statements (Budescu & Wallsten, 1990; Erev & Cohen, 1990). They are, however, more related to differences in outcome values than differences in probabilities, whereas numeric statements appear to emphasise more strongly the probability magnitudes (Gonzáles-Vallejo & Wallsten, 1992; Gonzáles-Vallejo, Erev & Wallsten, 1994). Decision efficiency appears to be improved when probability mode (verbal versus numerical) matches the source of the uncertainty (Olson & Budescu, 1997). With precise, external probabilities (gambles based on spinners), numbers were preferred to words; with vague, internal probabilities (general knowledge items), words were preferable.

These studies have, however, contrasted numerical with verbal probabilities as a group, and have not looked into the effect of using positive as opposed to negative verbal phrases. Our contention is that choice of term could also influence decisions.

Suppose that you have, against all odds, become the victim of the fictitious, but malignant PS, and are now looking for a cure. You are informed that only two treatment options exist, neither of them fully satisfactory. According to experts in the field, treatment A has "some possibility" of being effective, whereas the effectiveness of treatment B is "quite uncertain". Which treatment would you choose? If you (like us) opt for treatment A, what is the reason for your choice? Does "some possibility" suggest a higher probability of cure than does "quite uncertain", or is it rather that the positive perspective implied by the first formulation encourages action and acceptance, whereas the second, negative phrase more strongly indicates objections and hesitation?

To answer these questions, we presented the following scenario to five groups of Norwegian students (for details, see Teigen & Brun, 1999, Experiment 1).

> Marianne has periodically been suffering from migraine headaches, and is now considering a new method of treatment based on acupuncture. The treatment is rather costly and long-lasting. Marianne asks whether you think she should give it a try. Fortunately, you happen to know a couple of physicians with good knowledge of migraine treatment, whom you can ask for advice.
>
> They discuss your question and conclude that it is *quite uncertain* (group 1)/there is *some possibility* (group 2)/the probability is about *30–35 per cent* (group 3) that the treatment will be helpful in her case.
>
> On this background, would you advise Marianne to try the new method of treatment?

Two control groups were given the same scenario, but asked instead to translate the probability implied by *quite uncertain* (group 4) and *some possibility* (group 5) into numeric probabilities on a 0–100 per cent scale. They were also asked to indicate the highest and lowest probability equivalents that they would expect if they had asked a panel of 10 people to translate these verbal phrases into numbers.

The control group translations showed that "quite uncertain" and "some possibility" correspond to very similar probabilities (mean estimates 31.3 per cent and 31.7 per cent, respectively), with nearly identical ranges. Yet, 90.6 per cent of the respondents in the verbal positive condition recommended treatment, against only 32.6 per cent of the respondents in the verbal negative condition, who were told that the cure was "quite uncertain". The numerical condition ("30–35 per cent probability") led to 58.1 per cent positive recommendations, significantly above the negative verbal condition, but significantly below the positive verbal condition. These results demonstrate that the perspective induced by a positive or negative verbal phrase appears to have an effect on decisions, over and beyond the numeric probabilities these phrases imply.

NUMERIC PROBABILITIES REVISITED

The perspective analysis outlined in this chapter (as well as in Moxey and Sanford's work) indicates that verbal probability phrases should be placed in two complementary categories rather than along one single dimension. We now ask whether this insight can be used to improve our understanding of numeric probabilities as well.

Numeric probabilities are usually expressed as numbers between 0 and 1, or between 0 and 100 per cent on a probability scale. This scale is also, in a sense, directional, insofar as "probability" can be classified as a directionally positive term. In this respect, the probability scale is similar to other magnitude scales, such as scales of length, height, or age, which are usually named after the positive end of the scale. We ask how tall or old a person is rather than how small or young (Clark & Clark, 1977). This may, in turn, affect the way we talk and think of magnitudes. For instance, we may get a different answer from an author asked to justify the length of his chapter from what he or she would say when asked to justify its shortness. Which answer would we get if we, instead, asked the numerical question: How come your chapter is 20 pages? In this case, the author would probably need some additional linguistic hints: do you mean why it is *as many as* 20 pages, or why it is *only* 20 pages?

Inspired by the results of the sentence-completion task with verbal probability phrases, we performed a parallel study in which participants were asked to give reasons for statements containing numeric probabilities (Teigen & Brun, 2000). For instance, "it is a 70 per cent probability that people who wants to quit smoking, really succeed, because————", or "there is a 25 per cent probability of complications following appendix operations, because————". The sentences were chosen to describe both desirable outcomes, as in the first example, and undesirable outcomes, as in the second example. Furthermore, half of them described relatively high probabilities (70–75 per cent), whereas the other half described low probabilities (25–30 per cent). Finally, some outcomes had a high prior probability, estimated by a control group to be, on average, around 70–75 per cent (for example, the probability of SAS flights being on schedule, or the probability of HIV-infected persons developing AIDS), whereas others had a low prior probability, as in the smoking cessation and appendix complication examples. This implied that the numeric probabilities in some statements matched the participants' prior expectations, whereas in other cases they were either higher or lower. We also included statements containing lexical negations ("It is a 70 per cent probability that people who wants to quit smoking do *not* succeed, because————").

The reasons produced by the participants were coded as either positive (reasons in favour of the target outcome) or negative (reasons against the target outcome), as in the verbal probability study. In the appendix operation example, a pro-reason (why there are as many as 25 per cent complications) would be "because the operation is a difficult one", whereas a con-reason (why only 25 per cent complications) would be "because the surgeons are well trained for the job".

From the pattern of results, the following trends emerged:

1. *Directional ambiguity.* Sentences containing numeric probabilities are directionally ambiguous, giving rise to both pro- and con- reasons. It will be recalled that, in contrast, verbal phrases were found to be completely unambiguous, being completed by either positive or negative reasons, but not by both.

2. *Positive dominance.* There is an overall tendency to give more positive than negative reasons. About three-fourths of all reasons given were coded as explanations for why the target outcome would occur. Thus, even a 30 per cent probability often functions as a directionally positive expression. The positivity of numbers (unlike the positivity

of words) appears, however, to be moderated by several additional factors, as indicated below.

3. *Probability magnitude*. High probabilities (sentences containing probability values of 70–75 per cent) usually, but not exclusively, gave rise to positive explanations (in 83 per cent of the cases), whereas sentences containing low probabilities (25–30 per cent) were completed with fewer (68 per cent) negative reasons.

4. *Prior expectations*. Unexpected outcomes (target outcomes with low prior probabilities) were more often explained in positive terms (why this outcome might happen), whereas expected outcomes were more often given negative explanations (why it might not happen after all, or why it did not happen more often).

5. *Desirability*. Undesirable outcomes were more often explained with positive (pro) reasons than were desirable outcomes.

6. *Syntactic structure*. Negated outcomes (why some people are *not* successful, or why some operations do *not* have complications) were more often explained by supporting reasons than were than non-negated outcomes.

The last three points are in good agreement with previous research on causal thinking, which has concluded that people primarily search for explanations of unexpected and undesired events (Bohner et al., 1988). Point 6 confirms the linguistic intuition that negations tacitly imply (positive) expectations, which are then denied (Horn, 1989).

These results allow us to conclude that numeric probabilities, despite their precision, are directionally ambiguous. Being "probabilities" (rather than, for instance, "improbabilities" or "uncertainties"), they tend to bias the listener towards a positive perspective, but the strength of this bias is dependent not only upon the probability magnitude, but also upon contextual factors such as valence and prior expectations.

CONCLUSION

People use a rich vocabulary to characterise uncertain events. When these "verbal probabilities" are placed onto a probability dimension, they appear vague, and can be given widely different interpretations. There is, however, some method in this vagueness. Verbal and numeric estimates will sometimes differ because they do not always reflect the same probability concept. Numbers can be a result of analytic thinking and rule-based calculations, whereas verbal phrases appear to reflect more intuitive, non-distributional (perhaps causal) thinking. Verbal phrases are, furthermore, parts of ordinary language, and thus sensitive to conversational implicatures. So I may say that a particular outcome is somewhat uncertain, not because I think it has a low probability of occurring, but because I want to modify some actual, imagined or implied belief in its occurrence. Such modifications can go in two directions, either upwards or downwards on the probability scale. Verbal probability expressions can accordingly be categorised as having a positive or a negative directionality. They determine whether attention should be directed to the attainment or the non-attainment of the target outcome, and, in doing so, they have the ability to influence people's judgments and decisions in an unambiguous way. Words may be denotatively vague, but they are argumentatively precise. If you tell me that success is "possible", I know I am being encouraged, even if I do not know whether you have a probability of 30 per cent or of 70 per cent in mind. If you say it is "not certain", I know I am advised to be careful and to think twice. But if you tell me there is a 45 per cent probability I will not know what to think. The information is precise, but its pragmatic meaning is undecided. Do you mean uncertainty (I have *only* a 45 per cent chance) or possibility (at least I have a 45 per cent chance)? Likelihood or doubt? Or both?

Decision makers may not be prophets, but those who use verbal probabilities are voices in the wilderness warning against dangers and encouraging some actions above others. They are also able to claim, in hindsight, that they were right, and they may be blamed for being wrong. A forecaster saying that "T is not completely certain" will be praised for his foresight if T fails to appear, even if he had a substantial probability in mind (Teigen, 1988b; Teigen & Brun, 2003). Luckily, he framed it in a negative way. The numeric probability forecaster may, in comparison, be praised for his apparent expertise, but what exactly is it that he is trying to tell us?

The conclusion often drawn from the early research on verbal phrases was that words, because of their inherent variability and vagueness, are poor substitutes for numbers (e.g., Nakao & Axelrod, 1983). The research reviewed in the present chapter supports the complementary, and, in our opinion, equally valid conclusion that numbers do not exhaust the meaning of probability words. They may, however, be matched in the sense that some words describe some numbers better than others, and vice versa. The approach advocated by Budescu and Wallsten (1995) extends the idea of matching to the location, spread and shape of a word's membership function over the entire probability dimension. These authors have recently demonstrated that phrases with different directionality will have different and distinguishable membership functions, so that their directionality can be reliably predicted by the peak and the skewness of these functions (Budescu, Karelitz & Wallsten, 2000). This approach is, however, not designed to explain when and why a particular phrase is appropriate, for instance, why positive phrases are occasionally used to describe low probabilities, or when high probabilities will be described by a negative phrase. Verbal expressions of uncertainty and probability appear to perform both denotative and argumentative functions, reflecting speakers' beliefs as well as their communicative intentions. While this chapter has emphasised words' directionality, as well as their probability equivalents, future research may uncover other important dimensions; for instance, by distinguishing possibilities from probabilities, or uncertainties from doubts.

REFERENCES

Amer, T., Hackenbrack, K. & Nelson, M. (1994). Between-auditor differences in the interpretation of probability phrases. *Auditing: A Journal of Practice and Theory, 13*, 126–136.

Beyth-Marom, R. (1982). How probable is probable? A numerical translation of verbal probability expressions. *Journal of Forecasting, 1*, 257–269.

Black, M. (1937). Vagueness: An exercise in logical analysis. *Philosophy of Science, 4*, 427–455. Reprinted in M. Black (1949), *Language and Philosophy*. Ithaca, NY: Cornell University Press.

Bohner, G., Bless, H., Schwartz, N. & Strack, F. (1988). What triggers causal attributions? The impact of valence and subjective probability. *European Journal of Social Psychology, 18*, 335–345.

Brun, W. & Teigen, K. H. (1988). Verbal probabilities: Ambiguous, context-dependent, or both? *Organizational Behavior and Human Decision Processes, 41*, 390–404.

Bryant, G. D. & Norman, G. R. (1980). Expressions of probability: Words and numbers. *New England Journal of Medicine, 302*, 411.

Budescu, D. V. & Wallsten, T. S. (1985). Consistency in interpretation of probabilistic phrases. *Organizational Behavior and Human Decision Processes, 36*, 391–405.

Budescu, D. V. & Wallsten, T. S. (1990). Dyadic decisions with verbal and numerical probabilities. *Organizational Behavior and Human Decision Processes*, *46*, 240–263.

Budescu, D. V. & Wallsten, T. S. (1995). Processing linguistic probabilities: General principles and empirical evidence. *The Psychology of Learning and Motivation*, *32*, 275–318.

Budescu, D. V., Karelitz, T. & Wallsten, T. S. (2000). Predicting the directionality of probability words from their membership functions. Paper presented at the Psychonomic Society, 41st Annual Meeting, New Orleans.

Clark, D. A. (1990). Verbal uncertainty expressions: A review of two decades of research. *Current Psychology: Research and Reviews*, *9*, 203–235.

Clark, H. H. & Clark, E. V. (1977). *The Psychology of Language: An Introduction to Psycholinguistics*. New York: Harcourt, Brace.

Clarke, V. A., Ruffin, C. L., Hill, D. J. & Beamen, A. L. (1992). Ratings of orally presented verbal expressions of probability by a heterogeneous sample. *Journal of Applied Social Psychology*, *22*, 638–656.

Cliff, N. (1959). Adverbs as multipliers. *Psychological Review*, *66*, 27–44.

Cohen, B. L. & Wallsten, T. S. (1992). The effect of constant outcome value on judgments and decision making given linguistic probabilities. *Journal of Behavioral Decision Making*, *5*, 53–72.

Davidson, R. A. (1991). Practical difficulties encountered in selecting uncertainty words: The example of accounting standards. *Applied Psychology: An International Review*, *40*, 353–363.

Denes-Raj, V. & Epstein, S. (1994). Conflict between intuitive and rational processing: When people behave against their better judgment. *Journal of Personality and Social Psychology*, *66*, 819–829.

Erev, I. & Cohen, B. L. (1990). Verbal versus numerical probabilities: Efficiency, biases, and the preference paradox. *Organizational Behavior and Human Decision Processes*, *45*, 1–18.

Fillenbaum, S., Wallsten, T. S., Cohen, B. L. & Cox, J. A. (1991). Some effects of vocabulary and communication task on the understanding and use of vague probability expressions. *American Journal of Psychology*, *104*, 35–60.

González-Vallejo, C. C. & Wallsten, T. S. (1992). Effects of probability mode on preference reversal. *Journal of Experimental Psychology: Learning, Memory and Cognition*, *18*, 855–864.

González-Vallejo, C. C., Erev, I. & Wallsten, T. S. (1994). Do decision quality and preference order depend on whether probabilities are verbal or numerical? *American Journal of Psychology*, *107*, 157–172.

Hacking, I. (1975). *The Emergence of Probability*. Cambridge: Cambridge University Press.

Hamm, R. M. (1991). Selection of verbal probabilities: A solution for some problems of verbal probability expression. *Organizational Behavior and Human Decision Processes*, *48*, 193–223.

Hertwig, R. & Gigerenzer, G. (1999). The "conjunction fallacy" revisited: How intelligent inferences look like reasoning errors. *Journal of Behavioral Decision Making*, *12*, 275–305.

Horn, L. (1989). *A Natural History of Negation*. Chicago: University of Chicago Press.

Kahneman, D. & Tversky, A. (1982). Variants of uncertainty. *Cognition*, *11*, 143–157.

Karelitz, T., Budescu, D. & Wallsten, T. (2000). Validation of a new technique for eliciting membership functions of probability phrases. Poster presented at the Society for Judgment and Decision Making, Annual Meeting, New Orleans.

Kong, A., Barnett, G. O., Mosteller, F. & Youtz, C. (1986). How medical professionals evaluate expressions of probability. *New England Journal of Medicine*, *315*, 740–744.

Levin, P., Schneider, S. L. & Gaeth, G. J. (1998). All frames are not created equal: A typology and critical analysis of framing effects. *Organizational Behavior and Human Decision Processes*, *76*, 149–188.

Lichtenstein, S. & Newman, J. R. (1967). Empirical scaling of common verbal phrases associated with numerical probabilities. *Psychonomic Science*, *9*, 563–564.

McGlone, M. S. & Reed, A. B. (1998). Anchoring in the interpretation of probability expressions. *Journal of Pragmatics*, *30*, 723–733.

Moxey, L. M. & Sanford, A. J. (1987). Quantifiers and focus. *Journal of Semantics*, *5*, 189–206.

Moxey, L. M. & Sanford, A. J. (1993). *Communicating Quantities: A Psychological Perspective*. Hove: Erlbaum.

Moxey, L. M. & Sanford, A. J. (2000). Communicating quantities: A review of psycholinguistic evidence of how expressions determine perspectives. *Applied Cognitive Psychology*, *14*, 237–255.

Mullet, E. & Rivet, I. (1991). Comprehension of verbal probability expressions in children and adolescents. *Language and Communication*, *11*, 217–225.

Nakao, M. A. & Axelrod, S. (1983). Numbers are better than words. *American Journal of Medicine*, *74*, 1061–1063.

Olson, M. J. & Budescu, D. V. (1997). Patterns of preferences for numerical and verbal probabilities. *Journal of Behavioral Decision Making*, *10*, 117–131.

Reagan, R. T., Mosteller, F. & Youtz, C. (1989). Quantifying meanings of verbal probability expressions. *Journal of Applied Psychology*, *74*, 433–442.

Renooij, S. & Witteman, C. (1999). Talking probabilities: Communicating probabilistic information with words and numbers. *International Journal of Approximate Reasoning*, *22*, 169–194.

Reyna, V. F. (1981). The language of possibility and probability: Effects of negation on meaning. *Memory and Cognition*, *9*, 642–650.

Russell, B. A. W. (1923). Vagueness. *Australasian Journal of Philosophy and Psychology*, *1*, 84–92.

Sanbonmatsu, D. M., Posavac, S. S. & Stasney, R. (1997). The subjective beliefs underlying probability overestimation. *Journal of Experimental Social Psychology*, *33*, 276–295.

Sloman, S. A. (1996). The empirical case for two systems of reasoning. *Psychological Bulletin*, *119*, 3–22.

Sutherland, H. J., Lockwood, G. A., Tritchler, D. L., Sem, F., Brooks, L. & Till, J. E. (1991). Communicating probabilistic information to cancer patients: Is there "noise" on the line? *Social Science and Medicine*, *32*, 725–731.

Tavana, M., Kennedy, D. T. & Mohebbi, B. (1997). An applied study using the analytic hierarchy process to translate common verbal phrases to numerical probabilities. *Journal of Behavioral Decision Making*, *10*, 133–150.

Teigen, K. H. (1988a). When are low-probability events judged to be "probable"? Effects of outcome-set characteristics on verbal probability judgments. *Acta Psychologica*, *67*, 157–174.

Teigen, K. H. (1988b). The language of uncertainty. *Acta Psychologica*, *68*, 27–38.

Teigen, K. H. (1994). Variants of subjective probabilities: Concepts, norms, and biases. In G. Wright & P. Ayton (eds), *Subjective Probability* (pp. 211–238). London: Wiley.

Teigen, K. H. (2000). When equal chances = good chances. Verbal probabilities and the equiprobability effect. *Organizational Behavior and Human Decision Processes*, *85*, 77–108.

Teigen, K. H. & Brun, W. (1995). Yes, but it is uncertain: Direction and communicative intention of verbal probabilistic terms. *Acta Psychologica*, *88*, 233–258.

Teigen, K. H. & Brun, W. (1999). The directionality of verbal probability expressions: Effects on decisions, predictions, and probabilistic reasoning. *Organizational Behavior and Human Decision Processes*, *80*, 155–190.

Teigen, K. H. & Brun, W. (2000). Ambiguous probabilities: When does p = 0.3 reflect a possibility, and when does it reflect a doubt? *Journal of Behavioral Decision Making*, *13*, 345–362.

Teigen, K. H. & Brun, W. (2003). Verbal probabilities: A question of frame? *Journal of Behavioral Decision Making*, *16*, 53–72.

Trinkaus, J. (1989). How business students and faculty quantify probability expressions: Another look. *Perceptual and Motor Skills*, *68*, 97–98.

Tversky, A. & Kahneman, D. (1981). The framing of decisions and the psychology of choice. *Science*, *211*, 453–458.

Tversky, A. & Kahneman, D. (1983). Extensional versus intuitive reasoning: The conjunction fallacy in probabilistic reasoning. *Psychological Review*, *90*, 293–315.

Wallsten, T., Budescu, D. V., Rapoport, A., Zwick, R. & Forsyth, B. (1986). Measuring the vague meanings of probability terms. *Journal of Experimental Psychology*, *115*, 348–365.

Wallsten, T.S., Fillenbaum, S. & Cox, J. A. (1986). Base rate effects on the interpretations of probability and frequency expressions. *Journal of Memory and Language*, *25*, 571–587.

Wason, P. C. (1965). The contexts of plausible denial. *Journal of Verbal Learning and Verbal Behavior*, *4*, 7–11.

Weber, E. U. & Hilton, D. J. (1990). Contextual effects in the interpretation of probability words: Perceived base rate and severity of events. *Journal of Experimental Psychology: Human Perception and Performance*, *16*, 781–789.

Williamson, T. (1994). *Vagueness*. London: Routledge.

Windschitl, P. D. (2000). The binary additivity of subjective probability does not indicate the binary complementarity of perceived certainty. *Organizational Behavior and Human Decision Processes*, *81*, 195–225.

Windschitl, P. D. & Wells, G. L. (1996). Measuring psychological uncertainty: Verbal versus numeric methods. *Journal of Experimental Psychology: Applied*, *2*, 343–364.

Windschitl, P. D. & Wells, G. L. (1998). The alternative-outcomes effect. *Journal of Personality and Social Psychology*, *75*, 1411–1423.

CHAPTER 8

Possibilities and Probabilities

Paolo Legrenzi
University of Architecture, Venice, Italy
Vittorio Girotto
University of Provence, France; and University of Architecture, Venice, Italy
Maria Sonino Legrenzi
Formerly Padua University
and
Philip N. Johnson-Laird
Princeton University, New Jersey, USA

INTRODUCTION

Consider the following problem. If the president is in the office, her secretary is in the office, too. So, who is more likely to be in the office: the president or her secretary? A moment's thought should convince you that the probability that the secretary is in the office is greater than, or equal to, the probability that the president is in the office. The reason is that any time that the president is in the office her secretary will be, too, but her secretary could be in the office when the president is not. The answer is deductively valid; that is, given the truth of the premises, the conclusion must be true. What is mysterious is the nature of the mental processes that underlie such probabilistic reasoning.

The aim of this chapter is to make progress towards solving this mystery. Its solution matters because we are all confronted in daily life with questions about the likelihood of events, and, even though most of us are not experts in the probability calculus, we can usually come up with appropriate answers.

The chapter has three parts. First, it introduces some basic ideas and distinguishes between two ways of thinking about probabilities—one known as "extensional" and the other as "non-extensional". Second, it sketches the principles of a theory of reasoning based on mental models, and shows how it accounts for extensional reasoning. Third, it reviews some of the evidence that corroborates the model theory.

Thinking: Psychological Perspectives on Reasoning, Judgment and Decision Making. Edited by David Hardman and Laura Macchi.
© 2003 John Wiley & Sons, Ltd.

EXTENSIONAL AND NON-EXTENSIONAL REASONING

Human beings have been estimating probabilities at least since classical Greek times, but the calculus of probabilities was invented only in the seventeenth century. No one knows what caused the delay (Hacking, 1975). It shows, however, that for many purposes human reasoners do not need accurate numerical values for probabilities. An important distinction, which we owe to Danny Kahneman and the late Amos Tversky, who pioneered the study of probabilistic reasoning (see Kahneman, Slovic & Tversky, 1982), concerns its basis. To revert to the problem about the president and the secretary, suppose that you think about the different possibilities compatible with the conditional: if the president is in the office, the secretary is in the office. You think of the possibility of the president in the office, and so her secretary is in the office, too. You think about what happens if the president is not in the office: in one possibility, the secretary is in the office; in another possibility, the secretary is not in the office, either. You have envisaged the three possibilities that are compatible with the truth of the conditional assertion, which we summarize as follows, using the symbol "¬" to denote negation:

president in office	secretary in office
¬president in office	secretary in office
¬president in office	¬secretary in office

Following philosophers and logicians, we refer to such possibilities as the "extensions" of the conditional assertion, that is, the possibilities to which it refers (e.g., Montague, 1974). When individuals infer probabilities by considering the extensions of assertions, we shall say that they are reasoning *extensionally*.

You can tackle the problem about the president and her secretary in a different way. You know that presidents are unlikely to spend as much time in the office as their secretaries. This stereotype may have occurred to you as you were thinking about the problem, and you might have based your inference on it. When you think in this way, you do not consider the extensions of assertions; rather, you use some index—some evidence or knowledge—to infer a probability. We use "non-extensional" as an umbrella term to cover the many ways in which people can arrive at probabilities without thinking about extensions. Of course, you might think about a problem both extensionally and non-extensionally. But our focus in this chapter is on extensional reasoning, though we do say something about non-extensional reasoning.

The probability calculus is a branch of mathematics that concerns extensional probabilities. The calculus can be formulated in various equivalent ways. One such way depends on negation and such sentential connectives as "and" and "or", taken in their idealized, logical senses. The first assumption, or "axiom", of the calculus stipulates that probabilities are real numbers greater than or equal to 0. The second axiom states that the probability of a statement that is necessarily true is 1. The third axiom is the extensional principle that if two statements cannot both be true at the same time, the probability of their disjunction, A *or B*, is the sum of their respective probabilities.

The concept of a conditional probability is central to the calculus, that is, a probability that is conditional on the truth of some other proposition; for example, the probability that the secretary is in the office given that the president is in the office. The concept can be introduced into the calculus by an axiom stating that a conditional probability, which is written $p(A \mid B)$—the probability of A given the truth of B—corresponds to the subset of cases of B in which A also holds. In formal terms,

$$p(A \mid B) = \frac{p(A \text{ and } B)}{p(B)}$$

Given a problem about a set of events, you can consider its partition, that is, the exhaustive set of possible conjunctions of individual events. In the problem about the president and the secretary, there are four such possibilities, which comprise this "partition" for the problem:

president in office	secretary in office
president in office	¬secretary in office
¬president in office	secretary in office
¬president in office	¬secretary in office

Once you know the probabilities of each possibility in a partition, you know everything that is to be known from a probabilistic standpoint. So let us introduce some probabilities, which for convenience we state as chances out of a hundred:

president in office	secretary in office	50
president in office	¬secretary in office	0
¬president in office	secretary in office	30
¬president in office	¬secretary in office	20

You can now deduce the probability of any assertion about the domain, including conditional probabilities, such as, the probability that the president is not in the office given that the secretary is in the office is 30/80.

Bayes' theorem is a logical consequence of the axioms of the probability calculus. It is important because it allows conditional probabilities to be inferred from the values of other probabilities. The simplest version of the theorem can be expressed in terms of a hypothesis, H, and data, d:

$$p(H \mid d) = \frac{p(d \mid H)p(H)}{p(d)} \qquad \text{provided } p(d) \neq 0$$

Thus, the so-called *posterior* probability of a hypothesis, H, given data, d, depends on the conditional probability of the data given the truth of the hypothesis: $p(d \mid H)$, the prior probability of the hypothesis: $p(H)$, and the *prior* probability of the data: $p(d)$. For example, suppose that you want to deduce the probability that the secretary is in the office given that the president is in the office, and that you know only the following probabilities:

p(president in office	secretary in office)	5/8
p(secretary in office)		4/5
p(president in office)		1/2

The required probability follows from Bayes' theorem as follows:

$$p(\text{secretary} \mid \text{president}) = \frac{(5/8)(4/5)}{(1/2)} = \frac{(4/8)}{(1/2)} = 1$$

The probabilities in this example correspond to those in the partition above, and when you know the probabilities for a partition, you know everything. Hence, there is a more direct route to the required conditional probability. You merely examine the probabilities in the partition, and consider the subset of chances in which the secretary is in the office given those chances in which the president is in the office. The answer is that there are 50 chances of the secretary's being in the office in the 50 chances in which the president is in the office; that is, the conditional probability is once again 1.

The consequences of the probability calculus are often surprising (see Feller, 1957), and even Bayes' theorem is beyond the intuitions of naive individuals (Phillips & Edwards, 1966). It provides a normative answer, but when naive individuals try to infer posterior probabilities, they are most unlikely to be carrying out the calculations for Bayes' theorem (Edwards & Tversky, 1967). One controversial issue is whether people neglect the base rate of an event, that is, its prior probability, in assessing its posterior probability. Kahneman and Tversky (1973) showed that individuals can estimate base rates, but that they tend to be guided more by non-extensional aspects of problems than by their extensions. They judge the probability that something is a member of a particular category in terms of how "representative" it is of the category. In one of Kahneman and Tversky's (1973) studies, for example, the participants had to judge the probability that an individual was an engineer as opposed to a lawyer. They were much more influenced by a thumbnail sketch of the individual, which fitted their stereotype of engineers, than by the prior probability that the individual was an engineer; for example, he was selected at random from a sample of 30 engineers and 70 lawyers. These results suggested that people rely on their knowledge of typical engineers rather than on extensions.

Some authors have argued that the fallacy of ignoring the base rate has been exaggerated (e.g., Koehler, 1996). Others have argued that naive reasoners produce better extensional reasoning when problems are about frequencies rather than probabilities (see Gigerenzer & Hoffrage, 1995; Cosmides & Tooby, 1996). We will return to this "frequentist" hypothesis after we have considered an alternative account of probabilistic thinking. This account is based on the mental model theory, and so we now turn to a brief exposition of this theory.

THE THEORY OF MENTAL MODELS AND EXTENSIONAL PROBABILITIES

Craik (1943) proposed that the human mind builds internal models of the external world in order to anticipate events. This conjecture underlies an account of how individuals understand discourse and reason from it (e.g., Johnson-Laird & Byrne, 1991). The theory postulates that each mental model represents a possibility, and that its structure and content capture what is common to the different ways in which the possibility might occur. For example, when individuals understand that either the president or the secretary is in the office, but not both, they construct two mental models to represent the two possibilities:

president

        secretary

where each line represents an alternative model; "president" denotes a model of the president in the office, and "secretary" denotes a model of the secretary in the office. Likewise, a conjunction, such as:

The president is in the office and the secretary is in the office

has only a single mental model:

president   secretary

This model captures what is common to any situation in which the president and secretary are in the office, but it leaves out many aspects of the situation; for example, the size of the office, where they are in it and its location. In fact, mental models are more complicated than shown here, because models need to represent the individuals as *in* the office (Garnham & Oakhill, 1994).

Granted that individuals construct mental models to represent the possibilities described in assertions, they can reason by formulating a conclusion that holds in their mental models, and they can test its validity by checking whether it holds in all possible models of the discourse. They can establish the invalidity of a conclusion by finding a counterexample, that is, a model of the discourse in which the conclusion is false.

The theory makes a fundamental assumption: The principle of *truth*.

Individuals represent assertions by constructing sets of mental models in which, first, each model represents a true possibility, and, second, the clauses in the assertions, affirmative or negative, are represented in a mental model only if they are true in the possibility.

Consider an exclusive disjunction in which only one of the two clauses is true:

The president is not in the office or else the secretary is in the office.

The mental models of the disjunction represent only the two true possibilities, and within them, they represent only the two clauses in the disjunction when they are true within a possibility:

¬president
                secretary

The first model represents the possibility that the president is not in the office, but it does not represent explicitly that it is false that the secretary is in the office. The second model represents the possibility that the secretary is in the office, but it does not represent explicitly that it is false that the president is not in the office (that is, the president *is* in the office). Additional processes have to occur in order to recover information about what is false (e.g., Johnson-Laird & Byrne, 2002). In particular, mental models can be fleshed out into *fully explicit* models provided that individuals retain mental footnotes about what is false in models. For example, this procedure enables the mental models of the preceding disjunction to be fleshed out into the fully explicit models:

¬president   ¬secretary
 president   secretary

The mental models of conditionals are simple. For a conditional, such as if the president is in the office, then the secretary is in the office, the mental models represent explicitly only the possibility in which the two clauses are true, whereas the possibilities in which the antecedent clause (the president is in the office) is false are represented by a wholly implicit

Table 8.1 The mental models and the fully explicit models for four sentential connectives: the symbol "¬" denotes negation, and the ellipsis "..." denotes a wholly implicit model. Each line represents a model of a possibility

Connective	Mental models		Fully explicit models	
A and B	A	B	A	B
A or else B	A		A	¬B
		B	¬A	B
A or B, or both	A		A	¬B
		B	¬A	B
	A	B	A	B
If A then B	A	B	A	B
	...		¬A	B
			¬A	¬B

model (shown here as an ellipsis):

president   secretary

    ...

A mental footnote on the implicit model stipulates that the antecedent is false in the possibilities that this model represents. If individuals retain this footnote, they can construct fully explicit models:

  president   secretary
¬president   secretary
¬president   ¬secretary

We have developed a computer program that implements the theory, constructing both mental models and fully explicit models (e.g., Johnson-Laird & Savary, 1999). Table 8.1 summarizes the mental models and the fully explicit models for four major sentential connectives.

   Evidence supports the model theory. Reasoners can use counterexamples to refute invalid inferences (Bucciarelli & Johnson-Laird, 1999; Neth & Johnson-Laird, 1999), they search harder for counterexamples if they have inferred an unbelievable conclusion (Oakhill, Garnham & Johnson-Laird, 1990), and the frontal pole in the right frontal lobe appears to be particularly active during a search for counterexamples (Kroger, Cohen & Johnson-Laird, 2002). Deductions calling for multiple models are difficult, taking longer and leading to more errors (e.g., Byrne & Johnson-Laird, 1989; Schaeken, Johnson-Laird & d'Ydewalle, 1996; Bell & Johnson-Laird, 1998). Erroneous conclusions tend to correspond to single mental models of the premises (e.g., Bauer & Johnson-Laird, 1993). Indeed, reasoners model only what is minimally necessary (Ormerod, Manktelow & Jones, 1993; Sloutsky & Goldvarg, 2000). They tend to focus on what is explicit in their models and thus to be susceptible to various "focusing effects", including the influence of the verbal framing of premises on deductive reasoning (see Legrenzi, Girotto & Johnson-Laird, 1993). They therefore prefer information about a focal hypothesis to information about an alternative hypothesis—the phenomenon of "pseudodiagnosticity" (Girotto, Evans & Legrenzi, 1996). They succumb to illusory inferences that are a consequence of the failure to represent what is false (e.g., Johnson-Laird & Savary, 1999; Goldvarg & Johnson-Laird, 2000). These illusions, as we will see, also occur in probabilistic reasoning. They are perhaps the strongest sign of the use of mental models, because no other current theory—including theories based on formal rules of inference (Braine & O'Brien, 1998; Rips, 1994)—can account for them.

All the principal predictions of the model theory follow from the previous account. But, to explain probabilistic reasoning, it is necessary to make some additional assumptions (see Johnson-Laird, 1994; Johnson-Laird et al., 1999). An important assumption is the *equiprobability* principle. Each model represents an equiprobable possibility unless individuals have beliefs to the contrary, in which case they will assign different probabilities to the models representing the different possibilities. Shimojo and Ichikawa (1989) proposed a similar principle to account for Bayesian reasoning. The present principle differs from theirs in that it assigns equiprobability, not to actual events, but to mental models. Moreover, it applies only by default. An analogous principle of "indifference" or "insufficient reason" has a long history in classical probability theory (Hacking, 1975), but it is problematic because it applies to events.

The equiprobability principle works closely with the *proportionality* principle. Granted equiprobability, the probability of an event, A, depends on the proportion of models in which the event occurs; that is, $p(A) = n_A/n$, where n_A is the number of models containing A, and n is the number of models. Proportionality predicts that a description, such as "the president or her secretary, or both of them, are in the office" is compatible with three possibilities, which will each be assigned a probability of 1/3.

An analogous principle, applied to numerical probabilities, is the *numerical* principle. If assertions refer to numerical probabilities, their models can be tagged with the appropriate numerical values, and an unknown probability can be calculated by subtracting the sum of the remaining known probabilities from the overall probability of all the possibilities in the partition. The procedure is still extensional, but it generalizes to any sort of numerical values, including frequencies and probabilities expressed as fractions, decimals or percentages (see Stevenson and Over, 1995, who also postulate tagging models with probabilities).

How do naive individuals infer conditional probabilities, and, in particular, posterior probabilities? According to the model theory, they rely not on Bayes' theorem, but on a simple procedure: the *subset* principle. Granted equiprobability, a conditional probability, $p(A \mid B)$, depends on the subset of B that is A, and the proportionality of A to B yields the numerical value of the conditional probability.

For example, consider this problem. The chances that the president is in the office are 4 out of 10; on 3 out of these 4 cases her secretary is also in the office, but on 2 out of the 6 occasions when the president is not in the office, the secretary is in the office. Given that the secretary is in the office, what is the likelihood that the president is in the office? Naive individuals can build the appropriate equiprobable models:

president	secretary
president	secretary
president	secretary
president	¬secretary
¬president	secretary
¬president	secretary

. . .

where the implicit model represents cases in which neither the president nor the secretary is in the office. Reasoners may instead build numerical models:

		Chances
president	secretary	3
president	¬secretary	1
¬president	secretary	2
	. . .	4

Either set of models establishes that the chances that the secretary is in the office are 5 out of 10, and that the probability that the president is in the office, given the presence of the secretary, is 3 out of 5. In computing the value of the subset relation, reasoners can err in assessing either the numerator or, more likely, the denominator of the ratio.

These five principles (including the truth principle) make up the model theory of extensional reasoning about probabilities.

EXPERIMENTAL TESTS OF THE THEORY

Experimental tests have corroborated the model theory of extensional reasoning about probabilities. In one of these studies, the participants were given assertions about the contents of a box, and their task was to estimate the probabilities of various other assertions (Johnson-Laird et al., 1999). For example, given an exclusive disjunction, such as, "there is a box in which there is a either a yellow card or a brown card, but not both", individuals should construct models of the alternative possible contents of the box:

yellow card
                brown card

and so they should infer probabilities of 50 per cent for the following two assertions:

There is at least a yellow card in the box.
There is a yellow card in the box and there is not a brown card in the box.

The experiment examined three sorts of initial assertions:

exclusive disjunctions:	either A or B, but not both
inclusive disjunction:	A or B, or both
conditionals:	if A then B

Table 8.1 shows the mental models for each sort of these assertions, and they predict the probabilities that reasoners should assign to various categorical assertions presented after the initial assertions:

at least A
A and B
A and not B
neither A nor B

In the case of an inclusive disjunction, for instance, reasoners should assign a probability of 67 per cent to *at least* A, and a probability of 33 per cent to A *and* B. Because participants

Table 8.2 The predictions and the numbers of participants who made inferences within ±5 per cent of the predictions ($n = 22$) in Experiment 1 from Johnson-Laird et al. (1999)

	Types of judgment			
	$p(A)$	$p(A$ and $B)$	$p(A$ and not $B)$	$p($neither A nor $B)$
A or B, not both				
Predictions	50	0	50	0
No. of participants within ±5%	16	19	18	16
A or B, or both				
Predictions	67	33	33	0
No. of participants within ±5%	9	15	14	20
If A then B				
Predictions	50	50	0	50
No. of participants within ±5%	14	12	22	12

should construct certain models only when they are asked questions about the corresponding possibilities, particularly in the case of conditionals, they are likely to overestimate probabilities, so that the sum of their estimates of the different propositions in a partition should be greater than 100 per cent.

Table 8.2 presents the results of this study. The student participants estimated probabilities that tended to be within ±5 per cent of the predicted values. For every initial assertion, their estimates were closer to the prediction than one would expect by chance (sign tests varied from $p < .0005$ to $p < 1$ in 4 million). As the theory predicts, some participants appeared to forget the implicit model of the conditional; thus, four of them inferred a 100 per cent probability for *at least A*, and eight of them inferred a 100 per cent probability for *A and B*. The model theory also predicts that participants should tend to infer higher probabilities for *A and B* than for *neither A nor B*; both are possible for conditional and biconditional interpretations, but only the former corresponds to an initially explicit model. This difference was reliable. The inferences for *B and not-A*, which are not shown in Table 8.2, reflect the interpretation of the conditional: 12 participants inferred a probability of 0 per cent (the biconditional interpretation), four participants inferred a probability of 50 per cent (the conditional interpretation) and the remaining six participants inferred some other probability. In each case, we have inferences for all four possibilities in the partition, and they ought to sum to 100 per cent. A biconditional has fewer explicit models than a conditional, and those participants who made the biconditional interpretation tended to infer probabilities that summed correctly to 100 per cent, whereas those participants who made a conditional interpretation tended to infer probabilities that summed to more than 100 per cent. This difference was reliable. Reasoners failed to bring to mind all the models of the conditional, and so they overestimated the probability of the model that corresponds to the event for which they were trying to infer a probability (cf. the "subadditivity" predicted by Tversky and Koehler's [1994] theory of non-extensional reasoning).

The results supported the model theory. The participants appeared to infer probabilities by constructing models of the premises with the equiprobability principle, and assessing the proportion of models in which the events occur. Experts tend to baulk at the questions in our experiment or else to describe the range of possible probabilities. In contrast, naive individuals, such as those in our experiment, have intuitions about probability based on equiprobable possibilities. Both Shimojo and Ichikawa (1989) and Falk (1992) have also observed that their participants believed that if there were N possible events, the probability of any one of them was 1/N. The principles of equiprobability and proportionality are not unique to our theory, and they could be part of theories that do not rely on mental models. We now consider a prediction that is unique to the model theory.

The theory predicts the occurrence of systematic biases in extensional reasoning, because models represent what is true, not what is false. As readers will recall, this *principle of truth* applies at two levels: individuals construct models that make explicit only true possibilities, and these models make explicit only those clauses in premises that are true. It is important to bear in mind that what is omitted concerns falsity, not negation. A negative sentence can be true, in which case it will be represented in a mental model. For certain assertions, the failure to represent what is false should produce biased extensional inferences. The mental models of such assertions yield partitions that differ from the partitions corresponding to the fully explicit models of the assertions. The theory predicts that biased inferences should occur because they are based on mental models rather than fully explicit models. Other assertions, however, have mental models that yield partitions corresponding to the fully explicit models of the assertions. The theory predicts that inferences from these assertions should be unbiased. A computer program implementing the construction of mental models and fully explicit models searched systematically for both sorts of assertions in the vast space of possible assertions.

Consider the following problem:

The president at least is in the office, or else both the secretary and the chauffeur are in the office, but the three of them are not all in the office. What is the probability that the president and the chauffeur are in the office?

The mental models of the assertion are as follows:

president

        secretary   chauffeur

where "president" denotes a model of the president in the office, and so on. Reasoners should therefore infer that the probability of the president and the chauffeur's both being in the office is 0 per cent. The fully explicit models of the assertion, however, take into account that when it is true that the president is in the office, there are three distinct ways in which it can be false that both the secretary and the chauffeur are in the office:

president	secretary	¬chauffeur
president	¬secretary	chauffeur
president	¬secretary	¬chauffeur
¬president	secretary	chauffeur

It follows that the probability of the president and the chauffeur's being in the office is not 0 per cent. If each possibility is equiprobable, the probability is 25 per cent.

In general, an unbiased inference is one that applies the equiprobability principle to the alternatives corresponding to fully explicit models, which are the correct representation of the possibilities compatible with assertions. The following control problem should elicit an unbiased inference, because its mental models yield the same partition as its fully explicit models:

The president at least is in the office and either the secretary or else the chauffeur is in the office, but the three of them are not all in the office. What is the probability that the president and the chauffeur are in the office?

The assertion has the mental models

president   secretary
president   chauffeur

and so reasoners should respond, 50 per cent. The fully explicit models of the assertion are as follows

president   secretary   ¬chauffeur
president   ¬secretary   chauffeur

They support the same inference, and so it is an unbiased estimate. We carried out an experiment that investigated a set of nine experimental problems and nine control problems. The results corroborated the model theory's predictions (see Johnson-Laird et al., 1999, Experiment 3).

Conditional probabilities lie on the boundary of naive reasoning ability. Consider, for instance, the following problem (adapted from Bar-Hillel & Falk, 1982):

The president has two secretaries: A and B. One of them is a woman. What is the probability that the other is a woman?

If you have the stereotype that secretaries are women, you make a non-extensional inference of, say, 90 per cent. But, if you suppress this stereotype, you can draw the extensional conclusion that the probability is about 1/2. You assume that there are two possibilities for the other secretary:

woman
man

and equiprobability yields the conclusion. In fact, the problem calls for an estimate of a conditional probability, p(one secretary is a woman | other secretary is a woman). The partition is therefore as follows:

Secretary 1	Secretary 2
woman	woman
woman	man
man	woman
man	man

Because at least one secretary is a woman, we can eliminate the last of these four possibilities. Given that secretary 1 or 2 is a woman, it follows that the probability that the other secretary is a woman is 1/3. Readers will note that if the female secretary is identified in some way— for example, she is secretary 1—the probability that secretary 2 is a woman does indeed equal 1/2 (see Hilton, 1995; Nickerson, 1996, for subtleties influencing this analysis). Unfortunately, it is not always obvious that a problem concerns a conditional probability.

Now consider the following problem:

If the suspect is not guilty, the probability of a DNA match with the crime sample is 1 in a million. The suspect's DNA matches the crime sample. Is the suspect likely to be guilty?

Most people would say, yes. But, the information given in the problem does not specify the complete distribution of probabilities. In particular, it says nothing about the chances of a DNA match when the suspect is guilty. We can therefore complete these probabilities in, say, the following way:

		chances
¬guilty	DNA matches	1
¬guilty	¬DNA matches	999 999
guilty	DNA matches	1
guilty	¬DNA matches	0

The probability of a DNA match given that the suspect is not guilty is indeed 1 in a million. Given that the suspect's DNA matches the crime sample, however, the probability that the suspect is guilty is only 1/2. As we pointed out earlier, a conditional probability depends on a subset relation in models. The subset relation for one conditional probability, such as p(DNA match | not guilty), does not fix the subset relation for the converse conditional probability: p(not guilty | DNA match). Thus, your knowledge of one conditional probability tells you almost nothing about the value of the converse conditional probability.

Yet, naive individuals mistakenly infer one value from the other. They are likely to do so because they fail to build fully explicit models. They interpret the preceding problem in the following way:

		chances
¬guilty	DNA matches	1
	. . .	999 999

where they use only an implicit model for the second possibility. Their representation of the converse conditional probability is similar, and so they confuse the original conditional probability with its converse:

p(not guilty | DNA matches) = 1 in a million

Hence, they infer that the probability that the suspect is not guilty, given that the DNA matches, is very small; that is, the suspect is almost certainly guilty. The underlying difficulty here is a special case of the general difficulty of constructing fully explicit models, which overtaxes the processing capacity of working memory. The DNA problem is just one example of many that confuse naive reasoners (e.g., Eddy, 1982).

Previous studies of extensional probabilistic reasoning have focused on Bayesian problems. They have shown that naive individuals do not appear to use Bayes' theorem (see above), but rely on various beliefs (Shimojo & Ichikawa, 1989; Falk, 1992). The model theory is consistent with such claims, but, in addition, it specifies the nature of the mental representations that reasoners rely on. With some sorts of problems, naive reasoners are able to infer the correct posterior probabilities even though they do not use Bayes' theorem. The subset principle, which we outlined earlier, explains the underlying mental processes.

In our description of the subset principle, we used a simple example to demonstrate how it could be used to infer the posterior probability of the president's being in the office given that the secretary was in the office. The inference was drawn given a statement of the chances that the president was in the office, the chances that the secretary was in the office, and the chances that the secretary was in the office given that the president was in the office. We took pains to use an example about the chances of an individual event, but the subset principle can equally well be applied to problems about the relative frequencies of events. The crux is that, to infer a posterior probability, reasoners must be able to construct the relevant partition, together with the chances or frequencies of events, and to apply the subset principle.

Our reason for emphasizing unique events is that naive reasoners, and those who treat a probability as a degree of belief, readily assign probabilities to them (e.g., Kahneman & Tversky, 1996). Such probabilities, however, raise deep philosophical problems. For instance, the circumstances in which the following assertion is true are mysterious:

The chances that the president is in the office right now are 4 out of 10.

If the president is indeed in the office, is the assertion true? Likewise, if the president is not in the office, is the assertion false? It seems that the assertion can be true or false regardless of the whereabouts of the president. Psychologically speaking, however, the assertion is about the chances of various possibilities. The model theory allows that these possibilities can be represented either by a proportion of equiprobable models or by numerically tagged models, such as:

	Chances
President	4
¬President	6

If you assign this probability to a unique event, you should be prepared to pay $4 to win $10 if the president is in her office, or nothing if she is not.

Bayesian inference about unique events or about repeated events should be easier when three conditions hold: models allow reasoners to use the subset principle, the numerical values make for easy calculations, and the problem calls for separate estimates of the denominator and of the numerator corresponding to the conditional probability. Girotto and Gonzalez (2001) have shown that naive reasoners are able to solve problems with these three features. For example, most of their participants solved the following probability problem about a unique case:

A screening test of an infection is being studied. Here is the information about the infection and the test results. A person who was tested had 4 chances out of 100 of having the infection. Three of the 4 chances of having the infection were associated with a positive reaction to the test. Twelve of the remaining 96 chances of not having the infection were also associated with a positive reaction to the test.

Imagine that Pierre is tested now. Out of a total of 100 chances, Pierre has —— chances of having a positive reaction, —— of which will be associated with having the infection.

In contrast, few participants solved the following problem about the frequency of repeated events:

A screening test of an infection is being studied. Here is the information about the infection and the test results. Four of the 100 people tested were infected. Three of the 4 infected people had a positive reaction to the test. Twelve of the 96 uninfected people also had a positive reaction to the test. Among 100 people who had a positive reaction to the test, the proportion that have the infection will be equal to ——— out of ———.

The problem partitions a set of frequencies into exhaustive subsets, but it does not induce reasoners either to apply the subset principle or to compute separately the denominator and the numerator of the frequency ratio. Macchi (1995) had a similar idea: she showed that manipulating the statements expressing conditional probability, in problems that she defined as "partitive", helped the participants to infer more accurate posterior probabilities. These and other findings about Bayesian problems (Girotto & Gonzalez, 2000, 2001, in press) corroborate the model theory of extensional reasoning. Yet, they cannot be readily explained by the "frequentist" hypothesis (Gigerenzer & Hoffrage, 1995; Cosmides & Tooby, 1996), which postulates that evolution by natural selection has led to an innate "module" in the mind that makes Bayesian inferences about naturally occurring frequency data. It follows that naive reasoners should fail problems unique events.

CONCLUSIONS

The model theory is based on five principles about the extensions of probabilistic discourse: individuals should construct models of the true possibilities based on the premises (the truth principle); in the absence of contrary evidence, they should assume that the models represent equally probable alternatives (the equiprobability principle); they should infer the probability of an event, A, from the proportion of models in which A occurs (the proportionality principle) or from models tagged with numerical probabilities (the numerical principle); and they should infer the conditional probability of an event A, given an event B, from the subset of models of B in which A occurs (the subset principle).

On this account, naive individuals construct models of true possibilities, assume equiprobability by default, and infer probabilities from proportionality, from numerical values or from the subset principle. We have sketched some of the evidence that corroborates the theory (see also Johnson-Laird et al., 1999; Girotto & Gonzalez, in press). These results show that if mental models and the real alternatives (fully explicit models) diverge, naive reasoners tend to follow the mental models. In this sense, the present theory accommodates the earlier accounts of probabilistic reasoning by Shimojo and Ichikawa (1989) and Falk (1992).

How might mental models apply to probabilistic reasoning that is not extensional? General knowledge is readily triggered by any materials to which it seems relevant. Consider one last time our example about the president:

If the president is in the office, the secretary is, too.

Your knowledge of the typical hours that presidents and secretaries work, as we mentioned, may yield an answer to the question of who is more likely to be in the office. Tversky and Kahneman (1983) have shown that knowledge may also lead to a "conjunction fallacy" in which individuals rate a conjunction as having a higher probability than one of its conjuncts. For instance, given a description of a woman called Linda, which stressed her independence of mind and other features typical of feminists, individuals rated the conjunction:

Linda is a feminist and a bank teller

as more probable than its constituent proposition:

Linda is a bank teller.

They rated as most probable, however, its other constituent:

Linda is a feminist.

This pattern of ratings violates the general principle that a proposition has a probability greater than, or equal to, the probability of any conjunction in which it occurs.

Studies of the fallacy have shown that a conjunction is often rated as more probable than only *one* of its constituents (see Hertwig & Chase, 1998). In a recent unpublished study of non-extensional probabilistic reasoning, however, we have established a stronger version of the fallacy. The key to this phenomenon is the nature of causal explanations. We presented the participants with a series of logically inconsistent assertions, such as:

If a person pulls the trigger, the pistol will fire. Someone has pulled the trigger but the pistol did not fire. Why not?

The task was to rank order the probabilities of a series of putative explanations. One of the explanations was a causal chain consisting of a *cause* and an *effect*, where the effect in turn accounted for the inconsistency:

A prudent person had unloaded the pistol and there were no cartridges in the chamber.

This explanation was rated as having a higher probability than either the statement of the cause alone or the statement of the effect alone. The underlying mechanism in our view is the modulation of models of assertions by models in general knowledge—a mechanism that we have implemented in a computer program. Knowledge enables individuals to infer an effect from its cause, but it is harder to infer a cause from its effect, because effects may have other causes. Hence, the theory predicts the trend (for a similar account that anticipates our own, see Tversky and Kahneman, 1983, p. 305). Such modulations can occur even in extensional reasoning, and the mixture of extensional and non-extensional processes is typical in daily life.

The model theory dispels some common misconceptions about probabilistic reasoning. It is *not* necessarily an inductive process. The following sort of argument is deductively valid:

If the president is in the office, her secretary is in the office, too. Hence, the probability that the secretary is in the office is greater than, or equal to, the probability that the president is in the office.

Another misconception is that extensional reasoning depends on a tacit knowledge of the probability calculus, perhaps embodied in an innate inferential module that is triggered by premises that concern the natural frequencies of events (Gigerenzer & Hoffrage, 1995; Cosmides & Tooby, 1996). But, as the model theory predicts, and as Girotto and Gonzalez (2001, in press) have confirmed, naive individuals are able to infer posterior probabilities about the chances of unique events. Conversely, problems based on natural frequencies do not invariably elicit good Bayesian reasoning. The crux is the subset principle.

A final misconception is that cognitive illusions occur only in non-extensional reasoning and disappear in extensional reasoning. "Subadditivity" is a well-known phenomenon of non-extensional reasoning in which estimates of the probability of an implicit disjunctive category, such as "accidents", is less than the sum of its explicit disjuncts, such as "accidents in the home" and "accidents outside the home". According to Tversky and Koehler's (1994) "support" theory, the description of an event in greater detail recruits more evidence in favour of it and thus leads to a higher judged probability (see also Miyamoto, Gonzalez & Tu, 1995). But we described earlier an experiment showing that extensional reasoning can also yield subadditivity (Johnson-Laird et al., 1999, Experiment 3). The model theory predicted subadditivity on the grounds that reasoners have difficulty in calling to mind all the models of premises. The most striking cognitive illusions in extensional reasoning arise from the failure of reasoners to cope with falsity. As the model theory predicts, and as we also illustrated, individuals succumb to gross illusions about probabilities.

The model theory of probabilistic reasoning is based on a small number of simple principles. Reasoners make inferences from mental models representing what is true. By default, they assume that models represent equiprobable alternatives. They infer the probabilities of events from the proportions of models in which they hold. If the premises include numerical probabilities, reasoners tag their models with numerical probabilities, and use simple arithmetic to calculate probabilities. Problems that cannot be solved in these ways are probably beyond the competence of naive reasoners.

ACKNOWLEDGEMENTS

This research was supported in part by grants from MIUR (Italian Ministry of Universities and Research) and CNR (Italian National Council for Scientific Research) to the first two authors, and by a grant from the US National Science Foundation (Grant 0076287) to the last author to study strategies in reasoning. We thank Professor Jean-Paul Caverni for his hospitality to the authors at CREPCO, the University of Aix-en-Provence, and we thank Professor Alberto Mazzocco for his hospitality to the authors at the Department of Psychology, Padua University. We also thank Michel Gonzalez for his comments on a previous version of the chapter.

REFERENCES

Bar-Hillel, M.A. & Falk, R. (1982). Some teasers concerning conditional probabilities. *Cognition*, *11*, 109–122.
Bauer, M.I. & Johnson-Laird, P.N. (1993). How diagrams can improve reasoning. *Psychological Science*, *4*, 372–378.
Bell, V. & Johnson-Laird, P.N. (1998). A model theory of modal reasoning. *Cognitive Science*, *22*, 25–51.
Braine, M.D.S. & O'Brien, D.P. (eds) (1998). *Mental Logic*. Mahwah, NJ: Erlbaum.
Bucciarelli, M. & Johnson-Laird, P.N. (1999). Strategies in syllogistic reasoning. *Cognitive Science*, *23*, 247–303.
Byrne, R.M.J. & Johnson-Laird, P.N. (1989). Spatial reasoning. *Journal of Memory and Language*, *28*, 564–575.
Cosmides, L. & Tooby, J. (1996). Are humans good intuitive statisticians after all? Rethinking some conclusions from the literature on judgment under uncertainty. *Cognition*, *58*, 1–73.
Craik, K. (1943). *The Nature of Explanation*. Cambridge: Cambridge University Press.

Eddy, D.M. (1982). Probabilistic reasoning in clinical medicine: Problems and opportunities. In D. Kahneman, P. Slovic & A. Tversky (eds), *Judgment Under Uncertainty: Heuristics and Biases* (pp. 249–267). Cambridge: Cambridge University Press.

Edwards, W. & Tversky, A. (eds) (1967). *Decision Making*. Harmondsworth: Penguin.

Falk, R. (1992). A closer look at the probabilities of the notorious three prisoners. *Cognition, 43,* 197–223.

Feller, W. (1957). *An Introduction to Probability Theory and Its Applications*, 2nd edn. New York: Wiley.

Garnham, A. & Oakhill, J.V. (1994). *Thinking and Reasoning*. Oxford: Basil Blackwell.

Gigerenzer, G. & Hoffrage, U. (1995). How to improve Bayesian reasoning without instruction: Frequency format. *Psychological Review, 102,* 684–704.

Girotto, V. & Gonzalez, M. (2000). Strategies and models in statistical reasoning. In W. Schaeken, G. De Vooght, A. Vandierendonck & G. d'Ydewalle (eds) *Strategies in Deductive Reasoning* (pp. 267–285). Mahwah, NJ: Erlbaum.

Girotto, V. & Gonzalez, M. (2001). Solving probabilistic and statistical problems: A matter of question form and information structure. *Cognition, 78,* 247–276.

Girotto, V. & Gonzalez, M. (in press). Extensional reasoning about chances. In W. Schaeken, G. De Vooght, A. Vandierendonck & G. d'Ydewalle (eds), *Mental Model Theory: Extensions and Refinements*. Mahwah, NJ: Erlbaum.

Girotto, V., Evans, J.St.B.T. & Legrenzi, P. (1996). Pseudodiagnosticity in hypothesis testing: a focussing phenomenon. Paper presented at the 3rd International Conference on Thinking, British Psychological Society, University College London, August 1996.

Goldvarg, Y. & Johnson-Laird, P.N. (2000). Illusions in modal reasoning. *Memory and Cognition, 28,* 282–294.

Hacking, I. (1975). *The Emergence of Probability*. Cambridge: Cambridge University Press.

Hertwig, R. & Chase, V.M. (1998). Many reasons or just one: How response mode affects reasoning in the conjunction problem. *Thinking and Reasoning, 4,* 319–352.

Hilton, D. (1995). The social context of reasoning: Conversational inference and rational judgement. *Psychological Bulletin, 118,* 248–271.

Johnson-Laird, P.N. (1994). Mental models and probabilistic thinking. *Cognition, 50,* 189–209.

Johnson-Laird, P.N. & Byrne, R.M.J. (1991). *Deduction*. Hillsdale, NJ: Erlbaum.

Johnson-Laird, P.N. & Byrne, R.M.J. (2002). Conditionals: A theory of meaning, pragmatics, and inference. *Psychological Review, 109,* 646–678.

Johnson-Laird, P.N. & Savary, F. (1999). Illusory inferences: A novel class of erroneous deductions. *Cognition, 71,* 191–229.

Johnson-Laird, P.N., Legrenzi, P., Girotto, V., Legrenzi, M. & Caverni, J.-P. (1999). Naive probability: A model theory of extensional reasoning. *Psychological Review, 106,* 62–88.

Kahneman, D. & Tversky, A. (1996). On the reality of cognitive illusions: A reply to Gigerenzer's critique. *Psychological Review, 103,* 582–591.

Kahneman, D. & Tversky, A. (1973). On the psychology of prediction. *Psychological Review, 80,* 237–251.

Kahneman, D., Slovic, P. & Tversky, A. (eds) (1982). *Judgment Under Uncertainty: Heuristics and Biases*. Cambridge: Cambridge University Press.

Koehler, J.J. (1996). The base-rate fallacy reconsidered: Descriptive, normative and methodological challenges. *Behavioral and Brain Sciences, 19,* 1–53.

Kroger, J.K., Cohen, J.D. & Johnson-Laird, P.N. (2002). A double dissociation between logic and mathematics, Under submission.

Legrenzi, P., Girotto, V. & Johnson-Laird, P.N. (1993). Focussing in reasoning and decision-making. *Cognition, 49,* 37–66.

Macchi, L. (1995). Pragmatic aspects of the base-rate fallacy. *Quarterly Journal of Experimental Psychology, 48A,* 188–207.

Miyamoto, J., Gonzalez, R. & Tu, S. (1995). Compositional anomalies in the semantics of evidence. In J.R. Busemeyer, R. Hastie & D.L. Medin (eds), *Decision Making from the Perspective of Cognitive Psychology* (pp. 319–383). Psychology of Learning and Motivation, vol. 32. New York: Academic Press.

Montague, R. (1974). *Formal Philosophy: Selected Papers*. New Haven, CT: Yale University Press.

Neth, H. & Johnson-Laird, P.N. (1999). The search for counterexamples in human reasoning. In *Proceedings of the Twenty-First Annual Conference of the Cognitive Science Society*, p. 806.

Nickerson, S. (1996). Ambiguities and unstated assumptions in probabilistic reasoning. *Psychological Bulletin, 120*, 410–433.

Oakhill, J., Garnham, A. & Johnson-Laird, P.N. (1990). Belief bias effects in syllogistic reasoning. In K.J. Gilhooly, M.T.G. Keane, R.H. Logie & G. Erdos (eds), *Lines of Thinking*, vol. 1 (pp. 125–138). London: Wiley.

Ormerod, T.C., Manktelow, K.I. & Jones, G.V. (1993). Reasoning with three types of conditional: Biases and mental models. *Quarterly Journal of Experimental Psychology, 46A*, 653–678.

Phillips, L. & Edwards, W. (1966). Conservatism in a simple probability inference task. *Journal of Experimental Psychology, 72*, 346–354.

Rips, L. (1994). *The Psychology of Proof*. Cambridge, MA: MIT Press.

Schaeken, W.S., Johnson-Laird, P.N. & d'Ydewalle, G. (1996). Mental models and temporal reasoning. *Cognition, 60*, 205–234.

Shimojo, S. & Ichikawa, S. (1989). Intuitive reasoning about probability: Theoretical and experimental analyses of the "problem of three prisoners". *Cognition, 32*, 1–24.

Sloutsky, V.M. & Goldvarg, Y. (2000). Representation and recall of determinate and indeterminate problems. Under submission.

Stevenson, R.J. & Over, D.E. (1995). Deduction from uncertain premises. *Quarterly Journal of Experimental Psychology, 48A*, 613–643.

Tversky, A. & Kahneman, D. (1983). Extensional versus intuitive reasoning: The conjunction fallacy in probability judgment. *Psychological Review, 90*, 293–315.

Tversky, A. & Koehler, D.J. (1994). Support theory: A nonextensional representation of subjective probability. *Psychological Review, 101*, 547–567.

CHAPTER 9

The *Partitive* Conditional Probability

Laura Macchi
University of Milan, Italy

INTRODUCTION

"Consider the following two phrases:

(1) The death-rate among men is twice that for women;
(2) In the deaths registered last month there were twice as many men as women.

Are these two different ways of saying the same or are these different events? In fact, they are different events" (Lindley, 1985, p. 44). The two phrases describe two probabilities completely different connected to the same pair of events, respectively: p(Death/Men) and p(Men/Death).[1] In the first phrase, the uncertainty is about the mortality, given the gender, in the second one, the uncertainty is about the gender, given the mortality. While the second implies that p(M/D) is equal to 2/3, the first does not.[2] The confusion between these two notions is a very common phenomenon, and has great implications for reasoning and decision making. The main question is about the nature of this confusion and, consequently, the understanding and the use of the conditional probability. The aim of the present chapter is to investigate this phenomenon via another well-known and related phenomenon, the base-rate fallacy.

The study of conditional probability has been an important topic in the last few decades. One crucial experimental task consists of two types of information: the base rate (in the following example, the incidence of the illness) and likelihoods (hit rate and false alarms, based on the proportion of sick and healthy people with a positive mammography). An example of this kind of task (Gigerenzer & Hoffrage, 1995) is the disease problem, which follows:

---

[1] (1) p(D/M) = 2p(D/F);
  (2) P(M/D) = 2p(F/D)
P(M/D) = 2/3
but (1) does not imply p(D/M) = 2/3
[2] Except when the number of men and women is the same.

Thinking: Psychological Perspectives on Reasoning, Judgment and Decision Making. Edited by David Hardman and Laura Macchi.
© 2003 John Wiley & Sons, Ltd.

> The probability of breast cancer is 1% for women at age forty who participate in routine screening.
>   If a woman has breast cancer, the probability is 80% that she will get a positive mammography. If a woman does not have breast cancer, the probability is 9.6% that she will also get a positive mammography.
>   A woman in this age group had a positive mammography in a routine screening. What is the probability that she actually has breast cancer? ——%

To assess the requested probability, it is first necessary to consider 80 per cent (the probability that someone who has breast cancer will get a positive mammography, p(pos/ca)) of 1 per cent (the probability of having the breast cancer, p(ca)). It is then possible to determine the probability of getting a positive mammography and having breast cancer − p(pos & ca) = 0.8 per cent, or not having breast cancer − 9.6 per cent, p(pos/no ca), of 99 per cent, the p(no ca) = 9.5 per cent (p(pos & no ca)). Then consider the proportion of cases of breast cancer and positive mammography (0.8 per cent) among all of the cases of positive mammography (0.8 per cent + 9.5 per cent = 10.3 per cent, then 0.8/10.3 = 0.07). According to Bayes' theorem:

$$p(ca/pos) = \frac{p(pos/ca)\,p(ca)}{p(pos/ca)\,p(ca) + p(pos/no\ ca)\,p(no\ ca)}$$

$$= \frac{p(pos\ \&\ ca)}{p(pos\ \&\ ca) + P(pos\ \&no\ ca)} = \frac{(.80)(.01)}{(.80)(.01) + (.096)(.99)} = \frac{.008}{.103} = .077$$

In reasoning with problems of this type, people typically ignore the incidence of the disease and focus their attention on the likelihood of cancer given a positive test result, giving rise to the well-known phenomenon of base-rate neglect.

According to the heuristics and biases model, reasoning is guided by heuristic modes of thought that simplify judgments (Tversky & Kahneman, 1974). Heuristics may be useful in many circumstances, but also may cause a systematic departure from normatively correct performance, referred to as a "bias" (Kahneman, Slovic & Tversky, 1982; Bar-Hillel, 1983; Leddo, Abelson & Gross, 1984; Locksley & Stangor, 1984; Wells, 1985; Shafir, Smith & Osherson, 1990; Kahneman & Tversky, 1996). In this kind of task, the implicated heuristic principle could be said to be specificity (that is, more importance is given to specific information) and/or causality (that is, the base rate has no causal relevance) (Casscells et al., 1978; Eddy, 1982; Tversky & Kahneman, 1982; Bar-Hillel, 1990).

The traditional research programme supporting the heuristic thesis has been opposed by two main perspectives: the *frequentist* approach (Gigerenzer & Murray, 1987; Fiedler, 1988; Gigerenzer, Hell & Blank, 1988; Gigerenzer, 1991; Gigerenzer & Hoffrage, 1995; Cosmides & Tooby, 1996; Hertwig & Gigerenzer, 1999) and the *pragmatic* approach (Adler, 1984; Morier & Borgida, 1984; Ginossar e Trope, 1987; Macdonald & Gilhooly, 1990; Dulany & Hilton, 1991; Politzer & Noveck, 1991; Levinson, 1995; Macchi, 1995, 2000; Schwarz, 1996; Hilton, 1997; Mosconi & Macchi, 2001).

According to the frequentist approach the errors identified by the heuristics and biases programme are due to the fact that probability (percentage) is applied to single events or relative frequencies rather than to sequences of observable events. For example, in base-rate problems, the difference lies in the contrast between a statement such as "The probability that Mr X has the disease is 1 per cent " and "One out of the 100 people has the disease". The latter statement is frequentist and is considered to be much closer to the intuitive method of reasoning in conditions of uncertainty. Difficulties with base-rate problems are said to be caused by the probabilistic formulation of the single-case-oriented information. By giving classical problems a frequentist format, several authors have obtained a reduction in the number of classical errors (e.g., Gigerenzer & Hoffrage, 1995; Cosmides and Tooby, 1996). Similar reductions have been obtained for studies involving the conjunction fallacy (Fiedler, 1988; Reeves & Lockhart, 1993; Jones, Jones & Frisch, 1995; Hertwig & Gigerenzer, 1997).

The other critical approach, the pragmatic approach to the psychology of thinking and reasoning (for reviews, see Politzer, 1986; Hilton, 1995; Politzer & Macchi, 2000) has been able to change perspective and solve questions about old research paradigms (see Macchi, 1995, for Kahneman & Tversky's cab problem; Dulany & Hilton, 1991; Mosconi & Macchi, 2001; Politzer & Noveck, 1991, for the conjunction fallacy; Politzer, 2003, for conditional reasoning in context; van der Henst, Sperber & Politzer, 2002, for relational reasoning; Mosconi, 1990, for problem solving; Politzer, 1993, for the class inclusion question in children; Sperber, Cara & Girotto, 1995; Girotto et al., 2001, for Wason's selection task). By "pragmatic approach", we do not refer to the sheer acknowledgement of, or concern about, the effect of context or of world knowledge. It is now widely agreed that such factors affect performance (see, for instance, the meeting on "Pragmatics and Reasoning" of the British Psychological Society, London, 1996). Our view is more radical. We believe that every experimental task can be submitted to a pragmatic examination. It consists of an analysis of the perceptual[3] or linguistic stimuli that constitute the problem in order to make sure that they convey the meaning intended by the experimenter (particularized implicatures evoked in a specific context, or generalized implicatures as may occur when dealing with connectives or quantifiers (Grice, 1989). The analysis consists also of identifying the representation of the task, the intention and the state of knowledge of the experimenter, and of the skill that is required for the solution of the task. Thus, this latter analysis focuses on the special relationship between experimenter and participant. What is of interest to the experimenter (often the logical correctness) is not always clear to the participant; he or she may make attributions that lead to an experimental outcome that differs from the experimenter's expectations. If this occurs without being detected by the experimenter, the interpretation of the task by the participant will cause misinterpretation of the results by the experimenter (Politzer & Macchi, 2002). In particular, for the kind of problems mentioned above, a pragmatic analysis of the text has identified a particular discursive formulation of the likelihood term as the cause of the base-rate fallacy, rather than an intrinsic difficulty with Bayesian reasoning (Macchi, 1995, 2000; Macchi & Mosconi, 1998). Our own interpretation is also intended as a critical review of the heuristic approach and suggests a different explanation for the facilitation achieved with frequentist versions of base-rate tasks.

A PRAGMATICS PERSPECTIVE: THE PARTITIVE HYPOTHESIS

We propose that neither heuristic nor frequentist factors underlie the occurrence or elimination of the base-rate fallacy. What is crucial, given that all of the other elements of

---

[3] The information submitted to a pragmatic analysis is not necessarily linguistic, but it can also be visual stimuli (see, for instance, the studies by Mosconi on Mayer's virtual square (Mosconi, 1990)).

difficulty are the same (Macchi & Mosconi, 1998), is the presence or absence of a particular formulation of the likelihood information. This formulation, which I call *partitive*, consists of defining the set of which the datum (expressed in percentage or frequency terms) represents a part, and then relativizing its numerical content. Thus, the statement, "80 per cent of the people affected by the disease . . . have a positive mammography", defines the proportion (or subset) of the population with the disease (that is, the base-rate probability) and possessing particular properties (having a positive mammography). Specifically, this wording clearly indicates the relationships among the probabilities relating to the subsets that are a basic condition for Bayesian reasoning. This kind of formulation seems to express the intrinsic nature of a conditional probability, which conditions an event (A) to the occurrence of another one (B). Then it represents the cases in which, given the occurrence of B, A also happens. In other words, the subset which is the conjunction of two sets of events (A and B) indicates what is A and what is B without ambiguities.[4]

When such a formulation is used, be it in terms of percentages as relative frequencies, or ratio or natural sampling frequencies, it communicates the independence of the hit rate from the base rate. This is a crucial assumption for proper Bayesian analysis (Birnbaum, 1983), because the a posteriori probability P(H/D) is calculated on the basis of the base rate and is therefore dependent upon it. If the hit rate depended on the base rate, it would already include it and, if this were the case, we would already have the a posteriori probability, and it would be unnecessary to consider the base rate itself. This is what often underlies the base-rate fallacy, which consists of a failure to consider the base rate, as a result of the privileging of hit-rate information. In my view, the confusion sometimes generated between the hit rate and a posteriori probability is due to an ambiguous formulation of conditional probability or, in other words, to the absence of a partitive formulation.

If this is true, the partitive formulation has the triple effect of identifying the data reference set, eliminating confusion (by showing the independence of the data), and making it possible to perceive and make use of the relationships among the data. In this light, previous attempts to explain both shortcomings in Bayesian reasoning (Tversky & Kahneman, 1980) and correct Bayesian reasoning (Gigerenzer & Hoffrage, 1995) do not depend on the principles proposed by the authors (respectively, judgmental heuristics and frequency formats) but on the partitive expression of the hit rate.

Consistent with this perspective, we proposed the following four hypotheses:

(1) Partitive formulations prevent the confusion of probabilities (Macchi, 1995).
(2) There is no performance difference resulting from texts formulated in frequencies versus percentages (and also ratio terms), provided that these are partitive.
(3) Both frequencies (if partitive) and percentages (relative frequencies) lead to performances that are different and better than those obtained with versions relating to single events (Tversky & Kahneman, 1980) insofar as these are not partitive.[5]
(4) Even when probabilities are expressed in terms of frequency, the elimination of the partitive formulation leads to the re-emergence of reasoning errors.

---

[4] An ambiguity that, according to our hypotheses, is intrinsically connected to the single case expression of the likelihood.
[5] In this last case, an idea is given of the extent of effect or the impact of a property, but not of the relationship between them. This would explain the difficulties encountered in using Bayesian reasoning in the classical experiments based on this type of formula.

Table 9.1 Forecasts according to the theory of the partitive formulation

Partitive (Bayesian reasoning)

Probabilistic	Frequentist	Ratio
Problem type		
"15% of the cabs are blue... 80% of the blue cabs...".	"10 out of every 1000 cabs are blue 8 out of every 10 are..."	"Suicide attempts... Suicide attempts that result in death"
(Macchi, 1995)	(Gigerenzer & Hoffrage, 1995) "1 out of every 1000 50 out of every 1000" (Cosmides & Tooby, 1996)	(Tversky & Kahneman, 1980)

Non-partitive (base-rate fallacy)

Probabilistic	Frequentist	Ratio
Problem type		
"there is 80% probability that he/she...".	"10 out of every 1000 cabs are blue 80 out of every 100 are..."	"Suicide attempts... deaths by suicide"
(Tversky & Kahneman, 1980) (Casscells et al., 1978)	(Gigerenzer & Hoffrage, 1995)	(Macchi, 1995)
	"85 out of every 1000 50 out of every 1000" (Macchi & Mosconi, 1998)	

NON-PARTITIVE FORMULATIONS AS THE ORIGIN OF THE CONFUSION OF CONDITIONAL PROBABILITIES

Using the classical "cab" and "suicide" problems devised by Tversky and Kahneman (1980), it has been shown (Macchi, 1995) that the base-rate fallacy is much reduced (to 35 per cent of participants) or virtually disappears (to less than 10 per cent) when the the text makes clear which is the reference class for the relative frequency (the partitive formulation) (Table 9.1). This was achieved by modifying some of the textual elements hiding the independence of the data, without changing the specificity and causality (natural heuristics) of the information. Moreover, by introducing these textual elements into "causal" versions that normally do not produce the fallacy (Tversky & Kahneman, 1980), it was possible to generate the fallacy in causal problems.

Our analysis of the text problems used in the literature has identified differences that were not considered by the original researchers, but which can be held to be responsible for the appearance or otherwise of the fallacy.[6] On the basis of our research, we argued that the crucial factor for considering or neglecting the base rate is the diagnostic information— which, like conditional probabilities, can be confused with posterior probability (see Macchi, 1995, in relation to the "cab" and "suicide" problems) or random probability (cf. Macchi and Girotto, 1994, in relation to the "three boxes" problem).

---

[6] This chapter studies the textbook experimental paradigm, defined by Bar-Hillel (1983) as the study of problems in which both pieces of information are given: the base rate and the specific information. The case of the social judgment paradigm is different and deserves separate treatment.

According to the "confusion" hypothesis (Cohen, 1981; Eddy, 1982; Dawes, 1986; Hamm & Miller, 1988; Braine et al., 1990), participants confuse the conditional probability of the accuracy of a specific item of information (that is, the probability of observing a particular datum given that one hypothesis is true: P(D/H)) with the inverse conditional probability P(H/D), that is, that the focal hypothesis is true given that a particular datum has been observed). These authors attribute the confusion to people's inherent inability to understand the difference between these two conditional probabilities.

However, as participants are capable of distinguishing these two types of probability in many other contexts (cf. Bar-Hillel, 1990; Thuring & Jungermann, 1990), it can be argued that the confusion may depend less on a natural tendency to err and more on an ambiguous transmission of information due to the structure of the text (cf. Lindley, 1985). If there is a fundamental confusion, a textual variation that does not alter the nature of the conditional probability should not have any effect on the final evaluation of the participants.

In fact, it has been shown (Macchi, 1995) that diagnostic (specific) information concerning likelihood can be mistaken for a posterior probability as a consequence of: (i) the formulation of the question (when it refers only to the specific information); (ii) the formulation of the likelihood (as if it were already the result of its combination with the prior probability).

Here we shall consider only the formulation of the likelihood, some examples of which are given below.

Cab (short version of the original problem; non-partitive version)
[...] The witness made correct identifications in *80 per cent of the cases* and erred in 20 per cent of the cases.

Cab (partitive version)

[...] The witness recognized as blue *80 per cent of the blue cabs* and mistook 20 per cent of the green cabs for blue cabs.

Suicide (causal version by Tversky and Kahneman, 1980; partitive version)

In a population of adolescents, 80 per cent of *suicide attempts* are made by girls, and 20 per cent by boys. The percentage of *suicide attempts that result in death* is three times higher among boys than among girls.

Suicide (causal, non-partitive version)

In a population of *adolescents who attempted suicide*, 80 per cent are girls, and 20 per cent boys. The percentage of *deaths by suicide* is three times higher among boys who attempted suicide than among girls.

Macchi (1995) found that about 70 per cent of participants gave Bayesian answers with the partitive versions (74 per cent with the cab problem; 66 per cent with the suicide problem) compared to only about 30 per cent with the non-partitive versions (32 per cent with the cab problem; 27 per cent with the suicide problem).

A pragmatic analysis of the text problems used in the literature revealed differences between those problems which induce the bias and those problems which do not. These differences are not linked to the heuristics but concern the pragmatic structure of the texts; in particular, the text problems revealing bias (the non-partitive problems) seem to obscure the independence relation insofar as they do not clearly indicate the sets to which the data refer.

AN EXPERIMENTAL COMPARISON BETWEEN PARTITIVE AND NON-PARTITIVE TEXTS WITH DIFFERENT PROBABILISTIC FORMATS

EXPERIMENT—The Diploma Problem and the Diagnoses Problem

To test further the partitive hypothesis, we formulated (Macchi, 2000) the following problem:

Diploma Problem

Some 360 out of every 1000 students who sit their high-school diploma fail. Seventy-five per cent of the students who are not awarded a diploma fail the written Italian paper. However, 20 per cent of the students who are awarded a diploma also fail the written Italian paper. What percentage of those who fail the written Italian paper are not awarded a diploma?

Method

Participants

The problem was submitted to 180 undergraduates aged between 18 and 25 years. Participants received only one problem in booklet form, and were asked to give a written answer and explain their reasoning. There was no time limit.

Materials and procedure

Two groups of partitive and non-partitive versions of the same problem were created (see Appendix 9.1).

The *partitive* versions were as follows:

(1) a control frequency format text (partitive frequency [PF]) following the formulaic layout of the texts of Gigerenzer and Hoffrage (1995), which, on the basis of our analysis, has a partitive structure
   "[. . .] 270 out of every 360 students [. . .]"
(2) a partitive probabilistic version (partitive probability [PP]) involving relative frequency
   "[. . .] 75 per cent of the students who are [. . .]"
(3) a variation of the PP text (PPbis), in which also the base rate was given in percentage form in order to examine the effect of its form of expression (frequentist vs. percentage)
   "36 per cent of the students who sit their high-school diploma fail.
   75 per cent of the students who are not awarded a diploma fail the written Italian paper.
   [. . .]"
(4) a super partitive probability (SP) version—the formulation was "super-partitive" in the sense that it added a reference to the size of the sample ("75 per cent of the 360 students who fail") to the partitive formulation adopted in version PP ("75 per cent of the students

Table 9.2 Bayesian or quasi-Bayesian answers versus "other responses"

	Partitive		Super-P		Non-partitive	
	PF $n = 30$	PP $n = 30$	PPbis $n = 30$	SP $n = 30$	NPF $n = 30$	NPP $n = 30$
RB RQB	22 (74%)	21 (72%)	20 (68%)	27 (92%)	4 (13%)	9 (31%)
Other	8 (26%)	9 (28%)	10 (32%)	3 (8%)	26 (87%)	21 (69%)

Table 9.3 Solutions produced to non-partitive versus partitive versions

	Partitive		Super-P		Non-partitive	
	PF $n = 30$	PP $n = 30$	PPbis $n = 30$	SP $n = 30$	NPF $n = 30$	NPP $n = 30$
Bayesian answers	12	10	11	12	1	2
Pseudo-Bayesian answers	10	11	9	15	3	7
Base rate						3
Hit (freq. or rates)	2	2	3	1	4	5
False alarm						
Other	6	7	7	1	17	11
No answer				1	5	2

who fail"). The aim was to investigate the facilitating effect of indicating a numerical reference to the size of the sample given in text PF.

The *non-partitive* versions were as follows:

(1) a non-partitive frequency format (non-partitive frequency [NPF]) that was identical to the PF text except for its non-partitive formulation
"[. . .] 750 out of every 1000 students [. . .]"
(2) a non-partitive probabilistic (single-case) version NPP
"[. . .] there is a 75 per cent probability that he [. . .]".

Results

As shown in Tables 9.2 and 9.3, there was a significant difference (chi-square (1 df) = 47.06, $p < 0.001$) between the results obtained using the partitive and non-partitive texts, even though they should invoke the same heuristics, and regardless of whether or not they had a frequentist formulation. Our results do not support the approach that attributes the base-rate fallacy to certain heuristics (specificity, causality, etc.), but, like those of our previous studies (Macchi, 1995), they show that the use or otherwise of Bayesian reasoning to solve problems based on the same heuristics depends exclusively on the indicated partitive element. Furthermore, the fact that problems with a frequentist formulation in partitive format produced a high percentage of Bayesian responses, whereas, in non-partitive format, they produced a high percentage of *non*-Bayesian responses, implies that a frequentist formulation is not the crucial element for eliciting correct reasoning.

Table 9.2 shows the almost total coincidence of the percentages of Bayesian and quasi-Bayesian responses (that is, those demonstrating Bayesian reasoning even if the numerical answer is not correct,[7] cf. Cosmides & Tooby, 1996) in the partitive texts (PF, PP, PPbis). This occurred despite the fact that they differed in terms of their expression of probabilities as frequencies (PF), or percentages and probabilities (PP and PPbis). This confirms our second hypothesis, that there is no difference in performance between texts formulated in frequentist or percentage terms provided that these are partitive.

About 70 per cent (68–75 per cent) of the participants used Bayesian reasoning. In all three partitive groups, about one-half of this 70 per cent (see Table 9.2) gave the Bayesian answer ($270/270 + 128 = 270/398$), whereas the other half responded in a quasi-Bayesian manner. Between 25 and 30 per cent (just under 30 per cent) of the participants responded differently. None of them gave an answer corresponding only to the base rate, and one or two participants per group responded exclusively on the basis of the hit rate (a response that is very frequent in the case of participants who neglect the base rate because they confuse conditional probabilities). This confirms our first hypothesis, that partitive formulations prevent the confusion of probabilities.

About 20 per cent of the participants answered in a way that could only be included in a category called "other responses" because their heterogeneous nature meant that they could not be placed in any significant subgroupings (for details, see Macchi, 2000).

The PPbis condition was included in order to ensure that the predicted high percentage of Bayesian responses did not depend on the expression of the base rate as a frequency (see Hoffrage et al., in press), but on the use of a partitive formulation. According to Hoffrage et al., "providing the total sample (1000 women [or students]) serves as a starting point to mimic the procedure of natural sampling, thereby facilitating computational demands considerably" (p. 10). In reality, the results overlapped with those of PP, indicating that the use of a frequentist expression of the base rate was not responsible for Bayesian reasoning.

Finally, the SP text was considered super-partitive in the sense that it indicates the size of the samples (like the PF text), and adds this information to that already included in the formulation of PP, which clarifies which samples are to be considered. Almost all of the participants (92 per cent) solved the problem adequately, which shows that Bayesian reasoning can be used when the relationship between the different elements of information is clear (as in PP), but is facilitated when the numerical size of what were previously merely named samples is explicitly indicated. This indication is the same as that adopted by Gigerenzer and Hoffrage (1995) in the text formats that we reproduced in our PF text. It is interesting to note that, in contrast with the conclusions drawn by Gigerenzer and Hoffrage, the expression of probability in terms of percentages actually leads to better results than those obtained when the same information is given in terms of frequencies (SP vs. PF), despite the fact that SP involves an additional computational step.

Responses to the non-partitive texts were markedly different from responses to the partitive texts. The non-partitive frequency text (text NPF) elicited Bayesian responses from

---

[7] Bayesian were correct while "quasi-Bayesian" answers were those where the right combination of base rate and hit rate (D and H) and base rate and false alarms (D and not-H) were used, but without the final ratio (D and H/D).

Table 9.4   Verdicts and means for evidence strength, P(Source), and
P(Guilt) as a function of target and size of reference class: Experiment 1

Condition	Evidence strength (1–7)	P(source)	P(guilt)	Verdict (% guilty)
Single target				
Small reference class	3.9	.529	.514	.262
Large reference class	4.1	.592	.580	.204
Multi target				
Small reference class	3.9	.522	.496	.218
Large reference class	3.5	.340	.349	.094

Cell sizes range from 101 to 118.

just 11 per cent of respondents, thus confirming our fourth hypothesis that a frequency formulation is not sufficient to promote Bayesian reasoning. The non-partitive single-case text (NPP) elicited Bayesian solutions from just 31 per cent of respondents. This confirms our third hypothesis that the partitive frequentist (PF) and partitive percentage texts (PP) would lead to a higher proportion of correct answers than the single-case version (NPP) because the latter is not partitive, and not because it is probabilistic (as this is also a characteristic of text PP). Moreover, contrary to the claims of the frequentist approach, the use of percentages does not worsen but, if anything, slightly improves performance—as can be seen when we compare the proportion of Bayesian answers to texts NPF (11 per cent) and NPP (31 per cent).

Table 9.4 shows a breakdown of the answers classified as "other replies", and it is interesting to see that both texts led to a certain frequency of answers (respectively, 6 out of 17 and 6 out of 11), in which only the hit rate and false alarms were combined (by means of subtraction or addition), and the base rate was completely ignored. This appears to confirm the hypothesis that a non-partitive formulation hinders an appreciation of the independence of the two items of data, and, consequently, the need to consider the base rate is not appreciated. The failure to perceive the relationship between the data, and the consequent tendency to assume that they are dependent, means that the hit rates and false alarms may be added or subtracted, but the base rate is in any case ignored.

A further confirmation of these results is given by similar results obtained with the disease problem (see text problem at page 166). The comparison again was between a partitive probability and non-partitive probability text. As is shown in Table 9.4, the Bayesian answers were, respectively, 65 per cent and 15 per cent (see Appendix 9.2) (chi-square (1 df) $= 47.06$, $p < 0.001$).

CONSIDERATIONS ON FREQUENCY FORMAT AND NATURAL SAMPLING

By "natural sampling", Gigerenzer and Hoffrage mean: "The sequential acquisition of information by updating event frequencies without artificially fixing the marginal frequencies (e.g., of disease or no-disease cases)" (1995, p. 686). They consider the natural sampling (1995) or natural frequency (1999) to be only those frequencies that stem from one reference set, and they distinguish them from "normalized frequencies" (that is, fixing the marginal frequencies). In the disease problem, for instance, the initial base rate ("10 out of 1000 women have a disease") is progressively updated with the indication that 8 out of these "10 women" have a positive mammography, not considering another marginal frequency (different from 10).

The response of these authors to many criticisms of their model is that almost all the counterexamples shown in the literature are effective for the frequency format (marginal frequency), but not for the natural frequency or sampling format (Hoffrage et al., in press).

What I have shown here is that the natural frequency format is not essential to elicit Bayesian reasoning. Correct reasoning is obtained with partitive formats, whether probabilistic or frequentist, and what they call natural sampling is no different from a partitive frequency format (PF in our notation). An explanation given by Hoffrage et al. (in press) to the finding that partitive probability versions can be solved easily is that the base rate is expressed as a "definite one large sample" in frequencies. However, given that the same percentages of correct answers were obtained when the base rate was expressed in probabilities, clearly, this is not the case (see version PPbis of the reported experiment; see also Macchi, 1995).

Closer analysis of the texts themselves show that the partitive texts include differences that make the PP text (the one that adopts percentages and relative frequencies) more suitable for the study of Bayesian reasoning than frequentist texts of type PF ("natural sampling", in the words of Gigerenzer and Hoffrage, 1995), despite the fact that they produce the same percentage of correct answers. In the latter case, the relationships among the data are revealed by the fact that the coincident samples (or subsets) of natural sampling versions remove the need for computation. The data are actually *dependent* on the base rate because they are not provided in the form:

P(A/B) or P(A/not B)

to be multiplied by their related base rates

P(B) or P(not B)

but already as

P(A and B) = P(A/B) P(B)

The crucial part of the Bayesian calculation (and reasoning), which consists precisely of the need to weigh the data concerning the hit rate and the false alarm rate with their base rates of P(B) and P(not B), is eliminated. The base rate of P(B) is totally irrelevant when the data are given in the form P(A and B), because it is already "contained" in the received information, whereas the base rate is relevant in the case of problems such as version PP or NPP, which are generally used in studies of the base-rate fallacy (e.g., Tversky & Kahneman, 1980).

Gigerenzer and Hoffrage say that natural sampling is the intuitive method of reasoning, but if Bayesian reasoning can also be obtained with relative frequencies, this is no longer true. Rather, a positive result (a high percentage of Bayesian answers) does not depend on the natural sampling frequency formulation but on the partitive element it shares with PP.

Cosmides and Tooby (1996) have formulated another version of the disease problem which, while not even being in "natural sampling" format, still obtains quite a high ratio of Bayesian answers (about 70 per cent with experts and about 50 per cent with naive participants). The prevalence of the disease was described as "1 out of every 1000", and the hit rate was 100 per cent (all genuine cases are identified), but "out of every 1000 people who are perfectly healthy, 50 of them test positive for the disease". Note that if this problem was intended to convey natural frequencies, the false alarm rate should be "50 out of 999 healthy people" and not, as in the text, "50 out of 1000".

As with the text used by Gigerenzer and Hoffrage, what has been changed in comparison with the versions expressing percentage probabilities is not only the formulation of the probability (here given in frequencies), but also the provision of the formula P(D and H) rather than P(D/H).[8] This case is particularly delicate insofar as it requires the use of a proportion that takes the base rate into account

$$50 : 1000 = x : 999 \tag{1}$$

but, being a limit case, this is totally superfluous. If the base rate is equal to 1 out of 1000, 999 (the number of healthy people in relation to which the number of false positives must be recalculated) is so close to 1000 that it is possible to consider the number of false positives in the population as about 50, thus avoiding any calculation. Actually:

$$x = \frac{50 \times 999}{1000} = 49.9 \tag{2}$$

As in the case of Gigerenzer and Hoffrage, the sample to which the specific information relates concerning false alarms (50 out of *1000*) is almost identical to that of the base rate (*999*); given that we are dealing with frequencies, this makes use of the base rate virtually redundant. To distinguish the effect of a general frequency format from the effect of the particular frequency format which is represented by "natural sampling" (which, according to our thesis, is just a form of partitive frequency format), it was necessary to disentangle the two formats, creating versions in which the sizes of the marginal frequencies were not identical to those of the base rate. This aim was realized with two experimental tools: changing the base rate (version 1, Macchi & Mosconi, 1998) and changing the false alarms rates (version 2) (see Appendix 9.3).

If the base rate is not the limit case but, for instance, 85, instead of 1, out of 1000 (version 1), then the proportion has to be based on 915 (which is less close to 1000 than 999). This means that it is necessary to perform a computation that is in all senses equivalent to that which would need to be made in the case of percentages, and so it is possible to distinguish a correct Bayesian response from the other (apparently correct) responses— something that cannot be done with the problem used by Cosmides and Tooby:

$$50 : 1000 = X : 915 \tag{3}$$

$$X = \frac{50 \times 915}{1000} = 45.75 \tag{4}$$

This means that the number of false positives in a population of 915 healthy participants would be 46, and that the probability that a person with a positive test result is actually affected by the disease is

$$P((ca/pos) = \frac{85}{85 + 46} = \frac{85}{131} = 0.65 \text{ or "85 out of 131"} \tag{5}$$

---

[8] P(D and H) is "50 out of 1000" instead of P(D/H), which could have been, for instance, "5 out of 100".

With version 1, which—apart from the base rate—was identical to Cosmides and Tooby's original version (including the frequency format), the percentage of Bayesian answers to this version (3 per cent) was significantly lower than the 40 per cent observed in the case of Cosmides and Tooby's version (chi-square $= 6.2$; $p < .05$).

Version 1

85 out of 1000 Americans have disease X
[...]

This confirms the hypothesis that the increase in the number of Bayesian answers between the probabilistic original version of the problem (Casscells et al.) and Cosmides and Tooby's version 1 is not due to the use of frequentist phrasing, but to computational simplification, produced by natural sampling.

If the sets are changed,[9] the same situation is created as with version NPF of the diploma problem, in which the data have to be transformed into percentages. In version NPF, (P(D/H) = "80 out of 100"), or in the version 1 of Macchi and Mosconi (1998) (P(H) = "85 out of 1000"), the difficulty arises because the frequencies relate to apparently unrelated samples of different sizes, which implies the use of a proportion.[10]

This procedure is the same as should be done with the percentages, but the presence of the samples here makes the task more difficult because they should be transformed into percentages. Although the set to which the datum refers is indicated, it is a set that is difficult to identify in numerical terms because of the different ranges of the hit rate in comparison with the base rate.

In conclusion, the partitive formulation (that is, the identification of the set to which the datum refers) allows the information to be correctly combined when there are no elements breaking the link between the data (for example, by setting all of the data to 1000) and thus making it difficult to identify the relationship between the datum and the base rate.

The use of frequencies themselves does not facilitate the task and, although the use of natural sampling does help, this already includes the base rates and can therefore say nothing about the base-rate use and the base-rate fallacy.

ON THE COMPLEMENTARITY OF CONDITIONAL PROBABILITIES

According to some authors (Girotto & Gonzales, 2001), the partitive formulation of conditional probabilities should not be sufficient to produce a change in the representation of this kind of Bayesian problem. In a study (exp. 6) whose authors formulated the likelihood in terms of relative frequencies, the percentages of Bayesian answers was not better than with the single-case formulation.

The task was the following:

---

[9] $80:1000 = x:100$ (6)
to provide the percentage or
360 out of 1000   (7)
750 out of 1000   (8)
$1000 - 360 = 640$ (9)
$750:1000 = x:640$ (10)
[10] The base rate changed from "1" and "999" to "85" and "915".

Version 3

Four per cent of the people were infected.
Seventy-five per cent of the infected people had a positive reaction to the test.
Twenty-five per cent of the uninfected people also had a positive reaction to the test.
Among people having a positive reaction, —— out of —— will have the infection.

Participants demonstrated a very low performance that was even inferior to the results previously produced with this kind of problem in the literature (e.g., Tversky and Kahneman, 1980; Koehler, 1996).

This example, which at first sight could seem to be a critical case for the partitive hypothesis, seems to be a very predictable result if we consider the particular percentages used. As in other notorious problems (see, for instance, the cabs problem of Tversky and Kahneman, 1980), this problem involves two complementary percentages that could lead to the formation of an illusory set in participants' minds. In the Girotto and Gonzales (2001) problem, the complementary probabilities are the people who had the positive reaction to the test, 75 per cent of whom are actually infected and 25 per cent of whom are uninfected. The complementary percentages then could encourage confusion of the two conditional probabilities, P(pos/infected) and P(infected/pos), as already shown for other problems (Macchi, 1995), contrasting the effect of the partitive formulation. An indirect confirmation of this interpretation of the results is given by the fact that most of the participants gave the hit rate as their answer.

To test this hypothesis, we ran an experiment in which, leaving all the rest the same, we eliminated the complementarity of the hit rate and of the false alarms. The changed items of information were as follows.

Version 4

[…]
Seventy-five per cent of the infected people had a positive reaction to the test.
Ten per cent of the uninfected people also had a positive reaction to the test.
[…]

With this text (version 4) 64 per cent of Bayesian answers were obtained, as compared with 35 per cent of quasi-Bayesian answers with the original text (version 3).

AN APPLICATION: THE USE OF DNA EVIDENCE IN LEGAL DECISION MAKING

The weight that people attach to low-probability evidence has emerged as a significant concern in the courtroom. Scientists routinely testify about low probabilities in cases involving discrimination, deceptive trade practices and forensic science (Gastwirth, 2000), yet relatively little is known about the impact of this testimony on jurors (National Research Council, 1996, pp. 6–33). Perhaps the most important and pervasive low-probability evidence arises in cases involving DNA matches between a criminal suspect and trace evidence from a crime scene. In these cases, scientists provide a random match probability (RMP) that identifies the frequency that the genetic profile occurs in some reference population. Error rate issues aside, the objective strength of the DNA match for determining the source of trace evidence is inversely proportional to the size of the RMP. However, we claimed that the perceived value of the match evidence depends on whether or not exemplars are readily available to jurors, and that this depends on the way the information is formulated. We investigated this in the context of two legal-decision-making experiments (Koehler & Macchi, 2003).

In our studies, we varied the presentation of the RMP to promote or discourage exemplar generation by legal decision makers. The study employed a fully crossed 2 (target: single, multi-) X 2 (frame: probability, frequency) X 2 (reference class: small, large), between-participants design. Jurors were provided with a two-page summary of a murder case in which DNA evidence recovered from the crime scene matched a suspect (RMP = 1 in 100 000). The cases were identical across the eight conditions except for the size of the reference class (500 vs. 5 000 000) and the wording of the DNA match statistic. We distinguished sharply between the form or *frame* of the statistic (probability vs. frequency), and whether the statistic *targets* a single person or a broader class (the not partitive version vs. the partitive one). We predicted that some statistical presentation effects may be due more to target than to frame. Target is crucial because it identifies a problem-relevant reference class. In the context of DNA match evidence, single targets ("the probability that the suspect would match the blood drops [DNA] if he were not their source is 0.1 per cent") foreclose access to a broad reference class of alternative suspects. This discourages exemplar production and thereby reduces concern that someone other than the matching suspect is the source of the trace evidence.[11] On the contrary, multitargets (or the partitive formulation of the information) ("0.1 per cent of the people in the town who are not the source would nonetheless match the blood drops") provide access to a broader reference class and induce an outside perspective. However, an outside perspective alone, with very low probabilities, is not sufficient to cue DNA match exemplars. The reference class must be large enough relative to the RMP to suggest that there are others in the class who share the matching DNA profile. If the product of the RMP and reference class size is less than one, exemplars are probably not cued, and even jurors who hold an outside perspective are unlikely to worry about whether someone other than the matching suspect is the source of the DNA.

As predicted, when the evidence was exemplar-conducive (that is, multitarget plus large reference class), jurors were relatively less impressed with the evidence and overall case against the suspect. We found a target X reference class interaction for evidence strength ($F(1, 433) = 5.51$, $p = .019$), the two probability judgments ($F(2, 401) = 6.65$, $p = .001$) and verdict ($\chi^2 (1, n = 428) = 11.08$, $p = .002$). Follow-up univariate analyses on the probability judgments confirmed the interaction for P(source) ($F(1, 402) = 13.26$, $p < .001$) and P(guilt) ($F(1, 402) = 10.67$, $p = .001$). Conviction rates and the means for evidence strength, P(source) and P(guilt) for each condition appear in Table 9.4.

---

[11] This formulation, as those illustrated previously in this chapter (NPP), typically seems to induce a confusion with the posterior probability, and that produces the additional inference, according to which: given the RMP is 0.1 per cent, then the probability that he is the source of the blood drops not by chance (but because he is guilty) is 99.9 per cent.

The results supported our predictions and provide some insight into when and why people attach weight to low-probability events. Low-probability matching evidence that either invoked an inside view or that invoked an outside view but with a relatively small reference class, was treated as strong evidence. Jurors in these exemplar-unfriendly conditions generally believed that the defendant was the source of the DNA trace evidence and was guilty of the crime. This was not the case for jurors in the exemplar-friendly multitarget, large-reference-class conditions. Most of these jurors thought the defendant was not the source of the DNA and probably was not guilty of the crime. We suggest that this occurred because jurors in these groups realized that a 1 in 100 000 RMP, in combination with, for instance, a 5 000 000 member reference class, meant that there were almost certainly others in the population who would also match the DNA evidence. This theory received additional support from the jurors' written explanations which showed that jurors in the exemplar-friendly groups expressed more concern about others who might match the DNA than did jurors in the other groups.

We did not find that statistical frame (probability vs. frequency) interacted with reference class size to affect judgments. Our data support the fact that earlier reported differences between frequencies and single-event probabilities are probably due to differences in target rather than frame.

CONCLUSIONS

From the studies described here, the Bayesian use of conditional probabilities seems to be strictly connected to the formulation of them in terms of related partitions, as well as the partitive formulations. We suggest that it has not to be intended as a "cueing" or a facilitating way to express these data, but as a direct way to express them, intrinsically connected to the nature of this kind of probability and to its natural mental representation.

Actually, the comparison between partitive and non-partitive formulations shows that, regardless of whether the data are formulated in terms of percentages or frequencies (and using the same heuristic factors), the majority of the participants answer the partitive versions of the problem correctly and the non-partitive versions incorrectly. A chi-square test reveals that the association between correct responses and the partitive formulation is statistically significant ($p < 0.01$).

The results of this study indicate that the source of difficulty in certain types of probabilistic reasoning is related more to the structure of the text than to heuristic factors or the statistical format in which the probabilities are expressed (percentages vs. frequencies): that is, whether or not the text contains a *partitive* description of likelihood, which consists of defining the set of which the datum (expressed in percentage or frequency terms) represents a part, and then defining the proportion (or subset) of the population with particular properties (the base-rate probability). When such a formulation is used, be it in terms of percentages (relative frequencies), ratio or (natural sample) frequencies, it transmits the independence of the hit rate from the base rate. The partitive formulation thus has the triple effect of identifying the data reference set, eliminating confusion, and making it possible to perceive and make use of the relationships between the data.

We show here that there is no difference in performance between texts formulated in terms of frequencies, percentages or even ratios (see the suicide problem), provided that these are partitive. Both frequencies (if partitive) and percentages (relative frequencies) lead to performances that are different and better than those obtained using non-partitive versions relating to single events (Tversky & Kahneman, 1980). But even when probabilities are expressed in terms of frequency, the elimination of the partitive formulation leads to the re-emergence of error.

Indirect confirmation has been provided by Birnbaum and Mellers (1983), who showed that within-participant designs have a greater impact on the base rate than between-participant designs. In particular, in this case, the between-participant design uses what I would call a non-partitive text problem, whereas the within-participant design included it among a group of other texts that combined the use of frequencies with what I would call a partitive formulation of conditional probabilities. On the basis of my analyses, these earlier data indirectly confirm the effect of the partitive formulation.

In general, the idea that it is important to understand the relationship between items of information as parts of sets actually seems to be quite shared, although the explanations for it are very different (see Lewis & Keren, 1999; Mellers & McGraw, 1999; Krauss, Martignon & Hoffrage, 2000).

In a way which I feel to be very similar to my own approach, Krauss, Martignon and Hoffrage (2000) underline the importance of the relationships between subsets by speaking of the Markov frequencies that arise from the successive partitioning of a unique reference class. Markov frequencies allow Bayesian inference problems to be visualized even with an arbitrary number of cues. I would like to stress the convergence between our approaches if we consider the general idea of the "naturalness" of observing samples and their subsets. However, the partitive hypothesis seems to offer a more general explanation that is clearly consistent with this approach but can also explain the results obtained by use of probabilities, and this implies a reconsideration of their conclusion that frequency is more natural than probability.[12]

Lewis and Keren (1999) say that the use of frequency or probability statements, and the use of joint or conditional sampling information are examples of two different factors at work. They report an experiment with which they demonstrate that even with the use of frequency statements, Bayesian reasoning is more difficult with conditional than joint information. This is in line with my results (see text PF vs. NPF) but, also in this case, my explanation makes it possible to make forecasts even in relation to probabilistic versions. First of all, if, as Gigerenzer and Hoffrage (1999) reply, the explanation of the effect were joint statements, performance should also improve in the case of joint probabilities, but this does not happen. My explanation is that it is not a question of "joint" versus "standard", but partitive (which may be, *but is not necessarily*, in a "joint" format) versus non-partitive information. Consequently, if there is a joint statement in the probabilistic versions, but it is not clear which set is being referred to (something avoided by the use of a partitive formulation), the performances remain poor.

Finally, Mellers and McGraw (1999) argue that a natural sampling frequentist formulation facilitates understanding because it allows the construction of mental models of the elements of a set only in the case of rare events (that is, $p \leq 0.05$). In the case of more common

---

[12] Gigerenzer and Hoffrage (1995) argue that natural frequencies improve Bayesian performance because they carry information about the base rate and because computations are performed on natural numbers. In my present experiments, I got Bayesian performance *also* with percentages and without the base rate already contained in the information (see the PP case).

events, this difference does not exist and it is equally easy to construct relative mental models also with probabilities or systematic sampling (in which marginal frequencies differ from frequencies in the population). The obtained difference between probabilities and natural sampling using so-called rare events is once again not attributable to the difference between the frequentist and probabilistic formulations per se, but to a particular partitive frequentist formulation versus a particular non-partitive probabilistic formulation (corresponding to our versions PF vs. NPP).

On the basis of our results, we can also propose a final consideration concerning mental models theory. According to the theory, the difficulty also in probabilistic problems is related to the number of models and the degree to which the models are fleshed out, but, as the results of our experiment show, there are considerable differences in performance even when the number of models and the degree of their explicitness remain unchanged. The only differences in mental models for these problems are in the numerical tags attributed to the models. In the case of reasoning involving conditional probabilities, the theory hypothesizes another source of difficulty: "the need to represent the relation corresponding to a conditional probability. This problem is a special case of the general difficulty of constructing fully explicit models, which overtaxes the processing capacity of working memory" (Johnson-Laird et al., 1999, p. 42). Is it that grasping the relationship between models is an additional difficulty or is it a preliminary condition that causes an inability to "construct fully explicit models"? In other words, are the models not fully fleshed out because the relationships of their different elements are not correctly grasped, or is the failure to grasp their relationship due to the fact that the models are not fully fleshed out? In the second case, if the mental models are not fully fleshed out because reasoners do not represent the conditional relationship, this is not an explanation but a descriptive assertion: reasoning is difficult in the case of conditional probabilities because the conditional relation is not perceived or understood. The interesting question for me is why reasoners do not understand the conditional relationship, and whether this happens in general or only under certain conditions. In fact, it seems that this does not happen in general, and I have tried to indicate what I consider to be some of the crucial conditions governing the use of conditional probabilities.

APPENDIX 9.1 DIPLOMA PROBLEM

Partitive Texts

Partitive Frequency (PF)

Some 360 out of every 1000 students who sit their high-school diploma fail.
Some 270 out of every 360 students who are not awarded a diploma fail the written Italian paper.
However, 128 out of every 640 students who are awarded a diploma also fail the written Italian paper.
Here is a new representative sample of students who have failed the written Italian paper. How many of them do you expect not to be awarded a diploma? —— out of ——.

Partitive Probability (PP)

Some 360 out of every 1000 students who sit their high-school diploma fail.
Seventy-five per cent of the students who are not awarded a diploma fail the written Italian paper.
However, 20 per cent of the students students who are awarded a diploma also fail the written Italian paper.
What percentage of those who fail the written Italian paper are not awarded a diploma?

Super-Partitive (SP)

Some 360 out of every 1000 students who sit for their high-school diploma fail.
Seventy-five per cent of the 360 students who are not awarded a diploma fail the written Italian paper.
However, 20 per cent of the 640 students who are awarded a diploma also fail the written Italian paper.
What percentage of those who fail the written Italian paper are not awarded a diploma?

Non-Partitive Texts

Non-Partitive Frequency (NPF)

Some 360 out of every 1000 students who sit their high-school diploma fail.
Some 750 out of every 1000 students who are not awarded a diploma fail the written Italian paper.
However, 200 out of every 1000 students who are awarded a diploma also fail the written Italian paper.
Here is a new representative sample of students who have failed the written Italian paper.
How many of them do you expect not to be awarded a diploma? —— out of ——.

Non-Partitive Probability (NPP)

About 360 out of every 1000 students who sit their high-school diploma fail.
If a student is not awarded a diploma, there is a 75 per cent probability that he/she failed the written Italian paper.
However, even if a student is awarded a diploma, there is a 20 per cent probability that he/she failed the written Italian paper.
One student failed the written Italian paper. What is the probability that he or she was not awarded a diploma?

APPENDIX 9.2 DISEASE PROBLEM

Partitive Texts

Partitive Frequency (PF)

[. . .] 8 out of 10 women who have breast cancer will get a positive mammography. [. . .]

Partitive probability (PP)

[. . .] 80 per cent of women with breast cancer will get a positive mammography. [. . .]

Non-Partitive Texts

Non-Partitive Frequency (NPF)

[. . .] 80 of 100 women with breast cancer will get a positive mammography. [. . .]

Non-Partitive Probability (NPP)

[. . .] If a woman has breast cancer, the probability is 80 per cent that she will get a positive mammography. [. . .]

APPENDIX 9.3 DISEASE PROBLEM

Version 1

85 out of 1000 . . .
50 out of 1000 healthy . . .

Version 2

1 out of 1000 . . .
5 out of 100 healthy . . .

REFERENCES

Adler, J.E. (1984). Abstraction is uncooperative. *Journal for the Theory of Social Behavior*, *14*, 165–181.
Bar-Hillel, M. (1983). The base rate fallacy controversy. In R.W. Scholz (ed.), *Decision Making Under Uncertainty* (pp. 39–61). Amsterdam: Elsevier.
Bar-Hillel, M. (1990). Back to base rates. In R.M. Hogarth (ed.) *Insights in Decision Making* (pp. 200–216). Chicago, IL: University of Chicago Press.

Birnbaum, M.H. (1983). Base rates in Bayesian inference: signal detection analysis of the cab problem. *American Journal of Psychology*, *96*, 85–94.

Birnbaum, M.H. & Mellers, B.A. (1983). Bayesian inference: combining base rates with opinions of sources who vary in credibility. *Journal of Personality and Social Psychology*, *45*, 792–804.

Braine, M.D.S., Connel, J., Freitag, J. & O'Brien, D.P. (1990). Is the base-rate fallacy an instance of asserting the consequent? In K.L. Gilhooly, M.T.G. Leane, R.H. Logie & G. Erdos (eds), *Lines of Thinking* (vol. 1). Chichester: Wiley.

Brase, G.L. (2002). Ecological and evolutionary validity: comments on Johnson-Laird, Legrenzi, Girotto, Legrenzi, and Caverni's (1999) mental-model theory of extensional reasoning. *Psychological Review*, *109*, 722–728.

British Psychological Society–Cognitive Psychology Section (1996). 29–31 August, London.

Casscells, W., Schoenberger, A. & Graboys, T.B. (1978). Interpretation by physicians of clinical laboratory results. *New England Journal of Medicine*, *299*, 999–1001.

Cohen, L.J. (1981). Can human irrationality be experimentally demonstrated? *Behavioral and Brain Sciences*, *4*, 317–331.

Cosmides, L. & Tooby, J. (1996). Are humans good intuitive statisticians after all? Rethinking some conclusions from the literature on judgment under uncertainty. *Cognition*, *58*, 1–73.

Dawes, R.M. (1986). Representative thinking in clinical judgment. *Clinical Psychology Review*, *6*, 425–441.

Dulany, D.E. & Hilton, D.J. (1991). Conversational implicature, conscious representation, and the conjunction fallacy. *Social Cognition*, *9*, 85–110.

Eddy, D.M. (1982). Probabilistic reasoning in clinical medicine: problems and opportunities. In D. Kahneman, P. Slovic and A. Tversky (eds), *Judgement Under Uncertainty: Heuristics and Biases* (pp. 249–267). Cambridge: Cambridge University Press.

Fiedler, K. (1988). The dependence of the conjunction fallacy on subtle linguistic factors. *Psychological Research*, *50*, 123–129.

Gastwirth, J.L. (2000). *Statistical Science in the Courtroom*. New York: Springer.

Gigerenzer, G. (1991). On cognitive illusion and rationality. In E. Eells & T. Maruszewski (eds), *Reasoning and Rationality. Essays in Honour of L.J. Cohen*. Amsterdam: Rodopi.

Gigerenzer, G. (1994). Why the distinction between single-event probabilities and frequencies is important for psychology (and vice versa). In G. Wright & P. Ayton (eds), *Subjective Probability*. Chichester: Wiley.

Gigerenzer, G. and Hoffrage, U. (1995). How to improve Bayesian reasoning without instruction: frequency formats. *Psychological Review*, *102*, 684–704.

Gigerenzer, G. & Hoffrage, U. (1999). Helping people overcome difficulties in Bayesian reasoning: a reply to Lewis & Keren and Mellers & McGraw. *Psychological Review*, *106*, 425–430.

Gigerenzer, G. & Murray, D.J. (1987). Thinking: from insight to intuitive statistics. In *Cognition as Intuitive Statistics*. Hillsdale, NJ: Erlbaum.

Gigerenzer, G., Hell, W., & Blank, H. (1998). Presentation and content: the use of base rates as a continuous variable. *Journal of Experimental Psychology: Human Perceptions and Performance*, *14*, 513–525.

Ginossar, Z. & Trope, Y. (1987). Problem solving in judgment under uncertainty. *Journal of Personality and Social Psychology*, *52*, 464–474.

Girotto, V. & Gonzales, M. (2001). Solving probabilistic and statistical problems: a matter of information structure and question form. *Cognition*, *78*, 247–276.

Girotto, V., Kemmelmeier, M., van der Henst, J.B. & Sperber, D. (2001). Inept reasoners or pragmatic virtuosos? Relevance and the deontic selection task. *Cognition*, *81*, B69–B76.

Grice, P. (1989). *Studies in the Way of Words*. Cambridge, MA: Harvard University Press.

Hamm, R.M. & Miller, M.A. (1988). Interpretation of condition probabilities in probabilistic inference word problems. Unpublished manuscript.

Hertwig, R. & Gigerenzer, G. (1999). The "conjunction fallacy" revisited: how intelligent inferences look like reasoning errors. *Journal of Behavioral Decision Making*, *12*, 275–305.

Hilton, D. (1995). The social context of reasoning: conversational inference and rational judgment *Psychological Bulletin*, *118*, 248–271.

Hilton, D. (1997). The social context of reasoning: conversational inference and rational judgment, *Psychological Bulletin*, *118*, 248–271.

Hoffrage, U., Gigerenzer, G., Krauss, S. & Martignon, L. (in press). Representation facilitates reasoning: what natural frequencies are and what they are not. *Cognition*.

Johnson-Laird, P.N., Legrenzi, P., Girotto, V., Sonino Legrenzi, M. & Caverni, J-P. (1999). Naive probability: a mental model theory of extensional reasoning, *Psychological Review*, *106*, 62–88.

Jones, S.K., Jones Taylor, K. & Frisch, D. (1995). Biases of probability assessment: a comparison of frequency and single-case judgments. *Organizational Behavior and Human Decision Processes*, *61*, 109–122.

Kahneman, D. & Tversky, A. (1996). On the reality of cognitive illusions: a reply to Gigerenzer's critique. *Psychological Review*, *103*, 582–591.

Kahneman, D., Slovic, P. & Tversky, A. (eds) (1982). *Judgment under Uncertainty: Heuristics and Biases*. Cambridge: Cambridge University Press.

Koehler, J.J. (1996). The base rate fallacy reconsidered: descriptive, normative and methodological challenges. *Behavioral and Brain Sciences*, *19*, 1–17.

Koehler, J.J. & Macchi, L. (2003). Thinking about low probability events: an exemplar cueing theory. *Psychological Science*.

Krauss, S., Martignon, L. & Hoffrage, U. (2000). Simplifying Bayesian inference: the general case. In L. Magnani, N. Nersessian, and P. Thagard (eds), *Model-Based Reasoning in Scientific Discovery*. New York: Plenum Press.

Leddo, J., Abelson, R.P. & Gross, P.H. (1984). Conjunctive explanations: when two reasons are better than one. *Journal of Personality and Social Psychology*, *47*, 933–943.

Levinson, S.C. (1995). International biases in human thinking. In E.N. Goody (ed.), *Social Intelligence and Interaction* (pp. 221–260). Cambridge: Cambridge University Press.

Lewis C. & Keren G. (1999). On the difficulties underlying Bayesian reasoning: a comment on Gigerenzer and Hoffrage. *Psychological Review*, *106*, 411–416.

Lindley, D.V. (1985). *Making Decisions*. Chichester: Wiley.

Locksley, A. & Stangor, C. (1984). Why versus often: causal reasoning and the incidence of judgmental bas. *Journal of Experimental Social Psychology*, *20*, 470–483.

Macchi, L. (1995). Pragmatic aspects of the base rate fallacy. *Quarterly Journal of Experimental Psychology*, *48*A, 188–207.

Macchi, L. (2000). Partitive formulation of information in probabilistic problems: beyond heuristics and frequency format explanations. *Organizational Behavior and Human Decision Processes*, *82*, 217–236.

Macchi, L. & Girotto, V. (1994). Probabilistic reasoning with conditional probabilities: the three boxes paradox. Paper presented at the Society for Judgment and Decision Making Annual Meeting, St Louis, November.

Macchi, L. & Mosconi, G. (1998). Computational features vs. frequentist phrasing in the base-rate fallacy. *Swiss Journal of Psychology*, *57*, 79–85.

Macdonald, R.R. & Gilhooly, K.J. (1990). More about Linda or conjunction in context. *European Journal of Cognitive Psychological*, *2*, 57–70.

Mellers, B.A. & McGraw, A.P. (1999). How to improve Bayesian reasoning: comment on Gigerenzer and Hoffrage. *Psychological Review*, *106*, 417–424.

Morier, D.M. & Borgida, E. (1984). The conjunction fallacy: a task specific phenomenon? *Personality and Social Psychology Bulletin*, *10*, 243–252.

Mosconi, G. (1990). *Discorso e Pensiero* [Discourse and thought]. Bologna: Il Mulino.

Mosconi, G. & Macchi, L. (2001). The role of pragmatic rules in the conjunction fallacy. *Mind and Society*, *3*, 31–57.

Politzer, G. (1986). Laws of language use and formal logic. *Journal of Psycholinguistic Research*, *15*, 47–92.

Politzer, G. (2003). Premise interpretation in conditional reasoning. In D. Hardman & L. Macchi (eds), *Thinking: Psychological Perspectives on Reasoning, Judgment, and Decision Making* (pp. 77–94). Chichester: Wiley.

Politzer, G. & Macchi, L. (2000). Reasoning and pragmatics. *Mind and Society*, *1*, 73–94.

Politzer, G. & Macchi, L. (2003). The representation of the task: the case of the Lawyer-Engineer. In V. Girotto & P. N. Johnson-Laird (eds), *The Shape of Reason: Essays in Honor of Paolo Legrenzi*. Hove: Psychology Press.

Politzer, G. & Noveck, I.A. (1991). Are conjunction rule violations the result of conversational rule violations? *Journal of Psycholinguistic Research*, *15*, 47–92.

Reeves, T. & Lockhart, R.S. (1993). Distributional versus singular approaches to probability and errors in probabilistic reasoning. *Journal of Experimental Psychology: General, 122,* 207–226.

Schwarz, N. (1996). *Cognition and Communication: Judgmental Biases, Research Methods, and the Logic of the Conversation.* Hillsdale, NJ: Erlbaum.

Shafir, E.B., Smith, E.E. & Osherson, D.N. (1990). Typicality and reasoning fallacies. *Memory and Cognition, 18,* 229-239.

Sperber, D., Cara, F. & Girotto, V. (1995). Relevance theory explains the selection task. *Cognition, 57,* 31–95.

Sperber, D. & Wilson, D. (1986). *Relevance: Communication and Cognition.* Oxford: Basil Blackwell.

Thuring, M. & Jungermann, H. (1990). The conjunction fallacy: causality vs. event probability. *Journal of Behavioural Decision Making, 3,* 61–74.

Tversky, A. & Kahneman, D. (1974). Judgment under uncertainty: heuristics and biases. *Science, 185,* 1124–1131.

Tversky, A. & Kahneman, D. (1980). Causal schemata in judgments under uncertainty. In M. Fishbein (ed.), *Progress in Social Psychology* (vol. 1, pp. 49–72). Hillsdale, NJ: Erlbaum.

Tversky, A. & Kahneman, D. (1982). Evidential impact of base rates. In D. Kahneman, P. Slovic & A. Tversky (eds), *Judgment Under Uncertainty: Heuristics and Biases* (pp. 153–160). Cambridge: Cambridge University Press.

Van der Henst, J.-B., Sperber, D. & Politzer, G. (2002). When is a conclusion worth deriving? A relevance-based analysis of indeterminate relational problems. *Thinking and Reasoning, 8,* 1–20.

Wells, G.L. (1985). The conjunction error and the representativeness heuristic. *Social Cognition, 3,* 266–279.

CHAPTER 10

Naive and yet Enlightened: From Natural Frequencies to Fast and Frugal Decision Trees

Laura Martignon
Kassel University, Kassel, Germany
Oliver Vitouch
University of Klagenfurt, Austria
Masanori Takezawa
Max Planck Institute for Human Development, Berlin, Germany
and
Malcolm R. Forster
University of Wisconsin-Madison, Wisconsin, USA

10.1 INTRODUCTION

An evolutionary view of rationality as an adaptive toolbox of fast and frugal heuristics is sometimes placed in opposition to probability as the ideal of enlightened rational human inference. Indeed, this opposition has become the cornerstone of an ongoing debate between adherents to theories of normative as opposed to bounded rationality. On the one hand, it has been shown that probability provides a good approximation to human cognitive processing for tasks involving simple inferences, and humans actually are able to reason the Bayesian way when information is presented in formats to which they are well adapted (Gigerenzer & Hoffrage, 1995). On the other hand, it is clear that probabilistic inference becomes infeasible when the mind has to deal with too many pieces of information at once. Coping with resource limitations, the mind—as Gigerenzer, Todd and the ABC Research Group (1999) claim— adopts simple inference heuristics, often based on just one-reason decision making. Our aim is to present a unifying framework, based on the systematic use of trees for knowledge representation, both for fully Bayesian and for fast and frugal decisions.

Thinking: Psychological Perspectives on Reasoning, Judgment and Decision Making. Edited by David Hardman and Laura Macchi.
© 2003 John Wiley & Sons, Ltd.

Tree-structured schemes are ubiquitous tools for organizing and representing knowledge, and their history goes back to the third century, when Porphyry introduced a first version of the tree of life (Isagoge, around AD 305). We will show that both full Bayesian inference and one-reason decision making are processes that can be described in terms of tree-structured decision rules. A fully specified Bayesian model can be represented by means of the "full" or "maximal" tree obtained by introducing nodes for all conceivable conjunctions of events, whereas a one-reason decision rule can be represented by a "minimal" subtree of the maximal tree (with maximal and minimal reference to the number of paths connecting the root to the leaves). Subtrees of the full tree not containing any path from root to leaves are regarded as "truncated" since they necessarily truncate the access to available information; they will not be treated in this chapter. Minimal trees can be obtained by radically pruning the full tree. A minimal tree has a leaf at each one of its levels, so that every level allows for a possible decision. Indeed, when a radical reduction of complexity is necessary and when the environment is favorable, such a minimal tree will be extremely fast and frugal with negligible losses in accuracy. In this chapter, we introduce a name for such minimal trees, following the terminology used by Gigerenzer et al. (1999) for heuristics that very much resemble minimal trees. We will call them "fast and frugal trees".

While the construction by means of a radical pruning of the full tree serves theoretical purposes in order to understand the mathematical properties of fast and frugal trees, it seems unlikely that humans construct these trees in such a top-down fashion. Humans apparently use simple construction rules, without integrating information. They tend to ignore dependencies between cues, and their decision strategy is solely based on the ranking of these cues with respect to their "stand-alone" predictive usefulness.

We begin by describing how natural frequencies provide fully specified trees, which we will call "natural frequency trees", that carry and represent the statistical information required for Bayesian reasoning. We will then transform natural frequency trees into fully specified classification trees. We will proceed by describing how to prune radically a full classification tree, transforming it into a fast and frugal classification tree, which is then easily converted into a decision tree. We will show that fast and frugal trees are one-reason decision-making tools which operate as lexicographic classifiers.[1] Then we will approach the natural question: how do humans construct fast and frugal trees for classification and decision? We will propose simple construction rules, where all that matters is the ranking of cues. Once the ranking is established, the fast and frugal tree checks one cue at a time, and at each step, one of the possible outcomes of the considered cue is an exit node which allows for a decision. Finally, we will compare fast and frugal trees with an "optimizing" model from the general linear model framework, namely, logistic regression.

10.2   TREE-STRUCTURED REPRESENTATIONS IN CLASSIFICATION TASKS

Human classifications and decisions are based on the analysis of features or cues that the mind/brain extracts from the environment. There is a wide spectrum of classification schemes, varying in terms of the time scale they require, from almost automatic

---

[1] This corresponds to a characterization of fast and frugal trees as linear classifiers with non-compensatory weights (cf. Martignon & Hoffrage, 1999).

classifications the mind/brain performs without taking real notice, up to slow, conscious ones.

The literature on formalized schemes for processing cues aiming at object classification is vast, and it is beyond the scope of this chapter to give a comprehensive account. Among the diverse representational devices for classification, trees have been the most ubiquitous. Since the fourth century, trees representing sequential step-by-step processes for classification based on cue information have been common devices in many realms of human knowledge. These trees start from a root node and descend through branches connecting the root to intermediate nodes, until they reach final nodes or leaves.

A classification (also called categorization) tree is a graphical representation of a rule— or a set of rules—for making classifications. Each node of the tree represents a question regarding certain features of the objects to be classified or categorized. Each branch leading out of the node represents a different answer to the question. It is assumed that the answers to the question are exclusive (non-overlapping) and exhaustive (cover all objects). That is, there is exactly one answer to the question for each object, and each of the possible answers is represented by one branch out of the node. The nodes below a given node are called its "children", and the node above a node is called its "parent". Every node has exactly one parent except for the "root" node, which has no parent, and which is usually depicted at the top or far left. The "leaf" nodes, or nodes having no children, are usually depicted at the bottom or far right. In a "binary" tree, all non-leaf nodes have exactly two children; in general trees nodes may have any number of children. The leaf nodes of a classification tree represent a "partition" of the set of objects into classes defined by the answers to the questions. Each leaf node has an associated class label, to be assigned to all objects for which the appropriate answers are given to the questions associated with the leaf's ancestor nodes.

The classification tree can be used to construct a simple algorithm for associating any object with a class label. Given an object, the algorithm traverses a "path" from the root node to one of the leaf nodes. This path is determined by the answers to the questions associated with the nodes. The questions and answers can be used to define a "decision rule" to be executed when each node is traversed. The decision rule instructs the algorithm which arc to traverse out of the node, and thus which child to visit. The classification algorithm proceeds as follows:

Algorithm TREE-CLASS:
(1) Begin at root node.
(2) Execute rule associated with current node to decide which arc to traverse.
(3) Proceed to child at end of chosen arc.
(4) If child is a leaf node, assign to object the class label associated with node and STOP.
(5) Otherwise, go to (2).

10.2.1 Natural Frequency Trees

Natural frequency trees provide good representations of the statistical data relevant to the construction of optimal classification trees. In this section, we begin by recalling how natural frequency trees for complex classification tasks—that is, tasks involving several pieces of information—were introduced by Krauss et al. (2001), by generalizing the results

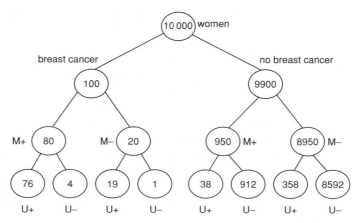

Figure 10.1 The natural frequency tree for classifying a patient as having or not having cancer, based on the results of a mammogram and an ultrasound test

of Gigerenzer and Hoffrage (1995). Krauss et al. showed empirically that the following problem is solved with ease by most participants:

> 100 out of every 10 000 women at age 40 who participate in routine screening have breast cancer.
> 80 of every 100 women with breast cancer will get a positive mammography.
> 950 out of every 9900 women without breast cancer will also get a positive mammography.
> 76 out of 80 women who had a positive mammography and have cancer also have a positive ultrasound test.
> 38 out of 950 women who had a positive mammography, although they do not have cancer, also have a positive ultrasound test.
> How many of the women who get a positive mammography and a positive ultrasound test do you expect to actually have breast cancer?

The (relative) frequencies in this task, for example, "38 out of 950", were called "natural frequencies" following Gigerenzer and Hoffrage (1995) and Kleiter (1994). In contrast, the traditional probability format of the task consisted of statements such as "For a woman with breast cancer, the probability of getting a positive mammogram is 80 percent." The important discovery was that the natural frequency format makes the task much easier to solve than the probabilistic format. The argument made by Gigerenzer and Hoffrage to explain the beneficial effects of natural frequencies was an evolutionary one. Since humans are used to counting and automatically sampling frequencies (see also Hasher & Zacks, 1984), they are also at ease when having to form simple proportions with these sampled frequencies.[2] Krauss et al. (2001) observed that some participants in their experiments drew trees like that in Figure 10.1 as an aid in solving the task.

Such a tree was called a "natural frequency tree". The numbers in the nodes indicate that the two tests are conditionally independent, given cancer. This is obviously an assumption.

---

[2] An alternative account of the effect of the natural frequency format is that the correct way of doing the partitioning of information becomes transparent from the instruction (cf. Macchi & Mosconi, 1998; Fiedler et al., 2000). Natural frequencies are a stable currency (80 cases equal 80 cases at every node of the tree), whereas 2 percent of A can be much more or much less than 2 percent of B.

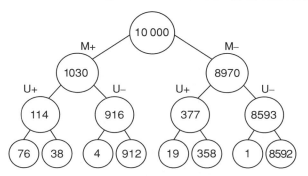

Figure 10.2   The natural frequency tree obtained from the tree in Figure 10.1, when the sampling order is mammogram → ultrasound → cancer

The reality of medical tests is that neither combined sensitivities nor combined specificities are reported in the literature; it is a frequent convention to assume tests' conditional independence, given the disease.

Observe that this natural frequency tree is *causally* organized. That is, the top node divides the universe of patients into those with cancer and those free of cancer. Successive nodes represent tests which are useful for diagnosing cancer because their outcomes are *caused* by the presence or absence of cancer. Thus, the patient's classification on the top node is a cause of the patient's classification on the lower nodes. Causal organization is useful for scientific evaluation of causal claims, but is less useful if the purpose is to facilitate rapid diagnosis. When a patient arrives at the doctor's office, it is not known whether she has cancer. Thus, it is not possible to follow the TREE-CLASS algorithm described in the previous section. The first decision—whether to trace the "breast cancer" or the "no breast cancer" arc—cannot be made from the information available to the doctor. For example, suppose a woman gets a positive mammogram (M+) and a positive ultrasound (U+). We cannot tell whether to trace the "breast cancer" or the "no breast cancer" link. In the first case, we would follow the U+ and M+ links to place her among the 76 women in the leftmost leaf node. In the second case, we would again follow U+ and M+ to place her among the 38 women in the fifth leaf node from the left. To calculate the probability that she has cancer, we need to trace each of these paths in turn and combine the results to form the ratio 76/(38 + 76). This calculation requires us to use information stored in widely separated parts of the tree. There are more practical natural frequency trees for diagnosis. They are obtained by inverting the order followed for the sequential partitioning of the total population (10 000 women) in Figure 10.1. Consider the tree in Figure 10.2.

Organizing the tree in the *diagnostic* direction produces a much more efficient classification strategy. An example of a diagnostic tree for the cancer task is shown in Figure 10.2. This tree has two major advantages over the tree in Figure 10.1 for a diagnostic task. First, we can follow the TREE-CLASS algorithm for the first two steps before becoming stuck at the second-to-last level above the leaf nodes. For example, for the hypothetical woman with M+ and U+ described above, we would be able to place her among the 114 women at the leftmost node on the third level from the top. Second, once we have placed a patient at a node just above the bottom of the tree, we can compute the probability of placing her at each of the two possible leaf nodes by using only local information. That is, the probability

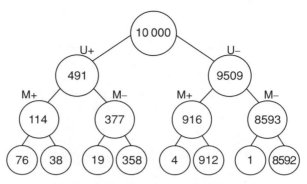

Figure 10.3   Natural sampling in the order ultrasound → mammography → cancer

our hypothetical woman has cancer can be computed by looking at the cancer node just below, discovering that there are 76 exemplars associated with that node, and dividing it by the 114 exemplars at the third level.

Comparing the leaves of Figures 10.1 and 10.2 reveals that they are the same; that is, they contain the same numbers, although their ordering is different, as is the topology of their connection to the rest of the tree. One might question whether a natural sampler would partition the population in the causal or the diagnostic direction. Pearl (e.g., 1988; see also Fiedler, 2000) argues that knowledge tends to be organized causally, and diagnostic inference is performed by means of inversion strategies, which, in the frequency format, are reduced to inverting the partitioning order as above (in the probability format, the inversion is carried out by applying Bayes' theorem; Bayes, 1763). Others (e.g., Chase, 1999) argue that ecologically situated agents tend to adopt representations tailored to their goals and the environment in which they are situated. Thus, it might be argued that a goal-oriented natural sampler performing a diagnostic task will probably partition the original population according to the cues first, and end by partitioning according to the criterion.

Now, consider another version of the diagnostic ordering of the cues, where, in the first phase, women are partitioned according to their ultrasound, and in the second phase, they are partitioned according to the mammograms and finally according to breast cancer. The tree is depicted in Figure 10.3.

Again, the numbers in the leaves coincide with those in the leaves of the trees in Figures 10.1 and 10.2. Partitioning is commutative: we obtain the same final cells no matter which partitioning order we follow.

10.2.2   From Natural Frequency Trees to Classification and Decision Trees

Remember that the decision maker has to decide what to do for each of the four combinations of cue values ([positive mammogram, positive ultrasound], [positive mammogram, negative ultrasound], [negative mammogram, positive ultrasound], [negative mammogram, negative ultrasound]). A fully specified classification tree would, for instance, look like the tree in Figure 10.3, without the lowest level. Its leaves would be labeled by the four combinations of cue values listed above. If, based on the statistical information provided by the natural

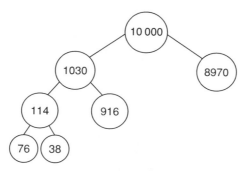

a   Radical pruning under M–

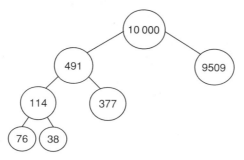

b   Radical pruning under U–

Figure 10.4   The trees resulting from radically pruning the fully specified tree

frequency tree, decision makers have to decide between "apply biopsy" or "send the patient home", they will try to reduce the number of *worst* errors, namely, sending women home who do have cancer, while trying to keep the number of biopsies on women without breast cancer low.

Radical Pruning

We now provide the construction rules for simple decision trees, starting from the fully specified natural frequency trees. There are, of course, many ways in which the complexity of the fully specified tree can be reduced. We will adopt the most radical one, by a sequential pruning which eliminates half of the remaining tree at every step. By observing the tree in Figure 10.2, we realize that if we send all women with a negative mammogram home with no further testing, we will miss 20 cancer cases out of the 10 000 women tested. This corresponds to pruning the children and grandchildren of the negative mammogram node in the tree. If we use ultrasound instead of mammogram as our "one-reason decision rule", we will miss five patients with the disease out of the 10 000 women tested (cf. Figure 10.3). Simplifying our trees even further, we can eliminate all children nodes of "positive mammogram and negative ultrasound" in Figure 10.2, obtaining the radically pruned trees in Figure 10.4a and b. Our error has become larger: twenty-four women with cancer will be declared healthy. The same error would arise if we prune the children of "positive ultrasound

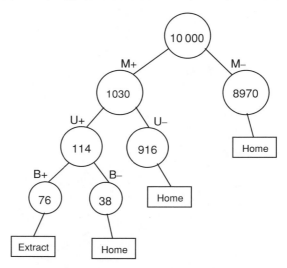

Figure 10.5   A fast and frugal decision tree in the "breast cancer" situation. The symbols B+ and B− stand for positive and negative biopsy

and negative mammogram" in Figure 10.3. In fact, the leaves left after pruning are the same in both cases, as shown in Figure 10.5.

The medical reality of the diagnosis and treatment of breast cancer is very close to the decision strategy resulting from this pruning procedure. If a woman with no symptoms has a negative mammogram, the doctor "sends her home". In routine screening, the mammogram is the first test taken, followed—if positive—by the ultrasound test. If both are positive, the doctor will tend to recommend a biopsy. Biopsy will (almost surely) detect the tumor if it exists and, after close laboratory examination, classify it as malignant or benign. A malignant tumor will be extracted "locally". In cases of extremely large tumors, amputation will be performed.

Medical decisions can usually not be based on the fully specified trees due to the costs involved in performing tests. These costs are not just in terms of the prices of the tests (mammograms and ultrasounds have comparable prices; modern biopsy can be twice as expensive); they are also to be seen as costs in time and, last but not least, in terms of the patient's health (Cousins, 1989; Gigerenzer, 2002). The medical tendency is to reduce the number of tests and biopsies to the minimum required for good diagnosis. When such constraints are taken into account, the radically simplified tree of Figure 10.5 becomes the viable strategy.

10.3   FAST AND FRUGAL TREES

A tree such as the one depicted in Figure 10.5 may be called a fast and frugal tree, according to the definition we present below. We formulate this definition for binary trees; that is, trees constructed with binary cues and a binary criterion. The generalization to other cases is straightforward. With the classification according to a binary criterion (for example, "cancer" or "no cancer"), we associate two possible decisions, one for each possible classification (for example, "biopsy" or "no biopsy"). An important convention has to be applied beforehand: cue profiles can be expressed as vectors of 0s and 1s, where a 1 corresponds to the value of the cue more highly correlated with the outcome of the criterion considered "positive" (for example, presence of cancer). The convention is that left branches are labeled with 1s and right branches with 0s. Thus, each branch of the fully specified tree can be labeled with a 1 or a 0, according to the cue value associated with the node at the end of the branch.

Definition

A fast and frugal binary decision tree is a decision tree with at least one exit leaf at every level. That is, for every checked cue, at least one of its outcomes can lead to a decision. In accordance with the convention applied above, if a leaf stems from a branch labeled 1, the decision will be positive (for example, "perform biopsy").

This definition cannot stand alone, that is, without a good characterization of fast and frugal trees as classifiers. Thus, the rest of this section is devoted to analytical characterizations that identify fast and frugal trees as very special types of classifiers. We begin by recalling that in any natural frequency tree organized in the diagnostic direction, as in Figures 10.2 and 10.3, each leaf represents the number of subjects in the population that have a given cue profile and have or do not have the disease. Again, according to our convention, we will encode "having the disease" with a 1, and "not having the disease" with a 0. If we have, say, three cues, the leaves of the full frequency tree will be labeled $(111,1)$, $(111,0)$, $(101,1)$, $(101,0)$, $(100,1)$, $(100,0)$, $(011,1)$, $(011,0)$, $(010,1)$, $(010,1)$, $(001,0)$, $(000,1)$, $(000,0)$, where the binary vectors will appear in decreasing lexicographic order from left to right. Observe that we have separated the cue profile from the state of the disease by a comma.

Since this ordering is similar to the ordering of words in a dictionary, it is usually called "lexicographic". Lexicographic orderings allow for simple classifications, by establishing that all profiles larger (in the lexicographic ordering) than a certain fixed profile will be assigned to one class, and all profiles smaller than the same fixed profile will be assigned to the other class. Let us pin this definition down.

Given a set of n binary cues, we say that L is a "lexicographic classifier" on the set of all possible cue profiles if there is a cue profile α such that L classifies all cue profiles larger than α (in the lexicographic ordering) as members of one class and all profiles smaller than α as members of the other. The profile α will be called the "splitting profile" of the classification (cf. Figure 10.6). The splitting profile α is classified according to its last bit. If this is 1, it will be assigned the same class as all profiles larger than α; it will be assigned the alternative class, if its last bit is 0.

A "lexicographic decision rule" makes one decision, say, D, for all profiles larger than a given, fixed profile, and the alternative decision, ¬D, for all profiles smaller than that same profile. The profile itself is assigned decision D if it ends with a 1, and decision ¬D if it ends with a 0.

A fast and frugal decision tree makes decisions *lexicographically*. This is what we prove in the following theorem.

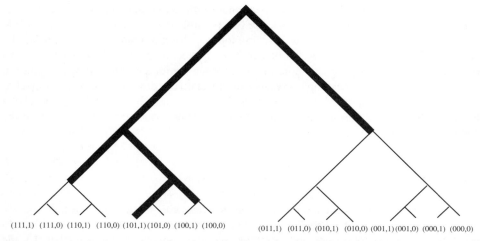

Figure 10.6 A lexicographic classifier determined by the path of profile (101), where the three bits are cue values and the last bit corresponds to the criterion (for example, having or not having the disease)

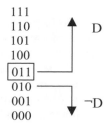

Figure 10.7 A lexicographic classifier that has the profile (011) as split

Theorem

Let T be the fast and frugal decision tree defined by the cue profile α. Denote by α the profile that coincides with α in all but the last cue value. Assume that α ends with a 1. Then T makes exactly the same decisions as a lexicographic decision rule that assigns the same decision D assigned to α to every profile $\beta > \alpha$, and the alternative decision $\neg D$ assigned to α to every $\beta < \alpha$ (cf. Figure 10.7).

Proof. Assume $\beta > \alpha$. This means, by definition of the lexicographic ordering, that for some k the first k cue values in the cue profile β coincide with those of α, but its $(k + 1)$-st cue value is 1, while the $(k + 1)$-st cue value of α is 0. By construction, this $(k + 1)$-st cue value labels a branch which terminates in a leaf, and, by convention, such a leaf must necessarily lead to decision D. This proves our assertion. An analogous argument proves that if $\beta < \alpha$, β will be assigned decision $\neg D$. Q.E.D.

At this point, we want to make a connection between fast and frugal decision trees and a well-established simple heuristic for comparison called "Take the Best". Take the Best, a heuristic for comparison proposed by Gigerenzer and Goldstein (1996), is a strategy for lexicographic comparison. In other words, if two objects have profiles of, say, (11101010) and (11110101), Take the Best will decide that the first one has a larger value on the criterion, simply because its cue profile is "larger" in the lexicographic sense.

The question is now: what makes a fast and frugal tree a "good" decision tree? In other words, given a set of cues, how do we know how to order them so as to minimize errors when constructing a fast and frugal tree? One thing is certain: the decision maker in a hurry does not have the time to construct the full tree and then choose the best ordering of cues by comparing the performances of possible orderings (see Section 4). The naive decision maker uses simple, naive ways for obtaining good fast and frugal trees. In the next section, we will illustrate some simple methods for constructing good fast and frugal trees with a real-life example.

10.3.1   Constructing Fast and Frugal Decision Trees

In order to illustrate the construction of a fast and frugal tree, we walk through an example extracted from the literature, where a simple tree—according to our definition, a fast and frugal tree—for medical diagnosis was constructed (Green & Mehr, 1997). Consider the following situation. A man is rushed into a hospital with severe chest pain. The doctors have to decide whether the patient should be assigned to the coronary care unit (CCU) or to a monitored nursing bed (NB). The cues on which a doctor bases such a decision are the following:

(1) ST segment elevation in the electrocardiogram (ECG)
(2) patient report of chest pain as most important symptom
(3) history of heart attack
(4) history of nitroglycerin use for chest pain
(5) pain in the chest or left arm
(6) ST segment barring
(7) T-waves with peaking or inversion.

Green and Mehr (1997) analyzed the problem of finding a simple procedure for determining an action based on this cue information. They began their project with the aim of implementing an existing logistic regression-based instrument proposed by Pozen et al. (1984), the Heart Disease Predictive Instrument, in a rural hospital. What they found was that by using the instrument, doctors quickly became sensitive to the important diagnostic cues (as opposed to pseudo-diagnostic or less valid ones). Even without the instrument with its exact beta weights at hand, they maintained the same level of performance. Inspired by the work of the ABC Research Group, this observation led Green and Mehr to construct a simple competitor. They reduced the seven cues to only three (creating a new cue formed by the disjunction of 3, 4, 6 and 7) and proposed the tree depicted in Figure 10.8.

Although Green and Mehr (1997) succeeded in constructing a fast and frugal decision tree with excellent performance, they did not reveal how they ended up with precisely this tree, nor did they provide any standard procedure to construct such trees. Our intention is to provide simple rules for their construction. Using the Green and Mehr task as an example, we will illustrate several methods for designing fast and frugal trees and then compare their performance.[3]

---

[3] In order to make the illustration simpler, we will treat the disjunction of cues (3, 4, 6, 7) as one cue instead of working with the four cues separately. Note that cue 5 (chest pain), which was included in the logistic regression model, is not included in the disjunctive cue (nor anywhere else in the tree), as it would be redundant with respect to the "higher-ranked" cue 2 (chest pain as chief symptom).

Table 10.1 Original data from the Green and Mehr (1997) study

C1, C2, C3	Infarction	No infarction
111	9	12
110	1	1
101	3	5
100	0	2
011	2	15
010	0	10
001	0	19
000	0	10

C1 = ST segment elevation; C2 = chest pain; C3 = any other cue of 3, 4, 6, 7. Columns 2 and 3 give the respective number of patients.

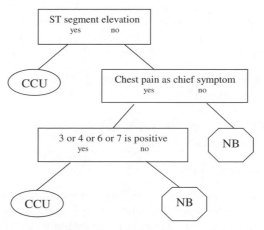

Figure 10.8 Green and Mehr (1997) tree for making decision D, "assign to CCU", or ¬D, "assign to NB"

10.3.2   Ordering of Cues

Table 10.1 shows a data subset from the Green and Mehr (1997) study. In order to construct a fast and frugal tree, one can, of course, test all possible orderings of cues and shapes of trees on the provided data set and optimize fitting performance; in the general case, this requires enormous computation if the number of cues is large. Another approach is to determine the "best" cue according to some given rule, and then determine the "second best" cue conditional on the first, and so on. But this again requires a fairly large number of computations.

In conceptual analogy to naive Bayes models, naive decision makers will not look into conditional dependencies and/or correlations between cues. Our conjecture is that they will basically have a good feeling of how well each cue alone predicts the criterion. They will sample natural frequency trees for each of the three cues individually. These trees are simple

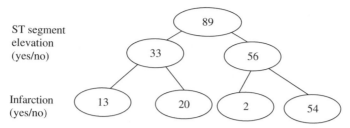

ST segment
elevation
(yes/no)

Infarction
(yes/no)

Figure 10.9a   Natural frequency diagnostic tree for ST segment elevation

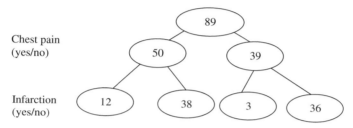

Chest pain
(yes/no)

Infarction
(yes/no)

Figure 10.9b   Natural frequency diagnostic tree for chest pain

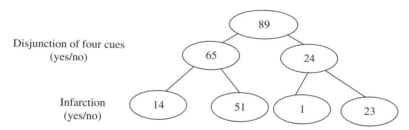

Disjunction of four cues
(yes/no)

Infarction
(yes/no)

Figure 10.9c   Natural frequency diagnostic tree for "disjunction of four cues"

enough as to be grasped/stored by our decision makers. They need a good feeling, however, of how the cues compare to each other (see Figure 10.9a–c). The question is: What is a good cue?

In what follows, we make a short digression to answer this question in detail. Let us consider the contingency table for an abstract criterion C over an abstract cue:

	C	¬C
cue	a	b
¬cue	c	d

Recall that a test can be good in more than one way. Its sensitivity, that is, the chances of obtaining a positive test result given that the patient has the disease (that is, $a/(a + c)$), can be very high. Or its specificity, that is, the chances of obtaining a negative result given that the patient does not have the disease (that is, $d/(d + b)$), can be very high. Another measure is based on the proportion of correct predictions. One can look at the correct predictions made by a positive test. This proportion (that is, $a/(a + b)$) is the "positive validity"—also called "positive predictivity"—of the test. Yet another measure is the proportion of correct predictions made by a negative test, or "negative validity" (that is, $d/(d + c)$), also called "negative predictivity". If, instead of separating into positive and negative parcels, we look at the global goodness of a test, we have diagnosticity (the average of sensitivity and specificity) and validity (the average of positive and negative validity). The diagnosticity of the cue is given by

$$\text{Diag(cue)} = P(\text{cue} \mid C)\, P(C) + P(\neg\text{cue} \mid \neg C)\, P(\neg C)$$

The validity (or predictivity) of the cue is given by

$$\text{Val(cue)} = P(C \mid \text{cue})\, P(\text{cue}) + P(\neg C \mid \neg\text{cue})\, P(\neg\text{cue})$$

Note that sensitivity and positive validity coincide only in the special case of equal marginals of the two-by-two table, as do specificity and negative validity. Their averages, however—validity and diagnosticity—necessarily coincide and are given by

$$P(C \cap \text{cue}) + P(\neg C \cap \neg\text{cue})$$

where $\cap$ denotes conjunction.

Here, we will focus on two different types of orderings: orderings based on (1) either sensitivity or specificity and (2) either positive or negative validity.

10.3.3   The Shape of Trees

As shown in Figure 10.10, there are four possible shapes, or branching structures, of fast and frugal trees for three cues.

Trees of type 1 and 4 are called "rakes" or "pectinates". As defined here, rakes have a very special property. They embody a strict conjunction rule, meaning that one of the two alternative decisions is made only if all cues are present (type 1) or absent (type 4). Trees of types 2 and 3 are called "zigzag trees". They have the property of alternating between positive and negative exits in the sequence of levels. Given a decision task and a set of cues, how can we choose one of these fast and frugal trees? We now list some simple, naive ways of ranking cues and deciding the shape of trees. Observe that all cues considered have the same technical cost once the electrocardiogram and the anamnesis have been performed; thus, procedural cost is not an issue when constructing the tree.

An important aspect is that, at least in the context of medical decision making, misses and false alarms differ in importance. Doctors' first priority is to reduce misses; their second priority is to reduce false alarms. This difference in gravity of errors will be discussed in more detail in Section 4, where we will focus on the performance of trees. This asymmetry will be reflected in the construction rules proposed, with the aim of achieving a large number of hits (correct assignments to coronary care unit) already at the first decisional level.

Let us first exhibit the contingency tables for the three cues in the Green and Mehr task (Table 10.2). Sensitivity and specificity of the cues are given in Table 10.3; positive and negative validities in Table 10.4.

Now we make use of this information in four different approaches to constructing a fast and frugal tree.

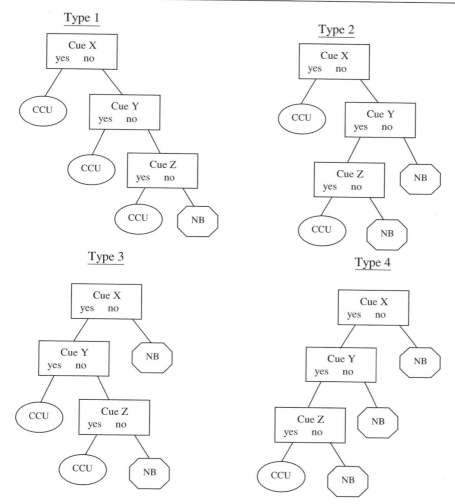

Figure 10.10   The four different shapes of fast and frugal trees with three cues

(1) *Max(sens, spec)*. We begin by picking the cue with maximal sensitivity. All remaining cues are then ranked by the maximum of (sensitivity, specificity). At each level, the larger value will determine the terminal decision. If the cue has been selected due to its sensitivity, we assign positive terminal decision to those members of the population for which the cue value is 1 (if cue value is 0, we proceed to check the next cue). If the cue has been selected due to its specificity, we assign the negative terminal decision to those members of the population for which the cue value is 0 (if cue value is 1, we proceed to check the next cue). In the case of the Green and Mehr data, the ranking obtained is then <any of four cues> → <ST segment> → <chest pain>. The resulting tree is of type 1.

(2) *Max (val+, val−)*. We begin by picking the cue with maximal positive validity. All remaining cues are then ranked by the maximum of (positive validity, negative validity). At each level, the larger value will determine the terminal decision. The ranking obtained is <ST segment> → <any of 4 cues> → <chest pain>. The resulting tree is of type 2.

Table 10.2 Contingency tables for "ST segment elevation", "chest pain", "any of 3, 4, 6, 7"

	Infarction	No infarction
ST segment = 1	13	20
ST segment = 0	2	54
Chest pain = 1	12	38
Chest pain = 0	3	36
(Any of 3, 4, 6, 7) = 1	14	51
(Any of 3, 4, 6, 7) = 0	1	23

Table 10.3 Sensitivity and specificity of each cue

	ST segment	Chest pain	Any of 3, 4, 6, 7
Sensitivity	.87	.80	.93
Specificity	.73	.49	.31

Table 10.4 Positive and negative validity of each cue

	ST segment	Chest pain	Any of 3, 4, 6, 7
Val+	.39	.24	.22
Val−	.96	.92	.96

(3) *Zigzag(sens, spec)*. We begin by picking the cue with maximal sensitivity, just as in the Max(sens, spec) case. In the next step, however, we proceed in zigzag and choose the cue with the highest specificity. We continue by switching directions again, producing an alternating sequence of (sens/spec) ruling the respective terminal decisions accordingly (for example, "sens" and cue value 1 ⇒ positive decision), until we have exhausted all cues. The ranking obtained is <any of four cues> → <ST segment> → <chest pain>. The resulting tree is of type 2.

(4) *Zigzag(val+, val−)*. We begin by picking the cue with maximal positive validity, just as in the Max(val+, val−) case. In the next step, we proceed in zigzag and choose the cue with the highest negative validity. We continue by switching directions again, producing an alternating sequence of (val+/val−), ruling the respective terminal decisions accordingly (for example, "val+" and cue value 1 ⇒ positive decision, until we have exhausted all cues. The ranking obtained is <ST segment> → <any of four cues> → <chest pain>. The resulting tree is of type 2.

The construction methods described above are simple. The first cue checked tends to guarantee a large number of hits from the very beginning. The rest is guided either by a strict maximum principle or by an alternating procedure that aims at counterweighting the previous decision at every new step. The "go for sensitivity and positive validity" prescription for the first level restricts the resulting trees (Figure 10.10) to type 1 and type 2; it excludes, by design, types 3 and 4, which would start with a terminal negative decision.

Table 10.5   The performance of all possible trees. Entries correspond to {no. misses, no. false positives}

	Type 1	Type 2	Type 3	Type 4
cue order 123:	{0, 64}	{0, 35}	{2, 18}	{6, 12}
132:	{0, 64}	{0, 35}	{2, 18}	{6, 12}
213:	{0, 64}	{0, 35}	{3, 28}	{6, 12}
231:	{0, 64}	{0, 43}	{3, 28}	{6, 12}
312:	{0, 64}	{0, 52}	{1, 32}	{6, 12}

Table 10.6   Performance of decision trees

	No. of infarctions sent to NB	No. of healthy patients sent to CCU	Total no. of errors
Max(sens, spec)	0	64	64
Max(val+, val–)	0	35	35
Zigzag(sens, spec)	0	52	52
Zigzag(val+, val–)	0	35	35
Green & Mehr, 1997	0	35	35

Total no. of patients = 89.

A core property of all procedures described above is that they follow simple principles, disregarding intercorrelations and conditional dependencies between cues. Thus, they are "naive" trees, in analogy to naive Bayesian strategies. Another property is that they allow for a terminal decision at every level, often stopping at an early stage. Thus, they deserve to be called "fast and frugal" trees, according to the concept of fast and frugal heuristics.

10.4   PERFORMANCE OF FAST AND FRUGAL DECISION TREES

How do the classifications of our trees compare? In order to compute the performance of different rankings, we begin by listing {no. of misses, no. of false positives} of all possible cue orderings for all possible fast and frugal trees (Table 10.5). Note that "pectinates" (types 1 and 4) are, by design, commutative. The ranking of cues has no influence on the partitioning and, hence, on their performance. Table 10.6 exhibits the performance of the decision trees constructed in Section 3.3. As intended, all resulting trees succeed in avoiding misses.

We now tackle the question of an adequate performance criterion. Theoretically, the costs of making misses and false positives might be identical. Looking at Table 10.5, we see that the best trees in this respect are different from those displayed in Table 10.6. If misses and false alarms were equally costly, the type 4 trees with a performance of {6, 12} would be best, and the type 1 trees would be worst. But in the context discussed here, it is obviously worse to assign an infarction patient to the nursing bed than to assign a healthy patient to the coronary care unit. This is the typical situation in medical diagnosis. We therefore need a context-specific definition concerning the order relation of diagnostic trees.

Definition

Let S and T be decision trees. We say that S "dominates" T if S has fewer misses than T. If both trees have the same number of misses, then S dominates T if S has fewer false positives than T. If S dominates T, we write S > T. Two trees are "equivalent" if they have the same number of misses and the same number of false positives.

This definition can be somewhat relaxed to allow for more flexibility and/or to penalize trees with an excessive number of false positives. One could, for instance, choose a positive threshold value α and establish T > S if $0 < (\text{sens}(S) - \text{sens}(T)) < \alpha$ and $\text{spec}(T) \gg \text{spec}(S)$. This means that a tree T would be chosen in favor of a tree S with somewhat higher sensitivity as soon as the sensitivity difference is negligible and T is *clearly* preferable in terms of specificity.

As becomes evident from Tables 10.5 and 10.6, the Green and Mehr tree, whose performance coincides with Max(val+, val–) and zigzag(val+, val–), dominates all other fast and frugal trees. This means that two of our construction rules succeeded in identifying a "locally optimal" solution (in the class of all possible trees) for our classification problem.

10.4.1   Comparing Fast and Frugal Decision Trees to Traditional Models

The next question arises here. Do fast and frugal trees perform well compared to rational and computationally demanding models? Let us compare the performance of logistic regression, a statistical tool widely used in expert systems of medical diagnostics. The performance of fitted logistic regression with various cutoff points compared to fast and frugal decision trees is illustrated in Figure 10.11.

We fitted a logistic regression model based on the three predictors exactly as used by the Green and Mehr tree (two single cues and the disjunction cue), and, for the sake of generality, we also fitted logistic regression with the whole set of the seven original cues. As evident

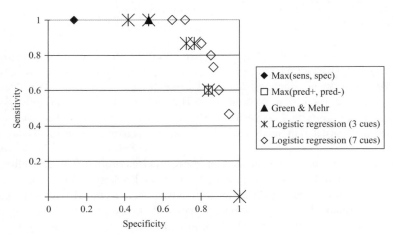

Figure 10.11   Performance (sensitivity and specificity) of logistic regression and the constructed fast and frugal trees

from the graph, logistic regression with all seven cues performs better than the best fast and frugal trees. It also achieves maximal sensitivity (avoiding all misses), and at the same time has a better specificity (two false positives less).[4] Note that our performance analysis covers only the *fitting* case, that is, modeling known data. The predictive accuracy of competing models (generalization to new data) can systematically differ from their success in fitting. As a guideline, simpler models tend to generalize better (see following section).

10.5   THE PRICE OF BEING NAIVE

Fast and frugal decision trees are constructed under the assumption that cues are all conditionally independent given the criterion. This naiveté, as we elucidate in this section, has its price. Indeed, full (Bayesian) trees have full classification power in many respects. Due to their unrestricted, unpruned and unsimplified structure, they do not structurally embody assumptions about certain cue–criterion relationships. They therefore are highly flexible in covering the whole possible range of different structures in the environment (including quite exotic ones). Full trees can, for instance, cover all sorts of cue interactions. Since every complete cue pattern has its own leaf, or "exit", in the bottom layer, and every exit can be freely linked to either of two consequences in the binary case, no assumptions about the general role or direction of cues have to be made. The same cue can be a positive indicator in the context of one cue pattern, and a negative indicator in the context of another pattern, that is, depending on the respective values of other cues. This is different for pruned trees. Imagine, for instance, a fast and frugal tree with four binary cues, c_1 to c_4. In this concrete tree, a cue value of $c_1 = 1$ in the first layer always prescribes a positive decision, D, whereas $c_1 = 0$ sends you deeper into the tree, to the second cue. (Decision D is chosen over not-D because it is the adequate reaction to the future event E, and from experience we know that $c_1 = 1$ is a good indicator for E to happen.) This means that cue patterns of the $\{1xxx\}$ type, with $x \in (0, 1)$, must all lead to the same decision, D. The chosen structure of the tree implements a strict order relation here. In all patterns of the $\{1xxx\}$ family, all possible values, and combinations of values, of c_2, c_3 and c_4 are *dominated* by the positive value of c_1. This simple structure obviously makes sense for data sets (environments) where the assumption of a strong correlation between $c_1 = 1$ and E *generally* holds over all possible $\{1xxx\}$ patterns, without stable major deviations from this contingency for specific patterns or subfamilies of patterns. For instance, the simplicity assumption would be contraindicated if c_1 is strongly correlated with E for all but one $\{1xxx\}$ pattern, but uncorrelated or even negatively correlated for, say, $\{1001\}$, given that $\{1001\}$ cases are not negligibly rare in the population. In this case, it would be wise to let the tree sprout into a structure that handles $\{1001\}$ cases differently from other $\{1xxx\}$ cases.

In the case of substantial cue interactions, pattern information does matter. Cue interactions go beyond the bivariate contingencies that are typically observed in the naive (unconditional) linear model framework. A straightforward demonstration of the interaction effect is given by what is now called "Meehl's paradox" (after its initial description by the clinician-statistician Paul E. Meehl, one of the pioneers in the field of clinical decision making; Meehl, 1950).

---

[4] The same performance can actually be achieved by a much simpler linear model here, namely, "tally" (count the number of 1s) with a threshold of 2: Allocate all patients with two or more positive cue values to the CCU (cf. Table 10.1).

Table 10.7   Meehl's paradox in the binary case

Criterion	Cue 1	Cue 2
1	1	1
1	0	0
1	1	1
1	0	0
1	1	1
1	0	0
0	0	1
0	1	0
0	0	1
0	1	0
0	0	1
0	1	0

Table 10.8   Correlations between cue 1 and the criterion in manifest subclasses indicated by cue 2

For cue 2 = 0		For cue 2 = 1	
0	3	3	0
3	0	0	3

For our purposes, imagine a fictitious data set with a binary event and two available binary cues for prediction (Table 10.7). The "paradoxical" nature of the given example is due to the fact that both single cues are essentially uncorrelated with the criterion from a bivariate perspective. Note also that the intercorrelation between cues is 0. Still, both cues together allow a perfect prediction of the criterion: the criterion value is present when *both* cues are either present or absent (the {11} and {00} cases), and absent if only one of them is present (the {10} and {10} cases, respectively). Both cues observed simultaneously contain predictive information that cannot be decomposed into an "additive" bivariate view. The dual-cue *pattern* cannot be reduced to the contributions of either cue alone.

Another way to put it is to look at one of the two cues as a *classifier* that discriminates between those cases where the correlation between the other cue and the criterion is positive and those where it is negative. The data set is a mixture of cases with either positive or negative intercorrelations between one cue and the criterion, with the other cue indicating the type of contingency (Table 10.8; cf. the concept of moderator effects in multivariate statistics). This, however, is the idealized, deterministic case of the paradox. While the extreme situation of a complete *reversal* of the contingency, with perfect predictability for both subtypes indicated by cue 2, will be unrealistic in most contexts, weaker forms of the paradox are more plausible. A bivariate cue–criterion correlation may be present in one subgroup but absent in another, or a strong correlation may hold for one subgroup only, but may be considerably weaker in the rest of the sample. Meehl's (1950) original formulation was meant to address the potential importance of cue interactions in clinical psychology, where

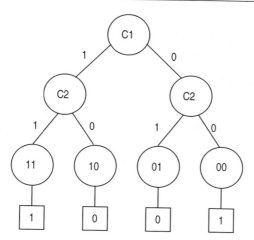

Figure 10.12   The representation of Meehl's paradox in a full tree, corresponding to the XOR property in network architectures

salient symptom patterns may go unnoticed if the focus is on statistical analysis within the standard multiple regression framework (where interaction terms are typically not included into the model). For instance, Jannarone and Roberts (1984) have shown that cue interactions in personality questionnaires can be a predictive source of information. Pattern effects of this kind are not restricted to bivariate cue interactions. In psychology, a method called "configural frequency analysis" (CFA) has been proposed (originally by Gustav A. Lienert in 1968) to analyze adequately data sets that may contain pattern information. The CFA identifies symptomatic "types" and "antitypes" by means of a χ^2-based analysis of cue–criterion patterns that occur more or less often than expected by chance (see von Eye, 1990).

Can decision trees handle Meehl's paradox? The basic answer is yes, of course, because pattern classification is what these trees have been designed for. However, the ability to represent cue interactions depends on the structure of the tree. A certain complexity of branching is required in order to implement the Meehl case. This is equivalent to the possibility of implementation of the "exclusive or" (XOR) statement in neural network architectures. XOR means that the output of a network should be set to a certain value (for example, "off", or 0) if either of two input nodes is active, but *not* if *both* are active. Just as XOR requires a "hidden layer" in the network where the signals of the input neurons interact, Meehl's paradox requires a (locally) fully branched structure of the tree (Figure 10.12). Again, the trick is that the values of one cue have different consequences conditional on the values of another cue. The decision crucially depends on "what happened before" in the tree, a situation that is structurally different from the splendid naiveté of "one-reason decision making" (Gigerenzer et al., 1999), as implemented in fast and frugal trees.[5]

This looks as if any pruning of the tree were a terrible negligence, and we should always stick to the full structure due to its marvelous flexibility. However, this unrestricted, finely

---

[5] In a fast and frugal tree, the Meehl case can be implemented only by applying a technical trick: the construction of compound cues. Two (or more) cues can always be recoded into a new cue such that the values of this cue embody the interaction information. This leads to the question of "natural" as opposed to artificially constructed representations of the environment ("What is a cue?").

branched flexibility comes with a flip side: questionable *stability* of the solution fitted to available data. As long as data sets are not sufficiently large to establish the validity of certain patterns in the lower levels of the tree (that is, as long as we do not have a large number of cases to sustain every possible pattern of cue combinations), it would be premature to pay too much attention to tiny differences between pattern details. Since the number of possible patterns is an exponential function of the number of cues, full trees quickly become intractable as the number of available cues increases. The fate of an overly complex tree is the same as for any complex model: it tends to *overfit* the available data, and therefore shows poor generalization if it comes to prediction with new data. This means that simpler models, and simpler trees, are typically more robust than more complex ones (Geman, Bienenstock & Doursat, 1992; Forster, 2000; Vitouch et al., 2001; Czerlinski et al., submitted).

CONCLUSION

Simple trees bet on a certain structure of the world, irrespective of the small fluctuations in a given set of available data. This can be a major advantage for generalization if the stable part of the process, which also holds for new data and new environments, is recognized and modeled. From a statistical point of view, it would, of course, be preferable to *test* empirically such assumptions instead of boldly implementing them in the model. But in real-life decision making, we usually do not have large numbers of data that are representative of the concrete decisional setting of interest at our disposal. For instance, even for large epidemiological trials in medicine, it often remains unclear whether the resulting databases allow good generalization to the situation in a particular hospital (due to special properties of local patients, insufficient standardization of measurements and diagnostic procedures, etc.). The fact that cue interactions *can* exist, and that they can be covered only by fully branched tree substructures, does not imply that they *must* exist; it says nothing about the frequency of their occurrence. Depending on the kind of the decision problem, there may be cases where we can make a reasonable guess about existing interactions on the substantial grounds of our knowledge of the problem domain. This may, for instance, be the case for interaction effects of drugs in medical treatment. The less we know, however, of a certain domain, the less reason we have to assume a priori that meaningful and stable interactions do exist. Indeed, the research program of the ABC Group has consistently shown that one-reason decision making, which, by definition, does not cover cue interactions, can work astonishingly well (Gigerenzer et al., 1999). In many decisional domains, we may be better off trusting the robust power of simple decision strategies rather than striving for full knowledge of brittle details.

REFERENCES

Bayes, T. (1763). An essay towards solving a problem in the doctrine of chances. *Philosophical Transactions*, *3*, 370–418. [Reprinted in W. E. Deming (ed.) (1963), *Two Papers by Bayes*. New York: Hafner.]

Chase, V. (1999). Where to look to find out why: Rational information search in causal hypothesis testing. Unpublished doctoral dissertation, University of Chicago.

Cousins, N. (1989). *The Biology of Hope*. New York: E. P. Dutton.

Czerlinski, J., Martignon, L., Gigerenzer, G. & Goldstein, D. G. (submitted). On the robustness of fast and frugal heuristics.

Fiedler, K. (2000). Beware of samples. *Psychological Review*, *107*, 659–676.

Fiedler, K., Brinkmann, B., Betsch, T. & Wild, B. (2000). A sampling approach to biases in conditional probability judgments: Beyond base rate neglect and statistical format. *Journal of Experimental Psychology: General*, *129*, 399–418.

Forster, M. R. (2000). Key concepts in model selection: Performance and generalizability. *Journal of Mathematical Psychology*, *44*, 205–231.

Geman, S., Bienenstock, E. & Doursat, R. (1992). Neural networks and the bias/variance dilemma. *Neural Computation*, *4*, 1–58.

Gigerenzer, G. (2002). *Calculated Risks: From Innumeracy to Insight*. New York: Simon & Schuster.

Gigerenzer, G. & Goldstein, D. G. (1996). Reasoning the fast and frugal way: Models of bounded rationality. *Psychological Review*, *4*, 650–669.

Gigerenzer, G. & Hoffrage, U. (1995). How to improve Bayesian reasoning without instructions: Frequency formats. *Psychological Review*, *102*, 684–704.

Gigerenzer, G., Todd, P. M. & ABC Research Group (eds) (1999). *Simple Heuristics That Make Us Smart*. New York: Oxford University Press.

Green, L. & Mehr, D. R. (1997). What alters physicians' decisions to admit to the coronary care unit? *Journal of Family Practice*, *45*, 219–226.

Hasher, L. & Zacks, R. T. (1984). Automatic processing of fundamental information: The case of frequency of occurrence. *American Psychologist*, *39*, 1372–1388.

Jannarone, R. J. & Roberts, J. S. (1984). Reflecting interactions among personality items: Meehl's paradox revisited. *Journal of Personality and Social Psychology*, *47*, 621–628.

Kleiter, G. D. (1994). Natural sampling. Rationality without base rates. In G. H. Fischer & D. Laming (eds), *Contributions to Mathematical Psychology, Psychometrics, and Methodology* (pp. 375–388). New York: Springer.

Krauss, S., Martignon, L., Hoffrage, U. & Gigerenzer, G. (2001). Bayesian reasoning and natural frequencies: A generalization to complex situations. MPI for Human Development, Berlin: Unpublished paper.

Macchi, L. & Mosconi, G. (1998). Computational features vs. frequentist phrasing in the base-rate fallacy. *Swiss Journal of Psychology*, *57*, 79–85.

Martignon, L. & Hoffrage, U. (1999). Why does one-reason decision making work? A case study in ecological rationality. In G. Gigerenzer, P. M. Todd & ABC Research Group (eds), *Simple Heuristics That Make Us Smart* (pp. 119–140). New York: Oxford University Press.

Meehl, P. E. (1950). Configural scoring. *Journal of Consulting Psychology*, *14*, 165–171.

Pearl, J. (1988). *Probabilistic Reasoning in Intelligent Systems*. San Francisco, CA: Morgan Kaufmann.

Pozen, M. W., D'Agostino, R. B., Selker, H. P., Sytkowski, P. A. & Hood, W. B. Jr. (1984). A predictive instrument to improve coronary-care-unit admission practices in acute ischemic heart disease. *New England Journal of Medicine*, *310*, 1273–1278.

Vitouch, O., Gigerenzer, G., Martignon, L. & Forster, M. R. (2001). Living on the safe side (vs. on the edge): The robust beauty of fast and frugal heuristics. MPI for Human Development, Berlin: Unpublished paper.

von Eye, A. (1990). *Introduction to Configural Frequency Analysis*. Cambridge: Cambridge University Press.

CHAPTER 11

More is not Always Better: The Benefits of Cognitive Limits

Ralph Hertwig

Max Planck Institute for Human Development, Berlin, Germany

and

Peter M. Todd

Max Planck Institute for Human Development, Berlin, Germany

THE LIABILITY VIEW OF COGNITIVE LIMITATIONS

Some of us ordinary mortals achieve extraordinary intellectual feats. For instance, the ancient Mithridates the Great (king of Pontus, a long and narrow strip of land on the southern coast of the Black Sea) is said to have learnt 22 languages, and to have been able in the days of his greatest power to transact business with the deputies of every tribe subject to his rule in their own peculiar dialect. Napoleon is known to have dictated 102 letters to successive teams of perspiring secretaries almost without pause, as he prepared the final details for the launching of his devastating campaign against Prussia (Chandler, 1997). One of the most celebrated physicists of our time was Richard Feynman, who won the 1965 Nobel Prize in physics for his many contributions to his field, especially for his work on quantum electrodynamics. Beyond being a brilliant thinker, on the bongos Feynman supposedly could play 10 beats with one hand against 11 with the other (Feynman, 1999; try it—you may decide that quantum electrodynamics is easier).

Despite numerous examples of people with prodigious abilities that we might otherwise have thought impossible, much of cognitive psychology rests on the premise that human information-processing capacity is rather severely bounded. In the words of Kahneman, Slovic and Tversky (1982), "cognitive psychology is concerned with internal processes, mental limitations, and the way in which the processes are shaped by the limitations" (p. xii). According to Cowan (2001), "one of the central contributions of cognitive psychology has been to explore limitations in the human capacity to store and process information" (p. 87). The list of documented limitations is long and includes the now classic thesis that the capacity of short-term memory is restricted to a limited number of chunks of information—"the magical number seven, plus or minus two" (Miller, 1956). Similarly, the ability to pursue multiple intentional goals at any one time (for example, driving a car, planning one's day at work and, simultaneously, listening to the latest scoop on the stock market) is thought to be restricted by a limited budget of strategic processing capacity (e.g., Shiffrin, 1988; Barsalou, 1992, Ch. 4).[1]

The premise that information-processing capacity is limited is usually accompanied by another ubiquitous assumption, namely, that these limitations pose a liability. They constrain our cognitive potential, this assumption holds, barring us from performing feats such as quickly computing the square roots of large numbers in our heads or reciting by heart all the entries of the Manhattan telephone book. Even more sinister, though, these cognitive limits are not only accused of hindering performance but are also suspected of being the culprit behind lapses of reasoning. In fact, the link between cognitive limitations and reasoning errors can be found in such disparate research programs as Piaget's theory of the cognitive development of children (e.g., Flavell, 1985), Johnson-Laird's mental model theory (1983; Johnson-Laird et al., 1999), and Kahneman and Tversky's heuristics-and-biases program (e.g., Kahneman, Slovic & Tversky, 1982).

Piaget, for instance, suggested that the still-immature mind of the preoperational child commits lapses of reasoning such as egocentrism (that is, the inability to take the perspective of another person) and animism (that is, ascribing lifelike qualities to inanimate objects). Only when cognitive development has reached its peak are children finally able to think in ways akin to those of scientists (for example, reasoning in accordance with the rules of logic and probability theory). The heuristics-and-biases program made a related point about the detriments of cognitive limits, but by challenging precisely the final stage of Piaget's developmental trajectory. In this research program's view, reasoning abilities that reflect the laws of probability and logic are *not* part of the intuitive repertoire of the adult human mind (e.g., Slovic, Fischhoff & Lichtenstein, 1976). Instead, due to their limited cognitive capacities, adults need to rely on quick shortcuts, or heuristics, when they reason about unknown or uncertain aspects of real-world environments. But this use of heuristics leaves adult human reasoning prone to "severe and systematic errors" (Tversky & Kahneman, 1974, p. 1124), some of them akin to the lapses in reasoning that Piaget's preoperational children suffered from (such as violation of class inclusion; see Hertwig, 2000).

What inspires the close link often made between bounds in cognitive capacity and lapses of reasoning, even irrationality? One speculative answer is that inferring this link naturally follows from a particular vision of rationality still embraced by many social scientists. This vision defines rational judgment and decision making in terms of *unbounded* rationality (see Gigerenzer & Todd, 1999). Unbounded rationality encompasses decision-making strategies that have little or no regard for humans' cognitive limitations and so are unfettered by concerns about decision speed or processing complexity. Theoretical frameworks such as subjective expected-utility maximization are often mathematically complex and computationally intractable; thus, they picture—implicitly or explicitly—the mind as if it were a supernatural being possessing unlimited powers of reason, boundless knowledge and endless time. Possibly, it is here that the link between limitations and irrationality suggests

---

[1] There are important exceptions such as parallel distributed memory models that disregard limited processing capacities by, for instance, assuming that search for a piece of information occurs simultaneously across multiple locations. In addition, there is evidence that the amount of information that can be held and processed in working memory can be greatly increased through practice (Kliegl et al., 1987; Ericsson & Kintsch, 1995), thus putting very narrow estimates of capacity limits somewhat into perspective.

itself to psychologists: being mere mortals, humans do not possess supernatural mental powers. Operating within the bounds of our cognitive limitations, we therefore must fall short of the norms defined by models of unbounded rationality.

The goal of this chapter is to challenge this obligatory link between cognitive limitations and human irrationality. While not doubting that limits can exact a price, we will question their exclusively negative status. Specifically, we put forth the thesis that limitations in processing capacity, as well as in other resources such as knowledge, can actually *enable* rather than *disable* important adaptive functions (*Thesis 1*). Secondly, we demonstrate that decision-making strategies that take limitations into account need not be less accurate than strategies with little or no regard for those limitations (*Thesis 2*). That is, we will show that accurate decision making does not necessitate supernatural mental powers, and thus that cognitive limitations need not be equated with inferior performance. Finally, we will challenge the assumption that simple decision-making strategies have evolved in response to the cognitive limitations of the human mind. We suggest the reverse causality and submit the thesis that capacity constraints may in fact be a byproduct of the evolution of simple strategies (*Thesis 3*).

THESIS 1: COGNITIVE LIMITATIONS CAN ENABLE IMPORTANT COGNITIVE FUNCTIONS

Because human beings are not omniscient, limitations in our knowledge are a ubiquitous fact—we differ only with regard to the domains in which we are more or less knowledgeable. In this sense, limited knowledge is an inevitable property of the *database* from which we derive inferences. Limitations in our knowledge, however, can be beneficial. We begin with an example of how limitations in knowledge can enable people to use a simple strategy to make surprisingly accurate inferences and predictions. But it is not just the data on which we base our decisions that are often limited—the *hardware* that we use to process those data and reach our conclusions is bounded as well. Hardware limitations—for instance, in terms of a limited working memory—also need not be a liability. In fact, as the later examples show, the limited capacity of human working memory can actually benefit learning and the vital inferences we make.

The Benefit of Limited Knowledge: The Recognition Heuristic

Most parents want their children to attend a good college. Unfortunately, the overwhelming variety of institutions of higher education makes the prospect of comparing them a daunting one. Just think of the many hundreds of US liberal arts colleges. How does one find out which are the good ones, or even just decide which of two colleges is the better one? Surprisingly, (partial) ignorance about the options in question can actually help people to make good choices. To see how limits in knowledge—in this case about colleges—can actually be beneficial, imagine the following scenario. Nearing the end of high school, three friends deliberate their choices of colleges. Because they are good students, they have applied only to liberal arts colleges that are ranked among the top 50 in the country. Eventually, each of the friends ends up with the choice between two colleges: *A* must choose between Middlebury and Vassar, *B* between Oberlin and Macalester, and *C* between Barnard and

Lafayette. Faced with these difficult choices, the friends turn to their parents for advice. Here is what they are told.

Student *A*'s parents have just moved to the USA. Thus, they know next to nothing about American colleges. In fact, they do not even recognize any of the colleges' names, and thus they can only guess which of the alternatives may be the better one. *B*'s parents also come from abroad—but they have already had the chance to absorb some knowledge about the American college system. Specifically, they recognize the names *Middlebury, Oberlin* and *Barnard* but do not recognize the names of the other contenders. Having no other knowledge to go on, they tell the three friends to go with those recognized alternatives. Finally, the friends turn to *C*'s mother, who happens to be a college professor. She has a lot of detailed knowledge about the colleges in question and can provide a plethora of information including the colleges' academic reputation, financial resources, student-to-faculty ratio, graduation rate and so on. Pressed to answer the question of which is the better college in each pair of choices, she responds: "It all depends!"

Although we all can resonate with the ideal that *C*'s mother represents, that knowing more about the alternatives in question is always better, such knowledge of multiple dimensions can create a predicament. In contrast to the convenient "common currency" assumption made by standard models of optimization (for example, translating everything into some amount of subjective expected utility), sometimes there is no way to compare all desires. Some things are incommensurable and thus difficult or impossible to convert into a single currency (Elster, 1979). For instance, should student *B* go to Oberlin because it has the higher academic reputation, or to Macalester because freshmen are more likely to return to campus the following year and eventually graduate (according to a recent college ranking published by *US NEWS*[2])? That is, should *B* strive to maximize the chance to get a good job or gain admission to a top graduate program, or should *B* try to maximize the chance of graduating by attending the school that may be offering the classes and services students need to succeed?

How can one escape this predicament of multiple, possibly incommensurable decision dimensions? Of course, one way to avoid it (later we will turn to another) is just to be ignorant about the intricacies of the choice situation—as was the case for *B*'s parents. But is this really a sensible path to take? Won't inferences based on pure recognition (and thus ignorance about other dimensions) be little more than random guesses? In fact, they can be a lot more. According to Goldstein and Gigerenzer (1999, 2002), choices based on recognition alone can be surprisingly accurate if exposure to different possibilities is positively correlated with their ranking along the decision criterion being used. They suggested that this is the case in environments involving competition (such as among colleges, baseball teams or companies). The decision task they focused on is a simple and common one: choose from two options (for example, colleges) the one that has a higher value on some criterion (for example, which one is older or more expensive). Akin to the strategy that *B*'s parents used, Goldstein and Gigerenzer proposed the recognition heuristic for this kind of task. Simply stated, this heuristic says: *If one of two objects is recognized and the other is not, infer that the recognized object has the higher value.*

This minimal strategy may not sound like much for a decision maker to go on, but there is often information implicit in the *failure* to recognize something, and this failure can be exploited by the heuristic. To find out how well the recognition heuristic would fare in our

---

[2] The college rankings can be found at *http://www.usnews.com/usnews/edu/college/rankings/natlibs/natliba2.htm*.

college example, we conducted a small-scale study in which we asked a group of Americans and a group of Germans (all familiar with the academic system of their own country) to indicate which of the 50 highest-ranked American liberal arts colleges (listed in the *US NEWS* reference ranking) they recognized. We expected to observe two effects: first, that the American group would recognize many more college names than the German group; second, that the recognition validity (that is, the percentage of correct choices among those pairs where one college is recognized and the other is not) would nonetheless be higher in the German group.

This is exactly what we found. With years of experience of the college system, the Americans recognized about three-quarters (75 percent) of the college names, while the Germans recognized slightly more than one-fifth (22 percent). In addition, we found that the average recognition validity was higher for the German group: .74 compared to .62 for the Americans. What this means is that if we had asked our participants to choose higher-ranking colleges out of pairs of college names, the Germans could have used the recognition heuristic to pick those they recognized over those they did not, and this would have resulted in reasonably good choices (58 percent correct). In contrast, the Americans, who recognized most college names, would have made fewer good choices (54 percent correct).

This sounds promising in theory, but do people actually use the recognition heuristic? Goldstein and Gigerenzer (1999, 2002) conducted a series of experimental studies that strongly suggested that the recognition heuristic is used. Consider an example. Which city has more inhabitants: San Diego or San Antonio? When students at the University of Chicago were asked to answer questions like this by picking the larger of two American cities (comparisons constructed from the 22 largest in the USA), they scored a median 71 percent correct inferences. Surprisingly, however, when quizzed on city pairs from the 22 largest cities in Germany, the same students increased their score to a median 73 percent correct inferences. This result is counterintuitive when viewed from the premise that more knowledge is always better. The students knew a lifetime of facts about US cities that could be useful for inferring population, but they knew little or nothing about the German cities beyond merely recognizing about half of them. The latter fact, however, is just what allowed them to employ the recognition heuristic to pick German cities that they recognized as larger than those they did not. The students could not use this heuristic for choosing between US cities, though, because they recognized all of them and thus had to rely on additional retriev-able information instead. Goldstein and Gigerenzer referred to this surprising phenomenon as the "less-is-more effect" and showed analytically and empirically that an intermediate amount of (recognition) knowledge about a set of objects can yield the highest proportion of correct answers—knowing (that is, recognizing) more than this will actually *decrease* the decision-making performance. We will return below to knowledge beyond recogni-tion and demonstrate that variants of the less-is-more effect also exist for other kinds of knowledge.

Common wisdom has it that more knowledge or information is always better and that ignorance stands in the way of good decision making. The recognition heuristic is a counterexample to this wisdom. It feeds on partial and non-random ignorance to make reasonable choices, and it works because our lack of recognition knowledge about, for instance, colleges, sports teams (Ayton & Önkal, 1997) and companies traded on a stock market (Borges et al., 1999), is often not random, but systematic and exploitable. Thus, it is limited knowledge that enables the success of this powerful and very simple decision heuristic.

The Benefit of a Limited Working Memory: Covariation Detection

Writers and scientists alike agree that "the impulse to search into causes is inherent in man's very nature" (Tolstoy, 1982/1869, p. 1168), and that "humans exhibit an almost obsessive urge to mold empirical phenomena conceptually into cause-effect relationships" (Pearl, 1988, p. 383). Whatever the reasons for this human "obsession" with causality, the key point for our discussion is that limitations in human cognitive capacity may lay the groundwork for inferences of causality in terms of the early detection of covariation. In a series of papers, Kareev (1995a,b, 2000; Kareev, Lieberman & Lev, 1997) advanced the argument that limitations of working-memory capacity force people to rely on small samples of information drawn from real-world environments (and from their long-term memory). Small samples of information, however, have a specific advantage: they maximize the chances for early detection of a correlation.

Kareev's argument runs as follows. To determine whether two variables covary (for example, does fleeing behavior trigger a predator's chase behavior), one typically relies on data sampled from one's environment (and prior expectations; see Alloy & Tabachnik, 1984). If the assessment of a covariation has to be made "on the fly", the limited capacity of working memory imposes an upper bound on the size of the information sample that can be considered at one time. What is the size of the working memory and consequently the size of the information sample from which inferences are drawn? As we all know, the classic estimate of short-term memory is 7 ± 2 chunks (Kareev uses the term "working memory", akin to the earlier concept "short-term memory", but see Baddeley, 2000, on the different meanings of the term "working memory"). Taking Miller's (1956) estimate as a starting point, Kareev et al. (1997; Kareev, 2000) suggested that the limited capacity of working memory increases the chances for early detection of a correlation.[3] Here is the rationale.

Drawing small data samples increases the likelihood of encountering a sample that indicates a stronger correlation than that of the population. To see why, imagine drawing many small data samples of two continuous variables (for binary variables, the argument works slightly differently; see Kareev, 2000). If, for each sample, one calculates the relationships between the two variables (the Pearson product-memory correlation) and plots the distribution of the correlation coefficients found in the samples, the resulting sampling distribution will have a characteristic shape. Unless the correlation in the population is zero, the sampling distribution of the correlation will be skewed, with both the *median* and the *mode* of the distribution more extreme than the population value (see Hays, 1963, p. 530). Moreover, the amount of skewedness is a function of the sample size: the smaller the sample, the more skewed the resulting distribution.

In other words, for small sample sizes, many more samples will exhibit a sample correlation higher than the correlation in the population. Thus, when drawing a random sample from a population in which a correlation exists, any random sample is more likely than

---

[3] In a recent review article, Cowan (2001) concluded that over 40 years after Miller's seminal paper, we are still uncertain about the nature of the storage limit. For instance, according to some theories, there is no limit in storage per se, but a limit on the time an item can remain in short-term memory without being rehearsed. Cowan also argued that the storage limit itself is open to considerable differences of opinion, but concluded that "the evidence provides broad support for what can be interpreted as a capacity limit of substantially fewer than Miller's 7 ± 2 chunks; about four chunks on the average" (p. 88).

not to indicate a correlation more extreme than that found in the population.[4] Thus, the limited working memory functions as an amplifier of correlations. Consistent with this thesis, Kareev et al. (1997) found that people with smaller working-memory capacity detected correlations faster and used them to make correct predictions better than people with larger working-memory capacity. Moreover, they observed that the detection of correlation improved when it was based on smaller samples.

This theoretical account and empirical observations suggest a new and interesting view of cognitive limitations in general. In Kareev's view, cognitive limitations in working memory are not a liability but, in fact, enable important adaptive functions such as the early detection of covariation. The ability to detect contingencies early seems particularly important in domains in which the benefits of discovering a contingency outweigh the costs of false alarms. (Note that the smaller the data sample from which the contingency is inferred, the greater the variability of the sampling distribution and, consequently, the danger of a false alarm.) Such domains include, for instance, threats in which misses would be extremely costly.

Another Benefit from a Limited Memory Span: Language Learning

Another domain where limitations are beneficial, possibly even a prerequisite for maximal success, is language learning. According to Newport (1990), lesser ability to process and remember form-meaning mappings in young children allows them to learn more accurately those mappings that they do acquire and then to build further upon these as language learning proceeds. Late language learners, in contrast, may falter when attempting to learn all at once the full range of semantic mappings with their mature mental capacities.

This situation has been studied concretely by Elman (1993) in a neural network model of language acquisition. When he tried to get a large, recurrent neural network with an extensive memory to learn the grammatical relationships in a set of several thousand sentences of varying length and complexity, the network faltered. It was unable to pick up such concepts as noun–verb agreement in embedded clauses, something that requires sufficient memory to keep embedded and non-embedded clauses disentangled. Instead of taking the obvious step of adding more memory to the model to attempt to solve this problem, though, Elman counterintuitively *restricted* its memory, making the network forget everything after every three or four words. He hoped in this way to mimic the memory restrictions of young children first learning language. This restricted-memory network could not possibly make sense of the long, clause-filled sentences it was exposed to. Its limitations forced it to focus on the short, simple sentences in its environment, which it did learn correctly, mastering the small set of grammatical relationships inherent in this subset of its input. Elman then increased the network's effective memory by forcing it to forget everything after five or six words. It was now able to learn a greater proportion of the sentences it was exposed to, building on the grammatical relationships it had already acquired. Further gradual enhancements of the

---

[4] This skewed distribution is related to the fact that correlation coefficients are truncated, with their absolute values not exceeding 1 or −1. Assume the correlation coefficient in the population is .8. Sample correlations can deviate in two directions from the population parameter: they can be larger or smaller. A deviation above, however, can at most be .2, while a deviation below can go as far as −1.8. To offset the (few) very large deviations in the downward direction, there must be many more (smaller) deviations in the upward direction. From this, it follows that one is more likely to encounter a sample correlation that amplifies the population value than a sample correlation that attenuates it.

network's memory allowed it ultimately to learn the entire corpus of sentences that the full network alone—without the benefit of starting small—had been unable to fathom.

Elman sees the restrictions of the developing mind as enabling accurate early learning about a small portion of the environment, which then provides a scaffold to guide learning and hypothesizing about the rest of the environment in fruitful, adaptive directions. Cognitive "constraints" are no longer a negative limitation of our (or our children's) ability to behave adaptively in our environment. Rather,

> the early limitations on memory capacity assume a more positive character. One might have predicted that the more powerful the network, the greater its ability to learn a complex domain. However, this appears not always to be the case. If the domain is of sufficient complexity, and if there are abundant false solutions [for example, local error minima in a neural network's solution space], then the opportunities for failure are great. What is required is some way to artificially constrain the solution space to just that region which contains the true solution. The initial memory limitations fill this role; they act as a filter on the input, and focus learning on just that subset of facts which lay the foundation for future success. (Elman, 1993, pp. 84–85)

Thus, a smaller memory span should not be seen as a *constraint* on language learning, but rather as an *enabler* of learning, as Cosmides and Tooby (1987, p. 301) have put it.

Let us conclude this section with a cautionary note. We should be careful not to extend these arguments automatically to every problem environment that humans face—language, after all, has evolved culturally to be something that our fast and frugal developing minds can readily learn. But further explorations beyond Kareev's and Elman's work should reveal other domains where limited memory enables rather than constrains inference or learning.

THESIS 2: COGNITIVE LIMITATIONS AND SIMPLE PROCESSING NEED NOT BE EQUATED WITH INFERIOR PERFORMANCE

Scientific theorizing, visions of rationality and common wisdom alike appear to share a mutual belief: the more information that is used and the more it is processed, the better (or more rational) the choice, judgment or decision will be. This belief is not just an inconsequential idea that people might have. It affects, for instance, how we set up our information environments. According to Andrew Dillon (1996), for instance, "the belief that enabling access to, and manipulation of masses of information . . . is desirable and will somehow increase learning (however measured) is ever-present in discussions on educational hypertext" (p. 31). In his view, however, "to date, the claims have far exceeded the evidence and few hypertext systems have been shown to lead to greater comprehension or significantly better performance. . . . This concern with vast information sources over real human needs betrays the technocentric values of its proponents even while they talk in user-centred terms" (p. 32).

What is the evidence that more information and more complex processing are, a priori, better, or, vice versa, that less information and less processing, a priori, impair performance? The research program that has most strongly advocated the view that less processing, via the use of simple cognitive heuristics (relying on simple psychological principles such as associative strengths), can yield severe and systematic errors is the heuristics-and-biases program

(Kahneman, Slovic & Tversky, 1982). Specifically, this program attributes numerous departures from classical probability norms in inductive reasoning—"cognitive illusions", such as overconfidence, base-rate neglect and the conjunction fallacy—to the application of heuristics (Kahneman & Tversky, 1996). Some have argued that these departures "should be considered the rule rather than the exception" (Thaler, 1991, p. 4), while others have shown that a simple change in the way statistical information is represented—from single-event probabilities to frequencies—substantially reduces those departures (e.g., Gigerenzer, 1991; Gigerenzer & Hoffrage, 1995; Hertwig & Gigerenzer, 1999; but see Mellers, Hertwig & Kahneman, 2001).

Are violations of rational norms really the rule, and is simple processing to be equated with inferior performance? Taken at face value, the research in the tradition of the heuristics-and-biases program suggests a positive answer. However, Kahneman and Tversky (1982, p. 124) themselves acknowledged that "although errors of judgment are but a method by which some cognitive processes are studied, the method has become a significant part of the message". It appears that as a consequence of the exclusive focus on errors, the original assessment of heuristics as "highly economical and usually effective" (Tversky & Kahneman, 1974, p. 1131) has been largely ignored, and research in the tradition of the heuristics-and-biases program has been silent on questions such as when and why simple heuristics yield good performance. Exactly these kinds of questions, however, are being addressed in a new research program that explores the performance of simple decision heuristics. The research program on fast and frugal decision heuristics (Gigerenzer, Todd & ABC Research Group, 1999) challenges the equating of simple processing with inferior performance.

Simple Heuristics That Make Us Smart

Earlier, we introduced one fast and frugal decision rule studied within this program, the recognition heuristic. It exploits the knowledge of whether or not an option (such as a college name) has ever been encountered before. Often, however, more than just this type of information is accessible. In what follows, we describe two more fast and frugal heuristics that can be applied if more than just recognition knowledge is available. To illustrate how they work, let us return to our introductory example—deciding which of two colleges is better.

How would a rational agent make this decision? Two commandments that are often taken as characteristics of rational judgments are *complete search* and *compensation* (see Gigerenzer & Goldstein, 1999). The former prescribes, "thou shalt find all the information available", while the latter says, "thou shalt combine all pieces of information" (that is, not rely on just one piece). Thus, to decide which college is better, the decision maker ought to retrieve all the information available (either from internal or external memories), and then somehow combine the pieces of information into a single judgment (typically, this implies that the information will first be weighted according to its predictive value for the decision criterion).

More or less the exact opposite of this "rational" approach is to rely on just a single dimension to make the decision. Such a strategy simultaneously violates the commandments of complete search and compensation. Here is how it would work. Imagine that the goal is to select one object (such as a college) from two possibilities, according to some criterion on which the two can be compared (such as ranking). Several decision dimensions (cues) could be used to assess each object on the criterion.[5] A one-reason heuristic that makes decisions on the basis of a single cue could then work as follows:

(1) Select a cue dimension and look for the corresponding cue values of each object.
(2) Compare the two objects on their values for that cue dimension.
(3) If they differ, stop and choose the object with the cue value indicating a greater value on the choice criterion.
(4) If the objects do not differ, return to the beginning of this loop (step 1) to look for another cue dimension.

Such a heuristic will often have to look up more than one cue before making a decision, but the simple stopping rule (in step 3) ensures that as few cues as possible will be sought, thus minimizing the information-searching time taken. Furthermore, ultimately only a single cue will be used to determine the choice, minimizing the amount of computation that must be done.

This four-step loop incorporates two of the three important building blocks of simple heuristics (as described in Gigerenzer & Todd, 1999): a stopping rule (step 3) and a decision rule (also step 3—deciding on the object to which the one cue points). To finish specifying a particular simple heuristic of this type, we must also determine just how cue dimensions are "looked for" in step 1. That is, we must pick a specific information search rule—the third building block. Two intuitive search rules are to search for cues in the order of their ecological validity (that is, their predictive power with regard to the decision criterion) or to select cues in a random order. In combination with the stopping and decision rules described above, the former search rule makes up the Take The Best heuristic, and the latter makes up the Minimalist heuristic (Gigerenzer & Goldstein, 1996).

Both heuristics disobey the commandments of complete search and compensation. Could such an unorthodox approach possibly work? To answer this question, Czerlinski, Gigerenzer and Goldstein (1999) used a set of 20 environments to test the heuristics' performance. The environments varied in number of objects and number of available cues, and ranged in content from high-school dropout rates to fish fertility. The decision accuracy of Take The Best and Minimalist were compared to those of two more traditional decision mechanisms that use all available information and combine it in more or less sophisticated ways: multiple regression, which weights and sums all cues in an optimal linear fashion, and Dawes's rule, which tallies the positive and negative cues and subtracts the latter from the former.

How did the two fast and frugal heuristics fare? They always came close to, and often matched, the performance of the traditional algorithms when all were tested on the data they were trained on—the overall average performance across all 20 data sets is shown in Table 11.1 (under "Fitting"). This surprising performance on the part of Take The Best and Minimalist was achieved even though they only looked through a third of the cues on average (and decided with only one of them), whereas multiple regression and Dawes's rule used them all (see Table 11.1, "Frugality"). The advantages of simplicity grew in the more important test of generalization performance, where the decision mechanisms were tested on a portion of each data set that they had not seen during training. Here, Take

---

[5] Cues can be either binary (is the college in the northeast of the USA?) or continuous (what is the student–faculty ratio?). For practical purposes, continuous variables can be dichotomized (for example, by a median split).

Table 11.1 Performance of different decision strategies across 20 data sets

Strategy	Frugality	Accuracy (% correct)	
		Fitting	Generalization
Minimalist	2.2	69	65
Take The Best	2.4	75	73
Dawes's rule	7.7	73	69
Multiple regression	7.7	77	68

Performance of two fast and frugal heuristics (Minimalist and Take The Best) and two linear strategies (Dawes's rule and multiple regression) across 20 data sets. The mean number of predictors available in the 20 data sets was 7.7. "Frugality" indicates the mean number of cues actually used by each strategy. "Fitting accuracy" indicates the percentage of correct answers achieved by the strategy when fitting data (test set = training set). "Generalization accuracy" indicates the percentage of correct answers achieved by the strategy when generalizing to new data (cross-validation, where test set ≠ training set) (data from Czerlinski, Goldstein & Gigerenzer, 1999).

The Best outperformed all three other algorithms by at least 4 percent (see Table 11.1, "Generalization").

To conclude, making *good* decisions need not rely on the standard rational approach of collecting all available information and combining it according to the relative importance of each cue—simply betting on one good reason, even one selected at random, can provide a competitive level of accuracy in a variety of environments. Of course, not all choices in life are presented to us as convenient pairs of options. Do the results on the efficacy of simple heuristics hold beyond the context of deliberated choices? The answer is yes. Limited processing of limited information can also suffice to perform such taxing tasks as estimating a precise criterion value (see Hertwig, Hoffrage & Martignon, 1999) and choosing the one category, from several possible, that a given object falls into (Berretty, Todd & Martignon, 1999). In short, psychological plausibility and precision are not irreconcilable, and simple processing need not be equated with inferior performance.

THESIS 3: COGNITIVE LIMITATIONS MAY BE A BYPRODUCT OF THE EVOLUTION OF SIMPLE STRATEGIES

Although there is little dispute that we humans often employ simple shortcuts or heuristics to reach decisions, there is much debate about *how* we use them—at our peril or to our advantage (e.g., Kahneman et al., 1982; Chase, Hertwig & Gigerenzer, 1998; Gigerenzer et al., 1999). An issue that seems equally important but, to date, has received hardly any attention is this: *why* is our mental machinery equipped with simple heuristics in the first place? One likely reason why this question is rarely addressed is that there is an apparently convincing straightforward answer: we rely on simple heuristics not because we choose to but because we have only limited processing capacities at our disposal. They, in turn, dictate the use of strategies that do not overtax our precious processing resources. Payne, Bettman and Johnson (1993), for instance, put this traditional argument very clearly: "Our basic thesis is that the use of various decision strategies [including simple heuristics] is an adaptive response of a limited-capacity information processor to the demands of complex task environments" (p. 9).

Why is this argument not necessarily as plausible as it appears at first glance? The reason (see also Todd, 2001) is that given sufficient adaptive pressure to succeed in complex tasks, evolution could have built complex and sophisticated information-processing structures so that human cognitive machinery would not need to rely on simple, sometimes erroneous, heuristics. In other words, cognitive limitations could have been circumvented over the course of evolution—certainly at a price, such as the considerable costs involved in bearing a large-headed, long-dependent human baby, or the costs of high-energy expenditure for maintaining the metabolism of a large brain. That a human mind, in theory, could have evolved to be less subject to bounds in its memory and processing capacity is evidenced both by the prodigious processing that evolution provided for the seemingly more elementary processes such as perception or motor coordination, and by the extraordinary abilities of a few exceptional individuals (some of whom we listed in the introduction; see also Sacks, 1995).

If, for a moment, we do not take cognitive limitations as a given, but conceive of cognitive capacity as a free parameter that has been adjusted in the course of evolution, then a bold alternative answer arises to the question of why humans are equipped with cognitive limitations. In contrast to the traditional view, heuristics may not be dictated by cognitive limitations; rather, the evolution of simple heuristics may have required the evolution of no more than a certain limited amount of cognitive capacity, namely, the amount that was needed to execute them. This view reverses the traditional causal direction—from limitations that lead to heuristics to heuristics that require a certain, limited amount of capacity. This argument, however, can work only if simple heuristics had a selective advantage over more complex cognitive strategies (that would have required more processing power). What could those advantage(s) have been? Being fully aware that any answer to this question is speculative, we suggest two plausible candidate advantages—speed and robustness.

The Importance of Speed

One of the most pressing concerns facing a variety of organisms in a variety of dynamic environmental situations is simply the passage of time. This pressure arises primarily through competition between organisms in two main ways. First, time is short: organisms have occasional speed-based encounters where the slower individual can end up at a serious disadvantage, for instance, being slowly digested by the faster. Second, time is money, or at least energy: beyond predator–prey or combative situations, the faster an individual can make decisions and act on them to accrue resources or reproductive opportunities, the greater adaptive advantage it will have over slower competitors.

The speed argument, however, faces an important objection. Speed is only a precious resource if one assumes that search for information and processing of the retrieved information occurs serially. If, however, our mental hardware operates in a parallel fashion, even extensive search for information and sophisticated processing of it can occur rapidly. In other words, in a parallel machine, time is not a limiting factor. How could the parallel processing argument be countered? While this argument may be valid (to the extent that our mind is a parallel machine) for processes within the mind, it is not applicable to processes outside the mind—in particular, the process of search for information (for example, the values of an object on various cue dimensions) in external sources. On an individual level, search for information in our environment occurs serially (ignoring the fact that our different senses can search in a parallel fashion). Following this reasoning, it is possible that many human decision heuristics were selected to achieve speed by seeking to use as little information from the environment as they could get away with.

All this is not to say that the entirety of human thought can be or should be characterized by simple heuristics—humans are uniquely able to set aside such mental shortcuts and engage in extensive cogitation, calculation and planning—but that we spend much of our time not taking the time to think deeply.

The Importance of Robustness

Learning means generalizing from the known to the unknown. This process of generalization has an element of gambling because the known information has both inherent structure and noise. Only the inherent structure, however, generalizes beyond the known information, and therefore this is what a learning model (for example, a decision strategy) should capture. Computationally powerful strategies (such as neural networks and multiple regression) aim to build a model of the known territory that is as perfect as possible, and thus to incorporate and account for as much of the known data as possible. Such a strategy is extremely successful if the known territory is large compared to the unknown, and if the known data include little noise. If the known territory, however, is small or includes much noise, trying to capture the known as precisely as possible turns out to be costly. Why? Because it means reliance not only on the inherent structure but also on the idiosyncrasies of the specific known information.

Take the US presidential election in 2000 as an example. Let us assume that the known data comprised only the election outcome in Florida, while the outcomes in the other states had to be predicted. As we all remember vividly, the outcome of the election in Florida was subject to many variables—some of them undoubtedly meaningful beyond Florida (for example, socioeconomic variables and the ethnic composition of Florida's constituency); others were relevant (if at all) only in the context of Florida's election turmoil (for example, poorly drafted "butterfly" ballots in one county and the secretary of state's interpretation of her "discretion"). Although across all 50 US states there is likely to be no true causal relationships between the election outcome and the variables idiosyncratic to Florida, the Florida sample of known data may (erroneously) indicate such relationships. Any inference model that tried to incorporate these idiosyncrasies to predict the election outcomes in the other states would be in danger of impairing its predictive power. In other words, it would "overfit" the known data.

How does the problem of "overfitting" relate to our thesis, namely, that simple heuristics may have had a selective advantage over more complex cognitive strategies? The argument we submit is that simple models are less prone to overfitting because they are parsimonious, using only a minimum number of parameters and thus reducing the likelihood of fitting noise (see Martignon & Hoffrage, 1999). Of course, there is a limit to simplicity, and there is "ignorant" simplicity (as in the case of that Minimalist heuristic, which randomly selects cues) and "smart" simplicity (as in the case of the Take The Best heuristic, which searches for one non-compensatory good reason, assuming that the structure of information is skewed in a non-compensatory way).

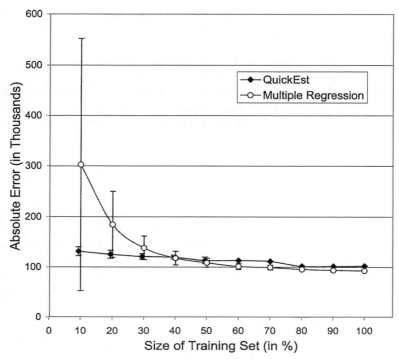

Figure 11.1 QuickEst's and multiple regression's mean absolute error (that is, absolute deviation between predicted and actual size) as a function of size of training set. Vertical lines represent standard deviations. Note that some of the points have been offset slightly in the horizontal dimension to make the error bars easier to distinguish, but they correspond to identical training set sizes

Are fast and frugal heuristics, in fact, robust—that is, do they generalize well from known to unknown territory? Using extensive simulations, we have consistently observed that simple heuristics are, in fact, more robust than computationally complex strategies (e.g., Czerlinski et al., 1999; Gigerenzer & Goldstein, 1999). Take the QuickEst heuristic (Hertwig, Hoffrage & Martignon, 1999) as an example. The QuickEst heuristic is designed to estimate the values of objects along some criterion (for example, how many people live in Maine?) using as little information as possible. QuickEst does this by betting that the environment follows a J-distribution, in which small values are common and big values are rare (here the "J" is rotated clockwise by 90 degrees). Such distributions characterize a variety of naturally occurring phenomena, including many formed by accretionary growth and phenomena involving competition (such as scientific productivity).

How well would QuickEst do if it were to learn cues from a small sample? QuickEst extracts from a learning sample only the order and sign of the cues, a very small amount of information compared to the information extracted by complex statistical procedures such as multiple regression (which extracts least-squares minimizing cue weights and covariances between cues). Which is the better policy? Figure 11.1 shows QuickEst competing with multiple regression at making generalizations from a training set to a test set. Each strategy estimated its respective parameters from a proportion (10 percent to 100 percent) of the

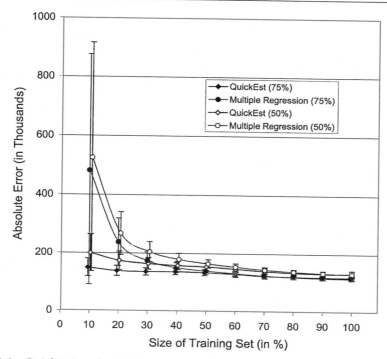

Figure 11.2 QuickEst's and multiple regression's mean absolute error (that is, absolute deviation between predicted and actual size) as a function of size of training set and of the amount of knowledge of cue values (75 percent and 50 percent). Vertical lines represent standard deviations

real-world environment of German cities with more than 100 000 inhabitants and values on eight ecological cues to population size (for example, is the city located in the industrial belt?), and made predictions about the complement.

Although (or because) QuickEst considers, on average, only 2.3 cues per estimate (out of 8 available cues), thus using only 32 percent of the information exploited by multiple regression, it exceeded the performance of multiple regression when the strategies had only scarce knowledge (that is, knew a third or fewer of the cities). When half of all cities were known, QuickEst and multiple regression performed about equally well. When the strategies had complete knowledge (all cities are known), multiple regression outperformed QuickEst by a relatively small margin. In other words, in the likely context of little to medium knowledge, QuickEst either matched the performance of multiple regression or outperformed it. Only when all knowledge was available—a situation that is rather unlikely to arise in most real-world domains—did multiple regression outperform QuickEst (by a small margin).

QuickEst's surprising performance is even more pronounced in a more difficult situation. Figure 11.2 shows the results for a simulation in which one-fourth or half of the cue values were eliminated from the environment (German cities) before the training and test sets were created, thus adding noise to the known data. Adding additional noise to the available information amplified QuickEst's edge over multiple regression. When only half of the cue values were known, QuickEst outperformed multiple regression throughout the training sets (except for the 100 percent training set), and again the advantage was particularly pronounced when the training sets were small.

The performance figures for QuickEst and for other fast and frugal strategies (e.g., Czerlinski et al., 1999; Gigerenzer & Goldstein, 1999) demonstrate that, on these data sets, simple heuristics are less prone to overfitting a known environment and are thus more robust when generalizing to new environments than are more complicated statistical procedures such as multiple regression.

To conclude, in combination with their speed, robustness under conditions of limited knowledge may have provided simple strategies with a selective advantage over more complicated strategies. Cognitive limitations could thus be the manifestation of the evolutionary success of simple strategies rather than their origin.

CONCLUSION

In this chapter, we proposed a different view of the role of cognitive limitations. In this view, cognitive limitations (regarding knowledge and processing capacity) are not a nemesis—rather, they can enable important adaptive functions. Secondly, we demonstrated that decision-making strategies that take limitations into account need not be less accurate than strategies with little regard for those limitations. In opposition to the traditional view, according to which cognitive limitations dictate the use of simple heuristics, we finally proposed that some cognitive limitations may follow from the evolution of simple strategies.

There are different ways to think about and analyze the possible functions of cognitive limitations. One approach we did not pursue is to think about how a mind equipped with *boundless* capacities would function in the real world. Others, however, have taken this approach. Conducting a literary *"Gedanken Experiment"*, the writer Jorge Luis Borges (1998) tells the story of Ireneo Funes, who, after a fall from a horse, found that his perception and memory had become essentially limitless. How did this man's perception of the world change as a function of his new abilities? Borges asserts that despite having an infinite memory, Funes is "not very good at thinking" (p. 137). Funes "was virtually incapable of general, platonic ideas . . . it irritated him that the 'dog' of three-fourteen in the afternoon, seen in profile, should be indicated by the same noun as the dog of three-fifteen, seen frontally" (p. 136). His mind consists of such perfect memory that no room exists for human creativity to link two dissimilar objects. In Borges' view, "to think is to ignore (or forget) differences, to generalize, to abstract" (p. 137), while Funes' memory is like a "garbage heap" (p. 135), which, whether he liked it or not, stored everything, the trivial and the important, indistinguishably.

Are these, in fact, the regrettable consequences of a perfect memory? Would we, as Borges suggests, become unable to function normally, because we were lost in a perpetual flux of unique instants of experience? Fortunately, we do not have to rely on our imagination (or on Borges' for that matter) to answer this question. There are real cases that approximate the *Gedanken Experiment* Borges engaged in; for instance, the wonderfully documented and fascinating case of S.V. Shereshevskii, a Russian memory-artist whose multisensory memory was studied over four decades by the neurologist A.R. Luria (1968/1987).

Resonating with Borges' portrayal of Funes, Luria described the most significant cost of possessing a memory that had "no distinct limits" (p. 11) as the inability to generalize, summarize and use abstractions. Shereshevskii told Luria: "I can only understand what I can visualise" (p. 130). He "was unable to grasp an idea unless he could actually see it, and so he tried to visualize the idea of 'nothing', to find an image with which to depict 'infinity'. And he persisted in these agonizing attempts all his life, forever coping with a basically adolescent conflict that made it impossible for him to cross that "'accursed' threshold to a higher level of thought" (p. 133).

To have "more memories than all mankind since the world began" (Ireneo Funes in Borges, 1998, p. 135) may not be so desirable after all.

ACKNOWLEDGEMENTS

We are grateful to Daniel Ames, Yaakov Kareev, Patricia Lindemann and Elke Weber for many helpful comments, and to the Deutsche Forschungsgemeinschaft for its financial support of the first author (Forschungstipendium He 2768/6-1).

REFERENCES

Alloy, L.B. & Tabachnik, N. (1984). Assessment of covariation by humans and animals: The joint influence of prior expectations and current situational information. *Psychological Review, 91*, 112–149.

Ayton, P. & Önkal, D. (1997). Forecasting football fixtures: Confidence and judged proportion correct. Unpublished paper.

Baddeley, A. (2000). The episodic buffer: A new component of working memory? *Trends in Cognitive Sciences, 4*, 417–423.

Barsalou, L.W. (1992). *Cognitive Psychology: An Overview for Cognitive Scientists*. Hillsdale, NJ: Erlbaum.

Berretty, P.M., Todd, P.M. & Martignon, L. (1999). Categorization by elimination: Using few cues to choose. In G. Gigerenzer, P.M. Todd & the ABC Research Group, *Simple Heuristics That Make Us Smart* (pp. 235–254). New York: Oxford University Press.

Borges, B., Goldstein, D.G., Ortmann, A. & Gigerenzer, G. (1999). Can ignorance beat the stock market? In G. Gigerenzer, P.M. Todd & the ABC Research Group, *Simple Heuristics That Make Us Smart* (pp. 59–72). New York: Oxford University Press.

Borges, J.L. (1998). *Collected Fictions*. New York: Penguin Books.

Chandler, D. (1997). Napoleon and death. *The Journal of the International Napoleonic Society, 1* (*http://www.napoleonicsociety.com/english/scholarship97/c_death.html*).

Chase, V.M., Hertwig, R. & Gigerenzer, G. (1998). Visions of rationality. *Trends in Cognitive Sciences, 2*, 206–214.

Cosmides, L. & Tooby, J. (1987). From evolution to behavior: Evolutionary psychology as the missing link. In J. Dupré (ed.), *The Latest on the Best: Essays on Evolution and Optimization* (pp. 277–306). Cambridge, MA: MIT Press.

Cowan, N. (2001). The magical number 4 in short-term memory: A reconsideration of mental storage capacity. *Behavioral and Brain Science, 24*, 87–185.

Czerlinski, J., Gigerenzer, G. & Goldstein, D.G. (1999). How good are simple heuristics? In G. Gigerenzer, P.M. Todd & the ABC Research Group, *Simple Heuristics That Make Us Smart* (pp. 97–118). New York: Oxford University Press.

Dillon, A.P. (1996). Myths, misconceptions and an alternative perspective on information usage and the electronic medium. In J.F. Rouet, J.J. Levonen, A.P. Dillon & R.J. Spiro (eds), *Hypertext and cognition* (pp. 25–42). Hillsdale, NJ: Erlbaum.

Elman, J.L. (1993). Learning and development in neural networks: The importance of starting small. *Cognition*, *48*, 71–99.

Elster, J. (1979). *Ulysses and the Sirens: Studies in Rationality and Irrationality*. Cambridge: Cambridge University Press.

Ericsson, K.A. & Kintsch, W. (1995). Long-term working memory. *Psychological Review*, *102*, 211–245.

Feynman, R.P. (1999). *The Pleasure of Finding Things Out: The Best Short Works of Richard P. Feynman*. Cambridge, MA: Perseus.

Flavell, J.H. (1985). *Cognitive Development*. Englewood Cliffs, NJ: Prentice-Hall.

Gigerenzer, G. (1991). How to make cognitive illusions disappear: Beyond "heuristics and biases". *European Review of Social Psychology*, *2*, 83–115.

Gigerenzer, G. & Goldstein, D.G. (1996). Reasoning the fast and frugal way: Models of bounded rationality. *Psychological Review*, *103*, 650–669.

Gigerenzer, G. & Goldstein, D.G. (1999). Betting on one good reason: The Take The Best heuristic. In G. Gigerenzer, P.M. Todd & the ABC Research Group, *Simple Heuristics That Make Us Smart* (pp. 75–95). New York: Oxford University Press.

Gigerenzer, G. & Hoffrage, U. (1995). How to improve Bayesian reasoning without instruction: Frequency formats. *Psychological Review*, *102*, 684–704.

Gigerenzer, G. & Todd, P.M. (1999). Fast and frugal heuristics: The adaptive toolbox. In G., Gigerenzer, P.M. Todd, & the ABC Research Group, *Simple Heuristics That Make Us Smart* (pp. 3–34). New York: Oxford University Press.

Gigerenzer, G., Todd, P.M. & the ABC Research Group (1999). *Simple Heuristics That Make Us Smart*. New York: Oxford University Press.

Goldstein, D.G. & Gigerenzer, G. (1999). The recognition heuristic: How ignorance makes us smart. In G. Gigerenzer, P.M. Todd & the ABC Research Group, *Simple Heuristics That Make Us Smart* (pp. 37–58). New York: Oxford University Press.

Goldstein, D.G. & Gigerenzer, G. (2002). Models of ecological rationality: The recognition heuristic. *Psychological Review*, *109*, 75–90.

Hays, W.L. (1963). *Statistics for Psychologists*. New York: Holt, Rinehart & Winston.

Hertwig, R. (2000). The questionable utility of "cognitive ability" in explaining cognitive illusions. *Behavioral and Brain Science*, *23*, 678–679.

Hertwig, R. & Gigerenzer, G. (1999). The "conjunction fallacy" revisited: How intelligent inferences look like reasoning errors. *Journal of Behavioral Decision Making*, *12*, 275–305.

Hertwig, R., Hoffrage, U. & Martignon, L. (1999). Quick estimation: Letting the environment do the work. In G. Gigerenzer, P.M. Todd & the ABC Research Group, *Simple Heuristics That Make Us Smart* (pp. 209–234). New York: Oxford University Press.

Johnson-Laird, P.N. (1983). *Mental Models*. Cambridge: Cambridge University Press.

Johnson-Laird, P.N., Legrenzi, P., Girotto, V., Legrenzi, M.S. & Caverni, J.-P. (1999). Naïve probability: A mental model theory of extensional reasoning. *Psychological Review*, *106*, 62–88.

Kahneman, D. & Tversky, A. (1982). On the study of statistical intuitions. *Cognition*, *11*, 123–141.

Kahneman, D. & Tversky, A. (1996). On the reality of cognitive illusions. *Psychological Review*, *103*, 582–591.

Kahneman, D., Slovic, P. & Tversky, A. (eds) (1982). *Judgment Under Uncertainty: Heuristics and Biases*. Cambridge: Cambridge University Press.

Kareev, Y. (1995a). Through a narrow window—working memory capacity and the detection of covariation. *Cognition*, *56*, 263–269.

Kareev, Y. (1995b). Positive bias in the perception of covariation. *Psychological Review*, *102*, 490–502.

Kareev, Y. (2000). Seven (indeed, plus or minus two) and the detection of correlations. *Psychological Review*, *107*, 397–402.

Kareev, Y., Lieberman, I. & Lev, M. (1997). Through a narrow window: Sample size and the perception of correlation. *Journal of Experimental Psychology: General*, *126*, 278–287.

Kliegl, R., Smith, J., Heckhausen, J. & Baltes, P.B. (1987). Mnemonic training for the acquisition of skilled digit memory. *Cognition and Instruction*, *4*, 203–223.

Luria, A.R. (1968/1987). *The Mind of a Mnemonist: A Little Book About a Vast Memory* (reprinted edn). Cambridge, MA: Harvard University Press.

Martignon, L. & Hoffrage, U. (1999). Why does one-reason decision making work? A case study in ecological rationality. In G. Gigerenzer, P.M. Todd & the ABC Research Group, *Simple Heuristics That Make Us Smart* (pp. 119–140). New York: Oxford University Press.

Mellers, B, Hertwig, R. & Kahneman, D. (2001). Do frequency representations eliminate conjunction effects? An exercise in adversarial collaboration. *Psychological Science, 12,* 269–275.

Miller, G.A. (1956). The magical number seven, plus or minus two: Some limits on our capacity for processing information. *Psychological Review, 63,* 81–97.

Newport, E.L. (1990). Maturational constraints on language learning. *Cognitive Science, 14,* 11–28.

Payne, J.W., Bettman, J.R. & Johnson, E.J. (1993). *The Adaptive Decision Maker.* New York: Cambridge University Press.

Pearl, J. (1988). *Probabilistic Reasoning in Intelligent Systems: Networks of Plausible Inference.* San Francisco, CA: Morgan Kaufmann.

Sacks, O. (1995). *An Anthropologist on Mars.* New York: Vintage Books.

Shiffrin, R.M. (1988). Attention. In R.C. Atkinson, R.J. Herrnstein, G. Lindzey & R.D. Luce (eds), *Stevens' Handbook of Experimental Psychology.* (Vol. 2. *Learning and Cognition,* pp. 739–811). New York: Wiley.

Slovic, P., Fischhoff, B. & Lichtenstein, S. (1976). Cognitive processes and societal risk taking. In J.S. Carroll & J.W. Payne (eds), *Cognition and Social Behavior* (pp. 165–184). Hillsdale, NJ: Erlbaum.

Thaler, R.H. (1991). *Quasi Rational Economics.* New York: Russell Sage Foundation.

Todd, P.M. (2001). Fast and frugal heuristics for environmentally bounded minds. In G. Gigerenzer & R. Selten (eds), *Bounded Rationality: The Adaptive Toolbox* (*Dahlem Workshop Report*) (pp. 51–70). Cambridge, MA: MIT Press.

Tolstoy, L. (1982/1869). *War and Peace.* London: Penguin.

Tversky, A. & Kahneman, D. (1974). Judgment under uncertainty: Heuristics and biases. *Science, 185,* 1124–1131.

CHAPTER 12

Correspondence and Coherence: Indicators of Good Judgment in World Politics

Philip E. Tetlock
University of California, Berkeley, USA

This chapter summarizes some research results on expert political judgment that bear on debates among experimental psychologists over alleged departures from rationality in human judgment (for more details, see Tetlock & Belkin, 1996; Tetlock, 1998, 1999; Tetlock & Lebow, 2001). The results derive from a 15-year research program tracking forecasting performance, and they should generally prove heartening to those in the judgment- and decision-making community who believe that demonstrations of systematic errors and biases are not just the artifactual byproducts of laboratory trickery performed on unmotivated undergraduate conscripts. The participants in all the studies reported here were seasoned professionals who made their living by analyzing and writing about political-economic trends. We shall discover that, even when seasoned professionals are making judgments about consequential real-world events within their domains of expertise, they often fall prey to such well-known errors or biases as the following:

(1) *Overconfidence*. There is frequently a large gap between the subjective probabilities that experts assign to outcomes and the objective probabilities of those outcomes materializing (Dawes, 1998).

(2) *Cognitive conservatism*. When we compare how much experts actually change their minds in response to new evidence to how much Bayes' theorem says they should change their minds, there are numerous indications that experts are too slow to update their beliefs (Slovic, Fischhoff & Lichtenstein, 1977; Einhorn & Hogarth, 1981).

(3) *Certainty of hindsight*. Experts sometimes deny mistakes altogether. They tend to recall assigning higher subjective probabilities to those political-economic outcomes that occur than they actually assigned before learning what occurred (Fischhoff, 1975; Hawkins & Hastie, 1990).

Thinking: Psychological Perspectives on Reasoning, Judgment and Decision Making. Edited by David Hardman and Laura Macchi.

(4) *Theory-driven standards of evidence and proof.* Experts generally impose higher standards of evidence and proof on dissonant claims than they do on consonant ones (Nisbett & Ross, 1980). This double standard is particularly noticeable in the reactions that political observers have to: (a) close-call counterfactuals that imply history could easily have gone down a different path and thus have implications for the validity of theoretical, ideological or policy stances; (b) historical discoveries that bear on the plausibility of these ideologically charged close-call counterfactuals.

(5) *Systematic evidence of incoherence in subjective probability judgments.* Political observers are highly susceptible to the subadditivity effects that Tversky and Koehler's (1994) support theory predicts should be the result of decomposing sets of possible futures or possible pasts into their exclusive and exhaustive components. In violation of the extensionality principle of probability theory, people often judge the likelihood of the whole to be less, sometimes far less, than the sum of its parts.

This chapter will, however, tell more than a tale about the real-world replicability of deviations from correspondence and coherence standards of good judgment. There will be some less familiar twists and turns of the argument.

(1) We shall discover how exasperatingly difficult it is to prove beyond a reasonable doubt in the political domain that experts have erred. This is true with respect to our empirical demonstrations of both overconfidence and cognitive conservatism. Experts can—and often do—defend overconfidence in their predictions of dramatic, low-base-rate outcomes as prudent efforts to call attention to the risks of war, nuclear proliferation and economic collapse. Experts also can—and often do—defend cognitive conservatism by invoking a variety of reasons for why, in light of intervening events, they should not be bound to change beliefs to the degree specified by reputational bets (likelihood ratios) they themselves made earlier.

(2) We shall discover more evidence of systematic individual differences in susceptibility to errors and biases than is customarily uncovered in experimental research programs. Cognitive style—the strength of respondents' preferences for explanatory closure and parsimony—moderated the magnitude of several effects. Specifically, respondents who valued closure and parsimony highly were more prone to biases that were rooted in excessive faith in the predictive and explanatory power of their preconceptions—biases such as overconfidence, cognitive conservatism, certainty of hindsight and selective standards of evidence and proof.

(3) We shall discover, however, that it is a mistake to suppose that high-need-for-closure experts were at a uniform disadvantage when it came to satisfying widely upheld standards of rationality within the field of judgment and decision making. There was one major class of judgmental bias—a violation of a basic coherence standard of rationality—that our more "open-minded", low-need-for-closure respondents were more prone to exhibit: namely, the subadditivity effect linked to unpacking classes of alternative counterfactual outcomes. Respondents who did not place a high value on parsimony and explanatory closure often wound up being too imaginative and assigning too much subjective probability to too many scenarios (with the result that subjective probabilities summed to well above 1.0).

(4) Susceptibility to subadditivity effects can, as Tversky and Fox (1995) noted, render people vulnerable to exploitation by shrewder competitors, who could design bets that capitalize on the resulting logical contradictions. But there is a silver lining of sorts. The imaginative capacity to transport oneself into alternative "possible worlds" confers a measure of protection against the theory-driven biases of hindsight and retrospective determinism.

In closing, I argue for the empirical robustness of many judgmental tendencies documented in laboratory research, but I also point out the normative contestability of automatic classifications of these judgmental tendencies as errors or biases in world politics. History poses distinctive challenges to normative theorists. The political observers studied here confront poorly understood (metacognitive) trade-offs as they struggle to make sense of historical flows of hard-to-classify events that unfold only once and that have difficult-to-determine numbers of branching points. My best guess is that the price of achieving cognitive closure in quirky path-dependent systems is often rigidity, whereas the price of open-mindedness in such systems is often incoherence.

METHODOLOGICAL BACKGROUND

The methodological details of the research program on political experts are documented in Tetlock (2002). Suffice it to say here that the program has involved soliciting conditional forecasts of a wide range of political and economic outcomes since the mid-1980s, with the most sustained data collection in 1988–89 and 1992–93. Roughly 200 professionals—from academia, government and international institutions—have participated in various phases of the project. Whenever possible, I ask experts not only to make predictions within their domains of expertise, but also to venture predictions outside those domains. For example, I pressed experts on China, India or the former Soviet Union to make predictions also about Canada, South Africa and Japan, and vice versa. The resulting data provide an instructive and usually humbling baseline for assessing the predictive skill conferred by many years of professional training and expertise.

The outcomes that experts have been asked to predict have also varied widely. Prediction tasks have included the following. Will this leader or political party still be in power in 5–10 years from now? Will civil or cross-border wars break out in the next 10–25 years? Will borders change in the next 10–25 years (as a result of secession/annexation, and will change be peaceful or violent)? Will GDP per capita grow faster, slower or at the same pace in the next 3 years as in the last 3 years? What about the central-government-debt-to-GDP ratio? Inflation? Unemployment? What about fiscal spending priorities? Will defense spending increase or decrease as a percentage of central-government expenditures (relative to the last 3 years)? The entities to be predicted have included the European Monetary Union (1992–93) and over 60 countries: the former Soviet Union (1988), South Africa (1988–89), North and South Korea (1988–89), Pakistan (1992), Poland (1991), Yugoslavia (1991–92), Canada (1992–93), China (1992–93), India (1992–93), Japan (1992–93), Saudi Arabia (1992–93), Mexico (1992–93), Nigeria (1992–93), Ethiopia (1992–93), Cuba (1992–93), Brazil (1992–93) and Argentina (1992–93). Experts were not, it should be stressed, asked to make point predictions. Their assignment was to assign subjective probability estimates (0–1.0) to broad classes of possible outcomes that had been carefully selected to be exclusive and exhaustive, and pass the clairvoyance test (easy to confirm or disconfirm *ex post*).

We also did not limit data collection to judgments of possible futures. Substantial effort went into soliciting judgments of possible pasts—experts' assessments of the plausibility of counterfactual conjectures bearing on how history could or would have unfolded under various contingencies. These judgments also covered a vast range of topics. Subgroups of experts judged counterfactuals that spanned several centuries: from the early 13th century ("If the Mongols had devastated Europe as they did the civilizations of China and Islam, the rise of European power would have been thwarted") to the mid- and late 20th century ("If Kennedy had heeded his hawkish advisers during the Cuban Missile Crisis, World War III would have been the result", or "If it were not for the pressure created by the Reagan arms buildup in the early 1980s, the USSR would still be with us today"). There is obviously no firm correspondence standard for judging the accuracy of these counterfactual conjectures, but careful analysis of these judgments does shed light on critical functional properties of expert political cognition.

BIAS NO. 1: OVERCONFIDENCE

Assessing the accuracy of subjective probability judgments of arguably unique events is problematic. If I claim that there is a 0.8 chance of Quebec's seceding from Canada between 1992 and 1997 or of the USSR's remaining intact between 1988 and 1993 or of South Africa's falling into civil war between 1989 and 1994, and those events do not materialize, I can always argue that I got the probabilities right, but the low-probability event just happened to occur. Only if I really go out on a limb, and assign the most extreme subjective probabilities on the scale, zero (x is impossible) or 1.0 (x is certain), can it be said that I have made a clearly falsifiable claim?

To get around this conundrum, calibration researchers have resorted to aggregation. It may not be possible to identify overconfidence in most individual cases, but it is possible across large numbers of forecasts. If we discover that, of all the predictions given 90 percent confidence, only 70 percent materialize, or of all those given 70 percent confidence, only 52 percent materialize, we would seem to have some warrant to claim a pattern of over-confidence. Using a number of computational procedures, including the proper quadratic scoring rule and Winkler's (1994) difficulty adjustments that control for variations across environments in the ease of predicting outcomes from simple extrapolation of base rates, we find that experts as a group tend to be overconfident. Figure 12.1 presents an illustrative calibration curve from the political-forecasting data that collapses data across 166 fore-casters, 20 countries, five criterion measures and two time periods. As can be seen, some experts were more prone to overconfidence than others. The best individual-difference pre-dictor of overconfidence was a 12-item scale that had been adapted from Arie Kruglanski's research program on the need for closure (Kruglanski & Webster, 1996) and included four additional questions that probed personal epistemologies (for example, the relative perils of overestimating or underestimating the complexity of the political world). Using a quartile split, experts with the strongest preferences for closure and parsimony were more prone than those with the weakest preferences to attach subjective likelihoods to their "most likely pos-sible futures" that substantially exceeded the average objective likelihood of those outcomes materializing.

It should, however, be noted that, even after the fact, some experts insisted that they were justified in affixing high subjective probabilities to relatively low base-rate events—such as cross-border or civil war, border shifts triggered by secession or annexation, regime shifts triggered by coups or revolutions, and the proliferation of weapons of mass destruction. They felt justified because false alarming on "x" (saying "x" will occur when it does not) was "by far the less serious error" than missing "x" (saying "x" will not occur when it does). To paraphrase one participant whom I had thoroughly debriefed: "Several false alarms do not offset the value of being ahead of the curve in calling the disintegration of the USSR

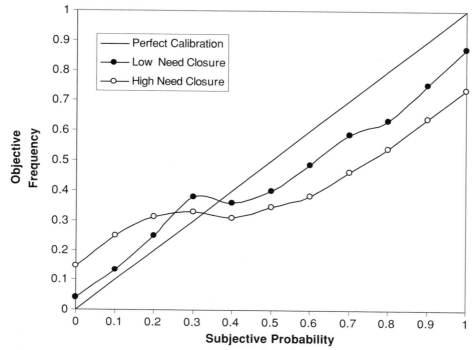

Figure 12.1 Calibration curves for experts derived by collapsing across political forecasting variables and nation-states within the 5-year forecasting frames for 1988 and 1992. Diagonal represents perfect calibration. The further a calibration curve falls below the diagonal, the greater the overconfidence

or Yugoslavia or in anticipating the nuclearization of the Indian subcontinent or the East Asian financial crisis. Who really cares if experts who are that prescient when it counts also predicted that Canada, Nigeria, Indonesia and South Africa would fall apart?" In this view, experts who hit the forecasting equivalent of home runs inevitably strike out a lot, but we should still want them on our team.

When we introduce statistical adjustments that treat "overprediction" errors as markedly less serious than "underprediction" errors for the specified outcome variables (from 1/2 to 1/4 to 1/8), the greater overconfidence effect among low-need-closure experts is significantly reduced. The effect does not, however, disappear.

BIAS NO. 2: COGNITIVE CONSERVATISM

Assessing how much experts should change their minds in response to subsequent events also raises daunting philosophical problems. Our solution took this form. For a subset of forecasting domains, experts were asked to make, *ex ante*, all the judgments necessary for constructing a reputational bet that would pit the predictive implications of their own assessments of political forces against the most influential rival perspective they cared to identify. We then plugged in Bayes' theorem to assess how much experts should have changed their minds upon learning that the outcomes either they or their rivals deemed most likely had occurred. The standard queries for this exercise were as follows:

(1) How likely do you think each of the following sets of possible futures is if your understanding of the underlying forces at work is correct? In the Bayesian belief-updating equations, these variables go by the designations p (x1/your hypothesis), p (x2/your hypothesis)... where x1, x2... refer to sets of possible futures, and your hypothesis refers to "your view of the underlying forces at work is correct".

(2) How much confidence do you have in the correctness of your understanding of the underlying forces at work? In Bayesian equations, this variable is p (your hypothesis).

(3) Think of the most influential alternative to your perspective on the underlying forces at work. How possible is it that this perspective might be correct? This variable is p (rival hypothesis).

(4) How likely do you think each set of possible futures is if this alternative view of the underlying forces at work is correct? These variables go by the designations p (x1/rival hypothesis), p (x2/rival hypothesis)....

Readers familiar with Bayesian probability theory will immediately recognize these judgments as critical inputs for computing diagnosticity ratios, the likelihood of B given A1 divided by the likelihood of B given A2, and for inferring experts' "priors", or their confidence in competing hypotheses bearing on underlying states of nature. I call these exercises "reputational bets" because they ask experts, in effect, to specify, as exactly as an odds-setting process would have to specify, competing predictions that are predicated on different views of reality. The amount of confidence one should retain in one's prior hypothesis (relative to the most plausible competing hypothesis) after learning what happened is known as the posterior odds. Bayes' theorem tells us precisely how to compute the posterior odds:

$$P \text{ (your hypothesis} / X_1 \text{ occurs)} = P (X_1 / \text{your hypothesis)} P \text{ (your hypothesis)}$$

$$P \text{ (rival hypothesis} / X_1 \text{ occurs)} \quad P (X_1 / \text{rival hypothesis)} P \text{ (rival hypothesis)}$$

Posterior odds = likelihood ratio × prior odds

We used this format in forecasts for the Soviet Union (1988), South Africa (1988–89), Canada (1992) and the European Monetary Union (1992).

Our full data set allowed us to answer three categories of questions:

(1) Do experts confronted by new evidence change their minds in the direction and to the approximate degree that Bayes' formula says they should have?
(2) When experts resist changing their minds, what types of justifications (or belief system defenses) do they invoke for holding their ground?
(3) Do systematic individual differences arise in the degree to which experts function like good Bayesian belief updaters?

Figure 12.2 indicates that across all forecasting domains in which we obtained measures of prior probabilities, diagnosticity ratios at the original forecasts, and posterior probabilities at the follow-up session, experts tended to take a "heads-I-win-and-tails-I-do-not-lose" attitude toward forecasting exercises. Experts whose most likely scenarios materialized generally claimed a measure of victory by increasing their confidence in their prior understanding of the underlying forces at work, but a large subgroup of experts whose most likely scenarios failed to materialize denied defeat by showing little inclination to decrease their understanding of the underlying forces at work. Figure 12.2 also shows that experts with

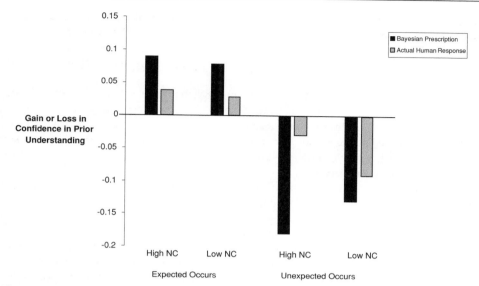

Figure 12.2 This graph shows how much low- and high-need-closure forecasters change their minds in response to expected or unexpected events and compares actual belief updating to the Bayesian-prescribed amount of belief updating

strong preferences for explanatory closure were more prone to resist changing their minds when unexpected outcomes occurred.

On first inspection, these findings would seem to replicate the well-known cognitive-conservatism bias in probabilistic reasoning which asserts that people generally do not change their minds as much as the ideal-type Bayesian would. The term "conservatism" carries, of course, no ideological connotation here, referring not to a particular point of view but rather to conserving existing mental structures or schemata. Liberals can be, and often are, as "guilty" of cognitive conservatism as conservatives.

Caution is, however, in order in drawing conclusions about rationality. Judging the appropriateness of belief updating in the political world is far more problematic than judging it in the classic context of sampling red and blue balls from urns. Experts invoked varying combinations of six strategies for protecting conditional forecasts that ran aground with troublesome evidence. These strategies should not, moreover, be written off as mere psychological defense mechanisms. On close inspection, many turn out to be logically and empirically defensible. We should not fall into the trap of supposing that it is merely a matter of arithmetic to determine whether people are good Bayesians. Some defenses can be viewed, for example, as thoughtful efforts to redefine the terms of reputational bets that, in a Bayesian framework, mandate how much belief change is warranted. The six strategies are as follows.

Strategy 1: The Close-Call Counterfactual Defense (I Was Almost Right)

History provides no control groups. We never know for sure what would have happened if this or that antecedent condition had taken on a slightly different value. Experts often take advantage of this causal ambiguity to argue that, although the predicted outcome did not occur, it "almost occurred", and it would have indeed occurred but for some inherently unpredictable, seemingly trivial, contingency. Examples of such "close-call counterfactuals" pop up in virtually every forecasting arena in which experts made reputational bets. Consider but the following two cases.

Observers of the former Soviet Union who, in 1988, thought the Communist Party would be firmly ensconced in the saddle of power 5 years hence were especially likely to believe that Kremlin hardliners almost overthrew Gorbachev in the coup attempt of August 1991, as they would have had the conspirators been more resolute and less inebriated, or had key military commanders obeyed orders to kill civilians challenging martial law or had Yeltsin not acted so bravely and decisively.

Experts who expected the European Monetary Union to collapse argued that the event almost happened in the wake of the currency crises of 1992, as, indeed, it would have but for the principled determination (even obstinacy) of politicians committed to the Euro cause and of the interventions of sympathetic central bankers. Given the deep conflict of interest between states that have "solid fundamentals" and those that "regularly resort to accounting gimmickery to make their budget deficits appear smaller", and given the "burbling nationalist resentment" of a single European currency, these experts thought it a "minor miracle" that most European leaders in 1997 were still standing by monetary union, albeit on a loophole-riddled schedule.

Strategy 2: The Just-Off-On-Timing Defense

This strategy moves us out of the murky realm of counterfactual worlds and back into this, the actual, world. Experts often insist that, although the predicted outcome has not yet occurred, it eventually will and we just need to be patient. This defense is limited, of course, in its applicability to political games in which the predicted outcome has not yet been irreversibly foreclosed. No one, for example, expected white-minority rule to be restored in South Africa or Al Gore suddenly to take George W. Bush's place in the White House in 2001. Those were done deals. But it is possible to argue, and experts often did, that a political trend that they deemed highly likely has merely been delayed, and that Canada still will disintegrate (the Parti Québécois will try again and prevail on its third attempt), that Kazakhstan will ultimately burst into a Yugoslav-style conflagration of interethnic warfare (demagogues on both sides of the border with Russia will eventually seize the opportunities for ethnic mobilization that Kazakhstan presents), that the European Monetary Union's misguided effort to create a common currency will some day end in tears and acrimony (the divergent interests of the prospective members will trigger crises that even determined leadership cannot resolve) and that nuclear war will ultimately be the fate of south Asia or the Korean peninsula. In effect, the experts admitted that they may have been wrong within my arbitrary time frames, but they will be vindicated with the passage of time.

Strategy 3: The "I-Made-the-Right-Mistake" Defense

This strategy concedes error, but, rather than trying to minimize the conceptual or empirical significance of the error, it depicts the error as the natural byproduct of pursuing the right moral and political priorities. As one conservative defiantly declared, "over-estimating the power of the Soviet Union in the 1980s, and the staying power of the Communist Party of the Soviet Union, was the prudent thing to do, certainly a lot more prudent than under-estimating those characters." A mirror-image variant of this defense was invoked by some liberals in the late 1990s in defense of International Monetary Fund (IMF) loans to Russia. Much of the money may have been wasted or misdirected into Swiss bank accounts, but, given the risks of allowing a nuclear superpower to implode financially, issuing the loans was, to paraphrase the second in command at the IMF, Stanley Fischer, the "prudent thing to do".

Strategy 4: Challenge Whether the Preconditions for Activating Conditional Forecasts Were Fulfilled

Each forecast was conditional on the correctness of the expert's understanding of the underlying forces at work. One does not need to be a logician or philosopher of science to appreciate that this is a complex form of "conditionality". Experts have the option of affixing responsibility for forecasting errors on the least ego-threatening and belief-destabilizing mistake that they made in sizing up the situation at the time of the original forecast.

We heard many variants of this refrain in policy debates. One side complains that the other side has unfairly and opportunistically stuck it with an idiotic prediction. The "wronged" side insists, for instance, that they were not mistaken about the efficacy of basic strategies of diplomatic influence, such as deterrence or reassurance, or about the efficacy of basic instruments of macroeconomic policy, such as shock therapy as opposed to gradualism. They merely failed to anticipate how maladroitly the policy would be implemented. Thus, experts could insist at various points between 1992 and 1997 that "if NATO had sent the Serbian leadership the right mix of deterrence-and-reassurance signals, we could have averted further escalation of the Yugoslavian civil war", or "if Yeltsin had practiced real shock therapy, the Russians need not have suffered through this renewed nasty bout of hyperinflation." It is worth noting that this belief-system defense has the net effect of transforming a conditional forecast (if x is satisfied, then y will occur) into an historical counterfactual ("if x had been satisfied, then y would have occurred). Counterfactual history often serves as a conceptual graveyard for conditional forecasts slain by evidence.

Strategy 5: The Exogenous-Shock Defense

All hypothesis testing in science presupposes a *ceteris paribus*, or "all-other-things-equal", clause. Conditional forecasters can thus argue that, although the conditions for activating the forecast were satisfied—their understanding of the underlying forces was correct—key background conditions (implicitly covered by *ceteris paribus*) took on bizarre forms that they could hardly have been expected to anticipate and that short-circuited the otherwise reliably deterministic connection between cause and effect. Theorists tend to be quite comfortable advancing this defense. They can explain away unexpected events by attributing them to plausible causal forces outside the logical scope of their theory. One realist, who was surprised by how far Gorbachev was prepared to go in making concessions on traditionally sensitive geopolitical and arms-control issues, commented: "I work at the level of relations among states. I am not a specialist on the Soviet Union. You are a psychologist and you should understand the distinction I am making. Would you count it as a failure against a theory of interpersonal relations if the theory predicts that a couple will stay married, the couple stays married for decades, and then suddenly the husband dies of a heart attack. Of course not. The failure, if there is one, lies in failing to check with the cardiologist. Well, my failure, if there was one, was in failing to pay adequate attention to warnings that the Soviet state was very sick."

Strategy 6: The Politics-Is-Hopelessly-Cloud-Like Defense

Finally, experts have the option of arguing that, although the relevant preconditions were satisfied, and the predicted outcome never came close to occurring and now never will, this failure should not be held against the framework that inspired the forecast. Forecasting exercises are best viewed as light-hearted diversions of no consequence because everyone knows, or else should know, that politics is inherently indeterminate, more cloud-like than clock-like. As Henry Kissinger wryly wrote Daniel Moynihan after the fragmentation of the Soviet Union, "Your crystal ball worked better than mine" (Moynihan, 1993, p. 23). On close inspection, of course, this concession concedes nothing.

BIAS NO. 3: HINDSIGHT BIAS

After the specified forecasting periods had elapsed, we asked a subset of experts in six domains to recall their original predictions. The results replicated the core finding in the large research literature on the certainty-of-hindsight effect (Fischhoff, 1975; Hawkins & Hastie, 1990). Experts claimed by an average margin of 0.16 (on a 0–1.0 scale) that they attached higher subjective probabilities to the observed outcomes than they actually did. The results also added the following two wrinkles to the hindsight effect:

(1) The tendency of experts to short-change the intellectual competition. When experts were also asked to recall the predictions they originally thought their most influential rivals would make, they imputed lower conditional likelihoods to the future that materialized than they did prior to learning what happened. In effect, experts claimed to know more about the future than they actually did, and gave less credit to their opponents for anticipating the future than they actually deserved.
(2) The tendency of experts who placed greater value on closure and parsimony to display stronger hindsight effects (cf. Campbell & Tesser, 1983).

BIAS NO. 4: THEORY-DRIVEN STANDARDS OF EVIDENCE AND PROOF

The data contained many examples in which experts applied higher standards of evidence and proof for dissonant than for consonant claims. One striking example was the shifting pattern of correlates of attitude toward close-call counterfactuals. We saw earlier that experts, especially those who valued explanatory closure, were more favorably disposed toward close-call scenarios that rescued conditional forecasts from falsification (the I-was-almost-right defense). This defense provided a convenient way of arguing that, although the predicted outcome did not occur, it almost did and would have but for theoretically irrelevant twists of fate: "Sure, I thought Canada would have disintegrated by now, and it nearly did", or "I thought South Africa would have lapsed into civil war by now, and it would have but for the remarkable coincidence of two remarkably mature leaders, emerging as leaders at the right moment."

In work on retrospective reasoning, we have found that, although the close-call counterfactual is a welcome friend of the theory-driven conditional forecaster, it is a nuisance at best, and a serious threat at worst to theory-driven thinkers who are on the prowl for ways of assimilating past events into favored explanatory frameworks. Consider the problem of the theorist who subscribes to the notion that the international balance of power is a self-equilibriating system. According to the theory of neorealist balancing, states are unified, rational, decision-making entities that seek to preserve their autonomy; states exist in a fundamentally anarchic interstate environment (no world government) in which, to paraphrase Thucydides, the strong do what they will and the weak accept what they must; therefore, whenever states perceive another state becoming too powerful, they coalesce against it. It was no accident from this point of view that would-be hegemonists—from Philip II of Spain to Napoleon to Hitler—have failed. The military outcomes were the inevitable result of the operation of a basic law of world politics. Not surprisingly, therefore, experts who endorse neorealist balancing theory, and prefer closure and parsimony, are especially likely to reject close-call counterfactuals that imply Napoleon or Hitler could have won if he had made better strategic decisions at various junctures. This theoretical-belief-by-cognitive-style interaction has now been replicated in four distinct conceptual domains (Tetlock & Lebow, 2001).

The most direct evidence for epistemic double-dealing emerges when we present experts with hypothetical discoveries from recently opened archives that either reinforce or undercut favored or disfavored close-call counterfactuals. For example, Sovietologists who subscribed to a monolithic totalitarian image of the Soviet Union cranked up the magnification in looking for flaws in historical work on new Kremlin archives purporting to show that the Communist Party came close to deposing Stalin in the late 1920s and to moving toward a kinder, gentler form of socialism. But the same experts accepted at roughly face value the same historical procedures when the procedures pointed to the more congenial conclusion that Stalinism was unavoidable (even without Stalin). By contrast, Sovietologists who subscribed to a more pluralistic image of the Soviet polity had the opposite reactions (Tetlock, 1999).

BIAS NO. 5: INCOHERENCE AND VIOLATIONS OF EXTENSIONALITY

The term "extensionality" may be forbiddingly technical, but the normative stipulation is simplicity itself. The likelihood of a set of outcomes should equal the sum of the likelihoods of the logically exhaustive and mutually exclusive members of that set. It is hard to imagine a more jarring violation of classic probability theory than the violation of extensionality.

The heuristics-and-biases literature warns us, however, to expect systematic violations of extensionality when people judge complex event sequences that require integrating two or more probabilistic linkages. The textbook illustration is the conjunction fallacy (Tversky & Kahneman, 1983). Imagine that one randomly constituted group is asked to judge the likelihood of a plausible conjunction of events, such as an earthquake causing a dam to rupture that, in turn, causes a flood killing more than 500 people in California. Imagine also that another randomly constituted group is asked to judge the likelihood of a flood (produced by any cause) killing more than 500 people in California. The likelihood judgments of the former group will typically exceed those of the latter group by a substantial margin, even though the former group is judging a subset of the class of outcomes being judged by the latter group.

Building on this work, Tversky and Koehler (1994) and Tversky and Fox's (1995) advanced support theory, which warns us to expect that psychologic will trump logic because people find it easier to mobilize mental support for highly specific possibilities than they do for the abstract sets that subsume these possibilities. For example, people will often judge the likelihood of an entire set of possibilities, such as any NBA team from a given league winning the championship, to be substantially less likely than the sum of the likelihood values that attach to the unpacking of the set's exclusive and exhaustive components (the individual teams that make up the league). The net result is thus that people judge the whole to be less than the sum of its parts (subadditivity) and wind up giving contradictory answers to logically equivalent versions of the same question.

Unpacking manipulations are understandably viewed as sources of cognitive bias on subjective-probability judgments of possible futures. They stimulate people to find too much support for too many possibilities. Returning to the basketball example, Tversky and Fox (1995) demonstrate that although binary complements at the league level generally sum to 1.0 (will the East or West win?), the subjective probabilities assigned to progressively more detailed or unpacked outcomes—the prospects of individual teams within leagues—substantially exceed 1.0. If people were to back up their unpacked bets with actual money, they would be quickly transformed into money pumps. It is, after all, logically impossible that each of four teams within an eight-team division could have a 0.4 chance of winning the championship the same year.

Unpacking manipulations may, however, help to debias subjective probability judgments of possible pasts by exactly the same mechanism. The key difference is that judgments of possible pasts, unlike those of possible futures, have already been contaminated by the powerful certainty-of-hindsight bias. Experimental work on this bias has shown that, as soon as people learn which one of a number of once-deemed possible outcomes happened, they quickly assimilate that outcome knowledge into their existing cognitive structures and have a hard time reconstructing their *ex ante* state of uncertainty (Hawkins & Hastie, 1990). Mental exercises that involve unpacking sets of possible pasts should have the net effect of checking the hindsight bias by bringing back to psychological life counterfactual possibilities that people long ago buried with deterministic "I-knew-it-had-to-be" thinking.

Our research on political experts is consistent with this debiasing hypothesis. In two sets of follow-up contacts with experts on China (1998) and North Korea (1998), randomly-assigned-to-treatment experts were less susceptible to hindsight when they had previously been encouraged to unpack the set of "alternative counterfactual outcomes" and to imagine specific ways in which "things could have worked out very

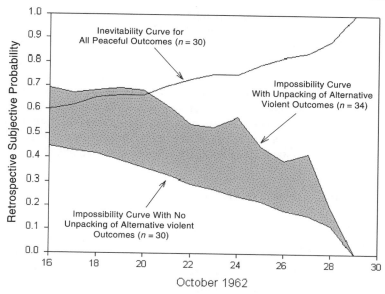

Figure 12.3 Inevitability and impossibility curves for the Cuban Missile Crisis. The inevitability curve displays gradually rising likelihood judgments of some form of peaceful resolution. The lower impossibility curve displays gradually declining likelihood judgments of all possible more violent endings. The higher impossibility curve was derived by adding the experts' likelihood judgments of six specific subsets of more violent possible endings. Adding values of the lower impossibility curve to the corresponding values of the inevitability curve yields sums only slightly above 1.0. Inserting values from the higher impossibility curve yields sums well above 1.0. The shaded area represents the cumulative effect of unpacking on the retrospective subjective probability of counterfactual alternatives to reality

differently" (Tetlock, 2002). Encouraging experts to unpack more temporally distant sets of historical possibilities has also been shown to have a pronounced influence on experts' judgments of the retrospective likelihood of possible outcomes of the Cuban Missile Crisis as well as of other even more remote historical processes. For example, Tetlock and Lebow (2001) report an experiment in which one-half of the participants were asked to imagine the set of alternative more violent endings of the Cuban Missile Crisis and judge the likelihood of the set as a whole on each day of the crisis. The other half were asked to break that set down into exclusive and exhaustive components, including subsets of scenarios in which violence is localized to the Caribbean or extends outside the Caribbean, and further subsets with casualties less than 100 or 100 or more—and then to judge the likelihood of each of these subsets on each day of the crisis. As support theory would lead one to expect, and as Figure 12.3 shows, the experts saw alternative more violent endings of the crisis as significantly more probable when they had performed the decomposition exercise, and this effect was significantly more pronounced among our more "open-minded", low-need-for-closure participants. As can also be inferred from Figure 12.3, when we add the judgments that experts made of the likelihood of some form of peaceful ending on each date (the inevitability curve) to the likelihood of alternative more violent endings taken as a whole set (the wholistic impossibility curve), the sum does not stray too far from 1.0 across dates (the binary-complementarity prediction of support theory). But when we add the points on the inevitability curve to the corresponding dates on the impossibility curve created by summing subjective probabilities of unpacked what-if scenarios, the sums for the two curves substantially exceed 1.0 on most dates (consistent with the subadditivity prediction of support theory).

Here, we confront another normative judgment that looks easy in laboratory settings but more problematic in the real world. From a strictly logical point of view, subadditivity is indefensible. If we believe, however, that historical reasoning is already biased by distortions of hindsight, there is a good case that encouraging experts to imagine counterfactual alternatives to reality, and inflating their subjective probability estimates beyond the bounds of reason, might be a reasonable thing to do if it checks the hindsight bias.

SOME CLOSING OBSERVATIONS

How should we balance these potentially endless arguments bearing on the rationality of professional observers of world politics? It is useful here to draw a sharp distinction between the descriptive and the normative; between the generalizability of purely empirical characterizations of particular judgmental tendencies and the generalizability of the normative characterizations of those judgmental tendencies as errors or biases. The studies reviewed in this chapter attest simultaneously to the empirical robustness and the normative contestability of error-and-bias claims in the hurly-burly of world politics. The case for empirical robustness is strong. Consider the following seven examples of how the real-world evidence reported here converges with the laboratory evidence in the mainstream literature:

(1) The overconfidence documented in political forecasts reaffirms a massive body of work on the calibration of subjective probability estimates of knowledge (Dawes, 1998).

(2) The selective activation of belief-system defenses by forecasters who "get it wrong" dovetails nicely with the classic dissonance prediction that people would most need defenses when they appear to have been wrong about something on which they were originally quite confident (Festinger, 1964).

(3) The skepticism that experts reserved for dissonant historical evidence and claims extended the work on theory-driven assessments of evidence and on the tendency for people to apply stringent "must-I-believe" tests to disagreeable evidence and much more lenient "can-I-believe" tests to agreeable discoveries (Griffin & Ross, 1991).

(4) Experts' generation of close-call counterfactuals in response to unexpected events is consistent with experimental work on norm theory and the determinants of spontaneous counterfactual thinking (Kahneman & Miller, 1986).

(5) The reluctance of experts to change their minds in response to unexpected events and in accord with earlier specified diagnosticity ratios parallels the excessive conservatism in belief revision often displayed by subjects in experiments that explicitly compare human judgment to Bayesian formulas (Edwards, 1968).

(6) The cognitive-stylistic differences in belief-system defense and belief underadjustment offer further evidence for the construct validity of the need-for-closure and integrative complexity measures (Kruglanski & Webster, 1996; Suedfeld & Tetlock, 2001).

(7) The subadditivity effects induced by encouraging experts to unpack counterfactual alternatives to reality is consistent both with Tversky's support theory and with work on the power of imagining alternative outcomes to check hindsight bias (Koehler, 1991).

In all seven respects, the current results underscore the generalizability of laboratory-based demonstrations of bounded rationality in more ecologically representative research designs. The psychological findings do hold up well when highly trained experts (as opposed to sophomore conscripts) judge complex, naturally occurring political events (as opposed to artificial problems that the experimenter has often concocted with the intent of demonstrating bias).

Curiously, though, empirical robustness coexists with normative contestability in the political realms surveyed here. Why should normative judgments of rationality become so much more problematic when the object of inquiry is political in content and historical in process? The answer appears to be at least threefold:

1. Politics is often defined as an organized competition for power in which rival communities of cobelievers warn of looming threats and advocate particular policies to avert threats and bring about consequences that most people deem desirable (for example, "We predict race riots if we don't adopt more egalitarian policies"; "We predict aggression by expansionist/revisionist states if we don't adopt stronger deterrence policies"). Therefore, it should not be surprising when experts representing competing theoretical or ideological camps place different values on avoiding type I as opposed to type II errors in predicting various outcomes. What looks like overconfidence within one camp will frequently look like a prudent effort to minimize the really serious type of error from the standpoint of the other camp.

2. Inasmuch as political cognition tends to occur in a highly adversarial environment, we should expect the players to be keenly aware that the other side will be prepared to pounce on potentially embarrassing errors. This helps to explain why it is difficult to persuade experts to make falsifiable forecasts even when they have been explicitly assured that all judgments will be absolutely confidential. Many participants in our studies work within professional cultures in which their reputations hinge on appearing approximately right most of the time and on never appearing clearly wrong. What looks like an error or bias from a Bayesian standpoint (an unwillingness to stick to reputational bets made earlier) can also be plausibly viewed as a strategic adaptation to the rhetorical demands of thrust and parry in highly partisan contest for power. As one expert told me, "You think we're playing the (hypothetico-deductive) game of science, and so you evaluate what is going on by those standards. But that is as silly as trying to apply the rules of football to baseball. In the game of politics, truth is secondary to persuasion."

3. Even granting this objection, the naive behavioral scientist might still wonder whether it is possible for rival communities of cobelievers to insulate themselves from falsification indefinitely. Surely, "truths"—to which everyone must be responsive—will slowly become undeniably apparent. This counterargument does not, however, adequately take into account the profound obstacles that arise in assessing historical causation. Sharp disagreements still exist over why World War I or, for that matter, the English Civil War of the 1640s broke out when and in the manner it did, and whether it could have been averted by this or that counterfactual alteration. It is not unusual for these sorts of disputes to persist for centuries, and even millennia (Tetlock, 2002).

Disagreements over causation are so intractable largely because all causal inference in history ultimately rests on speculative counterfactual judgments of how events would have unfolded if this or that antecedent condition, hypothesized to be relevant by this or that camp, had taken on a different value (Fogel, 1964; Fearon, 1991). The political observers in the current studies confronted the daunting task of making sense of constantly evolving path-dependent sequences of events with indeterminate numbers of branching points. The traditional scientific methods of causal inference—experimental and statistical control— just do not apply. Experimental control was not an option because history is a path-dependent system that unfolds once and only once. Statistical control was not an option because of the well-known problems of classifying complex, highly idiosyncratic events that many experts insist are categorically unique (and hence resistant to all classification), and that the remaining experts often insist on assigning to incompatible classificatory bins. Testing hypotheses about the effects of fuzzy-set concepts such as "deterrence" or "democracy" on war proneness requires, at minimum, agreement on when deterrence was or was not implemented, and on whether a given state qualifies as democratic.

In brief, our experts typically worked under loose reality constraints that made it easy to wriggle out of disconfirmation. We saw, for example, even with *ex ante* likelihood ratios in hand, how extraordinarily difficult it was to make a decisive case that any given individual was guilty of biased information processing or belief perseverance. History permits of too many explanations. Going backward in time, political partisans could always argue that they were not almost wrong, and, going forward in time, they could always insist that they were almost right. And who is to say for sure that anything is amiss. No one can visit these counterfactual worlds to determine which what-if assertions are defensive nonsense, and which ones are on target.

Although making accusations of irrational belief perseverance logically stick is extremely difficult, the studies reported here do still reveal ample grounds for concern that many political debates are equivalent to Einhorn and Hogarth's (1981) "outcome-irrelevant learning situations". Loose reality constraints coupled with the human propensity to theory-driven thinking make it easy for even sophisticated political observers to slip into tautological patterns of reasoning about history that make it well-nigh impossible for them ever to discover that they were wrong. For this reason, this chapter advances the argument that it is a mistake to treat subadditivity in judgments of alternative worlds as just a logical error; it is an error that can be put to good use in checking excessively theory-driven modes of making sense of history. We have seen that these theory-driven patterns of reasoning about historical outcomes, especially temporally distant ones, tend to be convergent. The focus is typically on explaining why what was had to be. The subadditivity effects appear, however, to be the product of divergent, imagination-driven thinking. The focus is (at least in the studies reported here) on what could have been. The theory-driven strategies confer the benefits of explanatory closure and parsimony by assuring us that we now know why things worked out as they did. But these strategies desensitize us to nuance, complexity and contingency. The imagination-driven strategies sensitize us to possible worlds that might or could have been, but the price can be increased confusion, self-contradiction and even incoherence.

One of the deepest conceptual challenges in historical reasoning may be that of striking a reasonable balance, a reflective equilibrium, between convergent theory-driven thinking and divergent imagination-driven thinking. On the one hand, historical observers need imagination-driven modes of thinking to check the powerful tendency to assimilate known outcomes into favorite causal schemata. On the other hand, observers need theory-driven modes of thinking to check runaway unpacking effects and to serve as plausibility pruners for cutting off speculation that would otherwise grow, like Topsy, beyond the bounds of probability. Of course, there is no single, well-defined equilibrium or normative solution. So there will be plenty of room for competing communities of cobelievers to stake out different theoretical and ideological standards for what counts as a reasonable balance. It is therefore a safe bet that setting standards of good political judgment will continue to be politically controversial.

REFERENCES

Campbell, J. D. & Tesser, A. (1983). Motivational interpretations of hindsight bias: an individual difference analysis. *Journal of Personality, 51*, 605–620.

Dawes, R. (1997). Judgment and choice. In D. Gilbert, S. Fiske & G. Lindzey (eds), *Handbook of Social Psychology*. New York: McGraw Hill.

Dawes, R. (1998). Judgment and Choice. In D. Gilbert, S. Fiske & G. Lindzey (eds), *Handbook of Social Psychology (Volume 1)* (pp. 497–548). New York: McGraw Hill.

Einhorn, H. & Hogarth, R. (1981). Behavioral decision theory: processes of judgment and choice. *Annual Review of Psychology, 31*, 53–88.

Edwards, W. (1968). Conservatism in human information processing. In B. Kleinmuntz (ed.), *Formal Representation of Human Judgment* (pp. 17–52). New York: Wiley.

Elster, J. (1978). *Logic and Society: Contradictions and Possible Worlds*. New York: Wiley.

Fearon, J. (1991). Counterfactuals and hypothesis testing in political science. *World Politics, 43*, 474–484.

Festinger, L. (ed.) (1964). *Conflict, Decision, and Dissonance*. Stanford, CA: Stanford University Press.

Fischhoff, B. (1975). Hindsight is not equal to foresight: the effect of outcome knowledge on judgment under uncertainty. *Journal of Experimental Psychology, 104*, 288–299.

Fogel, R. (1964). *Railroads and American Economic Growth: Essays in Econometric History*. Baltimore, MD: Johns Hopkins University Press.

Friedman, T. (1999). *The Lexus and the Olive Tree*. New York: Farrar, Straus, & Giroux.

Goldstein, W. & Hogarth, R. (eds) (1996). *Judgment and Decision Making: An Interdisciplinary Reader*. Cambridge: Cambridge University Press.

Griffin, D. & Ross, L. (1991). Subjective construal, social inference, and human misunderstanding. In M. Zanna (ed.), *Advances in Experimental Social Psychology* (volume 24, pp. 319–359). New York: Academic Press.

Hawkins, S. & Hastie, R. (1990). Hindsight: Biased judgment of past events after outcomes are known. *Psychological Bulletin, 107*, 311–327.

Kahneman, D., Slovic, P. & Tversky, A. (eds) (1982). *Judgment Under Uncertainty: Heuristics and Biases*. New York: Cambridge University Press.

Kahneman, D. & Miller, D. (1986). Norm theory: comparing reality to its alternatives. *Psychological Review, 93*, 136–153.

Koehler, D. (1991). Explanation, imagination, and confidence in judgment. *Psychological Bulletin, 110*(3), 499–519.

Kruglanski, A. & Webster, D. (1996). Motivated closing of the mind: seizing and freezing. *Psychological Review, 103*, 263–278.

Moynihan, D. P. (1993). *Pandemonium*. New York: Oxford University Press.

Nisbett, R. E. & Ross, L. (1980). *Human Inference: Strategies and Shortcomings of Social Judgment*. Englewood Cliffs, NJ: Prentice–Hall.

Slovic, P., Fischhoff, B. & Lichtenstein, S. (1977). Behavioral decision theory. *Annual Review of Psychology, 28*, 1–39.

Suedfeld, P. & Tetlock, P. E. (1999). Cognitive styles. In A. Tesser & N. Schwartz, *Blackwell International Handbook of Social Psychology: Intra-individual Processes* (vol 1 •••). London: Blackwell.

Suedfeld, P. & Tetlock, P. E. (2001). Cognitive styles. In A. Tesser & N. Schwartz, *Blackwell International Handbook of Social Psychology: Intra–individual Processes, (Vol 1)* (pp. 284–304). London: Blackwell Publishers.

Tetlock, P. E. (1991). Learning in U.S. and Soviet foreign policy: in search of an elusive concept. In George Breslauer & Philip Tetlock (eds), *Learning in U.S. and Soviet Foreign Policy*. Boulder, CO: Westview.

Tetlock, P. E. (1992). Good judgment in world politics: three psychological perspectives. *Political Psychology, 13*, 517–540.

Tetlock, P. E. (1998). Close-call counterfactuals and belief system defenses: I was not almost wrong but I was almost right. *Journal of Personality and Social Psychology, 75*, 230–242.

Tetlock, P. E. (1999). Theory-driven reasoning about possible pasts and probable futures: are we prisoners of our preconceptions? *American Journal of Political Science, 43*, 335–366.

Tetlock, P. E. (2002). Social-functionalist metaphors for judgment and choice: the intuitive politician, theologian, and prosecutor. *Psychological Review, 109*, 451–472.

Tetlock, P. E. & Belkin, A. (1996). *Counterfactual Thought Experiments in World Politics: Logical, Methodological, and Psychological Perspectives*. Princeton, NJ: Princeton University Press.

Tetlock, P. E. & Lebow, R. N. (2001). Poking counterfactual holes in deterministic covering laws: Alternative histories of the Cuban missile crisis. *American Political Science Review, 95*(4), 829–843.

Tversky, A. & Fox, C. (1995). Weighting risk and uncertainty. *Psychological Review, 102*(2), 269–83.

Tversky, A. & Kahneman, D. (1983). Extensional versus intuitive reason: the conjunction fallacy as probability judgment. *Psychology Review, 90*(2), 292–315.

Tversky, A. & Koehler, D. J. (1994). Support theory: A nonextensional representation of subjective probability. *Psychological Review, 101*, 547–567.

Winkler, R. L. (1994). Evaluating probabilities: asymmetric scoring rules. *Management Scence,40*, 1375–1405.

PART III

Decision Making

CHAPTER 13

Cognitive Mapping of Causal Reasoning in Strategic Decision Making

A. John Maule
University of Leeds, UK
Gerard P. Hodgkinson
University of Leeds, UK
and
Nicola J. Bown
University of Leeds, UK

INTRODUCTION

Strategic decisions are the basis on which organisations identify, clarify and act with respect to their medium- and longer-term goals. Over the last two decades there has been an explosion of interest in the application of concepts, theories and methods from the cognitive sciences to the analysis of such decisions, with a view to gaining a better understanding of the processes of strategy formulation and implementation, and developing interventions for facilitating these processes (e.g., Huff, 1990; Eden & Ackermann, 1998; Eden & Spender, 1998; Hodgkinson, 2001a,b; Hodgkinson & Sparrow, 2002; Huff & Jenkins, 2002). Researchers investigating strategic decision making from a cognitive perspective have generally adopted one of two complementary approaches.

The first approach has entailed the application of concepts from behavioural decision making in an attempt to clarify the ways in which individual strategists think and reason when making strategic choices (e.g., Barnes, 1984; Schwenk, 1984, 1985, 1986; Das & Teng, 1999). A large body of this work has drawn on the notion of heuristics and biases (Kahneman, Slovic and Tversky, 1982). According to researchers adopting this approach, in simplifying their reasoning in an effort to reduce the burden of information processing, strategists may make a number of errors, which, in turn, lead to poor decision making (for recent reviews, see Schwenk, 1995; Das & Teng, 1999; Hodgkinson, 2001b; Maule & Hodgkinson, 2002).

Thinking: Psychological Perspectives on Reasoning, Judgment and Decision Making. Edited by David Hardman and Laura Macchi.
© 2003 John Wiley & Sons, Ltd.

In addition to explaining aspects of strategic thinking, this body of research has provided a partial rebuttal of the criticism that the heuristics and biases may not generalise to situations outside the laboratory (Maule & Hodgkinson, 2002).

The second approach has entailed the use of various "cognitive mapping techniques" (e.g., Axelrod, 1976; Huff, 1990) to explore the structure and content of actors' mental representations of strategic problems, in a relatively direct fashion. This work is predicated on the assumption that actors construct simplified mental representations of reality and that strategic choices are ultimately informed by these representations. Drawing on the work of Bartlett (1932), Tolman (1932) and Johnson-Laird (1983), researchers adopting this approach have variously referred to these mental representations as "schemata", "cognitive maps" and "mental models" (e.g., Huff, 1990; Walsh, 1995; Reger & Palmer, 1996; Hodgkinson, 1997a). Hodgkinson and Sparrow (2002) note that despite being developed for different purposes, these terms have been used interchangeably to convey the general notion that actors develop internal representations of their worlds, which in turn, are linked to organisational action (see also Hodgkinson, 2003). Notwithstanding their differing origins, these terms are sufficiently similar in meaning to justify this general usage. In this chapter, therefore, we use "schemata", "cognitive maps" and "mental models" interchangeably, to capture the overarching idea that individuals internalise their knowledge and understanding of strategic issues and problems in the form of a simplified representation of reality.

The purpose of this chapter is to report one study from a programme of work that has brought together these two approaches to investigate the cognitive processes and accompanying mental representations of individual decision makers when they take strategic decisions. Using cognitive mapping techniques in conjunction with the experimental method, we have developed complex strategic choice problems for investigating several interrelated phenomena: cognitive inertia, the tendency for changes in actors' mental models of strategic issues and problems to lag significantly behind major changes in the wider task environment (Porac & Thomas, 1990; Reger & Palmer, 1996; Hodgkinson, 1997b), and the well-documented framing bias (Kahneman & Tversky, 1984; Hodgkinson et al., 1999) and escalation of commitment to a failing course of action (Staw, 1997). Specifically, we have employed a class of cognitive mapping techniques known as "causal mapping" (Axelrod, 1976; Huff, 1990), in an attempt to capture participants' mental representations of particular strategic problems, presented under varying experimental conditions, in the form of relatively elaborate case vignettes.

Within our system of causal mapping, the choice alternatives and the concepts used when thinking about the situation are represented as nodes (we call these "choice" and "concept" nodes, respectively) and the causal relations between these concepts are represented as links between the nodes. Each perceived relationship is signified by means of an arrowheaded pathway, the arrowhead depicting the direction of causality. A plus or minus sign indicates whether the perceived relationship is positive or negative. Our earlier work (Hodgkinson et al., 1999; Hodgkinson & Maule, 2002) and work by other authors (e.g., Green & McManus, 1995) suggests that this is a fruitful approach for capturing research participants' mental representations of causal reasoning.

In developing our approach, we fully recognise that the act of strategising in organisations takes place in a socio-political arena (Pettigrew, 1973, 1985; Mintzberg, 1983; Johnson, 1987; Schwenk, 1989) and that strategies are the product of a negotiated order (Walsh & Fahay, 1986), the consequence of which is that the conflicting cognitions of differing stakeholders must somehow be reconciled (Hodgkinson & Johnson, 1994; Forbes & Milliken, 1999). Nevertheless, our work has focused on the individual decision maker as the primary unit of analysis because a better understanding of individuals' judgment processes and belief systems is a vital prerequisite for better understanding the cognitive and behavioural dynamics of the strategy process at higher levels of analysis.

The primary purpose of this chapter is to illustrate our approach and the potential it has for furthering understanding of strategic choice and, more generally, as a basis for extending behavioural decision research. To achieve this purpose, the chapter is organised in the following way. First, we briefly outline our theoretical assumptions and use these to develop predictions about the nature of strategic choice. Then, we report an experiment testing these predictions and discuss the findings in terms of their implications for understanding strategic decision making and behavioural decision research in general.

THEORETICAL RATIONALE AND RESEARCH QUESTIONS

Our work is underpinned by a dual-process approach for describing the cognitive processes through which individual actors internally represent strategic problems and evaluate alternative courses of action during strategy making (Hodgkinson et al., 1998; Hodgkinson & Bown, 1999). This approach is based on theory and research within cognitive and social psychology suggesting that there are two different types of information-processing strategy—type I (heuristic) and type II (elaborative) (for reviews, see Fiske & Taylor, 1991; Moskowitz, Skurnik & Galinsky, 1999). Currently, researchers are divided in terms of the extent to which these processing strategies are more appropriately viewed as parallel functions, served by independent cognitive systems or, alternatively, as the bipolar extremes of a unidimensional continuum (see, for example, Chaiken & Trope, 1999; Hayes et al., 2003; Hodgkinson & Sadler-Smith, 2003a,b; Hodgkinson & Sparrow, 2002).

We employ the term "type I (heuristic) processing" to denote a largely automatic/semiconscious process in which strategic information is evaluated on the basis of its surface-level characteristics. There is a large volume of evidence showing that individuals engage in heuristic processing strategies during the course of strategic decision making (Schwenk, 1995; reviewed in Bazerman, 2002; Das & Teng, 1999; Hodgkinson, 2001b; Maule & Hodgkinson, 2002). While heuristic processing renders the world manageable (by reducing the information-processing requirements of the decision maker), it can on some occasions lead to errors and bias, reducing the effectiveness of strategic decision making. Type II (elaborative) processing, in contrast, entails a deeper level of stimulus analysis that occurs under conscious control. Type II processing is assumed to involve more effortful, analytical thought and is less likely to lead to error and bias, although it may sometimes also prove dysfunctional due to effects such as "paralysis by analysis", the tendency to become overwhelmed by too much information.

To the extent that our distinction between type I and type II processing is meaningful, we would expect to find that these different processing strategies are associated with differences in the structure and content of decision makers' mental representations of strategic issues and problems. Specifically, the complexity of an actor's mental representation of a problem should vary in accordance with the relative amounts of type I and type II processing deployed.

As noted by Schwenk (1988, p. 45), "The effects of cognitive heuristics and biases may be seen in decision-makers' assumptions about strategic problems." Citing the work of Mason and Mitroff (1981), Schwenk goes on to argue that these assumptions inform strategists' "frames of reference", or "world-views" which, in turn, are encoded as cognitive maps, or schemata, that is, cognitive structures which encapsulate the meaning and significance of the decision environment for the decision maker. Accordingly, we would also expect to find that actors choosing different strategic options would hold different mental representations of the situation.

In sum, our dual-process account of strategic cognition gives rise to two specific predictions:

(1) Differences in the relative amounts of type I and type II processing employed will affect the complexity of decision makers' mental representations of strategic problems, with greater amounts of type II processing resulting in relatively complex representations, and vice versa.
(2) Actors choosing different choice options will hold different mental representations of the strategic situation.

In this chapter, we present an experiment to test these predictions, using time pressure as a means of manipulating the relative amounts of each type of processing strategy. Several researchers have suggested that the introduction of time pressure increases the amount of type I at the expense of type II processing (see Fiske, 1993; Kruglanski & Webster, 1996). This is further supported by a large body of research showing that time pressure reduces the complexity of cognitive strategies underpinning decision making (see Maule & Edland, 1997). Maule and Hockey (1993) suggest that time pressure-induced reductions in the complexity of cognitive strategies may be relatively minor (for example, "filtration", involving small changes in the amount of problem-related information that is processed) or relatively major (for example, a change in the underlying decision rule that leads to relatively large changes in the amount of problem-related information that is processed).

In the present experiment, we employ time pressure in an attempt to increase the amount of type I relative to type II processing, predicting that this, in turn, will reduce the complexity of actors' mental representations of a decision problem. In addition, we investigate the form that this reduction in complexity might take. There are several ways in which time pressure might reduce the complexity of causal reasoning. For instance, participants may think about a smaller number of factors (that is, fewer concept nodes in a cognitive map), may make fewer causal connections between factors (that is, fewer links between concept nodes in a map) or both. Current dual-process approaches have little to say about how increases in type I processing affect an actor's representation of a problem. Hence, we investigate this issue in the present study.

While our second prediction, concerning the relation between actors' mental representations and choice, seems a highly plausible proposition, there has been surprisingly little research investigating this link. Our previous research has investigated this issue by making a distinction between the focal and peripheral regions of cognitive maps (Hodgkinson, Maule & Bown, 2000). The focal region includes the choice nodes and those concept nodes and links that are adjacent to the choice nodes. The peripheral region, by contrast, involves links and nodes that are not directly connected to the choice nodes. Maule et al. (2000) showed that the structure of causal reasoning is more important than its content in distinguishing between participants who choose different options. In particular, they found that all participants included similar concept nodes in their maps regardless of which option they chose. However, there were important differences in the structure of the focal region of their maps, with more causal reasoning around the option that they chose than the option they rejected. This finding is also consistent with recent suggestions by Svenson (1999), developed in the context of differentiation and consolidation theory. At the heart of this theory is the suggestion that individuals identify a promising alternative early in a decision process and then engage in a number of cognitive activities designed to differentiate this alternative from the others. This suggests an increased priority afforded to processing information relating to the chosen alternative, which in our experimental situation, based on cognitive mapping, should lead to a more elaborate network of causal reasoning around this alternative. A primary objective of the present study is to replicate our earlier work showing more elaborate causal reasoning around the chosen alternative, and to extend it in two ways.

First, in focusing just on the focal region of maps, our previous research had considered only those links and concept nodes adjacent to the choice nodes. In so doing, we recognised that we were failing to take account of potentially important chains of reasoning that lay outside this region. For instance, A may be causally linked to B, and B causally linked to a choice node. Restricting our analysis to the focal region of the map meant ignoring the indirect effect of concept A on the choice node. In the present study, we investigate these chains of reasoning by evaluating their frequency of occurrence and by looking for any regularities in how these chains, along with other links in the focal region, are structured around the chosen and rejected alternatives.

Second, we investigate the effects of a time pressure-induced increase in the proportion of type I processing on causal reasoning around the chosen and rejected alternatives. It is rather surprising that previous research has not specified how an increase in type I processing will affect an actor's mental representation of a problem, other than to postulate the rather general prediction that it will somehow lead to a decrease in complexity. A priori, we identified three ways in which increased type I processing might reduce the complexity of participants' cognitive maps. In the first place, it might lead to a reduction in causal reasoning restricted to the focal region of the map. Under this scenario, the effects would be similar in respect of both the chosen and rejected alternatives. Secondly, it might lead to a reduction in causal reasoning within the focal region, such that its effects are strongest in relation to the rejected alternative, given the reduced priority accorded to this alternative (cf. Svenson, 1999). Finally, it might lead to a reduction in causal reasoning in the peripheral region of the map. This third possibility takes account of the fact that time pressure is a stressor (Maule, Hockey & Bdzola, 2000) and that mild to medium levels of stress are known to reduce the processing of peripheral information while leaving focal information relatively unaffected (Eysenck, 1982).

THE STUDY

The research issues identified above were tested experimentally by presenting research participants with a strategic choice problem. Half the participants were given unlimited time, the other half a restricted amount of time, sufficient to induce time pressure. Having made their decision, all participants were given unlimited time to write down all the thoughts and ideas that went through their minds as they made their decision. These transcripts were then coded to produce causal cognitive maps. The maps were then coded in a form suitable for the testing of the main research hypotheses.

Method

Participants

The sample comprised $N = 118$ participants recruited from the postgraduate student population of the University of Leeds ($N = 67$ male; $N = 51$ female). The mean age of the sample was 27.7 years ($SD = 6.6$). Participation in the research was on an unpaid, voluntary basis.

Materials and Procedure

A strategic decision problem was constructed involving a choice between two job options for a graduating student. This situation was highly relevant to the participants, as most were close to leaving the university to take up jobs elsewhere.

The participants were asked to imagine that they were Alex, a computer science student, due to graduate in the very near future (Alex is a name used by both men and women, making the task relevant to both genders). All participants were presented with a strategic decision involving a choice between a safe option (taking up a job offer with a top software company) and a risky option (starting his/her own business). For the safe option, the career financial returns were highly predictable, such that by the end of the second year Alex would almost certainly be earning £15 000 a year. In contrast to this, the risky option was described in terms of two possible outcomes: (1) a successful outcome associated with financial returns considerably higher than the safe option (earning £45 000 a year by the end of the second year); (2) an unsuccessful outcome associated with financial returns considerably lower than the safe option (earning nothing because the business had failed). Participants were told that there was a probability of one-third that the successful outcome would occur, and two-thirds that the unsuccessful outcome would occur. The case information (about 1000 words) presented pro and contra arguments for both options in terms of Alex's personal needs and preferences as well as financial, organisational and commercial aspects of the decision. Participants were told that Alex aimed to be earning £45 000 by the end of his/her second year.

Design

Participants were allocated at random to one of two conditions distinguished in terms of the amount of time provided to make the decision. The control participants were run first, with the time taken to make a decision noted (mean time = 387.4 seconds; $SD = 126.2$). Having made their choices, these participants were then asked to provide a written narrative of all the thoughts and ideas that had occurred at the time they had made their decisions. The time-pressured group followed exactly the same procedure except that they had to make their decisions within a specified period. Adopting the procedure for inducing time

pressure suggested by Benson and Beach (1996), the time allowed was one standard deviation below the mean of the control group (261 seconds). The time-pressured group were
told how long they had to complete the task and were prompted 2 minutes and 1 minute
before the deadline ran out. To allow us to conduct a basic manipulation check, both groups
indicated how time-pressured they had felt during the decision-making exercise, using a
five-point Likert scale with end points "not at all" and "extremely". It is important to note that
both groups had unlimited time to provide a narrative of their thoughts while making their
decisions.

Coding the Cognitive Maps

Each narrative was analysed in three stages by two independent coders. First, each coder
independently identified all references to the choice alternatives (choice nodes) and all other
concepts (concept nodes) present in the narrative. Having completed the full set of maps,
coders compared their analyses, with all disagreement resolved by discussion. There was a
relatively high level of initial agreement (88 per cent) between the coders when identifying
these nodes, and the two coders had no difficulties in resolving disagreements. Next, in
stage two, the coders re-read the narratives and identified all casual relationships between
the previously agreed set of nodes. Again, there was a relatively high level of agreement
between the two coders (84 per cent), with disagreements resolved without difficulty. In
the third stage, the two coders re-read the narratives to determine the direction of causality
(which variable was the cause and which the effect) and the sign (whether there was a
positive or negative relationship) of the causal relations agreed at stage 2. Again the level
of agreement was high both for the direction of causality (95 per cent) and the sign of
the relationship (93 per cent). All disagreements were readily resolved. At the end of
this procedure, the coders drew a cognitive map for each participant. By way of further
clarification, we illustrate our coding process using a case example. Figure 13.1 presents
the narrative produced by one of our participants (number 15), and Figure 13.2 the cognitive
map derived using our coding process.

   In the first phase of the analysis, the coders identified a total of 10 nodes (shown as
boldface, italicised text in Figure 13.1). During the second phase, they identified 12 causal
links between these nodes and drew the map presented in Figure 13.2. Directions of causality
are denoted by the directions of the arrows, terminating in each case on the dependent
variable. The accompanying signs (+ or −) denote whether an increase in the independent
variable causes a concomitant increase or decrease in the dependent variable. In the case
of the link between "failure" and "damaging to career", the question mark ("?") conveys
the fact that there is uncertainty surrounding this particular relationship, as evidenced in the
accompanying narrative (Figure 13.1).

Mapping Measures

Having coded all narratives in this way, following Hodgkinson et al. (2000), we computed
the following series of measures of structural complexity:

(1) The number of choice and concept nodes in the map.
(2) The number of causal links in the map.

The main thoughts influencing my decision were concerning Alex's own personal satisfaction, regardless of the financial considerations.

If she set up *her own business*, she would be following her own *instincts and ambitions* as an independent and creative business person. But if she did not follow *her personal ambitions* and ended up in *a job* that she found *dull and undemanding*, she would *regret* that decision forever. If the *salary for the software company* had been higher (it was still below *her ideal target* by the second year), she would have had more to lose, but considering the *potential financial rewards* for each option, I thought it would be worth the risk involved.

Even if her *own business venture failed*, it would not necessarily be *very damaging* to her career, as it would reflect well on her *character* that she had the confidence and innovation to attempt to do so.

1. her own business
2. instincts and ambitions/personal ambitions (independent and creative business person)
3. a job/(salary for) the software company
4. dull and undemanding
5. regret
6. her ideal target
7. potential financial rewards (worth risk involved)
8. own business venture failed
9. very damaging
10. character (confidence and innovation).

Figure 13.1   Participant 15's narrative (coded nodes in italic boldface)

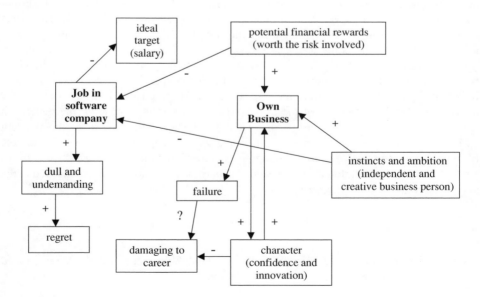

Figure 13.2   Participant 15's coded map

(3) The link-to-node ratio, suggested by Langfield-Smith and Wirth (1992) as a measure of complexity, calculated by dividing the number of links in a map by the number of nodes.

(4) Density, a metric suggested by Markoczy and Goldberg (1995). This is calculated by dividing the number of causal links present in a map by the maximum number possible, given the total number of nodes contained within the map. For example, given a total of four nodes, there is a maximum of 12 possible links (each variable/node can cause and/or be caused by the other three). Hence, if the map had just two links, the density would be is 0.17.

In addition, for the reasons noted earlier, we analysed the number of chains. For our purposes, a chain is a sequence of links involving three or more nodes that either begins or ends with a choice node (cf. Jenkins & Johnson, 1997a,b). For instance, in Figure 13.2, there are three chains: one emanating from "job in software company", involving "dull and undemanding" and "regret", and the others emanating from "own business", leading to "failure" and "damaging to career" and "character". While all of these examples highlighted happen to involve three nodes, chains may differ in terms of their length and whether they emanate *from* a choice node (as do the three examples in Figure 13.2) or terminate on a choice node. In the present study, there were too few chains to allow us to analyse at this level of detail. Instead, we simply counted the number of chains regardless of length or origin.

Thus, for the map presented in Figure 13.2, the number of nodes was 10, while the number of links was 11 or 12, depending on whether the aforementioned link characterised by uncertainty ("?") is tentatively regarded as a negative relationship or, alternatively, discounted. For present purposes, we have included this particular relationship. Hence, the density of the map is $12/90 = 0.133$, and the number of chains is 3.

Results

Choice Behaviour

Of the 59 participants in each condition, 25 chose the safe alternative under the control condition, and 23 chose this option under time pressure. A statistical analysis of these data indicated that time pressure did not affect preferences for the risky and safe options $(\chi^2 (1) = 0.15, p > 0.05$, n.s.).

Feelings of Time Pressure

The mean judgments of how time-pressured the two groups felt while making their choices, from not-at all (1) to extremely (5) are presented in the upper portion of Table 13.1. An analysis of these data revealed, as expected, a highly significant difference $(t(116) = 3.91, p < 0.001)$. While these findings show that our experimental manipulation was successful in inducing time pressure, the overall effect was relatively small, given that the experimental group mean is less than the mid-point of the scale.

Table 13.1 Mean perceived time pressure and the mean overall complexity of cognitive maps in terms of number of nodes, number of links, link-to-node ratio and number of chains for control and time-pressure groups

	Control	Time pressure
Perceived	1.83	2.63
time pressure	(1.12)	(1.10)
Nodes	11.05	9.10
	(3.71)	(2.94)
Link	10.01	7.76
	(4.63)	(3.51)
Link to node	0.91	0.82
	(0.20)	(0.19)
Density	0.20	0.22
	(0.08)	(0.07)
Chains	1.50	0.66
	(1.51)	(0.98)

Structural Complexity of Cognitive Maps

In this section, we first explore the structural complexity of the maps taken as a whole, then, following Hodgkinson et al. (2000), investigate focal complexity by comparing the amount of causal reasoning around each of the choice nodes.

As indicated earlier, the overall complexity of cognitive maps was assessed in terms of the number of nodes, the number of links, link-to-node ratio, density and the number of chains in participants' maps. The means and standard deviations associated with each measure under each condition are presented in the lower portion of Table 13.1. A multivariate analysis of variance of these data (using Wilks' criterion) indicated a significant effect of time pressure ($F(5,111) = 3.38, p < 0.01$), demonstrating, as predicted, that the time-pressured participants had less complex maps overall compared to their counterparts in the control group. Separate univariate analyses were undertaken in order to provide a more detailed understanding of the multivariate findings. These univariate analyses revealed significant effects of time pressure for the number of nodes ($t(115) = 3.15, p < 0.001$), the number of links ($t(115) = 2.97, p < 0.01$), the link-to-node ratio ($t(115) = 2.41, p < 0.01$) and the number of chains ($t(115) = 3.57, p < 0.001$). The map-density measure just failed to reach significance ($t(115) = 1.42, p < 0.08$). These findings support our prediction that time-pressured participants had simpler mental representations of the problem, relative to the control participants. In addition, we have clarified the nature of this simplification, showing that it involves a reduction in the number of concepts and links between concepts, a less dense pattern of causal reasoning (link-to-node ratio and map density) and fewer chains of causal reasoning.

Focal complexity was assessed by counting the number of links in to each choice node (called "in-degrees") and the number out from each choice node (called "out-degrees"). We then compared the numbers of in- and out-degrees to the nodes of the chosen and the rejected alternatives. Table 13.2 presents the means and standard deviations of these

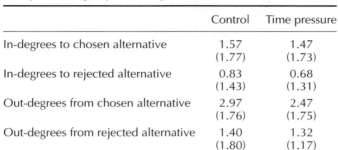

Table 13.2 The mean number of in- and out-degrees associated with the chosen and rejected alternatives for control and time-pressured groups (SDs in parentheses)

	Control	Time pressure
In-degrees to chosen alternative	1.57 (1.77)	1.47 (1.73)
In-degrees to rejected alternative	0.83 (1.43)	0.68 (1.31)
Out-degrees from chosen alternative	2.97 (1.76)	2.47 (1.75)
Out-degrees from rejected alternative	1.40 (1.80)	1.32 (1.17)

measures for the control and time-pressured groups of participants. Analysis of these data, using univariate analyses of variance, indicated that there were more links to the chosen than the rejected alternative ($F(1,115) = 68.78$, $p < 0.001$) and more out-degrees than in-degrees ($F(1,115) = 42.4$, $p < 0.001$). There was, however, no effect of time pressure ($F(1,115) = 2.00$, $p > 0.05$). In addition, none of the interactions was significant ($Fs(1,113) = 2.74$, n.s.).[1]

These findings replicate our earlier study (Hodgkinson et al., 2000) in showing more causal reasoning around the chosen alternative. However, there was no overall effect of time pressure, suggesting that the amount of causal reasoning in the focal region of the map was unaffected by time pressure.

Configuration of Causal Reasoning

In this section we investigate how causal reasoning is configured by looking for distinct patterns in how choice nodes and concept nodes are linked across the whole map. An initial inspection of participants' maps revealed three very distinct configurations. We were able to classify maps into one of these three types by applying two simple rules.

(1) Does the map have causal reasoning around both or just one choice node?
(2) If the map has causal reasoning around both choice nodes, are there any concept nodes linked to the two of them?

These rules led us to specify three types of map. Type A maps illustrated in Figure 13.3a, had causal reasoning around one of the choice nodes but nothing around the other. In all cases classified as this type, the causal activity was located around the chosen alternative, the rejected alternative being ignored altogether. Type B maps, illustrated in Figure 13.3b, had causal reasoning around both choice nodes, but with no concept nodes in common. Finally, type C maps, illustrated in Figure 13.3c, had causal reasoning around both choice nodes and at least one concept node linked to both choice alternatives. The maps of all but two participants could be readily classified into one of these three types. (The two maps

---

[1] This pattern of results occurs regardless of whether the data are analysed separately or jointly for subgroups whose chosen alternative is the safe or risky option.

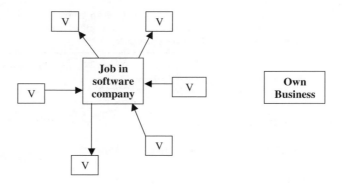

Figure 13.3a Type A map

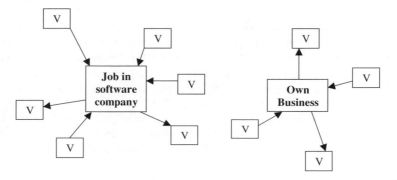

Figure 13.3b Type B map

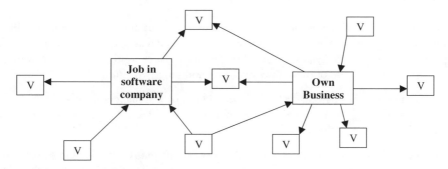

Figure 13.3c Type C map

that could not be so classified had no links to or from either choice node.) Having excluded these two "outliers", our analysis revealed that 23 per cent of the maps were type A, 37 per cent were type B and 40 per cent were type C. These different map types suggest rather different ways of conceptualising the strategic problem. To help clarify the implications of this classification, we undertook two further analyses.

First, we compared how frequently each map type was used by the control and time-pressure groups. This analysis revealed no differences (χ^2 (2) = 0.67, n.s.), suggesting that

Table 13.3 Mean perceived time pressure and the mean overall complexity of cognitive maps in terms of number of nodes, number of links, link-to-node ratio and number of chains for the three map structural types for control and time-pressure (TPress) groups (SDs in parentheses)

	Type A Single node		Type B Two separate nodes		Type C Two connected nodes	
	Control	TPress	Control	TPress	Control	TPress
Nodes	9.10 (2.88)	7.33 (2.01)	11.71 (3.76)	9.81 (3.14)	11.81 (3.93)	9.48 (2.87)
Links	7.5 (4.00)	5.42 (2.81)	10.52 (4.78)	7.57 (2.80)	11.43 (4.43)	9.28 (3.60)
Link/node	0.90 (0.23)	0.70 (0.20)	0.87 (0.19)	0.75 (0.12)	0.97 (0.16)	0.96 (0.12)
Density	0.24 (0.07)	0.23 (0.06)	0.18 (0.06)	0.19 (0.06)	0.20 (0.09)	0.18 (0.07)
Chains	1.33 (1.63)	0.58 (1.0)	1.67 (1.56)	0.67 (0.97)	1.53 (1.44)	0.72 (1.02)

the introduction of time pressure was not a factor in determining which of the three types of causal structure were adopted.

Second, we compared across the control and time-pressure groups the complexity of causal reasoning associated with each map type, using the global measures of structural complexity identified earlier. The means and standard deviations of these measures for the control and time-pressured groups of participants, broken down by the various map types, are presented in Table 13.3. A multivariate analysis of variance revealed significant effects of time-pressure ($F(5,105) = 3.86$, $p < 0.01$ and map type ($F (10,212) = 4.63$, $p < 0.001$). However, the map type by time-pressure interaction failed to reached significance ($F (10,212) = 1.45$, n.s.). The effects of time pressure are similar to those described earlier, when considering the maps as a whole (that is, prior to classifying them into the three subtypes). There is a general reduction in the overall complexity of all map types under time pressure. The map-type effect indicates that complexity is generally lowest for type A and highest for type C maps. Further clarification of these effects was undertaken using separate, univariate analyses. Again, the overall effects of time pressure were the same as those reported earlier, showing that time pressure reduced the complexity of cognitive maps in terms of the number of links, number of nodes, link-to-node ratio and number of chains ($F (1,109) = 10.38$, $p < 0.01$), but had no effect on map density ($F (1,109) = 1.33$, n.s.). The effects of map type showed significant differences in terms of number of links ($F (2,109) = 8.49$, $p < 0.001$), number of nodes ($F (2,109) = 5.93$, $p < 0.01$), link-to-node ratio ($F (2,109) = 11.91$, $p < 0.001$) and map density ($F (2,109) = 5.37$, $p < 0.01$). However, there were no significant differences in terms of the number of chains ($F (2,109) < 1$, n.s.). Further investigation of the significant effects associated with this particular set of analyses, using the Scheffe test, revealed that type A maps were significantly less complex than type B and type C maps in terms of the number of links ($p < 0.05$) and the number of nodes ($p < 0.05$). However, the differences between the type B and type C maps were not significantly different. The link-to-node ratio measure of structural complexity revealed that type A and type B maps were similar to one another, but both were significantly less complex than type C maps ($p < 0.05$). The pattern of findings was rather different for the density measure, with type A and type C maps being similar to one another, but both significantly more dense than type B maps ($p < 0.05$). Taken together, these effects support our earlier conclusion that for all measures except map density, the complexity of causal reasoning is generally lowest for type A and highest for type C maps.

In short, the overall pattern of these findings suggests that participants conceptualised the problem in very different ways, the varying map types reflecting key differences in terms of structural complexity and how the maps were configured.

Discussion

In this section, we first discuss the experimental findings and then consider the potential of our approach for theory and research on human decision making.

Interpretation of Our Findings

Our study was designed to investigate two predictions derived from our dual-process approach to describing the cognitive processes through which actors internally represent strategic decisions. Our first prediction, that an actor's mental representation of a problem becomes less complex as the amount of type I processing of problem information increases, was strongly supported. We demonstrated that time pressure, a manipulation believed to increase type I processing, decreased the overall complexity of participants' cognitive maps. In addition, we clarified the nature of this decrease in complexity, showing that it involves a reduction in (1) the number of nodes, (2) the number of causal links between nodes, (3) overall map density, (4) the link-to-node ratio and (5) the number of reasoning chains contained within the maps. A preliminary conclusion to be drawn from this pattern of findings is that increased type I processing induces mental representations that are less comprehensive, both in terms of the number of variables considered and the richness of the relations that are perceived to exist between these variables.

However, we failed to show an effect of time pressure when only the focal region of the maps was considered (that is, focal complexity). This suggests that time pressure exerted its primary effects on the peripheral elements of the participants' maps. We believe that this pattern of findings may have occurred because the experimental group was under mild time pressure. By definition, mild time pressure exerts only relatively minor effects. Such effects may well take the form of increased type I processing of less critical, peripheral information. Extreme time pressure effects, by contrast, might take the form of increased type I processing of focal information.

The lack of a time pressure effect on focal reasoning may explain why participants' choice behaviour was unaffected by time pressure. Since this aspect of reasoning is directly linked to the choice nodes, it would be expected to be more important in determining choice. External factors such as time pressure may induce changes in choice behaviour only if the focal region of an actor's mental representation is changed. Overall, our findings suggest that it is not only the amount of type I and type II processing that determines an actor's mental representation of a problem and their choice, but also which aspects of the problem information are processed under each type.

Our second prediction, that there are reliable differences in the mental representations of participants choosing different choice alternatives, was also supported. In particular, there was a richer causal network around the node of the chosen alternative than the rejected alternative, regardless of whether the safe or the risky option was chosen. This finding is consistent with a body of research on Differentiation and Consolidation theory, discussed earlier, showing that people process more attribute information describing chosen alternatives than rejected alternatives (Svenson, 1999). The present study extends this body of work by demonstrating that people also develop more elaborate representations of chosen than rejected alternatives when this is captured in terms of causal reasoning. However, in developing Differentiation and Consolidation theory, Svenson argues that the increased cognitive activity associated with the chosen alternative may occur prior to choice, so as to differentiate one alternative from the others, or after choice, in order to consolidate the chosen alternative, thereby sustaining the advantage it has over the rejected alternatives. Since our participants generated their narratives post-choice, we cannot, at this stage, be sure whether the more complex casual reasoning around the chosen alternative reflects pre-choice differentiation, post-choice consolidation or a combination of both. Svenson (1999) argued that consolidation processes usually take some time to build up, leading us to speculate that the reported differences between the chosen and rejected alternatives reflect differences in pre-choice causal reasoning. However, our approach has the potential to discriminate between these different explanations through a comparison of narratives generated by differing groups, before and after choice, and work is presently under way to investigate further these alternatives. Nevertheless, our study extends previous work by showing that the priority accorded to the chosen alternative, previously demonstrated in terms of attribute information processing, is also present in actors' causal representations of choice problems.

Our findings also revealed potentially important individual differences in respect of the configuration of causal reasoning, with the maps of all but two participants readily classified into one of three structural types. Type A maps were characterised by causal reasoning around just one of the choice alternatives (always the chosen), with no activity around the other. Type B and type C maps were similar to one another in that causal reasoning was evident around both choice nodes, but differed from one another, in that type B maps had no concept nodes linked to both choice nodes, whereas type C maps contained at least one such node. In addition, we showed that type A maps were characterised by the greatest structural simplicity and type C by generally the most complex. These different patterns of causal reasoning raise two questions.

The first question concerns why different participants map the problem in such different ways. One reason might be due to differences in the way participants interpret the mapping instructions, with some reporting only the more important aspects of their thinking, while others also report aspects of lesser importance. A second reason might reflect reliable individual differences in processing of problem-related information. For instance, previous work on need for cognition (Cacioppo & Petty, 1982) suggests that there are key differences in the extent to which people enjoy thinking. On the basis of this work, we would expect that such differences might have a bearing on the way in which individuals represent decision problems observed in the present study. At this point in time, we think that the differences in mental representation that we have observed are most likely to reflect reliable individual differences in processing styles and strategies, and we plan further work to investigate this.

The second question concerns what these different structural configurations might signify in terms of our dual-process model. In many ways, the characteristics of type A maps are consistent with what might be expected from a reliance on type I processing (for example, ignoring one alternative, fewer concepts considered or fewer causal connections). Similarly, the defining characteristics of type C maps (a more elaborate causal structure involving comparisons between different choice alternatives) seem more consistent with a reliance on type II processing. However, the proportion of participants with type A, B and C maps did not change under time pressure (recall that time pressure is assumed to increase the amount of type I processing). Consequently, in seeking to understand better the effects of changes in the relative amounts of type I and type II processing on problem representation, we are left with the dilemma of determining whether such effects are manifest primarily in terms of changes to the overall structural complexity of a cognitive map or in terms of changes to its configuration. We currently believe that the configuration of a map may be a more appropriate indicator of type I/type II processing strategies in use. Furthermore, we believe that the failure of time pressure to increase the number of participants modelling in terms of the simpler type A structure is due to the fact that our deadline manipulation induced only mild time pressure. As indicated earlier, mild time pressure is known to evoke filtration, a mode of adapting that involves minor modifications to the current cognitive strategy rather than a fundamental change in this strategy (Maule & Hockey, 1993). Thus, filtration would not be expected to lead to fundamental changes in type I/type II processing but should lead to a truncation of the existing strategy, a prediction that is broadly consistent with our findings showing an overall reduction in the structural complexity of maps.

This interpretation is further supported by our findings showing that time pressure primarily affected the peripheral, but not the focal, regions of the cognitive maps. Previous research has shown that filtration is focused primarily on the less important aspects of the problem information, which in our experimental situation would be expected to be represented in the peripheral region of the maps. Thus, we believe that the reduction in overall map complexity under time pressure, reported in our study, can be attributed to filtration rather than a change in strategy based on the amounts of type I/type II processing. We predict that under stronger time pressure, adapting through filtration would not be possible. Hence, participants would increase the amount of type I processing, leading to a concomitant increase in the number of participants modelling the problem in terms of the simpler type A configuration.

General Implications of Our Approach

A primary aim of this chapter was to outline our overall approach and to consider its potential, both as a basis for furthering our understanding of strategic choice and, more generally, as a basis for enriching the field of behavioural decision research. At the heart of our approach is the use of causal cognitive mapping as a means of opening up the "black box" of behavioural decision making, allowing us to formulate and test predictions about actors' representations of decision problems and their choice behaviours. Previous attempts to open up the "black box" have used verbal protocols and information boards to determine the thought processes that underlie human decision making (for a recent review, see Harte & Koele, 2001). We believe that causal cognitive mapping provides a third and hitherto under-used approach that is particularly useful when researchers wish to investigate an actor's mental model of a decision problem. Contemporary theories of human decision making often make assumptions about the nature of an actor's mental model (such as decision frames in prospect theory), yet these assumptions are rarely tested directly. Maule (1989) reported a study using verbal protocols to test assumptions about the decision frames associated in different versions of the Asian disease problem. He comments on difficulties in determining which aspects of the protocol capture research participants' representation of the problem at the moment of choice—there are often several different possibilities in long protocols. We believe that cognitive mapping, as illustrated in this chapter, overcomes this problem. Asking participants to provide a narrative of their thinking is more likely to elicit the "predominant" view, which, we believe, is the model of the problem most likely to inform choice behaviour. As noted in our introduction, we are currently working on a series of experiments that demonstrate the value of our approach for understanding the mental representations associated with the framing bias, escalation of commitment and cognitive inertia (see, for example, Hodgkinson et al., 1999, 2002; Maule et al., 2000; Hodgkinson & Maule, 2002).

Our approach has also highlighted and begun to resolve some hitherto neglected issues associated with current formulations of dual-process theory. For instance, we have highlighted the importance of specifying how increases in type I processing change an actor's mental representation of a problem, and have argued that this can be determined by the configuration of the map. Specifying these changes in detail has the potential to provide a way for future researchers to undertake a manipulation check, to determine whether changes in the relative amounts of type I and type II processing have actually occurred.

Finally, as noted above, our approach has added to an emerging view in decision research that individuals place a higher priority on processing problem-related information associated with chosen as compared with rejected alternatives. While earlier research focused on attribute information processing, our study demonstrates that these differences are also present in actors' causal mental representations of problems, with greater causal reasoning around the chosen alternative. These two approaches provide rather different ways of describing human decision making. Further research is now needed in order to understand the relationships between them.

ACKNOWLEDGEMENTS

The work reported in this chapter was funded by the UK Economic and Social Research Council (ESRC) under Phase II of its "Risk and Human Behaviour Programme" (Award Number L211 25 2042). The assistance of Neil Emmerson with the collection of data is gratefully acknowledged, as are the contributions of Keith W. Glaister and Alan D. Pearman.

REFERENCES

Axelrod, R. (1976). The mathematics of cognitive maps. In R. M. Axelrod (ed.), *Structure of Decision: The Cognitive Maps of Political Elites* (pp. 343–348). Princeton, NJ: Princeton University Press.
Barnes, J. H. (1984). Cognitive biases and their impact on strategic planning. *Strategic Management Journal*, 5, 129–137.

Bartlett, F. C. (1932). *Remembering: A Study in Experimental and Social Psychology*. London: Cambridge University Press.

Bazerman, M. H. (2002). *Judgment in Managerial Decision Making* (5th edn). New York: Wiley.

Benson, L. & Beach, L. R. (1996). The effects of time constraints on the pre-choice screening of decision options. *Organizational Behavior and Human Decision Processes*, 67, 222–228.

Cacioppo, J. T. & Petty, R. E. (1982). The need for cognition. *Journal of Personality and Social Psychology*, 42, 116–131.

Chaiken, S. & Trope, Y. (eds) (1999). *Dual-Process Theories in Social Psychology*. New York: Guilford.

Das, T. K. & Teng, B.-S. (1999). Cognitive biases and strategic decision processes. *Journal of Management Studies*, 36, 757–778.

Eden, C. & Ackermann, F. (1998). *Making Strategy: The Journey of Strategic Management*. London: Sage.

Eden, C. & Spender, J.-C. (eds) (1998). *Managerial and Organizational Cognition: Theory, Methods and Research*. London: Sage.

Eysenck, M. W. (1982). *Attention and Arousal: Cognition and Performance*. Berlin: Springer.

Fiske, S. T. (1993). Social cognition and social perception. *Annual Review of Psychology*, 44, 154–199.

Fiske, S. T. & Taylor, S. E. (1991) *Social Cognition* (2nd edn). New York: McGraw-Hill.

Forbes, D. P. & Milliken, F. J. (1999). Cognition and corporate governance: Understanding boards of directors as strategic decision-making groups. *Academy of Management Review*, 24, 489–505.

Green, D. W. & McManus, I. C. (1995). Cognitive structural models: The perception of risk and prevention in coronary heart disease. *British Journal of Psychology*, 86, 321–336.

Harte, J. M. & Koele, P. (2001) Modelling and describing human judgement processes. *Thinking and Reasoning*, 7, 29–50.

Hayes, J., Allinson, C. W., Hudson, R. S. and Keasey, K. (2003). Further reflections on the nature of intuition-analysis and the construct validity of the Cognitive Style Index. *Journal of Occupational and Organizational Psychology*, 76, 269–278.

Hodgkinson, G. P. (1997a). The cognitive analysis of competitive structures: A review and critique. *Human Relations*, 50, 625–654.

Hodgkinson, G. P. (1997b). Cognitive inertia in a turbulent market: The case of UK residential estate agents. *Journal of Management Studies*, 34, 921–945.

Hodgkinson, G. P. (2001a). The psychology of strategic management: Diversity and cognition revisited. In C. L. Cooper & I. T. Robertson (eds), *International Review of Industrial and Organizational Psychology* (vol. 16, pp. 65–119). Chichester: Wiley.

Hodgkinson, G. P. (2001b). Cognitive processes in strategic management: Some emerging trends and future directions. In N. Anderson, D. S. Ones, H. K. Sinangil & C. Viswesvaran (eds), *Handbook of Industrial, Work and Organizational Psychology* (vol. 2, pp. 416–440). London: Sage.

Hodgkinson, G. P. (2003). The interface of cognitive and industrial, work and organizational psychology. *Journal of Occupational and Organizational Psychology*, 76, 1–25.

Hodgkinson & Bown (1999). The individual in the strategy process: a cognitive model. Paper presented at the Annual Conference of the British Academy of Management, Manchester, UK, September.

Hodgkinson, G. P. & Johnson, G. (1994). Exploring the mental models of competitive strategists: The case for a processual approach. *Journal of Management Studies*, 31, 525–551.

Hodgkinson, G. P. & Maule, A. J. (2002). The individual in the strategy process: insights from behavioural decision research and cognitive mapping. In A. S. Huff & M. Jenkins (eds), *Mapping Strategic Knowledge* (pp. 196–219). London: Sage.

Hodgkinson, G. P., Maule, A. J. & Bown, N. J. (2000). Charting the mind of the strategic decision maker: A comparative analysis of two methodological alternatives involving causal mapping. Paper presented at the Annual Meeting of the Academy of Management, Toronto, Canada, August.

Hodgkinson, G. P. & Sparrow, P. R. (2002) *The Competent Organization: A Psychological Analysis of the Strategic Management Process*. Buckingham: Open University Press.

Hodgkinson, G. P. and Sadler-Smith, E. (2003a). Complex or unitary? A critique and empirical re-assessment of the Allinson-Hayes Cognitive Style Index. *Journal of Occupational and Organizational Psychology*, 76, 243–268.

Hodgkinson, G. P. and Sadler-Smith, E. (2003b). Reflections on reflections . . . on the nature of intuition, analysis and the construct validity of the cognitive style index. *Journal of Occupational and Organizational Psychology, 76*, 279–281.

Hodgkinson, G. P., Bown, N. J., Maule, A. J., Glaister, K. W. & Pearman, A. D. (1998). Dual information processing in strategic decision-making? A theoretical framework and some empirical data. Paper presented at the 18th Annual International Conference of the Strategic Management Society, Orlando, USA, November.

Hodgkinson, G. P., Bown, N. J., Maule, A. J., Glaister, K. W. & Pearman, A. D. (1999). Breaking the frame: An analysis of strategic cognition and decision making under uncertainty. *Strategic Management Journal, 20*, 977–985.

Hodgkinson, G. P., Maule, A. J., Bown, N. J., Pearman, A. D. & Glaister, K. W. (2002). Further reflections on the elimination of the framing bias in strategic decision making. *Strategic Management Journal, 23*, 1069–1076.

Huff, A. S. (ed.) (1990). *Mapping Strategic Thought*. Chichester: Wiley.

Huff, A. S. & Jenkins, M. (eds) (2002). *Mapping Strategic Knowledge*. London: Sage.

Jenkins, M. & Johnson, G. (1997a). Linking managerial cognition and organizational performance: A preliminary investigation using causal maps. *British Journal of Management, 8* (Special Issue), S77–S90.

Jenkins, M. & Johnson, G. (1997b). Entrepreneurial intentions and outcomes: A comparative causal mapping study. *Journal of Management Studies, 34*, 895–920.

Johnson, G. (1987). *Strategic Change and the Management Process*. Oxford: Blackwell.

Johnson-Laird, P. N. (1983). *Mental Models*. Cambridge: Cambridge University Press.

Kahneman D. & Tversky A. (1984). Choices, values and frames. *American Psychologist, 39*, 341–350.

Kahneman, D., Slovic, P. & Tversky, A. (eds) (1982). *Judgment Under Uncertainty: Heuristics and Biases*. Cambridge: Cambridge University Press.

Kruglanski, A. W. & Webster, D. M. (1996). Group members' reactions to opinion deviates and conformists at varying degrees of proximity to decision deadline and use of environmental noise. *Journal of Personality and Social Psychology, 61*, 212–225.

Langfield-Smith, K. & Wirth, A. (1992). Measuring differences between cognitive maps. *Journal of Operational Research Society, 43*, 1135–1150.

Markoczy, L. & Goldberg, J. (1995). A method for eliciting and comparing causal maps. *Journal of Management, 21*, 305–333.

Mason, R. & Mitroff, I. (1981). *Challenging Strategic Planning Assumptions*. New York: Wiley.

Maule, A. J. (1989). Positive and negative decision frames: A verbal protocol analysis of the Asian disease problem of Kahneman and Tversky. In H. Montgomery & O. Svenson (eds), *Process and Structure in Human Decision Making* (pp. 163–180). Chichester: Wiley.

Maule, A. J. & Edland, A. C. (1997). The effects of time pressure on judgement and decision making. In R. Ranyard, W. R. Crozier & O. Svenson (eds), *Decision Making: Cognitive Models and Explanation*. London: Routledge.

Maule, A. J. & Hockey, G. R. J. (1993). State, stress and time pressure. In O. Svenson & A. J. Maule (eds), *Time Pressure and Stress in Human Judgment and Decision Making* (pp. 83–101). New York: Plenum.

Maule, A. J. & Hodgkinson, G. P. (2002). Heuristics, biases and strategic decision making. *The Psychologist, 15*, 68–71.

Maule, A. J., Hockey, G. R. J. & Bdzola L. (2000). Effects of time pressure on decision making under uncertainty: Changes in affective state and information processing strategy. *Acta Psychologica, 104*, 283–301.

Maule A. J., Hodgkinson, G. P., Bown, N. J., Pearman, A. D. & Glaister, K. W. (2000). A cognitive mapping study of the relation between mental representations and choice behaviour in a strategic episode involving negative feedback. Paper presented to the Behavioral Decision Research in Management Conference, Tucson, Arizona, USA, May.

Mintzberg, H. (1983). *Power in and Around Organizations*. Englewood Cliffs, NJ: Prentice-Hall.

Moskowitz, G. B., Skurnik, I. & Galinsky, A. D. (1999). The history of dual-process notions, and the future of pre-conscious control. In S. Chaiken and Y. Trope (eds), *Dual-Process Theories in Social Psychology* (pp. 12–36). New York: Guilford.

Pettigrew, A. M. (1973). *The Politics of Organizational Decision Making.* London: Tavistock.

Pettigrew, A. M. (1985). *The Awakening Giant: Continuity and Change in Imperial Chemical Industries.* Oxford: Blackwell.

Porac, J. F. & Thomas, H. (1990). Taxonomic mental models in competitor definition. *Academy of Management Review, 15,* 224–240.

Reger, R. K. & Palmer, T. B. (1996). Managerial categorization of competitors: Using old maps to navigate new environments. *Organization Science, 7,* 22–39.

Schwenk, C. R. (1984). Cognitive simplification processes in strategic decision making. *Strategic Management Journal, 5,* 111–128.

Schwenk, C. R. (1985). Management illusions and biases: Their impact on strategic decisions. *Long Range Planning, 18,* 74–80.

Schwenk, C. R. (1986). Information, cognitive biases and commitment to a course of action. *Academy of Management Review, 11,* 298–310.

Schwenk, C. R. (1988). The cognitive perspective on strategic decision making. *Journal of Management Studies, 25,* 41–55.

Schwenk, C. R. (1989). Linking cognitive, organizational and political factors in explaining strategic change. *Journal of Management Studies, 26,* 177–187.

Schwenk, C. R. (1995). Strategic decision making. *Journal of Management, 21,* 471–493.

Staw, B. M. (1997). The escalation of commitment: An update and appraisal. In Z. Shapira (ed.), *Organizational Decision Making* (pp. 191–215). Cambridge: Cambridge University Press.

Svenson, O. (1999). Differentiation and consolidation theory: Decision making processes before and after a choice. In P. Juslin & H. Montgomery (eds), *Judgment and Decision Making: Neo-Brunswikian and Process-Tracing Approaches* (pp. 175–197). Mahweh, NJ: Erlbaum.

Tolman, E. C. (1932). *Purposive Behavior in Animals and Men.* New York: Century.

Walsh, J. P. (1995). Managerial and organizational cognition: Notes from a trip down memory lane. *Organization Science, 6,* 280–321.

Walsh, J. P. & Fahay, L. (1986). The role of negotiated belief structures in strategy making. *Journal of Management, 12,* 325–338.

CHAPTER 14

Belief and Preference in Decision Under Uncertainty*

Craig R. Fox

Anderson School of Management and Department of Psychology, UCLA, USA

and

Kelly E. See

Duke University, Fuqua School of Business, USA

14.1 INTRODUCTION

Most decisions in life are gambles. Should I speed up or slow down as I approach the yellow traffic light ahead? Should I invest in the stock market or in treasury bills? Should I undergo surgery or radiation therapy to treat my tumor? From mundane choices rendered with scarcely a moment's reflection to urgent decisions founded on careful deliberation, we seldom know in advance and with certainty what the consequences of our choices will be. Thus, most decisions require not only an assessment of the attractiveness of potential consequences, but also some appraisal of their likelihood of occurrence.

Virtually all decision theorists agree that values and beliefs jointly influence willingness to act under uncertainty. However, there is considerable disagreement about how to measure values and beliefs, and how to model their influence on decisions. Our purpose in this chapter is to bring into sharper focus the role of values and beliefs in decision under uncertainty and contrast some recent developments in the descriptive modeling of choice under uncertainty with the classical normative model.

14.1.1 The Classical Theory and the Sure-Thing Principle

The primitives of most decision theories are acts, states, and consequences (Savage, 1954; for an alternative approach, see Luce, 2000). An *act* is an action or option that yields one

---

* The view of decision making under uncertainty outlined in this chapter was heavily influenced by the late Amos Tversky. Of course, any errors or deficiencies of the present work are entirely the responsibility of the authors. We thank Jim Bettman, Rick Larrick, Bob Nau, John Payne, Shlomi Sher, Peter Wakker and George Wu for helpful comments on earlier drafts of this chapter. Most of the work on this chapter was completed while Craig Fox was at the Fuqua School of Business, Duke University, whose support is gratefully acknowledged.

Table 14.1   A decision matrix. Columns are interpreted as
states of the world, and rows are interpreted as acts; each
cell entry x_{ij} is the consequence of act i if state j obtains

		States				
		s_1	...	s_j	...	s_n
A	a_1	x_{11}	...	x_{1j}	...	x_{1n}
C	...	...	...	...	...	...
T	a_i	x_{i1}	...	x_{ij}	...	x_{in}
S	...	...	...	...	...	...
	a_m	x_{m1}	...	x_{mj}	...	x_{mn}

of a set of possible *consequences* depending on which future *state* of the world obtains.
For instance, suppose I am considering whether or not to carry an umbrella. Two possible
acts are available to me: carry an umbrella, or do not carry an umbrella. Two relevant states
of the world are possible: rain or no rain. The consequence of the act that I choose is a
function of both the act chosen (which governs whether or not I am burdened by carrying
an umbrella) and the state that obtains (which influences whether or not I will get wet).

More formally, let S be the set of possible states of the world, subsets of which are called
events. It is assumed that exactly one state obtains, which is unknown to the decision maker.
Let X be a set of possible consequences (also called "outcomes"), such as dollars gained
or lost relative to the status quo. Let A be the set of possible acts, which are interpreted as
functions, mapping states to consequences. Thus, for act $a_i \in A$, state $s_j \in S$, and consequence $x_{ij} \in X$, we have $a_i(s_j) = x_{ij}$. This scheme can be neatly captured by a decision
matrix, as depicted in Table 14.1.

In the classical normative model of decision under uncertainty, decision makers weight the
perceived attractiveness (utility) of each potential consequence by its perceived likelihood
(subjective probability). Formally, if $u(x_{ij})$ is the utility of outcome x_{ij} and $p(s_j)$ is the
subjective probability that state s_j will obtain, then the decision maker chooses the act that
maximizes subjective expected utility (SEU):

$$SEU(a_i) = \sum_{j=1}^{n} u(x_{ij})p(s_j). \tag{1}$$

Hence, the classical model segregates belief (probability) from value (utility). Subjective
expected utility theory (Savage, 1954) articulates a set of axioms that are necessary and
sufficient for the representation above, allowing subjective probability and utility to be
measured simultaneously from observed preferences.[1] For instance, if Alan is indifferent
between receiving $100 if it rains tomorrow (and nothing otherwise) or $100 if a fair coin
lands heads (and nothing otherwise), then we infer that he considers these target events to be
equally likely (that is, $p(\text{rain}) = p(\text{heads}) = 1/2$). If he is indifferent between receiving one of
these prospects or $35 for sure, we infer that $u(35) = 1/2\, u(100)$. It is important to emphasize
that Savage, following the tradition of previous theorists (e.g., Borel, 1924; Ramsey, 1931;

---

[1] For alternative axiomatic approaches that more explicitly distinguish the role of objective versus subjective probabilities, see
Anscombe and Aumann (1963) and Pratt, Raiffa and Schlaifer (1964).

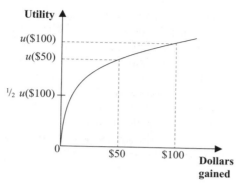

Figure 14.1   A concave utility function for dollars gained set to $u(0) = 0$

de Finetti, 1937), rejected direct judgments of likelihood in favor of a measure derived from observed preferences. In contrast, psychologists (e.g., Kahneman, Slovic & Tversky, 1982) give credence to direct expressions of belief and assume that they can be used to predict willingness to act under uncertainty.[2]

Expected utility theory was originally developed to explain attitudes toward risk. The lay concept of "risk" entails the threat of harm or loss. For instance, managers see risk as increasing with the likelihood and magnitude of potential losses (e.g., March & Shapira, 1987). Decision theorists, in contrast, see risk as increasing with variance in the probability distribution of possible outcomes, regardless of whether or not a potential loss is involved. For instance, a prospect that offers a .5 chance of receiving $100 and a .5 chance of receiving nothing is more risky than a prospect that offers $50 for sure—even though the "risky" prospect entails no possibility of losing money. *Risk aversion* is defined by decision theorists as a preference for a sure outcome over a chance prospect with equal or greater expected value.[3] Thus, the preference of $50 for sure over a 50–50 chance of receiving $100 or nothing is an expression of risk aversion. *Risk seeking*, in contrast, is defined as a preference for a chance prospect over a sure outcome of equal or greater expected value. It is commonly assumed that people are risk averse, and this is explained in expected utility theory by a concave utility function (see Figure 14.1). Such a shape implies, for example, that the utility gained from receiving $50 is more than half the utility gained from receiving $100; hence, receiving $50 for sure is more attractive than a 50–50 chance of receiving $100 or nothing.[4]

As stated earlier, Savage (1954) identified a set of preference conditions that are both necessary and sufficient to represent a decision maker's choices by the maximization of subjective expected utility. Central to the SEU representation (Equation (1)) is an axiom known as the "sure-thing principle" (also sometimes referred to as "weak independence"): if two acts yield the same consequence when a particular state obtains, then preference between acts should not depend on the particular nature of that common consequence

---

[2] Some statisticians, philosophers, and economists have been sympathetic to the use of direct probability judgment as a primitive for decision theories (e.g., DeGroot, 1970; Shafer, 1986; Karni & Mongin, 2000).
[3] The expected value of a gamble that pays $x with probability p is given by xp. This is the mean payoff that would be realized if the gamble were played an infinite number of times.
[4] In expected utility theory, utility is a function of the decision maker's aggregate wealth and is unique up to a positive affine transformation (that is, utility is measured on an interval scale). To simplify (and without loss of generality), we have set the utility of the present state of wealth, $u(W_0) = 0$.

(see Savage, 1954). To illustrate, consider a game in which a coin is flipped to determine which fruit Alan will receive with his lunch. Suppose that Alan would rather receive an apple if a fair coin lands heads and a *cantaloupe* if it lands tails (*a, H; c, T*) than receive a banana if the coin lands heads and a *cantaloupe* if it lands tails (*b, H; c, T*). If this is the case, Alan should also prefer to receive an apple if the coin lands heads and *dates* if the coin lands tails (*a, H; d, T*) to a banana if it lands heads and *dates* if it lands tails (*b, H; d, T*). In fact, the preference ordering over these prospects should not be affected at all by the nature of the common consequence—be it a cantaloupe, dates or a subscription to *Sports Illustrated*. The sure-thing principle is necessary to establish a subjective probability measure that is additive (that is, $p(s_1) + p(s_2) = p(s_1 \cup s_2)$).[5]

14.1.2 Violations of the Sure-Thing Principle

The sure-thing principle seems on the surface to be quite reasonable, if not unassailable. In fact, Savage (1954, p. 21) wrote, "I know of no other extralogical principle governing decisions that finds such ready acceptance." Nevertheless, it was not long before the descriptive validity of this axiom was called into question. Notably, two "paradoxes" emerged, due to Allais (1953) and Ellsberg (1961). These paradoxes pointed to deficiencies of the classical theory that have since given rise to a more descriptively valid account of decision under uncertainty.

Problem 1: The Allais Paradox

Choose between: (A) $1 million for sure; (B) a 10 percent chance of winning $5 million, an 89 percent chance of winning $1 million, and a 1 percent chance of winning nothing.

Choose between: (C) an 11 percent chance of winning $1 million; (D) a 10 percent chance of winning $5 million.

Problem 2: The Ellsberg Paradox

An urn contains 30 red balls, as well as 60 balls that are each either white or blue (but you do not know how many of these balls are white and how many are blue). You are asked to draw a ball from the urn without looking.

Choose between: (E) win $100 if the ball drawn is red (and nothing if it is white or blue); (F) win $100 if the ball drawn is white (and nothing if it is red or blue).

Choose between: (G) win $100 if the ball drawn is either red or blue (and nothing if it is white); (H) win $100 if the ball drawn is either white or blue (and nothing if it is red).

Maurice Allais (1953) presented a version of Problem 1 at an international colloquium on risk that was attended by several of the most eminent economists of the day. The majority of

---

[5] Savage's postulates P3 and P4 establish that events can be ordered by their impact on preferences and that values of consequences are independent of the particular events under which they obtain. In the context of P3 and P4, the sure-thing principle (Savage's P2) establishes that the impact of the events is additive (that is, that it can be represented by a probability measure). For an alternative approach to the derivation of subjective probabilities that neither implies nor assumes expected utility theory, see Machina and Schmeidler (1992).

Table 14.2 Visual representation of the Allais paradox. People typically prefer A over B but also prefer D over C, in violation of the sure-thing principle

	Ticket numbers		
	1	2–11	12–100
A	$1M	$1M	$1M
B	0	$5M	$1M
C	$1M	$1M	0
D	0	$5M	0

Table 14.3 Visual representation of the Ellsberg paradox. People typically prefer E over F but also prefer H over G, in violation of the sure-thing principle

	30 balls	60 balls	
	Red	White	Blue
E	$100	0	0
F	0	$100	0
G	$100	0	$100
H	0	$100	$100

these participants favored (A) over (B) and (D) over (C). Daniel Ellsberg (1961) presented a version of Problem 2 as a thought experiment to many of his colleagues, including some prominent decision theorists. Most favored (E) over (F) and (H) over (G). Both of these patterns violate the sure-thing principle, as can be seen in Tables 14.2 and 14.3.

Table 14.2 depicts the Allais problem as a lottery with 100 consecutively numbered tickets, where columns denote ticket numbers (states) and rows denote acts. Table entries indicate consequences for each act if the relevant state obtains. It is easy to see from this table that for tickets 1–11, acts C and D yield consequences that are identical to acts A and B, respectively. It is also easy to see that for tickets 12–100, acts A and B yield a common consequence (receive $1 million) and acts C and D yield a different common consequence (receive nothing). Hence, the sure-thing principle requires a person to choose C over D if and only if she chooses A over B. The modal preferences of A over B and D over C, therefore, violate this axiom.

Table 14.3 depicts the Ellsberg problem in a similar manner. Again, it is easy to see that the sure-thing principle requires a person to choose E over F if and only if he chooses G over H. Hence the dominant responses of E over F and H over G violate this axiom.

It should also be apparent that the sure-thing principle is implied by expected utility theory (see Equation (1)). To illustrate, consider the Allais problem above (see Table 14.2), and set $u(0) = 0$. We get:

$$SEU(A) = .11u(\$1M) + .89u(\$1M)$$
$$SEU(B) = .10u(\$5M) + .89u(\$1M).$$

Similarly,

$$SEU(C) = .11u(\$1M)$$
$$SEU(D) = .10u(\$5M).$$

Hence, the expected utilities of acts A and B differ from the expected utilities of acts C and D, respectively, only by a constant amount ($.89*u(\$1M)$). The preference orderings should therefore coincide (that is, A is preferred to B if and only if C is preferred to D). More generally, any time two pairs of acts differ only by a common consequence x that obtains with probability p, the expected utilities of these pairs of acts differ by a constant, $p*u(x)$. The preference ordering should therefore not be affected by the nature of this consequence (the value of x) or by its perceived likelihood (the value of p). Thus, when we consider the Ellsberg problem (see Table 14.3), we note that the preference between G and H should be the same as the preference between E and F, respectively, because the expected utilities of G and H differ from the expected utilities of E and F, respectively, by a constant amount, ($p(\text{blue})*u(\$100)$).

The violations of the sure-thing principle discovered by Allais and Ellsberg both cast grave doubt on the descriptive validity of the classical model. However, the psychological intuitions underlying these violations are quite distinct. In Problem 1, people typically explain the apparent inconsistency as a preference for certainty: the difference between a 100 percent chance and a 99 percent chance of receiving a very large prize (A versus B) looms much larger than does the difference between an 11 percent chance and a 10 percent chance of receiving a very large prize (C versus D). The pattern of preferences exhibited for Problem 2, in contrast, seems to reflect a preference for known probabilities over unknown probabilities (or, more generally, a preference for knowledge over ignorance). In this case, E and H afford the decision maker precise probabilities, whereas F and G present the decision maker with vague probabilities.

The Allais problem suggests that people do not weight the utility of consequences by their respective probabilities as in the classical theory; the Ellsberg problem suggests that decision makers prefer more precise knowledge of probabilities. Both problems draw attention to deficiencies of the classical model in controlled environments where consequences are contingent on games of chance, such as a lottery or a drawing from an urn. Most real-world decisions, however, require decision makers to assess the probabilities of potential consequences themselves, with some degree of imprecision or vagueness. An important challenge to behavioral decision theorists over the past few decades has been to develop a more descriptively valid account of decision making that applies not only to games of chance but also to natural events, such as tomorrow's weather or the outcome of an election.

Our purpose in this chapter is to review a descriptive model of decision making under uncertainty. For simplicity, we will confine most of our discussion to acts entailing a single positive consequence (for example, receive $100 if the home team wins and nothing otherwise). In Section 2, we take the Allais paradox as a point of departure and develop a psychological model of risky decision making that accommodates the preference for certainty. We extend these insights from situations where probabilities are provided to situations where decision makers must judge probabilities for themselves, and we develop a model that incorporates recent behavioral research on likelihood judgment. In Section 3, we take the Ellsberg paradox as a point of departure and describe a theoretical perspective that accommodates the preference for known probabilities. We extend this analysis to situations where consequences depend on natural events, and then modify the model developed in Section 2 to accommodate these new insights. Finally, in Section 4, we bring these strands together into a more unified account that distinguishes the role of beliefs, values and preferences in decision under uncertainty.

14.2 THE PREFERENCE FOR CERTAINTY: FROM ALLAIS TO THE TWO-STAGE MODEL

As we have observed, the Allais paradox violates the classical model of decision under uncertainty that weights utilities of consequences by their respective probabilities of occurrence. Moreover, numerous studies have shown that people often violate the principle of risk aversion that underlies much economic analysis. Table 14.4 illustrates a common pattern of risk aversion and risk seeking exhibited by participants in the studies of Tversky and Kahneman (1992). Let $C(x, p)$ be the "certainty equivalent" of the prospect (x, p) that offers to pay x with probability p (that is, the sure payment that is deemed equally attractive to the prospect). The upper left-hand entry in the table shows that the median participant is indifferent between receiving $14 for sure and a 5 percent chance of receiving $100. Because the expected value of the prospect is only $5, this observation reflects risk seeking.

Table 14.4 reveals a fourfold pattern of risk attitudes: risk seeking for low-probability gains and high-probability losses, coupled with risk aversion for high-probability gains and low-probability losses. Choices consistent with this pattern have been observed in several studies (e.g., Fishburn & Kochenberger, 1979; Kahneman & Tversky, 1979; Hershey & Schoemaker, 1980; Payne, Laughhunn & Crum, 1981). Risk seeking for low-probability gains may contribute to the attraction of gambling, whereas risk aversion for low-probability losses may contribute to the attraction of insurance. Risk aversion for high-probability gains may contribute to the preference for certainty in the Allais problem above (option A over option B), whereas risk seeking for high-probability losses is consistent with the common tendency to undertake risk to avoid facing a sure loss.

Table 14.4 The fourfold pattern of risk attitudes (adapted from Tversky & Kahneman, 1992). $C(x, p)$ is the median certainty equivalent of the prospect that pays x with probability p

	Gain	Loss
Low probability	$C($100, .05) = 14 risk seeking	$C(-$100, .05) = -8 risk aversion
High probability	$C($100, .95) = 78 risk aversion	$C(-$100, .95) = -84 risk seeking

14.2.1 Prospect Theory's Weighting Function

The Allais paradox (Problem 1) cannot be explained by the shape of the utility function for money because options A and B differ from options C and D by a common consequence. Likewise, the fourfold pattern of risk attitudes (Table 14.4) cannot be explained by a utility function with both concave and convex regions (Friedman & Savage, 1948; Markowitz, 1952) because this pattern is observed over a wide range of payoffs (that is, a wide range of utilities). Instead, these patterns suggest a nonlinear transformation of the probability scale (cf. Preston & Baratta, 1948; Edwards, 1962), as advanced in prospect theory (Kahneman & Tversky, 1979; Tversky & Kahneman, 1992; other models with nonadditive probabilities include Quiggin, 1982; Gilboa, 1987; Schmeidler, 1989; Luce & Fishburn, 1992). According to prospect theory, the value V of a simple prospect that pays \$$x$ with probability p (and pays nothing with probability $1 - p$) is given by:

$$V(x, p) = v(x)w(p),   \tag{2}$$

where v measures the subjective value of the consequence x, and w measures the impact of probability p on the attractiveness of the prospect. The value function, v, is a function of gains and losses relative to some reference point (usually the status quo), with $v(0) = 0$. The values of w are called decision weights; they are normalized so that $w(0) = 0$ and $w(1) = 1$. We pause to emphasize that w need not be interpreted as a measure of degree of belief—a person may believe that the probability of a fair coin landing heads is one-half but afford this event a weight of less than one-half in the evaluation of a prospect.

How might one measure the decision weight, $w(p)$? The simplest method is to elicit a person's certainty equivalent for a prospect that pays a fixed prize with probability p. For instance, suppose that Ann indicates that she is indifferent between receiving \$35 for sure, or receiving \$100 if a fair coin lands heads (and nothing if it lands tails). According to prospect theory (Equation (2)):

$$v(35) = v(100)w(.5)$$

so that

$$w(.5) = v(35)/v(100).$$

Now, to simplify our analysis, let us suppose that Ann's value function is linear,[6] so that $v(x) = x$. In this case:

$$w(.5) = .35.$$

Hence, in this example, a .5 probability receives a weight of .35 in the evaluation of the prospect, and Ann's risk aversion would be attributed not to the shape of the value function (as in expected utility theory—see Figure 14.1), but rather to the underweighting of a .5 probability.

According to prospect theory, the shapes of both the value function $v(.)$ and weighting function $w(.)$ reflect psychophysics of diminishing sensitivity: marginal impact diminishes with distance from the reference point. For monetary outcomes, the status quo generally serves as the reference point distinguishing losses from gains, so that the function is concave for gains and convex for losses (see Figure 14.2a). Concavity for gains contributes to risk aversion for gains (as we saw in the analysis of the concave utility function in Figure 14.1), and convexity for losses contributes to risk seeking for losses. The prospect theory value

---

[6] A more typical individual, as we shall see, can be characterized instead by a concave value function for gains; for example, $v(x) = x^{\alpha}$, $0 < \alpha < 1$. For relatively small dollar amounts such as those presented in this example, however, $v(x) = x$ is a reasonable first-order approximation, so that risk attitudes are driven primarily by the weighting of probabilities. However, the studies reviewed later in this chapter do not rely on such a simplifying assumption.

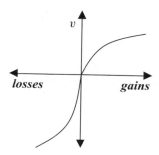

Figure 14.2a   Value function, v, for monetary gains and losses

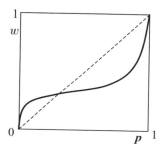

Figure 14.2b   Weighting function, w, for chance events that obtain with probability p

function is also steeper for losses than gains. This gives rise to risk aversion for mixed (gain-loss) gambles, so that, for example, people typically reject a gamble that offers a .5 chance of gaining $100 and a .5 chance of losing $100. As noted earlier, we will confine most of the analysis in this chapter to potential gains, so we will postpone a further discussion of losses until the conclusion.

For probability, there are two natural reference points: impossibility and certainty. Hence, diminishing sensitivity implies an inverse-S shaped weighting function that is concave near zero and convex near one, as depicted in Figure 14.2b. It explains the fourfold pattern of risk attitudes (Table 14.4), because low probabilities are overweighted (leading to risk seeking for gains and risk aversion for losses), and high probabilities are underweighted (leading to risk aversion for gains and risk seeking for losses).[7] It also accounts for the Allais paradox (Problem 1), because $w(1) - w(.99) >> w(.11) - w(.10)$. That is, increasing the probability of winning a large prize from .99 to 1 has more impact on the decision maker than increasing the probability of winning from .10 to .11. This inverse-S shaped weighting function seems to be consistent with a range of empirical findings (see Camerer & Ho, 1994; Wu & Gonzalez, 1996, 1998; Abdellaoui, 2000; Wakker, 2000; for parameterization of the weighting function, see Prelec, 1998; Gonzalez & Wu, 1999; for applications to decision analysis, see Bleichrodt & Pinto, 2000; Bleichrodt, Pinto & Wakker, 2001).

---

[7] As we stated in the previous paragraph, a value function that is concave for gains and convex for losses implies risk aversion for gains and risk seeking for losses. This pattern is reinforced by a weighting function that underweights moderate to large probabilities, but it is reversed by a weighting function that overweights low probabilities.

14.2.2   From Risk to Uncertainty: Measuring Diminished Sensitivity

The inverse-S shaped weighting function provides a parsimonious account of decision making in situations where outcome probabilities are known with precision by the decision maker. However, most decisions (as we have already observed) require the decision maker to assess probabilities herself, with some degree of imprecision or vagueness. Following Knight (1921), theorists distinguish between decisions under *risk*, where probabilities are known, and decisions under *uncertainty*, where probabilities are not known. The question arises of how to extend the analysis of decision weights from risk to uncertainty, because under uncertainty we can no longer describe decision weights as a transformation of the probability scale.

One approach to solving this problem is to formalize the notion of diminishing sensitivity for risk, and then extend this definition to uncertainty. Diminishing sensitivity means that the weight of an event decreases with distance from the natural boundaries of zero and one. Let p, q and r be numbers such that $0 < p, q, r < 1, p + q + r < 1$. Diminishing sensitivity near zero can be expressed as:

$$w(p) - w(0) \geq w(p + q) - w(q) \geq w(p + q + r) - w(q + r), \text{ and so forth.}$$

That is, adding probability p to an impossibility of winning a prize has a greater impact than adding p to some intermediate probability q, and this, in turn, has a greater impact than adding p to some larger probability $q + r$, and so forth. In general, this "diminishing" sensitivity is most pronounced near the boundaries (that is, the pattern expressed by the leftmost inequality above is more robust than the pattern expressed by subsequent inequalities). Hence, we will focus our attention on the "diminished" sensitivity to intermediate changes in outcome probabilities near zero. Noting that $w(0) = 0$, diminished sensitivity near zero can be expressed as:

$$w(p) \geq w(p + q) - w(q). \tag{3a}$$

Similarly, noting that $w(1) = 1$, diminished sensitivity near one can be expressed as:

$$1 - w(1 - p) \geq w(1 - q) - w(1 - q - p). \tag{3b}$$

To illustrate, suppose $p = q = .1$. The lower left-hand corner of Figure 14.3 illustrates "lower subadditivity". The impact of .1 is greater when added to 0 than when added to .1 (the length of segment A is greater than the length of segment B). For instance, consider a lottery with 10 tickets so that each ticket has a .1 chance of winning a fixed prize. Most people would pay more for a ticket if they did not have one (improving the probability of winning from 0 to .1) than they would pay for a second ticket if they already had one (improving the probability of winning from .1 to .2).[8] The upper right-hand corner in Figure 14.3 illustrates "upper subadditivity". The impact of .1 is greater when subtracted from 1 than when subtracted from .9 (the length of segment C is greater than the length of segment D). For instance, most people would pay more for the tenth ticket if they already had nine (improving the probability of winning from .9 to 1) than they would pay for a ninth ticket if they already had eight (improving the probability of winning from .8 to .9).[9]

This pattern of diminished sensitivity can be readily extended from risk to uncertainty. Again, let S be a set whose elements are interpreted as states of the world. Subsets of S are

---

[8] Such a pattern could be accommodated in expected utility theory only through a convex utility function for money.
[9] For an empirical demonstration similar to the lottery anecdote used here, see Gonzalez and Wu (1999).

called "events". Thus, S corresponds to the certain event, $\emptyset$ is the null event (that is, the impossible event), and $S - A$ is the complement of event A. A weighting function W (on S) is a mapping that assigns to each event in S a number between 0 and 1 such that $W(\emptyset) = 0$, $W(S) = 1$, and $W(A) \geq W(B)$ if A includes B. Note that the weighting function for uncertain events, W, should be distinguished from the weighting function for risky (chance) events, w. Thus, for uncertainty, we can rewrite Equation (2) so that the value of prospect (x, A) that offers $\$x$ if event A obtains and nothing otherwise is given by:

$$V(x, A) = v(x)\,W(A).$$

Equation (3a) can now be generalized as *lower subadditivity:*

$$W(A) \geq W(A \cup B) - W(B), \tag{4a}$$

provided A and B are disjoint (that is, mutually exclusive), and $W(A \cup B)$ is bounded away from one.[10] This inequality is a formal expression of the *possibility effect*: the impact of event A is greater when it is added to the null event than when it is added to some non-null event B. Equation (3b) can be generalized as *upper subadditivity:*

$$1 - W(S - A) \geq W(S - B) - W(S - A \cup B), \tag{4b}$$

provided $W(S - A \cup B)$ is bounded away from zero. Upper subadditivity[11] is a formal expression of the *certainty effect*: the impact of event A is greater when it is subtracted from the certain event S than when it is subtracted from some uncertain event $S - B$. Note that upper subadditivity can be expressed as lower subadditivity of the dual function, $W'(A) \equiv 1 - W(S - A)$. That is, upper subadditivity is the same as lower subadditivity where we transform both scales by subtracting events from certainty and decision weights from one (reversing both axes, as can be seen by viewing Figure 14.3 upside down).

Why the terms "lower subadditivity" and "upper subadditivity"? "Lower" and "upper" distinguish diminished sensitivity near zero (the lower end of the scale) from diminished sensitivity near one (the upper end of the scale), respectively. "Subadditivity" refers to the implication revealed when we rearrange terms of Equations (4a) and (4b):

$$W(A \cup B) \leq W(A) + W(B) \tag{i}$$

and

$$W'(A \cup B) \leq W'(A) + W'(B). \tag{ii}$$

Thus, when disjoint events are concatenated (added together) they receive less weight than when they are weighted separately and summed—W is a *sub-additive* function of events. The weighting function satisfies *bounded subadditivity*, or subadditivity (SA) for short, if it satisfies both (4a) and (4b).[12]

---

[10] The boundary conditions are needed to ensure that we always compare an interval that includes an endpoint (zero or one) to an interval that does not include an endpoint. See Tversky and Wakker (1995) for a more formal discussion.

[11] Note that if we define $B' = S - A \cup B$, then upper subadditivity can be expressed as $1 - W(S - A) \geq W(A \cup B') - W(B')$. Upper subadditivity has been previously presented in this form (Tversky & Fox, 1995; Tversky & Wakker, 1995; Fox & Tversky, 1998).

[12] For a more formal treatment of bounded subadditivity, see Tversky and Wakker (1995). For a more thorough account of diminishing sensitivity under risk that explores concavity near zero, convexity near one and diminishing marginal concavity throughout the scale, see Wu and Gonzalez (1996); for extensions to uncertainty, see Wu and Gonzalez (1999b).

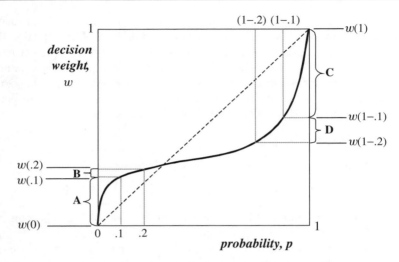

Figure 14.3 Visual illustration of bounded subadditivity. The lower left-hand corner of the figure illustrates lower subadditivity. The upper right-hand corner illustrates upper subadditivity

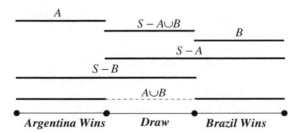

Figure 14.4 An event space for prospects defined by the result of a soccer match between Argentina and Brazil. Each row denotes a target event that defines a prospect

To illustrate bounded subadditivity more concretely, consider a soccer match between Argentina and Brazil. We can partition the state space into three elementary events (see Figure 14.4): Argentina wins (A), Brazil wins (B), or there is a draw $(S - A \cup B)$. Additionally, this partition defines three compound events: Argentina fails to win $(S - A)$, Brazil fails to win $(S - B)$, and there is a decisive game (that is, either Argentina or Brazil wins, $A \cup B$). Now suppose that we ask a soccer fan to price prospects that would pay $100 if each of these target events obtains. For instance, we ask the soccer fan what sure amount of money, C_A, she finds equally attractive to the prospect ($100, A$) that offers $100 if Argentina wins (and nothing otherwise). Let us suppose further, for simplicity, that this individual values money according to a linear value function, so that $v(x) = x$. In this case, $W(A) = C_A/100$.

Suppose our soccer fan prices bets on Argentina winning, Brazil winning, and a decisive match at $50, $40 and $80, respectively. In this case, we get $W(A) = .5$, $W(B) = .4$, and $W(A \cup B) = .8$, so that lower subadditivity (Equation (4a)) is satisfied because $.5 > .8 - .4$. Suppose further that our soccer fan prices bets on Argentina failing to win, Brazil failing to win, and a draw at $40, $50 and $10, respectively. In this case, we get $W(S - A) = .4$,

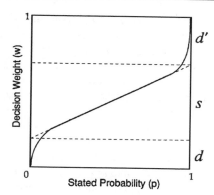

Figure 14.5 A weighting function that is linear except near the endpoints (*d* = "lower" intercept of the weighting function; *d'* = "upper" intercept of the weighting function; *s* = slope. Reproduced from Tversky & Fox, 1995)

$W(S - B) = .5$, and $W(S - A \cup B) = .1$, so that upper subadditivity (Equation (4b)) is satisfied because $1 - .4 > .5 - .1$.

We can determine the degree of subadditivity by assessing the magnitude of the discrepancy between terms on either side of inequalities (*i*) and (*ii*) above:

$$D(A, B) \equiv W(A) + W(B) - W(A \cup B)$$
$$D'(A, B) \equiv W'(A) + W'(B) - W'(A \cup B).$$

This metric provides a measure of the departures from additivity of the weighting function around impossibility (D) and certainty (D'). These measures are particularly useful because they do not require specification of objective probability. We can thus compare the degree of subadditivity between risk and uncertainty. More generally, we can compare the degree of subadditivity between different domains or *sources* of uncertainty, where a source of uncertainty is interpreted as a family of events that are traced to a common causal system, such as the roll of a die, the winner of an election or the final score of a particular soccer match.[13]

Suppose that an experimenter measures decision weights of several events so that she has multiple tests of upper and lower subadditivity for each individual. To obtain summary measures of subadditivity, let d and d', respectively, be the mean values of D and D' for a given respondent and source of uncertainty. To see how one might interpret the values of d and d', assume a weighting function that is approximately linear except near the endpoints (see Figure 14.5). It is easy to verify that within the linear portion of the graph, D and D' do not depend on A and B, and the values of d and d' correspond to the 0- and 1-intercepts of such a weighting function. Thus, d measures the magnitude of the impossibility "gap" and d' measures the magnitude of the certainty "gap". Moreover, we can define a global index of sensitivity, $s = 1 - d - d'$ that measures the slope of the weighting function—that is, a person's sensitivity to changes in probability. Prospect theory assumes that $d \geq 0$, $d' \geq 0$, and $s \leq 1$, whereas expected utility theory assumes $d = d' = 0$, and $s = 1$. An extreme instance in which $s = 0$ (and also $d > 0$, $d' > 0$) would characterize a three-valued logic in which a person distinguishes only impossibility, possibility and certainty.

---

[13] In decision under risk, we interpret uncertainty as generated by a standard random device; although probabilities could be realized through various devices, we do not distinguish between them and instead treat risk as a single source.

Tversky and Fox (1995) tested bounded subadditivity in a series of studies using risky prospects (for example, receive $150 with probability .2) and uncertain prospects with outcomes that depended on future temperature in various cities, future movement of the stock market, and the result of upcoming sporting events (for example, "receive $150 if the Buffalo Bills win the Super Bowl"). These authors estimated certainty equivalents by asking participants to choose between each prospect and a series of sure payments. For example, if a participant favored $35 for sure over a prospect that offered $150 with probability .2, and that participant also favored the prospect over receiving $30 for sure, then the certainty equivalent for the prospect was estimated to be $32.50 (midway between $30 and $35). The authors then estimated decision weights as $W(A) = v(C_A)/v(150)$, where the value function was estimated using data from another study. The results were very consistent: bounded subadditivity was pronounced for risk and all sources of uncertainty ($d > 0$, $d' > 0$ for a significant majority of participants). In addition, Tversky and Fox found that subadditivity was more pronounced for uncertainty than for risk. That is, values of d and d' were larger for uncertain prospects than for risky prospects.

Note that Figure 14.5, like Figures 14.2b and 14.3, is drawn so that the weighting function crosses the identity line below .5, and $d' > d$. This is meant to reflect the assumption under prospect theory that decision weights for complementary events generally sum to less than one, $W(A) + W(S - A) \leq 1$, or equivalently, $W(A) \leq W(S) - W(S - A)$. This property, called "subcertainty" (Kahneman & Tversky, 1979), accords with the data of Tversky and Fox (1995) and can be interpreted as evidence of more pronounced upper subadditivity than lower subadditivity; that is, the certainty effect is more pronounced than the possibility effect.

Figure 14.6 summarizes results from Tversky and Fox (1995), plotting the sensitivity measure s for risk versus uncertainty for all participants in their studies. Three patterns are worth noting. First, $s < 1$ for all participants under uncertainty (mean $s = .53$) and for all but two participants under risk (mean $s = .74$). Second, the value of s is smaller under uncertainty than under risk for 94 of 111 participants (that is, the large majority of points lie below the identity line). Third, there is a significant correlation between sensitivity to risk and sensitivity to uncertainty ($r = .37$, $p < .01$).

14.2.3   The Two-Stage Model

The observation that subadditivity is more pronounced under uncertainty than risk accords with the natural intuition that people could be less sensitive to changes in the target event when they do not have objective probabilities at their disposal but must instead make a vague assessment of likelihood. Fox and Tversky (1995) speculated that increased subadditivity under uncertainty might be directly attributable to subadditivity of judged probabilities. To test this conjecture, they asked participants in all of their studies to judge the probabilities of all target events. These researchers found that judged probability, $P(.)$, exhibited significant bounded subadditivity.[14] That is, if D_P and D'_P measure the degree of lower and upper subadditivity, respectively, of judged probabilities for disjoint events A and B, we get:

$$D_P(A, B) \equiv P(A) + P(B) - P(A \cup B) > 0$$

and

---

[14] Note that we distinguish judged probability, $P(.)$, from objective probability, p.

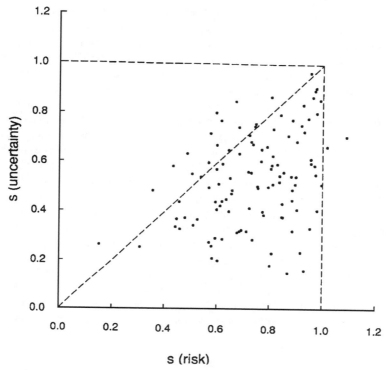

Figure 14.6 A plot of the joint distribution of the sensitivity measure s for risk and uncertainty for participants in the studies of Tversky and Fox (1995). Reproduced from Tversky and Fox (1995)

$$D'_P(A, B) \equiv P'(A) + P'(B) - P'(A \cup B) > 0$$

(where $P'(A) = 1 - P(S - A)$), for a significant majority of tests for all sources of uncertainty. Interestingly, the degree of subadditivity observed for direct judgments of probability was less than the degree of subadditivity observed for decision weights that were inferred from choices. This observation motivated Fox and Tversky (1995) to propose a two-stage model in which decision makers first judge the probability P of the target event A, and then transform this judged probability by the risky weighting function w. Thus, according to the two-stage model,

$$W(A) = w[P(A)]. \tag{5}$$

Indeed, when Fox and Tversky (1995) plotted the uncertain decision weight, $W(A)$, for each target event against the corresponding judged probability, $P(A)$, these plots closely resembled the plot of the risky weighting function, $w(p)$, against objective probability p for the same group of participants. The notion that risky decision weights are a constituent of uncertain decision weights may also explain the aforementioned finding of a significant positive correlation between sensitivity to risk and sensitivity to uncertainty (see Figure 14.6).

Further evidence for the two-stage model was obtained in a study of professional options traders who were surveyed on the floors of the Pacific Stock Exchange and Chicago Board Options Exchange by Fox, Rogers and Tversky (1996). Options traders are unique in that they are schooled in the calculus of chance and make daily decisions under uncertainty on which their jobs depend. Unlike participants in most studies, the majority of the options traders priced risky prospects by their expected value. This pattern is consistent with both a linear value function and linear risky weighting function.[15] However, when participants were asked to price uncertain prospects contingent on future stock prices (for example, "receive $150 if Microsoft stock closes below $88 per share two weeks from today"), their decision weights exhibited pronounced subadditivity. Furthermore, when these same participants were asked to judge the probability of each target event, they exhibited roughly the same degree of subadditivity as they had exhibited for decision weights. Thus, when decision weights were plotted against judged probabilities, points fell roughly along the identity line (that is, $W(A) = P(A)$). This pattern is consistent with the two-stage model, in which options traders first judge the probability of each target event—subadditively—and then weight the $150 prize by this judged probability.

Fox and Tversky (1998) elaborated the two-stage model (Equation (5)) and tested some of its implications. In this theory, both the uncertain weighting function, $W(.)$, and the risky weighting function, $w(.)$, are assumed to conform to prospect theory (that is, satisfy bounded subadditivity). In addition, judged probability, $P(.)$, is assumed to conform to support theory (Tversky & Koehler, 1994; Rottenstreich & Tversky, 1997), a descriptive model of judgment under uncertainty. To demonstrate how support theory accommodates subadditivity of judged probability and to highlight its novel implications for the two-stage model, we describe the key features of support theory in the section that follows.

Support Theory

There is abundant evidence from prior research that judged probabilities do not conform to the laws of chance (e.g., Kahneman, Slovic & Tversky, 1982). In particular, alternative descriptions of the same event can give rise to systematically different probability judgments (e.g., Fischhoff, Slovic & Lichtenstein, 1978), more inclusive events are sometimes judged to be less likely than less inclusive events (Tversky & Kahneman, 1983), and the judged probability of an event is typically less than the sum of judged probabilities of constituent events that are evaluated separately (e.g., Teigen, 1974). To accommodate such patterns, support theory assumes that judged probability is not attached to events, as in other theories, but rather to descriptions of events, called "hypotheses". Thus, two different descriptions of the same event may be assigned distinct probabilities. Support theory assumes that each hypothesis A has a non-negative support value $s(A)$ corresponding to the strength of evidence for that hypothesis. Support is assumed to be generated through heuristic processing of information or through explicit reasoning or computation (see also Sloman et al, 2003). The judged probability $P(A, \bar{A})$ that hypothesis A, rather than its complement $\bar{A}$, obtains is given by:

---

[15] Fox, Rogers and Tversky (1996) claimed that this pattern of results would be observed under cumulative prospect theory *if and only if* the value function and weighting function were both linear (p. 8, lines 15–18). Fox and Wakker (2000) observe that this assertion is not technically correct given the method by which the value function was elicited in that study, but that the conclusion is pragmatically reasonable and that the qualitative results reported in that paper are robust over a wide range of variations in the value function. For a method of measuring the shape of the value function that does not assume additive subjective probabilities, see Wakker and Deneffe (1996). A nonparametric algorithm for simultaneously estimating subjective value and decision weights from certainty equivalents of risky prospects was advanced by Gonzalez and Wu (1999).

$$P(A, \bar{A}) = s(A)/[s(A) + s(\bar{A})].\tag{6}$$

This equation suggests that judged probability can be interpreted as the balance of evidence for a focal hypothesis against its alternative. Hence, if the support for a hypothesis (for example, "rain tomorrow") and its complement (for example, "no rain tomorrow") are equal, the judged probability is one-half (that is, $P(\text{rain, no rain}) = .5$). As the support for the focal hypothesis increases relative to support for the alternative hypothesis, judged probability approaches one. Likewise, as support for the alternative hypothesis increases relative to support for the focal hypothesis, judged probability approaches zero.

The theory further assumes that (i) unpacking a hypothesis A (for example, "the winner of the next US presidential election will not be a Democrat") into an explicit disjunction of constituent hypotheses $A_1 \vee A_2$ (for example, "the winner of the next US presidential election will be a Republican or an independent candidate") generally increases support, and (ii) separate evaluation of the constituent hypotheses (for example, "the winner of the next US presidential election will be a Republican"; "the winner of the next US presidential election will be an independent candidate") generally gives rise to still higher total support. More formally,

$$s(A) \le s(A_1 \vee A_2) \le s(A_1) + s(A_2),\tag{7}$$

provided (A_1, A_2) is recognized as a partition (that is, exclusive and exhaustive constituents) of A.

The first set of consequences of support theory concerns the additivity of judged probabilities. Equation (6) implies *binary complementarity*: $P(A) + P(\bar{A}) = 1$. That is, the judged probability of A and its complement sum to unity.[16] For instance, the judged probability that the winner of the next election will be a "Democrat" plus the judged probability that the winner of the next election will "not be a Democrat" should sum to one. For finer partitions, however, Equations (6) and (7) imply *subadditivity*: $P(A) \le P(A_1) + P(A_2)$. That is, the probability of hypothesis A is less than or equal to the sum of probabilities of its disjoint components (note that this also implies that the judged probabilities of $n > 2$ exhaustive and exclusive hypotheses generally sum to more than one). For instance, the judged probability that the winner of the next election will "not be a Democrat" is less than or equal to the judged probability of "Republican" plus the judged probability of "an independent candidate". Such patterns have been confirmed in several studies reviewed by Tversky and Koehler (1994). Subadditivity and binary complementarity have also been documented in studies of physicians (Redelmeier et al., 1995), lawyers (Fox & Birke, 2002) and options traders (Fox, Rogers & Tversky, 1996); and subadditivity has been observed in published odds of bookmakers (Ayton, 1997). A within-subject test that traces the relationship between raw expression of support and judged probabilities is reported by Fox (1999; see also Koehler, 1996). For a demonstration of subadditivity in a classification learning task, see Koehler (2000). For exceptions to binary complementarity, see Brenner and Rottenstreich (1999), Macchi, Osherson and Krantz (1999) and Idson et al. (2001).

---

[16] In the studies that we will review here, participants are asked to evaluate a target hypothesis A (for example, judge the probability that "the Lakers win the NBA championship"), so that the alternative hypothesis is not explicitly identified (that is, participants are not asked to judge the probability that "the Lakers win rather than fail to win the NBA championship"). However, we assume that when evaluating the likelihood of a target event A, decision makers consider its simple negation $\bar{A}$ as the default alternative hypothesis. Moreover, to simplify our exposition, we abbreviate the expression $P(A, \bar{A})$ in our notation as $P(A)$, taking the negation of the focal hypotheses, $\bar{A}$, as implicit. Also, to simplify we use letters A, B, etc., henceforth to refer to hypotheses (that is, descriptions of events) rather than subsets of a state space.

A second important consequence of support theory is *implicit subadditivity*: $P(A) \leq P(A_1 \vee A_2)$. That is, the judged probability of a hypothesis generally increases when unpacked into an explicit disjunction of constituent hypotheses. For instance, the judged probability that the winner of the next election will "not be a Democrat" is less than or equal to the judged probability that the winner will be a "Republican or independent candidate". This pattern has been demonstrated empirically by Rottenstreich and Tversky (1997) and replicated by others (Redelmeier et al., 1995; Fox & Tversky, 1998; Fox & Birke, 2002; for counterexamples, see Sloman et al., 2003).

Because the two-stage model incorporates judged probabilities from support theory, it is a significant departure from other models of decision under uncertainty in two respects. First, subadditivity of the uncertain weighting function, $W(.)$, is partially attributed to subadditivity of judged probability. Traditional economic models of decision under uncertainty infer decision weights from observed choices and therefore cannot distinguish between belief and preference components of decision weights. Second, $W(.)$ allows different decision weights for distinct descriptions of a target event: $W(A) \leq W(A_1 \vee A_2)$. Thus, different descriptions of options can give rise to different preferences, in violation of the normative assumption of *description invariance* (see Tversky & Kahneman, 1986; Tversky, 1996).

The Partition Inequality

One of the most striking differences between the classical model of decision under uncertainty and the two-stage model can be observed directly from certainty equivalents for uncertain prospects. Suppose $(A_1, A_2, \ldots, A_n)$ is recognized as a partition of hypothesis A, and that $C(x, A)$ is the certainty equivalent of the prospect that pays \$x if hypothesis A obtains, and nothing otherwise. Expected utility theory assumes that the certainty equivalent of an uncertain prospect is not affected by the particular way in which the target event is described, so that:

$$C(x, A) = C(x, A_1 \vee \ldots \vee A_n) \tag{i}$$

for all real x, $n > 1$. For instance, a person's certainty equivalent for the prospect that pays \$100 if "there is measurable precipitation next April 1 in Chicago" should be the same as the certainty equivalent for the prospect that pays \$100 if "there is measurable rain or sleet or snow or hail next April 1 in Chicago".

Moreover, expected utility theory with risk aversion implies:

$$C(x, A) \geq C(x, A_1) + \cdots + C(x, A_n). \tag{ii}$$

That is, the certainty equivalent for a prospect is at least as large as the sum of certainty equivalents for subprospects that are evaluated separately (for a derivation, see Fox & Tversky, 1998, p. 882, Footnote 6). To illustrate, note that for a risk-averse individual the certainty equivalent of a prospect that pays \$100 if a fair coin lands heads will be less than its expected value of \$50. Likewise, for this same individual the certainty equivalent of a prospect that pays \$100 if a fair coin lands tails will be less than \$50. Hence the aggregate price of the subprospects, evaluated separately by this risk-averse individual, will be less than the price of the prospect that pays \$100 for sure.

Taken together, (*i*) and (*ii*) above imply the following *partition inequality*:[17]

$$C(x, A) = C(x, A_1 \lor \ldots \lor A_n) \geq C(x, A_1) + \ldots + C(x, A_n). \tag{8}$$

If decision makers act in accordance with the two-stage model (Equation (5)), then the partition inequality will not generally hold. In particular, situations can arise where:

$$C(x, A) < C(x, A_1 \lor \ldots \lor A_n) < C(x, A_1) + \ldots + C(x, A_n).$$

The equality (*i*) in Equation (8) is especially likely to fail when the explicit disjunction reminds people of possibilities that they may have overlooked or makes compelling possibilities more salient. The inequality (*ii*) in Equation (8) is especially likely to fail when the target event is partitioned into many pieces so that subadditivity of judged probability and subadditivity of the risky weighting function are more pronounced than concavity of the value function.

14.2.4 Tests of the Two-Stage Model

We now present evidence from several previous studies that test the two-stage model against the classical model (expected utility with risk aversion). We begin with tests of the partition inequality, and then proceed to more direct tests of the relative fit of these models.

Tests of the Partition Inequality

To date, only partial tests of the entire partition inequality (Equation (8)) have been published. In this section, we begin by presenting evidence from previous studies for violations of description invariance (part (*i*)) and risk aversion (part (*ii*)), and then present evidence from new studies that simultaneously test the entire pattern in Equation (8) within-subject.

Violations of Description Invariance

There have been only a few documented tests of unpacking effects (implicit subadditivity) against the description invariance assumption of expected utility theory (part (*i*) of Equation (8)). Johnson et al. (1993) reported that consumers were willing to pay more for an insurance policy that covered hospitalization due to "any disease or accident" ($47.12) than hospitalization for "any reason" ($41.53). Similarly, Fox and Tversky (1998) found that participants valued the prospect offering $75 if "Chicago or New York or Indiana or Orlando" wins the National Basketball Association (NBA) playoffs more highly than the prospect offering $75 if an "Eastern Conference" team wins the NBA playoffs, despite the fact that the teams listed in the former prospect were only a (proper) subset of the teams comprising the Eastern Conference.

In a more extensive investigation, Wu and Gonzalez (1999a) observed that participants favored "unpacked" prospects over "packed" prospects, even though the latter dominated the former. For instance, most participants said they would rather receive a sure payment

---

[17] This version of the partition inequality extends Equation (4) from Fox and Tversky (1998).

Table 14.5 Subadditivity and violations of the partition inequality

				Certainty equivalents		Judged probability	
Study	N	Source of uncertainty	Atoms	ΣC	$\Sigma C(A_i) > C(S)$	$P(A) + P(S-A)$	ΣP
Tversky & Fox (1995)							
NBA fans	27	a. NBA playoffs	6	1.40	93%	0.99	1.40
		b. San Francisco temperature	6	1.27	77%	0.98	1.47
NFL fans	40	c. Super Bowl	6	1.31	78%	1.01	1.48
		d. Dow Jones	6	1.16	65%	0.99	1.25
Stanford students	45	e. San Francisco temperature	6	1.98	88%	1.03	2.16
		f. Beijing temperature	6	1.75	82%	1.01	1.88
Fox et al. (1996)							
Options traders (Chicago)	32	g. Microsoft	4	1.53	89%	1.00	1.40
		h. GE	4	1.50	89%	0.96	1.43
Options traders (SF)	28	i. IBM	4	1.47	82%	1.00	1.27
		j. Gannett Co.	4	1.13	64%	0.99	1.20
Fox & Tversky (1998)							
NBA fans	50	k. NBA playoffs	8	2.08	82%	1.02	2.40
Stanford students	82	l. Economic indicators	4	1.14	41%	0.98	1.14
Median				1.44	82%	1.00	1.42

Note: Adapted from Fox and Tversky (1998, Table 8). The first three columns identify the participant population, sample size and sources of uncertainty. The fourth column lists the number of elementary events (*atoms*) in the finest partition of the state space (S) available in each study. The fifth and sixth columns present the median sum of normalized certainty equivalents for an *n*-fold partition of S, and the proportion of participants who reported certainty equivalents that summed to more than the amount of the prize. The last two columns present the median sum of judged probabilities for binary partitions of S and an *n*-fold partition of S.

of $150 than a prospect that offered $*240 if the Bulls win more than 65 games (and nothing otherwise)*. However, when the prospect was modified so that it offered $*240 if the Chicago Bulls win between 65 and 69 games and $220 if the Bulls win more than 70 games (and nothing otherwise)*, most participants instead favored the prospect over a sure payment of $150. Apparently, unpacking the target prospect increased its attractiveness even though the unpacked prospect is dominated by the packed prospect (note that the unpacked version offers $20 less if the Bulls win more than 70 games). Wu and Gonzalez (1999a) obtained a similar pattern of results for prospects drawn from diverse domains such as election outcomes and future temperatures. Although, strictly speaking, Wu and Gonzalez's demonstrations do not entail a violation of description invariance, they do suggest that unpacking the target event into a separate description of constituent events (each with similar consequences) can increase the attractiveness of a prospect.

Violations of Risk Aversion

There have been a number of published studies testing (lower) subadditivity against expected utility with risk aversion (part (*ii*) of Equation (8)). Table 14.5 summarizes these results, showing a pattern that consistently favors the two-stage model. First, consider certainty equivalents. The column labeled ΣC presents the median sum of normalized certainty equivalents (that is, certainty equivalents divided by the amount of the relevant prize) for the finest partition of S available in each study, and the column labeled $\Sigma C(A_i) > C(S)$ presents the corresponding percentage of participants who violated part (*ii*) of the partition inequality for the finest partition of S. In accord with the two-stage model, the majority of participants in every study violated the partition inequality, and the sum of certainty equivalents was often substantially greater than the prize. For instance, in Fox and Tversky's (1998) sample of NBA fans, participants priced prospects that offered $160 if a particular team would win the NBA playoffs (eight teams remained in contention at the time of the study). The median participant reported certainty equivalents for the eight teams that sum to 2.08 times the $160 prize (that is, $330). Moreover, 82 percent of respondents violated part (*ii*) of the partition inequality by reporting certainty equivalents that exceed $160.

Next, consider probability judgment. The column labeled $P(A) + P(S-A)$ presents the median sum of judged probabilities for binary partitions of the state space. The column labeled ΣP presents the median sum of judged probabilities for the finest partition of S. The results conform to support theory: sums for binary partitions are close to one, whereas sums for finer partitions are consistently greater than one. For instance, in Fox and Tversky's (1998) study of NBA fans, the median sum of probabilities that the "Western Conference" would win the NBA championship and the "Eastern Conference" would win the NBA championship was 1.02. However, when these same participants separately judged the probabilities that each of the eight teams remaining would win the NBA championship, the median participant reported numbers that summed to 2.40.

Violations of the Partition Inequality

In a new set of studies, we (Fox & See, 2002) have documented violations of the entire partition inequality (Equation (8)), including tests of both description invariance (part (*i*)) and risk aversion (part (*ii*)). We replicated the methods of Fox and Tversky (1998), adding elicitation of explicit disjunctions (the middle term in Equation (8)) so that the entire pattern predicted by support theory and the two-stage model could be tested simultaneously and within-subject.

The data presented here are drawn from two studies. In the first study, Duke University undergraduates were asked to price prospects that offered $160 depending on which team would win the Atlantic Coast Conference (ACC) men's college basketball tournament (a topic that Duke students follow closely), and then judge probabilities of all target events. The ACC consists of nine schools in the southeastern USA. Schools were categorized according to geographic subregion ("inside North Carolina" versus "outside North Carolina") and funding ("private school" versus "public school").[18] In the second study, Brown University students first learned the movement of economic indicators in a hypothetical economy (interest rates and unemployment, which could each move either "up" or "down" in a given period). Next they were asked to price prospects that offered $160 depending on the direction in which indicators would move in the following period. Finally, participants were asked to judge probabilities of all target events. Participants in

---

[18] The results presented here from Fox and See (2002) are a subset of results from this study in which we relied on a hierarchical partition of the state space. Participants were also asked to price prospects contingent on the final score of an upcoming game (a dimensional partition) and prospects contingent on the conjunction of results in two upcoming games (a product partition). The results of these latter tasks were consistent with the two-stage model, but did not yield significant implicit subadditivity in either judgment or choice.

Table 14.6 Mean certainty equivalents for joint events, explicit disjunction, and sums

Study	N	Source of uncertainty		Implicit (A)		Explicit $(A_1 \vee A_2)$		Sum $(A_1 + A_2)$
Fox & See (2002)								
Duke basketball	51	Basketball	$P(.)$	0.56	**	0.65	**	0.81
fans			$C(.)$	0.53	**	0.61	**	0.76
Brown students	29	Economic	$P(.)$	0.52	**	0.55	*	0.68
		indicators	$C(.)$	0.42	†	0.52	**	0.63

† $p < .10$; * $p < .05$; ** $p < .005$.
The first three columns identify the participant population, sample size and sources of uncertainty. The fourth column indicates the relevant dependent variable (judged probability or normalized certainty equivalent). The remaining columns list the mean judged probabilities and normalized certainty equivalents for implicit disjunctions, explicit disjunctions and constituent events that were evaluated separately and summed. Asterisks and dagger indicate significance of differences between adjacent entries.

both studies were also asked to price risky prospects and complete a task that allowed us to estimate the shape of their value function for monetary gains.

Table 14.6 presents the mean judged probabilities and normalized certainty equivalents for participants in the studies of Fox and See (2002). The column labeled (A) presents the mean normalized certainty equivalent and judged probability for simple events, or "implicit disjunctions" in the language of support theory (for example, "interest rates go up"). The column labeled ($A_1 \vee A_2$) presents the mean normalized certainty equivalent and judged probability for the same events described as explicit disjunctions (for example, "interest rates go up and unemployment goes up, or interest rates go up and unemployment goes down"). The column labeled ($A_1 + A_2$) presents the mean sum of normalized certainty equivalents and judged probabilities for the same constituent events when assessed separately (for example, "interest rates go up and unemployment goes up"; "interest rates go up and unemployment goes down"). Judged probabilities reported in Table 14.6 accord perfectly with support theory, and certainty equivalents clearly violate both parts of the partition inequality (Equation (8)), consistent with the two-stage model.

Table 14.7 lists the proportion of participants in each of the Fox and See (2002) studies that violate various facets of the partition inequality (Equation (8)), as well as the proportion of participants whose judged probabilities follow an analogous pattern. The last column displays the proportion of participants whose certainty equivalents and judged probabilities exhibit subadditivity. Just as we saw in the studies summarized in Table 14.5 (see column 6), a large majority of participants in the Fox and See studies violated risk aversion (part (*ii*) of Equation (8)), exhibiting subadditivity of certainty equivalents. Moreover, a large majority of participants showed an analogous pattern of subadditivity among judged probabilities.

The fourth and fifth columns of Table 14.7 display tests of the more refined predictions of the partition inequality (Equation (8)). The results in column 4 show that a majority of participants reported higher certainty equivalents when events were described as explicit disjunctions (violating the first part of Equation (8)). A similar pattern appeared among judged probabilities (satisfying "implicit subadditivity" in the language of support theory; see Rottenstreich & Tversky, 1997). Finally, the results in column 5 show that a large majority of participants reported higher certainty equivalents when constituent prospects were evaluated separately and summed than when evaluating a single prospect whose target event was described as an explicit disjunction of the same constituent events (violating

Table 14.7   Percentage of participants violating the partition inequality

Study	N	Source of uncertainty		Implicit < Explicit $A < A_1 \vee A_2$	Explicit < Sum $A_1 \vee A_2 < A_1 + A_2$	Implicit < Sum $A < A_1 + A_2$
Fox & See (2002)						
Duke basketball	51	Basketball	$P(.)$	63%†	78%**	86%**
fans			$C(.)$	65%*	84%**	94%**
Brown students	29	Economic	$P(.)$	69%*	66%†	83%**
		indicators	$C(.)$	59%	62%	66%†

† $p < .10$; * $p < .05$; ** $p < .005$.
The first three columns identify the participant population, sample size and sources of uncertainty. The fourth column indicates the relevant dependent variable (judged probability or normalized certainty equivalent). The remaining columns list the percentage of participants who violate the designated facet of the partition inequality (for certainty equivalents) and satisfy the designated prediction of support theory (for judged probability); asterisks and dagger indicate the statistical significance of the percentage.

the second part of Equation (8)). A similar pattern was exhibited for judged probabilities (satisfying "explicit subadditivity" in the language of support theory).

Fitting the Two-Stage Model

The two-stage model can be tested more directly against expected utility theory by comparing the fit of both models to empirical data. To fit the two-stage model, we did the following. For each target event, A, we observed its median judged probability $P(A)$. We next searched for the median certainty equivalent C of the risky prospect (x, p), where $p = P(A)$ (recall that these studies also asked participants to price risky prospects). Hence,

$C(x, A)$ is estimated by $C(x, p)$ where $p = P(A)$.

To illustrate, consider the study of basketball fans reported by Fox and See (2002). One of the prospects presented to these participants offered \$160 if Duke won its upcoming game against the University of North Carolina (UNC). To fit the two-stage model, we first observed that the median judged probability of the target event was .8. Next we found that the median certainty equivalent of this same population for the prospect that offered \$160 with probability .8 was \$119. The median certainty equivalent for the prospect that offered \$160 if Duke won its game against UNC was \$120. Thus, the error in this case was \$120−\$119 = \$1, or 0.6 percent.

To fit the classical theory, let C_A be the certainty equivalent of the prospect (\$160, A). Setting $u(0) = 0$, the classical theory yields $u(C_A) = u(160)P(A)$, where u is concave and $P(A)$ is an additive subjective probability measure.[19] Hence, $P(A) = u(C_A)/u(160)$. Previous studies (e.g., Tversky, 1967; Tversky & Kahneman, 1992) have suggested that the utility function for small to moderate gains can be approximated by a power function: $v(x) = x^\alpha$, $\alpha > 0$. Thus, risk aversion (a concave utility function) is modeled by $\alpha < 1$, risk neutrality (a linear utility function) is modeled by $\alpha = 1$, and risk seeking (a convex utility function) is modeled by $\alpha > 1$. An independent test of risk attitudes of these same participants yielded an estimate of α, assuming expected utility theory.

---

[19] Note that the additive subjective probability measure $P(.)$ should be distinguished from judged probability $P(.)$ and objective probability p.

Table 14.8 Comparison of data fit for two-stage model and classical theory

| | | | | Mean absolute error | | |
| | | | | --- | --- | --- |
Study	N	α	Source of uncertainty	Two-stage model	Classical theory	Superior fit of 2SM
Fox & Tversky (1998)						
NBA fans	50	0.83	Basketball	0.04	0.15	90%**
Stanford students	82	0.80	Economic indicators	0.04	0.08	61%*
Fox & See (2002)						
Duke basketball fans	51	0.63	Basketball	0.13	0.18	74%**
Brown students	29	0.87	Economic indicators	0.12	0.43	97%**

* $p < .05$; ** $p < .01$.
The first two columns identify the participant population and sample size. The third column lists the median value of alpha (α) estimated for participants in each sample. The fourth column identifies the relevant source of uncertainty. The fifth and sixth columns indicate the mean absolute error in fitting median data to the two-stage model and classical theory, respectively. The final column lists the percentage of participants for whom the fit of the two-stage model was superior to the fit of the classical theory; asterisks indicate the statistical significance of the percentage.

As anticipated, participants in the studies of Fox and Tversky (1998) and Fox and See (2002) exhibited risk-averse utility functions under expected utility theory. Median estimates of α for each of these studies, listed in the fourth column of Table 14.8, range from 0.63 to 0.87. Moreover, a significant majority of participants in these studies exhibited $\alpha \leq 1$ (92 percent of NBA fans, 98 percent of Stanford University students, 94 percent of Duke University basketball fans and 83 percent of Brown University students; $p < .001$ for all samples). This confirms our earlier assertion that part (*ii*) of the partition inequality would be expected to hold for most participants under expected utility theory.

Subjective probabilities were estimated as follows. For each target event A, we computed $(C_A/160)^{\alpha}$ and divided these values by their sum to ensure additivity. Fits of both the two-stage model and classical theory for the studies of Fox and Tversky (1998) and also Fox and See (2002) are listed in Table 14.8. Based on the median certainty equivalents obtained in the studies listed, the fit of the two-stage model was consistently better than the fit of the classical theory. The mean absolute error for the two-stage model ranges from one-quarter to one-half of the mean absolute error of expected utility theory. Moreover, when this analysis was replicated for each participant, the two-stage model fit the data better than the classical theory for a significant majority of participants in all four studies.

14.2.5 From Allais to the Two-Stage Model: Summary

The Allais (1953) paradox and fourfold pattern of risk attitudes (see Table 14.4) suggest that consequences are not weighted by an additive probability measure. Instead, it seems that consequences are weighted by an inverse-S shaped transformation that overweights small probability consequences and underweights moderate to large probability consequences. This weighting function reflects diminished sensitivity to events between the natural boundaries of impossibility and certainty, which is formally expressed as *bounded subadditivity*. Numerous empirical studies have documented significant bounded subadditivity for chance bets (risk) and a more pronounced degree of subadditivity for bets contingent on natural events (uncertainty). This reduced sensitivity to uncertainty can be attributed to subadditivity of judged probability. According to the two-stage model (Tversky & Fox, 1995; Fox & Tversky, 1998), decision makers first judge the probability of the target event (consistent with support theory), and then weight that probability by an inverse-S shaped function (as in prospect theory). This two-stage model is a radical departure from previous models because it allows decision weights to violate both the assumptions of additivity and description invariance.

Evidence from a number of studies suggests that the two-stage model generally provides a better fit to the data than does the classical model. Moreover, both prospect theory and the two-stage model accommodate the Allais pattern in Problem 1, which reflects a preference for certainty. We now turn to the Ellsberg paradox illustrated in Problem 2. As we observed in Section 1, the Ellsberg pattern also violates the classical theory. However, the two-stage model cannot accommodate the Ellsberg paradox, because the two-stage model attaches the same weight to all events with probability p, regardless of their source. Hence, under the two-stage model, a prize that obtains with probability 1/3 should be equally attractive, regardless of whether the probability is clear (for example, option E in Problem 2) or vague (option F). Similarly, a prize that obtains with probability 2/3 should be equally attractive, regardless of whether the probability is clear (option H) or vague (option G). This prediction is contradicted by modal preferences exhibited in the Ellsberg problem.

In order to develop a more satisfactory account of decision under uncertainty, we must first gain a deeper understanding of the Ellsberg phenomenon: the empirical results that have been documented and how they might be interpreted. At that point, we will be ready to extend the two-stage model to accommodate this phenomenon.

14.3 THE PREFERENCE FOR KNOWLEDGE: FROM ELLSBERG TO THE COMPARATIVE IGNORANCE HYPOTHESIS

Recall that the violation of the sure-thing principle observed in the Allais paradox (Problem 1) was explained by diminished sensitivity to changes in probability away from zero and one. The violation observed in the Ellsberg paradox (Problem 2) resonates with a very different intuition: people prefer to bet on known rather than unknown probabilities. This interpretation is brought into sharper focus in a simpler, two-color problem that was also advanced by Ellsberg (1961). Imagine two urns, both containing red and black balls. Urn I contains 50 red balls and 50 black balls, whereas Urn II contains 100 red and black balls in an unknown proportion. Suppose that your task is to guess a color, and then draw a ball from one of the urns without looking. If you draw the color that you had guessed, you win a prize, say, $10. Most people would rather bet on drawing a black ball from the known probability urn than a black ball from the unknown probability urn, and most people would likewise rather bet on drawing a red ball from the known probability urn than a red ball from the unknown probability urn. This pattern violates expected utility theory because it implies that the subjective probabilities for red and black are greater for the 50—50 urn than for the unknown probability urn and therefore cannot sum to one for both urns.

The Ellsberg problem has garnered much attention because in real-world contexts decision makers are seldom provided with precise probabilities of potential consequences. Ellsberg (1961, 2001) argued that willingness to act under uncertainty is governed not only by the perceived likelihood of target events and the attractiveness of potential consequences, but also the *ambiguity* of the information on which the likelihood judgment is based (that is, the degree of uncertainty concerning probabilistic information). Ellsberg observed that people generally find ambiguity aversive. More generally, we say that people prefer to bet on sources of uncertainty for which events have known rather than unknown probabilities.[20]

In this section, we begin with a review of the empirical study of ambiguity and source preference. Second, we describe ways in which researchers can establish that a decision maker prefers one source of uncertainty to another. Third, we discuss the psychological interpretation of ambiguity aversion and source preference. Finally, we outline ways in which source preference can be incorporated into the two-stage model that was developed in the previous section.

14.3.1 The Empirical Study of Ambiguity Aversion

Although Ellsberg presented no experimental evidence, the preference to bet on known rather than unknown probabilities has been demonstrated in numerous empirical studies using variations of Ellsberg's original problems (for a review of the literature on ambiguity aversion, see Camerer & Weber, 1992). In particular, a number of researchers have provided participants with either precise information concerning probabilities or no information concerning probabilities, as in the original Ellsberg problems. These studies provide empirical support for the predicted pattern of choices in the Ellsberg two-color problem (Raiffa, 1961; Becker & Brownson, 1964; Yates & Zukowski, 1976; Kahn & Sarin, 1988; Curley & Yates, 1989; Eisenberger & Weber, 1995) and three-color problem (Slovic & Tversky, 1974; MacCrimmon & Larsson, 1979).

Numerous studies have extended the exploration of ambiguity aversion by examining the effect of increasing the degree of second-order uncertainty (that is, uncertainty about probability). Traditionally, researchers have relied on four different methods for manipulating what they interpret to be "ambiguity". First, some experimenters have varied the width of a *range* of possible probabilities. For example, participants might be asked to price gambles with probabilities of (a) .5, (b) somewhere between .4 and .6, or (c) somewhere between .3 and .7 (Becker & Brownson, 1964; Curley & Yates, 1985, 1989; Kahn & Sarin, 1988). Second, some researchers have *endowed* participants with a probability and a qualitative degree of second-order uncertainty (Einhorn & Hogarth, 1986; Kahn & Sarin, 1988; Hogarth, 1989; Hogarth & Kunreuther, 1989; Hogarth & Einhorn, 1990; Kunreuther et al., 1995). For example, Kunreuther et al. (1995) manipulate ambiguity in the context of underwriter decision making by telling participants either that "all experts agree that the probability of a loss is [*p*]" or that the experts' best estimate of the probability of a loss is [*p*], but "there is wide disagreement about this estimate and a high degree of uncertainty among experts" (p. 11). Third, some researchers have provided participants with small and large random *samples* of information with identical proportions (Chipman, 1960; Beach & Wise, 1969; Gigliotti & Sopher, 1996). For instance, Chipman (1960) had participants choose between betting on a box with a known proportion of 100 match stems and heads versus

---

[20] Tversky and Wakker (1995, p. 1270) define sources of uncertainty as families of events that are assumed to be closed under union and complementation (that is, if events A_1 and A_2 are members of source **A**, then so are $A_1 \cup A_2$, $S - A_1$, and $S - A_2$). This assumption is satisfactory with one salient exception: in the Ellsberg three-color example (Problem 2), we might interpret known probability events {red, white $\cup$ blue} as one source of uncertainty and unknown probability events {white, blue, red $\cup$ white, red $\cup$ blue} as a second source of uncertainty. Hence, for our purposes, it is the fundamental character of the information on which judgment is based that defines a source.

a box with an unknown proportion of 100 stems and heads from which 10 items had been sampled (yielding a matched proportion of stems and heads). Finally, some researchers have manipulated ambiguity by providing participants with a *game of chance* entailing a multistage lottery in which the outcome probability is determined by a first-stage drawing (Yates & Zukowski, 1976; Larson, 1980; Bowen & Qui, 1992). For instance, in a study by Larson (1980), the proportion of winning poker chips in a container was to be determined by a number written on a card to be randomly drawn from a deck with 20 cards. Pairs of decks were constructed with fixed means and normal distributions surrounding those means; half the decks had a relatively large variance, and half had a relatively small variance.

Studies using the methods discussed above seem to provide broad empirical support for the notion that the attractiveness of a prospect generally decreases as second-order uncertainty increases. Many of these studies have also claimed to find "ambiguity seeking" for low probability gains. However, an important caveat is in order when evaluating the results of any study using one of these methods for manipulating ambiguity: they do not necessarily control for variations in subjective probability. Heath and Tversky (1991; see especially Table 4, p. 24) provide evidence that subjective probabilities associated with higher variance or less reliable estimates of p may be less extreme (that is, closer to .5) than those associated with lower variance or more reliable estimates of p. This pattern is also consistent with a model in which people anchor on an "ignorance prior" probability of one-half, and then adjust according to information provided them, with greater adjustment in response to more precise probabilistic information (cf. Fox & Rottenstreich, 2003). Hence, when participants learn that the best estimate of probability is .1 but "there is wide disagreement about [the] estimate and a high degree of uncertainty among experts", they may adopt a posterior probability that is higher than participants who learn that the best estimate is .1 and "all experts agree" (cf. Hogarth & Kunreuther, 1989). Such a pattern would mimic "ambiguity seeking" for low probability gains, but, in fact, it merely reflects a variation in subjective probability. In sum, although the studies using the foregoing methods (range, endowment, sampling and games of chance) make a persuasive case for ambiguity aversion in situations where there are clear and vague probabilities of .5, the interpretation of ambiguity seeking for low-probability gains should be regarded with some skepticism. In order to establish ambiguity aversion (or seeking), one must be careful to control for unintended variations in belief that may be introduced by the manipulation of ambiguity. Before turning to a discussion of how one might interpret these empirical observations, we must first address the question of how to distinguish ambiguity aversion—or more generally, the preference to bet on one source of uncertainty over another—from an account that can be attributed to differences in belief.

14.3.2 Establishing Source Preference

Two methods for establishing source preference can be defended, which we will call (1) probability matching and (2) complementary bets. Although we use games of chance (such as balls drawn from an urn) to illustrate these methods, the two methods allow us to extend the study of ambiguity to the domain of natural events, such as the future outcome of an election or future close of the stock market.

The probability matching method can be formalized as follows. Let **A** and **B** be two different sources of uncertainty. For instance, source **A** might be the color of a ball drawn from an urn containing 50 red and 50 black balls, whereas source **B** might be the color of a ball drawn from an urn containing 100 red and black balls in unknown proportion. A decision maker is said to prefer source **A** to source **B** if for any event A in **A** and B in **B**, $P(A) = P(B)$ implies $W(A) \geq W(B)$ or equivalently, $P(A) = P(B)$ implies $C(x, A) \geq C(x, B)$ for all $x > 0$. Thus, a person who says event A and event B are equally likely, but strictly prefers to bet on A, exhibits a preference for source **A** over source **B**. For instance, suppose a person says the probability of "black from the 50−50 urn" is .5 and the probability of "black from the unknown probability urn" is also .5. If this person prefers betting on black from the known probability urn to black from the unknown probability urn, then she has exhibited ambiguity aversion that cannot be readily attributed to differences in belief.

One could potentially object to the probability matching method on the grounds that it relies on an expression of judged probability rather than a measure of belief that is inferred from preferences. A second method for establishing source preference does not rely on judged probability. A decision maker is said to prefer source **A** to source **B** if for any event A in **A** and B in **B**, $W(A) = W(B)$ implies $W(S−A) \geq W(S− B)$, or equivalently, $C(x, A) = C(x, B)$ implies $C(x, S−A) \geq C(x, S−B)$ for all $x > 0$. Thus, a person who would rather bet on event A (for example, drawing a black ball from the 50−50 urn) than on event B (for example, drawing a black ball from the unknown probability urn) and would rather bet against A (that is, drawing a red ball from the 50–50 urn) than against B (that is, drawing a red ball from the unknown probability urn) exhibits source preference that cannot be readily attributed to differences in belief.[21]

14.3.3 Interpreting Ambiguity Aversion

Most of the aforementioned empirical studies of ambiguity aversion have manipulated ambiguity through vagueness of probabilities. Indeed, Ellsberg (1961) himself proposed to model ambiguity aversion in terms of probability vagueness (that is, the range of possible probabilities), and most models of ambiguity that followed Ellsberg have parameterized features of a second-order probability distribution (for a review, see Camerer & Weber, 1992, pp. 343–347). However, Ellsberg originally characterized ambiguity aversion not as vagueness aversion per se, but rather as reluctance to bet in situations where the decision maker perceives that he lacks adequate information or expertise:

> An individual ... can always assign relative likelihoods to the states of nature. But how does he *act* in the presence of uncertainty? The answer to that may depend on another judgment, about the reliability, credibility, or adequacy of his information (including his relevant experience, advice and intuition) as a whole. (Ellsberg, 1961, p. 659)

In recent years, many behavioral researchers have returned to the original interpretation of ambiguity aversion as driven by the decision maker's confidence in his or her knowledge, skill or information (e.g., Frisch & Baron, 1988; Heath & Tversky, 1991). That is, ambiguity aversion might be attributed to reluctance to bet in situations where the decision maker feels relatively ignorant.

---

[21] This pattern could be attributed to differences in belief if the sum of probabilities of complementary events is lower for the less familiar source of uncertainty. Recall that support theory (Tversky & Koehler, 1994; Rottenstreich & Tversky, 1997) holds that judged probabilities of complementary events generally sum to one. Numerous studies provide evidence supporting this prediction (for a review of evidence, see Tversky & Koehler, 1994; Table 14.5 of this chapter). For counterexamples, see Brenner and Rottenstreich (1999); Macchi, Osherson and Krantz (1999) and Idson et al. (2001).

Vagueness Aversion Versus Ignorance Aversion

Under most circumstances, the ignorance versus vagueness conceptions are confounded: when a decision maker feels less knowledgeable, her judged probabilities are less precise. In order to tease apart these two accounts, we must find a circumstance in which vagueness aversion and ignorance aversion imply different patterns of choice. Heath and Tversky (1991) conducted a series of experiments comparing people's willingness to bet on their uncertain beliefs to their willingness to bet on chance events. Contrary to the vagueness-aversion hypothesis, Heath and Tversky found that people prefer to bet on their vague beliefs in situations where they feel especially knowledgeable or competent—though they prefer to bet on chance when they do not feel especially knowledgeable or competent. For instance, in one study, participants were asked to order their preferences among bets contingent on three sources of uncertainty: chance events, the winner of various professional football games and the winner of various states in the 1988 presidential election. Participants who rated their knowledge of football to be high and their knowledge of politics to be low preferred betting on football games to chance events that they considered equally probable. However, these participants preferred betting on chance events to political events that they considered equally probable. Analogously, participants who rated their knowledge of football to be low and their knowledge of politics to be high favored bets on politics to chance and chance to football.

The foregoing demonstration provides evidence for the ignorance-aversion hypothesis and casts doubt on the vagueness-aversion hypothesis. This demonstration relies on the probability matching method described in Section 14.3.2. In other studies using the complementary bets method, Heath and Tversky (1991) found that participants were willing to pay more to bet both for and against familiar events (for example, "more than 85 percent of undergraduates at [your university] receive on-campus housing") than for or against matched events that were less familiar (for example, "more than 70 percent of undergraduates at [a less familiar university] receive on-campus housing"). The preference to bet on more familiar events has since been replicated by a number of researchers using both the probability matching method (Taylor, 1995; Taylor & Kahn, 1997) and the complementary bets method (Keppe & Weber, 1995; Tversky & Fox, 1995).

The perspective we are advancing is that the ambiguity-aversion phenomenon is driven by the decision maker's perception of her level of knowledge concerning the target event, rather than by features of the second-order probability distribution. Heath and Tversky (1991) provided support for this interpretation by identifying situations where decision makers preferred to bet on their vague assessments of familiar events rather than bet on chance events with matched probability. We are not arguing that perceptions of one's own competence influence probability vagueness or that vagueness influences perceived competence. Rather, characteristics of a source of uncertainty influence both the precision with which likelihood can be assessed by the decision maker and the decision maker's subjective perception of her own competence judging likelihood. However, it is the perception of competence that drives willingness to act under uncertainty. Indeed, Heath and Tversky (1991) found that two-thirds of participants preferred to bet on their guess of whether a randomly picked stock would go up or down the next day rather than bet on their guess of whether a randomly picked stock had gone up or down the previous day. Clearly, the vagueness of one's judgment is unlikely to be influenced by whether the stock is picked from yesterday's or tomorrow's paper (if anything, participants could have more precise knowledge of yesterday's stock movement). However, when betting on yesterday's close, participants may feel relatively ignorant because they can already be wrong at the time of "postdiction" (see also Brun & Teigen, 1990).

The Comparative Ignorance Hypothesis

The ignorance-aversion hypothesis asserts that source preference is driven by the decision maker's subjective appraisal of his or her knowledge concerning target events rather than some second-order measure of probability vagueness. Fox and Tversky (1995) extended this account by asking what conditions produce ignorance aversion. They conjectured that a decision maker's confidence betting on a target event is enhanced (diminished) when he contrasts his knowledge of the event with his inferior (superior) knowledge about another event, or when he compares himself with less (more) knowledgeable individuals. According to the "comparative ignorance hypothesis", ambiguity aversion is driven by a comparison with more familiar sources of uncertainty or more knowledgeable people and is diminished in the absence of such a comparison. Three nuances of this account are worth emphasizing: (1) source preference increases with the salience of contrasting states of knowledge; (2) source preference is relative rather than absolute; (3) source preference is a function of decision makers' appraisal of their relative *knowledge* rather than their *information*.

The Salience of Contrasting States of Knowledge

Virtually every empirical study of ambiguity aversion reported before Fox and Tversky (1995) relied on a within-subject design in which all participants evaluated multiple sources of uncertainty (for example, in which each participant priced bets drawn from both clear and vague probability urns). In a series of experiments, Fox and Tversky (1995) docu-mented pronounced ambiguity aversion in *comparative* contexts in which each participant evaluated lotteries with both clear and vague probabilities, but they found the effect was greatly diminished—or disappeared entirely—in *noncomparative* contexts in which differ-ent groups of participants evaluated the lotteries in isolation. For instance, participants in a comparative condition said they were willing to pay $24.34, on average, for a bet that offered $100 if they correctly guessed the color drawn from an urn containing 50 red balls and 50 black balls, but they would pay only $14.85, on average, for a bet that offered $100 if they correctly guessed the color drawn from an urn containing 100 red and black balls in an unknown proportion. In contrast, participants who priced the 50–50 bet in isolation were willing to pay $17.95, on average, whereas participants who priced the unknown probability bet in isolation were willing to pay $18.42, on average. Hence, the Ellsberg result seemed to disappear when the experiment was run as a between-subject design rather than a within-subject design. A similar pattern was observed in a follow-up study in which participants evaluated prospects contingent on the future temperature in San Francisco (a familiar city) and/or Istanbul (an unfamiliar city). Chow and Sarin (2001) replicated the finding that source preference greatly diminishes in noncomparative contexts, though in some of their studies it did not disappear entirely. Further evidence from market studies has shown that the pronounced difference in prices for clear versus vague bets, observed when both bets are traded together, diminishes or disappears when these bets are traded in separate markets (Sarin & Weber, 1993).

The comparative ignorance hypothesis asserts that source preference is driven by the salience of contrasting states of knowledge. It applies not only to the contrast in a decision maker's knowledge of two different sources of uncertainty but also to the contrast between a decision maker's knowledge and that of other people. Fox and Tversky (1995) showed that participants who were told that more knowledgeable people would be making the same choice were much less likely to bet on their prediction than participants who were not told about such experts. For instance, in one study, psychology undergraduates were asked whether they thought that a particular stock would close higher in its next day of trading, and then asked whether they would prefer to receive $50 for sure or $150 if their prediction was correct. In this case, most favored the uncertain prospect. However, when a second group of participants was told that the survey was also being presented to economics graduate students and professional stock analysts, most favored the sure payment. In a similar vein, Chow and Sarin (1999) found that the preference for known over unknown probabilities is amplified when participants pricing a single bet (for example, a draw from a 50–50 urn) are made aware of the fact that another participant or group of participants is evaluating a different bet that offers a contrasting degree of information about probabilities (for example, a draw from an unknown probability urn).

Relative Versus Absolute Knowledge

Fox and Tversky (1995) emphasized that the distinction between comparative and non-comparative assessment refers to the state of mind of the decision maker rather than the experimental context. The studies cited above facilitated such comparisons by juxtaposing a known probability or familiar prospect with an unknown probability or unfamiliar prospect, or by explicitly mentioning other people who were more (or less) knowledgeable. More recently, Fox and Weber (2002) have shown that the comparative state of mind that drives source preference can be manipulated without resorting to this "joint–separate" evaluation paradigm. For instance, participants in one study were less willing to bet on their prediction of the outcome of the upcoming Russian election (a modestly familiar event) when they had been previously asked a question concerning the upcoming US election (a more familiar event) than when they had been previously asked a question concerning the upcoming Dominican Republic election (a less familiar event). This demonstration also provides evidence that when a state of comparative ignorance is induced (by reminding people of alternative states of knowledge), willingness to act is governed by the decision maker's *relative* knowledge judging the target event rather than some measure of *absolute* knowledge.[22]

Knowledge Versus Information

Fox and Weber (2002) also demonstrated that comparisons can be facilitated even in a decision context that is not explicitly comparative. In particular, when people are provided with information they do not know how to use, this may remind them of their ignorance relative to experts who do know how to use that information. For instance, in one study, psychology students were less willing to bet on their assessment of the inflation rate in the Netherlands if they had been provided information concerning the country's gross domestic product

---

[22] For a demonstration in the context of strategic uncertainty, see also Fox and Weber (2002), study 5.

growth, unemployment rate and prevailing interest rate than if they had been provided no such information. This demonstration also suggests that comparative ignorance effects are governed by the decision maker's perception of her relative *knowledge* concerning the target event rather than the absolute amount of relevant *information* that she has available.

14.3.4   Incorporating Source Preference into the Two-Stage Model

The comparative ignorance effect presents serious modeling challenges. In particular, demonstrations using the joint–separate evaluation paradigm show that strict source preference sometimes disappears when prospects are evaluated separately, rather than jointly. This violates the principle of *procedure invariance*, according to which strategically equivalent elicitation procedures should produce the same preference ordering (Tversky, Sattath & Slovic, 1988; see also Tversky, 1996). More troubling still is the problem that the comparative ignorance phenomenon is inherently subjective and context-dependent. To predict source preference *ex ante*, one must somehow parameterize (1) the decision maker's sense of his or her relative knowledge regarding the events in question and (2) the salience of alternative states of knowledge.

These caveats notwithstanding, it would certainly be valuable to incorporate source preference into the two-stage model. Recall that according to the two-stage model, a decision maker first judges probabilities, consistent with support theory, and then transforms these probabilities in a way that accords with his or her weighting of chance events. Hence, the original specification of the two-stage model does not allow for source preference. Although the model presented in Equation (5) may provide a reasonable first-order approximation of people's decision behavior under uncertainty, it is important to note that this specification will fail when source preference is especially pronounced.

Fox and Tversky (1998) acknowledged this limitation and proposed that their model could be extended to accommodate source preference while preserving the segregation of belief (that is, judged probability) and preference (that is, decision weights). They suggested generalizing Equation (5) by letting $W(A) = F[P(A)]$, so that the transformation F of probability depends on the source of uncertainty. They assume that F, like the risky weighting function, w, is a subadditive transformation of P (see Tversky & Fox, 1995; Tversky & Wakker, 1995; Wakker, in press). One convenient parameterization may be defined by

$$W(A) = (w[P(A)])^{\theta}, \tag{9}$$

where $\theta > 0$ is inversely related to the attractiveness of the particular source of uncertainty. A second approach is to vary a parameter of the probability weighting function that increases weights throughout the unit interval. For instance, one could vary the parameter δ of Prelec's (1998) two-parameter weighting function, $w(p) = \exp(-\delta(-\ln p)^{\gamma})$, where $\delta > 0$ is inversely related to the attractiveness of the source. This latter scheme has the advantage of manipulating "elevation" (that is, source preference) independently of the degree of "curvature" (that is, source sensitivity). It also allows for the possibility of differences in sensitivity to probabilities drawn from different sources of uncertainty that can be modeled through changes in the parameter γ. Such a decrement in sensitivity was recently documented for an extremely unfamiliar domain by Kilka and Weber (2001).

An approach that allows for differences in curvature of probability weights may have a second application. The two-stage model, like most normative and descriptive models of decision under uncertainty, presumes that (weighted) beliefs and (the subjective value of) consequences can be segregated into separate terms that are independent of one another. Recently, the generality of even this basic principle has been called into question. Rottenstreich and Hsee (2001) observed that the weighting function may exhibit greater curvature for more "affect-rich" outcomes, such as the possibility of receiving an electrical shock or a kiss from a favorite movie star, than for "affect-poor" outcomes, such as money. For instance, these researchers report that their participants found an electric shock about as unattractive as a penalty of $20. However, participants were willing to pay seven times as much to avoid a 1 percent chance of an electric shock as they were to avoid a 1 percent chance of losing $20. This phenomenon begs further study—in particular, a more tightly circumscribed definition and independent measure of "affect richness" would be useful. In any case, the phenomenon can easily be accommodated by the extended two-stage model if we allow the curvature parameter of the probability weighting function to vary with the degree of affect richness of the target outcome.

14.3.5   From Ellsberg to the Comparative Ignorance Hypothesis: Summary

The Ellsberg paradox and similar demonstrations have established that willingness to act under uncertainty depends not only on the degree of uncertainty but also on its source. The empirical study of decision under uncertainty has suggested that the aversion to ambiguity does not reflect a reluctance to bet on vaguer probabilities, but rather a reluctance to act when the decision maker feels less knowledgeable. Moreover, it appears that the awareness of relative ignorance occurs only to the extent that contrasting states of knowledge are especially salient to the decision maker, an account known as the "comparative ignorance hypothesis". Source preference can be accommodated by the two-stage model through a generalization that weights judged probabilities by a subadditive function F, the elevation of which depends on the source of uncertainty.

14.4   SUMMING UP: A BEHAVIORAL PERSPECTIVE ON DECISION UNDER UNCERTAINTY

The Allais and Ellsberg paradoxes present challenges to the classical theory of decision under uncertainty that are so robust and so fundamental that they appear in most introductory texts of microeconomics (e.g., Kreps, 1990), decision analysis (e.g., von Winterfeldt & Edwards, 1986) and behavioral decision theory (e.g., Baron, 2001). The implications of these anomalies continue to preoccupy decision theorists to this day. Although modal preferences in both problems violate the sure-thing principle, the violations seem to reflect a distinct psychological rationale: the preference for certainty (Allais) versus the preference for knowledge (Ellsberg). Nevertheless, both patterns can be accommodated by a nonlinear weighting function that models source sensitivity through its degree of curvature and source preference through its elevation.

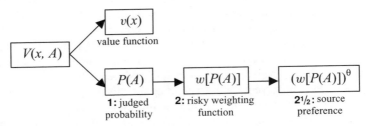

Figure 14.7   Visual depiction of the extended two-stage model, as parameterized in Equation (9). $V(x, A) = v(x)W(A) = v(x)(w[P(A)])^\theta$, where $V(x, A)$ is the value of the prospect that pays \$x if event A obtains (and nothing otherwise), $v(.)$ is the value function for monetary gains, $P(.)$ is judged probability, $w(.)$ is the risky weighting function, and θ is the source preference parameter

The two-stage model bridges two of the most influential strains of research in behavioral decision theory. It integrates the analysis of decision under risk and uncertainty articulated in prospect theory (Kahneman & Tversky, 1979; Tversky & Kahneman, 1992) with work on heuristics and biases in judgment under uncertainty (e.g., Kahneman, Slovic & Tversky, 1982) that can be formalized through support theory (Tversky & Koehler, 1994; Rottenstreich & Tversky, 1997). The resulting model extends prospect theory by teasing apart the role of belief (that is, judged probability) and preference (that is, source sensitivity and source preference) in the weighting of events. It departs markedly from previous models by allowing decisions to differ depending on the way in which target events are described.

14.4.1   Value, Belief and Preference in Decision Under Uncertainty

We began this chapter with the observation that values and beliefs are key inputs in choice under uncertainty. However, we have identified systematic deficiencies of the classical approach in which values and beliefs are neatly segregated into utilities and subjective probabilities. In particular, we have observed that the weight decision makers afford uncertain events can be decomposed into judged probabilities that are weighted according to an inverse-S shaped function, the curvature of which reflects the decision maker's sensitivity to the particular source of uncertainty, and the elevation of which reflects the decision maker's preference to act on that source. A summary of our perspective on the role of value, belief and preference in decision under uncertainty, according to the extended two-stage model (as parameterized in Equation (9)), is presented in Table 14.9 and illustrated in Figure 14.7.

First, willingness to act under uncertainty is influenced in this model by the subjective value of the target outcome, $v(x)$. This value function is characterized by *reference dependence:* that is, it is a function of losses and gains relative to a reference point (usually, the status quo) rather than absolute states of wealth as in expected utility theory. The function is *concave for gains,* giving rise to some risk aversion for gains, just as in expected utility theory (see Figure 14.1). However, the function is also *convex for losses,* giving rise to some risk seeking for losses, contrary to expected utility theory (see Figure 14.2a). Finally, the function is *steeper for losses than for gains,* giving rise to "loss aversion" that can appear

Table 14.9 Summary of the role of value, belief and preference in decision under uncertainty according to the extended two-stage model[a]

Function/ Parameter	Interpretation	Characteristics	Empirical implications	Key references
$v(.)$	Value function	1) Reference dependence	1) Framing effects	Kahneman & Tversky (1984)
		2) Concave for gains; convex for losses	2) Risk seeking for gains; risk aversion for losses	Tversky & Kahneman (1986) Kahneman, Knetsch & Thaler (1990)
		3) Steeper for losses than gains	3) Loss aversion	Tversky & Kahneman (1991)
$P(.)$	Judged probability	1) Subadditivity	1) $P(A) \leq P(A_1) + P(A_2)$	Tversky & Koehler (1994)
		2) Description-dependence	2) $P(A) \leq P(A_1 \vee A_2)$	Rottenstreich & Tversky (1997)
$w(.)$	Risky weighting function	1) Bounded subadditivity	1) Fourfold pattern of risk attitudes	Tversky & Fox (1995)
		2) Subcertainty	2) More risk aversion than risk seeking	Tversky & Wakker (1995) Wu & Gonzalez (1996) Prelec (1998) Gonzalez & Wu (1999)
θ	Source preference parameter	Source preference varies with salience and nature of contrasting states of knowledge	Comparative Ignorance Effect	Heath & Tversky (1991) Fox & Tversky (1995) Fox & Weber (2002)

[a]Fox & Tversky (1998); see also Tversky & Kahneman (1992); Kahneman & Tversky (1979).

as risk aversion.[23] For instance, most people would reject a bet that offered a .5 chance of winning $100 and a .5 chance of losing $100, because a potential loss of $100 has a greater psychological impact than a potential gain of the same amount. In fact, most people would require a .5 chance of gaining at least $200 to compensate for a .5 chance of losing $100.

Second, willingness to act under uncertainty is influenced in this model by the perceived likelihood that the target event will occur, which can be quantified as a judged probability, $P(A)$. Judged probabilities are characterized by *subadditivity*: the probability of an uncertain event is generally less than the sum of probabilities of constituent events. This may contribute to violations of the partition inequality that mimic risk-seeking behavior. Moreover, judged probabilities are *description dependent*: as the description of the target event is unpacked into an explicit disjunction of constituent events, judged probability may increase. This phenomenon gives rise, for example, to a greater willingness to pay for an

---

[23] In fact, risk aversion over modest stakes for mixed (gain-loss) prospects cannot be explained by a concave utility function because it implies an implausible degree of risk aversion over large stakes. See Rabin (2000).

insurance policy that covers hospitalization due to "accident or disease" than a policy that covers hospitalization for "any reason" (Johnson et al., 1993).

Third, willingness to act under uncertainty is influenced in this model by the risky weighting function, $w(.)$. The curvature of this weighting function provides an index of a person's diminishing sensitivity to changes in probability between the natural boundaries of zero and one, and the elevation of this weighting function provides an index of a person's overall risk preference. The risky weighting function is generally characterized by *bounded subadditivity:* a probability p has more impact on decisions when added to zero or subtracted from one than when added to or subtracted from an intermediate probability q.

This inverse-S shaped weighting function implies a fourfold pattern of risk attitudes: people tend to be risk averse for gains and risk seeking for losses of moderate to high probability (underweighting of moderate to high probabilities reinforces the risk attitudes implied by the shape of the value function), but they tend to be risk seeking for gains and risk averse for losses of low probability (overweighting of low probabilities reverses the risk attitudes implied by the shape of the value function).

The risky weighting function is also generally characterized by *subcertainty:* $w(p) + w(1-p) \leq 1$. Visually, subcertainty manifests itself as a weighting function that crosses the identity line below .5, and weighting functions with lower elevation are associated with more pronounced degrees of subcertainty. It is important to note that there are large individual differences in both the curvature and elevation of measured weighting functions, so that some people might exhibit pronounced bounded subadditivity and no subcertainty, some might exhibit little subadditivity and pronounced subcertainty, and others might exhibit both or neither (for a detailed investigation, see Gonzalez & Wu, 1999).

Finally, willingness to act under uncertainty is influenced in this model by the source preference parameter, θ. Source preference reflects a person's eagerness or reluctance to act on one source of uncertainty (for example, invest in the domestic stock market) rather than another (for example, invest in a foreign stock market). Decision makers prefer to act in situations where they feel relatively knowledgeable or competent to situations in which they feel relatively ignorant or incompetent, but only to the extent that comparative states of knowledge are salient. We suspect that the original formulation of the two-stage model is adequate in most environments, where a contrasting state of knowledge does not occur to the decision maker. Indeed, the research reviewed in this chapter suggests that the perception of comparative ignorance, when it does occur, is subjective, transitory and context-dependent.

14.4.2   Judged Probability Versus Subjective Probability

In the classical model of decision under uncertainty, direct judgments of probability are rejected in favor of a measure of belief that is inferred from choices between bets. This approach yields an elegant axiomatic theory that allows for the simultaneous measurement of utility and subjective probability. Unfortunately, the price of this parsimony is a set of restrictions on subjective probability that are descriptively invalid. In particular, the data reviewed in this chapter suggest that outcomes are weighted in a manner that violates both the assumptions of additivity and description invariance. Perhaps it was the observation of incoherent judged probabilities that led early theorists to reject direct expressions of belief in their development of a normative theory of choice. However, empirical studies reviewed in this chapter demonstrate persuasively that judged probabilities are, in fact, diagnostic of choices and therefore can be fruitfully incorporated into a *descriptive* model of decision under uncertainty. Moreover, support theory provides a formal framework for predicting departures from additivity and description invariance in judged probability. Thus, the descriptive theory of decision making under uncertainty may be informed and facilitated by a deeper understanding of judgment under uncertainty.[24]

14.4.3 Concluding Comments

In this chapter, we have reviewed a descriptive account of decision making under uncertainty. The picture that has emerged accommodates a wide range of empirical data that have been collected in recent decades and explains several puzzles in the literature. The (extended) two-stage model teases apart the role of value, belief and preference underlying willingness to act under uncertainty. Of course, the story presented here is incomplete, and a great deal of continuing research is called for. The present account accommodates the observation that real-world decisions require people to judge probabilities for themselves, with some degree of second-order uncertainty. However, we have confined most of the present discussion to prospects involving a single positive outcome, such as a bet that pays a fixed prize if the home team wins a sporting event (and nothing otherwise). Decisions in the real world often involve a host of multiple potential outcomes, some of which may entail losses. Although the cumulative version of prospect theory accommodates multiple uncertain outcomes entailing both gains and losses, further research is needed to determine an appropriate decomposition of decision weights into belief and preference terms in rank- and sign-dependent models (for an early attempt, see Wu & Gonzalez, 1999b).

Another promising avenue for future research is to develop tools for helping decision makers make more rational decisions. The present account suggests that several violations of rational choice theory can be avoided if the decision maker merely calculates the expected value of each option and is willing to bind her actions to the principle of expected value maximization. This simple procedure will eliminate inconsistencies in: (1) risk preference attributed to nonlinearity of the value function v; (2) risk preference attributed to nonlinearity of the risky weighting function w; (3) source preference attributed to the comparative ignorance effect and modeled by the parameter θ. However, the present account suggests that a final source of departures from rational choice—those attributed to incoherence of belief—are not so readily purged. The aforementioned study of options traders (Fox, Rogers & Tversky, 1996) is especially relevant in this respect. Options traders in this sample did indeed price chance prospects by their expected value, based on objective probabilities provided by the experimenter. Likewise, these experts priced uncertain prospects by their *apparent* expected value, based on probabilities they had judged for themselves. However, because these judged probabilities exhibited subadditivity, selling prices for uncertain prospects were also subadditive. It appears that even experts whose careers depend on their ability to make rational decisions under uncertainty have difficulty avoiding subadditivity in

---

[24] Note that according to the two-stage model, applying the inverse risky weighting function to uncertain decision weights will recover judged probabilities; that is, $w^{-1}(W(A)) = P(A)$, where w^{-1} is the inverse of w (cf. Wakker, in press).

their judgment and decision making. Because belief-based departures from rational choice cannot be eliminated by a simple act of volition, future prescriptive work might seek a better understanding of the psychological mechanisms underlying belief formation so that appropriate corrective measures might be developed.

REFERENCES

Abdellaoui, M. (2000). Parameter-free elicitation of utility and probability weighting functions. *Management Science, 11*, 1497–1512.

Allais, M. (1953). Le comportement de l'homme rationnel devant le risque, critique des postulates et axiomes de l'école américaine. *Econometrica, 21*, 503–546.

Anscombe, F.J. & Aumann, R.J. (1963). A definition of subjective probability. *Annals of Mathematical Statistics, 34*, 199–205.

Ayton, P. (1997). How to be incoherent and seductive: Bookmakers' odds and support theory. *Organizational Behavior and Human Decision Processes, 72*, 99–115.

Baron, J. (2001). *Thinking and Deciding* (3rd edn). Cambridge: Cambridge University Press.

Beach, L.R. & Wise, J.A. (1969). Subjective probability and decision strategy. *Journal of Experimental Psychology, 79*, 133–138.

Becker, S.W. & Brownson, F.O. (1964). What price ambiguity? On the role of ambiguity in decision making. *Journal of Political Economy, 72*, 2–73.

Bleichrodt, H.B. & Pinto, J.L. (2000). A parameter-free elicitation of the probability weighting function in medical decision analysis. *Management Science, 46*, 1485–1496.

Bleichrodt, H., Pinto, J.L. & Wakker, P.P. (2001). Making descriptive use of prospect theory to improve the prescriptive use of expected utility. *Management Science, 46*, 1498–1514.

Borel, É. (1924/1964). Apropos of a treatise on probability. In H. Kyburg & H. Smokler (eds), *Studies in Subjective Probability* (pp. 46–60). New York: Wiley.

Bowen, J. & Qui, Z. (1992). Satisficing when buying information. *Organizational Behavior and Human Decision Processes, 51*, 471–481.

Brenner, L.A. & Y. Rottenstreich (1999). Focus, repacking, and judgment of grouped hypotheses. *Journal of Behavioral Decision Making, 12*, 141–148.

Brun, W. & Teigen, K. (1990). Prediction and postdiction preferences in guessing. *Journal of Behavioral Decision Making, 3*, 17–28.

Camerer, C.F. & Ho, T.H. (1994). Violations of the betweenness axiom and nonlinearity in probability. *Journal of Risk and Uncertainty, 8*, 167–196.

Camerer, C.F. & Weber, M. (1992). Recent developments in modeling preferences: Uncertainty and ambiguity. *Journal of Risk and Uncertainty, 5*, 325–370.

Chipman, J.S. (1960). Stochastic choice and subjective probability. In D. Willner (ed.), *Decision, Values, and Groups* (vol. 1, pp. 70–85). Oxford, UK: Pergamon.

Chow, C.C. & Sarin, R.K. (2001). Comparative ignorance and the Ellsberg paradox. *Journal of Risk and Uncertainty, 2*, 129–139.

Chow, C.C. & Sarin, R.K. (1999). Choices under uncertainty: Known, unknown, and unknowable. Unpublished paper, University of California at Los Angeles.

Cohen, M., Jaffray, J.Y. & Said, T. (1985). Individual behavior under risk and under uncertainty: An experimental study. *Theory and Decision, 18*, 203–228.

Curley, S.P. & Yates, J.F. (1985). The center and range of the probability interval as factors affecting ambiguity preferences. *Organizational Behavior and Human Decision Processes, 36*, 272–287.

Curley, S.P. & Yates, J.F. (1989). An empirical evaluation of descriptive models of ambiguity reactions in choice situations. *Journal of Mathematical Psychology, 33*, 397–427.

deFinetti, B. (1937). La prévision: Ses lois logiques, ses sources subjectives. English translation in H.E. Kyburg & H.E. Smokler (eds) [1964], *Studies in Subjective Probability* (pp. 93–158). New York: Wiley.

DeGroot, M.H. (1970). *Optimal Statistical Decisions*. New York: McGraw-Hill.

Edwards, W.D. (1962). Dynamic decision theory and probabilistic information processing. *Human Factors, 4*, 59–73.

Einhorn, H.J. & Hogarth, R.M. (1986). Decision making under ambiguity. *Journal of Business, 59*, 225–249.

Eisenberger, R. & Weber, M. (1995). Willingness-to-pay and willingness-to-accept for risky and ambiguous lotteries. *Journal of Risk and Uncertainty, 10*, 223–233.

Ellsberg, D. (1961). Risk, ambiguity, and the Savage axioms. *Quarterly Journal of Economics, 75*, 643–669.

Ellsberg, D. (2001). *Risk, Ambiguity and Decision*. New York: Garland.

Fischhoff, B., Slovic, P. & Lichtenstein, S. (1978). Fault trees: Sensitivity of estimated failure probabilities to problem representation. *Journal of Experimental Psychology: Human Perception and Performance, 4*, 330–344.

Fishburn, P. & Kochenberger, G. (1979). Two-piece Von Neumann–Morgenstern utility functions. *Decision Sciences, 10*, 503–518.

Fox, C.R. (1999). Strength of evidence, judged probability, and choice under uncertainty. *Cognitive Psychology, 38*, 167–189.

Fox, C.R. & Birke, R. (2002). Lawyers exhibit subadditivity when forecasting trial outcomes. *Law and Human Behavior, 26*, 159–173.

Fox, C.R. & Rottenstreich, Y. (2003). Partition priming in judgment under uncertainty. *Psychological Science, 13*, 195–200.

Fox, C.R. & See, K.E. (2002). Testing the two-stage model in decision under uncertainty. Unpublished data, Fuqua School of Business, Duke University.

Fox, C.R. & Tversky, A. (1995). Ambiguity aversion and comparative ignorance. *Quarterly Journal of Economics, 110*, 585–603.

Fox, C.R. & Tversky, A. (1998). A belief-based account of decision under uncertainty. *Management Science, 44*, 879–895.

Fox, C.R. & Wakker, P.P. (2000). Value elicitation in Fox, Rogers & Tversky (1996): The method is flawed but the results are robust. Unpublished paper, University of Amsterdam.

Fox, C.R., Rogers, B.A. & Tversky, A. (1996). Options traders exhibit subadditive decision weights. *Journal of Risk and Uncertainty, 13*, 5–17.

Fox, C.R. & Weber, M. (2002). Ambiguity aversion, comparative ignorance, and decision context. *Organizational Behavior and Human Decision Processes, 88*, 476–498.

Friedman, M. & Savage, L.J. (1948). The utility analysis of choices involving risk. *Journal of Political Economy, 56*, 279–304.

Frisch D. & Baron, J. (1988). Ambiguity and rationality. *Journal of Behavioral Decision Making, 1*, 149–157.

Gigliotti, G. & Sopher, B. (1996). The testing principle: Inductive reasoning and the Ellsberg paradox. *Thinking and Reasoning, 2*, 33–49.

Gilboa, I. (1987). Expected utility with purely subjective non-additive probabilities. *Journal of Mathematical Economics, 16*, 65–88.

Gonzalez, R. & Wu, G. (1999). On the shape of the probability weighting function. *Cognitive Psychology, 38*, 129–166.

Heath, C. & Tversky, A. (1991). Preference and belief: Ambiguity and competence in choice under uncertainty. *Journal of Risk and Uncertainty, 4*, 5–28.

Hershey, J.C. & Schoemaker, P.J. (1980). Prospect theory's reflection hypothesis: A critical examination. *Organizational Behavior and Human Decision Processes, 25*, 395–418.

Hogarth, R.M. (1989). Ambiguity and competitive decision making: Some implications and tests. *Annals of Operations Research, 19*, 31–50.

Hogarth, R.M. & Einhorn, H.J. (1990). Venture theory: A model of decision weights. *Management Science, 36*, 780–803.

Hogarth, R.M. & Kunreuther, H. (1989). Risk, ambiguity, and insurance. *Journal of Risk and Uncertainty, 2*, 5–35.

Idson, L.C., Krantz, D.H., Osherson, D. & Bonini, N. (2001). The relation between probability and evidence judgment: An extension of support theory. *Journal of Risk and Uncertainty, 22*, 227–249.

Johnson, E.J., Hershey, J., Meszaros, J. & Kunreuther, H. (1993). Framing, probability distortions, and insurance decisions. *Journal of Risk and Uncertainty, 7*, 35–51.

Kahn, B.E. & Sarin, R.K. (1988). Modeling ambiguity in decisions under uncertainty. *Journal of Consumer Research, 15,* 265–272.

Kahneman, D. & Tversky, A. (1979). Prospect theory: An analysis of decision under risk. *Econometrica, 4,* 263–291.

Kahneman, D. & Tversky, A. (1984). Choices, values, and frames. *American Psychologist, 39,* 341–350.

Kahneman, D., Knetsch, J. & Thaler, R. (1990). Experimental tests of the endowment effect and the Coase theorem. *Journal of Political Economy, 98,* 1325–1348.

Kahneman, D., Slovic, P. & Tversky, A. (eds) (1982). *Judgment Under Uncertainty: Heuristics and Biases.* Cambridge: Cambridge University Press.

Karni, E. & Mongin, P. (2000). On the determination of subjective probability by choices. *Management Science, 46,* 233–248.

Keppe, H.J. & Weber, M. (1995). Judged knowledge and ambiguity aversion. *Theory and Decision, 39,* 51–77.

Kilka, M. & Weber, M. (2001). What determines the shape of the probability weighting function under uncertainty? *Management Science, 47,* 1712–1726.

Knight, F.H. (1921). *Risk, Uncertainty, and Profit.* Boston, MA: Houghton-Mifflin.

Koehler, D.J. (1996). A strength model of probability judgments for tournaments. *Organizational Behavior and Human Decision Processes, 66,* 16–21.

Koehler, D.J. (2000). Probability judgment in three-category classification learning. *Journal of Experimental Psychology: Learning, Memory, and Cognition, 26,* 28–52.

Kreps, D.M. (1990). *A Course in Microeconomic Theory.* Princeton, NJ: Princeton University Press.

Kunreuther, H., Meszaros, J., Hogarth, R.M. & Spranca, M. (1995). Ambiguity and underwriter decision processes. *Journal of Economic Behavior and Organization, 26,* 337–352.

Larson, J.R., Jr. (1980). Exploring the external validity of a subjectively weighted utility model of decision making. *Organizational Behavior and Human Performance, 26,* 293–304.

Luce, R.D. (2000). *Utility for Gains and Losses: Measurement-Theoretical and Experimental Approaches.* New York: Erlbaum.

Luce, R.D. & Fishburn, P.C. (1992). A note on deriving rank-dependent utility using additive finite first-order gambles. *Journal of Risk and Uncertainty, 11,* 5–16.

Macchi, L., Osherson, D. & Krantz, D. (1999). A note on superadditive probability judgment. *Psychological Review, 106,* 210–214.

MacCrimmon, K.R. (1968). Descriptive and normative implications of the decision-theory postulates. In K. Borsch & J. Mossin (eds), *Risk and Uncertainty* (pp. 3–32). London: Macmillan.

MacCrimmon, K.R. & Larsson, S. (1979). Utility theory: Axioms versus "paradoxes". In M. Allais & O. Hagen (eds), *Expected Utility and the Allais Paradox* (pp. 27–145). Dordrecht: D. Reidel.

Machina, M.J. & Schmeidler, D. (1992). A more robust definition of subjective probability. *Econometrica, 60,* 745–780.

March, J.G. & Shapira, Z. (1987). Managerial perspectives on risk and risk-taking. *Management Science, 33,* 1404–1418.

Markowitz, H. (1952). The utility of wealth. *Journal of Political Economy, 60,* 151–158.

Payne, J.W., Laughhunn, D.J. & Crum, R. (1981). Further tests of aspiration level effects in risky choice. *Management Science, 27,* 953–958.

Pratt, J.W., Raiffa, H. & Schlaifer, R.O. (1964). The foundations of decision under uncertainty: An elementary exposition. *Journal of the American Statistical Association, 59,* 353–375.

Prelec, D. (1998). The probability weighting function. *Econometrica, 66,* 497–527.

Preston, M. & Baratta, P. (1948). An experimental study of the auction-value of an uncertain outcome. *American Journal of Psychology, 61,* 183–193.

Quiggin, J. (1982). A theory of anticipated utility. *Journal of Economic Behavior and Organization, 3,* 323–343.

Rabin, M. (2000). Risk aversion and expected utility theory: A calibration theorem. *Econometrica, 68,* 1281–1292.

Raiffa, H. (1961). Risk, ambiguity, and the Savage axioms: Comment. *Quarterly Journal of Economics, 75,* 690–694.

Ramsey, F.P. (1931). Truth and probability. In R.B. Braithwaite (ed.), *The Foundations of Mathematics and Other Logical Essays by F.P. Ramsey* (pp. 158–198). New York: Harcourt, Brace.

Redelmeier, D.A., Koehler, D.J., Liberman, V. & Tversky, A. (1995). Probability judgment in medicine: Discounting unspecified possibilities. *Medical Decision Making, 15*, 227–230.

Rottenstreich, Y. & Hsee, C.K. (2001). Money, kisses, and electric shocks: An affective interpretation of probability weighting function. *Psychological Science, 12*, 185–190.

Rottenstreich, Y. & Tversky, A. (1997). Unpacking, repacking, and anchoring: Advances in support theory. *Psychological Review, 2*, 406–415.

Sarin, R.K. & Weber, M. (1993). Effects of ambiguity in market experiments. *Management Science, 39*, 602–615.

Savage, L.J. (1954). *The Foundation of Statistics*. New York: Wiley.

Schmeidler, D. (1989). Subjective probability and expected utility without additivity. *Econometrica, 57*, 571–587.

Shafer, G. (1986). Savage revisited. *Statistical Science, 1*, 463–501.

Sloman, S.A., Rottenstreich, Y., Hadjichristidis, C., Steibel, J.M. & Fox, C.R. (2003). Unpacking implicit probability judgment. Working paper, Brown University, Department of Cognitive and Linguistic Sciences.

Slovic, P. & Tversky, A. (1974). Who accepts Savage's axiom? *Behavioral Science, 19*, 368–373.

Taylor, K. (1995). Testing credit and blame attributions as explanation for choices under ambiguity. *Organizational Behavior and Human Decision Processes, 54*, 128–137.

Taylor, K. & Kahn, B. (1997). An investigation of consumer reactions to ambiguity: The effects of knowledge, control, and accountability. University of Pennsylvania, Wharton School, Working Paper 96–006.

Teigen, K.H. (1974). Subjective sampling distributions and the additivity of estimates. *Scandinavian Journal of Psychology, 24*, 97–105.

Tversky, A. (1967). Utility theory and additivity analysis of risky choices. *Journal of Experimental Psychology, 75*, 27–36.

Tversky, A. (1996). Contrasting rational and psychological principles of choice. In R.J. Zeckhauser, R.L. Keeney & J.K. Sebenius (eds), *Wise Choices* (pp. 5–21). Boston, MA: Harvard Business School Press.

Tversky, A. & Fox, C.R. (1995). Weighing risk and uncertainty. *Psychological Review, 102*, 269–283.

Tversky, A. & Kahneman, D. (1983). Extensional versus intuitive reasoning: The conjunction fallacy in probability judgment. *Psychological Review, 90*, 293–314.

Tversky, A. & Kahneman, D. (1986). Rational choice and the framing of decisions. *Journal of Business, 59*, 251–278.

Tversky, A. & Kahneman, D. (1991). Loss aversion in riskless choice: A reference dependent model. *Quarterly Journal of Economics, 106*, 1039–1061.

Tversky, A. & Kahneman, D. (1992). Advances in prospect theory: Cumulative representation of uncertainty. *Journal of Risk and Uncertainty, 5*, 297–323.

Tversky, A. & Koehler, D.J. (1994). Support theory: A nonextensional representation of subjective probability. *Psychological Review, 101*, 547–567.

Tversky, A. & Wakker, P.P. (1995). Risk attitudes and decision weights. *Econometrica, 63*, 1255–1280.

Tversky, A., Sattath, S. & Slovic, P. (1988). Contingent weighting in judgment and choice. *Psychological Review, 95*, 371–384.

von Winterfeldt, D. & Edwards, W. (1986). *Decision Analysis and Behavioral Research*. Cambridge: Cambridge University Press.

Wakker, P.P. (2001). Testing and characterizing properties of nonadditive measures through violations of the sure-thing principle. *Econometrica, 69*, 1039–1059.

Wakker, P.P. (in press). On the composition of risk preference and belief. *Psychological Review*.

Wakker, P.P. & Deneffe, D. (1996). Eliciting von Neumann–Morgenstern utilities when probabilities are distorted or unknown. *Management Science, 42*, 1676–1690.

Wu, G. & Gonazalez, R. (1996). Curvature of the probability weighting function, *42*, 1676–1690.

Wu, G. & Gonzalez, R. (1998). Common consequence effects in decision making under risk. *Journal of Risk and Uncertainty, 16*, 113–135.

Wu, G. & Gonzalez, R. (1999a). Dominance violations and event splitting in decision under uncertainty. Unpublished paper, University of Chicago.

Wu, G. & Gonzalez, R. (1999b). Nonlinear decision weights in choice under uncertainty. *Management Science, 45*, 74–85.

Yates, J. & Zukowski, L.S. (1976). Characterization of ambiguity in decision making. *Psychological Science, 21*, 19–25.

CHAPTER 15

Medical Decision Scripts: Combining Cognitive Scripts and Judgment Strategies to Account Fully for Medical Decision Making

Robert M. Hamm

University of Oklahoma, Oklahoma, USA

I. INTRODUCTION: SCRIPTS OR HEURISTIC STRATEGIES?

This chapter presents both the cognitive science and the judgment and decision making approaches to the psychology of clinical reasoning and medical decision making. The field of cognitive psychology and cognitive science has produced a general model of how people apply knowledge in practice (Anderson, 1993; Kintsch, 1998a), characterized by rapid recognition of complex representations. Although some researchers have used this framework in studying the psychology of medical decision making (Custers, Regehr & Norman, 1996; Norman, 2000), its potential has not been fully realized. The psychological research approach most closely associated with medical decision making—the field of judgment and decision making (JDM)—has used the general cognitive psychology model only superficially. In its comparisons of medical decision making behavior with decision theoretic norms, it has identified important phenomena (Chapman & Elstein, 2000). However, in practice, it has had limitations as a description of medical decision making and as a guide for improving it. Cognitive psychology's general model, represented by the "script" metaphor (Schank & Abelson, 1977), offers a powerful descriptive framework (Abernathy & Hamm, 1995) which, in combination with decision theory's normative framework, promises new progress for attempts to improve medical decision making (Goldstein & Weber, 1995; Hamm et al., 2000).

A wide variety of psychologists, educators, behavioral scientists, physicians and other health-care providers do research on the psychology of clinical reasoning and medical

Thinking: Psychological Perspectives on Reasoning, Judgment and Decision Making. Edited by David Hardman and Laura Macchi.
© 2003 John Wiley & Sons, Ltd.

decision making. This chapter will focus on their research on how *physicians* think while managing patients. Other providers, of course, think and make decisions in the same manner.

The chapter focuses on cognition during decision making, as the physician investigates the particular patient's problem and takes actions for the patient. "Decision making" is interpreted broadly, to include any examinations or tests selected in order to establish a diagnosis and prognosis, as well as the development of treatment plans and the choice among alternative treatments. Its scope also includes conversations for gathering information, sharing the decision making and giving instructions. Additionally, decision making for a particular patient can extend through time: information may not be available immediately, the situation may be changing, and some strategies may put off treatments, or even additional decision making, until later.

As will be described in Section II, psychologists using the general cognitive model to explain clinical reasoning have most commonly viewed diagnosis as a categorization process (see Custers et al., 1996; Norman, 2000). Their work describes the structure of knowledge, the recognition process, and the changes involved in learning, but has seldom addressed physician decision making. "What to do" is assumed to be part of the knowledge structure activated when the diagnosis is achieved (Charlin, Tardif & Boshuizen, 2000). Section III will describe the psychology of the deliberative aspects of medical decision making—comparing competing treatment options, considering the probability that a diagnosis is true or a treatment will have a satisfactory result, and assessing the utility of possible outcomes. These have received attention from the JDM psychologists (Elstein, 2000), working closely with physicians seeking to use decision theory to guide medical practice (Chapman & Elstein, 2000). The work on how physicians judge and interpret probabilities and use them when taking action addresses an essential component of medical decision making, uncertainty. This approach, however, has tended to focus on deviations from the use of normative principles when the physicians deliberate about unfamiliar questions (even if the content of the cases about which the unfamiliar questions are asked is familiar), and has neglected accounting for how physicians make decisions in their daily practice, particularly nondeliberative decisions. Section IV will advocate extending the cognitive psychology approach from medical categorization and diagnosis to medical decision making, in what might be called a "decision-script" approach. It is hoped that the former approach's realistic account of how people represent the world can sharpen the accuracy and broaden the applicability of our descriptions of the important phenomena of physician judgment and decision making.

II. SCRIPTS: THE COGNITIVE PSYCHOLOGY APPROACH TO MEDICAL DIAGNOSIS

Psychologists and medical educators studying clinical reasoning have adopted the most powerful of the cognitive psychology approaches to describe how physicians use knowledge to make a diagnosis. This framework incorporates the elements of associative memory, recognition, complex memory structures, rules, operations, search and so on, under a variety of names, to account for experts' use of knowledge in applied situations. I will use the term "script" to refer to the expert knowledge characterized by this approach. This was one of the concepts used by Schank and Abelson (1977) to describe how ambiguous sentences about everyday situations are understood through the listener's knowledge of such situations. For example, if a "restaurant script" were activated, it would allow someone to interpret a sentence such as "After they were seated, no one showed up until they started slapping the big, plastic-covered cards on the table", in terms of inattentive waiters and menus. Although many other terms refer to different aspects of people's knowledge and various theories about how it is organized, "script" has recently been used in medical psychology to refer to complex mental representations that are used by the experienced physician in making a decision about a patient (Feltovich, Spiro & Coulson, 1989; Schmidt, Norman & Boshuizen, 1990; Abernathy & Hamm, 1994, 1995; Charlin, Tardif et al., 2000). I will use the term "script" to refer to the approach generally, covering research by authors who did not use the term.

Cognitive Psychology's General Model: Rules Embodied in, and Applied to, a Semantic Network

The general cognitive psychology model is based on the image that knowledge is stored as a semantic network (Quillian, 1968; Johnson-Laird, 1988), with a node representing a particular concept connected to other nodes representing associated concepts. Thus, the node representing the idea of a disease might have connections to the nodes representing the symptoms associated with the disease (Pauker et al., 1976), the conditions that make people likely to catch the disease (Schmidt et al., 1990) and the treatments used for the disease. While a node is active, activation spreads along the connections to associated nodes. The degree of node activity can vary. The more active the node, the more likely the idea it represents is to be involved in the ongoing thinking. A node may need stimulating inputs from several sources before it is activated enough to influence other nodes.

Theorists using the semantic network metaphor have mapped the nodes not just to elementary facts (for example, features of a disease being connected to the name of the disease) but also to other levels of knowledge, including propositions, predicate-argument structures (Kintsch, 1998b), cases (Riesbeck & Schank, 1989), strategies, schemes and scripts (Greeno & Simon, 1988; Lesgold, 1988; Anderson, 1990). Custers et al. (1996) review the researchers in medical diagnosis who have favored analysis with each of these forms of knowledge.

Though the semantic network is assumed to be embodied in the brain's neurons, it is often modeled in terms of rules that have the form "If (condition), then (action)". If the nodes that represent the conditions of the rule are active enough, associated nodes that represent the rule's action will become active. This can be considered an internal, cognitive "pattern-recognition" process. The "action" nodes of the first rule may be, in turn, the "conditions" for other such rules, which now become active. A system with these characteristics can serve as a general purpose computer (Newell & Simon, 1972), and so this description is powerful enough to account for any thinking. This approach has been used to produce general models of human cognition (Newell, 1990; Anderson, 1993), and it is natural to apply it to medicine (Gilhooly, 1990; Schmidt et al., 1990; Abernathy & Hamm, 1995; Custers et al., 1996; Norman, 2000).

One of the strengths of the approach is its ability to model learning, the change in knowledge with experience (Anderson, 1990). Links can be strengthened, such that activation becomes more likely to spread along them. Nodes that are frequently activated at the same time tend to develop stronger mutual links. Thus, the medical student rehearsing a disease's symptoms, or seeing that many patients with those symptoms receive the label of that disease, establishes strong links between the presenting symptom nodes and the diagnosis nodes. This type of mechanism can also account for nodes being strengthened through confirmation of expectations, or through the experience of good outcomes. With such mechanisms of reinforcement, these models have the capability of internal, cognitive operant learning: ideas that have been reinforced in a situation come more quickly to mind in that situation.

Another significant feature of this type of model is the development of larger, more complicated knowledge structures ("chunks"). Through such a mechanism, all the knowledge a physician needs to represent the typical presentation of a disease can be activated at once (Feltovich, 1983), on the basis of one or two key symptoms seen in context (Elstein, Shulman & Sprafka, 1978). This can account for the rapidity of expert thought, for a node encoding a complex unit of knowledge can be activated with the same speed as a node representing a simple fact. It also can account for the difficulty experts have in explaining their thinking. When the complex knowledge units incorporate many elementary nodes, the included nodes may not be accessible to awareness. It also may explain the difficulty physicians have in changing their practices "at will". Nodes have to be active or in awareness in order to be amenable to being changed through the establishment of new links. One can learn a fact that logically implies one should do a new behavior in a situation, but this does not mean that fact will be active enough to influence behavior when next in that situation.

Application of Cognitive Psychology's Semantic Network Model to Medical Reasoning

The impetus for applying the general cognitive psychology model, with the central role it assigns to recognition, to medical reasoning was the evident inadequacy of an earlier approach, the theory that physicians apply general problem-solving strategies in order to do hypothetico-deductive reasoning when they make diagnoses. Several detailed studies of physician diagnostic reasoning in the 1970s showed that in diagnosis physicians use rapid pattern recognition to access their knowledge, rather than deliberate hypothetico-deductive reasoning (Elstein et al., 1978; Deber & Baumann, 1992; Elstein, 1992). This led researchers to explain medical reasoning in terms of the physicians' knowledge, rather than their reasoning skill: content rather than process. This parallels the insight from computer science which led to the "expert systems" movement: the recognition that it may be more effective to develop specialized knowledge structures than to use general problem-solving routines (Regehr & Norman, 1996).

Subsequent research focused on understanding how knowledge is learned, organized in memory and accessed later to solve problems (Norman, 2000, p. S127). Researchers have considered several different ways of organizing medical knowledge: hierarchies, networks, matrices, propositions, semantic axes and individual exemplars (Norman, 2000). Custers et al. (1996) compare the advantages and disadvantages of three types of memory organization theory. Accounts in terms of 1) prototypical combinations of features, or 2) collections of instances, can explain some important phenomena but fall short both empirically and conceptually. The third type, which includes semantic-network, schema and script models, is the only approach to modeling the structure of memory which can support diagnostic reasoning in addition to yes/no pattern recognition (Custers et al., 1996). Working within this framework, Patel, Evans and Groen (1989) observed the use of basic science knowledge in medical students' and physicians' reasoning about hypothetical patients, noting the features that changed with experience. McGaghie et al., (1996) used a Pathfinder scaling algorithm to represent the cognitive structure of students' concepts, before and after instruction. They observed that the students' structures became more similar to the structure of experts' knowledge, and those whose structures were most similar to the experts' tended to have higher scores on the test.

A recent paper on the effect of prior knowledge on diagnostic judgment illustrates the approach. Hatala, Norman and Brooks (1999) studied students', residents' and cardiologists' diagnoses of electrocardiograms (ECGs). Each of 10 ECGs was accompanied by a) no history (the control) or by a brief clinical history suggestive of either b) the correct diagnosis, or c) the most plausible alternative diagnosis. The history affected the subjects' diagnostic reading, increasing their probability for the suggested disease as well as the probability that they saw the features consistent with that disease. The results can be explained in terms of the prior activation of the disease concept influencing the subsequent processing of the ECG evidence pertinent to that disease. The clinical implications of the study are disturbing, of course. The physician managing such a patient and consulting another physician for interpretation of the ECG ideally wants the ECG results to be an independent piece of evidence that can be used to revise a prior probability. If the consultant's ECG interpretation is based on the referring physician's pre-existing beliefs, its contribution to the referring physician's diagnostic accuracy is greatly diminished. Hatala's results support the inseparable role of knowledge and context in what is ostensibly a pattern-recognition process based on visual features. The activation of the concepts is influenced by any knowledge the physician has, not solely by the information from the visual channel. This mechanism is also involved in the influence of pharmaceutical company representatives' quick pitches (Wazana, 2000), even when the physician intends not to be swayed (Reeder, Dougherty & White, 1993; Shaughnessy, Slawson & Bennett, 1995).

An important event in this field is Schmidt, Norman and Boshuizen's (1990) account of the development of medical knowledge, from statements of facts, to causal models of patho-physiological systems, to illness scripts which represent the disease knowledge activated by patients' clinical presentations, and finally to collections of case representations that collectively cover all possible clinical presentations. The sequence may indicate increased efficiency and complexity, or merely reflect the content of medical education. While each individual physician's knowledge may not develop through this exact sequence, the metaphor of the multiple representations, with different levels being available in the areas where one has different experience, is compelling.

Another key metaphor is that backward-search and forward-search strategies are available for diagnostic problem solving (Patel & Groen, 1986). For cases where the physician has much experience, the connection between case presentation and diagnosis involves activation flowing from case features to disease category. For cases where the physician has less experience, or that do not clearly match any disease category, the physician can reason backward from the known features of possible diseases, to the observable features of the case, in explicit hypothetico-deductive reasoning. Gilhooly (1990) suggests that experts actually use a mixture of the forward and backward reasoning.

A recent study claimed to find support for a scripts account of expertise, by using the theory to devise a measure of physician competence. Earlier studies using credentialing tests (Bordage et al., 1996), as well as tests of mastery of decision theoretic concepts (Berwick, Fineberg & Weinstein, 1981), had suggested the paradoxical result that physicians get less competent with years of experience. Charlin, Brailovsky and colleagues (2000) created tests based on what experts do. They let the most common answer on a test item define the right answer, an approach justified by Batchelder and Romney (1988). The test presented clinical scenarios and asked what should be done. All response options were plausible. The option chosen most often by a panel of experienced physicians was defined as the best response (with decreasing partial credit for the answers that were not quite as popular with the experts). On this test, more experienced physicians had higher scores. Although one might object to the "Panglossian" (Stanovich & West, 2000) assumptions of this approach—that the experts must be right because they are experts—this form of testing can be used to measure the extent to which physicians have adopted any given script. For example, the answer key could be based not on the script most popular with the experts, but on a script explicitly based on scientific evidence.

Custers et al. (1996) summarize the advantages of the scripts and semantic networks approach to medical diagnostic reasoning. Such models, which are more robust than the prototype or exemplar models, can account for reasoning as well as pattern recognition. They can explain the development of expertise, covering a variety of empirical observations, such as that physicians with intermediate levels of knowledge may do worse on "classic presentations" than those with little knowledge or those with high knowledge (Lesgold, 1984). They can also explain the reverse pattern, that those with intermediate knowledge may have better memory for cases than those with little, or high, knowledge (Green & Gilhooly, 1992; Schmidt & Boshuizen, 1993; van de Wiel, Schmidt & Boshuizen, 1998). Script models may be viewed as more relevant to what people actually do than an approach which insists that people get as close as possible to the conclusions that could be drawn by analytical use of statistical data (Norman, 2000). They can account for flexibility in physicians' reasoning, because of the multiple representations and multiple reasoning strategies that they acknowledge are available. Computational simulations can be made to test the assumptions and predictions of the models.

Custers et al. (1996) note, however, that the approach has several disadvantages. Most importantly, it may be too powerful (Johnson-Laird, Herrmann & Chaffin, 1984). There are so many different forms of representation, and processes for reasoning with them, that it is difficult to refute the general form of the model. Moreover, it is not enough to show that a theory predicts some aspect of behavior; one must also show that other theories do not predict it. Second, when descriptions done within this framework are not sufficiently precise, any experimental result can be fitted post hoc into a network, schema or script model. Colliver (2000) has emphasized this issue:

> It really isn't clear what knowledge networks are and it isn't clear what it means to say they are activated, and it certainly isn't clear what activates them and how much and whether different stimuli activate the networks in different amounts... [E]ducational theory and its basic research, on close examination, seem to be nothing more than metaphor and demonstration, nothing that taps into the underlying substrate of learning that would allow prediction and control. (p. 265)

Third, researchers characterizing the structure of medical knowledge should be cautious in interpreting verbal reports, because so much cognitive processing occurs without conscious awareness (Elstein, 2000). Fourth, when researchers model individual experts' knowledge structures, these are very different from each other. While this may be consistent with the notion that automatization leads to unawareness, such evidence cannot prove the automatization model correct. Fifth, doing research on the scripts requires both detailed observation and extensive inference, using previously developed models. This presents an imposing barrier to many researchers otherwise attracted to work in this area. Even those who have well-developed computer models of cognition find themselves searching for shortcut methods (Kintsch, 1998b). Finally, there has been little work applying the scripts approach of cognitive psychology to the important phenomena of medical decision making under uncertainty, other than "deciding" on a diagnosis.

III. THE JDM RESEARCHERS' APPROACH TO MEDICAL DECISION MAKING

While the researchers who applied the cognitive science approach to physicians' reasoning have focused primarily on diagnosis, the JDM researchers have addressed diagnosis, prediction and decision making. This difference in scope arises from the different tasks they consider physicians to be doing. For the first group, the physician's task is to use knowledge to solve the problem of what category to put the patient in, while the second group assumes the physician is making decisions under conditions of uncertainty (Elstein, 2000; Norman, 2000). While the first group is concerned about diagnostic accuracy, of course—how does the physician find the right disease?—the second group has explicit standards for good diagnosis and decision making against which to compare physicians' performance. This characteristic relationship with the standards is both the source of the JDM approach's powerful descriptive models and important findings, and a reason for its limitations.

In the JDM researchers' view, physicians' decisions are important because the wrong actions can lead to bad outcomes as well as wasting resources. Diagnoses, predictions and decisions are made in uncertain situations. Therefore, the question is not only, "Did the physician make the right diagnosis or decision in this case?" but also, "If the physician diagnoses or decides in this manner for every case, will there be as many good outcomes as there potentially could have been?"

The standard for optimal diagnosis in uncertain conditions is Bayes' theorem for using test results to adjust pre-existing degrees of belief (probabilities) about the possible diseases, as modified by receiver operating characteristic (ROC) analysis' considerations of the relative costs of the two distinct types of error, false positives and false negatives (Swets, Dawes & Monahan, 2000). The psychological questions here include the following. Can physicians judge those prior probabilities? If given diagnostic test results, can they adjust the probabilities appropriately, without neglecting the base rates? Can they interpret and use information about test sensitivity, specificity, likelihood ratio or ROC curve?

The standard for choosing alternative medical treatments is expected utility, which is the sum of the utilities of the consequences that could follow from the treatment, each weighted by their probability of occurrence (Weinstein & Feinberg, 1980). The standard for allocating limited resources among different needs is cost-effectiveness, which is the difference in cost due to the treatment, divided by the difference in effect due to the treatment (Mandelblatt et al., 1997). The corresponding questions are the following. Can physicians judge these utilities, costs and probabilities? Can they interpret and use information about probability, utility, cost, expected utility or cost effectiveness? Can they combine such information appropriately into an overall judgment of the preferability of a treatment?

The standard for a physician's prediction of a future outcome or estimate of an unobservable characteristic of the patient, based on an integration of the observable features of the patient, is to compare the physician's use of those features with the relative weights the features have in predicting the outcome or characteristic in a multivariate statistical model (Elstein, 1976; Stewart, 1988; Dawes, Faust & Meehl, 1989). The researchers' questions are the following. Can physicians judge the patient features accurately, whether these be categories or extents? Can they give appropriate weight to the various available cues when making their judgments? How reliably do physicians follow a judgment policy? Can they interpret and use information about relative weights, judgment accuracy and judgment consistency?

The JDM researchers, then, study how—and how well—physicians do each of the tasks that it is presumed they must do (consciously or unconsciously) in order to diagnose, predict or treat in an uncertain world. A variety of methodologies and designs are used for describing physician performance and comparing it to the standard. A prominent subset of these studies seeks to replicate in the medical realm phenomena observed in previous research on "heuristics and biases". Whether studying medical reasoning for itself or as an additional demonstration of known heuristic strategies, this body of research has made a number of significant findings.

The JDM research on medical decision making has been reviewed in numerous papers (Detmer, Fryback & Gassner, 1978; Dawson & Arkes, 1987; Sox et al., 1988; Elstein, 1992; Tape, Kripal & Wigton, 1992; Dawson, 1993; Wigton, 1996; Elstein, 1999; Chapman & Elstein, 2000; Dawson, 2000; Hamm et al., 2000) and books (Dowie & Elstein, 1988; Bergus & Cantor, 1995; Chapman & Sonnenberg, 2000). I now give examples of this approach, covering the different tasks required for decision making under uncertainty.

Perhaps the most fundamental task for medical diagnosis, prognosis and decision making is the judgment of probability. Because the probability that a patient has a disease is a necessary component of the formal analysis of diagnosis, it is assumed to be a key element of diagnostic reasoning. In one study, Poses, Cebul and Wigton (1995) studied physicians' judgments of the probabilities that their patients' sore throats were due to streptococcal infections. The probability judgments were high compared to laboratory-verified prevalence. There was also great variation, among physicians, in the role of different symptoms in the diagnosis. Green and Yates (1993, 1995) studied physicians' probabilities that patients in the emergency room concerned about chest pain actually have had a heart attack. The physicians' use of patient information was compared to the weight that a large study had shown should be given to the information. The physicians tended to underweight the diagnostic tests that best predict current heart attacks, and instead to rely on patient history information (such as smoking, hypertension and high cholesterol) which predicts the development of heart disease, but has very little relation to whether the patient is currently having a heart attack. Because it was plausible that these cues would help to diagnose heart attacks, though, in fact, they did not, Green and Yates (1993) called this an example of "pseudodiagnosticity" (Kern & Doherty, 1982; Wolf, Gruppen & Billi, 1988).

Accurate diagnosis requires that physicians change their degree of belief in a hypothesized disease appropriately when new information (about symptoms or test results) is received. For diseases where the physician typically uses one test at a time, as in AIDS or strep throat, it is possible to use Bayes' theorem to calculate the probability that the patient has the disease after the test results are known. This requires information about 1) the pre-test probability of the disease, 2) sensitivity, the likelihood the test will be accurate if the patient has the disease, and 3) specificity, the likelihood the test will be accurate if the patient does not have the disease (Weinstein & Feinberg, 1980). For a positive test,

$$\text{post-test probability} = \frac{\text{pretest probability} \times \text{sensitivity}}{\text{pretest probability} \times \text{sensitivity} + (1 - \text{pretest probability}) \times (1 - \text{specificity})}$$

Bergus and colleagues (Bergus et al., 1995; Chapman, Bergus & Elstein, 1996) studied primary care physicians' use of diagnostic information in a case of suspected stroke. The method was to give a booklet with new information on each page, and to ask for the physician's updated probability that the patient had a stroke, after each piece of information. Some respondents' booklets presented first the information favoring stroke and then the information making stroke unlikely. Other booklets presented the same information but in the reverse order. At each point, the answer could be compared to the Bayes' theorem answer (with realistic assumptions), and there was little systematic difference (though there was large variability). However, in comparing different presentation orders of the same two conflicting test results, a recency effect (see Hogarth & Einhorn, 1992) was revealed—the physicians' final probability was most influenced by the test result they had seen last.

In not finding that the physicians neglected base rate, this study contradicts a common finding in other domains (Bar-Hillel, 1980; Koehler, 1996) as well as two studies with medical content. Hamm and Miller (1988) showed that college students neglect base rate with hypothetical diseases and tests. They explained the neglect of base rate with reference to the subjects' confusion between the question, p(disease | test result), and the test sensitivity, p(test result | disease), which is the reverse conditional probability (Eddy, 1982; Dawes et al., 1993). A study by Hoffrage and Gigerenzer (1998) showed this same confusion, leading to base-rate neglect, in physicians thinking about hypothetical breast cancer screening cases. Using an alternative presentation of the same information, however, these medical decision makers made better use of the prior probability. The alternative presentation used "absolute" or "natural" frequencies rather than conditional probabilities. The multiplications and divisions of Bayes' theorem (see above) had already been done with reference to a particular reference population. Unfortunately, preparing this helpful display ahead of time could be misleading if the prior probability of the disease were different (as indeed may happen when women with high- or low-risk factors get screening mammography [Elmore et al., 1998]). Responses with absolute frequency displays are not always more accurate than responses with probabilities (Griffin & Buehler, 1999).

Accurate diagnosis also requires that physicians understand the potential value of the available information so that they can seek the most useful information when they ask questions (Gruppen, Wolf & Billi, 1991). Wolf, Gruppen and Billi (1985) studied first-year residents' choice of which information to request concerning the rate at which a symptom occurred with a disease, in an abstract diagnosis task. The physicians did not ask for all the needed information. In particular, they commonly neglected information on how often the observed symptom occurred in conjunction with the competing disease. Curley and colleagues (Connelly et al., 1990; Curley, Connelly & Rich, 1990) looked at physicians' use of sources for medical information pertinent to their patients' presentations (not test results, but information about the possible diseases) and found that physicians use the easily available information sources even though they recognize the information is of lower quality.

Decision making requires consideration of the probability a patient will experience an outcome if treated, or if not treated. Dawson (2000) reviewed a number of studies of physicians' accuracy in making judgments about future outcomes for actual patients. The accuracy, expressed as the area under the ROC curve, ranged from .63 to .89 (where .50 would be random, and 1.0 completely accurate). The calibration ranged from "small underestimation" to "large overestimation", depending in part on the prevalence of the outcome. Among the most accurate were expert intensive care unit (ICU) physicians' probability estimates that patients would survive their ICU stay. Indeed, these physicians were slightly more accurate than the predictions of the APACHE II model, a prediction rule derived from the data about a large number of patients (McClish & Powell, 1989). Among the least accurate, with moderate underestimation, were emergency department physicians' estimates of the probability of congestive heart disease patients' survival for 90 days (Poses et al., 1997). Poses has also observed that physicians' prognostic probabilities do not adjust sufficiently to new information (Poses et al., 1990) and that their judgments are swayed by irrelevant considerations (Poses & Anthony, 1991; Poses et al., 1991). The ways in which the accuracy of physicians' probability estimates depends on domain and task are not yet understood. Certainly, an important factor is the inherent predictability of the outcome from the available information.

Predictability is addressed by another approach to studying physicians' probability judgments that focuses on the use of information, comparing their judgments not just to the actual patient outcome, but to a best-fit model of how the outcome is related to the information. In this research, physicians make predictive probability judgments when given information about only the important features of the case, measured on an objective scale. These studies allow the researcher to analyze the sources of the physician's accuracy (and inaccuracy). For example, lens model analysis (Hammond et al., 1975; Stewart, 1988; Garb & Schramke, 1996; Wigton, 1996) can be done when information is available about the true state of the case in addition to the true cue measures and the physician's judgment. It permits the agreement between the physician's judgments and the true state to be partitioned into its sources in the physician's knowledge and judgmental consistency. Several studies have done lens model analysis of prognostic probability judgments (Stevens et al., 1994; Poses et al., 1997). This technique is particularly useful for identifying differences between individuals in their use of information (Kirwan et al., 1983).

The second elemental concept pertinent to medical decision making is the utility of the outcomes the patient may experience. The standard to compare the physician's judgments against—the patient's utilities—is difficult to assess, whether through conversation or formal measurement (Bursztajn & Hamm, 1982; Hamm, Clark & Bursztajn, 1984). Patient utilities measured with different methods do not fully agree (van der Donk et al., 1995; Law, Pathak & McCord, 1998; Lenert & Kaplan, 2000). It is unclear whether to give credence to the perspective of the patient before, during or after experiencing an outcome (Christensen-Szalanski, 1984; van der Donk et al., 1995; Gabriel et al., 1999). Nonetheless, when making decisions on behalf of a particular patient, the physician should understand the patient's evaluations of the possible outcomes. This is particularly important for those decisions which are driven by the individual patient's utilities, such as treatment for localized prostate cancer (Cowen et al., 1998) or for anticoagulation for atrial fibrillation (Protheroe et al., 2000). Some studies have shown that physicians are not very accurate in judging their patient's utilities or treatment preferences (Holmes et al., 1987; Druley et al., 1993; Teno et al., 1995; Hamm, Hicks & Bemben, 1996; Coppola et al., 2001). Family members, too, judge patients' preferences inaccurately (Sulmasy et al., 1998).

Presumably, physicians would judge utilities, for themselves or their patients, in the same manner that JDM research has shown that nonphysicians do. Prospect theory (Kahneman & Tversky, 1979; Tversky & Kahneman, 1992) holds that people evaluate gains and losses with reference to the status quo. This means their evaluations can be influenced by manipulating their reference point (Kahneman & Tversky, 1984), changing whether the outcomes are described as gains or losses. This has been demonstrated with a hypothetical Asian disease (Kahneman & Tversky, 1984) and the decision whether to treat a cancer with surgery or radiation (McNeil et al., 1982). However, the phenomenon has not proven robust in the medical realm. Framing effects were not found in communication about breast cancer to patients (Siminoff & Fetting, 1989), nor in 10 new contexts (Christensen et al., 1995) presented to physicians.

A prominent feature of health outcomes is the time when they occur. The closer an outcome is to the present, the more of an impression it makes (Chapman, 2000). This holds both for health states in the past (Redelmeier & Kahneman, 1992; Ariely & Zauberman, 2000) and for the anticipation of health states in the future. Changes in the evaluation of a future health state as a function of when it occurs are described with the concept of "discounting", in which value is a declining function of the time until the health state is experienced. Experimental psychologists favor using a hyperbolic function to characterize peoples' (Loewenstein & Prelec, 1992; Green, Fristoe & Myerson, 1994; Roelofsma & Read, 2000) or animals' (Ainslie, 1975; Mazur, 2001) discount rate,

$$\text{utility}_{\text{if experienced in future}} = \frac{\text{utility}_{\text{if experienced now}}}{1 + d \times t},$$

where d = the hyperbolic discount rate and t is the time delay. However, medical decision making researchers discount with the exponential function,

$$\text{utility}_{\text{if experienced in future}} = \frac{\text{utility}_{\text{if experienced now}}}{(1 + d)^t},$$

where d = the exponential discount rate, because it is consistent with the way economists discount money and calculate interest (Chapman & Elstein, 1995). There have been few studies of physicians' discount rates. Presumably, they would be similar to nonphysicians' discount rates for health states, which have been shown to vary greatly between people, to range (between elicitation methods, and between individuals) from very highly positive (Cairns, 1992; Chapman & Elstein, 1995; Chapman, 1996) to slightly negative (Loewenstein & Prelec, 1993; Hamm & Sieck, 2000), to be higher for short delays than long delays (Bleichrodt & Johannesson, 2001) (possibly due to the researchers' use of the exponential rather than the hyperbolic function), and to be influenced by factors which should be irrelevant, such as gains versus losses, small magnitude versus large magnitude, the domain of the outcome (health versus money) (Chapman, 1996), and the way the assessment method clarifies the extension of the health state through time (Hamm & Sieck, 2000).

Other explanations of temporal effects propose that time affects different aspects of the outcome in different ways. For example, Busemeyer et al. (2000) suggest that some reversals of preference as a decision nears are due to the negative attributes of the outcome being discounted more steeply than the positive attributes. Though an option was attractive when far in the future, as it nears, its disadvantages loom larger. Trope and Liberman (2000) discard the notion that people discount, suggesting instead that the distribution of the person's attention over the important and unimportant attributes of outcomes may vary with temporal distance. Attention is distributed broadly over all aspects when the outcome is in the near future, but distributed narrowly, to only the most important attributes, when it is far in the future.

Within the JDM framework, one may evaluate physicians not only on how accurately they judge probabilities and utilities, but also on how they combine these in decision making. The medical treatments physicians choose are not always those that a decision analysis using their own probabilities and utilities would prescribe. For example, Elstein and colleagues (Elstein et al., 1986; Elstein, Dod & Holzman, 1989) constructed decision-analytic models of the decision whether to prescribe estrogen after menopause, based on individual physicians' beliefs. Estrogen (with progesterone) promises to protect against osteoporosis and heart disease, but it also threatens to increase the probability of breast cancer. The physicians stated their probabilities for the good and bad outcomes, as well as their utilities for the outcomes. They also stated whether they would recommend hormone replacement for each of 12 hypothetical women patients. The physicians indicated for many patients that they would not recommend hormone replacement, although the decision analyses based on their probabilities and utilities indicated hormone replacement was preferred. Analysis of their reasons indicated that the physicians were most concerned about avoiding causing cancer, similar to the motivations for the "omission bias" (Ritov & Baron, 1990). A general "practice style" may govern physicians' decisions more than the perceived benefit in the particular case (Elstein et al., 1999).

A similar inconsistency has been found between *patients'* preferences and physicians' treatment decisions (Protheroe et al., 2000). Atrial fibrillation patients' preferences regarding the risk and benefits of treatment with warfarin underwent individualized decision analysis. Warfarin can prevent ischemic stroke (due to clots blocking blood vessels), but also can make hemorrhagic stroke (due to bleeding) more likely. Patients' stroke risks and the effect of warfarin on those risks were derived by applying rules derived from previous studies. Patients judged the utilities of the possible outcomes by the time trade-off method. There was substantial inconsistency between the recommendations of the individualized decision analyses and the treatments the patients actually received. Given the within-physician inconsistency demonstrated in the estrogen-replacement study (Elstein et al., 1986), and patients' reported aversion to any risk of cancer (Lydakis et al., 1998) and underestimation of risk of cardiovascular disease (Holmes-Rovner et al., 1996), it is not clear whether explicit analysis of individual risks and preferences, and communication about their implications, would change this physician–patient inconsistency.

According to the principle of "regularity", the way physicians integrate the probabilities and utilities about treatment options should not change if an additional option is made available. Redelmeier and Shafir (1995) demonstrated a violation of this principle. Family physicians were given a hypothetical vignette describing a patient with osteoarthritis of the hip, who has tried several nonsteroidal anti-inflammatory drugs (NSAIDs) without success. In the vignette shown to some physicians, the patient is considering whether to get a hip operation or try another NSAID. Other participants' vignette was identical, except that a second new NSAID was also considered. Among those physicians offered just two treatments, 53 percent chose the operation and 47 percent the NSAID. Offered the operation and two different NSAIDS, 72 percent chose the operation and 28 percent one of the NSAIDs. The fact that adding a treatment option increased the proportion choosing one of the original options violates the principle of regularity. Chapman and Elstein (2000) hypothesized that the physicians chose the operation to avoid having to think about choosing between the two similar NSAIDs.

The studies reviewed above illustrate how physicians do the various tasks whose importance is recognized by the general JDM framework—the components of rational decision making. The studies have some characteristics in common: they articulate a standard for a situation, observe physicians' behavior and compare it to the standard. Some of them simply count right and wrong answers, just enough to show that physicians, too, manifest a familiar bias (for example, Redelmeier & Shafir, 1995), or do not (Christensen-Szalanski & Beach, 1982; Hoffrage & Gigerenzer, 1998). Others used more elaborate methodologies to describe what the physicians do in the situation (e.g., Wigton, Hoellerich & Patil, 1986; Bergus et al., 1995). Some studies showed physicians' performance to be of high quality (McClish & Powell, 1989; Hoffrage & Gigerenzer, 1998), while others showed it to be inaccurate or inconsistent (Elstein et al., 1986; Poses & Anthony, 1991). Some studies demonstrated that the phenomena of the heuristics and biases school are useful for explaining what physicians do (e.g., McNeil et al., 1982), but in others the expected biases were not observed (e.g., Christensen et al., 1995).

A theme of this chapter is that the JDM approach to medical decision making has not made sufficient use of key concepts from cognitive psychology concerning the representation and utilization of knowledge. At the same time, it is well known that the approach is grounded in cognitive psychological theory. Indeed, both in its founding metaphors (Simon, 1956; Tversky, 1973) and in its ongoing practice, the approach has referred to cognitive psychology ideas, and there have been frequent interaction and mutual influence between JDM and the broader field (Hastie, 1991). A brief review of the main forms of explanation used in JDM research can clarify the degree to which cognitive psychology has been used in explaining the psychology of medical decision making. The cognitive processes that have been central to research on decision making, including medical decision making, are the role of associative memory in judgment, the mechanisms for judging unidimensional and multidimensional stimuli, the hard or easy strategies people may use to accomplish a decision-making task and the multiple modes of cognition, including affect. Although the role of complex, automated knowledge structures—scripts—has received little attention in JDM research, the field has long worked with many of its components.

Associative Memory

In an insightful review, Arkes (1991) identified association-based errors as one of the key process explanations invoked by JDM researchers. Judgment errors induced by automated recall mechanisms are one of the costs of our otherwise highly adaptive system of associations within semantic memory. An example is the availability heuristic—overestimation of the likelihood of possible events, or diagnostic categories, when instances come easily to mind because they are frequently publicized, they happened recently or they were originally intensely experienced (Tversky, 1973). In response to the criticism that many heuristics and biases "remain nothing more than informally worded verbal descriptions of psychological processes" (p. 180), Dougherty, Gettys and Ogden (1999) developed an explicit, associative memory-based theory of likelihood judgments. Simulations that express this theory in terms of the strength of traces in episodic memory provided plausible explanations for 10 familiar JDM biases, including availability and base-rate neglect, as well as for some expert–novice differences. Such a memory model for deliberate probability judgment by reference to the traces of similar past experiences is an important part of the total explanation of medical decision making, though, of course, it is distinct from a script representation accounting for expert expectations in routine situations, and from the representation-building that is characteristic of the expert physician deliberating about nonroutine cases.

Psychophysical Judgments

Psychologists studying sensory processes ask people to rate qualities or intensities of physical stimuli, such as light or sound. Comparison of these numerical judgments to the numerical measures of the physical stimulus allows the derivation of a psychophysical function. The subjects' numerical judgments are presumably a function of the intensity of neural activity subsequent to the transduction of the physical energy.

Arkes (1991) pointed out that the psychophysical judgment metaphor underlies many of the JDM theories, and Chapman and Elstein (2000) identified examples in medical decision-making research. For example, prospect theory (Kahneman & Tversky, 1979) assumes that when people form their preferences for "prospects"—options that have specified probabilities that outcomes with specified gains or losses will occur—they apply an "uncertainty weight" function to the probabilities. This function underestimates the higher probabilities and overestimates the lower ones. The revised cumulative prospect theory's uncertainty weights (Tversky & Kahneman, 1992; Wakker & Stiggelbout, 1995; Fennema & Wakker, 1997; Bayoumi & Redelmeier, 2000; Miyamoto, 2000) differ only in that the impact of the probability of an outcome is a function of the probabilities of all the more attractive (for gains) or less attractive (for losses) outcomes as well. Both prospect theories also posit a "value function" in which the amount of good or bad in each outcome is evaluated with respect to a reference point, the status quo usually, and there are separate concave value functions for losses and gains (Kahneman & Tversky, 1979; Lenert, Treadwell & Schwartz, 1999; Treadwell & Lenert, 1999).

Judgment Based on Multiple Cues

A third psychological process explicitly studied by the JDM approach is the integration of multiple pieces of information into an overall judgment. This is applicable to medical tasks such as judging the probability of a diagnosis from a number of features (Speroff, Connors & Dawson, 1989), judging the importance of a symptom in signaling a patient has a disease (Price & Yates, 1993), judging the utility of an outcome from multiple features (de Bock et al., 1999) or judging the expected utility of a treatment from the utilities of the outcomes weighted by the probabilities those outcomes will occur. Researchers describing physicians' performance of these tasks use statistical models fit to judgments of multiple cases to characterize the relation between the input and output, such as analysis of variance (Anderson, 1970), multiple regression (Wigton, 1988) or discriminant analysis (Carson et al., 1999).

Strategy Choice

Another key explanatory mechanism from JDM research that is helpful for explaining medical decision making is the optional use of strategies for processing the available information to accomplish the given task. Recognition that the physician has more than one way to deliberate about the patient's symptoms in estimating the probability of a disease, for example, leads researchers to compare the performance of the available strategies and to explain why a particular strategy is chosen. Thus, Wolf et al. (1985) invoked the strategy concept to explain how residents selected information in a diagnostic task. The task's goal was to learn which of two novel diseases was the likely cause of a hypothetical patient's illness. The patient had two symptoms, and the sensitivity of one symptom for one disease was given. The resident could select one more piece of information from three options: the sensitivity of that symptom for the other disease, or the sensitivity of the other symptom for either disease. Only 24 percent of the residents consistently selected the sensitivity of the first symptom for the second disease, which was the best answer because it allowed them to compare the sensitivity of one known symptom for both diseases. About 97 percent of those who used this strategy, the "competing hypotheses heuristic", got the right answer, while only 53 percent of those who used a different strategy did. This study is typical of the strategy approach. It defined a very simple information-processing strategy, characterized physicians as users or nonusers of the strategy, and showed that using the strategy affects the accuracy of decision making. The task, being novel, invited conscious choice of strategy and conscious strategy execution. In other situations, both choice and execution may be done unconsciously or automatically.

Affect or Emotion

Medical decision making may be influenced by the physician's affect. Emotions differ from modes of cognition mainly in that they also have a feeling component. Isen and colleagues have demonstrated that positive affect facilitates medical problem solving (Isen, Daubman & Nowicki, 1987; Isen, Nygren & Ashby, 1988; Isen, Rosenzweig & Young, 1991), and have linked affect to the activation of brain systems (Ashby, Isen & Turken, 1999). The classic conception of anxiety as an aversive state can explain physicians' avoidance of anxiety-provoking hypotheses (Di Caccavo & Reid, 1995; Allison et al., 1998), conversations (Annunziata et al., 1996), treatments (Bradley, 1992) or stages of problem solving in which there is a large amount of uncertainty (Bursztajn et al., 1990; Allison et al., 1998) or risk (Loewenstein et al., 2001), as well as their practice of "anxiety-based medicine" (Mold & Stein, 1986) when they should be practicing "evidence-based medicine". Stress can be thought of as an attention narrower (Easterbrook, 1959) or a stimulus to adopt simpler response rules, but also as a performance disrupter (Hammond, 1999). There has been little attention to these concepts in medical decision-making research, other than observations of the effects of residents' sleep deprivation on performance (Deaconson et al., 1988; Laine et al., 1993).

IV. DECISION SCRIPTS

This section will sketch a "decision-scripts" approach to the psychology of medical decision making. This holds that to understand physician decision making it is necessary to consider the physician's knowledge of the disease, which is best described by the general cognitive psychology model, taking a scripts approach, as described in Section II. It contrasts with the notion that physicians have a general decision-making procedure which they apply to each decision they must make, a procedure based on the perception of the degree of probability of possible events and the degree of value of the possible consequences (Goldstein & Weber, 1995). Cognitive psychology's general model of how people apply knowledge in practice can complement the past work done within the JDM approach in helping us understand the way physicians make decisions, just as it provides a good account of how they make diagnoses (see Abernathy & Hamm, 1995; Patel, Arocha & Kaufman, 1999; Norman, 2000). The relations and boundaries between the two approaches to medical decision making have been explored in several recent papers (Regehr & Norman, 1996; Elstein, 2000; Norman, 2000).

The decision-scripts approach cannot stand alone in accounting for decision-making behavior. However, the JDM approach has often left something out. It has not adequately dealt with the fact that most "decisions" physicians make are routine. Doctors hear the patient's complaint, recognize the problem as a familiar one and treat it in the usual way. The physician does not deliberate about probabilities and utilities to decide which alternative is best. Nor does the physician quickly and intuitively process the probabilities and utilities, using heuristic strategies. Rather, the decision to treat is built into the knowledge structure that has been activated; in most cases, the action is taken without any activation of decision-theoretic concepts (Hamm et al., 2000). Furthermore, in that minority of cases where the physician acknowledges the need to consider diagnostic or prognostic uncertainties, or trade-offs among benefits and side effects, the more elaborate decision-making process starts with the memory representation activated by that same recognition process (Crozier & Ranyard, 1997). Just as diagnosis usually works at the syndrome-recognition level (see symptoms S; identify disease D), but can open up to biomedical reasoning when pattern recognition fails to supply an answer (Feltovich et al., 1989; Schmidt et al., 1990), so also does treatment choice usually work at the syndrome level (for disease D, do treatment T), but can open up to decision-making reasoning when needed. Such reasoning attends, in some way, to the likelihood of disease (dependent on test accuracies and disease prevalence) and of good or bad outcomes (dependent on treatment efficacies and patient robustness), and to the value of the possible outcomes, and it integrates conflicting considerations into a decision.

In the general decision-script view, the physician's default approach when first the pa-tient's situation is recognized is a function of both the situation and the physician's knowl-edge. The content of the decision script, the features of the patient and the match between the features and the script jointly determine whether the physician simply performs a treat-ment or engages in a decision-making process. That is, a sequence of thoughts, questions, judgments and statements that we would recognize as "a physician making a decision with decision theory" can be part of a decision script in the same way that a sequence of ques-tions, tests and treatment actions that we would call "a routine response to a recognized pattern of symptoms" can. The expert's script includes the initial response, the alternative backup responses and what to do when none of the responses is quite appropriate. The use of reasoning about the decision—option seeking, estimating the uncertainties (possi-bly measuring the probabilities), considering the consequences (possibly measuring them) and making overall assessments of, and comparisons among, options—could be a part of a physician's decision script. Whether it is depends on training, personal preference for decision style, situational expectations and constraints, and all the other factors that create the expert's knowledge.

Another element of expert reasoning that is essential to the decision-script account, but that cannot be called part of a decision script per se, is reflection. This is involved in monitoring whether the current understanding of the situation is adequate, and in judging whether one of the script's options is likely to be effective in the situation. This reflection helps the physician become aware of the need to make changes in the approach to the current situation, and provides the conditions for the development of new responses (changes in script). When the physician becomes aware of a mismatch between the script's pattern and the patient, it is an opportunity to seek more information or engage in more effortful deliberation (Hamm, 1988; Payne, Bettman & Johnson, 1993; Klein, 1997). Learning— change or development of decision scripts—is accomplished by incorporating a successful solution—a newly figured out variant of patient presentation and the appropriate response to it—into the decision script, available for future use (Anderson, 1990; Abernathy & Hamm, 1995). Reflecting on one's script may depend on the physician's having spare working-memory capacity (Abernathy & Hamm, 1995), a factor which is influenced by the degree to which the knowledge necessary for processing the situation has been condensed into efficient chunks, by the availability of "long-term working memory" for temporary storage of information about the situation (Ericsson & Kintsch, 1995), by the lack of competing distractions in the environment, by the level of stress or arousal (Hammond, 1999) and by the individual's breadth of working-memory capacity (Lohse, 1997; Engle et al., 1999).

JDM researchers working in areas other than medicine have recognized the importance of the decision maker's memory representation for the particular domain. Klein (1997) and Beach (1990) have developed broad theories based on the person's knowledge, incorporating contingent decision-making strategies. Similarly, the approaches of Shanteau (1992), Gigerenzer (2000) and Hogarth (2001) refer to people's knowledge in their accounts of judgment and decision making in realistic situations, in particular to explain adequate performance in the absence of analytic effort.

Perhaps the most useful framework is that of Goldstein and Weber (1995). They emphasized the importance of content, what the decision is about. People use different representations and decision processes when deliberating about different types of options; for example, gambles, stocks, personal relationships (see also Rettinger & Hastie, 2001) or medical treatments. The factors that content may affect include encoding and representation of the information, domain-specific rules for manipulating the encoded information and the effects of attention mechanisms that may be different in different situations. They describe four modes of decision making in which there are distinct memory representations and processes of deliberation.

"Nondeliberative decision making" is a mechanism by which decisions may be made in repeatedly encountered situations. "[T]he decision maker recognizes the alternative or situation as a member of a category for which a judgment or action has already been stored. There may have been deliberation on previous occasions, but if judgment or action is required subsequently, it is only retrieved" (Goldstein & Weber, 1997, p. 594). In common with the scripts approach to medical diagnosis (Section II), this account of decision making speaks of the person having a large number of categories (for physicians, previous care episodes; Weber et al., 1993), the rapid recognition of situations by activating a category and the easy retrieval of actions associated with the categories.

Goldstein and Weber distinguish three modes of deliberative decision making. "Associative deliberation" is a process of paying attention to the various aspects of the situation unsystematically. "Each successive consideration inclines the decision maker toward a particular course of action, either augmenting or counteracting the effects of previous considerations. The decision is resolved when the cumulative effects of the considerations sufficiently incline the decision maker toward a course of action" (Goldstein & Weber, 1997, p. 595). "Rule-based deliberation", in contrast, processes the features of the situation systematically, because the person is following a set of rules, stored in some sort of procedure memory. This use of procedure memory may be conscious or unconscious, depending on the person's history and the demands of the situation (Goldstein & Weber, 1995). This would describe a physician who was following a sequence of steps for producing a decision, whether it be the arithmetic calculations needed for a decision-theoretic measure of the expected utility of a decision, or a sequence of yes/no judgments as laid out in a clinical algorithm (Nichols, Hyslop & Bartlett, 1991).

The highest level in Goldstein and Weber's typology is "schema-based deliberation", in which the decision maker works with the representation of the situation. The distinguishing characteristics are "(1) that judgments and choices proceed by fitting a pre-existing knowledge structure to the available information and by fleshing it out with inferred information and relations, and (2) that the judgments and choices themselves depend partly on an assessment of the adequacy of the resulting instantiated structure as an organization of the information" (Goldstein & Weber, 1997, p. 598). While this mode is inspired by Pennington and Hastie's (1988) account of jury deliberation, Goldstein and Weber (1995) suggest the organizing structures need not be causes (as in a narrative that explains a defendant's role in a crime), but could also be categories (such as diseases) or activities (such as plans for managing diseases).

Goldstein and Weber's (1995) description of four distinct modes by which decisions are made offers a full framework for understanding the role of content knowledge in medical decision making. Its building blocks are all three main types of long-term memory—declarative, episodic and procedural—and it includes conscious and unconscious processes, as well as analysis and intuition. For full coverage of the scope of the "decision-scripts" metaphor, it needs to account for which modes of decision-making deliberation physicians use in which conditions. It must articulate why different ways of using knowledge structures in decision making may appear for different diseases (within individual physician), for the same physician and the same disease at different points in time (changing with increased experience, with increased time pressure or just as a matter of momentary preference), or as a characteristic of a field/specialty that differs between locations or schools and changes over time. Studies verifying this prediction of different decisions in different situations would provide support for the general notion that the decision-making process depends on content. Given the current state of the field, this would be useful, but it would serve mainly as an invitation for the more detailed work of characterizing the modes and the conditions under which they are adopted.

As demonstrations that the physicians' knowledge is relevant to our understanding of medical decision-making, the studies to be reviewed next have a consistent theme. Each provides evidence of different decision making processes, according to the degree of the decision maker's medical expertise about the content. Many of these results surprised the researchers, but they are consistent with a decision-scripts account.

Ignoring Decision-Relevant Information in Familiar Situations

Elstein et al. (1999) showed critical care clinicians six realistic case vignettes, and asked them to assess the benefits of several treatments and to select treatments for the patients. Each case was given (to different respondents) in two versions, varying the probability of survival. Respondents indicated which of a list of possible management options they recommended, and estimated the probability of survival given their recommended treatment(s). Surprisingly, neither treatment choice nor perceived treatment benefit depended on the manipulated prognostic probability. The physicians simply followed their practice style—high treatment versus low treatment—on all six cases. This is consistent with each vignette activating a decision script. When following their scripts, these physicians did not process information, such as probabilities, that we would consider highly relevant to the decision, but instead responded with their script's standard response. Perhaps with a different education, physicians could learn to use the probability information. The cross-vignette consistency is a phenomenon that should be explored. Is it that the physician has learned one general "critical care" script, or learned multiple scripts but in the same learning environment? Or is it that the physician, possessing a stable degree of tolerance for uncertainty, tends to construct scripts that handle uncertainty in a similar manner?

Ubel, Jepson and Asch (2000) showed physicians hypothetical patient scenarios, and asked them to decide whether to recommend that the patient get the described cancer-screening procedure. The scenario was varied among the physicians. Some scenarios described a familiar screening procedure, for which there is a well-established script (breast, cervical and colorectal cancers), while the others did not activate a script (gastric cancer, cervical cancer with a novel screening procedure and an unlabeled cancer). The vignette also provided one of several types of information about the cost-effectiveness of the screening procedure: its cost per year of life saved, compared to no screening; the incremental cost-effectiveness ratio (extra cost per extra year of life saved, compared to the costs and effects of a basic screening program); or no cost information. In familiar scenarios, the cost information had no effect on the physician's willingness to recommend screening. In unfamiliar scenarios, physicians were less willing to recommend more expensive screening, especially when incremental cost-effectiveness ratios (which tend to be very high) were given as compared to raw cost-effectiveness. The authors' explanation, that physicians are "set in their ways", can be restated in decision-script terms. Physicians have a well-learned script for familiar screening decisions, which is not affected by cost-effectiveness information, since they follow the script instead of "making a decision". But when the screening situation is unfamiliar, they have no basis for a response other than to think about its advantages and disadvantages, and hence they use the cost-effectiveness information.

A third example of physicians ignoring decision-relevant information (probability) when it does not fit in their pre-existing way of managing a situation (end-of-life care) is the unexpected failure of the SUPPORT study (SUPPORT Principal Investigators, 1995), which was discussed by Hamm et al. (2000).

Not Making Heuristic-Based Errors in Familiar Situations

Bergus and colleagues (Bergus et al., 1995; Chapman et al., 1996) found that physicians thinking about hypothetical patients in a familiar, realistic diagnosis vignette did not neglect the disease's base rate (despite some order effects, described above). This contrasts with the base-rate neglect shown by nonphysicians and by physicians asked to revise probabilities after diagnostic tests in vignettes about hypothetical diseases (Casscells, Schoenberger & Graboys, 1978). A possible explanation is that the decision script for a familiar diagnostic situation imposes a structure on the representation of the situation that does not permit the physician to confuse the meaning of the conditional probabilities, the sensitivity (probability of finding given disease) and the post-test probability (probability of disease given finding). That is, they know enough about the situation that they can take the information in the problem presentation and put it in the appropriate place as they build a representation of the situation (Koehler, 1996). This prevents them from making the one major error that drives the usual base-rate neglect demonstrations, the confusion of p(disease|sign) and p(sign|disease) (Dawes et al., 1993; Hamm, 1996).

A similar result was found with vignettes that presented people with a choice to continue investing in a course of action that now has a very low chance of success or to cut losses. People generally have difficulty in ignoring the "sunk costs". Vignettes with medical content (whether to continue the current, ineffective medical management strategy) and nonmedical content (whether to continue with prepaid music lessons one does not enjoy) were presented to undergraduate students and to physicians in residency training. The residents were less likely than the undergraduates to exhibit the sunk cost "bias" when dealing with the four medical vignettes, but they showed it equally as often with the four nonmedical vignettes (Bornstein, Emler & Chapman, 1999). Chapman and Elstein (2000) attribute this to "decision rules specific to medicine, such as choosing the most effective treatment", which enable physicians "to override the sunk cost fallacy in the medical domain" (Chapman and Elstein, 2000, p. 195). An alternative explanation may be that the script generally used for managing the particular disease includes responses for when the initial treatment does not work. Such a script need not include "decision rules" that explicitly assess and choose the most effective treatment. Decision scripts typically consist of specific "what to do when" rules rather than general "how to make a good decision" rules.

Physicians should choose the same treatment, independent of changes in how the options are described. But it has been shown that changing the "frame"—the reference point implicit in the description of the outcomes—can change people's preference between treatments for hypothetical or real diseases (McNeil et al., 1982; Kahneman & Tversky, 1984). Christensen et al. (1995) explored the generality of this framing effect with 12 medical vignettes, with physician subjects. They replicated the framing effect with the hypothetical Asian disease (Kahneman & Tversky, 1984), but the frame did not influence the choice in the expected direction for any of the 11 realistic diseases. This is consistent with the notion that the familiar scripts may prevent the simple manipulation of the frame from influencing physicians' preferences. It has not been established whether (a) physicians' understanding of the situation, embodied in their scripts, is so good that they cannot be misled by the framing manipulation, or (b) their scripted understanding is such a strong determinant of what to do that they do not even make the judgment that would be influenced by the frame.

O'Connor and colleagues (O'Connor et al., 1985; O'Connor, 1989; Sullivan et al., 1996) found that patients' and nonpatients' preferences for hypothetical cancer treatments were influenced by whether the outcomes were framed in terms of survival rate or death rate. A similar study was done for patients with chronic lung disease considering whether to receive an influenza vaccine, where it was possible to observe the patients' actual vaccination decisions. Framing had no influence in this nonhypothetical decision in which the patients were considerably involved (O'Connor, Pennie & Dales, 1996). Siminoff and Fetting (1989) similarly found no framing effects with breast cancer patients' actual treatment decisions.

Learning a Script by Exposure to Analytic Aids—So the Aids are not Needed

Green and Mehr (1997) made a heart attack diagnosis decision aid available in emergency rooms, to see whether it would enable physicians to distinguish more accurately those patients with chest pain who had a high probability of heart attack. The goal was to reduce the number of low-probability patients who were being unnecessarily admitted to hospital. However, before the study started, the researchers explained the key features that the decision aid worked with to the physicians, as part of the process of securing their participation in the study. The behavior of the physicians underwent an abrupt change at the time of the lecture, rather than changing as an effect of the presence or absence of the decision aid. A plausible explanation is that they learned the basic decision script from the lecture.

Wellwood, Johannessen and Spiegelhalter (1992) showed that a computer-based clinical decision support system designed to improve the diagnosis of abdominal pain (de Dombal et al., 1972) was effective at training physicians, due to its requirement for structured data input. Novice clinicians using the computer program learned to collect the relevant data, thus improving their unaided diagnostic accuracy to a level comparable to that of their computer-aided diagnosis. After this demonstration, enthusiasm for using the decision aid declined. Hence, unfortunately, the training advantage was lost (Hamm et al., 2000). The decision aid, like Green and Mehr's (1997) lecture, provided training in "what to pay attention to" for the problem of diagnosing abdominal pain, as well as showing what diagnosis is given for various combinations of features. It can be viewed as an effective way to teach the physician the script.

These examples support the claim that the content of physicians' knowledge is important for understanding their decisions. Physicians responded one way when asked to think about novel decisions, but differently when examples with the same structure were constructed with real medical decisions. Physicians did not use decision-relevant information that was provided with the intent of improving their decision making. Decision aids did not improve physicians' decision making each time they were used, because they improved the decision making on the first few exposures. Decision scripts offered a plausible explanation for each of these phenomena.

Assessment of the Decision-Scripts Approach

The decision-scripts approach has several strengths. The concept has face validity. As shown above, it could account for results that were anomalous when observed by those working within the JDM research framework. The approach has already had some success in a different domain, accounting for the phenomena of medical diagnosis, where it has emerged in a leading position from several decades of competition among alternative approaches, all of which dealt with how medical knowledge is represented in memory (see Section II, above). The decision-scripts metaphor also has much in common with approaches that have been advocated in the JDM field in other domains than medical decision making (cf. Goldstein & Weber, 1995).

The concept of "decision script" needs more development and testing to see whether it indeed offers the best explanation for physician decision making. The argument presented here has not specified a model in detail. The structures sketched by Goldstein and Weber (1995) or by Schmidt, Norman, and Boshuizen (1990) need sharper definition before serious hypothesis testing can be done. At a general level of description, decision scripts can make broad predictions concerning behavioral differences as well as side effects. These could include the type of information that physicians will find easy to learn (Mandin et al., 1997), the kind of information physicians will retain with time since medical school (Charlin et al., 2000) or the amount of memory capacity required to use knowledge while making a decision. We have already discussed some studies that confirm the prediction that people with medical scripts would make decisions differently than people without scripts.

Another possible type of prediction that has considerable practical importance concerns methods for changing physician decision-making behavior. One could design interventions to improve medical decision making, guided by a decision-script account of how people make decisions, rather than by the hope that people can carry out decision-theoretic analyses if trained, or by the notion that informing people about the errors that may be caused by heuristic strategies for estimating probability or value will enable them to use their heuristic strategies more judiciously. For example, Hamm et al. (2000) proposed the following approach for changing physician behavior by changing decision scripts.

> 1. Discover the physicians' particular decision-making scripts, and understand how their use is rewarded and how they compete with each other in this context.
> 2. Analyze the scripts and the situation to see how the unsatisfactory outcomes are produced. How would the script and/or the situation need to be different in order to lead to better outcomes?
> 3. Develop new scripts and/or new ways for the system to work so that a physician using those scripts in this situation would make satisfactory decisions.
> 4. Test to verify that the redesigned scripts and situations can work.
> 5. Implement a change by explicitly training all relevant people to use the new scripts, along with needed system changes. (Hamm et al., 2000, p. 409)

For any of these types of prediction that the decision-scripts approach may make, researchers can choose to invest in a study based on an appealing metaphor that has not been specified or verified, or to do the theoretical and empirical work to ensure that the metaphor has validity. Gambling that the decision-script account is correct may produce useful results quickly, but it may waste time and resources.

The work to assess the validity of this framework will need methods for describing physicians' decision scripts, their complex knowledge about the problems of their daily experience. By definition, this knowledge is different from that which can be induced in an hour's work on a novel task in a laboratory. Some work has taken the decision maker's self-report as an indication of the kind of processing and representation that is involved (e.g., Goldstein & Weber, 1995; Rettinger & Hastie, 2001). Physicians' explanations have even been published verbatim as "scripts" (Abernathy & Hamm, 1994), though this was intended to educate specialist physicians rather than as a scientifically valid description of a decision script. A serious effort to characterize the processes that operate on knowledge representations in the course of medical decision making will need to use cognitive modeling, perhaps computer simulation, and to verify the models by developing accounts for behavior in specific situations and testing the details through experimental studies. An example of this kind of analysis was work by Patel et al. (1989) to determine the forms of knowledge related to diagnostic reasoning.

This chapter has reviewed two substantial accounts of the psychology of medical decision making—one based on cognitive psychology's descriptions of knowledge and applied most frequently to physicians' diagnostic behavior (Section II), and the other based on JDM research's descriptions of the production and use of decision relevant information (probabilities and utilities) and applied most often to physicians' decision-making behavior (Section III). It has proposed that the theoretical framework of the first account be applied to the content of the second account (Section IV). An implication of this proposal is that those who study the psychology of medical decision making need to pay more attention to the role of the physicians' knowledge of the particular problem. The organized structure of the physicians' knowledge, the recognition process through which it is activated and the active process by which the representation is adjusted until it adequately describes the patient should be explicitly recognized as background for any description of medical decision making. The exercise of making these explicit may lead to different types of explanation for physicians' decisions, and to the discovery of new phenomena.

REFERENCES

Abernathy, C. M. & Hamm, R. M. (1994). *Surgical Scripts*. Philadelphia, PA: Hanley and Belfus.

Abernathy, C. M. & Hamm, R. M. (1995). *Surgical Intuition*. Philadelphia, PA: Hanley and Belfus.

Ainslie, G. (1975). Specious reward: A behavioral theory of impulsiveness and impulse control. Psychological Bulletin, *82*, 463–496.

Allison, J. J., Kiefe, C. I., Cook, E. F., Gerrity, M. S., Orav, E. J. & Centor, R. (1998). The association of physician attitudes about uncertainty and risk taking with resource use in a Medicare HMO. *Medical Decision Making, 18*, 320–329.

Anderson, J. R. (1990). *Cognitive Psychology and Its Implications* (2nd edn). New York: W.H. Freeman.

Anderson, J. R. (1993). *Rules of the Mind*. Hillsdale, NJ: Erlbaum.

Anderson, N. H. (1970). Functional measurement and psychophysical judgment. *Psychological Review, 77*, 153–170.

Annunziata, M. A., Talamini, R., Tumolo, S., Rossi, C. & Monfardini, S. (1996). Physicians and death: Comments and behaviour of 605 doctors in the north-east of Italy. *Support Care Cancer, 4*, 334–340.

Ariely, D. & Zauberman, G. (2000). On the making of an experience: The effects of breaking and combining experiences on their overall evaluation. *Journal of Behavioral Decision Making, 13*, 219–232.

Arkes, H. R. (1991). Costs and benefits of judgment errors: Implications for debiasing. *Psychological Bulletin, 110*, 486–498.

Ashby, F. G., Isen, A. M. & Turken, A. U. (1999). A neuropsychological theory of positive affect and its influence on cognition. *Psychological Review, 106*, 529–550.

Bar-Hillel, M. (1980). The base rate fallacy in probability judgments. *Acta Psychologica, 44*, 211–233.

Batchelder, W. H. & Romney, A. K. (1988). Test theory without an answer key. *Psychometrika, 53*, 71–92.

Bayoumi, A. M. & Redelmeier, D. A. (2000). Decision analysis with cumulative prospect theory. *Medical Decision Making, 20*, 404–412.

Beach, L. R. (1990). *Image Theory: Decision Making in Personal and Organizational Contexts*. Chichester: Wiley.

Bergus, G. R. & Cantor, S. B. (1995). *Medical Decision Making* (vol. 22). Philadelphia, PA: W.B. Saunders.

Bergus, G. R., Chapman, G. B., Gjerde, C. & Elstein, A. S. (1995). Clinical reasoning about new symptoms despite preexisting disease: Sources of error and order effects. *Family Medicine, 27*, 314–320.

Berwick, D. M., Fineberg, H. V. & Weinstein, M. C. (1981). When doctors meet numbers. *American Journal of Medicine, 71*, 991–998.

Bleichrodt, H. & Johannesson, M. (2001). Time preference for health: A test of stationarity versus decreasing timing aversion. *Journal of Mathematical Psychology, 45*, 265–282.

Bordage, G., Brailovsky, C. A., Cohen, T. & Page, G. (1996). Maintaining and enhancing key decision-making skills from graduation into practice: An exploratory study. In A. J. J. A. Scherpbier, C. P. M. van der Vleuten & J.-J. Rethans (eds), *Advances in Medical Education I* (pp. 128–130). Dordrecht: Kluwer Academic.

Bornstein, B. H., Emler, A. C., & Chapman, G. B. (1999). Rationality in medical treatment decisions: Is there a sunk-cost effect? *Social Science and Medicine, 49*, 215–222.

Bradley, C. P. (1992). Uncomfortable prescribing decisions: A critical incident study. *British Medical Journal*, *304* (6822), 294–296.

Bursztajn, H. & Hamm, R. M. (1982). The clinical utility of utility assessment. *Medical Decision Making*, *2*, 161–165.

Bursztajn, H. J., Feinbloom, R. I., Hamm, R. M. & Brodsky, A. (1990). *Medical Choices, Medical Chances: How Patients, Families, and Physicians Can Cope with Uncertainty*. New York: Routledge.

Busemeyer, J. R., Weg, E., Barkan, R., Li, X. & Ma, Z. (2000). Dynamic and consequential consistency of choices between paths of decision trees. *Journal of Experimental Psychology: General*, *129*, 530–545.

Cairns, J. (1992). Discounting and health benefits: another perspective. *Health Economics*, *1*, 76–79.

Carson, A. D., Bizot, E. B., Hendershot, P. E., Barton, M. G., Garvin, M. K. & Kraemer, B. (1999). Modeling career counselor decisions with artificial neural networks: Predictions of fit across a comprehensive occupational map. *Journal of Vocational Behavior*, *54*, 196–213.

Casscells, W., Schoenberger, A. & Graboys, T. B. (1978). Interpretation by physicians of clinical laboratory results. *New England Journal of Medicine*, *299*, 999–1001.

Chapman, G. B. (1996). Temporal discounting and utility for health and money. *Journal of Experimental Psychology. Learning, Memory, and Cognition*, *22*, 771–791.

Chapman, G. B. (2000). Preferences for improving and declining sequences of health outcomes. *Journal of Behavioral Decision Making*, *13*, 203–218.

Chapman, G. B. & Elstein, A. S. (1995). Valuing the future: Temporal discounting of health and money. *Medical Decision Making*, *15*, 373–386.

Chapman, G. B. & Elstein, A. S. (2000). Cognitive processes and biases in medical decision making. In G. B. Chapman & F. A. Sonnenberg (eds), *Decision Making in Health Care: Theory, Psychology, and Applications* (pp. 183–210). New York: Cambridge University Press.

Chapman, G. B. & Sonnenberg, F. (eds) (2000). *Decision Making in Health Care: Theory, Psychology, and Applications*. New York: Cambridge University Press.

Chapman, G. B., Bergus, G. R., & Elstein, A. S. (1996). Order of information affects clinical judgment. *Journal of Behavioral Decision Making*, *9*, 201–211.

Charlin, B., Tardif, J. & Boshuizen, H. P. (2000). Scripts and medical diagnostic knowledge: Theory and applications for clinical reasoning instruction and research. *Academic Medicine*, *75*, 182–190.

Charlin, B., Brailovsky, C., Roy, L., Goulet, F. & Vleuten, C. v. d. (2000). The script concordance test: A tool to assess the reflective clinician. *Teaching and Learning in Medicine*, *12*, 189–195.

Christensen, C., Heckerling, P., Mackesy-Amiti, M. E., Bernstein, L. M. & Elstein, A. S. (1995). Pervasiveness of framing effects among physicians and medical students. *Journal of Behavioral Decision Making*, *8*, 169–180.

Christensen-Szalanski, J. J. J. (1984). Discount functions and the measurement of patients' values. Women's decisions during childbirth. *Medical Decision Making*, *4*, 47–58.

Christensen-Szalanski, J. J. J. & Beach, L. R. (1982). Experience and the base rate fallacy. *Organizational Behavior and Human Decision Processes*, *29*, 270–278.

Colliver, J. A. (2000). Effectiveness of problem-based learning curricula: Research and theory. *Academic Medicine*, *75*, 259–266.

Connelly, D. P., Rich, E. C., Curley, S. P. & Kelly, J. T. (1990). Knowledge resource preferences of family physicians. *Journal of Family Practice*, *30*, 353–359.

Coppola, K. M., Ditto, P. H., Danks, J. H. & Smucker, W. D. (2001). Accuracy of primary care and hospital-based physicians' predictions of elderly outpatients' treatment preferences with and without advance directives. *Archives of Internal Medicine*, *161*, 431–440.

Cowen, M. E., Miles, B. J., Cahill, D. F., Giesler, R. B., Beck, J. R. & Kattan, M. W. (1998). The danger of applying group-level utilities in decision analyses of the treatment of localized prostate cancer in individual patients. *Medical Decision Making*, *18*, 376–380.

Crozier, W. R. & Ranyard, R. (1997). Cognitive process models and explanations of decision making. In R. Ranyard, W. R. Crozier & O. Svenson (eds), *Decision Making: Cognitive Models and Explanations* (pp. 5–20). London: Routledge.

Curley, S. P., Connelly, D. P. & Rich, E. C. (1990). Physicians' use of medical knowledge resources: Preliminary theoretical framework and findings. *Medical Decision Making*, *10*, 231–241.

Custers, E. J., Regehr, G. & Norman, G. R. (1996). Mental representations of medical diagnostic knowledge: A review. *Academic Medicine, 71*(Suppl. 10), S55–61.

Dawes, R. M., Faust, D. & Meehl, P. E. (1989). Clinical versus actuarial judgment. *Science, 243* (4899), 1668–1674.

Dawes, R. M., Mirels, H. L., Gold, E. & Donahue, E. (1993). Equating inverse probabilities in implicit personality judgments. *Psychological Science, 4*, 396–400.

Dawson, N. V. (1993). Physician judgment in clinical settings: Methodological influences and cognitive performance. *Clinical Chemistry, 39*, 1468–1480.

Dawson, N. V. (2000). Physician judgments of uncertainty. In G. B. Chapman & F. A. Sonnenberg (eds), *Decision Making in Health Care: Theory, Psychology, and Applications* (pp. 211–252). New York: Cambridge University Press.

Dawson, N. V. & Arkes, H. R. (1987). Systematic errors in medical decision making: Judgment limitations. *Journal of General Internal Medicine, 2*, 183–187.

Deaconson, T. F., O'Hair, D. P., Levy, M. F., Lee, M. B., Schueneman, A. L. & Codon, R. E. (1988). Sleep deprivation and resident performance. *Journal of the American Medical Association, 260*, 1721–1727.

Deber, R. B. & Baumann, A. O. (1992). Clinical reasoning in medicine and nursing: Decision making versus problem solving. *Teaching and Learning in Medicine, 4*, 140–146.

de Bock, G. H., Reijneveld, S. A., van Houwelingen, J. C., Knottnerus, J. A. & Kievit, J. (1999). Multiattribute utility scores for predicting family physicians' decisions regarding sinusitis. *Medical Decision Making, 19*, 58–65.

de Dombal, F. T., Leaper, D. J., Staniland, J. R., McCann, A. P. & Horrocks, J. C. (1972). Computer-aided diagnosis of acute abdominal pain. *British Medical Journal, 2*, 9–13.

Detmer, D. E., Fryback, D. G. & Gassner, K. (1978). Heuristics and biases in medical decision-making. *Journal of Medical Education, 53*, 682–683.

Di Caccavo, A. & Reid, F. (1995). Decisional conflict in general practice: Strategies of patient management. *Social Science and Medicine, 41*, 347–353.

Dougherty, M. R. P., Gettys, C. F. & Ogden, E. E. (1999). MINERVA DM: A memory processes model for judgments of likelihood. *Psychological Review, 106*, 180–209.

Dowie, J. & Elstein, A. S. (eds) (1988). *Professional Judgment: A Reader in Clinical Decision Making*. Cambridge: Cambridge University Press.

Druley, J. A., Ditto, P. H., Moore, K. A., Danks, J. H., Townsend, A. & Smucker, W. D. (1993). Physicians' predictions of elderly outpatients' preferences for life-sustaining treatment. *Journal of Family Practice, 37*, 469–475.

Easterbrook, J. A. (1959). The effect of emotion on cue utilization and the organization of behavior. *Psychological Review, 66*, 183–201.

Eddy, D. M. (1982). Probabilistic reasoning in clinical medicine: Problems and opportunities. In D. Kahneman, P. Slovic & A. Tversky (eds), *Judgment Under Uncertainty: Heuristics and Biases* (pp. 249–267). Cambridge: Cambridge University Press.

Elmore, J. G., Barton, M. B., Moceri, V. M., Polk, S., Arena, P. J. & Fletcher, S. W. (1998). Ten-year risk of false positive screening mammograms and clinical breast examinations. *New England Journal of Medicine, 338*, 1089–1096.

Elstein, A. S. (1976). Clinical judgment: Psychological research and medical practice. *Science, 194*, 696–700.

Elstein, A. S. (1992). Paradigms for research on clinical reasoning: A researcher's commentary. *Teaching and Learning in Medicine, 4*, 147–149.

Elstein, A. S. (1999). Heuristics and biases: Selected errors in clinical reasoning. *Academic Medicine, 74*, 791–794.

Elstein, A. S. (2000). Clinical problem solving and decision psychology: Comment on "The epistemology of clinical reasoning". *Academic Medicine, 75*(Suppl. 10), S134–136.

Elstein, A. S., Dod, J. & Holzman, G. B. (1989). Estrogen replacement decisions of third-year residents: Clinical intuition and decision analysis. In D. A. Evans & V. L. Patel (eds), *Cognitive Science in Medicine: Biomedical Modeling* (pp. 21–52). Cambridge, MA: MIT Press.

Elstein, A. S., Shulman, L. S. & Sprafka, S. A. (1978). *Medical Problem Solving: An Analysis of Clinical Reasoning*. Cambridge, MA: Harvard University Press.

Elstein, A. S., Christensen, C., Cottrell, J. J., Polson, A. & Ng, M. (1999). Effects of prognosis, perceived benefit, and decision style on decision making in critical care. *Critical Care Medicine*, *27*, 58–65.

Elstein, A. S., Holzman, G. B., Ravitch, M. M. et al. (1986). Comparison of physicians' decisions regarding estrogen replacement therapy for menopausal women and decisions derived from a decision analytic model. *American Journal of Medicine*, *80*, 246–258.

Engle, R. W., Tuholski, S. W., Laughlin, J. E. & Conway, A. R. A. (1999). Working memory, short-term memory and general fluid intelligence: A latent variable approach. *Journal of Experimental Psychology: General*, *128*, 309–331.

Ericsson, K. A. & Kintsch, W. (1995). Long-term working memory. *Psychological Review*, *102*, 211–245.

Feltovich, P. J. (1983). Expertise: Reorganizing and refining knowledge for use. *Professions Education Research Notes*, *4*, 5–9.

Feltovich, P. J., Spiro, R. J. & Coulson, R. L. (1989). The nature of conceptual understanding in biomedicine: The deep structure of complex ideas and the development of misconceptions. In D. A. Evans & V. L. Patel (eds), *Cognitive Science in Medicine: Biomedical Modeling* (pp. 113–172). Cambridge, MA: MIT Press.

Fennema, H. & Wakker, P. (1997). Original and cumulative prospect theory: A discussion of empirical differences. *Journal of Behavioral Decision Making*, *10*, 53–64.

Gabriel, S. E., Kneeland, T. S., Melton, L. J., III, Moncur, M. M., Ettinger, B. & Tosteson, A. N. A. (1999). Health-related quality of life in economic evaluations for osteoporosis: Whose values should we use? *Medical Decision Making*, *19*, 141–148.

Garb, H. N. & Schramke, C. J. (1996). Judgment research and neuropsychological assessment: A narrative review and meta-analyses. *Psychological Bulletin*, *120*, 140–153.

Gigerenzer, G. (2000). *Adaptive Thinking: Rationality in the Real World*. New York: Oxford University Press.

Gilhooly, K. J. (1990). Cognitive psychology and medical diagnosis. *Applied Cognitive Psychology*, *4*, 261–272.

Goldstein, W. M. & Weber, E. U. (1995). Content and discontent: Indications and implications of domain specificity in preferential decision making. In J. Busemeyer, D. L. Medin & R. Hastie (eds), *Decision Making from a Cognitive Perspective* (vol. 32, pp. 83–136). San Diego, CA: Academic Press.

Goldstein, W. M. & Weber, E. U. (1997). Content and discontent: Indications and implications of domain specificity in preferential decision making. In W. M. Goldstein & R. M. Hogarth (eds), *Research on Judgment and Decision Making: Currents, Connections, and Controversies* (pp. 566–617). New York: Cambridge University Press.

Green, A. J. K. & Gilhooly, K. J. (1992). Empirical advances in expertise research. In M. T. Keane & K. J. Gilhooly (eds), *Advances in the Psychology of Thinking* (vol. I, pp. 45–70). Hemel Hempstead: Harvester Wheatsheaf.

Green, L. A. & Mehr, D. R. (1997). What alters physicians' decisions to admit to the coronary care unit? *Journal of Family Practice*, *45*, 219–226.

Green, L. A. & Yates, J. F. (1993). Influence of pseudodiagnostic information in acute chest pain admission decisions. *Medical Decision Making*, *13*, 387.

Green, L. A. & Yates, J. F. (1995). Influence of pseudodiagnostic information on the evaluation of ischemic heart disease. *Annals of Emergency Medicine*, *25*, 451–457.

Green, L., Fristoe, N. & Myerson, J. (1994). Temporal discounting and preference reversals in choice between delayed outcomes. *Psychonomic Bulletin and Review*, *1*, 383–389.

Greeno, J. G. & Simon, H. A. (1988). Problem solving and reasoning. In R. C. Atkinson, R. J. Herrnstein, G. Lindzey & R. D. Luce (eds), *Stevens' Handbook of Experimental Psychology*. vol. 2. *Learning and Cognition* (2nd edn, pp. 589–672). New York: Wiley.

Griffin, D. & Buehler, R. (1999). Frequency, probability, and prediction: easy solutions to cognitive illusions? *Cognitive Psychology*, *38*, 48–78.

Gruppen, L. D., Wolf, F. M. & Billi, J. E. (1991). Information gathering and integration as sources of error in diagnostic decision making. *Medical Decision Making*, *11*, 233–239.

Hamm, R. M. (1988). Moment by moment variation in experts' analytic and intuitive cognitive activity. *IEEE Transactions on Systems, Man, and Cybernetics*, *18*, 757–776.

Hamm, R. M. (1996). Physicians neglect base rates, and it matters (Comment on Koehler). *Behavioral and Brain Sciences, 19*, 25–26.

Hamm, R. M. & Miller, M. A. (1988). *Interpretation of Conditional Probabilities in Probabilistic Inference Word Problems* (Publication no. 88–15). Boulder, CO: Institute of Cognitive Science, University of Colorado.

Hamm, R. M. & Sieck, J. P. (2000). Anomalies revealed using a novel method for assessing intertemporal discount rates [Meeting abstract]. *Medical Decision Making, 20*, 489.

Hamm, R. M., Clark, J. A. & Bursztajn, H. (1984). Psychiatrists' thorny judgments: Describing and improving decision making processes. *Medical Decision Making, 4*, 425–448.

Hamm, R. M., Hicks, R. J. & Bemben, D. A. (1996). Antibiotics and respiratory infections: Are patients more satisfied when expectations are met? *Journal of Family Practice, 43*, 56–62.

Hamm, R. M., Scheid, D. C., Smith, W. R. & Tape, T. G. (2000). Opportunities for applying psychological theory to improve medical decision making: Two case histories. In G. B. Chapman & F. A. Sonnenberg (eds), *Decision Making in Health Care: Theory, Psychology, and Applications* (pp. 386–421). New York: Cambridge University Press.

Hammond, K. R. (1999). *Judgments Under Stress*. New York: Oxford University Press.

Hammond, K. R., Stewart, T. R., Brehmer, B. & Steinmann, D. (1975). Social judgment theory. In M. Kaplan & S. Schwartz (eds), *Human Judgment and Decision Processes*. New York: Academic Press.

Hastie, R. (1991). A review from a high place: The field of judgment and decision making as revealed in current textbooks. *Psychological Science, 2*, 135–138.

Hatala, R., Norman, G. R. & Brooks, L. R. (1999). Impact of a clinical scenario on accuracy of electrocardiogram interpretation. *Journal of General Internal Medicine, 14*, 126–129.

Hoffrage, U. & Gigerenzer, G. (1998). Using natural frequencies to improve diagnostic inferences. *Academic Medicine, 73*, 538–540.

Hogarth, R. M. (2001). *Educating Intuition*. Chicago, IL: University of Chicago Press.

Hogarth, R. M. & Einhorn, H. J. (1992). Order effects in belief updating: The belief-adjustment model. *Cognitive Psychology, 24*, 1–55.

Holmes, M. M., Rovner, D. R., Rothert, M. L. et al. (1987). Women's and physicians' utilities for health outcomes in estrogen replacement therapy. *Journal of General Internal Medicine, 2*, 178–182.

Holmes-Rovner, M., Padonu, G., Kroll, J. et al. (1996). African-American women's attitudes and expectations of menopause. *American Journal of Preventive Medicine, 12*, 420–423.

Isen, A. M., Daubman, K. A. & Nowicki, G. P. (1987). Positive affect facilitates creative problem solving. *Journal of Personality and Social Psychology, 52*, 1122–1131.

Isen, A. M., Nygren, T. E. & Ashby, F. G. (1988). Influence of positive affect on the subjective utility of gains and losses: It is just not worth the risk. *Journal of Personality and Social Psychology, 55*, 710–717.

Isen, A. M., Rosenzweig, A. S. & Young, M. J. (1991). The influence of positive affect on clinical problem solving. *Medical Decision Making, 11*, 221–227.

Johnson-Laird, P. (1988). *The Computer and the Mind: An Introduction to Cognitive Science*. Cambridge, MA: Harvard University Press.

Johnson-Laird, P. N., Herrmann, D. J. & Chaffin, R. (1984). Only connections: A critique of semantic networks. *Psychological Bulletin, 96*, 292–315.

Kahneman, D. & Tversky, A. (1979). Prospect theory: An analysis of decision under risk. *Econometrica, 47*, 263–291.

Kahneman, D. & Tversky, A. (1984). Choices, values, and frames. *American Psychologist, 39*, 341–350.

Kern, L. & Doherty, M. E. (1982). "Pseudodiagnosticity" in an idealized medical problem-solving environment. *Journal of Medical Education, 57*, 100–104.

Kintsch, W. (1998a). *Comprehension: A Paradigm for Cognition*. New York: Cambridge University Press.

Kintsch, W. (1998b). The representation of knowledge in minds and machines. *International Journal of Psychology, 33*, 411–420.

Kirwan, J. R., Chaput de Saintonge, D. M., Joyce, C. R. B. & Currey, H. L. F. (1983). Clinical judgment analysis: Practical application in rheumatoid arthritis. *British Journal of Rheumatology, 22*, 18–23.

Klein, G. (1997). The recognition-primed decision (RPD) model: Looking back, looking forward. In C. E. Zsambok & G. Klein (eds), *Naturalistic Decision Making* (pp. 285–292). Mahwah, NJ: Erlbaum.

Koehler, J. J. (1996). The base rate fallacy reconsidered: Normative, descriptive and methodological challenges. *Behavioral and Brain Sciences, 19,* 1–53.

Laine, C., Goldman, L., Soukup, J. R. & Hayes, J. G. (1993). The impact of a regulation restricting medical house staff working hours on the quality of patient care. *Journal of the American Medical Association, 269,* 374–378.

Law, A. V., Pathak, D. S. & McCord, M. R. (1998). Health status utility assessment by standard gamble: A comparison of the probability equivalence and the lottery equivalence approaches. *Pharmaceutical Research, 15,* 105–109.

Lenert, L. & Kaplan, R. M. (2000). Validity and interpretation of preference-based measures of health- related quality of life. *Medical Care, 38* (Suppl. 9), II, 138–150.

Lenert, L. A., Treadwell, J. R. & Schwartz, C. E. (1999). Associations between health status and utilities implications for policy. *Medical Care, 37,* 479–489.

Lesgold, A. (1988). Problem solving. In R. J. Sternberg & E. E. Smith (eds), *The Psychology of Human Thought* (pp. 188–213). New York: Cambridge University Press.

Lesgold, A. M. (1984). Human skill in a computerized society: Complex skills and their acquisition. *Behavior Research Methods, Instruments, and Computers, 16,* 79–87.

Loewenstein, G. & Prelec, D. (1992). Anomalies in intertemporal choice: Evidence and an interpretation. *Quarterly Journal of Economics, 107,* 573–597.

Loewenstein, G. & Prelec, D. (1993). Preferences for sequences of outcomes. *Psychological Review, 100,* 91–108.

Loewenstein, G. F., Weber, E. U., Hsee, C. K. & Welch, N. (2001). Risk as feelings. *Psychological Bulletin, 127,* 267–286.

Lohse, G. L. (1997). The role of working memory on graphical information processing. *Behavior and Information Technology, 16,* 297–308.

Lydakis, C., Kerr, H., Hutchings, K. & Lip, G. Y. (1998). Women's awareness of, and attitudes towards, hormone replacement therapy: Ethnic differences and effects of age and education. *International Journal of Clinical Practice, 52,* 7–12.

Mandelblatt, J. S., Fryback, D. G., Weinstein, M. C., Russell, L. B. & Gold, M. R. (1997). Assessing the effectiveness of health interventions for cost-effectiveness analysis. Panel on Cost-Effectiveness in Health and Medicine. *Journal of General Internal Medicine, 12,* 551–558.

Mandin, H., Jones, A., Woloschuk, W. & Harasym, P. (1997). Helping students learn to think like experts when solving clinical problems. *Academic Medicine, 72,* 173–179.

Mazur, J. E. (2001). Hyperbolic value addition and general models of animal choice. *Psychological Review, 108,* 96–112.

McClish, D. K. & Powell, S. H. (1989). How well can physicians estimate mortality in a medical intensive care unit? *Medical Decision Making, 9,* 125–132.

McGaghie, W. C., Boerger, R. L., McCrimmon, D. R. & Ravitch, M. M. (1996). Learning pulmonary physiology: Comparison of student and faculty knowledge structures. *Academic Medicine, 71,* S13-S15.

McNeil, B. J., Pauker, S. G., Sox, H. C., Jr. & Tversky, A. (1982). On the elicitation of preferences for alternative therapies. *New England Journal of Medicine, 306,* 1259–1262.

Miyamoto, J. M. (2000). Utility assessment under expected utility and rank-dependent utility assumptions. In G. B. Chapman & F. A. Sonnenberg (eds), *Decision Making in Health Care: Theory, Psychology, and Applications* (pp. 65–109). Cambridge: Cambridge University Press.

Mold, J. W. & Stein, H. F. (1986). The cascade effect in the clinical care of patients. *New England Journal of Medicine, 314,* 512–514.

Newell, A. (1990). *Unified Theories of Cognition.* Cambridge, MA: Harvard University Press.

Newell, A. & Simon, H. A. (1972). *Human Problem Solving.* Englewood Cliffs, NJ: Prentice-Hall.

Nichols, R. L., Hyslop, N. E., Jr. & Bartlett, J. G. (1991). *Decision Making in Surgical Sepsis.* Philadelphia, PA: B.C. Becker.

Norman, G. R. (2000). The epistemology of clinical reasoning: Perspectives from philosophy, psychology, and neuroscience. *Academic Medicine, 75*(Suppl. 10), S127–S133.

O'Connor, A. M. (1989). Effects of framing and level of probability on patients' preferences for cancer chemotherapy. *Journal of Clinical Epidemiology, 42*, 119–126.

O'Connor, A. M., Pennie, R. A. & Dales, R. E. (1996). Framing effects on expectations, decisions, and side effects experienced: The case of influenza immunization. *Journal of Clinical Epidemiology, 49*, 1271–1276.

O'Connor, A. M., Boyd, N. F., Tritchler, D. L., Kriukov, Y., Sutherland, H. & Till, J. E. (1985). Eliciting preferences for alternative cancer drug treatments: The influence of framing, medium, and rater variables. *Medical Decision Making, 5*, 453–463.

Patel, V. L. & Groen, G. J. (1986). Knowledge-based solution strategies in medical reasoning. *Cognitive Science, 10*, 91–116.

Patel, V. L., Arocha, J. F. & Kaufman, D. R. (1999). Medical cognition. In F. T. Durso (ed.), *Handbook of Applied Cognition* (pp. 663–693). Chichester: Wiley

Patel, V. L., Evans, D. A. & Groen, G. J. (1989). Biomedical knowledge and clinical reasoning. In D. A. Evans & V. L. Patel (eds), *Cognitive Science in Medicine: Biomedical Modeling* (pp. 53–112). Cambridge, MA: MIT Press.

Pauker, S. G., Gorry, G. A., Kassirer, J. P. & Schwartz, W. B. (1976). Towards the simulation of clinical cognition: Taking a present illness by computer. *American Journal of Medicine, 60*, 981–996.

Payne, J. W., Bettman, J. R. & Johnson, E. G. (1993). *The Adaptive Decision Maker*. New York: Cambridge University Press.

Pennington, N. & Hastie, R. (1988). Explanation-based decision making: Effects of memory structure on judgment. *Journal of Experimental Psychology: Learning, Memory, and Cognition, 14*, 521–533.

Poses, R. M. & Anthony, M. (1991). Availability, wishful thinking, and physicians' diagnostic judgments for patients with suspected bacteremia. *Medical Decision Making, 11*, 159–168.

Poses, R. M., Cebul, R. D. & Wigton, R. S. (1995). You can lead a horse to water: Improving physicians' knowledge of probabilities may not affect their decisions. *Medical Decision Making, 15*, 65–75.

Poses, R. M., Bekes, C., Copare, F. J. & Scott, W. E. (1990). What difference do two days make? The inertia of physicians' sequential prognostic judgments for critically ill patients. *Medical Decision Making, 10*, 6–14.

Poses, R. M., McClish, D. K., Bekes, C., Scott, W. E. & Morley, J. N. (1991). Ego bias, reverse ego bias, and physicians' prognostic judgments. *Critical Care Medicine, 19*, 1533–1539.

Poses, R. M., Smith, W. R., McClish, D. K. et al. (1997). Physicians' survival predictions for patients with acute congestive heart failure. *Archives of Internal Medicine, 157*, 1001–1007.

Price, P. C. & Yates, J. F. (1993). Judgmental overshadowing: Further evidence of cue interaction in contingency judgment. *Memory and Cognition, 21*, 561–572.

Protheroe, J., Fahey, T., Montgomery, A. A. & Peters, T. J. (2000). The impact of patients' preferences on the treatment of atrial fibrillation: Observational study of patient based decision analysis. *British Medical Journal, 320* (7246), 1380–1384.

Quillian, M. R. (1968). Semantic memory. In M. L. Minsky (ed.), *Semantic Information Processing* (pp. 227–270). Cambridge, MA: MIT Press.

Redelmeier, D. A. & Kahneman, D. (1992). The pain of invasive procedures: An evaluation of patients' experiences and memories of colonoscopy (Meeting abstract). *Medical Decision Making, 12*, 338.

Redelmeier, D. A. & Shafir, E. (1995). Medical decision making in situations that offer multiple alternatives. *Journal of the American Medical Association, 273*, 302–305.

Reeder, M., Dougherty, J. & White, L. J. (1993). Pharmaceutical representatives and emergency medicine residents: A national survey. *Annals of Emergency Medicine, 22*, 1593–1596.

Regehr, G. & Norman, G. R. (1996). Issues in cognitive psychology: implications for professional education. *Academic Medicine, 71*, 988–1001.

Rettinger, D. A. & Hastie, R. (2001). Content effects on decision making. *Organizational Behavior and Human Decision Processes, 85*, 336–359.

Riesbeck, C. K. & Schank, R. C. (1989). *Inside Case-Based Reasoning*. Hillsdale, NJ: Erlbaum.

Ritov, I. & Baron, J. (1990). Reluctance to vaccinate: Omission bias and ambiguity. *Journal of Behavioral Decision Making, 3*, 263–277.

Roelofsma, P. H. M. P. & Read, D. (2000). Intransitive intertemporal choice. *Journal of Behavioral Decision Making, 13*, 161–177.

Schank, R. C. & Abelson, R. P. (1977). *Scripts, Plans, Goals and Understanding: An Inquiry into Human Knowledge Structures.* Hillsdale, NJ: Erlbaum.

Schmidt, H. G. & Boshuizen, H. P. (1993). On the origin of intermediate effects in clinical case recall. *Memory and Cognition, 21,* 338–351.

Schmidt, H. G., Norman, G. R. & Boshuizen, H. P. A. (1990). A cognitive perspective on medical expertise: Theory and implications. *Academic Medicine, 65,* 611–621.

Shanteau, J. (1992). The psychology of experts: An alternative view. In G. Wright & F. Bolger (eds), *Expertise and Decision Support* (pp. 11–23). New York: Plenum.

Shaughnessy, A. F., Slawson, D. C. & Bennett, J. H. (1995). Teaching information mastery: Evaluating information provided by pharmaceutical representatives. *Family Medicine, 27,* 581–585.

Siminoff, L. A. & Fetting, J. H. (1989). Effects of outcome framing on treatment decisions in the real world: Impact of framing on adjuvant breast cancer decisions. *Medical Decision Making, 9,* 262–271.

Simon, H. A. (1956). Rational choice and the structure of the environment. *Psychological Review, 63,* 129–138.

Sox, H. C., Jr., Blatt, M. A., Higgins, M. C. & Marton, K. I. (1988). *Medical Decision Making.* Boston, MA: Butterworths.

Speroff, T., Connors, A. F., Jr. & Dawson, N. V. (1989). Lens model analysis of hemodynamic status in the critically ill. *Medical Decision Making, 9,* 243–252.

Stanovich, K. E. & West, R. F. (2000). Individual differences in reasoning: Implications for the rationality debate? *Behavioral and Brain Sciences, 23,* 645–726.

Stevens, S. M., Richardson, D. K., Gray, J. E., Goldmann, D. A. & McCormick, M. C. (1994). Estimating neonatal mortality risk: An analysis of clinicians' judgments. *Pediatrics, 93*(6 Pt 1), 945–950.

Stewart, T. R. (1988). Judgment analysis: Procedures. In B. Brehmer & C. R. B. Joyce (eds), *Human Judgment: The SJT View* (pp. 41–73). Amsterdam: Elsevier.

Sullivan, K. E., Hebert, P. C., Logan, J., O'Connor, A. M. & McNeely, P. D. (1996). What do physicians tell patients with end-stage COPD about intubation and mechanical ventilation? *Chest, 109,* 258–264.

Sulmasy, D. P., Terry, P. B., Weisman, C. S. et al. (1998). The accuracy of substituted judgments in patients with terminal diagnoses. *Annals of Internal Medicine, 128,* 621–629.

SUPPORT Principal Investigators (1995). A controlled trial to improve care for seriously ill hospitalized patients: The Study to Understand Prognoses and Preferences for Outcomes and Risks of Treatments (SUPPORT). *Journal of the American Medical Association, 274,* 1591–1598.

Swets, J. A., Dawes, R. M. & Monahan, J. (2000). Psychological science can improve diagnostic decisions. *Psychological Science in the Public Interest, 1,* 1–25.

Tape, T. G., Kripal, J. & Wigton, R. S. (1992). Comparing methods of learning clinical prediction from case simulations. *Medical Decision Making, 12,* 213–221.

Teno, J. M., Hakim, R. B., Knaus, W. A. et al. & the SUPPORT Investigators (1995). Preferences for cardiopulmonary resuscitation: Physician–patient agreement and hospital resource use. *Journal of General Internal Medicine, 10,* 179–186.

Treadwell, J. R. & Lenert, L. A. (1999). Health values and prospect theory. *Medical Decision Making, 19,* 344–352.

Trope, Y. & Liberman, N. (2000). Temporal construal and time-dependent changes in preference. *Journal of Personality and Social Psychology, 79,* 876–889.

Tversky, A. & Kahneman, D. (1973). Availability: A heuristic for judging frequency and probability. *Cognitive Psychology, 5,* 207–232.

Tversky, A. & Kahneman, D. (1992). Advances in prospect theory: Cumulative representation of uncertainty. *Journal of Risk and Uncertainty, 5,* 297–323.

Ubel, P. A., Jepson, C. & Asch, D. A. (2000). Cost-effectiveness information and screening recommendations: Are physicians set in their ways? *Journal of General Internal Medicine, 15*(Suppl. 1), S151.

van de Wiel, M. W., Schmidt, H. G. & Boshuizen, H. P. (1998). A failure to reproduce the intermediate effect in clinical case recall. *Academic Medicine, 73,* 894–900.

van der Donk, J., Levendag, P. C., Kuijpers, A. J. et al. (1995). Patient participation in clinical decision-making for treatment of T3 laryngeal cancer: A comparison of state and process utilities. *Journal of Clinical Oncology, 13,* 2369–2378.

Wakker, P. & Stiggelbout, A. (1995). Explaining distortions in utility elicitation through the rank-dependent model for risky choices. *Medical Decision Making, 15,* 180–186.

Wazana, A. (2000). Physicians and the pharmaceutical industry: Is a gift ever just a gift? *Journal of the American Medical Association, 283,* 373–380.

Weber, E. U., Bockenholt, U., Hilton, D. J. & Wallace, B. (1993). Determinants of diagnostic hypothesis generation: Effects of information, base rates, and experience. *Journal of Experimental Psychology. Learning, Memory, Cognition, 19,* 1151–1164.

Weinstein, M. C. & Feinberg, H. V. (1980). *Clinical Decision Analysis.* Philadelphia, PA: W.B. Saunders.

Wellwood, J., Johannessen, S. & Spiegelhalter, D. J. (1992). How does computer-aided diagnosis improve the management of acute abdominal pain? *Annals of the Royal College of Surgeons of England, 74,* 40–46.

Wigton, R. S. (1988). Use of linear models to analyze physicians' decisions. *Medical Decision Making, 8,* 241–252.

Wigton, R. S. (1996). Social judgment theory and medical judgment. *Thinking and Reasoning, 2,* 175–190.

Wigton, R. S., Hoellerich, V. L. & Patil, K. D. (1986). How physicians use clinical information in diagnosing pulmonary embolism: An application of conjoint analysis. *Medical Decision Making, 6,* 2–11.

Wolf, F. M., Gruppen, L. D. & Billi, J. E. (1985). Differential diagnosis and the competing-hypotheses heuristic: A practical approach to judgment under uncertainty and Bayesian probability. *Journal of the American Medical Association, 253,* 2858–2862.

Wolf, F. M., Gruppen, L. D. & Billi, J. E. (1988). Use of the competing-hypotheses heuristic to reduce "pseudodiagnosticity". *Journal of Medical Education, 63,* 548–554.

CHAPTER 16

On the Assessment of Decision Quality: Considerations Regarding Utility, Conflict and Accountability

Gideon Keren
Eindhoven University of Technology, The Netherlands

and

Wändi Bruine de Bruin
Carnegie Mellon University, Pittsburgh, USA

During the course of their lives, people are faced with many decisions—covering a wide variety of contexts and ranging in importance. Common decision-making topics include career moves, whether to get married (and, if so, to whom and when), what house to rent (or buy), where to shop for groceries and what to have for dinner. The need for making a good decision grows as the importance of the context increases. Unfortunately, it is often not obvious what constitutes a good decision.

At the bottom line, the question of decision quality is the essence of decision sciences: a main goal of researchers in the discipline is to help improve people's decision making. Yet, with few exceptions (e.g., Edwards et al., 1984; Lipshitz, 1989, 1995; Hershey & Baron, 1992, 1995; Frisch & Jones, 1993; Frisch & Clemen, 1994), this topic has received relatively little attention in the literature. Several reasons may account for the reluctance to treat it directly. First, the topic may be seen as too broad and ill-defined, rendering it virtually impossible to be treated in a systematic and concise manner. A second, related, reason may be that various classes of decisions can be defined, each requiring different judgment criteria (e.g., von Winterfeldt, 1980). Third, the discussion of "decisions about decisions" introduces the concept of second-order decision making. In turn, this would expose third-, fourth-, and fifth-order decisions, and so on ad infinitum. A similar problem was identified

Thinking: Psychological Perspectives on Reasoning, Judgment and Decision Making. Edited by David Hardman and Laura Macchi.
© 2003 John Wiley & Sons, Ltd.

with the subject of second-order probabilities (Goldsmith & Sahlin, 1982). Finally, some may claim that a satisfactory answer to the question does not yet exist. Pessimists may extend this claim to the future.

Despite the difficulties associated with assessing decision quality, some researchers have attempted to address the issue. Perhaps the most fundamental question has been whether decisions should be judged by the *process* (by which they were derived) or by *outcome* (and the associated consequences). Most have taken a process-oriented approach, often basing their advice on one version of utility theory or another (Savage, 1954; Luce & Raiffa, 1957), and discussing how a good decision should be structured and modeled (Edwards et al., 1984; Lipshitz, 1989). The main argument for this process-based approach is that most, if not all, decisions are made under uncertainty. "A decision is therefore a bet, and evaluating it as good or not must depend on the stakes and the odds, not on the outcome" (Edwards et al., 1984, p. 7). Given the structure and numbers that enter into a decision problem, the task of decision making itself should, in principle, be trivial. The difficulty lies in obtaining the appropriate structure and problem space, reflecting all possible outcomes, the degree to which they fulfill one's goals, the contingencies between decision and outcome, and the probability of occurrence of different outcomes. The "right" decision, then, is to choose the option with the highest chance of accomplishing the decision maker's goals. The underlying assumption is that, in the long run, good decision processes are more likely to generate good outcomes.

Thus, the process-oriented approach evaluates a decision's quality by its structure, including how well it represents the decision maker's goals. As a result, it is easier to assess the quality of well- than ill-defined decision problems (Simon, 1973). When judging ill-defined problems, the focus often remains on the inadequate problem formulation rather than on the decision itself.

Most real-life decisions are vague and ill-defined (Fischhoff, 1996). Decision makers may, for example, hold multiple and ambiguous goals, making it difficult to judge what would be the best decision. Yet, process-oriented students of decision making would argue that half of the solution involves appropriate structuring of the decision problem.

Baron (1994) notes that people have difficulty in following this process-oriented approach. Normatively, the decision structure should incorporate potential outcomes, because only these affect the fulfillment of the decision maker's goals—a requirement known as "consequentialism". Even if it does not affect the consequences of a decision (in terms of their goals), people are sensitive to the *manner* in which an outcome has been obtained. Baron and his colleagues (e.g., Spranca, Minsk & Baron, 1991; Ritov & Baron, 1992) have shown that decisions with identical outcomes are judged as worse when they result from acts of commission than acts of omission. For example, most people are reluctant to vaccinate children against a potentially lethal flu when side effects of the vaccine can cause death. Faced with a flu epidemic that is expected to kill 10 out of 10 000 children, most people are not willing to accept a 9 out of 10 000 risk of death from vaccination, and the median acceptable maximum risk is 5 in 10 000. Apparently, killing a child with a vaccination (that is, an act of commission) is perceived as worse than causing its death by failing to vaccinate (that is, an act of omission) (Ritov & Baron, 1990). This pattern of results poses a violation of consequentialism, unless feelings of guilt (resulting from commission but not from omission) may be included in the definition of "consequence". Indeed, some argue that strong emotional responses should be considered as part of the decision outcome (see commentaries included in Baron, 1994).

After the outcome of a decision is known, people are even less likely to follow the guidelines provided by the process-based literature. Instead, when judging decision quality, they tend to focus on the outcome rather than the process (Baron & Hershey, 1988; Jones, Yurak & Frisch, 1997). Referring to an operation as successful *after* the patient has died remains unsatisfactory for most laypersons. The simple reason underlying this emphasis on the outcome is that, at the end of the day, the consequences of a decision are more salient than the process that produced them.

Some researchers of behavioral decision making have defended the focus on outcomes. Hershey and Baron (1992, 1995) point out that if a good decision process is more likely to lead to a good outcome, it follows logically that good outcomes are more likely to stem from good decision processes.[1] Frisch and Clemen (1994) take this argument further, treating the question of decision quality as entirely empirical. Any feature of the decision process that increases the probability of obtaining a good outcome thus improves the quality of the decision—even if it violates the process-oriented approach.

Yet, the majority of researchers emphasize that the process, rather than the outcome, should be the object of evaluation. Their theories are considered "normative", prescribing how people should make, and judge, decisions. "Descriptive" research, which describes how decisions are actually made, shows that people focus on decision outcomes. Normative and descriptive considerations are deeply interrelated, and there is an ongoing interplay between the two perspectives (Coombs, Dawes & Tversky, 1970; Keren, 1996). To assess decision quality, it is important to examine both normative and descriptive facets of the relevant issues. A common procedure is to use normative benchmarks to which the actual process and outcome are compared.[2] An alternative option, and the one that we recommend, is what Keeney and Raiffa (1976) termed the "prescriptive" approach. It offers guidelines to decision makers who search for optimization, yet takes into account their limited capacity for memory and information processing that makes them vulnerable to human error, reasoning biases and swaying emotions.

Which specific considerations prevail in the process of assessing decision quality depends, to a large extent, on the decision-making model that is adopted by the judge. In the following, the problem of decision quality is examined within three, broadly defined, different approaches to the study of decision making. The first is the so-called gambling paradigm, which has been the dominating metatheory in the field of decision making since its inception. Its main underlying assumption is that every decision problem can be translated into a choice between gambles, relying heavily on utility theory (e.g., Luce & Raiffa, 1957; Keeney & Raiffa, 1976; Schoemaker, 1982). The second approach is the conflict model, which considers a decision to be the resolution of an emotional conflict, in which to choose one option means to forego another (e.g., Janis & Mann, 1977; Coombs, 1987). The third and last approach is the accountability model (Tetlock, 1991; Lerner & Tetlock, 1999), which asserts that the decision maker's major goal is to defend decisions convincingly—if held accountable. Although the latter two models were not intended to be normative, each offers implicit guidelines to judge decision quality, assigning different (relative) weights to the outcome- and process-oriented approach.

This chapter emphasizes that the judge of the decision and the decision maker may not use the same framework to evaluate the decision—and, hence, may disagree. Evaluations may even vary between judges who endorse different perspectives and different models. For

---

[1] Hershey and Baron's argument that P(good outcome/good decision) corresponds "logically" to P(good decision/good outcome) actually holds only under the assumption that "bad" decisions are not more likely than "good" decisions.
[2] Note that normative guidelines may vary depending on the assumptions one wants to adopt. Often, specifically with complex decisions, an unequivocal solution does not exist.

example, patients and colleagues may take a different approach to judging the quality of a physician's decision. While the colleagues may emphasize the decision process, the patients will probably focus on the outcome. As suggested before, the latter will be more likely to consider a decision to operate wrongly if it leads to a death. Whatever the perspective taken, a perfectly neutral judge rarely, if ever, exists.

How a decision is assessed also depends on whether the judge focuses on the decision or the decision maker—the product or the producer. For example, a jury could judge the crime or the criminal—considering, among other things, the number of offenses. Although the two are closely linked, they are by no means the same. A focus on the decision maker may involve a review of that person's decision-making history, which incorporates multiple, repeated, decisions. Judging only a specific decision, in contrast, treats it as unique, inspiring a more narrow view. Formal normative theories (specifically different versions of utility theory, to be discussed later in this chapter) assume that there is no fundamental difference (e.g., Coombs, Dawes & Tversky, 1970). In both cases, good decision processes have a higher chance of producing good outcomes. There is mounting empirical evidence, however, that, in practice, the decision maker's choice patterns (and, possibly, judgments of these decisions) under unique and repeated choice conditions are not necessarily the same (e.g., Lopes, 1981; Keren, 1991a; Redelmeier & Tversky, 1992, to mention just a few). People may be hesitant to take a gamble (with positive expected value) once, but be willing to take it repeatedly (Samuelson, 1963).

Whether a decision is perceived as unique or repeated is often determined by the manner in which the decision is framed, and by who the decision maker is. For instance, a patient (or one of her relatives) who has to judge the quality of a medical treatment will naturally focus solely on the particulars of her own case, thus adopting a unique perspective. In contrast, physicians will probably tend to take into account distributional information. The dispute concerning statistical as opposed to clinical judgment (Dawes, Faust & Meehl, 1989) suggests that while the former approach is normatively superior, most people cling to the latter. A fundamental disagreement between the decision maker and the judge may arise when one adopts the clinical while the other adopts the statistical approach (or vice versa).

In sum, the judgment of decision quality depends on the perspective taken by the judge—whether focusing on outcome or process, the decision or the decision maker, a statistical or a clinical judgment. In the rest of this chapter, we first examine pros and cons associated with the outcome- and process-oriented approach to the assessment of decision quality. We then consider the evaluation of decision quality as envisaged within each of the three metatheories mentioned above, taking into account the perspective of different judges as well as the decision maker. In the final section, we briefly summarize the different arguments and discuss the implications for daily life and future research.

OUTCOME VERSUS PROCESS DELIBERATIONS IN THE EVALUATION OF DECISION QUALITY

As mentioned, whether decisions are judged by outcome or by process may depend on the perspective of the judge. It can hardly be denied that decision processes and the corresponding outcomes are strongly interrelated. As noted by Frisch and Clemen (1994), "to evaluate decision quality, researchers need to identify those decision processes that tend to lead to desirable outcomes" (p. 48). Imminent decisions, then, should follow the most successful process, as apparent *before* they are made (that is, in foresight). However, *after* the decision has been made, people often mistakenly reassess the decision process in light of the outcome (Baron & Hershey, 1988).

Indeed, knowledge of the outcome may alter perceptions of the decision, including the quality of its process. In hindsight, people consistently overestimate what could have been anticipated in foresight (Fischhoff, 1975): events that appeared irrelevant beforehand, seem to have caused the outcome after it has emerged. As a result, an unfortunate surprise outcome makes an unlucky decision maker seem incompetent, as in the case of the unforeseen (but, in hindsight, obvious) attack on Pearl Harbor (Wohlstetter, 1962). Outcome knowledge may affect the assessment of what the decision maker should have known (for example, possible outcomes and corresponding probabilities), evoking criticism especially when the outcome is disadvantageous.

Evaluation both by process and by outcome may be vulnerable to the hindsight bias. In retrospect, people may be good at constructing counterfactuals (Roese & Olson, 1995) of how both the decision process and the corresponding outcome could have been better. In particular, "close" counterfactuals, showing that an alternative outcome "almost" happened (Kahneman & Varey, 1990), may affect judgment and evaluation in different ways. The existence of close counterfactuals may suggest to a lenient judge that the decision maker almost got it right, whereas for a strict judge, the closeness may highlight the failure of the decision maker.

A danger of taking into account decision outcomes is that they are asymmetrical (Jones & Nisbett, 1972). While the decision maker takes credit for good outcomes, others may not even pay attention. Bad outcomes, in contrast, lead to public outcry. Before a disastrous explosion (May, 2000) in a fireworks depot that obliterated an entire neighborhood from the map of Enschede (The Netherlands), only one citizen had formally questioned the location of the depot. The authorities refuted his objections, and the decision went unnoticed. Even if, today, the decision makers maintain that they followed a good decision process, the Dutch public holds them responsible for the horrendous disaster.

Another fundamental problem that is often manifested in using outcomes for judgment of decision quality is addressed by Einhorn and Hogarth (1978). Given a decision between two or more options, one can know for sure only the outcome (and the corresponding consequences) of the chosen option. However, the exact consequences of options that were rejected remain uncertain. Assuming, for instance, the existence of a well-defined criterion to assess job candidates, we will never know how well the rejected ones would have done. Without that outcome information, the evaluation of our decision contains an inherent component of uncertainty (which may be assessed differently by the decision maker and the judge).

The strategies underlying the decision process determine not just the outcome but can influence the evaluation of the decision itself. Specifically, Higgins (1998, 2000) proposed that decisions could occur under two different modes, which he termed "promotion" and "prevention". The focus under the former is the attainment of positive optimal outcomes, whereas the focus under the latter is the preclusion of total failures. Hence, the same outcome may be perceived differently depending on the mode adopted: the fact that a potential negative outcome was averted may be considered as a success under the prevention mode, yet as not sufficiently satisfactory under the promotion mode. Consequently, disagreements may arise if the decision maker and the judge have tacitly adopted different modes.

We have briefly touched on some key issues concerning the judgment of a decision by process or by outcome. A most important factor that would determine the manner by which decisions are evaluated would depend on the global perspective adopted by the judge, as encapsulated in the three frameworks for decision making mentioned in the introduction—the gambling paradigm, the accountability model and the conflict model. We now examine the merits and drawbacks associated with each of the three perspectives. Our goal is to show the multiple—normatively, often unsupported—objectives held by real-world decision makers and their judges. Some readers may argue that, whatever the goal, it can be stated in terms of subjective expected utility. Because this decision-making model does not *explicitly* deal with conflict and accountability, we chose to discuss these models separately.

THE ROLE OF PROCESS AND OUTCOME WITHIN THE GAMBLING PARADIGM

The predominant framework within decision making has been the "gambling paradigm", the origins of which can be traced to early studies of gambling in the 17th century. The basic tacit assumption of this model is that any decision can be represented as a choice between gambles, with decision options expressed in terms of probabilities and utilities. It further assumes that the decision maker is a rational agent who will choose the option that offers the most advantageous bet.

Utility theory, which serves as the cornerstone of the gambling paradigm, was originally conceived as a normative theory, and therefore provides clear advice for evaluating decision quality. The guiding principle underlying this framework, as dictated by utility theory (e.g., Luce & Raiffa, 1957; Schoemaker, 1982), is maximization of expected utility. A decision maker who follows this rule is expected to be consistent, thus fulfilling a basic tenet of a rational agent. Specifically, it provides an algorithm by which each option should be structured as a gamble, and includes a subjective utility assessment of the possible outcomes and the corresponding assessed probabilities for each outcome. The two components should be expressed numerically, so that their multiplication provides the subjective expected utility of a gamble.

According to utility theory, the decision maker should maximize subjective expected utility by selecting the option with the highest value. The theory is normative, because it postulates that strictly following the above algorithm will result in the best decision. Hence, a strict interpretation of utility theory implies that in the long run, decision quality can be equally assessed by either process or outcome. Unlike the conflict and the accountability models (treated below), the gambling paradigm provides, at least theoretically, an unambiguous standard for judging decision quality.

Broadly speaking, most decisions are based on three components: (1) obtaining relevant information (either from memory or from the external world), (2) construction of the problem (or decision) space and inserting the relevant information appropriately in the decision problem structure, and (3) assessing the values and likelihoods of different outcomes. Utility theory omits advice on how to conduct the first two stages, implying that there are no transparent criteria for evaluating the performance of the decision maker on these two facets. Decision analysis (von Winterfeldt & Edwards, 1986) provides some guidelines regarding the elicitation of the relevant utilities and probabilities. However, it is not an inherent part of the theory, and whether the method really yields valid and consistent responses has not been established empirically.

There is ample research showing that the assessment of the relevant utilities and probabilities is subject to a large number of pitfalls. For example, utility theory adopts the philosophy of "articulated values" (Fischhoff, 1991), postulating that people possess well-differentiated values (and thus, the only problem concerns reliable and accurate methods for eliciting these values). However, people's preferences are often unstable (Fischhoff, Slovic & Lichtenstein, 1980; Slovic, 1995). A more realistic approach is expressed by the philosophy of "basic values", according to which people do not possess a priori values for most decision problems, except for a few broad and general principles (Fischhoff, 1991). According to this view, much of the observed instability in preferences can be accounted for by the fact that judgments and choices are most often made online, that is, during the process of elicitation (Slovic, 1995).

Valuations derived from basic values use inferential processes that are subject to different framing effects. For instance, beef described as 75 percent lean should, according to utility theory, be equally attractive if presented as 25 percent fat. However, diners under the first description reported a significantly higher eating pleasure (Levin & Gaeth, 1988). Such framing effects violate utility theory's principle of procedure invariance, according to which preferences should not depend on the description of the options or the method of elicitation. It goes without saying that different frames may constitute a major source of discrepancy between the decision maker and the judge.

Beside the difficulties associated with assessment and measurement, the term "utility" remains vague, at least with regard to its temporal nature. Specifically, Kahneman, Wakker and Sarin (1997) proposed to distinguish between "remembered", "experienced" and "predicted" utility, thus referring to the past, the present and the future, respectively. This distinction has an important implication for our context: whereas the utility envisaged by a decision maker (at the time of making the decision) can be interpreted only in the last sense, namely, as a forecast, the judgment of the decision is based on either experienced or remembered utilities. Without knowing the decision maker's preferences, a decision is difficult to judge. If judges use their own preferences to assess decision quality, they may (at least in the view of the decision maker) erroneously condemn the decision. Attempting to reconstruct the decision maker's preferences is an extremely difficult task in itself. Moreover, it creates the danger that any decision can be justified, and deemed optimal—by constructing preferences not beforehand, as prescribed by the subjective expected utility model, but afterwards (Schoemaker, 1991).

Note that the judgment of decision quality within the gambling paradigm can be carried out in two fundamentally different ways. Under one approach, the judge would try to assess as accurately as possible the goals, values and utilities of the decision maker, judging whether the decision maker followed the basic maxims of rational behavior. Under an alternative approach, the judge's task is to evaluate not just the decision maker's rationality, but also whether the decision maker's goals and the utilities attached to different outcomes are "acceptable".[3]

If we turn to the uncertainty component encapsulated in the utility model, subjective probabilities seem to be one of the less realistic features of utility theory, and of the gambling

---

[3] The term "acceptable" is obviously subjective and often ill-defined. Acceptability may be determined by social norms, or by the norms adopted by the judge.

paradigm in general. In real life, probabilities are usually ambiguous and imprecise. Furthermore, extensive empirical research indicates that people are often poorly calibrated (e.g., Keren, 1991b), and that probability assessments are vulnerable to different biases (e.g., Kahneman, Slovic & Tversky, 1982). For instance, as a result of the availability heuristic, salient outcomes are more likely to be remembered, and seem more likely to occur (Tversky & Kahneman, 1973). At an even more fundamental level, people have strong preferences for deterministic definitive (yes/no) predictions (Keren & Teigen, 2001), casting doubt on whether people think probabilistically at all.

Finally, there is overwhelming evidence that, contrary to one of the basic assumptions of utility theory, the assessments of utilities and probabilities are not independent (see Weber, 1994, for an excellent review). Current theorizing suggests that rank-order utilities may provide the best description of people's choice behavior. However, even if this description accurately describes the underlying choice processes, it is highly questionable whether people are entirely aware of it.[4] Since rank-order dependence is not intuitive, it is doubtful whether judges of the decision process would adopt it in their judgment of the decision quality.

It is beyond the scope of the present chapter to provide even a brief evaluation of the pros and cons of the gambling paradigm in general, and of utility theory in particular. The question we are addressing here is the extent to which the gambling paradigm provides an adequate and sensible framework for the evaluation of decision quality.

The appealing aspect of the gambling paradigm as a basis for judging decision quality is that, unlike the other two models (treated below), it provides an apparently unambiguous procedure for evaluating decisions. However, as we noted already, because of their inherently subjective nature, there are serious difficulties associated with the assessment of both subjective probability and subjective utility.

The gambling paradigm, which largely relies on subjective expected utility theory, resembles a bookkeeping activity, in which the probabilities and utilities (and their products) of the different options are balanced against each other. In that respect, the gambling paradigm offers judges a convenient method by which they can evaluate the decision or the decision maker. Despite the measurement problems briefly reviewed above, it seems to be a neutral and systematic method by which decisions may be evaluated. In reality, however, people are not accountants, and bookkeeping is usually not the way by which they make their decisions. The gambling model may be adequate for some, but certainly not all, economic decisions. The most serious shortcoming of the gambling model may be its neglect of the emotional impact on the decision process (e.g., Lopes, 1987), specifically when the consequences are of major importance for the decision maker. It considers solely what Janis and Mann (1977) refer to as "cold" decisions. A judge who follows the conflict model, which is discussed next, will treat decisions as "hot"—taking emotions into account.

DECISION EVALUATION BY PROCESS OR OUTCOME—THE CONFLICT MODEL

An alternative perspective to the one offered by the gambling paradigm is to view a decision between two (or more) options as a conflict resolution (Coombs, 1987). Janis and Mann

---

[4] If the principles associated with rank-dependent utility theory were transparent, it stands to reason that the originators of utility theory would probably be aware of it.

(1977) were among the first to propose a framework in which conflict[5] is central. Because choosing one option means giving up another, it implies an internal conflict in which the decision maker expects to experience regret regardless of what is decided. A decision can thus be described as a competition between different selves, each advocating one of the possible options.

Such an internal conflict may have the decision maker torn between normative considerations, on the one hand, and contradicting emotions, on the other hand (e.g., Sloman, 1996; Haidt, 2001). While the conflict model has no clear prescriptions and offers mainly a descriptive perspective, a judge who follows the conflict model understands that powerful emotions may, under some circumstances, override rational considerations. Although relatively little is known about how exactly emotions affect the decision process,[6] it is nevertheless widely accepted that much behavior is (to some degree) non-volitional, even after substantial deliberations (e.g., Loewenstein, 1998).

Indeed, most judicial systems in Western culture would take into account the emotional circumstances under which a decision has been reached or an action conducted. A murder committed in cold blood will usually receive harsher punishment than one that "just happened" in the heat of the moment. This example illustrates that conflict-minded judges are not blind to the outcome of a decision. Circumstances may alleviate the harshness of the judgment, but not change its valence: killing is always wrong.

While emotions may compete with "rational" decision making, they may also contradict each other. A woman with a family history of breast cancer may experience conflicting anticipated and anticipatory emotions when considering whether to take a test for the breast cancer gene (e.g., Loewenstein et al., 2001). Anticipated emotions arise from the possible negative consequences, like those expected as a result of a positive test outcome (for example, the knowledge that one carries the gene). Anticipatory emotions are those experienced during the decision process, and they reflect the aversive feelings associated with uncertainty (for example, the possibility that one might, at some point, develop breast cancer). After a positive test outcome, anticipatory emotions can be so powerful that women with a family history of breast cancer decide to reduce their uncertainty by undergoing a preventive mastectomy.

The internal struggle evoked by a difficult decision may be described as an approach–avoidance conflict (e.g., Miller & Kraeling, 1953). While part of the decision maker may want to avoid the conflict (by procrastinating or shifting the responsibility to others), another part may want to "get it over with". Approach strategies include bolstering the chosen alternative by emphasizing its good aspects (Janis & Mann, 1977), and taking the decision in small steps to make the responsibility seem less overwhelming (Sunstein & Ullmann-Margalit, 1998). While "conflict model" judges may understand the emotions for both approach and avoidance, the first may be more effective in terms of reducing conflict in the long run. Moreover, people judging their distant past tend to harbor more regrets about inactions than those pertaining to actions (Gilovich & Medvec, 1995).

Judges using the conflict model should also be aware that decision makers may change their minds as circumstances and related emotions change. For example, most pregnant

---

[5] In the present context, conflict refers exclusively to an internal conflict (or conflict between different selves). Conflict among two or more individuals (or organizations) is not considered here.

[6] Elster (1998) correctly notes that, by and large, most psychological studies on emotions have focused on the proximate or ultimate causes of the emotions, relatively undermining issues regarding how emotions *generate* behavior. Indeed, the latter is the more important facet of emotions relevant to judgment of decision quality.

women prefer to avoid anesthesia during childbirth when asked one month before giving birth. However, during active labor, the preferences of many shifted toward avoiding pain. When they were evaluated one month postpartum, their preferences tended to return to avoiding anesthesia. Thus, the conflict between bearing the pain and maximizing the new-born's safety is resolved differently at various points in time (Christensen-Szalanski, 1984). Fear tends to increase as the time between the decision and the realization of the outcome gets smaller (Loewenstein et al., 2001).

Observing such inconsistencies in intertemporal choice may lead a judge who follows the gambling paradigm to conclude that the decision is an "anomaly" (Loewenstein & Prelec, 1992). Even a judge following the conflict model may have difficulty in understanding the decision maker. After all, if the decision maker cannot predict, in foresight or in hindsight, the emotions experienced at the time of the decision, a judge may have even more difficulty in doing so.

Thus, considering emotions complicates decisions as well as the corresponding judgments of their quality. Under the conflict model, neither is as straightforward and unequivocal as is the case under the gambling paradigm. It is difficult to articulate any clear course of action for either decision maker or judge as to how decisions should be made except for general (and hence vague) guidelines. Decisions under the conflict model are often guided by what Damasio (1994) termed the "somatic marker", a sensational gut feeling (visceral and non-visceral) that may strongly affect both judgment and choice. For the present context, it is important to emphasize that even the decision maker will have difficulty in exactly articulating the somatic marker effects, let alone the judge.

Judges who adopt the conflict model may have difficulty in reliably reconstructing the emotional conditions and the particular internal conflict the decision maker was facing at the time of decision. It is generally difficult, sometimes impossible, to separate emotions from "rational" arguments, and decide on what should be their relative weights. Using the conflict model, then, is not as straightforward as the use of the gambling model.

ACCOUNTABILITY—BY PROCESS OR BY OUTCOME

Elster (1989) pointed out two opposing approaches in the social sciences that he referred to as *Homo economicus* and *Homo sociologicus*. The former is outcome-oriented and guided by considerations of instrumental rationality, as reflected in the gambling paradigm. The latter emphasizes the broader social context in which a decision takes place. Indeed, the (moral, social and legal) norms, conventions and traditions which constitute the cornerstones of the *Homo sociologicus* perspective play a central role in the assessment of decision quality. The accountability model, proposed by Tetlock and his associates (e.g., Tetlock, 1991; Lerner & Tetlock, 1999), is a manifestation of the *Homo sociologicus* approach within the domain of decision making.

The accountability model posits that people do not face their decisions within a social vacuum (see Lerner & Tetlock, 1999, for an overview), but rather as part of a social struc-ture. Decision makers resemble politicians, because they depend on approval and respect from others to maintain their position. The ultimate goal of a decision, therefore, is sat-isfying or getting approval of "relevant" others and establishing a good reputation. They need to take regular "opinion polls" of the relevant audience's beliefs, and incorporate the results in their decisions. Bolstering may be used to frame the decision in terms of others' preferences—even if they are not actually taken into account. Emphasizing existing support from other groups may sway an audience to approve a decision.

The powerful effects of social influence on human decisions have been empirically demonstrated by two of the most seminal sets of experiments in the psychological sciences—the conformity studies by Asch (1951, 1956) and the obedience studies by Milgram (1974). First, consider the experiments by Asch. He made his subjects believe that they were participating in a visual perception study. They were instructed to judge which of three lines was the same length as a standard line. The subject was seated together with a number of other participants (who were all confederates of the experimenter), and gave her judgment after the others. The differences between the three lines were sufficiently large so that, under normal conditions, they could be detected (practically) 100 percent of the time. On some of the trials, however, Asch instructed his confederates to give a wrong answer. His main finding was that a substantial number of his genuine subjects were unable to resist the group pressure and conformed by giving the wrong answer, too. From a strictly normative viewpoint, the decision to provide the incorrect answer should certainly be judged to be inappropriate. From a broader viewpoint, in judging decision quality, the circumstances under which the decision was made should not be ignored.[7]

The obedience experiments conducted by Milgram demonstrated that people find it difficult to disobey authority, even when its rules are unequivocally conflicting with universal moral norms. Specifically, participants were instructed to deliver electric shocks to a learner, whenever he made an error. Although the extreme laboratory setup employed by Milgram may be artificial, such situations are not entirely uncommon in real life. For example, should soldiers in the battlefield blindly accept the orders given to them by their commanders?[8] Note that within the accountability framework a conflict may arise as to which authority the decision maker is accountable. This conflict may emerge either within or outside the organization. In the first case, the question may arise to which superior the decision maker is accountable, while in the second situation one may ask whether one is accountable to the organization (for example, the army) or to the larger community (in which case, the decision maker should act according to other norms). In judging a decision, a dispute may arise between the decision maker and the judge as to what authority the decision maker is accountable. Authority in this context should be interpreted in the broadest way: hence, a fundamental clash between the decision maker and the judge could arise because of disagreement about the appropriate authority for values and moral norms (for example, the authority of different religions).

More generally, it is important to realize whether the decision maker and the judge possess similar perspectives and share compatible views with regard to what constitutes a good decision. Decision makers who fail to understand a judge's beliefs may miss the opportunity to convince her. As a result of differences in jargon, knowledge base and social norms, interactions with people from backgrounds other than the decision maker's may lead to unfortunate misunderstandings. In order to be accountable, one may want to take the perspectives of the judges in order to assess their opinions. This requires decision makers to abandon, if only momentarily, their own perspective and be careful not to fall into the well-known confirmation bias (Wason, 1960)—the tendency to select information that confirms their own beliefs.

---

[7] Indeed, in a similar vein, most judicial systems (especially when determining the punishment) take into account the circumstances under which the decision to commit wrongdoing was made.

[8] The major argument of Adolf Eichmann, as well as many other Nazi war criminals, was that he simply followed orders from his superiors.

The metaphor underlying the accountability model is that of politicians who should always be able to produce reasons to justify their choice to a judge. Thus, decisions under the accountability model are more likely to follow a reason-based than a rule-based mode (Shafir, Simonson & Tversky, 1993).

In contrast to the gambling model, which is based on a strictly rational analytical reasoning mode, the accountability framework is more flexible, and arguments that are based on intuitive narrative considerations (e.g., Denes-Raj & Epstein, 1994) are acceptable as long as they sound sufficiently convincing.

There are several aspects of the decision process that are highlighted within the accountability framework. First, a decision maker who is mainly motivated by accountability considerations would tend to examine the justification for each and every decision. Especially on decisions associated with important consequences, it will be difficult to justify poor outcomes by claiming that the decision strategy employed is the optimal one in the long run. A judge evaluating a decision would usually focus only on the current outcome. In other words, in most circumstances, judges of decisions would tend to adopt a clinical rather than a statistical or actuarial approach (e.g., Dawes, Faust & Meehl, 1989), eventually leading to zero tolerance of errors, even when allowing errors may, in the long run, be the policy with the best results (Einhorn, 1986).

Decision makers sensitive to being accountable, may be particularly susceptible to certain heuristics and decision pitfalls. For instance, they may prefer the current status quo to a new course of action (Samuelson & Zeckhauser, 1988), refrain from taking action, thus exhibiting the omission bias (e.g., Ritov & Baron, 1990, 1992), and continue current projects even if they are no longer profitable—ignoring sunk costs (Arkes & Blumer, 1985).[9] Many people mistakenly feel that each of these strategies offers the "safer" decision. Because judges are also subject to these biases, following them may help decision makers to minimize the risks of being held accountable for any negative unwanted outcomes.

To be accountable, a decision maker should appear to be trustworthy. Building trust may increase the odds that the judge will exhibit an empathic attitude when evaluating the decision maker. Those in favor of impeaching President Bill Clinton focused on his lies about his affair with Monica Lewinsky—*not* on the affair itself. A main argument for impeachment was that trust in the president had been lost. A major component in the buildup of trust is intentionality (Snijders & Keren, 2001). The problem with intentionality, especially in real-life situations, is that it is usually prone to a subjective judgment and can only be inferred.

SUMMARY AND CLOSING COMMENTS

By the time we completed this chapter, we asked ourselves whether we had made the correct decision in undertaking to write an essay about a diffused and controversial question. Examining the process by which we reached our decision, we thought that regardless of the difficulties involved, the issue is too central to be ignored, and thus we were willing to meet the challenge. (We omit here our considerations regarding the possible risk in terms of loss of reputation.) As far as the outcome is concerned, we leave the judgment to the reader.

---

[9] Hence, Senator Jeremiah Denton may have saved his position by stating that "to terminate a project in which $1.1 billion has been invested represents an unconscionable mishandling of the taxpayers' dollars" (4 November 1981, quoted in Dawes, 1988).

Our review survey suggests that there is no unequivocal answer to the question of how to judge decision goodness; in particular, whether it should be based on process or on outcome. It would depend on the perspective adopted by the decision maker and the judge in terms of goals, whether short- or long-term considerations are emphasized (among other things, whether one views the decision as a unique case or as one out of many similar repeated decisions), and on the implicit model underlying the decision. We briefly discussed three possible frameworks in which the decision can be made and judged. The gambling paradigm, with subjective utility theory at its core, prescribes that rational decision makers trade off the possible positive and negative consequences of options to match their preferences. The conflict model views decisions as a source of conflict, in which the major goal is to resolve it in a manner that would reduce tension and stress. The accountability framework sees decision makers as politicians wanting to maintain their position. A good decision therefore pleases relevant others. While each model takes a different approach to decision making, each highlighting specific aspects, they are not necessarily always incompatible. One common feature shared by all the three approaches is that decision makers should select the option that is most likely to serve their best interest—whether optimizing personal profit, reducing conflict or maintaining social support.

It should be emphasized that the three frameworks discussed in this chapter do not exhaust all possible views, and other paradigms or subtypes of paradigms are conceivable. For instance, the decision maker or the judge may adopt a "rule-based" view, according to which a decision is good when it conforms to certain "acceptable" rules of conduct. Another example refers to, the distinction between adapting a promotion or a prevention outlook (Higgins, 1998) may be a major source of discrepancies in judging decision quality.

The question of which model the judge (or the decision maker) should adopt is a question that obviously cannot be answered unequivocally. The major problem underlying the judgment of decision quality is largely a question of compatibility between the decision maker and the judge (who performs a second-order decision). There are two major facets for which the compatibility between the decision maker and the judge can be assessed. First, there is the question whether both employ similar frameworks in structuring the decision problem. For instance, discrepancies between the decision maker and the judge may arise if the former was motivated by emotional considerations associated with conflict, whereas the latter, in making her judgment, was solely guided by utility theory. Even a judge who uses the same model as the decision maker may not entirely understand the decision maker's position at the time the decision was made. It is difficult, if not impossible, to ignore outcome knowledge when attempting to assess in retrospect the decision maker's situation. Similarly, differences between the decision maker and the judge may come about from different interpretations of the decision problem at hand. Indeed, framing effects probably constitute the most ubiquitous phenomenon of decision making. Thus, gaps may simply result from different framing of the decision problem by the decision maker and the judge. Besides such "perceptual" discrepancies that can lead to diverging interpretations, differences may also stem from differences in the tacit assumptions underlying the conduct of communication, as has been convincingly shown by Schwarz (1998).

The second source of possible disagreements between the decision maker and the judge may stem from differences in their value systems. Decision-making theory, however, is not set up to deal with differences in tastes and values. Indeed, the three theoretical frameworks tacitly assume different basic principles and values. For instance, the gambling paradigm endorses consequentialism, which is not necessarily the ultimate criterion for the other two paradigms.

The above two issues lead to a fundamental question: what exactly is meant by a good decision? Students of decision making would correctly claim that examining decision quality should be restricted to the first facet, the way the problem has been structured and the extent to which this structuring lends itself to acceptable solutions given the decision maker's goals. In practice, however, decisions and judgments are often strongly influenced by the underlying basic value system. Hence, judgments along the two facets mentioned above may often be confounded. More specifically, the perspective adopted by judges to assess the first facet may be strongly biased by their stand on the second facet.

In this chapter, we briefly touched upon some of the central controversies associated with judging decision quality. Our inquiry leads us to conclude that there are no unequivocal standards or guidelines for judging decision quality. Like the sentence and the verdict of the courtroom, the judgment of decision quality may sometimes be controversial and not always withstand scrutiny. Whether the judgment is "reasonable" (and we are aware that, like decision quality, "reasonable" is not well defined) would depend not only on the final verdict, but also on the arguments that justify the verdict. At the end of the day, it is probably the case that, at least in practice, the justification of a decision or its judgment is mainly driven by the strength of the supporting arguments (Shafir et al., 1993). Such a conclusion is probably most compatible with the accountability model of decision making. The fact that those who assess and judge decision makers (for instance, committees assessing decisions made by societal decision makers) frequently adopt one or the other version of an accountability model should not be taken as normative evidence for the superiority of the model.

REFERENCES

Arkes, H.R. & Blumer, C. (1985). The psychology of sunk cost. *Organizational Behavior and Human Performance*, *35*, 129–140.

Asch, S.E. (1951). Effects of group pressure upon the modification and distortion of judgment. In H. Guetzkow (ed.), *Groups, Leadership, and Men* (pp. 177–190). Pittsburgh: Carnegie Press.

Asch, S.E. (1956). Studies of independence and conformity: A minority of one against a unanimous majority. *Psychological Monographs*, *70*, 70.

Baron, J. (1994). Nonconsequentialist decisions. *Behavioral and Brain Sciences*, *17*, 1–42.

Baron, J. & Hershey, J.C. (1988). Outcome bias in decision evaluation. *Journal of Personality and Social Psychology*, *54*, 569–579.

Christensen-Szalanski, J.J.J. (1984). Discount functions and the measurement of patients' values: Women's decisions during childbirth. *Medical Decision Making*, *4*, 47–58.

Coombs, C.H. (1987). The structure of conflict. *American Psychologist*, *42*, 355–363.

Coombs, C.H., Dawes, R.M. & Tversky, A. (1970). *Mathematical Psychology. An Elementary Introduction*. Englewood Cliffs, NJ: Prentice-Hall.

Damasio, A.R. (1994). *Descartes' Error: Emotion, Reason, and the Human Brain*. New York: Avon Books.

Dawes, R.M. (1988). *Rational Choice in an Uncertain World*. San Diego, CA: Harcourt Brace Janovich.

Dawes, R.M., Faust, D. & Meehl, P.E. (1989). Clinical vs. actuarial judgment. *Science*, *243*, 1668–1674.

Denes-Raj, V. & Epstein, S. (1994). Conflict between intuitive and rational processing: When people behave against their better judgment. *Journal of Personality and Social Psychology*, *66*, 819–829.

Edwards, W., Kiss, I., Majone, G. & Toda, M. (1984). What constitutes "a good decision"? *Acta Psychologica*, *56*, 5–27.

Einhorn, H. (1986). Accepting error to make less error. *Journal of Personality Assessment*, *50*, 387–395.

Einhorn, H.J. & Hogarth, R.M. (1978). Confidence in judgment: Persistence of the illusion of validity. *Psychological Review*, *85*, 395–418.

Elster, J. (1989). *The Cement of Society: A Study of Social Order*. Cambridge: Cambridge University Press.

Elster, J. (1998). Emotions and economic theory. *Journal of Economic Literature*, *36*, 47–74.

Fischhoff, B. (1975). Hindsight ≠ foresight: The effect of outcome knowledge on judgment under uncertainty. *Journal of Experimental Psychology: Human Perception and Performance*, *1*, 288–299.

Fischhoff, B. (1991). Value elicitation: Is there anything in there? *American Psychologist*, *46*, 835–847.

Fischhoff, B. (1996). The real world: What good is it? *Organizational Behavior and Human Decision Processes*, *65*, 232–248.

Fischhoff, B., Slovic, P. & Lichtenstein, S. (1980). Knowing what you want: Measuring labile values. In Wallsten, T. (ed.), *Cognitive processes in choice and decision behavior* (pp. 117–141). Hillsdale, NJ: Erlbaum.

Frisch, D. & Clemen, R.T. (1994). Beyond expected utility: Rethinking behavioral decision research. *Psychological Bulletin*, *116*, 46–54.

Frisch, D. & Jones, S.K. (1993). Assessing the accuracy of decisions. *Theory and Psychology*, *3*, 115–135.

Gilovich, T. & Medvec, V.H. (1995). The experience of regret: What, when, and why. *Psychological Review*, *102*, 379–395.

Goldsmith, R.W. & Sahlin, N.E. (1982). The role of second-order probabilities in decision making. In P.C. Humphreys, O. Svenson & A. Vari (eds), *Analysing and Aiding Decision Processes* (pp. 455–467). Amsterdam: North-Holland.

Haidt, J. (2001). The emotional dog and its rational tail: A social intuitionist approach to moral judgment. *Psychological Review*, *108*, 814–834.

Hershey, J.C. & Baron, J. (1992). Judgment by outcomes: When is it justified? *Organizational Behavior and Human Decision Processes*, *53*, 89–93.

Hershey, J.C. & Baron, J. (1995). Judgment by outcomes: When is it warranted? *Organizational Behavior and Human Decision Processes*, *62*, 127.

Higgins, E.T. (1998). Promotion and prevention: regulatory focus as a motivational principle. In M.P. Zanna (ed.), *Advances in Experimental Social Psychology*, *30*, 1–46.

Higgins, E.T. (2000). Making a good decision: Value from fit. *American Psychologist*, *55*, 1217–1227.

Janis, I.L. & Mann, L. (1977). *Decision Making: A Psychological Analysis of Conflict, Choice, and Commitment*. New York: Free Press.

Jones, E.E. & Nisbett, R.E. (1972). The actor and the observer: Divergent perceptions of the causes of behavior. In E.E. Jones, D.E. Kanouse, H.H. Kelley, R.E. Nisbett, S. Valins & B. Weiner (eds), *Attribution: Perceiving the Causes of Behavior* (pp. 79–94). Morristown, NJ: General Learning Press.

Jones, S.K., Yurak, T.J. & Frisch, D. (1997). The effect of outcome information on the evaluation and recall of individuals' own decisions. *Organizational Behavior and Human Decision Processes*, *71*, 95–120.

Kahneman, D. & Varey, C. (1990). Propensities and counterfactuals: The loser that almost won. *Journal of Personality and Social Psychology*, *59*, 1101–1110.

Kahneman, D., Slovic, P. & Tversky, A. (1982). *Judgment Under Uncertainty: Heuristics and Biases*. Cambridge: Cambridge University Press.

Kahneman, D., Wakker, P.P. & Sarin, R. (1997). Back to Bentham? Explorations of experienced utility. *Quarterly Journal of Economics*, *112*, 375–405.

Keeney, R.L. & Raiffa, H. (1976). *Decisions with Multiple Objectives: Preferences and Value Tradeoffs*. New York: Wiley.

Keren, G. (1991a). Additional tests of utility theory under unique and repeated conditions. *Journal of Behavioral Decision Making*, *4*, 297–304.

Keren, G. (1991b). Calibration and probability judgments: Conceptual and methodological issues. *Acta Psychologica, 77*, 217–273.

Keren, G. (1996). Perspectives of behavioral decision making: Some critical notes. *Organizational Behavior and Human Decision Processes, 65*, 169–178.

Keren, G. & Teigen, K.H. (2001). Why is p = .90 better than p = .70? Preference for definitive predictions by lay consumers of probability judgments. *Psychonomic Bulletin and Review, 8*, 191–202.

Lerner, J.S. & Tetlock, P.E. (1999). Accounting for the effects of accountability. *Psychological Review, 125*, 255–275.

Levin, I.P. & Gaeth, G.J. (1988). How consumers are affected by the framing of attribute information before and after consuming the product. *Journal of Consumer Research, 15*, 374–378.

Lipshitz, R. (1989). "Either a medal or a corporal": The effects of success and failure on the evaluation of decision making and decision makers. *Organizational Behavior and Human Decision Processes, 44*, 380–395.

Lipshitz, R. (1995). Judgment by outcomes: Why is it interesting? A reply to Hershey and Baron: "Judgment by outcomes: When is it justified?" *Organizational Behavior and Human Decision Processes, 62*, 123–126.

Loewenstein, G. (1998). Out of control: Visceral influences on behavior. *Organizational Behavior and Human Decision Processes, 65*, 272–292.

Loewenstein, G. & Prelec, D. (1992). Anomalies in intertemporal choice: Evidence and interpretation. *Quarterly Journal of Economics, 107*, 573–597.

Loewenstein, G., Weber, E., Hsee, C. & Welch, N. (2001). Risk as feelings. *Psychological Bulletin, 127*, 267–286.

Lopes, L.L. (1981). Decision making in the short run. *Journal of Experimental Psychology: Human Learning and Memory, 7*, 377–385.

Lopes, L.L. (1987). Between hope and fear. The psychology of risk. In L. Berkowitz (ed.), *Advances in Experimental Social Psychology* (vol. 20, pp. 255–295). New York: Academic Press.

Luce, R.D. & Raiffa, H. (1957). *Games and Decisions*. New York: Wiley.

Milgram, S. (1974). *Obedience to Authority*. New York: Harper and Row.

Miller, N.E. & Kraeling, D. (1953). Displacement: Greater generalization of approach than avoidance in a generalized approach-avoidance conflict.

Redelmeier, D.A. & Tversky, A. (1992). On the framing of multiple prospects. *Psychological Science, 3*, 191–193.

Ritov, I. & Baron, J. (1990). Reluctance to vaccinate: Omission bias and ambiguity. *Journal of Behavioral Decision Making, 3*, 263–277.

Ritov, I. & Baron, J. (1992). Status-quo and omission bias. *Journal of Risk and Uncertainty, 5*, 49–61.

Roese, N.J. & Olson, J.M. (1995). *What Might Have Been: The Social Psychology of Counterfactual Thinking*. Mahwah, NJ: Erlbaum.

Samuelson, P.A. (1963). Risk and uncertainty: A fallacy of large numbers. *Scientia, 98*, 108–113.

Samuelson, W. & Zeckhauser, R. (1988). Status quo bias in decision making. *Journal of Risk and Uncertainty, 1*, 7–59.

Savage, L.J. (1954). *The Foundations of Statistics*. New York: Wiley.

Schoemaker, P.J.H. (1982). The expected utility model: Its variants, purposes, evidence, and limitations. *Journal of Economic Literature, 20*, 529–563.

Schoemaker, P.J.H. (1991). The quest for optimality: A positive heuristic of science? *Behavioral and Brain Sciences, 14*, 205–245.

Schwarz, N. (1993). *Cognition and Communication*. Mahwah, NJ: Erlbaum.

Shafir, E., Simonson, I. & Tversky, A. (1993) Reason-based choice. *Cognition, 49*, 11–36.

Simon, H. (1973). The structure of ill-structured problems. *Artificial Intelligence, 4*, 181–201.

Sloman, S.A. (1996). The empirical case for two systems of reasoning. *Psychological Bulletin, 119*, 3–22.

Slovic, P. (1995). The construction of preference. *American Psychologist, 50*, 364–371.

Snijders, C. & Keren, G. (2001). Do you trust? Whom do you trust? When do you trust? *Advances in Group Processes, 18*, 129–160.

Spranca, M., Minsk, E. & Baron, J. (1991). Omission and commission in judgment and choice. *Journal of Experimental Social Psychology, 27*, 76–105.

Sunstein, C.R. & Ullman-Margalit, E. (1998). Second-order decisions. Discussion paper no. 178, Center for Rationality and Interactive Decision Theory, Hebrew University of Jerusalem.

Tetlock, P.E. (1991). An alternative metaphor in the study of judgment and choice: people as politicians. *Theory and Psychology*, *1*, 451–475.

Tversky, A. & Kahneman, D. (1973). Availability: A heuristic for judging frequency and probability. *Cognitive Psychology*, *5*, 207–232.

von Winterfeldt, D. (1980). Structuring decision problems for decision analysis. *Acta Psychologica*, *45*, 71–93.

von Winterfeldt, D. & Edwards, W. (1986). *Decision Analysis and Behavioral Research*. Cambridge: Cambridge University Press.

Wason, P.C. (1960). On the failure to eliminate hypotheses in a perceptual task. *Quarterly Journal of Experimental Economics*, *12*, 129–140.

Weber, E.U. (1994). From subjective probabilities to decision weights: The effect of asymmetric loss functions on the evaluation of uncertain outcomes and events. *Psychological Bulletin*, *115*, 228–242.

Wohlstetter, R. (1962). *Pearl Harbor: Warning and Decision*. Stanford, CA: Stanford University Press.

Author Index

Note: This index includes co-authors who may on some pages be included in "*et al.*" citations.

ABC Research Group, 189–90, 199, 209–10, 221
Abdellaoui, M., 281
Abelson, R.P., 166, 315–16
Abernathy, C.M., 315, 317, 330–1, 336
Ackermann, F., 253
Adams, E., 101
Adler, J.E., 166
Ahn, W., 67
Ainslie, G., 325
Alexander-Forti, D., 324
Alibali, M.W., 32
Alksnis, O., 10, 66, 86, 96, 102, 104, 107–10
Allais, M., 276, 296
Allen, J.L., 12
Allinson, C.W.A., 255
Allison, J.J., 329
Alloy, L.B., 218
Amer, T., 126
Andersen, C., 32
Anderson, A.R., 98
Anderson, J.R., 47, 56, 101, 315, 317, 331
Anderson, N.H., 328
Annunziata, M.A., 329
Anscombe, F.J., 274
Anscombre, J.-C., 82
Anthony, M., 324, 327
Arena, P.J., 323
Ariely, D., 325
Arkes, H.R., 322, 327–8, 358
Arocha, J.F., 330
Asch, D.A., 333
Asch, S.E., 357
Ashby, F.G., 329
Aumann, R.J., 274
Austin, G.A., 5, 6
Axelrod, R.M., 254
Axelrod, S., 142
Ayton, P., 217, 289

Baddeley, A.D., 47, 218
Ball, L.J., 8
Baltes, P.B., 214
Bara, B.G., 11
Baratta, P., 280

Bar-Hillel, M.A., 157, 166, 169–70, 323
Barkan, R., 325
Barnes, J.H., 253
Barnett, G.O., 126, 132
Baron, J., 27, 35, 72, 300, 305, 326, 347–9, 351, 358
Barsalou, L.W., 214
Barston, J.L., 11, 27
Bartlett F.C., 254
Bartlett, J.G., 332
Barton, M.B., 323
Barton, M.G., 328
Barwise, J., 50–1
Batchelder, W.H., 320
Bauer, M.I., 152
Baumann, A.O., 318
Bayes, T., 194
Bayoumi, A.M., 328
Bazerman, M.H., 255
Bdzola, L., 257
Beach, L.R., 259, 298, 327, 331
Beamen, A.L., 126
Beck, J.R., 324
Beck, M.A., 96, 113–14, 119
Becker, S.W., 298
Bekes, C., 324
Belkin, A., 233
Bell, V., 152
Beller, S., 67
Belnap, N.D., 98
Bemben, D.A., 324
Bennett, J.H., 319
Benson, L., 259
Ben-Zeev, T., 67
Bergus, G.R., 322–3, 327, 333
Bernstein, L.M., 325, 327, 334
Berretty, P.M., 223
Berwick, D.M., 319
Betsch, T., 192
Bettman, J.R., 223, 331
Beyth-Marom, R., 126–7, 132
Bienenstock, E., 210
Billi, J.E., 322–3, 329
Birke, R., 289–90

Birnbaum, M.H., 168, 181
Bisanz, J., 25
Bizot, E.B., 328
Bjorklund, D.F., 25
Black, M., 127
Blank, H., 166
Blatt, M.A., 322
Bleichrodt, H.B., 281, 325
Bless, H., 141
Blumer, C., 358
Bockenholt, U., 331
Boerger, R.L., 319
Bohner, G., 141
Bonini, N., 289
Bordage, G., 319
Borel, É., 274
Borges, B., 217
Borges, J.L., 228–9
Borgida, E., 166
Bornstein, B.H., 334
Boshuizen, H.P., 316–17, 319–20, 330, 335
Bowen, J., 299
Bown, N.J., 254–6, 259, 262–3, 269
Boyd, N.F., 334
Bradley, C.P., 329
Brailovsky, C., 319–20, 335
Braine, M.D.S., 10–11, 16, 26, 76, 84, 87–8, 98, 153, 170
Brase, G.L., 182
Breer, L., 326
Brehmer, B., 324
Brenner, L.A., 300
Brinkmann, B., 192
Brodsky, A., 329
Brooks, L., 126
Brooks, L.R., 319
Brooks, P.G., 6
Brown, A., 25
Brownson, F.O., 298
Brun, W., 126–7, 131–40, 142, 302
Bruner, J.S., 5–6
Bryant, G.D., 126
Bucciarelli, M., 12, 37, 152
Buck, E., 12, 96, 114–19
Budescu, D.V., 127, 138–9, 142
Buehler, R., 323
Bursztajn, H., 324, 329
Busemeyer, J.R., 325
Byrne, R.M.J., 4, 7, 9–11, 13–16, 24, 26, 28–9, 37, 46, 64, 66, 79, 84–5, 88, 95–6, 100, 104–5, 107, 109–11, 150–2

Cacioppo, J.T., 267
Cahill, D.F., 324
Cairns, J., 325
Camerer, C.F., 281, 298, 300
Campbell, A., 242
Cantor, S.B., 322
Cara, F., 7, 64, 82, 116–17, 167

Carson, A.D., 328
Casscells, W., 166, 169, 177, 333
Caverni, J-P., 153–5, 157, 160, 162, 167, 182, 214
Cebul, R.D., 322
Centor, R., 329
Chaffin, R., 320
Chaiken, S., 255
Chan, D., 85, 101, 112
Chandler, D., 213
Chapman, G.B., 315–16, 322–3, 325–328, 333–4
Chaput de Saintonge, D.M., 324
Charlin, B., 316–17, 320, 335
Chase, V.M., 161, 194, 223
Chase, W.G., 47
Chater, N., xiii, 8–9, 64, 73, 95–96, 101, 103–4, 106–8, 110–12, 114, 116–17, 119–20
Cheng, P.W., 27, 65, 67, 76
Chi, M.T.H., 56
Chipman, J.S., 298
Chow, C.C., 302–3
Christensen, C., 325–7, 332, 334
Christensen-Szalanski, J.J.J., 31, 324, 327, 356
Chua, F., 85, 101, 112
Clark, D.A., 126
Clark, E.V., 133, 140
Clark, H.H., 47, 133, 140
Clark, J.A., 324
Clark, K.L., 100
Clarke, D.D., 89
Clarke, V.A., 126
Clemen, R.T., 347, 349–50
Clemo, F.L., 324
Clibbens, J., 14
Cliff, N., 130
Codon, R.E., 329
Cohen, B.L., 128, 138
Cohen, J.D., 152
Cohen, L.J., 170
Cohen, T., 319
Colenda, C.C., 3rd, 324
Colliver, J.A., 320
Comrie, B., 102, 115, 118
Coney, J., 29
Connell, J., 84, 87–8, 170
Connelly, D.P., 323
Connors, A.F., Jr., 328
Conway, A.R.A., 331
Cook, E.F., 329
Cook, S.A., 329
Coombs, C.H., 349–50, 354
Cooper, L.A., 23, 30, 33
Copare, F.J., 324
Coppola, K.M., 324
Cosmides, L., 65, 76, 150, 160–1, 166–7, 169, 173, 175–7, 220
Costa, G., 90
Cottrell, J.J., 326, 332
Coulson, R.L., 317, 330
Cousins, N., 196

Cowan, N., 213, 218
Cowen, M.E., 324
Cox, J.A., 127–8
Cox, R., 45, 51–2
Craik, K., 150
Cressie, N.A.C., 105
Crowley, K., 24, 30, 32, 36–7
Crozier, W.R., 330
Crum, R., 279
Cummins, D.D., 10, 65, 86, 88, 96, 102, 104,
    107–10
Curley, S.P., 298, 323
Currey, H.L.F., 324
Custers, E.J., 315–18, 320
Czerlinski, J., 210, 222–3, 226, 228

D'Agostino, R.B., 199
Dales, R.E., 334
Damasio, A.R., 356
Danks, J.H., 324
Das, T.K., 253, 255
Daubman, K.A., 329
Davidson, R.A., 126
Dawes, R.M., 170, 233, 246, 321–3, 334, 349–50,
    358
Dawson, N.V., 322–3, 328
de Bock, G.H., 328
de Dombal, F.T., 335
De Vooght, G., 24
Deaconson, T.F., 329
Deber, R.B., 318
deFinetti, B., 275
DeGroot, M.H., 275
Deneffe, D., 288
Denes-Raj, V., 128, 358
Dennis, I., 8, 87
Detmer, D.E., 322
Di Caccavo, A., 329
Dickstein, L., 28
Dieussaert, K., 29
Dillon, A., 220
Ditto, P.H., 324
Dod, J., 326
Doherty, M.E., 6, 322
Donahue, E., 323, 334
Dougherty, J., 319
Dougherty, M.R.P., 327
Douglas, G., 30
Doursat, R., 210
Dowie, J., 322
Doyle, J., 100
Dragan, W., 6
Druley, J.A., 324
Dulany, D.E., 166–7
d'Ydewalle, G., 24, 29, 152

Easterbrook, J.A., 329
Eddy, D.M., 158, 166, 170, 323
Eden, C., 253

Edgington, D., 14
Edland, A.C., 256
Edwards, W., 150, 246, 280, 305, 347–8, 352
Einhorn, H.J., 233, 248, 298, 323, 351, 358
Eisenberger, R., 298
Ellis, C.E., 14
Ellis, M.C., 87
Ellsberg, D., 276, 297, 300
Elman, J.L., 219–20
Elmore, J.G., 323
Elstein, A.S., 315–16, 318, 320–3, 325–8, 330,
    332–334
Elster, J., 216, 355–6
Emler, A.C., 334
Engle, R.W., 331
Epstein, S., 128, 358
Erev, I., 138
Ericsson, K.A., 33, 214, 331
Espino, O., 96, 110
Etchemendy, J., 50–1
Ettinger, B., 324
Evans, D.A., 318, 336
Evans, J. St. B.T., 3–4, 6–18, 25, 27–8, 37, 58,
    63–4, 76, 79, 87, 95–6, 113–19, 152
Eysenck, M.W., 257

Fairley, N., 67–72, 74, 76, 86, 88–9
Fahay, L. 254
Fahey, T., 324, 326
Falk, R., 156–8, 160
Faust, D., 322, 350, 358
Fearon, J., 247
Feinberg, H.V.,321–2
Feller, W., 150
Fellows, B.J., 29
Feltovich, P.J., 56, 317–18, 330
Fennema, H., 328
Festinger, L., 246
Fetting, J.H., 325, 334
Feynman, R.P., 213
Fiedler, K., 166–7, 192, 194
Fillenbaum, S., 80, 127–8
Fineberg, H.V., 319
Fischhoff, B., 214, 233, 242, 288, 348, 351,
    353
Fishburn, P.C., 279–80
Fiske, S.T., 255–6
Flavell, J.H., 214
Fletcher, S.W., 323
Fodor, J., 3
Fogel, R., 247
Forbes, D.P., 254
Ford, M., 29, 45–7, 49, 53
Forster, M.R., 210
Forsyth, B., 127
Fox, C.R., 234, 244, 283, 285–97, 299, 301–4,
    307, 309
Freitag, J., 170
Friedman, M., 280

Frisch, D., 167, 300, 347, 349–50
Fristoe, N., 325
Fryback, D.G., 321–2

Gabriel, S.E., 324
Gaeth, G.J., 136, 353
Galinsky, A.D., 255
Galotti, K.M., 27, 35
Garb, H.N., 324
Garcia-Mila, M., 32
Garnham, A., 13, 151–2
Garvin, M.K., 328
Gassner, K., 322
Gastwirth, J.L., 178
Geis, M.L., 83
Geman, S., 210
George, C., 86, 101, 112
Gerrity, M.S., 329
Gettys, C.F., 327
Giesler, R.B., 324
Gigerenzer, G., 8, 65, 67, 128, 150, 160–1, 165–9,
    171, 173–6, 181–2, 189–92, 196, 198, 209–10,
    214, 216–17, 221–3, 226, 228, 323, 327, 331
Gigliotti, G., 298
Gilboa, I., 280
Gilhooly, K.J., 28–9, 166, 317, 319–20
Gilmore, D.J., 27, 29–30, 33–6, 39–40, 45–7
Gilovich, T., 355
Ginossar, Z., 166
Ginsberg, M.L., 97
Girotto, V., 7–8, 12, 14–15, 64, 76, 82, 96, 114–17,
    119, 152–5, 157, 159–62, 167, 169, 177–8, 182,
    214
Gjerde, C., 323, 327, 333
Glaister, K.W., 254, 255–6, 269
Glaser, R., 33, 56
Glass, A., 30
Gold, E., 323, 334
Gold, M.R., 321
Goldberg, J., 261
Goldman, L., 329
Goldmann, D.A., 324
Goldsmith, R.W., 348
Goldstein, D.G., 8, 198, 210, 216–17, 221–3, 226,
    228
Goldstein, W.M., 315, 329, 331–2, 335
Goldvarg, Y., 152–3
Gonzalez, M., 159–62, 177–8
Gonzalez, R., 281–3, 288, 291–2, 307–9
González-Vallejo, C.C., 132, 138
Goodman, N., 81
Goodnow, J.J., 5–6
Gorry, G.A., 317
Goulet, F., 335
Graboys, T.B., 166, 169, 177, 333
Graham, L.M., 67
Grainger, B., 95, 114
Gray, J.E., 324
Green, A.J.K., 320

Green, D.W., 254
Green, L., 325
Green, L.A., 199–200, 202–3, 206, 322, 334–5
Greeno, J.G., 317
Grice, H.P. 167
Griffin, D., 246, 323
Griggs, R.A., 37, 39, 64
Groen, G.J., 318–19, 336
Gross, P.H., 166
Gruppen, L.D., 322–3, 329

Ha, Y.W., 6
Habbema, J.D., 324
Hackenbrack, K., 126
Hacking, I., 128, 148, 153
Hadjichristidis, C., 288, 290
Haidt, J., 355
Hakim, R.B., 324
Haller, K.B., 324
Hamm, R.M., 126, 170, 315, 317, 322–5, 330–1,
    333–6
Hammond, K.R., 324, 329
Handley, S.H., 12–18, 29, 96, 114–19
Harasym, P., 335
Harnishfeger, K.K., 25
Harper, C., 13
Harte, J.M., 269
Hasher, L., 192
Hastie, R., 233, 242, 244, 327, 331, 332, 336
Hatala, R., 319
Hawkins, S., 233, 242, 244
Hayes, J.G., 329
Hayes, P., 97, 255
Hays, W.L., 218
Heath, C., 299–301, 307
Hebert, P.C., 334
Heckerling, P., 325, 327, 334
Heckhausen, J., 214
Hell, W., 166
Hendershot, P.E., 328
Herrmann, D.J., 320
Hershey, J.C., 279, 291, 308, 347, 349, 351
Hertwig, R., 128, 161, 166–7, 214, 221, 223, 226
Hicks, R.J., 324
Higgins, E.T., 359
Higgins, M.C., 322, 351
Hill, D.J., 126
Hilton, D.J., 89, 128, 157, 167, 331
Hirtle, S.C., 56
Ho, T.H., 281
Hockey, G.R.J., 256–7, 268
Hodgkinson, G.P., 253–6, 259, 262–3, 269
Hoellerich, V.L., 327
Hoffrage, U., 150, 160–1, 165–9, 171, 173–6,
    181–2, 189–92, 221, 223, 225–6, 323, 327
Hogarth, R., 233, 248, 298, 299, 323, 331, 351
Holmes, M.M., 324
Hood, W.B. Jr., 199
Holmes, M.M., 324

Holmes-Rovner, M., 326
Holyoak, K.J., 27, 65, 67, 76
Holzman, G.B., 326–7
Hoppe, R.B., 326–7
Horn, L., 131, 141
Horn, L.R., 83
Horrocks, J.C., 335
Hsee, C.K., 305, 329
Huber, E.C., 324
Hudson, R.R., 255
Huff, A.S., 253–4
Hug, K., 65, 67
Hunt, E.B., 23, 29–31, 46–7
Hutchings, K., 326
Hyslop, N.E., Jr., 332

Ichikawa, S., 153, 156, 158, 160
Idson, L.C., 289, 300
Isen, A.M., 329

Janis, I.L., 349, 354–5
Jannarone, R.J., 209
Jaspars, J.M.F., 89
Jenkins, E.A., 24, 31–2, 34, 36–7
Jenkins, M., 253, 261
Jepson, C., 333
Johannessen, S., 335
Johannesson, M., 325
Johnson, E.J., 223, 291, 308, 331
Johnson, G., 254, 261
Johnson-Laird, P.N., 4, 7, 10–15, 17–18, 24, 26,
  37, 46, 66, 76, 80, 96, 100, 114, 150–5, 157,
  160, 162, 167, 182, 214, 254, 317, 320
Jones, A., 335
Jones, E.E., 351
Jones, G.V., 152
Jones, K.T., 167
Jones, S.K., 167, 347, 349
Joyce, C.R.B., 324
Jungermann, H., 170

Kahn, B.E., 298, 301
Kahneman, D., xi, 128, 136–7, 148, 150, 159–161,
  166–70, 175, 178, 181, 213–14, 221, 223, 244,
  246, 253–4, 275, 279–80, 286, 288, 290, 295,
  306–7, 324–5, 328, 334, 351, 353–4
Kaplan, R.M., 324
Kareev, Y., 218–20
Karelitz, T., 127, 142
Karmiloff-Smith, A., 36
Karni, E., 275
Kassirer, J.P., 317
Kattan, M.W., 324
Kaufman, D.R., 330
Keasey, K., 255
Keeney, R.L., 349
Kelly, J.T., 323
Kemmelmeier, M., 167
Kennedy, D.T., 126

Keppe, H.J., 301
Keren G., 181, 349–50, 354, 358
Kern, L., 322
Kerr, H., 326
Kiefe, C.I., 329
Kievit, J., 328
Kilka, M., 304
Kintsch, W., 214, 315–17, 331
Kirwan, J.R., 324
Kiss, I., 347–8
Klauer, K.C., 12
Klayman, J., 6
Klein, G., 331
Kleiter, G.D., 192
Kliegl, R., 214
Knaus, W.A., 324
Kneeland, T.S., 324
Knetsch, J., 307
Knight, F.H., 282
Knottnerus, J.A., 328
Kochenberger, G., 279
Koedinger, K.R., 56
Koehler, D.J., 155, 162, 234, 244, 246, 288–90,
  300, 306–7
Koehler, J.J., 150, 178–9, 323, 333
Koele, P., 269
Kong, A., 126, 132
Kraeling, D., 355
Kraemer, B., 328
Krantz, D.H., 289, 300
Krauss, S., 173, 175, 181, 191–2
Kreps, D.M., 305
Kripal, J., 322
Kripke, S., 98
Kriukov, Y., 334
Kroger, J.K., 152
Kroll, J., 326
Kruglanski, A., 236, 246, 256
Kuhn, D., 24, 29, 32, 36
Kuijpers, A.J., 324
Kunreuther, H., 291, 298–99, 308
Kyllonen, P.C., 23, 32, 49

Laine, C., 329
Langfield-Smith, K., 261
Larkin, J., 101, 103–4, 106–8, 110–12, 116,
  119–20
Larkin, J.H., 59
Larson, J.R., Jr., 299
Larsson, S., 298
Laughhunn, D.J., 279
Laughlin, J.E., 331
Law, A.V., 324
Layde, P., 324
Leaper, D.J., 335
Lebow, R.N., 233, 243, 245, 247
Leddo, J., 166
Lee, M.B., 329
LeFevre, J., 25

Legrenzi, M.S., 153–5, 157, 160, 162, 167, 182, 214
Legrenzi, P., 8, 12, 14–15, 76, 80, 152–5, 157, 160, 162, 167, 182, 214
Lehmann, A.C., 33
Lemaire, P., 29
Lenert, L., 324, 328
Lerner, J.S., 349, 356
Lesgold, A., 317, 320
Lev, M., 218–19
Levendag, P.C., 324
Levesque, H.J., 48
Levin, I.P., 353
Levin, P., 136
Levine, M., 5
Levinson, S., 118, 166
Levy, M.F., 329
Lewis, C., 181
Lewis, C.I., 98
Lewis, D., 98, 101
Li, X., 325
Lichtenstein, S., 126, 214, 233, 288, 353
Liberman, V., 289–90, 325
Lieberman, I., 218–19
Lilje, G.W., 83
Lindley, D.V., 165, 170
Lip, G.Y., 326
Lipshitz, R., 347–8
Liu, I., 101, 110
Lo, K., 101, 110
Lockhart, R.S., 167
Locksley, A., 166
Lockwood, G.A., 126
Loehle, C., 105
Loewenstein, G., 325, 329, 355–6
Logan, J., 334
Logie, R.H., 28–9
Lohman, D.F., 23, 32, 49
Lohse, G.L., 331
Lopes, L.L., 350, 354
Lowe, E.J., 64
Lubart, T., 10, 66, 86, 96, 102, 104, 107–10
Luce, R.D., 273, 280, 348–9, 352
Luria, A.R., 228–9
Lydakis, C., 326
Lynn, J., 324

Ma, Z., 325
Macchi, L., 160, 166–73, 175–9, 192, 289, 300
MacCrimmon, K.R., 298
Macdonald, R.R., 166
Machina, M.J., 276
Mackesy-Amiti, M.E., 325, 327, 334
MacLeod, C.M., 23, 29–31, 46–7
Mackie, J.L., xiii, 80–2
Majone, G., 347–8
Mandelblatt, J.S., 321
Mandin, H., 335

Manktelow, K.I., 4, 6, 8, 63–72, 74, 76, 79, 86, 88–9, 152
Mann, J., 10
Mann, J.M., 96, 113
Mann, L., 349, 354–5
March, J.G., 275
Marquer, J.M., 47
Markoczy, L., 261
Markowitz, H., 280
Markovits, H., 87–8
Marr, D., 101, 103
Martignon, L., 173, 175, 181, 190–2, 210, 223, 225–6
Marton, K.I., 322
Mason, R., 256
Matalon, B., 80
Mathews, N.N., 23, 29, 30–31, 46–7
Maule, A.J., 253–7, 259, 262–3, 268–9
May, E.R., 351
Mazur, J.E., 325
Mazzocco, A., 96, 114–15, 119
McCann, A.P., 335
McCarthy, J.M., 97, 100
McClish, D.K., 324, 327
McCord, M.R., 324
McCormick, M.C., 324
McCrimmon, D.R., 319
McDermott, D., 100
McGaghie, W.C., 319
McGlone, M.S., 128
McGraw, A.P., 181
McKeithen, K.B., 56
McManus, I.C., 254
McNeely, P.D., 334
McNeil, B.J., 325, 327, 334
Medvec, V.H., 355
Meehl, P.E., 207–9, 322, 350, 358
Meeuwis, C.A., 324
Mehr, D.R., 199–200, 202–3, 206, 334–5
Mellers, B.A., 181, 221
Melton, L.J., III, 324
Meszaros, J., 291, 298, 308
Metheny, W.A., 326–7
Miles, B.J., 324
Milgram, S., 357
Miller, D., 246
Miller, D.J., 324
Miller, G.A., 214, 218
Miller, M.A., 170, 323
Miller, N.E., 355
Milliken, F.J., 254
Minsk, E., 348
Mintzberg, H., 254
Mirels, H.L., 323, 334
Mitroff, I., 256
Miyamoto, J.M., 162, 328
Moceri, V.M., 323
Mohebbi, B., 126
Mold, J.W., 329

Monaghan, P., 50, 53, 59
Monahan, J., 321
Moncur, M.M., 324
Monfardini, S., 329
Mongin, P., 275
Montague, R., 148
Montgomery, A.A., 324, 326
Moore, K.A., 324
Morier, D.M., 166
Morley, J.N., 324
Mosconi, G., 166–9, 176–7, 192
Moskowitz, G.B., 255
Mosteller, F., 126, 132
Moxey, L.M., 129, 131–2, 136, 139
Moynihan, D.P., 242
Muir-Broaddus, J.E., 25
Mullet, E., 126
Mumaw, R.J., 23, 30
Murray, D.J., 166
Musch, J., 12
Myerson, J., 325
Mynatt, C.R., 6

Nakao, M.A., 142
National Research Council, 178
Naumer, B., 12
Nelson, M., 126
Neth, H., 152
Newell, A., 8, 34, 317
Newman, J.R., 126
Newport, E.L., 219
Newstead, S.E., 7, 12, 14, 15, 28, 37, 39, 64, 79, 87, 95–6, 113
Newton, E.J., 27, 29, 30, 32–6, 40
Ng, M., 326, 332
Nguyen-Xuan, A., 65
Nichols, R.L., 332
Nickerson, S., 157
Nisbett, R.E., 234, 351
Norman, G.R., 126, 315–21, 330, 335
Noveck, I.A., 166–7
Nowicki, G.P., 329
Nygren, T.E., 329

Oaksford, M., xiii, 8–9, 64, 73, 95–6, 101, 103–4, 106–8, 110–12, 114, 116–17, 119–20
Oakhill, J., 13, 151–2
Oberlander, J., 45, 48, 51–2
O'Brien, D.P., 11, 16, 26, 76, 90, 153, 170
O'Brien, T.C., 80
O'Connor, A.M., 334
Ogden, E.E., 327
O'Hair, D.P., 329
Olson, J.M., 351
Olson, M.J., 139
Önkal, D., 217
Orav, E.J., 329
Ormerod, T.C., 8, 152

Ortmann, A., 217
Osherson, D.N., 166, 289
Over, D.E., 3–4, 6, 8–11, 14, 63, 65–7, 76, 85, 101, 111–12, 153, 300
Overton, W.F., 90

Padonu, G., 326
Page, G., 319
Paivio, A., 47
Palmer, T.B., 254
Pask, G., 52
Patel, V.L., 318–19, 330
Pathak, D.S., 324
Patil, K.D., 327
Pauker, S.G., 317, 325, 327, 334
Payne, J.W., 223, 279, 331
Pearl, J., 101, 105, 194, 218
Pearman, A.D., 254–6, 269
Pearsall, S., 24, 32
Pennie, R.A., 334
Pennington, N., 332
Pereira, M., 47
Peters, T.J., 324, 326
Pettigrew, A.M., 254
Petty, R.E., 267
Phillips, L., 150
Phillips, R.S., 324
Pinto, J.L., 281
Politzer, G., 10, 65, 80, 166–7
Polk, S., 323
Pollard, P., 11–12, 27
Polson, A., 326, 332
Porac, J.F., 254
Posavac, S.S., 137
Poses, R.M., 322, 324, 327
Powell, S.H., 324, 327
Pozen, M.W., 199
Pratt, J.W., 274
Prelec, D., 281, 304, 307, 325, 356
Preston, M., 280
Price, P.C., 328
Protheroe, J., 324, 326
Pylyshyn, Z., 47, 99

Qui, Z., 299
Quiggin, J., 280
Quillian, M.R., 317
Quinn, S., 88
Quinton, G., 29

Rabin, M., 307
Raiffa, H., 274, 298, 348–9, 352
Ramsey, F.P., 81, 274
Ranyard, R., 330
Rapoport, A., 127
Ravitch, M.M., 319, 326–7
Read, D., 325
Read, T.R.C., 105
Reagan, R.T., 126, 132

Reber, A.S., 3
Redelmeier, D.A., 289–90, 325–8, 350
Reder, L.M., 25, 31–32
Reed, A.B., 128
Reeder, M., 319
Reeves, T., 167
Regehr, G., 315–18, 320, 330
Reger, R.K., 254
Reid, F., 329
Reijneveld, S.A., 328
Reiter, R., 100
Reitman, J.S., 56
Renooij, S., 126
Rettinger, D.A., 331, 336
Reyna, V.F., 131
Rich, E.C., 323
Richardson, D.K., 324
Riding, R.J., 30
Riesbeck, C.K., 317
Rips, L.J., 11, 16, 24, 26, 76, 96, 100, 153
Rist, R., 10, 66, 86, 96, 102, 104, 107–10
Ritov, I., 326, 348, 358
Rivet, I., 126
Roberge, J.J., 113, 119
Roberts, M.J., 24–30, 32–7, 39–40, 45–7, 50
Roberts, J.S., 209
Roelofsma, P.H.M.P., 325
Roese, N.J., 351
Roest, F.H., 324
Rogers, B.A., 287–89, 292, 309
Romney, A.K., 320
Rood, B., 14
Rosenzweig, A.S., 329
Ross, L., 234
Rossi, C., 329
Rothert, M.L., 324
Rottenstreich, Y., 288, 290, 294, 299–300, 305–7
Rovner, D.R., 324
Roy, L., 335
Rueter, H.H., 56
Ruffin, C.L., 126
Rumain, B., 84, 87–8
Russell, B.A.W., 127
Russell, L.B., 321

Sabini, J.P., 27, 35
Sacks, O., 224
Sadler-Smith, E., 255
Sahlin, N.E., 348
Samuelson, P.A., 350
Samuelson, W., 358
Sanbonmatsu, D.M., 137
Sanford, A.J., 129, 131–2, 136, 139
Santamaria, C., 96, 110
Sarin, R.K., 298, 302–3, 353
Sattath, S., 304
Savage, L.J., 273–6, 280, 348
Savary, F., 7, 152–3
Schaeken, W., 13, 24, 29, 152

Schank, R.C., 315–17
Scheid, D.C., 315, 322, 330, 333, 335–6
Schiano, D.J., 33
Schiavo, M.D., 6
Schlaifer, R.O., 274
Schmeidler, D., 276, 280
Schmidt, H.G., 317, 319–20, 330, 335
Schmitt, B.P., 324
Schmitz, P.I., 324
Schneider, S.L., 136
Schneider, W., 25
Schoenberger, A., 166, 169, 177, 333
Schoemaker, P.J., 279, 349, 352–3
Schoenfeld, A.H., 25
Schramke, C.J., 324
Schroyens, W., 29
Schueneman, A.L., 329
Schunn, C.D., 25, 31–2, 107
Schwartz, C.E., 328
Schwartz, N., 141, 166, 359
Schwartz, W.B., 317
Schwenk, C.R., 253–6
Scott, B.C.E., 30
Scott, W.E., 324
See, K.E., 293–6
Selker, H.P., 199
Sem, F., 126
Shafer, G., 275
Shafir, E.B., 166, 326–7, 358, 360
Shanteau, J., 331
Shapira, Z., 275
Shapiro, D., 64
Shaughnessy, A.F., 319
Shiffrin, R.M., 214
Shimojo, S., 153, 156, 158, 160
Shin, S., 57
Shoam, Y., 100
Shotter, J., 29
Shrager, J., 24, 30, 32, 36
Shulman, L.S., 318
Sieck, J.P., 325
Siegler, R.S., 24–5, 29–32, 34–7, 39
Siminoff, L.A., 325, 334
Simon, H.A., xi, 8, 33, 59, 317, 327, 348
Simonson, I., 358, 360
Skurnik, I., 255
Slawson, D.C., 319
Sloman, S.A., 58, 67, 128, 288, 290, 355
Sloutsky, V.M., 152
Slovic, P., xi, 148, 166, 213–14, 221, 223, 253, 275, 288, 298, 304, 306, 353–4
Smith, E.E., 166
Smith, J., 214
Smith, W.R., 315, 322, 324, 330, 333, 335–6
Smucker, W.D., 324
Snijders, C., 358
Snow, R.E., 49–50
Sonnenberg, F., 322
Sopher, B., 298

Soukup, J.R., 329
Sox, H.C., Jr., 322, 325, 327, 334
Spada, H., 67
Sparrow, P.R., 253–5
Spender, J.-C., 253
Sperber, D., 7, 64, 82, 116–17, 167
Speroff, T., 328
Spiegelhalter, D.J., 335
Spiro, R.J., 317, 330
Sprafka, S.A., 318
Spranca, M., 298, 348
Staller, A., 67
Stallings, R.Y., 324
Stalnaker, R., 98
Stangor, C., 166
Staniland, J.R., 335
Stanovich, K.E., 3, 4, 58, 64, 320
Stasney, R., 137
Staudenmayer, H., 80
Staw, B.M., 254
Steibel, J.M., 288, 290
Stein, H.F., 329
Steinmann, D., 324
Stenning, K., 45, 48, 50–53, 55–7, 96
Stern, E., 25, 39
Sternberg, R.J., 23, 29, 30
Stevens, S.M., 324
Stevenson, R.J., 10, 85, 101, 111–12, 153
Stewart, T.R., 321, 324
Stiggelbout, A., 328
Strack, F., 141
Suedfeld, P., 246
Sullivan, K.E., 334
Sulmasy, D.P., 324
Sunstein, C.R., 355
SUPPORT Investigators, 324, 333
Sutherland, E.J., 66
Sutherland, H.334
Sutherland, H.J., 126
Svenson, O., 257, 267
Swets, J.A., 321
Sykes, E.D.A., 27
Sytkowski, P.A., 199

Tabachnik, N., 218
Talamini, R., 329
Talarczyk, G., 326
Tape, T.G., 315, 322, 330, 333, 335–6
Tardif, J., 316–317
Tasso, A., 96, 114–15, 119
Tavana, M., 126
Taylor, K., 301
Taylor, S.E., 255
Teigen, K.H., 126–9, 131–40, 142, 288, 302, 354
Teng, B.-S., 253, 255
Teno, J.M., 324
Terry, P.B., 324
Tessler, J., 242
Tetlock, P.E., 233–4, 242, 245–7, 349, 356

Thaler, R., 221, 307
Thomas, H., 254
Thompson, V.A., 10, 67, 86, 88, 96,110, 113
Thuring, M., 170
Till, J.E., 126, 334
Tobin, R., 52
Toda, M., 347–8
Todd, P.M., 8, 189–90, 209–10, 214, 221–4
Tolman, E.C., 254
Tolstoy, L., 218
Tooby, J., 150, 160–1, 166–7, 169, 173, 175–7, 220
Tosteson, A.N.A., 324
Townsend, A., 324
Treadwell, J.R., 328
Trinkaus, J., 126
Tritchler, D.L., 126, 334
Trope, Y., 166, 255, 325
Tu, S., 162
Tuholski, S.W., 331
Tumolo, S., 329
Turken, A.U., 329
Tversky, A., xi, 128, 136–7, 148, 150, 155,
    159–162, 166–70, 175, 178, 181, 213–14, 221,
    223, 234, 244, 246, 253–4, 275,
    279–80, 283, 285–304, 306–7, 309,
    324–5, 327–8, 334, 349–50, 354, 358,
    360
Tweney, R.D., 6
Twyman-Musgrove, J., 87

Ubel, P.A., 333
Ullman-Margalit, E., 355

van der Auwera, J., 83
van der Donk, J., 324
van der Henst, 167
van de Wiel, M.W., 320
van Houwelingen, J.C., 328
Vandierendonck, A., 24
VanLehn, K., 34
Varey, C., 351
Veltman, F., 98
Vettese, M.A., 324
Vitouch, O., 210
Vleuten, C. v.d., 335
von Eye, A., 209
von Winterfeldt, D., 305, 347, 352

Wakker, P.P., 281, 283, 288, 298, 304, 307, 309,
    328, 353
Wallace, B., 331
Wallach, D., 107
Wallsten, T.S., 127–8, 132, 138, 142
Walsh, J.P., 254
Wason, P.C., 6, 8, 10, 63–4, 74, 79–80, 95, 103,
    167, 357
Wazana, A., 319
Weber, E.U., 128, 315, 329, 331–2, 335–6, 354
Weber, M., 298, 300–4, 307

Webster, D., 236, 246, 256
Weg, E., 325
Weil, E.M., 29
Weinstein, M.C., 319, 321–2
Weisman, C.S., 324
Welch, N., 329
Wells, G.L., 128, 138, 166
Wellwood, J., 335
Wenger, N.S., 324
West, R.F., 320
Wetherick, N.E., 28–9
White, L.J., 319
Wigton, R.S., 322, 324, 327–8
Wild, B., 192
Wiley, J., 56
Wilkins, M.C., 63
Williamson, T., 127
Wilson, D., 7
Windschitl, P.D., 128, 138
Winkler, 236
Wirth, A., 261
Wise, J.A., 298
Witteman, C., 126
Wohlstetter, R., 351

Wolf, F.M., 322–3, 329
Wolfram, S., 105
Woloschuk, W., 335
Wood, D.J., 27, 29–30, 33–6, 39–40,
   45–7
Wu, A.W., 324
Wu, G., 281–3, 288, 291, 307–8
Wu, J., 101, 110,
Wynn, V., 28–9

Yates, J.F., 298, 299, 322, 328
Young, M.J., 329
Youtz, C., 126, 132
Yule, P., 45, 55
Yurak, T.J., 349

Zacks, R.T., 192
Zauberman, G., 325
Zeckhauser, R., 358
Zhang, H.C., 33
Zohar, A., 32
Zukowski, L.S., 298–9
Zwick, R., 127
Zwicky, A.M., 83

Subject Index

accountability model, 347–63
Allais paradox, 276–81, 296–7, 305
alternative causes/antecedents, 66–77, 83–4,
   87–91, 96–113
ambiguity aversion, 297–305
aptitude-treatment interactions, 49–59
atmosphere heuristic, 28, 39
availability heuristic, 354

base rate neglect/base rate fallacy, 150, 165–87,
   221, 321, 323, 327, 333–4
Bayes' theorem/Bayesian thinking, 5, 10, 64,
   149–50, 153, 158–62, 165–87, 189–94, 207,
   233, 237–9, 246–7, 321–3
belief bias, 12–13, 19, 63
bounded rationality, 8

causal field, 80–1, 89
causal inference, 66–77, 79–91, 218
certainty effect, 278–97, 305
cognitive inertia
cognitive mapping, 253–72
cognitive style, 30, 234, 243, 246
comparative ignorance see ignorance aversion
compass-point directions task, 28–9, 32–7, 40,
   46–7
complementary necessary conditions (CNC),
   81–91
conditional field, 81–3, 89, 91
confirmation bias, 6, 357
conflict model, 347–63
confusion hypothesis, 170
conjunction fallacy, 136–7, 160–1, 167, 221
consequentialism, violations of, 348
content effects, 63–77, 80, 89, 91, 100
conservativism, 232–4, 237–9, 246
correspondence bias
counterfactual thinking, 234–236, 239, 241–9,
   351
covariation detection, 218–19

Dawes' rule, 222–3
decision aids, 334–5
   see also decision trees
decision quality, 347–63
decision trees, 189–211

deontic thinking, 64–7, 70–1, 74–7, 95
   obligations, 70
   permissions, 65–6, 70, 86, 89, 113
Differentiation and Consolidation Theory, 257,
   267
disabling conditions, 10, 66–70, 86, 89
discounting see temporal effects
dual processes, 3–5
   heuristic-analytic theory, 4
   implicit processes, 3–4, 7, 9, 32, 58–9
   explicit processes, 3–5, 9, 58–9
   system 1 vs. system 2 thinking, 3–4, 58
   type 1 vs. type 2 thinking, 255–7, 266–9

Ellsberg paradox, 276–8, 297–8, 302, 305
emotions, 349, 354–6
equiprobability effect/equiprobability principle see
   principles
escalation of commitment, 269
Euler circles, 52–9
expected utility theory see utility
explicit thinking see dual processes
extensionality (incl. violations of), 147–62, 234–46

fast and frugal heuristics, 8, 221–23, 225–29
   fast and frugal decision trees, 189–211
frame problem, 7, 99
framing bias, 254, 269, 324–25, 334
frequencies/frequentist approach, 150, 153,
   159–61, 165–87, 221, 323
fundamental computational bias, 3, 4, 58–9
fundamental reasoning mechanism, 24–6, 45–6

gambling paradigm, 349, 352–4, 356, 358–60

heuristic-analytic theory see dual processes
hindsight bias, 233–4, 242, 244–5
Hyperproof, 50–5
hypothetical thinking, 3–21

ignorance aversion, 278, 297, 301–10
illusory inferences, 152–7, 162
implicit thinking see dual processes
information gain, 95–120

less-is-more effect, 217

Meehl's paradox, 207–10
membership function, 127–8, 142
mental logic, 11, 16, 18, 19, 26, 96–7, 100
mental models, 10–18, 26, 46, 96–7, 100, 147–62,
    167, 181–2, 214 254, 269
Minimalist heuristic, 222, 225

natural sampling, 168, 173–7, 180–2
need for closure, 234–6, 238–9, 242–3, 245–6,
    248
need for cognition, 267
negative conclusion bias, 95–6, 103, 115, 117, 120
non-monotonic reasoning, 9, 97, 99–100, 104, 119

order effects, 96, 113–20
overconfidence, 221, 233–4, 236–7, 246

partitive hypothesis, 160, 165–87
permission rules see deontic thinking
perspective effects, 64–7
possibility effect, 283, 286
pragmatic approach, 166–70
principles
    description invariance, 290–5, 297, 308–9
    equiprobability principle, 128–9, 153–7, 160
    numerical principle, 153–4, 158–62
    procedure invariance, 304
    proportionality principle, 153–4, 156, 160
    regularity, 326
    relevance principle, 4–5, 7–8, 13
    satisficing principle, 4–5, 8–10
    semantic principle, 11, 15
    singularity principle, 4–7, 9, 11–14
    subset principle, 153–4, 158–61
    superordinate principles (or SuperP), 63–77
    sure-thing, 273–9, 297, 305
    truth principle, 7–8, 15–16, 151–3
Prospect Theory, 269, 279–88, 297, 306–10,
    324–5, 328
    Cumulative Prospect Theory, 309, 328
pseudodiagnosticity, 6, 152, 322

QuickEst heuristic, 226–8

rarity assumption, 103–4
recognition heuristic, 215–17, 221
regularity principle see principles
relevance logic, 97–100
relevance principle see principles
representativeness, 136–7, 150
risk attitudes, 279–81, 295–7, 307–8

satisficing principle see principles
schemas
    domain-specific, 65–6, 76–7
    pragmatic reasoning, 67, 76–7
scripts, 315–45
sentence-picture verification task, 46–9
singularity principle see principles
social contract algorithm, 65, 76–7

source preference, 298–310
spatial representations see strategies
strategic decisions, 253–272
strategy/strategies, 23–43
    availability of, 29, 33–7
    broad definitions, 24–6
    development of, 23–43
    discovery, 23–43
    expansion, 36
    narrow definitions, 25
    reduction, 36
    selection, 25, 29–33, 37, 328–9
    see also principles
strategy types
    cancellation, 27, 32–8, 40
    coping, 27–8, 30, 37–9, 41
    deduction as a strategy, 12
    first-and-last, 37
    first-two, 37
    min-, 31–2, 34
    reductio ad absurdum, 16–18
    spatial, 26–33, 35, 38–9, 46–9, 54–5, 58–9
    task-specific short-cuts, 27–9, 35, 37–9, 41
    verbal, 26–31, 38, 46–9, 54–6
subadditivity, 155–7, 162, 234, 244–6, 248,
    282–95, 307–10
subjective expected utility theory see utility
sunk cost, 334
SuperP or superordinate principles see principles
support theory, 234, 244–6, 288–90, 293–9, 303,
    306, 309
suppositional reasoning, 16–18
suppression effects, 96, 101–13, 115, 119
sure-thing principle see principles
syllogisms
    categorical, 11–13, 27–9, 33, 35, 37–9, 45–7,
        52–9
    linear, 29, 39, 46, 48, 55–6
System 1 vs. System 2 thinking see dual
    processes

Take The Best heuristic, 222–3
temporal effects, 325
time pressure, 256–69
truth table task, 7–8, 14–16, 89–91
two-stage model (of decisions under uncertainty),
    279–98, 304–6, 308
    extended two-stage model, 305–7
Type 1 vs. Type 2 thinking see dual processes

universal reasoning theory, 24
utility, 347–63

vagueness, 127–8, 138–9, 141–2
verbal probabilities, 125–45

Wason
    2 4 6 task, 6
    selection task, 8, 14–15, 63–6, 74, 79–80, 167
    THOG task, 6